BELLAMY & CHILD

European Union Law of Competition

D1584759

BELLAMY & CHILD

European Union Law of Competition

THIRD CUMULATIVE SUPPLEMENT TO THE SEVENTH EDITION

LAURA ELIZABETH JOHN

Monckton Chambers

JON TURNER QC
CONSULTANT EDITOR
Monckton Chambers

OXFORD
UNIVERSITY PRESS

OXFORD
UNIVERSITY PRESS

Great Clarendon Street, Oxford, OX2 6DP,
United Kingdom

Oxford University Press is a department of the University of Oxford.
It furthers the University's objective of excellence in research, scholarship,
and education by publishing worldwide. Oxford is a registered trade mark of
Oxford University Press in the UK and in certain other countries

Published in the United States of America by Oxford University Press
198 Madison Avenue, New York, NY 10016, United States of America

British Library Cataloguing in Publication Data
Data available

Library of Congress Control Number: 2016930489

ISBN 978–0–19–877861–5

Printed in Great Britain by
Ashford Colour Press Ltd, Gosport, Hampshire

CONTENTS

PREFACE AND HIGHLIGHTS OF THE THIRD CUMULATIVE SUPPLEMENT TO THE 7TH EDITION

Since the 7th Edition of *Bellamy & Child* was published OUP has launched the online service, *Oxford Competition Law*. This supplement is available in online format, as well as the traditional paper format, together with the 7th Edition itself and the Materials Volume. It covers the legislative and jurisprudential developments that have occurred in the 37 months since the date at which the law is stated in the 7th Edition.

We are indebted to the Editors of the 7th Edition, Vivien Rose (now Mrs Justice Rose, Judge of the Chancery Division of the High Court), and David Bailey, for setting aside their time to guide us through the task of updating this comprehensive work. Sincere thanks also go to Andrew Macnab for his ongoing dedication to ensuring that the materials continue to be comprehensive and user-friendly, and to the contributors who at various points have assisted with updates: Alistair Lindsay (Chapter 4), John Boyce, Claire Jeffs and Ingrid Lauwers (Chapter 8), Oke Odudu (Chapter 9), Brendan McGurk (Chapter 10), Ligia Osepciu (Chapter 12), Julianne Kerr Morrison (Chapter 14) and Alan Bates (Chapter 17). Thanks also go to Ruth Anderson, Gemma Parsons and Francesca Halstead, and their respective teams at Oxford University Press, for their inextinguishable patience, support and good humour.

We have endeavoured to ensure the updated text is correct as at 31 August 2015. As the updating will be an ongoing exercise, we would be happy for any reader who notices any errors or omissions to contact us in Chambers and draw them to our attention.

Note on Citation

On 24 March 2014 the European Case Law Identifier ('ECLI') was introduced for all judgments of the European Courts and opinions of the Advocates General. The references below therefore include the new ECLI numbers, which are composed as follows: [code for the Member State court or tribunal concerned, or for the EU]:[abbreviation for the Court that gave the decision – the abbreviation for the Court of Justice is 'C', and for the General Court 'T']:[year of the decision]:[order number]. For example, the ECLI of the judgment in Case C-213/89 *Factortame* is EU:C:1990:257. The Court has assigned an ECLI to all decisions delivered by the European Union Courts since 1954, and to the Opinions of the Advocates General.

Highlights

The following paragraphs refer to the main developments affecting each chapter of the 7th Edition.

Chapter 1: EU Competition Law and its Territorial Reach

On 1 July 2013, Croatia joined the EU, bringing the number of Member States to 28.

On the Commission's jurisdiction over undertakings established outside the EEA, the Court of Justice dismissed a complaint in Case C-231/14P *Innolux v Commission (Liquid Crystal Displays)*, EU:C:2015:451, that the Commission had acted in breach of the territoriality principle, as articulated in Joined Cases 89/85, etc, *Ahlström Osakeyhtiö and Others v Commission* [1988] ECR 5193, 'Woodpulp', in the method it had used to calculate the fine imposed in its decision in COMP/39309 *Liquid Crystal Displays*, decision of 8 December 2010. The Commission had calculated the undertakings' value of sales on the basis of direct sales of the cartelised LCD product into the EEA, and in addition a proportion of the value of the sales made by different companies within the same undertakings, into the EEA, of finished products into which the cartelised LCD product had been incorporated. The Court dismissed a complaint that the Commission's approach effectively brought into account sales that were made to subsidiary companies outside the EEA, and that in doing so it exceeded its jurisdiction. Disagreeing with the Opinion of Advocate General Wathelet, EU:C:2015:292, the Court held that the Commission had jurisdiction to apply Article 101 to the cartel, because the cartelists made direct sales of the cartelised product into the EEA, and that the appropriate method for determining the fine to be imposed in respect of that cartel was a separate question to jurisdiction. The General Court also held in Case T-286/09 *Intel v Commission*, EU:T:2014:547, [2014] 5 CMLR 270 at paras 231 et seq, that jurisdiction can be established on the basis of the undertakings' conduct being implemented in the EU, following *Woodpulp*, or on the basis of their conduct having immediate, substantial and foreseeable effects within the EU, following Case T-102/96 *Gencor v Commission* [1999] ECR II-753. These are alternative approaches, not cumulative, and the Commission does not have to establish implementation within the EU if it can demonstrate that the conduct will have immediate, substantial and foreseeable effects within the EU. The General Court also held that the immediate, substantial and foreseeable effects do not have to be actual effects that have already materialised: para 251. For completeness the Court also considered whether, in that case, jurisdiction could also be established on the basis of the conduct being implemented within the EU. It held that direct sales by the addressee are not the only means of implementation within the EU, and in that case, which concerned an abuse of dominance contrary to Article 102, implementation could comprise conduct in the EU by the dominant undertaking's customer, by which the customer implemented an agreement between it and the dominant undertaking: paras 296 et seq. On further appeal, Case C-413/14P, not yet decided.

The Court of Justice has confirmed that, although it is not always necessary to define the relevant market in order to determine whether there is an appreciable effect on trade between Member States, in the context of verifying whether market share thresholds have been exceeded it is by definition necessary to define the market: Cases C-429/11P *Portielje and Gosselin v Commission*, EU:C:2013:463, [2013] 5 CMLR 37; and C-439/11P *Ziegler v Commission*, EU:C:2013:514, [2013] 5 CMLR 36.

The EU has concluded a fifth agreement on competition matters, with the Swiss Confederation: Agreement between the European Union and the Swiss Confederation concerning cooperation on the application of their competition laws, OJ 2014 L347/3, which entered into force on 1 December 2014: Press Release IP/14/2245 (28 November 2014). On 26 September 2014 the EU published the agreed text of a Comprehensive and Economic Free Trade Agreement with Canada, which remains subject to ratification. Negotiations are ongoing with the US regarding a Transatlantic Trade and Investment Partnership. The EU signed Association Agreements with Ukraine (27 June 2014; OJ 2014 L161/3), Georgia (22 July 2014; OJ 2014 L261/4) and Moldova (27 June 2014; OJ 2014 L260/4), which introduce a preferential trade regime called the Deep and Comprehensive Free Trade Area. DG Competition signed a Memorandum of Understanding with the Competition Commission of India in November 2013: see Press Release IP/13/1143 (21 November 2013).

Chapter 2: Article 101(1)

(i) Undertakings

On the concept of an 'undertaking', the Court of Justice confirmed in Case C-440/11P *Commission v Portielje and Gosselin*, EU:C:2013:514, [2013] 5 CMLR 37 that if a company holds all the capital, or almost all the capital, in a subsidiary company that is a sufficient basis for the application of the presumption of decisive influence. It is not necessary to consider whether the parent company is also itself engaged in an economic activity and individually constitutes an undertaking, if it is part of the same undertaking as the subsidiary. It upheld the Commission's appeal, and overturned the judgment in Cases T-208&209/08

Gosselin Group v Commission [2011] ECR II-03639, [2013] 4 CMLR 671 in which the General Court had held that the Commission had not established that a parent company was itself an undertaking, relying on the judgment in Case C-222/04 *Cassa di Risparmio* [2006] ECR I-289, [2008] 1 CMLR 705 that mere holding of shares is not itself an economic activity.

The Court of Justice also confirmed, in Cases C-179/12P *Dow Chemical Company v Commission*, EU:C:2013:605, [2014] 4 CMLR 6; and C-172/12P *El du Pont de Nemours v Commission*, EU:C:2013:601, [2014] 4 CMLR 7, that two parent companies and the joint venture in which they each have a 50 per cent shareholding can be considered to be a single undertaking for the purposes of establishing liability for participation in an infringement of competition law, provided that the factual evidence demonstrates the actual exercise of decisive influence.

On the activities of an agent, the General Court held in Case T-418/10 *Voestalpine v Commission*, EU:T:2015:516 that an agent who acted on behalf of two principals, both of which participated in the cartel, could be considered to be part of the same undertaking as one of them. It is not relevant for the purposes of establishing liability that the principal is unaware of the agent's participation in anti-competitive conduct; the acts of the agent can be imputed to the principal just as those of an employee may be imputed to an employer. That imputation extends to finding the principal liable for participating in a single and continuous infringement on the basis that it is considered to have been aware, through its agent, of the conduct of the other undertakings in pursuit of the same overall plan.

In Case C-413/13 *FNV Kunsten Informatie en Media v Staat der Nederlanden*, EU:C:2014:2411 the Court of Justice outlined the factors that are relevant in considering whether a person is an 'employee' or self-employed and an undertaking.

(ii) Agreements, decisions and concerted practices

The General Court's judgments in the appeals against the Commission's decision in COMP/38698 *CISAC*, decision of 16 July 2008, are particularly significant on the concept of a 'concerted practice'. The General Court upheld the Commission's conclusion that the membership clause in the collecting societies' agreements infringed Article 101 (Cases T-392/08 etc, EU:T:2013:170, [2013] 5 CMLR 15) but considered that the Commission did not have sufficient evidence also to establish a concerted practice. It held that the need for the collecting societies to monitor the use of copyrighted material provided a plausible explanation for their parallel behaviour, and the decision was therefore partially annulled: eg Case T-442/08, EU:T:2013:188, [2013] 5 CMLR 536.

The Court of Justice dismissed the appeals in Joined Cases C-239/11P, etc, *Siemens v Commission (Gas Insulated Switchgear)*, EU:C:2013:866, [2014] 4 CMLR 606. It upheld the General Court's conclusion that the evidence was sufficient to establish the existence of a common understanding that the European and Japanese manufacturers would not enter each other's territories, and in particular it noted that the existence of an information exchange mechanism between the undertakings supported the General Court's conclusion that the Japanese manufacturers were credible 'potential competitors' on the European markets: para 114. It confirmed that in those circumstances there was no need to examine whether there was an alternative plausible explanation for the undertakings' conduct (such as, as was argued in that case, the existence of alleged technical and economic barriers to entry into the European markets): paras 219 et seq. There was also no need to consider whether the common understanding was complementary to the agreement that the European manufacturers had reached between themselves, in order to conclude that there was a single and continuous infringement, as the two formed part of the same overall plan: paras 241 and 247–248. The judgment is also significant for its consideration of the credibility of statements made by a leniency applicant (see Chapter 5, below).

In C-455/11P *Solvay v Commission*, EU:C:2013:796, [2014] 4 CMLR 581, at paras 39 et seq, the Court of Justice held that in a highly concentrated oligopolistic market, the exchange of commercial information between competitors will itself allow operators to know the market positions and strategies of their competitors, and the exchange of such information in preparation for an anti-competitive agreement therefore suffices to prove the existence of a concerted practice. It is not necessary to establish that the competitors formally undertook to adopt a particular course of conduct, or that the competitors colluded over their future conduct on the market. The Court also dismissed Solvay's appeal against the General Court's conclusion that it had not rebutted the presumption that it had acted on the information it had received. The Court held that data illustrating the competitive nature of the market and decreases in market prices is not sufficient to rebut the presumption, because it does not show that the undertaking determined its conduct without reference to the information it had received, or that uncertainties regarding its conduct in the market had not been eliminated by the receipt of that information.

The Court of Justice considered further the concept of a single and continuous infringement in Case C-441/11P *Commission v Verhuizingen Coppens*, EU:C:2012:778, [2013] 4 CMLR 312, where it held that if an undertaking did not participate in the single and continuous infringement found by the Commission, it must still be held liable for the parts of the infringing behaviour in which it did participate.

On decisions by associations of undertakings, the Court of Justice dismissed the further appeal in Case C-382/12P *MasterCard v Commission*, EU:C:2014:2201 and upheld the General Court's conclusion that MasterCard continued to operate, after its listing on the stock exchange, as 'an institutionalised form of coordination of the conduct of the banks'. The Court confirmed that commonality of interests between undertakings is not the exclusive criterion for determining whether a body is an association of undertakings. It held, however, that the General Court's findings of fact that the banks continued collectively to exercise decision-making powers in respect of the essential aspects of the operation of the organisation, and that the multilateral interchange fees ('MIFs') reflected the aligned interests of MasterCard, its shareholders and the banks, were both relevant and sufficient for the purposes of assessing whether MasterCard could still be considered an 'association of undertakings': paras 68–73.

(iii) Prevention, restriction or distortion of competition

The Court of Justice and the General Court have considered several cases on 'object' infringements. Of particular significance, in Case C-67/13P *Groupement des cartes bancaires v Commission*, EU:C:2014:2202, at paras 57–58, the Court held '... the essential legal criterion for ascertaining whether coordination between undertakings involves such a restriction of competition "by object" is the finding that such coordination reveals in itself a sufficient degree of harm to competition' and the concept of a restriction by object must be interpreted restrictively. In that case, it confirmed that in considering all relevant aspects of the economic and legal context of the agreement it is immaterial whether those aspects relate to the relevant market or to other markets, particularly in a case concerning related markets and the more so in a case concerning a two-sided system: paras 78–79. It overturned the General Court's judgment that there was infringement by object, as it had not explained in what respect the restriction of competition revealed a sufficient degree of harm so as to be characterised as an object infringement: paras 55 et seq. In view of the General Court's findings of fact, first, that in a two-sided card payment system the issuing and acquiring activities are essential to one another and to the operation of the system, and, secondly, that the agreements in question sought to maintain a certain ratio between the issuing and acquiring activities of the group's members, the most that could be inferred from the terms of the agreements was that they had as their object the combatting of 'free-riding'. That objective is legitimate, and not harmful to the proper functioning of competition: paras 72–75. In addition, on 'object' infringements see the Court of Justice's judgments in Case C-32/11 *Allianz Hungária Bistozitó*, EU:C:2013:160, [2013] 4 CMLR 25 (vertical agreements that were likely to affect two markets); Case C-68/12 *Protimonopolný úrad v Slovenská sporitel'ňa*, EU:C:2013:71, [2013] 4 CMLR 491 (an agreement intended to exclude a competitor that had been operating illegally on the market); and Case C-286/13P *Dole Food Company v Commission* EU:C:2015:184, [2015] 4 CMLR 967 (concerted practice which had an anticompetitive object); and the General Court's judgments in the appeals against the *CISAC* decision, finding that the membership and exclusivity clauses in the societies' model contract were a restriction by object: eg, Case T-401/08 *Säveltäjäin Tekijänoikeustoimisto Teosto v Commission*, EU:T:2013:170, [2013] 5 CMLR 15.

On 'effect' infringements, the Court of Justice in Case C-382/12P *MasterCard v Commission*, EU:C:2014:2201 confirmed that, for the purpose of assessing effects, it is necessary to consider as a counterfactual what would actually have happened in the absence of the agreement: paras 164 et seq. The General Court in that case had erred by assessing the effects of MasterCard's MIFs against a counterfactual in which the MasterCard system was operated using a prohibition on *ex post* pricing (in which issuing banks would be prohibited from setting the amount of the interchange fee after the cardholder had already made its purchase from the merchant) without considering how realistic that counterfactual was. That counterfactual was appropriate in the context of assessing whether the agreement was an objectively necessary ancillary restraint, but assessing the impact of the agreement on competition requires an assessment of the competition in question within the actual context in which it would occur in the absence of the agreement. On the facts of that case, however, the Court went on to find that it had not been contended before the General Court that the MasterCard system would have collapsed without the MIFs, and the only alternative before the Court was the *ex post* pricing prohibition. This was therefore the only plausible and likely alternative to the MIFs before the General Court, and the judgment could be upheld on alternative grounds.

The Commission decision in COMP/39839 *Telefónica and Portugal Telecom*, decision of 23 January 2013, is of particular interest in respect of ancillary restraints (on appeal, Cases T-208/13 *Portugal Telecom v Commission* and T-216/13 *Telefónica v Commission*, not yet decided).

(iv) Appreciable effect

On the concept of 'appreciability', the judgment in Case C-226/11 *Expedia Inc*, EU:C:2012:795, [2013] 4 CMLR 439 confirms that although NCAs may take account of the market share thresholds set by the Commission's *De Minimis* Notice when determining whether an agreement has an appreciable effect on competition, they are not required to do so. The Court also held that an agreement that may affect trade between Member States and that has an anti-competitive object constitutes, by its nature and independently of any concrete effects that it may have, an appreciable restriction of competition. On 30 August 2014 the Commission adopted a revised *De Minimis* Notice to take account of this judgment: OJ 2014 C291/1.

Chapter 3: Article 101(3)

In Case C-382/12P *MasterCard v Commission*, EU:C:2014:2201 the Court of Justice confirmed that, in the case of a two-sided system, to determine whether an agreement meets the first condition of Article 101(3) it is necessary to take into account all the objective advantages flowing from it. That includes not only the advantages on the market on which the restriction is established but also on the other market where there is another group of consumers associated with the system. This is particularly important where there is interaction between the two sides of the system: para 237. However, the Court also confirmed that where the restrictive effects are felt only on one of the markets, the first condition of Article 101(3) can only be satisfied where some of the benefits are enjoyed by consumers on the market on which the restrictive effects are felt; if the benefits are entirely felt in the separate but connected market then they cannot, in themselves, compensate for the disadvantages of the agreement in the relevant market. It therefore upheld the General Court's conclusion that even if the MIFs lead to some benefit to cardholders, the absence of any benefits to merchants is sufficient to preclude the application of Article 101(3): paras 237 et seq.

The General Court has dismissed a number of appeals against decisions in which the Commission concluded that the criteria of Article 101(3) were not met. The Article 101(3) analysis in the Commission's *CISAC* decision was upheld in Case T-451/08 *Föreningen Svenska Tonsättares Internationella Musikbyrå v Commission*, EU:T:2013:189, [2013] 5 CMLR 577 (the only judgment in which the finding of a concerted practice was upheld, and in which the Court therefore went on to consider the application of Article 101(3)); the analysis in COMP/39188 *Bananas*, decision of 15 October 2008, was upheld in Case T-587/08 *Fresh Del Monte Produce v Commission*, EU:T:2013:129, [2013] 4 CMLR 30; and Case T-588/08 *Dole Food Company v Commission*, EU:T:2013:130, [2013] 4 CMLR 31 (further appeals dismissed in Joined Cases C-293&294/13P *Fresh Del Monte Produce*, EU:C:2015:416, [2015] 5 CMLR 513 and C-286/13P *Dole Food Company*, EU:C:2015:184, [2015] 4 CMLR 967); and the analysis in COMP/38606 *Cartes Bancaires*, decision of 17 October 2007, was upheld in Case T-491/07 *CB v Commission*, EU:T:2012:633 (the General Court's judgment was overturned by the Court of Justice, on other grounds, in Case C-67/13P *Groupement Cartes Bancaires v Commission*, EU:C:2014:2202 (see Chapter 2, above), and has been remitted).

The Commission concluded in COMP/39839 *Telefónica and Portugal Telecom*, decision of 23 January 2013, that the requirement of indispensability was not met (on appeal, Cases T-208/13 *Portugal Telecom v Commission* and T-216/13 *Telefónica v Commission*, not yet decided).

Chapter 4: Market Definition

The Court of Justice's judgment in Case C-457/10P *Astra Zeneca v Commission*, EU:C:2012:770, [2013] 4 CMLR 233, upheld the General Court's conclusions on market definition in the context of its dominance analysis. In Case C-439/11P *Ziegler v Commission*, EU:C:2013:514, [2013] 5 CMLR 36, the Court confirmed that it is necessary to define the relevant market in order to apply a market share criterion (in that case, to determine whether there was an appreciable effect on trade between Member States in that market).

In addition, a number of decisions in the merger field that contain detailed market definition analyses have been published, including: M.5830 *Olympic/Aegean Airlines* (26 January 2011); M.6166 *Deutsche Börse/NYSE Euronext* (1 February 2012) (upheld in Case T-175/12 *Deutsche Börse v Commission*, EU:T:2015:148, [2015] 4 CMLR 1187); M.6541 *Glencor/Xsrata* (22 November 2012); M.6690 *Syniverse/Mach* (29 May 2013); M.6944 *Thermo Fisher/Life Technologies* (26 November 2013); M.7292 *DEMB/Mondelez/Charger Opco* (5 May 2015); and M.6800 *PRSfM/STIM/GEMA/JV* (16 June 2015).

Chapter 5: Cartels

The discussion in the main text of the Commission's decision in *Bananas*—in particular, in section 1(c) of Chapter 5 on arguments typically used to justify cartels, and section 2 on prices and pricing restrictions—should now be read alongside the General Court's judgments in Cases T-587/08 *Fresh Del Monte Produce v Commission*, EU:T:2013:129, [2013] 4 CMLR 30; and T-588/08 *Dole Food Company v Commission*, EU:T:2013:130, [2013] 4 CMLR 31, which uphold the Commission's analysis on liability (further appeals dismissed in Joined Cases C-293&294/13P *Fresh Del Monte Produce*, EU:C:2015:416, [2015] 5 CMLR 513, and Case C-286/13P *Dole Food Company v Commission* EU:C:2015:184, [2015] 4 CMLR 967). In addition, on pricing restrictions, the Commission's decisions in COMP/39847 *E-books*, decision of 12 December 2012 (OJ 2012 C283/7), and of 25 July 2013 (OJ 2013 C378/25) accept commitments from five publishing companies, and Apple, *inter alia* not to enter into most favoured nation clauses for five years. The Commission has opened a similar investigation into the arrangements between Amazon and publishers: COMP/40153 *E-book MFNs*, and Press Release IP/15/5166 (11 June 2015). See also M.6458 *Universal Music Group/ EMI Music* (21 September 2012), in which the Commission cleared a merger upon Universal committing *inter alia* not to include most favoured nation clauses in its licensing agreements with digital music services in the EEA for five years. The UK's OFT and the German Bundeskartellamt have closed their investigations into Amazon's pricing parity clauses, which prevented sellers who use Amazon's retail platform from offering their products more cheaply on any other online sales channel, after Amazon agreed to remove these clauses from its contracts (ECN Brief 05/2013, p30). The Bundeskartellamt has found that most favoured nation pricing clauses in contracts between a hotel booking platform and hotels breach Article 101 and national competition law (on appeal to the Düsseldorf Higher Regional Court): ECN Brief 01/2014, p6.

On the credibility of statements made by a leniency applicant, in Joined Cases C-239/11P, etc, *Siemens v Commission (Gas Insulated Switchgear)*, EU:C:2013:866, [2014] 4 CMLR 606, the Court of Justice considered various detailed arguments relating to the credibility of witness evidence which had been adduced on behalf of a leniency applicant, and relied upon by the General Court, to establish the existence of a common understanding. It dismissed as inadmissible a complaint that the General Court should not have relied upon the witness evidence of the leniency applicant because of 'established knowledge relating to the functioning of the memory and the psychology of witnesses', and the possibility that an individual may have had an interest in maximising the unlawful conduct of competitors and minimising their own liability. It upheld the General Court's conclusion that the leniency applicant's evidence was credible, in particular as its representative would have been aware of the potential negative consequences of submitting inaccurate information: para 138; and the applicant itself had acted against its own interests in applying for leniency, because of the risk of damages actions being brought against it in national courts: para 141. The other cartelists' evidence, on the other hand, was correctly assessed as being less credible as they had sought to deny the existence of the common understanding and therefore were not acting against their own interests. It also upheld the conclusion that evidence corroborating a leniency statement does not have to be contemporaneous documentation but can comprise other statements made with a view to obtaining leniency: para 191.

The General Court confirmed that where an alleged cartel includes an exchange of commercially sensitive information, it is necessary that the recipient of the information should be active on the cartelised market, such that there is potential for that recipient to modify its behaviour as a result of receiving the information, in order for the exchange to breach Article 101: Case T-380/10 *Wabco Europe v Commission (Bathroom Fittings)*, EU:T:2013:449, [2014] 4 CMLR 4, at paras 79 and 98–99; and Joined Cases T-379&381/10 *Keramag Keramische Werke and Others (Bathroom Fittings) v Commission*, EU:T:2013:457, [2014] 4 CMLR 3, at paras 92 and 221 (on further appeal, Case C-613/13P, not yet decided). The General Court distinguished its judgment in Joined Cases T-456&457/05 *Gütermann and Zwicky v Commission* [2010] ECR II-1443, upon which the Commission had relied, which it held would apply to a disclosure of commercially sensitive information with a view to restricting competition in the market on which the recipient of the information is active, by a disclosing party that is not itself active on that market, whereas in the decision under appeal, COMP/39092 *Bathroom Fittings*, decision of 23 June 2010, the Commission had (as the Court held, wrongly) found that the purpose of the disclosure was to restrict competition in a market on which the disclosing party was active but the recipient was not.

In the UK, the cartel offence in section 188 of the Enterprise Act 2002 has been amended by the Enterprise and Regulatory Reform Act 2013 which entered into force in April 2014.

Chapter 6: Non-Covert Horizontal Cooperation

The discussion in the main text of the Commission's decision in *Bananas* should be read alongside the General Court's judgments in Cases T-587/08 *Fresh Del Monte Produce v*

Commission, EU:T:2013:129, [2013] 4 CMLR 30; and T-588/08 *Dole Food Company v Commission*, EU:T:2013:130, [2013] 4 CMLR 31, which uphold the Commission's analysis on liability (further appeals dismissed in Joined Cases C-293&294/13P *Fresh Del Monte Produce*, EU:C:2015:416, [2015] 5 CMLR 513, and Case C-286/13P *Dole Food Company v Commission*, EU:C:2015:184, [2015] 4 CMLR 967).

On the concept of unlawful 'information exchanges', as noted above in respect of Chapter 2, the Court of Justice in C-455/11P *Solvay v Commission*, EU:C:2013:796, [2014] 4 CMLR 581, at paras 39 et seq, held that in a highly concentrated oligopolistic market, the exchange of commercial information between competitors will itself allow operators to know the market positions and strategies of their competitors, and the exchange of such information in preparation for an anti-competitive agreement therefore suffices to prove the existence of a concerted practice. In addition, as noted above in respect of Chapter 5, the General Court held in Case T-380/10 *Wabco Europe v Commission (Bathroom Fittings)*, EU:T:2013:449, [2014] 4 CMLR 4, at paras 79 and 98–99; and Joined Cases T-379&381/10 *Keramag Keramische Werke and Others (Bathroom Fittings) v Commission*, EU:T:2013:457, [2014] 4 CMLR 3, at paras 92 and 221 (on further appeal, Case C-613/13P, not yet decided), that there will only be a breach of Article 101 where the recipient of the information is active on the relevant market.

In the UK, the Competition Appeal Tribunal judgment in *Tesco v OFT* [2012] CAT 31 discusses the state of mind required to satisfy the test laid down by the Court of Appeal in *Argos, Littlewoods v OFT and JJB v OFT* [2006] EWCA Civ 1318, for unlawful 'hub and spoke' arrangements.

On 6 May 2015 the Commission launched an inquiry into the e-commerce sector: see Press Release IP/15/4921 (6 May 2015). A preliminary report is expected in mid-2016, and the final report in the first quarter of 2017.

(i) Banking and payments services

There have been a number of developments in the banking and payments services sector, discussed in section 9(b) of Chapter 6.

A number of legislative measures have been adopted in order to regulate the sector. Regulation 260/2012 establishing technical and business requirements for credit transfers and direct debits in euros and amending Regulation 924/2009, OJ 2012 L94/22, was adopted on 12 March 2012 and requires a move to the new Single Euro Payment Area systems established by the European Payments Council. The EU has also adopted Directive 2015/2366 on Payment Services, OJ 2015 L337/35, and Regulation 2015/751 on Interchange Fees for Card-Based Payment Transactions, OJ 2015 L123/1, which includes a cap on interchange fees.

On the application of Article 101 to the sector, the Commission settled with eight undertakings for their participation in cartels in the markets for financial derivatives, through the setting of benchmark interest rates for interest rate derivative trading, and imposed fines totalling €1.71 billion: COMP/39861 *Yen Interest Rate Derivatives ('YIRD')*, decision of 4 December 2013. On 4 February 2015 it issued a decision that another undertaking, which provides broker services, had facilitated six of the seven infringements: COMP/39861 *Yen Interest Rate Derivatives ('YIRD')*, decision of 4 February 2015. In respect of the manipulation of Swiss franc interest rates, it settled with two undertakings in COMP/39924 *Swiss Franc Interest Rate Derivatives (CHF LIBOR)*, decision of 21 October 2014, and with four undertakings in COMP/39924 *Swiss Franc Interest Rate Derivatives (Bid Ask Spread Infringement)*, decision of 21 October 2014. At the time of writing, a number of other investigations are also ongoing, including COMP/39745 *CDS – Information Market* in which a statement of objections has been issued (Press Release IP/613/630 (1 July 2013)); and COMP/39730 *CDS – Clearing*.

On MIFs in particular, in addition to the Court of Justice's judgments in Case C-67/13P *Groupement des cartes bancaires v Commission*, EU:C:2014:2202; and Case C-382/12P *MasterCard*, EU:C:2014:2201, referred to above, the Commission has accepted commitments from Visa Europe regarding its MIFs on consumer credit card transactions: COMP/39398 *Visa MIF*, decision of 26 February 2014. This follows its earlier decision on 8 December 2010 accepting commitments in respect of Visa Europe's MIFs on consumer debit card transactions. In particular, Visa Europe has agreed to cap its credit card MIFs at 0.3 per cent for all consumer credit card transactions in the EEA where Visa Europe sets the rate. This level is the same as that to which MasterCard undertook to reduce its fees, pending its appeal against the decision in COMP/34579 *MasterCard*, decision of 19 December 2007. It represents a reduction of 40–60 per cent of Visa Europe's MIFs. The French Autorité de la Concurrence has also accepted commitments by both Visa and Mastercard to reduce the level of their fees in France on payments/withdrawals on their Visa and MasterCard 'only' cards (ie those outside the Cartes Bancaires system): Decision 13-D-17 of 20 September 2013 (MasterCard), and Decision 13-D-18 of 20 September 2013 (Visa); also ECN Brief 05/2013, p7. The Polish Court of Competition and Consumer Protection has upheld a decision that the Visa and MasterCard systems breach national and EU competition law: ECN Brief 05/2013, p13.

At the time of writing, the Commission's proceedings are ongoing in respect of the international inter-bank fees applied to transactions by card holders from outside the EEA at merchants within the EEA by Visa Inc (see COMP/39398 *Visa MIF*); and in respect of the rules on cross-border acquiring, and international inter-bank fees applied to transactions by card holders from outside the EEA at merchants within the EEA, by MasterCard (see COMP/40049 *MasterCard II*; a statement of objections was sent on 9 July 2015: see Press Release IP/15/5323 (9 July 2015)).

Chapter 7: Vertical Agreements Affecting Distribution or Supply

On the issue of sales by a distributor via the internet, the Irish High Court in *SRI Apparel v Revolution Workwear and others* [2013] IEHC 289 held that the use by a distributor of the website Amazon was active selling rather than passive, and that an agreement to restrict such activity was within the scope of Article 4(b)(i) of the Vertical Block Exemption. In the UK, the OFT concluded in its decision CE/9578-12 '*Roma-branded mobility scooters: prohibitions on online sales and online price advertising*', decision of 5 August 2013, that an agreement or concerted practice in which a manufacturer prevented the distributors in its selective distribution system from selling its products online, or advertising their prices online, was a restriction of competition by object.

The Commission has accepted commitments in COMP/39847 *E-books*, decision of 12 December 2012 (OJ 2012 C283/7) and of 25 July 2013 (OJ 2013 C378/25) from five publishing companies, and Apple, under which they have agreed to terminate their agency agreements, which the Commission considered in its preliminary assessment were entered into on a coordinated basis in order to implement a common strategy in the EEA. Under the commitments, the publishers are required to allow retailers full discretion to set their e-book prices for at least two years, and not to enter into most favoured nation clauses for five years. The Commission has opened a similar investigation into the arrangements between Amazon and publishers: COMP/40153 *E-book MFNs*, and Press Release IP/15/5166 (11 June 2015).

Chapter 8: Merger Control

(i) Legislation

The Commission has adopted a number of measures simplifying procedures under the Merger Regulation. Commission Implementing Regulation 1269/2013 amends the Implementing Regulation, and includes a revised Form CO, Short Form, and Form RS (OJ 2013 L336/1). The Notice on a simplified procedure for treatment of certain concentrations under Council Regulation (EC) No 139/2004 (OJ 2013 C366/5) revises the Simplified Procedures Notice. The most significant changes include revising the categories of cases in which the simplified procedure is available, and redefining what is considered to be an 'affected market'. The revised Form CO encourage parties voluntarily to submit a description of the data that each of the undertakings collects and holds in cases where a quantitative economic analysis of the affected markets is likely to be useful, and voluntarily to submit a list of any non-EEA competition authorities that are also reviewing the concentration in order to facilitate the Commission's discussions with those authorities.

(ii) European Court judgments

The General Court judgment in Case T-332/09 *Electrabel v Commission*, EU:T:2012:672, ruled for the first time on a Commission decision to impose a fine for implementing a concentration without prior notification and approval. The judgment in particular considers various factors said to bear upon the proportionality of the fine, and holds that the Commission was correct to conclude that a failure to notify is a serious infringement of EU merger law. The Court of Justice dismissed the further appeal, in Case C-84/13P *Electrabel v Commission*, EU:C:2014:2040, as partly inadmissible and partly unfounded.

The Court of Justice has handed down judgments in the parallel appeals in *Éditions Odile Jacob*, regarding the significance of warehousing arrangements for the clearance of concentrations, and the role of trustees in approving purchasers of divested assets. In Case C-551/10P *Éditions Odile Jacob v Commission*, EU:C:2012:681, [2013] 4 CMLR 11 the Court dismissed the appeal regarding the clearance of the concentration, and held that even if the General Court had erred (in Case T-279/04 *Éditions Odile Jacob v Commission*, [2010] ECR II-0185) in its conclusion that the transaction was within Article 3(5)(a) Merger Regulation, that did not bear upon whether the concentration was compatible with the common market, only upon whether the notification was late or the concentration implemented prematurely. In Cases C-553&554/10P *Commission v Éditions Odile Jacob*, EU:C:2012:682, [2013] 4 CMLR 55, the Court disagreed with Advocate General Mazák and upheld the General Court judgment (in Case T-452/04 *Éditions Odile Jacob v Commission* [2010] ECR II-4713) regarding the approval of a purchaser of the assets to be divested. The Court discusses the requirement for trustees to be independent, and confirms that any lack of independence does not need to be shown to have affected a trustee's choice of purchaser for its decision to be annulled.

On the significance of market shares in conducting a substantive appraisal, the General Court upheld the Commission's decision in M.6281 *Microsoft/Skype* (7 October 2011) clearing the concentration at Phase I, because notwithstanding the merged entity would have a combined market share of 80–90 per cent, and would lead to a very high degree of market concentration, the characteristics of the market were such that the merged entity would not have the ability significantly to impede competition on the market. The Court observed in particular that the market was characterised by short innovation cycles, in which large market shares could pass quickly, and that the Commission was right also to consider it relevant that the services were provided for free, such that any attempt to charge, or a failure to innovate, would be likely to lead to consumer switching in the absence of technical or economic constraints upon them doing so. It also upheld the Commission's assessment that the merger would not have conglomerate effects: Case T-79/12 *Cisco Systems and Messagenet v Commission*, EU:T:2013:635, paras 65–74.

(iii) Commission decisions

The Commission has issued two prohibition decisions since the main text was published: M.6570 *UPS/TNT Express* (30 January 2013) (on appeal, Case T-194/13 *United Parcel Service v Commission*, not yet decided); and M.6663 *Ryanair/Aer Lingus III* (27 February 2013) (on appeal, Case T-260/13 *Ryanair v Commission*, not yet decided).

It has accepted a failing firm defence in M.6360 *Nynas/Shell/Harburg* (2 September 2013); and M.6796 *Aegean/Olympic II* (9 October 2013).

On the Commission's jurisdiction, the decision in M.7217 *Facebook/Whatsapp* (3 October 2014) illustrates the operation of the relevant turnover thresholds. Facebook acquired Whatsapp for USD19 billion. However, because Whatsapp (which provides a free service in most Member States and does not sell advertising space) had a turnover that did not reach the €100 million threshold, the Commission found that it did not have jurisdiction to consider the merger. It was able to consider the transaction only by virtue of the parties requesting a referral under Article 4(5) of Merger Regulation.

Five significant decisions on the substantive appraisals of concentrations have been published: M.6690 *Syniverse/Mach* (29 May 2013); M.7047 *Microsoft/Nokia* (4 December 2013); M.6905 *INEOS/Solvay/JV* (8 May 2014); M.7009 *Holcim/Cemex West* (5 June 2014); and M.7332 *BSkyB/Sky Deutschland/Sky Italia* (11 September 2014). In M.6690 *Syniverse/Mach* (29 May 2013), the Commission considered a proposed merger between the largest and second largest operators in a number of markets for roaming technology services provided to telecommunications companies, such as data clearing and financial settlement, that would have created a dominant player with virtual monopoly market shares. The Commission considered detailed arguments from the parties that the relevant markets were characterised by contestable 'Bertrand' competition, such that the presence of only two players in the market did not lead to coordination and higher prices, and market shares and concentration levels should not be relied upon: see paras 211 et seq. The Commission did not agree that the markets were in fact contestable, and in particular concluded that the barriers to expansion that would be faced by smaller competitors in a post-merger situation were such that they would not be credible threats to the merged entity. It cleared the concentration after accepting commitments at Phase II to divest a significant part of Mach's assets in the EEA. The decision in M.7047 *Microsoft/Nokia* (4 December 2013) includes significant analyses of vertical effects. The Commission considered that any possible competition concerns that might arise from the conduct of Nokia following the transaction, which certain respondents were concerned would lead to the removal of various competitive constraints to which Nokia had previously been subject on the exploitation of its patent portfolio, were outside the scope of the Merger Regulation. Nokia's future conduct would be governed by Article 102, and by its obligation to license its standard essential patents ('SEPs') on fair, reasonable, and non-discriminatory ('FRAND') terms. The Commission did analyse the likely future conduct of Microsoft, as part of the merged entity, and concluded that Microsoft's upstream position would not be strengthened as a result of the merger, as it would not acquire any SEPs as a result of the transaction and its exposure to third party intellectual property rights would increase through its need to renew Nokia's existing licensing agreements on their expiry. M.6905 *INEOS/Solvay/JV* (8 May 2014), paras 702 et seq and Annex A, is an unusual example of the Commission being able to analyse likely effects, *ex ante*, by considering the effects which previous mergers in the same sector had had *ex post*. It used transaction data and costs and margins data to conduct a differences-in-differences analysis of INEOS' prices following two previous mergers in which it had participated, and concluded that INEOS had been able to increase its prices to a greater extent than its competitors following the second of those mergers. In M.7009 *Holcim/Cemex West* (5 June 2014) the Commission analysed whether coordinated effects were likely to arise as a result of the concentration. The market under consideration had already been cartelised in the past, and the Commission could not exclude that there was a degree of coordination in the markets today. It concluded however that the proposed merger would not itself have the effect of facilitating that coordination, or of making it more stable or more effective. In M.7332 *BSkyB/Sky Deutschland/Sky Italia* (11 September 2014), paras 130 et seq, the Commission considered potential conglomerate effects where the parties have market power in geographically neighbouring markets. It considered whether the concentration of parties with significant market power in the UK and Ireland, Germany and Austria, and Italy, respectively, could increase BSkyB's negotiating power in relation to licensors of audio-visual content and TV channel suppliers, by combining negotiations and contracts in different EEA territories; or could result in other distributors being *de facto* cut out of the negotiation process for key content.

On remedies, two decisions are of particular interest. In M.7275 *Novartis/ Glaxosmithkline Oncology Business* (28 January 2015), paras 285 et seq, the Commission accepted a structural remedy designed to accommodate third party contractual rights. The divestment assets consisted primarily of two of Novartis' pipeline pharmaceutical products, one of which was owned by a third party, Array, and was being developed by Novartis under an exclusive licence. Under the commitments, Novartis agreed to return the licence to Array; to divest the other product also to it; and to oblige Array to negotiate an agreement with a fourth party, to be approved by the Commission, for the development and commercialisation of the products failing which a licence to develop and commercialise the products would be assigned to a divestiture trustee for sale. In parallel, Novartis and Array entered into a contractual agreement mirroring the commitments. In M.7252 *Holcim/ Lafarge* (15 December 2014), a divestiture remedy was required, and in view of the scale of the business to be divested the Commission accepted that divestiture could take place either by selling the divestiture business to an approved purchaser in the conventional manner, or by selling at least 50 per cent of the shares in the business to an approved purchaser with the balance being sold through capital markets.

(iv) National judgments

On the reference by the UK OFT to the Competition Commission of Ryanair's acquisition of a minority shareholding in Aer Lingus, referred to in the main text, the Competition Commission decided in *Ryanair Holdings and Aer Lingus Group*, decision of 28 August 2013, that the acquisition of a minority shareholding in Aer Lingus had led, or might be expected to lead, to a substantial lessening of competition in the markets for air passenger services between Great Britain and the Republic of Ireland, and ordered partial divestiture; and in *Ryanair Holdings v Competition and Markets Authority* [2014] CAT 3 the Competition Appeal Tribunal dismissed an application for review of that decision. In particular, it held that ordering divestiture, while Ryanair's appeal to the General Court was pending (Case T-260/13 *Ryanair v Commission*, appeal subsequently withdrawn) against M.6663 *Ryanair/ Aer Lingus III* (27 February 2013), did not breach the duty of sincere cooperation under Article 4(3) TEU as the decision concerned Ryanair's existing minority shareholding rather than the proposed acquisition that was under consideration by the European Commission and was at that time before the General Court.

Chapter 9: Intellectual Property Rights

The politically charged issue of moving towards harmonisation of the laws governing intellectual property rights took a step forward in Cases C-274&295/11 *Spain & Italy v Council*, EU:C:2013:240, [2013] 3 CMLR 623, in which the Court of Justice upheld the legality of the Council's decision authorising the use of the enhanced cooperation procedure in Article 20 TEU in the area of the creation of a unitary patent (Council Decision 2011/167/EU of 10 March 2011).

The General Court's judgments in the appeals against the Commission's *CISAC* decision, and the Court of Justice's judgment in Case C-457/10P *AstraZeneca*, EU:C:2012:770, [2013] 4 CMLR 233, discussed above are particularly significant in respect of the application of competition law to intellectual property rights.

The Court of Justice has handed down a number of significant judgments on the interpretation of the Copyright Directive. On the concept of 'communication to the public' in Article 3(1), it has held that this is limited to situations where the public is not present at the place where the performance or direct presentation takes place (Case C-283/10 *Circul Globus București*, EU:C:2011:772, [2011] ECR I-12031). It has considered the application of Article 3(1) to a company that captures television broadcasts and retransmits them via the internet in real time, holding that the original broadcast does not exhaust the right to communicate to the public, and retransmission via the internet constitutes a 'communication to the public' within Article 3(1) that the right holder is entitled to prohibit (Case C-607/11 *ITV Broadcasting and others*, EU:C:2013:147, [2013] 3 CMLR 1). It has also confirmed that providing hyperlinks to another website which contains protected works is an act of 'communication' within the scope of the Directive; however, if that other website can be accessed without restriction by members of the public, then the provision of a hyperlink is not a new communication of the protected works that the rights holder is entitled to prohibit, because the person providing the hyperlink is a member of the public to whom the works have already been communicated by the first website (Case C-466/12 *Svensson v Retriever Sverige*, EU:C:2014:76). On distribution rights, the Court has clarified that where goods are sold in a Member State through an online sales website, from a country outside the EU where the intellectual property right holder's rights are not protected, that sale is a form of 'distribution to the public' under Article 4 of the Copyright Directive, or 'use in the course of trade' under Article 5 of the Trademark Directive. It is not necessary to show that the goods were offered for sale, or advertised, to consumers of that Member State (Case C-98/13 *Blomqvist v Rolex*, EU:C:2014:55). Similarly, there is an infringement of the right of exclusive distribution where a trader who does not hold the copyright engages in a commercial act, such as offering for sale or advertising, in the territory of the Member State in which works are protected and it is not necessary that there should be a transfer of ownership to a purchaser on the basis of an offer for sale, in order for the rights holder's rights to be infringed (Case C-516/13 *Dimensione Direct Sales v Knoll International*, EU:C:2015:315, paras 26 et seq).

Following the pharmaceutical sector inquiry, the Commission has continued to monitor patent settlements between originator and generics companies, and it published its Third Report of 25 July 2012 covering the period January to December 2011, Fourth Report of 9 December 2013 covering the period January to December 2012, and Fifth Report of 5 December 2014 covering the period January to December 2013. It has issued decisions in COMP/39226 *Lundbeck* (Press Release IP/13/563 (19 June 2013)) (on appeal, Cases T-460/13, etc, not yet decided); COMP/39685 *Johnson & Johnson and Novartis* (Press Release IP/13/1233 (10 December 2013); and COMP/39612 *Perindopril (Servier)* (Press Release IP/14/799 (9 July 2014)) (on appeal, Case T-691/14, not yet decided). In France, the Autorité de la concurrence has taken a number of decisions against originator companies for adopting strategies of denigrating their generic competitors. On 14 May 2013 it fined Sanofi-Aventis €40.6 million for abuse of dominance by denigrating the generic versions of clopidogrel, an anti-platelet medication used to prevent relapses of serious cardiovascular diseases: Decision 13-D-11 of 14 May 2013 (see also ECN Brief 03/2013, p8); appeal to the Cour d'Appel de Paris dismissed, 18 December 2014. On 19 December 2013 it fined Schering-Plough €15.3 million for abuse of dominance by denigrating the generic version of buprenorphine, used to treat opiate addiction: Decision 13-D-21 of December 2013 (see also ECN Brief

01/2014, p5); appeal to the Cour d'Appel de Paris dismissed, 26 May 2015. It is still investigating a possible breach in respect of fentanyl, an analgesic.

In the area of standards essential patents ('SEPs'), the Court of Justice in Case C-170/13 *Huawei v ZTE*, EU:C:2015:477 confirmed that a refusal by the proprietor of a SEP to grant a licence on fair, reasonable, and non-discriminatory ('FRAND') terms, in circumstances where the patent has acquired SEP status as a result of the proprietor having irrevocably undertaken to the standard-setting body that it will license on FRAND terms, may in principle be contrary to Article 102: para 53. The proprietor's undertaking does not, however, deprive it of its right to bring an action before the courts of a Member State to enforce its patent, so long as it complies with specific requirements, set out in detail by the Court, when it does so. These are to notify the alleged infringer of the SEP and its breach; to make a specific, written offer of a licence on FRAND terms specifying the royalty and the way in which it has been calculated. The alleged infringer must respond in good faith, and without delay. If it does not accept the offer, it must promptly make a written counter-offer that corresponds to FRAND terms, and if its counter-offer is rejected and it is using the teachings of the SEP then from the point of rejection it must provide appropriate security. The parties may agree to submit the determination of the amount of the royalty to a third party. If the proprietor has complied with the requirements incumbent upon it, or if the alleged infringer has failed to comply with the requirements incumbent upon it, then it is not an abuse of the proprietor's dominant position for it to commence litigation to enforce its patent. See also the Commission's investigation into alleged abusive conduct in relation to IPR used in international telecoms standards. In COMP/39985 *Motorola – enforcement of ETSI standards essential patents*, decision of 29 April 2014 (Press Release IP/14/489 (29 April 2014)) the Commission found that Motorola breached Article 102 by seeking an injunction in Germany against Apple for breach of its SEPs, in circumstances where it had committed to license on FRAND terms, and where Apple was willing to enter into a licence agreement and to be bound by a determination by the German Court of the FRAND terms. However, in view of the novelty of the infringement finding, no fine has been imposed. The Commission accepted commitments from Samsung in COMP/39939 *Samsung – enforcement of ETSI standards essential patents*, decision of 29 April 2014. In its preliminary assessment, the Commission considered that Samsung had infringed Article 102 by seeking injunctions against Apple in several Member States to enforce its SEPs, where Samsung had committed to license on FRAND terms. The Commission has accepted commitments under which Samsung agrees, in essence, for a period of five years not to seek an injunction before any court or tribunal in the EEA for infringement of its SEPs implemented in mobile devices against a potential licensee that agrees to, and complies with, a particular framework set out in the commitments decision for determining the terms of a licence.

In the UK, the High Court in *Unwired Planet International v Huawei and others* [2015] EWHC 2097 (Pat) considered the application of Article 101 to an agreement transferring SEP rights. It struck out a defence to an infringement action in which it had been contended that the agreement to transfer the SEPs to Unwired Planet, a 'patent assertion entity', was void under Article 101 for failing fully and effectively to confer on potential licensees the right to obtain from the transferee a licence on FRAND terms; or for failing to transfer the FRAND obligation previously undertaken by the transferor, as opposed to requiring the transferee to offer a new FRAND undertaking (meaning, in particular, that the transferee would not need to have regard to the terms on which the transferor had hitherto licensed commercial parties under those patents, as part of the obligation to offer terms that are non-discriminatory). The Court refused to strike out two further defences under Article 101. Under the first, Samsung argued that the agreement to transfer the SEPs was void under Article 101 as it permitted the transferor to retain a substantial share in the licensing revenue generated by the transferee and to achieve higher royalties. Under the second, the agreement was alleged to be unlawful and void as it contained payment terms encouraging or requiring the transferee to charge higher royalties. The decision to strike out the first defence is on appeal to the Court of Appeal, not yet decided.

On 21 March 2014, the Commission adopted Regulation 316/2014 on the application of Article 101(3) TFEU to categories of technology transfer agreement (OJ 2014 L93/17), and replacement guidelines (OJ 2014 C89/3). These apply from 1 May 2014.

Chapter 10: Article 102

In addition to the decisions discussed in connection with Chapter 9, above, also of significance in respect of the interaction between Article 102 and intellectual property rights is the Court of Justice judgment in Case C-457/10P *AstraZeneca*, EU:C:2012:770, [2013] 4 CMLR 233. On the issue of dominance, the Court discusses the arguments raised as to the relevance of a patent holder's first-mover status, its financial resources, and its intellectual property rights, as well as the relevance of the powers of the State as a monopsonist purchaser and as a price regulator. On the issue of abuse, the Court considers the circumstances in which an undertaking abuses its dominant position by making objectively wrong representations to patent offices. While it leaves open the question of where the line should be drawn between abusive and non-abusive behaviour, it confirms that deliberately to mislead patent authorities is abusive, whereas innocently to misrepresent is not, provided that the representations are withdrawn immediately upon the undertaking realising that they are not correct.

On rebate arrangements, the General Court in Case T-286/09 *Intel v Commission*, EU:T:2014:547, [2014] 5 CMLR 270 distinguished three types of rebates, all of which it held require different analysis under Article 102: (a) Quantity rebates: rebates linked solely to the volume of purchases made from the dominant undertaking, which are presumed to be linked to efficiencies and economies of scale and are generally considered not to have foreclosure effects: para 75; (b) Exclusivity rebates: rebates which are conditional upon the purchaser obtaining all, or most, of its requirements from the dominant undertaking. These are designed to prevent customers from obtaining their supplies from competing producers and are by their very nature capable of restricting competition. It is not necessary to consider the individual circumstances of the case to determine whether they have a foreclosure effect: paras 76 et seq. It is also not necessary to consider whether there might be other reasons for the purchaser obtaining all, or most, of its requirements from the dominant undertaking; the relevant question is whether the level of the rebates is conditional upon exclusivity: eg paras 539 et seq; and (c) Non-exclusive rebates, which may nonetheless have loyalty-inducing effects: rebates which are granted on a basis other than volume of purchases, or exclusivity. These require a consideration of all the circumstances, in particular the criteria for determining whether the rebate is granted, to analyse whether they tend to remove or restrict the buyer's freedom to choose his supplier, to bar competitors from accessing the market, or to strengthen the supplier's dominant position: paras 78 et seq. The General Court held that Intel's rebate arrangements were exclusivity arrangements, and that it was therefore not necessary to consider their effects. It went on, however, to conclude that even if it were necessary to consider the effects of the rebates in question, it would still not be necessary to do so by means of an 'as efficient competitor' or 'AEC' test. An AEC test would establish whether access to the market had been made impossible by the conduct in question, but it would not rule out the possibility that it had been made more difficult and it would not therefore rule out that there had been a foreclosure effect: paras 142 et seq. The Court distinguished the case law requiring an analysis of the circumstances of the case, and the application of an AEC test, as being concerned with pricing practices: paras 99 and 152 respectively. It also held that the Guidance on the Commission's enforcement priorities in applying Article 82 of the EC Treaty to abusive exclusionary conduct by dominant undertakings, OJ 2009 C45/7, sets priorities for the Commission's future enforcement activities; it does not apply to proceedings that had already been initiated before it was published, even if it was published prior to the adoption of the contested decision in those proceedings. The Guidance therefore did not affect its conclusion that it was not necessary for the Commission to conduct an AEC test: paras 154–156. On further appeal, Case C-413/14P, not yet decided.

In the UK, the Competition Appeal Tribunal has considered how to quantify damages caused by a margin squeeze in *Albion Water v Dŵr Cymru's Cyfyngedig* [2013] CAT 6. The Tribunal rejected Dŵr Cymru's argument that it had to determine the highest price that could lawfully have been charged, and held that a counterfactual should be constructed using a figure in the middle of the range of potential lawful prices.

(i) *Refusal to supply*

The High Court of England and Wales has considered a number of cases regarding refusal to supply. On the issue of refusal to satisfy demand for parallel trade, the High Court in *Chemistree Homecare v Abbvie* [2013] EWHC 264 (Ch) considered the test laid down in Cases C-468/06, etc, *Sot Lelos kai Sia v GlaxoSmithKline* [2008] ECR I-7139 of whether orders are 'ordinary'. It held that where a pharmaceutical company organises its business around supplying only to retailers, orders placed by a customer for the undisclosed purpose of reselling the product on the wholesale market are not ordinary (upheld on other grounds by the Court of Appeal, *Chemistree Homecare v Abbvie* [2013] EWCA Civ 1338, concluding that dominance could not be established). More generally, in *Arriva the Shires v London Luton Airport* [2014] EWHC 64 (Ch), the High Court held that a refusal to supply can be an abuse even in circumstances where the dominant undertaking is neither present in the downstream market, nor restricting the ability of its upstream competitors to access a downstream market. It considered that the General Court judgment in Case T-128/98 *Aéroports de Paris v Commission* [2000] ECR II-3929 at para 173 establishes that it is not necessary for a dominant undertaking to obtain a commercial benefit from its conduct in order for that conduct to be considered abusive, and that that case is not confined to discriminatory pricing complaints. In the alternative, the Court held that if it did have to be shown that the dominant undertaking obtained a commercial benefit, that benefit need not be obtained as a result of the dominant undertaking being present on the downstream market. It could be obtained from the dominant undertaking having an interest in the downstream market, such as, in that case, by it receiving revenues from the grant of an exclusive right to downstream operators. The Court concluded that, in that case, granting an exclusive right to access the Luton airport bus station, in order to operate coach journeys between Luton Airport and London, for a period of seven years was anti-competitive and distorted competition between coach operators. The grant of that right was analogous to the grant considered by the European Commission in Case COMP/38173 *Joint Selling of the media rights for the FA Premier League*, decision of 22 March 2006.

(ii) *Other forms of abuse*

In addition to the recent decisions against pharmaceutical companies for adopting strategies to denigrate generic competitors, discussed in connection with Chapter 9, above, the French Autorité de la concurrence has fined the electricity provider EDF for abuse of dominance by allowing one of its subsidiaries, operating in the emerging market for photovoltaic solar power, to market its services under the EDF brand (including using a similar logo and trademark to EDF) and using the EDF customer database to access customers for marketing purposes. Competitors were adversely affected, because consumers confused the subsidiary with EDF itself, and competitors could not replicate the advantages that the subsidiary enjoyed. Decision 13-D-20 of 17 December 2013; appeal to the Cour d'Appel de Paris dismissed, 9 April 2014 (also ECN Brief 01/2014, p7).

Chapter 11: The Competition Rules and the Acts of Member States

The Court of Justice in Case C-553/12P *Commission v DEI*, EU:C:2014:2083, [2014] 5 CMLR 945 has overturned the General Court's *Greek Lignite* judgment (Case T-169/08 *DEI v Commission*, EU:T:2012:448). In order to establish an infringement of Article 106 in conjunction with Article 102 it is not necessary for the Commission to show that a former monopolistic undertaking, which continues to hold a dominant position, has in fact abused that dominant position. An infringement will arise where inequality of opportunity between operators, and thus distorted competition, arises as a result of a State measure.

On Article 106(2), in a number of judgments the General Court has held that an analysis of the proportionality of the rights granted must be conducted. In Joined Cases T-533/10&151/11 *DTS and Telfónica v Commission*, EU:T:2014:629 it held that the rights granted will fall outside Article 106(2) if they 'affect trade and competition significantly and to an extent which is manifestly disproportionate to the objectives pursued by the Member States'. On further appeal, Case C-449/14P, not yet decided. Further, in Case T-57/11 *Castelnou Energía v Commission* EU:T:2014:1021, at paras 163–164 it held that where Article 106(2) is relied on in respect of a measure which is State aid, the measure will by definition give rise to distortions, and it can only be considered to fall outside of Article 106(2) therefore where the distortions in question are 'substantially and manifestly disproportionate'.

The Commission has issued a Staff Working Document on the interaction between Article 106(2), State aid and public procurement *'Guide to the application of the European Union rules on state aid, public procurement and the internal market to services of general economic interest, and in particular to social services of general interest'*.

Chapter 12: Sectoral Regimes

(i) Electronic communications

In the field of electronic communications, the Court of Justice has confirmed that Member States may lawfully impose spectrum use renewal fees under the Authorisation Directive (Case C-375/11 *Belgacom v Belgium*, EU:C:2013:185, [2013] 3 CMLR 185), and that an undertaking is 'affected' by a NRA decision, for the purposes of Article 4(1) of the Framework Directive, in circumstances where it provides electronic communications networks or services; is a competitor of the undertaking which is party to a procedure for the authorisation of a transfer of rights to use radio frequencies and the addressee of the decision; and its position in the market is likely to be impacted by the decision (Case C-282/13 *T-Mobile Austria v Telefon-Kontrol-Kommission*, EU:C:2015:24). The

Commission has considered a number of significant mergers, including a full-function JV established by three of the leading UK MNOs (M.6314 *Telefónica UK/Vodafone UK/EE/JV* (4 September 2012), creating a JV to operate in the nascent 'mCommerce' sector). In the UK, in *Recall Support Services and others v Secretary of State for Culture, Media and Sport* [2013] EWHC 3091 (Ch), the High Court held that the UK's decision to impose a specific licence requirement, going beyond a general authorisation, on the commercial provision of communications services to multiple users through GSM gateway devices, was justified on grounds of public security.

(ii) Energy

In the electricity sector, the Commission has accepted commitments in COMP/39727 *CEZ* that include CEZ divesting itself of generation capacity. It has taken two infringement decisions against national power exchanges. In COMP/39984 *OPCOM/Romanian Power Exchange*, decision of 5 March 2014, it fined the Romanian Power Exchange, OPCOM, for breaching Article 102 by requiring electricity traders to be VAT registered in Romania in order to participate in the Exchange. The Commission considered that this created an artificial barrier to entry for non-Romanian EU traders, and reduced liquidity on the Romanian wholesale electricity market. See Press Release IP/14/214 (5 March 2014). In COMP/39952 *Power Exchanges*, decision of 5 March 2014, it fined two European spot power exchanges, EPEX Spot and Nord Pool Spot, for breaching Article 101 by entering into a market allocation agreement along the lines of national boundaries. It has also sent a number of statements of objection to undertakings operating in the sector in Eastern Europe: COMP/39816 *Upstream gas supplies in Central and Eastern Europe*, Press Release IP/15/4828 (22 April 2015); and COMP/39767 *BEH Electricity*, Press Release IP/14/922 (12 August 2014).

In the gas sector, the High Court of Ireland has considered the methodology by which tariffs for the use of, and access to, the transmission system and pipeline network are to be calculated. In *Shannon LNG and another v Commission for Energy Regulation and others* [2013] IEHC 568, the Court held that the Third Gas Directive does not require that an 'interconnector' be treated separately from the transmission pipeline for tariff-setting purposes; nor does Article 13 of that Directive (which states that tariffs must 'reflect actual costs incurred') require that a tariff be set by reference to specific parts of the infrastructure, rather than by reference to the revenue required to maintain, operate and develop the transmission system as a whole. The Court also rejected a complaint that the methodology adopted by the regulator would lead to the transmission operator abusing its dominant position contrary to Article 102, and would constitute an unlawful State aid contrary to Article 106. No actual tariffs had yet been set, so it could not be said that the regulator's methodology would necessarily bring about either abusive conduct or an advantage to the transmission operator.

(iii) Postal services

In the postal sector, the General Court upheld the Commission's decision in COMP/39562 *Slovakian postal legislation relating to hybrid mail services*, decision of 7 October 2008, in Case T-556/08 *Slovenská pošta v Commission*, EU:T:2015:189, [2015] 4 CMLR 1024. It confirmed the Commission's conclusion that hybrid mail services in Slovakia was a separate product market from traditional postal services, and that the calculations put forward for the costs of providing a universal service in Slovakia did not justify the re-monopolisation of the hybrid mail services. On further appeal, Case C-293/15P, not yet decided.

The Commission prohibited the proposed merger in M.6570 *UPS/TNT Express* (30 January 2013).

(iv) Agriculture

On 17 December 2013, the Parliament and Council adopted Regulation 1308/2013 establishing a common organisation of the markets in agricultural products, OJ 2013 L347/671, replacing Regulation 1234/2007.

(v) Transport

In the railway transport sector, Directive 2012/34/EU establishing a single European railway area was adopted on 21 November 2012.

In the maritime transport sector, the Commission has not renewed the Maritime Transport Guidelines, which expired on 26 September 2013. It has extended the maritime consortia block exemption regulation (Regulation 906/2009 (OJ 2009 L256/31)), which expired on 25 April 2015, for a further five years to April 2020: Press Release IP/14/717 (24 June 2014).

On the application of Article 102 to the sector, the Commission has accepted commitments from Deutsche Bahn in COMP/39678 *Deutsche Bahn I*, decision of 18 December 2013, regarding the pricing structure adopted by companies in its group for supplying traction current, which is used to power locomotives, which the Commission considered may have restricted access to the markets for the provision of rail freight and long-distance passenger transport services in Germany by imposing a margin squeeze. Deutsche Bahn is the sole owner of the specific electricity grid required to distribute the traction current, and operates downstream rail services. It has agreed to alter its pricing structure, so that the discounts it offers can in practice be obtained by companies other than its own downstream entities.

Chapter 13: Enforcement and Procedure

(i) Impact of the Charter on Fundamental Rights

The impact of the entry into force of the Charter on Fundamental Rights ('the Charter'), following the Lisbon Treaty, has been reflected in the judgments handed down in appeals raising procedural questions.

A number of cases have considered the application of Articles 41 and 47 of the Charter in particular: see, for example, Case C-501/11P *Schindler v Commission (Elevators and Escalators)*, EU:C:2013:522, [2013] 5 CMLR 39 (the imposition of fines by the Commission, rather than by a court, is compatible with Article 47); Case C-439/11P *Ziegler v Commission*, EU:C:2013:513, [2013] 5 CMLR 36 (it is the principle of good administration in Article 41 that applies to administrative proceedings before the Commission); Case T-286/09 *Intel v Commission*, EU:T:2014:547, [2014] 5 CMLR 270 (on the scope of the Commission's obligation, under Article 41, to accede to requests by undertakings to obtain additional documents during the course of its investigation, and to record the information it receives during meetings or telephone conversations in the course of its investigation); and Case C-199/11 *Europese Gemeenschap v Otis*, EU:C:2012:684, [2013] 4 CMLR 141 (there is no breach of Article 47 if the Commission brings a civil action in a Member State to seek to recover the damages it has itself suffered as a result of a cartel). In addition, in Joined Cases C-239/11P, etc, *Siemens v Commission (Gas Insulated Switchgear)*, EU:C:2013:866, [2014] 4 CMLR 606, the Court of Justice confirmed that the Commission's, and the General Court's, discretion whether to require the attendance of a witness for examination is compatible with the right to a fair hearing and Article 6(3)(d) of the ECHR, and that it is for an applicant to apply for witnesses to be examined; the General Court cannot be criticised for not having heard a witness of its own motion.

(ii) *Powers of investigation*

On powers of investigation under Article 18 of Regulation 1/2003, the General Court largely upheld the Commission decision in Case COMP/39520 *Cement and related products*, decision of 30 March 2011, ordering the provision of information under Article 18(3) by various cement producers. In Case T-306/11 *Schwenk Zement v Commission*, EU:T:2014:123 it confirmed that it must be proportionate for the Commission to take a decision under Article 18(3) rather than to make a request under Article 18(2): para 49; but in that case held that the use of Article 18(3) had been proportionate (on further appeal, Case C-248/14P *Schwenk Zement v Commission*, not yet decided). In Case T-296/11 *Cementos Portland Valderrivas v Commission*, EU:T:2014:121, at the applicant's request, the General Court adopted measures of inquiry and reviewed the evidence in the Commission's possession on which it had based its decision to conduct an investigation. The Court held that the Commission must be in possession of sufficiently serious evidence, consistent with the suspicion of an infringement, to justify adopting a decision under Article 18(3), and if an applicant puts forward factors that cast doubt on the sufficiently serious nature of the evidence then the General Court will examine the evidence on review: paras 40 et seq. On the facts of that case, the Court held that the Commission's evidence was consistent with a reasonable suspicion of infringement, and upheld the decision. The General Court also held in *Schwenk* that the time limit that the Commission imposes for compliance with a decision under Article 18(3) must be adequate to allow the undertaking to ensure that the information it provides is accurate, complete and not misleading: para 73. In that case, a time limit of two weeks for a response to a certain set of questions was disproportionately short, and the decision was annulled to that extent.

The General Court also considered detailed complaints about the Commission's conduct of its investigation in Case T-286/09 *Intel v Commission*, EU:T:2014:547, [2014] 5 CMLR 270. In response to a complaint that the Commission had failed to obtain documents that the undertaking alleged would have been exculpatory, the Court held that in principle it is for the Commission to decide how it wishes to conduct the investigation, what documents it must collect in order to have a sufficiently complete picture of the case, and when the documents it has gathered are sufficient. It is not appropriate to impose on the Commission an obligation to obtain as many documents as possible in order to ensure that it obtains all potentially exculpatory material. If an undertaking requests that the Commission obtain additional documents, the Commission has a margin of discretion in deciding whether to accede to it. However, Article 41 of the Charter entails a duty to examine carefully and impartially all aspects of the case. The General Court held that the Commission will be obliged to obtain documents at an undertaking's request in exceptional circumstances, and it outlined the conditions under which such an obligation will arise: paras 340 et seq. In response to a complaint that the Commission had failed to make adequate records of voluntary interviews it had conducted, the Court held that the Commission has a discretion whether it conducts interviews on a voluntary basis, or under Article 19 of Regulation 1/2003, and where it decides to conduct an interview on a voluntary basis the requirements of Article 3 of Regulation 773/2004 do not apply: paras 615 and 618. Article 41 of the Charter imposes on the Commission a duty to examine carefully and impartially all the relevant aspects of the individual case, but the existence, nature and extent of a duty to record the information the Commission receives during meetings or telephone conversations depends on the content of that information. It must establish adequate documentation, in the file to which the undertakings concerned have access, on the essential aspects of the investigation including all information 'of a certain importance and which bears an objective link with the subject-matter of an investigation, irrespective of whether it is incriminating or exculpatory': para 620. The General Court also held that if there had been an irregularity, in the circumstances of the case the criteria for determining whether the undertaking's rights of defence had been affected were the same as those for determining whether an applicant's rights of defence are affected by non-disclosure of documents on the file. Thus the applicant must adduce *prima facie* evidence that the Commission failed to record exculpatory evidence, which was at variance with the thrust of the documentary evidence on which the Commission relied or at least which sheds different light on it: paras 626–629.

On powers of inspection under Article 20 of Regulation 1/2003, and the review-ability of the Commission's exercise of those powers, in Case T-135/09 *Nexans and Nexans France v Commission*, EU:T:2012:596, [2013] 4 CMLR 195 the General Court held that Article 20(2) contains powers to take measures to implement inspection decisions, such as copying documents and asking representatives of the investigated undertaking for explanations of facts and documents, and that the exercise of one of these powers does not have binding legal effects, separate from the inspection decision. As such, the exercise of these powers cannot itself be the subject of an annulment application before the General Court, but can only be examined in the context of an appeal against an infringement decision under Article 101, or an appeal against a decision imposing a penalty for refusing to co-operate with the inspection. The appeal, on other grounds, was dismissed in Case C-37/13P *Nexans v Commission*, EU:C:2014:2030, [2014] 5 CMLR 642. In Case T-410/09 *Almamet v Commission*, EU:T:2012:676, [2013] 4 CMLR 788 the General Court further held that if the Commission has followed the procedures in Article 20 for gathering evidence, it is only the addressee from whom evidence has been gathered who can complain of irregularities in the way in which the process has been carried out.

In respect of Article 20(4), the General Court accepted in Joined Cases T-289/11, etc, *Deutsche Bahn and others v Commission*, EU:T:2013:404, that the exercise of the Commission's powers of inspection under Article 20(4) is a 'clear interference' with the right to respect for private and family life under Article 8 of the ECHR/Article 7 of the Charter, but held that the absence of a requirement for prior judicial authorisation does not render it a disproportionate interference (further appeal dismissed, Case C-583/13 *Deutsche Bahn v Commission* EU:C:2015:404, [2015] 5 CMLR 341, para 25). In Case T-402/13 *Orange v Commission*, EU:T:2014:991 the General Court held that although it will determine whether a decision to conduct an inspection is arbitrary in circumstances where an undertaking puts forward arguments liable to cast doubt on the reasonableness of grounds relied upon by the Commission, it can also conduct a review by examining the statement of reasons set out in the inspection decision and conclude that the decision was not arbitrary on the sole basis of those reasons: para 93. In that case, the Commission was entitled to adopt an inspection decision even though the French NCA had accepted commitments in respect of the conduct in question, because the Commission is not bound by the NCA decision, and because the NCA had not itself conducted an inspection but had only considered documents submitted voluntarily.

On refusal to submit to inspections ordered by decision, or producing the required records of a business in incomplete form, the General Court in Case T-272/12 *Energetický a průmyslový v Commission*, EU:T:2014:995 upheld the Commission's decision imposing a fine of €2.5 million on two Czech companies for negligently allowing an individual to access his email account after the Commission had requested it be blocked, and for intentionally diverting incoming emails to a server, during the course of the Commission's inspection. It was not necessary to show that the contents of the email accounts were deleted or manipulated, or that a back-up to the server had not taken place such that the contents of the account could not be verified: paras 39 et seq. Nor was it necessary to show that the diverted emails were not available on the server: paras 50–51. The Court also upheld the amount of the fine. It upheld the Commission's finding that a failure to render email accounts completely inaccessible to account holders is by its very nature a serious infringement of an undertaking's procedural obligations during an inspection. It is necessary to take into consideration the need to ensure a sufficient deterrent effect, and the deterrent effect is all the more important in respect of electronic files as they are much easier and quicker to manipulate, and inspectors do not know whether the electronic data to which they have access is complete and intact: para 108.

(iii) Formal Procedure Prior to an Adverse Decision

In Case T-27/10 *AC-Treuhand v Commission*, EU:T:2014:59, at paras 170 et seq, the General Court held that an undertaking should be notified at the preliminary investigation stage of the object and purpose of the Commission's investigation, in order to ensure that its ability to exercise its rights of defence at the *inter partes* stage is not compromised by the passage of time between the two stages. In that case, although AC-Treuhand had not been notified of the Commission's investigation into its role until a few weeks before the statement of objections was issued, it had received adequate notification of the object and purpose of the Commission's investigation at the preliminary investigation stage through receiving an information request under Article 18 of Regulation 1/2003. On further appeal, Case C-194/14P *AC-Treuhand v Commission*, not yet decided. In a separate appeal against the same decision, the General Court dismissed a complaint that the Commission notifying different undertakings of its investigation at different stages of the investigation breaches the principle of equal treatment: Case T-46/10 *Faci v Commission*, EU:T:2014:138, [2014] 4 CMLR 930, at para 148. On further appeal, Case C-291/14P, not yet decided.

In Case T-286/09 *Intel v Commission*, EU:T:2014:547, [2014] 5 CMLR 270, in response to a complaint that the Commission had failed to conduct a second oral hearing after issuing a supplementary statement of objections, and a letter of facts, the General Court held that the Commission is not required to hold a hearing on a supplementary statement of objections where the undertaking has not made a request within the timeframe stipulated by the Commission in accordance with Articles 10(2) and 12 of Regulation 773/2004, and that there is no right to a hearing under Article 12 of Regulation 773/2004 in respect of a letter of facts: paras 325–327. On further appeal, Case C-413/14P, not yet decided.

In Case T-47/10 *GEA Group v Commission*, EU:T:2015:506, [2015] 5 CMLR 617, paras 309 et seq the General Court dismissed a complaint that the undertaking's rights of defence had been breached by the six-year delay to the administrative proceedings which resulted from the dispute between it and the Commission over the seizure of documents. It found, however, that the Commission had breached the principle of equal treatment by reducing the fine imposed on all the undertakings, except the applicant, on account of the delay. The Commission's argument that the applicant was in an objectively different situation as it was responsible for the dispute was not compatible with the principle of effective judicial protection, and would deter undertakings from exercising their right to bring judicial proceedings while they were involved in an investigation by the Commission. On further appeal, Case C-515/15P, not yet decided.

There have also been a number of judgments concerning the publication of the Commission's decisions. The General Court has held that if the Commission accepts an undertaking's request for confidentiality, the Hearing Officer does not have power to reject it (Case T-462/15 *Pilkington v Commission*, EU:T:2015:508, para 31); and the Hearing Officer is not competent to hear objections to publication based on the principles of legitimate expectations or equal treatment (Case T-341/12 *Evonika Degussa v Commission*, EU:T:2015:51, para 44; on further appeal, Case C-162/51P, not yet decided). It has also held that publishing the parts of a decision which set out the facts constituting an infringement would not result in the communication to third parties of requests for leniency submitted by the applicant to the Commission, of minutes recording oral statements made by the applicant pursuant to the leniency programme, or of documents which the applicant voluntarily submitted to the Commission during the investigation. The Commission is entitled to publish such parts of its decisions, because of the public interest in knowing as fully as possible the reasons behind any Commission action; the interests of economic operators in knowing the sort of behaviour for which they are liable to be penalised; and the interest of persons harmed by the infringement in being informed of the details so that they can assert their right to compensation (Case T-341/12 *Evonika Degussa v Commission*, EU:T:2015:51, para 107; on further appeal, Case C-162/51P, not yet decided). Information identifying the infringing undertakings' customers can be published in circumstances where the undertakings themselves supplied each other with the identities of their customers as part of the infringement; where the market under consideration was characterised by a degree of transparency; and where that information was included in the decision as part of the narrative account of the infringement (Case T-465/12 *AGC Glass Europe v Commission*, EU:T:2015:505, paras 36 et seq, on further appeal, Case C-517/15P, not yet decided; and Case T-462/15 *Pilkington v Commission*, EU:T:2015:508, paras 56 et seq). As to publication under Regulation 1049/2001, the Commission must disclose, within the mandatory time frame, all parts of its decision in respect of which requests for confidential treatment are not still outstanding (Case T-534/11 *Schenker v Commission*, EU:T:2014:854, paras 137–138). The Commission has published Guidance on the preparation of public versions of Commission Decisions adopted under Articles 7–10, 23 and 24 of Regulation

1/2003, which sets out the kinds of information the Commission will redact, and the procedures to be followed in requesting redactions. The guidance is available on the DG Comp website.

(iv) Commitments and settlements

The General Court held in Case T-456/10 *Timab Industries*, EU:T:2015:296, [2015] 5 CMLR 7 that if a settlement involves some, but not all, of the participants in an infringement (either because one or more parties have withdrawn from the settlement discussions, or because the Commission terminates the discussions with one or more parties) then the Commission must observe the principle of equal treatment as between addressees of the decision taken under the settlement procedure and the addressees of the decision taken under the Regulation 773/2004 procedure.

The Commission exercised its power under Article 23(2)(c) of Regulation 1/2003 for the first time in COMP/39530 *Microsoft – Tying*, decision of 6 March 2013, for Microsoft's failure to comply with the commitments decision of 16 December 2009. It imposed a fine of €561 million.

In Case T-342/11 *Confederación Española de Empresarios de Estaciones de Servicio ('CEEES') v Commission*, EU:T:2014:60, at paras 47 et seq, the General Court confirmed that if an undertaking breaches its commitments the Commission is not obliged either to re-open its investigation, or to impose a fine under Article 23(2) (c), or to impose daily penalty payments under Article 24(1)(c). It has a discretion, and in exercising that discretion it is required to have regard to the same factors as when it is considering whether to reject a complaint about an alleged breach of Articles 101 and 102. It may also take into account any steps taken by NCAs in respect of the undertaking's conduct.

On 5 March 2014 the Commission issued guidance 'To commit or not to commit? Deciding between prohibition and commitment' (2014) 3 EU Competition Policy Brief, outlining the relevant considerations and criteria that it will take into account in deciding whether it would be appropriate to deal with a case by way of a prohibition decision under Article 7 of Regulation 1/2003, or a commitments decision under Article 9.

(v) Review by the General Court

On the ability of non-addressees to challenge Commission decisions, the General Court judgment in Case T-442/08 *International Confederation of Societies of Authors and Composers (CISAC) v Commission*, EU:T:2013:188, [2013] 5 CMLR 536, stands in contrast with the approach taken by the General Court in Case T-358/06 *Wegenbouwmaatschappij J. Heijmans v Commission*, Order of 4 July 2008. Like Heijimans, CISAC was an addressee of the Commission's statement of objections, but not of the decision. Unlike Heijimans, CISAC is a non-profit non-governmental organisation whose principal task is representing the entities that were addressed by the Commission decision, and facilitating cooperation between them. In *CISAC* the General Court considered that the decision was of direct and individual concern to CISAC, as its activities would be relevant to assessing whether the addressees were bringing to an end the concerted practice found in the decision, and as the decision affected its role as a facilitator of cooperation (particularly in mediating between the societies on issues relating to the grant of multi-territorial licences).

On the admissibility of evidence in proceedings before the Courts, the General Court has drawn a distinction between the admissibility of evidence in the context of a review of an infringement decision, and in the context of a review of the amount of a penalty. A document on which the Commission did not rely in its decision is inadmissible for the purposes of the substantive review of legality, but it can be taken into account in the exercise of the Court's unlimited jurisdiction regarding fines: Case T-462/07 *Galp Energía España v Commission*, EU:T:2013:459, [2014] 4 CMLR 272. On further appeal, Case C-603/13P, not yet decided.

The judgment in Case C-441/11P *Commission v Verhuizingen Coppens*, EU:C:2012:778, [2013] 4 CMLR 312 considers the question of partial annulment/severance in circumstances where the Commission has found a single and continuous infringement.

Chapter 14: Fines for Substantive Infringements

Significant judgments have been handed down on the procedure for reviewing the Commission's decisions on fines. The Court of Justice has confirmed that the 2006 Fining Guidelines do not impose a more onerous obligation on the Commission to state reasons for its fining decisions than did the 1998 Guidelines (Cases C-444/11P *Team Relocations v Commission*, EU:C:2013:464, [2013] 5 CMLR 38; and C-439/11P *Ziegler v Commission*, EU:C:2013:513, [2013] 5 CMLR 36). The General Court has held that Article 49 of the Charter of Fundamental Rights requires that the penalties imposed for an infringement must be proportionate (eg Case T-418/10 *Voestalpine v Commission* EU:T:2015:516, paras 442 et seq). The Court of Justice has also held that the 'manifest error' test, applied by the General Court to reviewing the exercise of the Commission's discretion to assess an undertaking's cooperation under the Leniency Notice, does not meet the requirements of Article 47 of the Charter on Fundamental Rights. The General Court cannot rely on the Commission's margin of discretion as a basis for not conducting an in-depth review of the law and facts (Case C-510/11P *Kone v Commission*, EU:C:2013:696, [2014] 4 CMLR 10).

A substantial number of judgments have been handed down on substantive appeals against the fines imposed by the Commission. Of particular interest are the following:

Value of sales in the EEA: The General Court confirmed that an undertaking's value of sales within the EEA can be determined by reference to its sales invoiced in the EEA, rather than sales delivered in the EEA, provided that that reflects the reality of the market: Case T-146/09 *Parker ITR and Parker-Hannifin v Commission (Marine Hoses)*, EU:T:2013:258, [2013] 5 CMLR 712 (partially annulled, on other grounds on further appeal, in Case C-434/13P *Commission v Parker Hannifin Manufacturing and Parker-Hannifin* EU:C:2014:2456, [2015] 4 CMLR 179). On the meaning of 'the EEA', the General Court held in Case T-286/09 *Intel v Commission*, EU:T:2014:547, at para 1577, that the relevant year for determining the undertaking's value of sales is normally the last full business year of its infringement, and the scope of the EEA is to be determined by reference to that year. It dismissed an argument that the Commission is required to consider the value of sales in the EEA by reference to the Member States comprising the EEA at different stages of the infringement. On further appeal, Case C-413/14P, not yet decided.

Value of sales includes indirect sales: The Court of Justice upheld the Commission's approach in its decision in COMP/39309 *Liquid Crystal Displays*, decision of 8 December 2010, discussed in the main text at paragraph 14.020: Case C-231/14P *Innolux v Commission (Liquid Crystal Displays)*, EU:C:2015:451; and Case C-227/14P *LG Display v Commission (Liquid Crystal Displays)*, EU:C:2015:258, [2015] 4 CMLR 1165. The Commission had calculated the undertakings' value of sales on the basis not only of direct sales of the cartelised product into the EEA, but had also taken into account a proportion of the value of the sales made by different companies within the same undertakings, into the EEA, of products into which the cartelised product had been incorporated. The Court in particular dismissed a complaint that the latter should have been excluded on the basis that Commission's findings of infringement did not extend to finished products incorporating LCDs. It held that although the finished products were sold onto a separate downstream market from the cartelised products, nonetheless sales of the finished products by a vertically integrated cartel participant were liable to affect competition in that downstream market, either because the cartelist would pass on the price increase on the cartelised product, or it would obtain a cost advantage by not doing so: *Innolux*, paras 56-57. Those sales were therefore properly considered to be related to the infringement, within Paragraph 13 of the Fining Guidelines. The Court also rejected the contention that the Commission had thereby exceeded its territorial jurisdiction (see Chapter 1, above). In Case C-580/12P *Guardian Industries v Commission*, EU:C:2014:2363 the Court confirmed that the principle of equal treatment requires that the Commission should take into account internal sales in identifying an undertaking's value of sales, and the General Court's judgment in Case T-82/08 *Guardian Industries v Commission*, EU:T:2012:494, [2012] 5 CMLR 1234 was set aside.

Multiplier for duration: In Case T-566/08 *Total Raffinage Marketing v Commission (Candle Waxes)*, EU:T:2013:423, at paras 549 et seq, the General Court held that the Commission must comply with the principle of equal treatment in determining the multiplier for duration, and that a practice of rounding part years to the nearest whole number can breach the principle by treating the different situations of undertakings in the same way. On further appeal, Case C-634/13P, not yet decided. In Case T-540/08 *Esso v Commission*, EU:T:2014:630, [2014] 5 CMLR 507, at paras 102 et seq, the General Court held that the Commission breached the principle of equal treatment by imposing a fine which did not reflect the fact that prior to a merger between two entities only one of them had participated in the infringement. The Commission had applied a multiplier for the full duration of the cartel to the value of sales of the merged entity, which the General Court held did not reflect the economic reality of the years preceding the merger.

Recidivism: In two cases the Court of Justice considered the requirements to which the Commission is subject if it is to impose an uplift for recidivism. In Case C-508/11P *Commission v Eni*, EU:C:2013:289, [2013] 5 CMLR 607 it held that the Commission must provide an adequate explanation of the capacity in which, and the extent to which, the allegedly recidivist undertaking is considered to have participated in a previous infringement. In Joined Cases C-93&123/13P *Commission v Eni & Versalis (Chloroprene rubber)*, EU:C:2015:150, [2015] 45 CMLR 727, at para 91, it confirmed that to impose an uplift for recidivism on a parent company it is not necessary for that parent company to have been the subject of an earlier infringement decision, but only that it should have been part of the same undertaking as the infringing subsidiary at the time of the earlier infringement. The parent company's rights of defence are met by the opportunity afforded to it in the subsequent proceedings to dispute the allegation of recidivism.

Provision of misleading information: In Case T-99/11 *Innolux v Commission (Liquid Crystal Displays)*, EU:T:2014:92, [2014] 4 CMLR 798, at para 172, the General Court adjusted the fine imposed on Innolux on account of an error that had been made in the data submitted to the Commission. A third party consultant had submitted sales data to the Commission on behalf of Innolux, and in error had included data on non-cartelised products. The Court held, in the exercise of its unlimited jurisdiction as to fines, that this should not be considered an aggravating circumstance for the purposes of setting the fine. Although Innolux had been negligent in the instructions it had given to its consultants, it had not sought to mislead the Commission, nor did it have any interest in doing so. The further appeal, on other grounds, was dismissed in Case C-231/14P *Innolux v Commission (Liquid Crystal Displays)*, EU:C:2015:451.

Reduction of fine for delay: The Court of Justice in Case C-50/12P *Kendrion v Commission*, EU:C:2013:771, [2014] 4 CMLR 454, at paras 91 et seq, refused to reduce the fine imposed on the undertaking on account of the delay in the Court's process, and did not follow the approach set out in Case C-185/95P *Baustahlgewebe v Commission* [1998] ECR I-8417, [1999] 4 CMLR 1203. The Court held that a claim for damages against the EU under Article 268 TFEU and the second paragraph of Article 340 TFEU is an effective remedy. In that case, the proceedings before the General Court had taken five years and nine months, which the Court of Justice considered breached Article 47 of the Charter, and to be a sufficiently serious breach of a rule of law intended to confer rights on individuals to sound in damages. However, it rejected the undertaking's appeal seeking a reduction in the fine, holding that a separate action must be brought before the General Court to recover those damages.

Inability to pay: The Court of Justice in Case C-439/11P *Ziegler v Commission*, EU:C:2013:513, [2013] 5 CMLR 36, considered the Commission's powers under paragraphs 35 and 37 of the Fining Guidelines to reduce the amount of the fine. An inability or reduced ability to pay under paragraph 35 cannot be sufficient alone to give rise to a reduction in the fine under paragraph 37, but an inability to pay may be relevant to determining whether to make a reduction under paragraph 37: paras 171–174. In addition, the General Court considered the issue of inability to pay and the impact of the Commission deciding to reduce the fine imposed on one among several undertakings on that basis, but not the others, in the appeals against the Commission's decision in COMP/39396 *Calcium carbide and magnesium based reagents*, decision of 22 July 2009 (Case T-410/09 *Almamet v Commission*, EU:T:2012:676, [2013] 4 CMLR 788; Case T-352/09 *Nováčke chemické závody v Commission*, EU:T:2012:673, [2013] 4 CMLR 734; and Case T-392/09 *1. garantovaná v Commission*, EU:T:2012:674, further appeal dismissed in Case C-90/13P, EU:C:2014:326, [2014] 5 CMLR 79).

Cap on fines: In Case C-50/12P *Kendrion v Commission*, EU:C:2013:771, [2014] 4 CMLR 454, the Court of Justice held that the cap on fines, of 10 per cent of the undertaking's turnover, can be applied separately to the infringing parent and subsidiary companies where those entities have ceased to form part of the same undertaking. In that case, the former subsidiary company had benefitted from the application of the cap, and the former parent company had been held liable for the full amount. The Court dismissed the argument that because liability was imposed on a joint and several basis, Kendrion could not be held liable for a larger fine than its former subsidiary: para 57. It also held that Kendrion and its subsidiary ceasing to be part of the same undertaking was a factor that differentiated Kendrion from the other parent companies addressed by the Commission's decision, and that justified Kendrion being fined for a larger amount than its subsidiary where the other parent company addressees had not been: paras 66 et seq.

Fines for different infringing parties: The Court of Justice considered the distinction between the Commission's powers to determine the fine to be imposed on different infringing undertakings, under Article 23(2) of Regulation 1/2003, and to determine the proportions that particular legal entities within an undertaking should contribute towards payment of that fine, in Joined Cases C-231/11P, etc,

Commission v Siemens and others, EU:C:2014:256, at paras 55 et seq. The Court held that although the Commission must necessarily address its decision to particular legal entities, its powers do not extend to determining the shares to be paid by different legal entities within an undertaking. That is a matter for the national courts to determine, applying national law to the dispute in a manner consistent with EU law.

Parental liability: The issue of parental liability continues to be raised in a large proportion of the cases considered by the Courts. The Court of Justice confirmed in Joined Cases C-628/10P&C-14/11P *Alliance One v Commission*, EU:C:2012:479, [2012] 5 CMLR 738 that the Commission can lawfully rely on a 'dual basis' method of attribution, which assesses evidence of actual exercise of decisive influence as well as relying upon the presumption of decisive influence, but that there would be a breach of the principle of equal treatment if the Commission relied on evidence of actual exercise of decisive influence in order to attribute responsibility to some parent companies, but sought to rely solely on the presumption of decisive influence as a basis for attribution in respect of others. In Case C-247/11P *Areva v Commission*, EU:C:2014:257, [2014] 4 CMLR 31, it further considered the requirements with which the Commission must comply if it relies on this 'dual basis' method. It held that the Commission fulfils its obligation to state reasons in respect of a finding of actual exercise of decisive influence if it conducts a 'global assessment' of the arguments put forward by the parent company to rebut the evidence: para 42. The Commission does not have to show that the parent company actually used the organisational, economic and legal links that characterise its relationship with the subsidiary by reference to particular actual conduct on the relevant market, as that would render the presumption ineffective: para 91.

In Case C-286/11P *Commission v Tomkins*, EU:C:2013:29, [2013] 4 CMLR 466, the Court of Justice held that where a parent company's liability is wholly derived from that of its subsidiary, and where both companies have brought actions before the European Courts seeking a reduction in their fines on the same basis (in this case, on the basis of the duration of the infringement), then the fine imposed on the parent company can be recalculated on account of the outcome of the appeal by the subsidiary. It is not necessary for the scope of their actions, or the arguments deployed, to be identical.

In Case T-343/06 *Shell Petroleum v Commission*, EU:T:2012:478, [2012] 5 CMLR 1064 the General Court upheld the Commission's conclusion that conduct could be attributed to a parent company which held only 40 per cent of the shares in the infringing subsidiary, because at the time of the infringement the subsidiary was owned by two parent companies, both within the Shell undertaking, and the Court agreed that the situation was analogous to that in which a single parent company fully controls the subsidiary.

On the liability of parent companies for the conduct of joint ventures, in addition to the Court of Justice's judgments in Cases C-179/12P *Dow Chemical Company v Commission*, EU:C:2013:605, [2014] 4 CMLR 6; and C-172/12P *El du Pont de Nemours v Commission*, EU:C:2013:601, [2014] 4 CMLR 7, referred to in respect of Chapter 2, above, in Case T-541/08 *Sasol v Commission (Candle Waxes)*, EU:T:2014:628, [2014] 5 CMLR 729, at paras 40 et seq, the General Court considered the circumstances in which the conduct of a joint venture can be imputed to one parent company alone. The Commission had attributed liability to Sasol, which owned two-thirds of the shares in the joint venture, using evidence of its ability to exercise decisive influence without finding that it had actually exercised decisive influence. The Court held that the Commission can establish actual decisive influence by way of an abstract analysis of the documents signed before a joint venture began to operate, along the lines of the analysis conducted under Regulation 139/2004 (the Merger Regulation) to determine whether the company is able to 'control' the joint venture, in as much as the Commission may presume that the legislation and provisions of agreements relating to the operation of that undertaking, in particular the joint venture's articles of association and the shareholder and voting rights agreement, have been implemented and complied with: para 49. However, it is open to the Commission and the undertaking concerned to adduce evidence that the joint venture's commercial decisions were taken by procedures other than those apparent from the mere abstract examination of the agreements, and in particular that they were taken by several or all of the parent companies unanimously: para 50.

Liability of successor undertakings: The Court of Justice in Case C-247/11P *Areva v Commission*, EU:C:2014:257, [2014] 4 CMLR 31 at paras 129 et seq held that it is unlawful for the Commission to adopt a 'cascade' method of determining the fines to be imposed on successive parent companies for the infringing conduct of their subsidiaries. The Commission had imposed a fine on the successor parent, jointly and severally with the subsidiary, and had incorporated that fine in its entirety in the fine imposed on the original parent. The Court of Justice held that this approach breached the principle that penalties must be specific to the offender and the offence, and the principle of legal certainty. It confirmed that the Commission must determine the fine separately for each undertaking involved in the infringement.

Leniency: The Court of Justice confirmed in Joined Cases C-293&294/13P *Fresh Del Monte Produce*, EU:C:2015:416, [2015] 5 CMLR 513, paras 180 et seq, that the assistance provided by an undertaking may only be taken into account for the purposes of determining the fine where it has been provided without the Commission having asked for it. If information is provided in response to a request under Article 18(2) of Regulation 1/2003, then irrespective of the fact that the undertaking was not legally obliged to provide it (in contrast to a decision under Article 18(3) of Regulation 1/2003), it is not information provided voluntarily. The General Court held in Case T-655/11 *FSL v Commission*, EU:T:2015:383, para 149, that in circumstances where an immunity application reveals facts which the Commission considers constitute two separate infringements, such that the Commission conducts two separate investigations, the duty of cooperation requires the immunity applicant to cooperate in both investigations and to continue to do so even after securing final immunity with regard to one of the infringements covered by one of the investigations. On further appeal, Case C-469/15P, not yet decided.

The ECN has issued a revised Model Leniency Programme. The main changes are that all undertakings applying to the Commission for leniency in cases concerning more than three Member States will be able to submit a summary application to national competition authorities, where previously only the first applicant, ie the immunity applicant, was entitled to use summary applications under the model leniency programme; and the ECN has agreed on a standard template for summary applications, which can be used in all Member States.

Chapter 15: The Enforcement of the Competition Rules by National Competition Authorities

Litigants have continued to dispute whether, and if so at what point, national proceedings should be stayed pending investigations by the Commission, and appeals to the European courts by the addressees of Commission decisions. On the issue of the impact of pending Commission investigations, the Court in *Secretary of State for Health v Servier* [2012] EWHC 2761 (Ch) granted a stay until after the oral hearing before the Commission in COMP/39612 *Perindopril (Servier)*, but refused to extend the stay until a decision was issued; and the Court in *Infederation v Google* [2013] EWHC 2295 (Ch) refused a stay other than on one issue and otherwise ordered disclosure while the Commission investigation in COMP/39740 *Google* was ongoing. On the impact of pending appeals to the European courts, in *WM Morrison Supermarkets v Mastercard and others* [2013] EWHC 1071 (Comm) the High Court followed *National Grid* and refused to stay damages proceedings that were brought in reliance on the decision in COMP/34579 *Mastercard I*, decision of 19 December 2007; and in *CDC Project 14 v Shell and others*, judgment of 1 May 2013, Case No. C/09/414499/HA ZA 12-293, the District Court of the Hague refused to stay proceedings before pleadings had closed in a claim brought in reliance on the decision in COMP/39181 *Candle Wax*, decision of 1 October 2008.

The General Court has handed down three judgments of particular significance on the cooperation between the Commission and NCAs. In Case T-201/11 *Si. mobil v Commission*, EU:T:2014:1096, [2015] 4 CMLR 329, it dismissed a challenge to the Commission's decision to reject a complaint on the basis that a NCA was already investigating. It held that the Network Notice does not create rights for individuals to have complaints dealt with by any particular authority, and even if the Commission were to have been 'best placed' to deal with the case the applicant would not have had a right to have its complaint dealt with by the Commission: para 40. The General Court also held that to be satisfied that a NCA is 'dealing with the case' the Commission must ascertain that the NCA is actually investigating it, as opposed merely to having received a complaint or having opened a case of its own initiative, but the Commission does not have to assess whether the NCA is taking a well-founded approach to the case, or that it has the institutional, financial and technical means available to it to accomplish the tasks entrusted to it: paras 47 et seq. In the other two judgments, the General Court confirmed that a NCA decision accepting commitments does not preclude the Commission from investigating, as the Commission is not bound by the NCA's decision, and the fact that the Commission did not exercise its discretion under Article 11(6) of Regulation 1/2003 to relieve the NCA of its jurisdiction to apply Articles 101 and 102 does not render an inspection decision inappropriate (Case T-402/13 *Orange v Commission*, EU:T:2014:991); and a NCA decision rejecting a complaint on grounds of administrative priorities renders a complaint already dealt with for the purposes of Article 13(2) of Regulation 1/2003 such that the Commission is not required to accept the complaint (Case T-355/13 *easyJet v Commission*, EU:T:2015:36, paras 25 et seq).

On the exchange of information between ECN members, in Case T-655/11 *FSL (Exotic fruit) v Commission*, EU:T:2015:383, paras 71 et seq, the General Court dismissed an argument that the protections afforded to an undertaking by Article 12 of Regulation 1/2003 should apply, by analogy, to information gathered by the Commission from national regulatory authorities other than the relevant NCA. On further appeal, Case C-469/15P, not yet decided.

On the cooperation between the Commission and national courts, as part of the ongoing modernisation of the State aid regime the Commission has been given powers to transmit information, or opinions, to national courts considering State aid cases in the same way as under Article 15 of Regulation 1/2003 in Article 101/ 102 cases: Regulation 734/2013, amending Regulation 659/99, adopted on 22 July 2013 (OJ 2013 L204/15). This is discussed in the updates to Chapter 17.

The ECN published reports on Investigative Powers and on Decision-Making Powers, on 31 October 2012, which contain a comparative analysis of the enforcement powers conferred on NCAs in different Member States, and identify areas of divergence. It has subsequently, in December 2013, endorsed a series of recommendations on key investigative and decision-making powers that it considers NCAs should have available in their competition toolbox.

Chapter 16: Litigating Infringements in the National Courts

(i) Legislation

There have been a number of significant legislative developments in the field of private enforcement of competition law.

A recast Brussels Regulation ('Brussels II'; Regulation 1215/2012) was adopted on 20 December 2012, and applies from January 2015.

Directive 2014/104 on certain rules governing actions for damages under national law for infringements of the competition law provisions of the Member States and of the European Union, OJ 2014 L349/1, was adopted on 26 November 2014. The deadline for national implementation is 27 December 2016.

On 11 June 2013, the Commission also adopted a Recommendation on common principles for injunctive and compensatory collective redress mechanisms in the Member States concerning violations of rights granted under Union law, OJ 2013 L201/60.

In the United Kingdom, the Consumer Rights Act 2015 grants the Competition Appeal Tribunal power to grant injunctions; introduces mechanisms for collective redress; and aligns the time limits for bringing damages claims in the Competition Appeal Tribunal with those in the High Court. The Tribunal's rules have been updated to include collective proceedings and collective settlements: Competition Appeal Tribunal Rules 2015 (SI/2015/1648).

(ii) Jurisdiction

Questions have continued to arise on the application of Brussels I to cross-border competition cases.

The Court of Justice in Case C-352/13 *Cartel Damage Claims Hydrogen Peroxide (CDC) v Evonik Degussa and others*, EU:C:2015:335, [2015] 5 CMLR 285 provided detailed guidance on the application of Brussels I to follow-on damages actions brought against defendants domiciled in different Member States, and relying upon a decision from the European Commission finding that those defendants participated in a single and continuous infringement of competition law. For the purposes of Article 5(3) of Brussels I, the Court held that (a) the place of the event giving rise to damage is the place at which the cartel was concluded; or, if the cartel consisted of a number of collusive agreements and there was one particular agreement which was the sole cause of damage to the claimant, the place at which that agreement was concluded: para 50; and (b) the place where the harmful event occurred, when the damage is an alleged overcharge, is in general the place at which the claimant's registered office is located. For the purposes of Article 6 of Brussels I, the Court confirmed that there would be a risk of irreconcilable judgments if separate actions were to be brought against those defendants in different Member States: para 25. In respect of a valid jurisdiction in a contract for the supply of goods, the Court held that such a clause is to be given effect if it excludes the jurisdiction that the court would otherwise have under Article 5(3) and/or Article 6; however, the national court must determine whether the clause in question binds the parties to the proceedings before it, and whether the clause, properly interpreted, does in fact derogate from the court's jurisdiction.

In particular, a clause which abstractly refers to all disputes arising from contractual relationships must be regarded as not extending to a dispute relating to the tortious liability that results from an infringement of competition law, and as not validly derogating from the court's jurisdiction, whereas a clause which does refer to disputes concerning liability that results from an infringement of competition law will constitute a valid derogation: paras 57 et seq.

In the UK, in *Deutsche Bahn and others v Morgan Crucible and others* [2013] EWCA Civ 1484 (refusing permission to appeal in a reasoned judgment by two Lord Justices) the Court of Appeal dismissed an argument that damage suffered by indirect purchasers was not capable of founding jurisdiction under Article 5(3) of Brussels I. In *Bord Na Mona Horticulture v British Polythene Industries* [2012] EWHC 3346 (Comm) the High Court considered the 'centre of interest' for the purposes of Article 5(3), and the application of Article 6 where the action against an anchor defendant was inadmissible. On the nature of the cause of action, the Court of Appeal in *WH Newson Holding and others v IMI and others* [2013] EWCA Civ 1377 confirmed that proceedings in England and Wales do not have to be brought as a claim for breach of statutory duty, and that a claim could be available for the tort of unlawful means conspiracy, provided the requisite element of intent to cause loss could be established. In that case, which concerned follow-on proceedings brought in the Competition Appeal Tribunal, the Court held that the Commission decision relied upon did not contain findings of the requisite intent to injure the particular claimants; and in *Air Canada and others v Emerald Supplies* [2015] EWCA Civ 1024, which concerned stand-alone proceedings brought in the High Court, it held that the requisite intent to injure the particular claimants could not be established where it was possible that the alleged victims would be in a position to pass on any overcharges imposed on them, thereby avoiding any loss themselves. In *Ryanair v Esso Italiana* [2013] EWCA Civ 1450 the Court of Appeal rejected an attempt to characterise a claim for repayment of an overcharge as a claim for breach of contract. It held that the relevant contract must be capable, on a proper construction, of encompassing a claim based on a breach of competition law, and the contract at issue in that case was not capable of encompassing such a claim. The Court also refused to imply a term into the contract that prices would not be inflated as a result of breaches of competition law. On that occasion the Court of Appeal was concerned with jurisdiction under Article 23 of Brussels I, rather than Article 5(1), but its approach to the breach of contract claim appears equally applicable to an analysis under Article 5(1).

(iii) Access to documents

In Case C-365/12P *Commission v EnBW Energie Baden-Württemberg* ('*EnBW*'), EU:C:2014:112, [2014] 4 CMLR 30, at paras 79 et seq, the Court of Justice has overturned the General Court's judgment regarding access to documents on the Commission's file under Regulation 1049/2001. By analogy with the approach taken in respect of requests for documents on merger proceedings (Case C-404/10 P *Commission v Éditions Odile Jacob*, EU:C:2012:808, [2013] 4 CMLR 11; and Case C-477/10 P *Commission v Agrofert Holding*, EU:C:2012:394, [2012] 5 CMLR 510, discussed in paragraph 8.184 of the main text), and on State aid proceedings (Case C-139/07P *Commission v Technische Glaswerke Ilmenau* [2010] ECR I-5885, discussed in paragraphs 16.046 et seq of the main text), the Commission is entitled to apply a general presumption that disclosure of documents on its file in an antitrust investigation would undermine the protection of the commercial interests of the undertakings involved in those proceedings, as well as the protection of the purpose of investigations relating to such proceedings, within the meaning of the first and third indents of Article 4(2) of Regulation No 1049/2001. Otherwise, the restrictive rules on access to the file in Regulation 1/2003 and Regulation 773/2004 could be undermined: paras 88–90. It is not necessary to examine each document individually and determine the application of the exceptions to each: para 93. It is also entitled to apply a presumption that disclosure of its internal documents (such as background notes on the evidence, correspondence with other competition authorities, and consultations with other departments in the Commission) would seriously undermine the Commission's decision-making process, within the meaning of the second paragraph of Article 4(3) of Regulation 1049/2001, in circumstances where an appeal against the Commission's decision is still ongoing, and the possibility remains that the Commission may be called upon to re-open its investigation: para 114. The presumption can be rebutted if there is evidence that it would be in the public interest to disclose the documents, but a general statement that disclosure is required for the purposes of bringing a claim for compensation in the national courts will not suffice: a requestor would have to establish that particular documents are necessary for that purpose in order for its rights to compensation to constitute an overriding public interest in disclosure.

The General Court has upheld the Commission's refusal to provide access to various documents under Regulation 1049/2001, including information exchanged between ECN members (Case T-623/13 *Unión de Almacenistas de Hierros de España v Commission*, EU:T:2015:268); the Commission's internal documents prepared in the course of merger control proceedings (Case T-561/12 *Beninca v Commission*, EU:T:2013:558, [2014] 4 CMLR 549); documents on the Commission's file in a State aid investigation (Case T-456/13 *Sea Handling v Commission*, EU:T:2015:185, para 63); an undertaking's responses to the Commission's questionnaires regarding its ability to pay, and to the Commission's second questionnaire (Case T-181/10 *Reagens v Commission*, EU:T:2014:139, [2014] 4 CMLR 960).

(iv) Actions for damages

The Court of Justice confirmed in Case C-557/12 *Kone v ÖBB-Infrastruktur*, EU:C:2014:1317, that Article 101 precludes a provision of national law which categorically excludes a claim for damages being brought by a claimant that purchased from a non-infringing undertaking, in circumstances where the cartel has enabled the non-infringing undertaking to charge higher prices than it would have done in conditions of normal competition (known as 'umbrella pricing'), on the basis that there is an inadequate causal link between the cartel and the pricing decision of the non-infringing undertaking. The Court held that a victim of umbrella pricing must be able to claim damages from the infringing undertaking(s) where it is established that (a) in the circumstances of the case and, in particular given the specific aspects of the relevant market, the cartel at issue was liable to have the effect of enabling the non-infringing undertakings to offer higher prices than they would have done under conditions of normal competition; and (b) those circumstances, and the specific aspects of the relevant market, could not be ignored by the members of that cartel. It is for the national court to determine whether those conditions are satisfied.

On the quantification of damages, the Commission has adopted a Communication on quantifying harm in actions for damages based on breaches of Article 101 or 102 TFEU (COM(2013) 3440, OJ 2013 C167/19), and an accompanying Practical Guide (SWD(2013) 205) ('Quantification Guide'). The Competition Appeal Tribunal's judgment in *Albion Water v Dŵr Cymru Cyfyngedig* [2013] CAT 6 is a useful, detailed illustration of the quantification of competition law damages. Following its earlier judgments finding that Dŵr Cymru had engaged in unfair pricing and margin squeeze, the Tribunal determined what non-abusive price would have been charged absent the abusive conduct (a figure in the middle of a range of lawful prices, not the highest that could lawfully have been charged) and fed that price into a detailed counterfactual that looked at what Albion's input costs would have been, and what price it could have charged its customers. The Tribunal also allowed Albion to recover for the loss of a chance to bid successfully on an additional contract, although it rejected the claim for exemplary damages.

The developments regarding the enforcement of standard essential patents, discussed in respect of Chapter 9, above, are relevant to the issue of reliance on Articles 101 and 102 as a defence.

Chapter 17: State Aids

(i) Legislation

The State aid modernisation programme has continued apace, and there have been a large number of legislative measures adopted. Particular developments include:

- On 22 July 2013, the Council adopted Regulation 733/2013, amending Regulation 994/98 (the Enabling Regulation) and increasing the categories of aid in respect of which the Commission is able to adopt block exemption regulations (OJ 2013 L217/28) and Regulation 734/2013, amending Regulation 659/99 (the Procedural Regulation) (OJ 2013 L204/15). Significant reforms include powers for the Commission to request information from Member States other than the notifying Member State, or from an undertaking or association of undertakings; to conduct sector inquiries in the same way as in Article 101/ 102 cases; and to transmit information, or opinions, to national courts in the same way as under Article 15 of Regulation 1/2003 in Article 101/102 cases. On 29 April 2015, the Commission opened its first sector inquiry using its new powers. It is investigating measures adopted by Member States to ensure that adequate capacity to produce electricity is available at all times, in order to avoid blackouts: see Press Release IP/15/4891 (29 April 2015).

• On 18 December 2013, the Commission adopted Regulation 1407/2013 on the application of Articles 107 and 108 of the Treaty on the Functioning of the European Union to *de minimis* aid (OJ 2013 L352/1). The new *De Minimis* Regulation retains the existing threshold of €200,000, repayable within three years, and is extended to include aid granted to firms in difficulty.

• On 17 June 2014, following the expansion in Regulation 733/2013 of the list of categories of aid which the Commission has power to exempt, the Commission adopted a new General Block Exemption Regulation ('the Revised GBER'), Regulation 651/2014, OJ 2014 L187/1. Regulation 800/2008 (the General Block Exemption Regulation, 'GBER') was prolonged until 30 June 2014, after which the Revised GBER entered into force. The Revised GBER extends the categories of aid covered. The Commission also adopted, on 18 December 2013, a new block exemption for *de minimis* aid in the agricultural sector: Commission Regulation 1408/2013, OJ 2013 L352/9; and on 1 July 2014 a new block exemption regulation for State aid in the agricultural and forestry sectors and in rural areas: Commission Regulation 702/2014, OJ 2014 L193/1.

• A new framework for State aid for research and development and innovation ('R&D&I Framework') was published in June 2014, OJ 2014 C198/1.

The Commission has also revised a number of its guidelines; including: on 19 June 2013, the Guidelines on regional State aid for 2014–2020 (OJ 2013 C209/1); on 19 December 2012, the Guidelines on Short-term Export-credit Insurance (OJ 2012 C392/1); on 26 January 2013, the Guidelines on the application of State aid rules in relation to the rapid deployment of broadband networks (OJ 2013 C25/1); on 13 November 2013, the Guidelines on the criteria for assessing State aid for films and other audiovisual works (OJ 2013 C332/1); on 15 January 2014, the Guidelines on State aid to promote risk finance investments (OJ 2014 C19/4); on 20 February 2014, the Guidelines on State aid to airports and airlines (OJ 2014 C93/3); on 9 April 2014, the Guidelines on State aid for environmental protection and energy 2014–2020 (OJ 2014 C200/01); on 21 May 2014, a Communication amending the Communications from the Commission on EU Guidelines for the application of State aid rules in relation to the rapid deployment of broadband networks, on Guidelines on regional State aid for 2014–2020, on State aid for films and other audiovisual works, on Guidelines on State aid to promote risk finance investments and on Guidelines on State aid to airports and airlines (OJ 2014 C198/30), to ensure that the transparency requirements in each are consistent with one another; on 20 June 2014, a Communication on the criteria for the analysis of the compatibility with the internal market of State aid to promote the execution of important projects of common European interest, OJ 2014 C188/4; and on 1 July 2014, Guidelines for State aid in the agricultural and forestry sectors and in rural areas 2014 to 2020: OJ 2014 C204/1.

(ii) *The concept of an aid, and compatibility with the internal market*

The Court of Justice considered several cases on the constituent elements of a State aid, including the application of the market economy investor principle to partial payment of tax debts (Case C-73/11P *Frucona Košice v Commission*, EU:C:2013:32, [2013] 2 CMLR 28) and to decisions taken by the State as a shareholder in a 'bailed out' bank (Case C-224/12P *Commission v Netherlands and ING Group*, EU:C:2014:213, [2014] 3 CMLR 987); the engagement of State resources where an offer of a shareholder loan is made publicly, to the undertaking's economic advantage, but is never actually taken up (Cases C-399/10P&C-401/10P *Bouygues Télécom v Commission*, EU:C:2013:175, [2013] 3 CMLR 6); the engagement of State resources where an obligation is imposed on undertakings to purchase wind-generated electricity at a price higher than the market price, and the undertakings are compensated for the cost of meeting the obligation by charges imposed by the State on all consumers of electricity in the Member State, the charges being administered by a public body and the amount being determined by the Minister for Energy (Case C-26212 *Vent de colère*, EU:C:2013:851, [2014] 2 CMLR 35); the selectivity of a measure made available equally to all undertakings at one point in time, which confers an advantageous position on those who have taken it up when the market situation subsequently changes (Case T-499/10 *MOL v Commission*, EU:T:2013:592, paras 64 et seq; upheld on further appeal, Case C-15/14P *Commission v MOL*, EU:C:2015:362); the degree of discretion that can be afforded to authorities in determining whether to grant the benefit of a tax exemption if that exemption is not to be considered selective (Case C-6/12 *P Oy*, EU:C:2013:525); and the provision of support for the construction of infrastructure (Case C-288/11P *Mitteldeutsche Flughafen and Flughafen Leipzig-Halle v Commission*, EU:C:2012:821, [2013] 2 CMLR 18).

The General Court has considered three cases on the lawfulness of a Commission decision under Article 107(3)(b), following the 2008 financial crisis and in pursuance of the Commission's various communications on the application of the State aid rules to measures adopted in response to the crisis. In Case T-391/11 *ABN Amro v Commission*, EU:T:2014:186, the General Court dismissed an appeal against the conditions imposed by the Commission on its approval of the aid. The objective of the prohibition on ABN Amro making any further acquisitions (other than of a specified type and specified size), for a period of three years, extended to five years if the Dutch State continues to own more than 50 per cent of ABN Amro at the end of the three-year period, was consistent with the Commission's communications and with the principle of proportionality. In Case T-457/09 *Westfälisch-Lippischer Sparkassen- und Giroverband v Commission*, EU:T:2014:683, paras 196 et seq, the General Court confirmed that the Rescue Guidelines (OJ 2004 C244/2) can be applied in circumstances where a firm is in difficulty as a result of a serious disturbance in the economy, provided it meets the definition of being 'in difficulty'. The Court dismissed a complaint that the Commission erred in considering the Rescue Guidelines when determining whether Article 107(3)(b) was met. In Case T-487/11 *Banco Privado Português v Commission*, EU:T:2014:1077 the General Court upheld a decision requiring Portugal to recover aid granted pursuant to a guarantee it had provided, as the condition upon which the Commission authorised the aid, under the Rescue Guidelines, was not met and the aid had been extended beyond the maximum six month period. The Commission was therefore justified in concluding that the aid did not meet Article 107(3)(b). In a parallel reference made to the Court of Justice for a preliminary ruling, by the Portuguese national court, the Court likewise confirmed, in Case C-667/13 *Estado português v Banco Privado Português*, EU:C:2015:151, para 74, that the temporal limitation on rescue aid and the obligation to notify the Commission of subsequent extensions are necessary conditions for aid to be declared compatible with the internal market and are not mere procedural requirements.

On the authorisation powers of the Council, the Court of Justice held that a decision to authorise a specific measure does not oust the power of the Commission to examine whether or not that measure constitutes State aid to its beneficiaries, if the authorisation decision is not taken pursuant to Article 108(2): see Case C-272/12P *Commission v Ireland*, EU:C:2013:812, [2014] 2 CMLR 895, at paras 49–50, reversing the General Court's judgment in Cases T-50/06, etc, *RENV v Commission*, EU:T:2012:134. The Court held that the Council's authorisation of certain Member States' excise duty exemptions, pursuant to its powers under EU legislation harmonising such duties, did not preclude the Commission from subsequently examining whether or not those exemptions constituted State aid to the undertakings that benefited from them.

(iii) Supervision under Article 108

A number of judgments have considered the issue of recovery. In Case T-473/12 *Aer Lingus v Commission*, EU:T:2015:78, paras 97 et seq, the General Court accepted that in some cases the actual value of the benefit received from the aid by the beneficiary will not necessarily be the same as the full value of the unlawful aid. In the circumstances of that case, it was necessary to determine the extent to which the economic benefit of being charged an excise duty at a lower rate than other undertakings was passed on by the beneficiary to its customers, in order to identify the economic benefit it had enjoyed. On further appeal, Case 164/15P, not yet decided. In Case C-69/13 *Mediaset v Ministero dello Sviluppo economico*, EU:C:2014:71,

[2014] 3 CMLR 169 the Court of Justice confirmed that where the Commission has taken a final decision that an aid measure was unlawful, but has not specified in the decision the recipients of the aid and/or the amounts to be recovered from each of them, a national court called upon to determine those matters will be bound by the Commission's decision, but not by any subsequent statements that the Commission has made in the execution of that decision. On the availability of the defence of impossibility, the Court of Justice held in Case C-63/14 *France v Commission*, EU:C:2015:458, paras 52 et seq, that where recovering an unlawful aid might lead to social unrest, and jeopardise public order, a Member State can rely upon a defence of absolute impossibility only where it could not cope with the consequences of that unrest using all the means at its disposal. The Commission has accepted a defence of impossibility in SA.20829 *Scheme concerning the municipal real estate tax exemption granted to real estate used by non commercial entities for specific purposes*, decision of 19 December 2012, OJ 2013 L166/24 (difficulty in assessing retrospectively the proportion of each property that was used for economic activities and therefore the extent of the unlawful aid); and SA.33083 *Aid measures linked to the 1990 earthquake in Sicily and the 1994 floods in Northern Italy*, decision of 14 August 2015 (impossible to assess the extent of unlawful aid granted more than 10 years ago as national law does not require undertakings to retain business and accounting records for more than 10 years).

In addition, a number of recent decisions illustrate the Commission considering whether there is economic continuity between the recipient of aid and a subsequent purchaser of the recipient's assets, such that recovery could be sought from the purchaser: see SA.315501 *Nürburgring*, decision of 1 October 2014, paras 231 et seq; and SA.35546 *Restructuring aid to Viana shipyards*, decision of 7 May 2015, paras 146 et seq.

(iv) Judicial remedies

In Case T-517/12 *Alro v Commission*, EU:T:2014:890, para 44, the General Court held that although a decision to initiate the formal investigation procedure in relation to a measure which is already being implemented can itself be challenged under Article 263 TFEU, a decision to initiate a formal investigation in relation to a measure which is no longer in the course of implementation does not produce binding legal effects and therefore is not challengeable.

On standing to bring appeals to the General Court against a State aid decision, in Case C-274/12P *Telefónica v Commission*, EU:C:2013:852; and Case 132/12P *Stichting Woonpunt v Commission*, EU:C:2014:100, and Case C-133/12P *Stichting Woonlinie v Commissioner*, EU:C:2014:105, the Court of Justice considered the applicability of the fourth paragraph of Article 263 TFEU, which permits challenges to regulatory acts which do not entail implementing measures and are of direct concern to the applicant, to a State aid decision. In *Telefónica* the Court of Justice held that even though the applicant was a beneficiary of the aid in question, the part of the Commission's decision under challenge did not identify it as such or order recovery from it, and the decision would therefore require implementing measures. In *Stichting Woonpunt* and *Stichting Woonlinie* the Commission had decided that an existing aid was compatible with the internal market, subject to amendments proposed by the Member State. The Court of Justice held that the decision under challenge therefore entailed the Member State implementing its proposed amendments to the scheme. In Case T-601/11 *Dansk Automat Brancheforening v Commission*, EU:T:2014:839, paras 58–60, the General Court applied this case to a situation in which the Commission had declared a new aid to be compatible with the internal market as notified. It held that as the decision under challenge entailed the Member State enacting, and implementing, legislation the applicants did not have standing under the fourth paragraph of Article 263 TFEU. On further appeal, Case C-563/14P, not yet decided. The General Court has also held that where the person bringing the appeal against a refusal to open a formal complaint seeks not only to secure the procedural rights available under Article 108(2), but also challenges the merits of a decision which finds an aid to be compatible with the internal market, he must establish that he is directly and individually concerned within the meaning of that test laid down in Case C-25/62 *Plaumann v Commission* [1963] ECR 95, [1964] CMLR 29 if the latter arguments are to be admissible: eg Case T-57/11 *Castelnou Energía v Commission* EU:T:2014:1021, paras 28 et seq.

The Courts have considered several cases on the factors relevant to determining whether the Commission's initial review revealed serious difficulties with the aid in question, such that it should have opened a formal investigation, including Case C-646/11P *Falles Fagligt Forbund (3F) v Commission*, EU:C:2013:36, at para 32 (the Commission's preliminary examination being of longer duration than two months is relevant, but is not, of itself, sufficient); Case T-304/08 *Smurfit Kappa Group v Commission*, EU:T:2012:351, para 26 (the sufficiency or completeness of the Commission's examination is relevant); Case T-58/13 *Club Hotel Loutraki v Commission*, EU:T:2015:1, paras 41–44 (the fact that the Member State offered commitments to modify the aid should not be interpreted as meaning that the Commission had serious doubts about its compatibility with the internal market) (on further appeal, Case C-131/15, not yet decided); and Case T-57/11 *Castelnou Energía v Commission*, EU:T:2014:1021, paras 81 et seq (the number and seriousness of objections raised against an aid at national level is not relevant, but the nature of those objections may be).

On proceedings before national courts in respect of new aids, in Case C-284/12 *Deutsche Lufthansa v Flughafen Frankfurt-Hahn*, EU:C:2013:755, [2014] 2 CMLR 20, the Court of Justice held that where the Commission has issued a decision under Article 108(2) formally to investigate an aid, the national court must adopt all necessary measures with a view to drawing the appropriate conclusions from an infringement of the obligation to suspend implementation of the measure, and to that end it may suspend implementation and order recovery of payments already made. If it doubts whether the measure in question constitutes an aid, or whether the decision under Article 108(2) is valid, or how the decision under Article 108(2) is to be interpreted, it may seek clarification from the Commission or refer to the Court of Justice for a preliminary ruling.

On the role of Member States in recovering unlawfully paid aid, the Court of Justice has imposed a fine of €20 million on Spain for its long-standing failure to recover aid that the Court ordered ten years previously it should recover, and a daily fine of €50,000 until it is recovered (Case C-610/10 *Commission v Spain*, EU:C:2012:781). It has also held that, if a national court has difficulties in quantifying the amount of aid to be recovered, it may contact the Commission for assistance, and although the Commission's views on quantum will not be binding, the principle of good faith cooperation in Article 4(3) TEU will require the national court to take them into account (Case C-69/13 *Mediaset*, EU:C:2014:71, paras 30–31).

Laura Elizabeth John, Editor
Jon Turner QC, Consultant Editor
31 December 2015

ALPHABETICAL TABLE OF EU CASES AND DECISIONS

TABLE OF EUROPEAN COURT OF HUMAN RIGHTS AND NATIONAL CASES

TABLE OF EU AND EEA NOTICES, GUIDELINES AND OTHER INFORMAL TEXTS

TABLES OF TREATIES AND LEGISLATION

TABLE OF EU DIRECTIVES

TABLE OF NATIONAL LEGISLATION

Ireland

UK

TABLE OF INTERNATIONAL TREATIES AND CONVENTIONS

1

EU COMPETITION LAW AND ITS TERRITORIAL REACH

1. Introduction

Plan of this Chapter. There are now 28 Member States, Croatia having joined **1.002**
the EU on 1 July 2013.

2. The EU Treaties

Expiry of the ECSC Treaty. **1.004**
Fn 10 The General Court dismissed the appeals against the Commission's findings of infringement in COMP/37956 *Concrete reinforcing bars*, decision of
30 September 2009, but upheld three undertakings' appeals in respect of the
fine: Cases T-472/09, etc, *SP v Commission* EU:T:2014:1040.

The Charter of Fundamental Rights. The Court of Justice held that the **1.008**
Commission is bound by Article 41 of the Charter on Fundamental Rights
when conducting investigations into potential breaches of competition law: Case
C-439/11P *Ziegler v Commission*, EU:C:2013:513, [2013] 5 CMLR 1217, para 154.

3. EU Competition Law

(b) The aims of the EU competition rules

Competition policy and productivity. On 27 July 2015 the Commission issued **1.016**
a study entitled 'Improving competition in the Member States to boost growth'
(2015) 5 EU Competition Policy Brief, analysing the effects that increased competition in Member States, including the removal of remaining obstacles to competition, would have on growth.

1.017 **Competition policy and the liberalisation of markets.** On 27 July 2015 the Commission issued a study entitled 'Improving competition in the Member States to boost growth' (2015) 5 EU Competition Policy Brief, analysing the effects that increased competition in Member States, including the removal of remaining obstacles to competition, would have on growth.

(c) The interpretation of the EU competition rules

1.020 The effectiveness of the competition rules.
Fn 70 See also Case C-536/11 *Bundeswettbewerbsbehörde v Donau Chemie*, EU:C:2013:366, [2013] 5 CMLR 658.

(d) The EU Competition Rules

1.028 **Articles 107–109.** Regulation 994/98, which enables the Commission to adopt block exemption regulations for State aids, was amended on 22 July 2013 by Council Regulation 733/2013: OJ 2013 L217/28. On the same day Regulation 659/99 which sets out general procedural rules for State aid notifications was amended by Regulation 734/2013: OJ 2013 L204/15. The amendments are discussed in detail in the updates to paragraphs 17.070 and 17.075, below.

(e) Other provisions of the TEU and TFEU

1.038 **Other relevant Treaty provisions.** The Commission's decision in COMP/ 38698 *CISAC Agreements*, decision of 16 July 2008, [2009] 4 CMLR 577, was partially annulled by the General Court: Cases T-392, 398, 401, 410, 411, 413–422, 425, 428, 432–434, 442/08, judgments of 12 April 2013. Only one appellant contended that the Commission had erred in its conclusions as to the impacts of the territorial restrictions in the licences on cultural diversity, and this appeal was dismissed: Case T-451/08 *Föreningen Svenska Tonsättares Internationella Musikbyrå*, EU:T:2013:189, [2013] 5 CMLR 577, paras 73 et seq (the appellant had not pleaded that the Commission had insufficient evidence to establish a concerted practice, which was the argument which succeeded in the other appeals).

4. The Institutional Structure of the EU

(a) The EU institutions

1.041 The official languages of the EU. Following Croatia's joining the EU, on 1 July 2013, there are 24 official languages of the EU, Croatian having been added.

1.042 The European Parliament. Following Croatia's joining the EU on 1 July 2013, membership of the European Parliament stands at 751.

The European Commission.   Following Croatia's joining the EU on 1 July **1.044**
2013, there are 28 members of the Commission.

(c) The EU and EFTA Courts

The Court of Justice of the European Union.   Following Croatia's joining the **1.050**
EU on 1 July 2013, there are 24 official languages of the EU.

As well as the numbering of cases before the Court of Justice with 'C-', and before
the General Court with 'T-', in April 2014 the European Case-Law Identifier
('ECLI') was created for all judgments of the European Courts, reflecting the fact
that the European Court Reports are no longer produced in hard copy. The ECLI
numbers are composed as follows: [code for the Member State court or tribunal
concerned, or for the EU]:[abbreviation for the Court that gave the decision—the
abbreviation for the Court of Justice is 'C', and for the General Court 'T']:[year
of the decision]:[order number]. For example, the ECLI of the judgment in Case
C-213/89 *Factortame* is EU:C:1990:257.

Composition and procedure of the Court of Justice.   The procedure of the Court **1.053**
of Justice is now governed by Supplementary Rules, issued on 1 February 2014,
as well as by the Statute of the Court of Justice and the Rules of Procedure: OJ
2014 L32/37.

(d) The Directorate-General for Competition

(iii) Enforcement through investigation and decision

Sectoral inquiries.   The most recent sector inquiry is in the e-commerce sector, **1.069**
announced on 6 May 2015, which remains ongoing: see Press Release IP/15/4921
(6 May 2015). A preliminary report is expected in mid-2016, and the final report
in the first quarter of 2017.

The Commission also now has power, under Article 20a of Regulation 659/99 as
amended by Regulation 734/2013 (OJ 2013 L204/15), to conduct general inquiries into any economic sector, or type of aid instrument, to consider their compatibility with the EU rules on State aid, Articles 107 and 108 TFEU, similarly to its
power in respect of Articles 101 and 102.

The European Competition Network. **1.071**
Fn 263 In respect of the NCAs applying the procedures and powers provided by
national law when applying Articles 101 and 102, see also the ECN's Report on
Investigative Powers and Report on Decision-Making Powers, both of 31 October
2012, which contain comparative analyses of the enforcement powers conferred on
NCAs in different Member States, and identify areas of divergence. Subsequently,
the ECN has published a series of Recommendations on key investigative and
decision-making powers that it considers NCAs should have available in their competition toolbox. All are available on the ECN section of the DG Comp website.

Fn 264 A revised Model Leniency Programme, available on the ECN section of the DG Comp website, was issued in November 2012, in particular to extend the concept of summary applications to NCAs to all leniency applicants, not just the first to approach the Commission.

1.072 **Enforcement by national courts.** As well as asking the Commission for information or its opinion on questions concerning the application of Articles 101 and 102, national courts may now also ask the Commission for information or its opinion on questions concerning the application of Articles 107 or 108 TFEU: Regulation 734/2013, amending Regulation 659/99 and adding Article 23(a): OJ 2013 L204/15.

Fn 270 A recent example of the Commission submitting observations to the United Kingdom courts is *Deutsche Bahn v Morgan Crucible Company* [2014] UKSC 24, in which the Commission submitted observations on the question of the legal status of a Commission infringement decision addressed to a party being sued in a civil claim for damages, in circumstances where the Commission decision has been the subject of successful appeals by other addressees to the European Courts (discussed in paragraph 13.093 of the main text, and the update thereto). The Commission's observations are available on the *Amicus Curiae* section of the DG Comp website.

(v) Guidelines and guidance

1.074 **Purpose of Commission notices and guidelines.**
Fn 275 On 21 March 2014 the Commission issued revised Guidelines on the application of Article 101 of the Treaty on the Functioning of the European Union to technology transfer agreements, OJ 2014 C89/3 ('Revised Technology Transfer Guidelines'). These accompany Regulation 316/2014 on the application of Article 101(3) of the Treaty on the Functioning of the European Union to categories of technology transfer agreements, OJ 2014 L93/17. Regulation 316/2014 entered into force on 1 May 2014, and replaces Regulation 772/2004, which expired on 30 April 2014.

Fn 278 The reference to para 131 of the Technology Transfer Guidelines should be read as para 156 of the Revised Technology Transfer Guidelines.

1.076 **Legal status of Commission notices and guidelines.**
Fn 283 The Court of Justice held in Case C-226/11 *Expedia Inc*, EU:C:2012:795, [2013] 4 CMLR 439, at para 31, that a national competition authority may take into account the Commission's *De Minimis* Notice, but it is not required to do so.

1.077 **Guidance on the Commission's enforcement activities.** The Guidance on the Commission's enforcement priorities in applying Article 82 of the EC Treaty to abusive exclusionary conduct by dominant undertakings, OJ 2009 C45/7, sets priorities for the Commission's future enforcement activities, and it does not apply to proceedings that had already been initiated before it was published, even if it was published prior to the adoption of the Commission's decision in those proceedings: Case T-286/09 *Intel v Commission*, EU:T:2014:547, [2014] 5 CMLR 270 at paras 155–156 (on further appeal, Case C-413/14P, not yet decided).

Fn 288 On 30 August 2014 the Commission adopted a revised *De Minimis* Notice to take account of the Court of Justice's judgment in Case C-226/11 *Expedia Inc*, EU:C:2012:795, [2013] 4 CMLR 439: OJ 2014 C291/1. The revised Notice is discussed in the updates to paragraphs 2.164 et seq, below.

Fn 289 On 30 August 2014 the Commission adopted a revised *De Minimis* Notice to take account of the Court of Justice's judgment in Case C-226/11 *Expedia Inc*, EU:C:2012:795, [2013] 4 CMLR 439: OJ 2014 C291/1. The revised Notice is discussed in the updates to paragraphs 2.164 et seq, below.

5. Territorial Ambit of EU Competition Rules

(a) The Member States: enlargement

Becoming 27 Member States.   Following Croatia's joining the EU on 1 July **1.086**
2013, there are now 28 Member States.

Candidate countries.   Croatia joined the EU on 1 July 2013.   **1.087**

(c) EFTA and the EEA

Allocation of jurisdiction under the EEA Agreement.   **1.095**
Fn 351 The Commission's decision in COMP/38698 *CISAC Agreements*, decision of 16 July 2008, [2009] 4 CMLR 577, has been partially annulled by the General Court, on other grounds: Cases T-392, 398, 401, 410, 411, 413–422, 425, 428, 432–434, 442/08, judgments of 12 April 2013.

(d) Agreements between the EU and third countries

Competition cooperation agreements with other States.   The EU has con- **1.102**
cluded a fifth cooperation agreement on competition matters, with the Swiss Confederation: Agreement between the European Union and the Swiss Confederation concerning cooperation on the application of their competition laws, OJ 2014 L347/3. It entered into force on 1 December 2014: Press Release IP/14/2245 (28 November 2014).

Association agreements between the EU and other states.   **1.104**
Fn 403 On 26 September 2014 the EU published the agreed text of a Comprehensive and Economic Free Trade Agreement with Canada, which remains subject to ratification. Negotiations are ongoing with the US regarding a Transatlantic Trade

and Investment Partnership. The EU signed Association Agreements with Ukraine (27 June 2014; OJ 2014 L161/3), Georgia (22 July 2014; OJ 2014 L261/4) and Moldova (27 June 2014; OJ 2014 L260/4), which introduce a preferential trade regime called the Deep and Comprehensive Free Trade Area.

Fn 405 The General Court dismissed a complaint that the Commission decision in COMP/39180 *Aluminium Fluoride*, decision of 25 June 2008, was issued in breach of the EU's obligations under Article 36 of the Euro-Mediterranean Agreement establishing an association between the European Communities and their Member States, of the one part, and the Republic of Tunisia, of the other part (OJ 1998 L97/2): see T-406/08 *Industries chimiques du fluor v Commission*, EU:T:2013:322, paras 208 et seq. (further appeal, on other grounds, dismissed in Case C-467/13P, *Industries chimiques du fluor v Commission*, EU:C:2014:2274).

1.105 **Cooperation between the Commission and enforcement bodies in other States.** A memorandum to increase cooperation between DG Competition and the Competition Commission of India was signed on 21 November 2013: see Press Release IP/13/1143 (21 November 2013).

6. The Territorial Jurisdiction of the EU Institutions

(a) Trade into the EU from third countries

1.109 **Agreements on imports into the EU.**
Fn 419 The Court of Justice dismissed the further appeals in Joined Cases C-239/11P, etc, *Siemens v Commission (Gas Insulated Switchgear)*, EU:C:2013:866, [2014] 4 CMLR 606.

(b) Trade from EU to third countries

1.113 **Imports into the EU: *de minimis*.**
Fn 440 The Court of Justice dismissed the further appeals in Joined Cases C-239/11P, etc, *Siemens v Commission (Gas Insulated Switchgear)*, EU:C:2013:866, [2014] 4 CMLR 606.

(c) Jurisdiction over undertakings outside the EU

1.115 **Agreements involving undertakings located in third countries.** In Case T-286/09 *Intel v Commission*, EU:T:2014:547, [2014] 5 CMLR 270 at paras 231 et seq, the General Court held that the Commission's jurisdiction was established on the basis that the conduct in question would have immediate, substantial and foreseeable effects in the EU (see the update to paragraph 1.116, below), but for completeness at paras 296 et seq the Court considered whether jurisdiction could also be established on the basis of the conduct being implemented within the EU. The Court considered that direct sales by the addressee are not the only means of implementation within the EU. In that case, which concerned an abuse of dominance contrary to Article 102, implementation could comprise conduct in the EU by the dominant undertaking's customer, by which the customer implemented an agreement between it and the dominant undertaking. On further appeal, Case C-413/14P, not yet decided.

In Case C-231/14P *Innolux v Commission (Liquid Crystal Displays)*, EU:C:2015:451, the Court of Justice dismissed a complaint that the Commission had acted in breach of the territoriality principle, as articulated in Joined Cases 89/85, etc, *Ahlström Osakeyhtiö and Others v Commission* [1988] ECR 5193, '*Wood Pulp I*', in the method it had used to calculate the fine imposed. In its decision in COMP/39309 *Liquid Crystal Displays*, decision of 8 December 2010, discussed in the main text at paragraph 14.020, the Commission had calculated the undertakings' value of sales on the basis of direct sales of the cartelised LCD product into the EEA, and in addition a proportion of the value of the sales made by different companies within the same undertakings, into the EEA, of finished products into which the cartelised LCD product had been incorporated. The Court dismissed a complaint that the Commission's approach effectively brought into account sales that were made to subsidiary companies outside the EEA, and that in doing so it exceeded its jurisdiction. Disagreeing with the Opinion of Advocate General Wathelet, EU:C:2015:292, the Court held that the Commission had jurisdiction to apply Article 101 to the cartel, because the cartelists made direct sales of the cartelised product into the EEA, and that the appropriate method for determining the fine to be imposed in respect of that cartel was a separate question to jurisdiction: paras 73 et seq. On the method of setting the fine, see the update to paragraph 14.020, below.

The General Court dismissed a complaint that the Commission's decision in COMP/39180 *Aluminium Fluoride*, decision of 25 June 2008, which was addressed to an undertaking established in Tunisia, was issued in breach of the EU's obligations under Article 36 of the Euro-Mediterranean Agreement establishing an association between the European Communities and their Member States, of the one part, and the Republic of Tunisia, of the other part (OJ 1998 L97/2): see Case T-406/08 *Industries chimiques du fluor v Commission*, EU:T:2013:322, paras 208 et seq (further appeal, on other grounds, dismissed in Case C-467/13P, *Industries chimiques du fluor v Commission*, EU:C:2014:2274).

Fn 447 The General Court dismissed the appeals against the Commission's findings of infringement in COMP/39181 *Candle Waxes*, decision of 1 October 2008, but reduced the fine imposed on five of the undertakings. The appeals were dismissed in: Case T-548/08 *Total v Commission*, EU:T:2013:434 (on further appeal, Case C-597/13P, not yet decided); Case T-551/08 *H&R ChemPharm v Commission*, EU:T:2014:1081 (on further appeal, Case C-95/15P, not yet decided); Case T-550/08 *Tudapetrol Mineralölerzeugnisse Nils Hansen v Commission* EU:T:2014:1079 (on further appeal, Case C-94/15P, not yet decided); Case T-562/08 *Repsol YPF Lubricantes y especialidades*, EU:T:2014:1078; and Case T-544/08 *Hansen & Rosenthal and H&R Wax Company Vertrieb v Commission*, EU:T:2014:1075 (on further appeal, Case C-90/15P, not yet decided). The fines were reduced, but the appeals otherwise dismissed, in: Case T-566/08 *Total Raffinage Marketing*, EU:T:2013:423 (fine reduced on grounds of duration) (on further appeal, Case C-634/13P, not yet decided); Case T-540/08 *Esso v Commission*, EU:T:2014:630, [2014] 5 CMLR 507 (fine reduced on grounds of duration of involvement of entities that merged during the infringement period); Case T-541/08 *Sasol v Commission*, EU:T:2014:628, [2014] 5 CMLR 729 (fine reduced on grounds of incorrect attribution of conduct by a joint venture); and Case T-543/08 *RWE v Commission*, EU:T:2014:627 (fine reduced on grounds of incorrect attribution of conduct by a joint venture); and Case T-558/08 *Eni v Commission*, EU:T:2014:1080 (fine reduced on grounds of incorrect application of an uplift for recidivism).

1.116 *Gencor:* **EU law must comply with public international law.** In Case T-286/09 *Intel v Commission*, EU:T:2014:547, [2014] 5 CMLR 270 at paras 231 et seq, the General Court held that jurisdiction can be established over undertakings outside the EU based on their conduct being implemented in the EU, following Joined Cases 89/85, etc, *Ahlström Osakeyhtiö and Others v Commission* [1988] ECR 5193, '*Woodpulp*' (discussed in paragraph 1.115 of the main text) or based on their conduct having immediate, substantial and foreseeable effects within the EU, following Case T-102/96 *Gencor v Commission* [1999] ECR II-753. These are alternative approaches, not cumulative, and the Commission does not have to establish implementation within the EU if it can demonstrate that the conduct will have immediate, substantial and foreseeable effects within the EU. The commentary in the main text should be read in the light of this judgment. The General Court also held that the immediate, substantial and foreseeable effects do not also have to be actual effects that have already materialised: para 251. It went on to conclude that the criteria were met on the facts of that case. On further appeal, Case C-413/14P, not yet decided.

1.117 **International comity.** The General Court dismissed a complaint that the Commission decision in COMP/39180 *Aluminium Fluoride*, decision of 25 June 2008, which was addressed to an undertaking established in Tunisia, was issued in breach of the EU's obligations under Article 36 of the Euro-Mediterranean Agreement establishing an association between the European Communities and their Member States, of the one part, and the Republic of Tunisia, of the other part (OJ 1998 L97/2) and of international comity: see Case T-406/08 *Industries chimiques du fluor v Commission*, EU:T:2013:322, paras 208 et seq (further appeal, on other grounds, dismissed in Case C-467/13P, *Industries chimiques du fluor v Commission*, EU:C:2014:2274).

7. Effect on Trade between Member States

(a) Generally

The Effect on Trade Guidelines.   **1.122**
Fn 471 The Court of Justice dismissed the further appeals against the Commission's decision in COMP/38620 *Hydrogen Peroxide and Perborate*, decision of 3 May 2006: see, eg, Case C-455/11P *Solvay v Commission*, EU:C:2013:796, [2014] 4 CMLR 581.

Trade.   **1.123**
Fn 472 The Court of Justice in Case C-440/11P *Commission v Portielje and Gosselin*, EU:C:2013:514, [2013] 5 CMLR 1291, upheld the Commission's appeal on other grounds, and has overturned the General Court judgment in Cases T-208&209/08 *Gosselin Group v Commission* [2011] ECR II-03639, [2013] 4 CMLR 671. The appeal, also on other grounds, in Case C-429/11P *Portielje and Gosselin v Commission*, EU:C:2013:463, was dismissed.

Fn 478 The Commission's decision in COMP/38698 *CISAC Agreements*, decision of 16 July 2008, [2009] 4 CMLR 577, has been partially annulled by the General Court, on other grounds: Cases T-392, 398, 401, 410, 411, 413–422, 425, 428, 432–434, 442/08, judgments of 12 April 2013.

Fn 487 See also Case C-1/12 *Ordem dos Técnicos Oficiais de Contas v Autoridade da Concorrência*, EU:C:2013:127, [2013] 4 CMLR 651 regarding the professional services of chartered accountants.

Fn 489 The General Court judgment annulling the Commission's decision in COMP/38700 *Greek Lignite and Electricity Generation*, decision of 5 March 2008, was overturned by the Court of Justice in Case C-553/12P *Commission v DEI*, EU:C:2014:2083, [2014] 5 CMLR 945.

Alteration of the pattern of trade.   **1.125**
Fn 504 The Court of Justice dismissed the further appeals in Joined Cases C-239/11P, etc, *Siemens v Commission (Gas Insulated Switchgear)*, EU:C:2013:866, [2014] 4 CMLR 606.

Potential effect.   **1.128**
Fn 520 The Court of Justice has dismissed the appeal on other grounds in Case C-181/11P *Compañía española de tabaco en rama v Commission*, EU:C:2012:455.

Fn 528 See also Case T-519/09 *Toshiba v Commission (Power Transformers)*, EU:T:2014:263, [2014] 5 CMLR 219, at para 243, in which the General Court dismissed a complaint that trade between Member States had not been affected by a market-sharing arrangement as there were insurmountable barriers to Japanese manufacturers entering the European market. On further appeal, Case C-373/14P, not yet decided.

1.129 **Indirect effects.**
Fn 533 The Court of Justice has dismissed the appeal on other grounds in Case C-181/11P *Compañía española de tabaco en rama v Commission*, EU:C:2012:455.

1.132 **Application of the 'NAAT-rule'.**
Fn 547 On the requirement to define the relevant market for these purposes, see also Cases C-429/11P *Portielje and Gosselin v Commission*, EU:C:2013:463; and C-439/11P *Ziegler v Commission*, EU:C:2013:514, [2013] 5 CMLR 1291; in particular see para 65 of *Portielje and Gosselin*, and para 63 of *Ziegler*.

Fn 549 The Court of Justice dismissed the further appeal in Case C-439/11P *Ziegler v Commission*, EU:C:2013:514, [2013] 5 CMLR 1291.

Fn 550 The Court of Justice dismissed the further appeal in Case C-439/11P *Ziegler v Commission*, EU:C:2013:514, [2013] 5 CMLR 1291. The Commission requested that the Court substitute new grounds for the General Court's judgment insofar as it held that turnover generated as a subcontractor could be excluded for these purposes, but the Court held there was no need to rule on this request: paras 35 and 89.

1.133 **NAAT-rule is a rebuttable presumption.** In respect of NCAs and national courts not being bound by the Commission's guidance documents, the Court of Justice has confirmed, on the reference for a preliminary ruling from the French Cour de Cassation, that although NCAs may take account of the market share thresholds set by the Commission's *De Minimis* Notice when determining whether an agreement has an appreciable effect on competition, they are not required to do so: Case C-226/11 *Expedia Inc*, EU:C:2012:795, [2013] 4 CMLR 439, para 31.

1.134 **Presumption of appreciable effect in relation to certain agreements.** The Court of Justice in Cases C-429/11P *Portielje and Gosselin v Commission*, EU:C:2013:463; and C-439/11P *Ziegler v Commission*, EU:C:2013:514, [2013] 5 CMLR 1291, held that the Commission had in fact provided a sufficiently detailed description of the services with which its decision was concerned to constitute a definition of the market for these purposes: paras 67–73 of *Portielje and Gosselin* and paras 71–77 of *Ziegler*. In any event it considered that there were factors including in particular the geographic scope of the cartel and the cross-border nature of the services affected that supported the conclusion that there was an appreciable effect on trade: para 99.

(b) **Particular aspects of effect on trade**

1.135 **Effect of agreement as a whole in Article 101 cases.**
Fn 556 The Court of Justice dismissed the further appeals in Joined Cases C-239/11P, etc, *Siemens v Commission (Gas Insulated Switchgear)*, EU:C:2013:866, [2014] 4 CMLR 606.

Effect of conduct in Article 102 cases.　　　　　　　　　　　　　　　**1.136**

Fn 562 The Court of Justice in Case C-457/10P *AstraZeneca v Commission*, EU:C:2012:770, [2013] 4 CMLR 233, upheld the General Court's judgment and dismissed the further appeals.

Agreements or practices confined to a single Member State.　　See also Case　**1.138** C-172/14 *ING Pensii* EU:C:2015:484, [2015] 5 CMLR 820, paras 49–52. The Court of Justice held that an agreement regarding the allocation of customers of pensions services was capable of affecting trade within the EU in circumstances where the agreement extended over the entire territory of Romania; where the customers might be located in other Member States and the pension providers might be subsidiaries of companies in other Member States; and where the requirement that pension providers be registered in Romania made it more difficult for companies established outside Romania to enter the market.

2

ARTICLE 101(1)

2. Undertakings

(a) Generally

Undertakings. See also Joined Cases C-231/11P, etc, *Commission v Siemens and* **2.003**
others, EU:C:2014:256, [2014] 5 CMLR 7, at paras 55 et seq, in which the Court
of Justice upheld the Commission's appeal and confirmed that the Commission
has no power to determine the proportions that particular legal entities within
an undertaking should contribute towards payment of a fine. The Court stated
at para 55:

> 'While it is true that a Commission decision imposing fines must necessarily be
> addressed to the legal persons comprising an undertaking, that limitation, which
> is of a purely practical nature, does not mean that, where the Commission makes
> use of its power to hold a number of legal entities jointly and severally liable for
> payment of a fine, as they formed a single undertaking at the time the infringement
> was committed, the rules and principles of EU competition law are to be applied
> not only to the undertaking concerned but also to the legal persons of which the
> undertaking is made up.'

Economic activity. **2.005**
Fn 13 The Court of Justice confirmed, in Case C-288/11P *Mitteldeutsche Flughafen
and Flughafen Leipzig Halle v Commission*, EU:C:2012:821, [2013] 2 CMLR 483,
the General Court's conclusion in Joined Cases T-443&455/08 *Freistaat Sachsen
and Land Sachsen-Anhalt v Commission* [2011] ECR II-1311, that the operation of
an airport constitutes an economic activity (such that financial assistance granted
to enable the building of an additional runway at the airport could constitute a
State aid).

Fn 15 The Court of Justice upheld the Commission's appeal in Case C-440/11P
Commission v Portielje and Gosselin, EU:C:2013:514, [2013] 5 CMLR 1291,
at paras 41–46, and overturned the General Court judgment in Joined Cases
T-208&209/08 *Gosselin Group v Commission* [2011] ECR II-03639, [2013]
4 CMLR 671: see the update to paragraph 2.011, below. The appeal in Case
C-429/11P *Portielje and Gosselin v Commission*, EU:C:2013:463, was dismissed.

2.010 **Individuals as undertakings.** Chartered accountants have also been held to be undertakings, see C-1/12 *Ordem dos Técnicos Oficiais de Contas v Autoridade da Concorrência*, EU:C:2013:127, [2013] 4 CMLR 651, para 38.

Fn 31 The Commission's decision in COMP/39510 *Ordre National des Pharmaciens en France (ONP)*, decision of 8 December 2010, was upheld as to liability in Case T-90/11 *ONP v Commission* EU:T:2014:1049. See in particular paras 344 et seq.

2.011 **Shareholders as undertakings.** The Court of Justice upheld the Commission's appeal in Case C-440/11P *Commission v Portielje and Gosselin*, EU:C:2013:514, [2013] 5 CMLR 1291, and overturned the General Court judgment in Joined Cases T-208&209/08 *Gosselin Group v Commission* [2011] ECR II-03639, [2013] 4 CMLR 671. The Court confirmed that if a company holds all the capital, or almost all the capital, in a subsidiary company that is sufficient basis for the application of the presumption of decisive influence: para 41. It is not relevant to consider whether the parent company is also itself engaged in an economic activity and individually constitutes an undertaking, if it is part of the same undertaking as the subsidiary: paras 42–46. The Court also overturned the General Court's conclusion that Portielje had rebutted the presumption of decisive influence: paras 65–73. The appeal in Case C-429/11P *Portielje and Gosselin v Commission*, EU:C:2013:463, was dismissed.

(b) The State as an undertaking

2.014 **Distinction between economic activity and State functions.** In Case C-327/12 *SOA Nazionale Costruttori*, EU:C:2013:827, at paras 27 et seq, the Court of Justice held that private bodies providing certification services under a statutory certification scheme are engaged in an economic activity. The Court noted in particular that the bodies did not perform any standardisation tasks, or make decisions connected with the exercise of public powers.

2.020 **Regulatory bodies.** See also Case C-1/12 *Ordem dos Técnicos Oficiais de Contas v Autoridade da Concorrência*, EU:C:2013:127, [2013] 4 CMLR 651, paras 46 et seq, regarding the body that regulates chartered accountants in Portugal.

In Case C-327/12 *SOA Nazionale Costruttori*, EU:C:2013:827, at paras 27 et seq, the Court of Justice held that private bodies providing certification services under a statutory certification scheme are engaged in an economic activity. The Court noted in particular that the bodies did not perform any standardisation tasks, or make decisions connected with the exercise of public powers.

Fn 89 The Commission's decision in COMP/39510 *Ordre National des Pharmaciens en France (ONP)*, decision of 8 December 2010, was upheld as to liability in Case T-90/11 *ONP v Commission* EU:T:2014:1049.

(c) Treatment of economically linked legal entities

Group of companies as a single undertaking. The focus of EU law on economic rather than legal identity was underlined by the Court of Justice in Joined Cases C-231/11P, etc, *Commission v Siemens and others*, EU:C:2014:256, [2014] 5 CMLR 7, at paras 55 et seq, upholding the Commission's appeal and confirming that the Commission has no power to determine the proportions that particular legal entities within an undertaking should contribute towards the payment of a fine. The Court stated at para 55: **2.024**

> 'While it is true that a Commission decision imposing fines must necessarily be addressed to the legal persons comprising an undertaking, that limitation, which is of a purely practical nature, does not mean that, where the Commission makes use of its power to hold a number of legal entities jointly and severally liable for payment of a fine, as they formed a single undertaking at the time the infringement was committed, the rules and principles of EU competition law are to be applied not only to the undertaking concerned but also to the legal persons of which the undertaking is made up.'

The determination that an undertaking is jointly and severally liable for a fine does not extend to determining the shares to be paid by legal entities within the undertaking, which is a matter for the national courts applying national law to the dispute in a manner consistent with EU law.

Arrangements within a group of companies. **2.025**
Fn 105 On 21 March 2014 the Commission adopted Regulation 316/2014 on the application of Article 101(3) of the Treaty on the Functioning of the European Union to categories of technology transfer agreements, OJ 2014 L93/17. It entered into force on 1 May 2014, and replaces Regulation 772/2004 which expired on 30 April 2014. The reference to Article 2 of Regulation 772/2004 should be read as Article 2 of Regulation 316/2014.

Attribution to a parent company of the conduct of wholly owned subsidiaries. **2.026**
In Case T-399/09 *HSE v Commission (Calcium Carbide)*, EU:T:2013:647, [2014] CMLR 738 the General Court observed that the case law on the concept of economic unity applies equally to companies which are owned, directly or indirectly, by the State: para 48. It also applies to holding companies, whose ownership of a subsidiary is only temporary: para 59.

Fn 106 The Court of Justice dismissed the further appeal in Case C-50/12P *Kendrion v Commission*, EU:C:2013:771, [2014] 4 CMLR 454; see in particular para 34.

Parent company and partly-owned subsidiaries. The General Court in Case **2.027**
T-587/08 *Fresh Del Monte Produce*, EU:T:2013:129, [2013] 4 CMLR 1091, upheld the Commission's decision in COMP/39188 *Bananas*, decision of 15 October 2008, discussed in the main text, in which the Commission held Del Monte

liable for the conduct of Weichert: paras 50 et seq. The Court of Justice dismissed the further appeal in Joined Cases C-293&294/13P *Fresh Del Monte Produce*, EU:C:2015:416, [2015] 5 CMLR 513: paras 75 et seq.

In Case C-343/06 *Shell Petroleum v Commission*, EU:T:2012:478, [2012] 5 CMLR 1064, at paras 45–51, the General Court upheld the Commission's decision that two parent companies could be held liable for the conduct of a subsidiary, based on a presumption of decisive influence, where the two parent companies were within the same undertaking and together owned all of the shares in the subsidiary. The infringing subsidiary, Shell Nederland Verkoopmaatschappij ('SNV') was owned, indirectly, by Shell Transport and Trading ('STT') and Koninklijke Nederlandsche Petroleum Maatschappij ('KNPM'), who held 40 per cent and 60 per cent shares respectively in the holding company that owned SNV. The General Court held that in the light of the structure of the Shell group the situation was analogous to SNV being held by a single parent company, and the Commission was entitled to rely on a presumption that the two companies STT and KNPM exercised a decisive influence over SNV's conduct. The further appeal, in Case C-585/12P, was withdrawn: Order of 11 April 2013.

Fn 115 See also Case T-399/09 *HSE v Commission (Calcium Carbide)*, EU:T:2013:647, [2014] CMLR 738 upholding the Commission's findings that HSE was liable for the conduct of its subsidiary on the basis of a 74.44 per cent shareholding and evidence of the actual exercise of decisive influence.

2.028 **Parent companies and joint ventures.** The Court of Justice dismissed the further appeals against the Commission's decision in COMP/38629 *Chloroprene Rubber*, decision of 5 December 2007 (at footnote 118 of the main text), in Cases C-179/12P *Dow Chemical Company v Commission*, EU:C:2013:605, [2014] 4 CMLR 220; and C-172/12P *El du Pont de Nemours v Commission*, EU:C:2013:601, [2014] 4 CMLR 236. Provided the factual evidence demonstrates the actual exercise of decisive influence, there is no error of law in holding two parent companies and the joint venture in which they each have a 50 per cent shareholding to be a single undertaking for the purposes (and only for the purposes) of establishing liability for participation in an infringement of competition law: see in particular *Dow*, para 58 and *du Pont*, para 47.

In Case T-541/08 *Sasol v Commission (Candle Waxes)*, EU:T:2014:628, [2014] 5 CMLR 729, at paras 40 et seq, the General Court has considered the circumstances in which the conduct of a joint venture can be imputed to one parent company alone. The Commission had attributed liability to Sasol, which owned two-thirds of the shares in the joint venture, using evidence of its ability to exercise decisive influence without finding that it had actually exercised decisive influence. The Court held that the Commission can establish actual decisive influence by way of an abstract analysis of the documents signed before a joint venture began to operate, along the lines of the analysis conducted under Regulation 139/2004 (the Merger Regulation) to determine whether the company is able to 'control' the joint venture, in as much as the Commission may presume that the legislation and provisions of agreements relating to the operation of that undertaking, in particular the joint venture's articles of association and the shareholder and voting rights agreement, have been implemented and complied with: para 49. However, it is open to the Commission and the undertaking concerned to adduce evidence that the joint venture's commercial decisions were taken by procedures other than those apparent from the mere abstract examination of the agreements, and in particular that they were taken by several or all of the parent companies unanimously: para 50. In that case, the General Court held that the Commission had made an error of assessment in dismissing the evidence that the other parent company of the joint venture exercised decisive influence jointly with the one to which liability had been attributed. See also Case T-543/08 *RWE v Commission (Candle Waxes)*, EU:T:2014:627, at paras 99 et seq, in which the General Court considered the joint attribution of liability to both parents of a joint venture on the basis of ability to exercise decisive influence.

Agents.   It is not relevant that the principal is unaware of the agent's participa- **2.030** tion in anti-competitive conduct. The acts of the agent can be imputed to the principal just as those of an employee may be imputed to an employer: Case T-418/10 *Voestalpine v Commission*, EU:T:2015:516, para 175. That imputation extends to finding the principal liable for participating in a single and continuous infringement on the basis that it is considered to have been aware, through its agent, of the conduct of the other undertakings in pursuit of the same overall plan: paras 389 et seq.

Fn 126 See, however, Case T-418/10 *Voestalpine v Commission*, EU:T:2015:516, paras 149 et seq. The General Court held that an agent who acted on behalf of two principals, both of which participated in the cartel, could be considered to be part of the same undertaking as one of them. In such a situation, the relevant question is whether the agent acts as an independent trader free to determine his own business strategy, or whether the functions he carries out on behalf of the principal in question are an integral part of the latter's activities.

Fn 127 For a recent example, see Case T-418/10 *Voestalpine v Commission*, EU:T:2015:516, paras 142 et seq.

Fn 128 For a recent example, see Case T-418/10 *Voestalpine v Commission*, EU:T:2015:516, paras 142 et seq.

Employees and trade unions.   On whether a person is an 'employee' or self- **2.031** employed and an undertaking, see also Case C-413/13 *FNV Kunsten Informatie en Media v Staat der Nederlanden*, EU:C:2014:2411. The Court of Justice considered whether a collective labour agreement between a body representing musicians and a body representing orchestras, which covered the hiring of substitute members of orchestras both under contracts of employment and also under contracts for services, was within the scope of Article 101(1). The Court held that it is for a national court to decide, on the facts of a given case, whether a person is an employee under EU law notwithstanding his classification as self-employed under national law, because his independence is merely notional and he enjoys no more independence or flexibility than an employee performing the same activity. In that regard, it is relevant to consider whether he acts under the direction of his employer in respect of, in particular, his freedom to choose the time, place and content of his work; whether he shares in the employer's commercial risks; and, for the duration of their relationship, whether he forms an integral part of the employer's undertaking, so forming an economic unit with that undertaking. If the person performs the same activities as the employer's employed workers, then a provision in a collective labour agreement setting minimum fees for his services falls outside the scope of Article 101(1).

3. Agreements, Decisions and Concerted Practices

(a) Agreements

2.034 **Proof of an agreement.**
Fn 151 The Court of Justice dismissed the undertakings' further appeals in Joined Cases C-239/11P, etc, *Siemens v Commission (Gas Insulated Switchgear)*, EU:C:2013:866, [2014] 4 CMLR 606. See the update to paragraph 2.064, below.

2.035 **Agreements may be informal.** The General Court upheld the Commission's decision in COMP/38698 *CISAC Agreements*, decision of 16 July 2008, insofar as it found the membership clause in the collecting societies' agreements infringed Article 101: Cases T-392, 401, 422, 432/08, EU:T:2013:170, [2013] 5 CMLR 15. It partially annulled the decision on other grounds in Cases T-392, 398, 401, 410, 411, 413–422, 425, 428, 432–434, 442/08, judgments of 12 April 2013.

2.036 **Agreements may be incomplete.**
Fn 160 The General Court dismissed the appeals against the Commission's findings of infringement in COMP/39181 *Candle Waxes*, decision of 1 October 2008, but reduced the fine imposed on five of the undertakings. On the alleged failure to implement the cartel, see Case T-558/08 *Eni v Commission*, EU:T:2014:1080, paras 132–133. The General Court held that it is sufficient for the Commission to establish a concurrence of wills between the undertakings as to the principle of fixing or aligning prices, without it being necessary for it to establish further that any price increases were, or could, be implemented.

2.037 **Agreements made under duress.**
Fn 165 See also Case T-154/09 *Manuli Rubber Industries v Commission (Marine Hoses)*, EU:T:2013:260, paras 182 et seq, in which the General Court rejected a

contention that the undertaking maintained contact with the other cartelists in order to give the impression that it had an interest in re-launching the cartel, and to protect itself against reprisals. At paras 233 et seq, the General Court rejected a contention that this could bear upon the gravity of the infringement for the purpose of determining the percentage of relevant sales on which to set the fine, and at paras 285 et seq it rejected the contention that the Commission should have considered this a factor mitigating the fine.

Authority to enter into agreements. In Case T-146/09 *Parker ITR and Parker-* **2.038** *Hannifin v Commission (Marine Hoses)*, EU:T:2013:258, [2013] 5 CMLR 712, paras 151 et seq, the General Court held that the fact that an individual established a fraudulent scheme to allow him, and the companies which he controlled or to which he was linked, to benefit from the illegal gains of the cartel, did not affect the undertaking's liability for the infringement found in COMP/39406 *Marine Hoses*, decision of 28 January 2009, since the individual was authorised to act on the undertaking's behalf irrespective of whether he was acting with its knowledge (the General Court's judgment was partially overturned, on other grounds on further appeal, in Case C-434/13P *Commission v Parker Hannifin Manufacturing and Parker-Hannifin*, EU:C:2014:2456, [2015] 4 CMLR 179; see the update to paragraph 14.101, below). See also Case T-551/08 *H&R ChemPharm v Commission (Candle Waxes)*, EU:C:2014:1081, para 133, in which the General Court held that it was irrelevant that a particular individual, who acted with the undertaking's authority, devoted only 30 per cent of his working time to the undertaking. Even very brief periods of time spent in contact with the undertaking would enable the individual to communicate information that he had obtained during the anti-competitive meetings. On further appeal, Case C-95/15P, not yet decided.

In Case T-418/10 *Voestalpine v Commission*, EU:T:2015:516, para 175, the General Court held that the acts of the agent, who participates in anti-competitive conduct of which his principal is not aware, can be imputed to the principal just as those of an employee may be imputed to an employer in such circumstances. That imputation extends to finding the principal liable for participating in a single and continuous infringement, on the basis that it is considered to have been aware, through its agent, of the conduct of the other undertakings in pursuit of the same overall plan: paras 389 et seq.

Fn 166 See also Case C-68/12 *Protimonopolný úrad v Slovenská sporitel'ňa*, EU:C:2013:71, [2013] 4 CMLR 491, para 28, where the Court of Justice held 'it is not necessary to demonstrate personal conduct on the part of a representative authorised under the undertaking's constitution or the personal assent, in the form of a mandate, of that representative to the conduct of an employee of the undertaking who has participated in an anti-competitive meeting'.

Fn 168 The General Court dismissed the appeals against the Commission's findings of infringement in COMP/39181 *Candle Waxes*, decision of 1 October 2008, but reduced the fine imposed on five of the undertakings. On the authority of the individual who participated in the anti-competitive meetings to make price-setting decisions, see Case T-551/08 *H&R ChemPharm v Commission (Candle Waxes)*, EU:C:2014:1081, paras 126 et seq. On further appeal, Case C-95/15P, not yet decided.

2.040 **Acquiescence to a unilateral policy.** The Supreme Court of Lithuania has referred to the Court of Justice for a preliminary ruling questions concerning undertakings' participation in a common computerised information system, and in particular whether the participating undertakings agree, expressly or tacitly, to a restriction on price discounts when the system includes a notice stating that discounting is restricted, and there are technical restrictions on discounting via the system: Case C-74/14 *UAB Eturas*, not yet decided. The undertakings have been fined by the Lithuanian Competition Council for a concerted practice in their online sales.

2.043 **Incorporation of terms in an agreement.**
Fn 191 The General Court upheld the Commission's decision in COMP/38698 *CISAC Agreements*, decision of 16 July 2008, insofar as it found the membership clause in the collecting societies' agreements infringed Article 101: Cases T-392, 401, 422, 432/08 judgments of 12 April 2013, [2013] 5 CMLR 15. It partially annulled the decision on other grounds in Cases T-392, 398, 401, 410, 411, 413–422, 425, 428, 432–434, 442/08, judgments of 12 April 2013.

2.046 **Government measures.**
Fn 200 The Commission's decision in COMP/39510 *Ordre National des Pharmaciens en France (ONP)*, decision of 8 December 2010, was upheld as to liability in Case T-90/11 *ONP v Commission*, EU:T:2014:1049. See paras 344 et seq.

2.047 **Infringement actions and rights delimitation agreements.** On the application of Article 101 to agreements settling infringement actions, see the Commission's enforcement action in the pharmaceutical sector following the sector inquiry report (discussed in paragraph 9.061 of the main text). Lundbeck and four groups of generics companies have been fined for infringing Article 101 by entering into 'reverse payment' settlement agreements, in respect of the antidepressant drug citalopram: COMP/39226 *Lundbeck*, decision of 19 June 2013: see Press Release IP/13/563 (19 June 2013). The decision is under appeal: Cases T-460/13, etc, not yet decided. In COMP/39685 *Johnson & Johnson and Novartis*, decision of 10 December 2013, the Commission found that a 'co-promotion' agreement under which Novartis' Dutch subsidiary, Sandoz, had strong financial incentives to refrain from entering the Netherlands market for the analgesic drug fentanyl infringed Article 101: see Press Release IP/13/1233 (10 December 2013). In COMP/39612 *Perindopril (Servier)*, decision of 9 July 2013, as well as finding that reverse payment settlement agreements between Servier and five generics companies breached Article 101, the Commission found that Servier's conduct infringed Article 102. It considered that by holding a number of secondary patents for the ACE inhibitor drug perindopril and acquiring the most advanced source of non-protected technology, and then by entering into reverse payment settlement agreements with the five generics companies that sought to enter the market, Servier had abused its dominant position in the market. On appeal, Case T-691/14, not yet decided.

Similar concerns regarding patent settlements have arisen in the United States, and the US Supreme Court judgment in *Federal Trade Commission v Actavis and others*, of 17 June 2013, 570 U.S. (2013) clarified that in the United States a 'rule of reason' approach is to be applied to antitrust scrutiny of such agreements, that is, the courts will consider in the light of all the relevant facts and circumstances whether a particular agreement has overall pro-competitive or anti-competitive effects on the relevant market (see further paragraphs 2.104 et seq of the main text).

On the application of Article 102, see the Court of Justice in Case C-170/13 *Huawei v ZTE*, EU:C:2015:477 in which the Court considered whether it was contrary to Article 102 for a dominant undertaking to bring proceedings before a Member State court to enforce a standard essential patent ('SEP'), in circumstances where the patent has acquired SEP status as a result of the proprietor having irrevocably undertaken to the standard-setting body that it will license on fair, reasonable, and non-discriminatory ('FRAND') terms. The Court held that to bring such proceedings may in principle be contrary to Article 102. The proprietor's undertaking to the standard-setting body does not deprive it of its right to bring an action before the courts of a Member State to enforce its patent, but it must comply with specific requirements when it does so. These are to notify the alleged infringer of the SEP and its breach; to make a specific, written offer of a licence on FRAND terms specifying the royalty and the way in which it has been calculated. The alleged infringer must respond in good faith, and without delay. If it does not accept the offer, it must promptly make a written counter-offer that corresponds to FRAND terms, and if its counter-offer is rejected and it is using the teachings of the SEP then from the point of rejection it must provide appropriate security. The parties may agree to submit the determination of the amount of the royalty to a third party. If the proprietor has complied with the requirements incumbent upon it, or if the alleged infringer has failed to comply with the requirements incumbent upon it, then it is not an abuse of the proprietor's dominant position for it to commence litigation to enforce its patent. See also COMP/39985 *Motorola – enforcement of ETSI standards essential patents*, decision of 29 April 2014 (Press Release IP/14/489 (29 April 2014)) in which the Commission found that Motorola had breached Article 102 by seeking an injunction in Germany against Apple for breach of its SEPs (which were essential to meeting the European Telecommunications Standardisation Institute's (ETSI) GPRS standard, part of the GSM standard, which is a key industry standard for mobile and wireless communications), in circumstances where it had committed to license on FRAND terms, and where Apple was willing to enter into a licence agreement and to be bound by a determination by the German

Court of the FRAND terms. However, in view of the novelty of the infringement finding, no fine has been imposed. The Commission accepted commitments from Samsung in COMP/39939 *Samsung – enforcement of ETSI standards essential patents*, decision of 29 April 2014. In its preliminary assessment, the Commission considered that Samsung had infringed Article 102 by seeking injunctions against Apple in several Member States to enforce its patents that were essential to complying with ETSI's 3G UMTS standard (a key standard for mobile and wireless communications), and that Samsung had committed to license on FRAND terms. The Commission accepted commitments under which Samsung agrees, in essence, for a period of five years not to seek an injunction before any court or tribunal in the EEA for infringement of its SEPs implemented in mobile devices against a potential licensee that agrees to, and complies with, a particular framework set out in the commitments decision for determining the terms of a licence.

2.048 **Assignments and licences of intellectual property rights.**
Fn 209 On 21 March 2014 the Commission adopted Regulation 316/2014 on the application of Article 101(3) of the Treaty on the Functioning of the European Union to categories of technology transfer agreements, OJ 2014 L93/17. It entered into force on 1 May 2014, and replaces Regulation 772/2004 which expired on 30 April 2014. The new Regulation is discussed in the updates to Chapter 9, below.

2.049 **Terminated or 'spent' agreements.** The General Court upheld the Commission's decision in COMP/38698 *CISAC Agreements*, decision of 16 July 2008, discussed in the main text, insofar as it found the exclusivity clause in the collecting societies' agreements infringed Article 101: Case T-401/08 *Säveltäjäin Tekijänoikeustoimisto Teosto v Commission*, EU:T:2013:170, [2013] 5 CMLR 15. It partially annulled the decision on other grounds in Cases T-392, 398, 401, 410, 411, 413–422, 425, 428, 432–434, 442/08, judgments of 12 April 2013.

Fn 212 See also Case C-70/12P *Quinn Barlo v Commission* ('*Methacrylates*'), EU:C:2013:351, [2013] 5 CMLR 637, para 40, in which the Court of Justice held that an infringement may be found throughout the period in which unlawful prices were applied by an undertaking even though the unlawful contacts formally have come to an end; and Case T-540/08 *Esso v Commission*, EU:T:2014:630, [2014] 5 CMLR 507, at paras 81–85, in which the General Court held that even if representatives of an undertaking did not participate in certain unlawful meetings nonetheless the undertaking could be presumed throughout the period preceding those meetings to have taken account of information already exchanged with its competitors in determining its conduct on the market. It therefore upheld the Commission's findings as to the duration of the cartel.

The Court of Justice dismissed the undertakings' further appeals, on other grounds, Joined Cases C-231/11P, etc, *Commission v Siemens and others*, EU:C:2014:256, [2014] 5 CMLR 7. The Commission's appeal was upheld: see the update to paragraph 2.024, above.

Judicial settlements and compromise of litigation. As part of the **2.050**
Commission's ongoing enforcement action following the pharmaceutical
sector inquiry, Lundbeck and four groups of generics companies have been
fined for infringing Article 101 by entering into 'reverse payment' settlement
agreements, in respect of the antidepressant drug citalopram: COMP/39226
Lundbeck, decision of 19 June 2013: see Press Release IP/13/563 (19 June 2013).
The decision is under appeal: Cases T-460/13, etc, not yet decided. In COMP/
39685 *Johnson & Johnson and Novartis*, decision of 10 December 2013, the
Commission found that a 'co-promotion' agreement under which Novartis'
Dutch subsidiary, Sandoz, had strong financial incentives to refrain from entering the Netherlands market for the analgesic drug fentanyl infringed Article
101: see Press Release IP/13/1233 (10 December 2013). In COMP/39612
Perindopril (Servier), decision of 9 July 2013, as well as finding that reverse
payment settlement agreements between Servier and five generics companies
breached Article 101, the Commission found that Servier's conduct infringed
Article 102. It considered that by holding a number of secondary patents for
the ACE inhibitor drug perindopril and acquiring the most advanced source
of non-protected technology, and then by entering into reverse payment settlement agreements with the five generics companies that sought to enter the
market, Servier had abused its dominant position in the market. On appeal,
Case T-691/14, not yet decided.

Collective labour relations agreements. In Case C-413/13 *FNV Kunsten* **2.051**
Informatie en Media v Staat der Nederlanden, EU:C:2014:2411 the Court of
Justice considered whether a collective labour agreement between a body representing musicians and a body representing orchestras, which covered the hiring
of substitute members of orchestras both under contracts of employment and also
under contracts for services, was within the scope of Article 101(1). The Court
held that it is for a national court to decide, on the facts of a given case, whether
a person is an employee under EU law, notwithstanding his classification as self-
employed under national law, because his independence is merely notional and
he enjoys no more independence or flexibility than an employee performing the
same activity. In that regard, it is relevant to consider whether he acts under the
direction of his employer as regards, in particular, his freedom to choose the time,
place and content of his work; does not share in the employer's commercial risks;
and, for the duration of their relationship, forms an integral part of the employer's
undertaking, so forming an economic unit with that undertaking. If the person
performs the same activities as the employer's employed workers, then a provision in a collective labour agreement setting minimum fees for his services falls
outside the scope of Article 101(1).

Agreements made prior to date of accession to the EU. **2.054**
Fn 241 The General Court dismissed the appeals against the Commission's findings of infringement in COMP/39181 *Candle Waxes*, decision of 1 October 2008,

but reduced the fine imposed on five of the undertakings. MOL, the undertaking to whom the Commission's findings in this regard were addressed, did not appeal the decision.

(b) Concerted practices

2.055 Generally.
Fn 245 The Commission's decision in COMP/39188 *Bananas,* decision of 15 October 2008, finding an unlawful concerted practice was upheld in Case T-587/08 *Fresh Del Monte Produce v Commission,* EU:T:2013:129, [2013] 4 CMLR 1091, paras 295 et seq (further appeal, on other grounds, dismissed in Joined Cases C-293&294/13P *Fresh Del Monte Produce,* EU:C:2015:416, [2015] 5 CMLR 513); and in Case T-588/08 *Dole Food Company v Commission,* EU:T:2013:130, paras 53 et seq (further appeal dismissed in Case C-286/13P *Dole Food Company v Commission* EU:C:2015:184, [2015] 4 CMLR 967).

2.058 Concertation or cooperation between undertakings. In Case C-455/11P *Solvay v Commission,* EU:C:2013:796, [2014] 4 CMLR 581, at paras 39 et seq, the Court of Justice held that in a highly concentrated oligopolistic market the exchange of commercial information between competitors will itself allow operators to know the market positions and strategies of their competitors, and the exchange of such information in preparation for an anti-competitive agreement therefore suffices to prove the existence of a concerted practice. It is not necessary to establish that the competitors formally undertook to adopt a particular course of conduct, or that the competitors colluded over their future conduct on the market.

Fn 265 The General Court upheld the Commission's decision in COMP/ 39188 *Bananas,* decision of 15 October 2008, applying the judgment in *British Sugar* discussed in the main text (Case T-202/98, etc, *Tate & Lyle v Commission* [2001] ECR II-2035), in Case T-587/08 *Fresh Del Monte Produce v Commission,* EU:T:2013:129, [2013] 4 CMLR 1091 (reducing the fine but dismissing the appeal on liability), para 369 (further appeal, on other grounds, dismissed in Joined Cases C-293&294/13P *Fresh Del Monte Produce,* EU:C:2015:416, [2015] 5 CMLR 513); and Case T-588/08 *Dole Food Company v Commission,* EU:T:2013:130, para 403 (further appeal dismissed in Case C-286/13P *Dole Food Company v Commission,* EU:C:2015:184, [2015] 4 CMLR 967).

2.059 Conduct on the market. In Case C-455/11P *Solvay v Commission,* EU:C:2013:796, [2014] 4 CMLR 581, at paras 39 et seq, the Court of Justice held that in a highly concentrated oligopolistic market the exchange of commercial information between competitors will itself allow operators to know the market positions and strategies of their competitors, and the exchange of such information in preparation for an anti-competitive agreement therefore suffices to prove the existence of a concerted practice. It is not necessary to establish that the competitors formally undertook to adopt a particular course of conduct, or that the competitors colluded over their future conduct on the market.

The presumption may apply to a meeting on a single occasion. The General 2.061
Court applied the approach set out by the Court of Justice in Case C-8/08 *T-Mobile Netherlands v Commission* [2009] ECR I-4529, [2009] 5 CMLR 11 in its judgments upholding the Commission's decision in COMP/39188 *Bananas*, decision of 15 October 2008: see Case T-587/08 *Fresh Del Monte Produce v Commission*, EU:T:2013:129, [2013] 4 CMLR 1091, paras 351–352 (further appeal, on other grounds, dismissed in Joined Cases C-293&294/13P *Fresh Del Monte Produce*, EU:C:2015:416, [2015] 5 CMLR 513); and Case T-588/08 *Dole Food Company v Commission*, EU:T:2013:130, paras 368 et seq (further appeal dismissed in Case C-286/13P *Dole Food Company v Commission*, EU:C:2015:184, [2015] 4 CMLR 967). See also Case T-655/11 *FSL (Exotic fruit) v Commission*, EU:T:2015:383, paras 447–448 (on further appeal, Case C-469/15P, not yet decided).

Proof of a concerted practice.   2.063
Fn 282 See also the General Court's approach in its judgments partially annulling the Commission's decision in COMP/38698 *CISAC Agreements*, decision of 16 July 2008, in which it had found an unlawful concerted practice: for example, Case T-442/08 *CISAC v Commission*, EU:T:2013:188, [2013] 5 CMLR 536, paras 92–94.

Documentary evidence of a concerted practice. In Joined Cases C-239/11P, 2.064
etc, *Siemens v Commission (Gas Insulated Switchgear)*, EU:C:2013:866, [2014] 4 CMLR 606, the Court of Justice held that the existence of an information exchange mechanism in the agreement between European and Japanese manufacturers supported the General Court's conclusion that the Japanese manufacturers were credible 'potential competitors' on the European markets: para 114. As the Commission had established evidence of the existence of a concerted practice, it was not necessary to examine whether there was an alternative plausible explanation for the undertakings' conduct such as the existence of alleged technical and economic barriers to entry into the European markets: paras 219 et seq. The Court also considered the credibility of leniency statements, and the corroborative evidence required where other cartelists contest the contents of a leniency statement, as evidence of a concerted practice: see paragraphs 5.027 and 5.028 of the main text, and the updates thereto below. Similarly, see Case T-519/09 *Toshiba v Commission (Power Transformers)*, EU:T:2014:263, [2014] 5 CMLR 219, at paras 229–235 (on further appeal, Case C-373/14P, not yet decided).

In C-455/11P *Solvay v Commission*, EU:C:2013:796, [2014] 4 CMLR 581, at paras 39 et seq, the Court of Justice held that in a highly concentrated oligopolistic market the exchange of commercial information between competitors will itself allow operators to know the market positions and strategies of their competitors, and the exchange of such information in preparation for an anti-competitive agreement therefore suffices to prove the existence of a concerted practice. It is not necessary to establish that the competitors formally undertook to adopt a particular course of conduct, or that the competitors colluded over their future conduct on the market.

2.065 **Relying on conduct as evidence of a concerted practice.** The Commission's decision in COMP/38698 *CISAC Agreements*, decision of 16 July 2008, discussed in the main text was partially annulled by the General Court: Cases T-392, 398, 401, 410, 411, 413–422, 425, 428, 432–434, 442/08, judgments of 12 April 2013. It held that the Commission did not have sufficient evidence to establish the existence of a concerted practice, and that the need for monitoring the use of copyrighted material did provide a plausible explanation for the parallel behaviour of collecting societies within the EEA.

2.066 **Alternative explanations for parallel behaviour.** See also the General Court's judgments partially annulling the Commission's decision in COMP/38698 *CISAC Agreements*, decision of 16 July 2008, discussed in the update to paragraph 2.065, above.

2.067 **Disclosure of pricing information from retailers to suppliers.** The state of mind required to satisfy the test laid down by the Court of Appeal in *Argos & Littlewoods and JJB Sports v Office of Fair Trading* [2006] EWCA Civ 1318, para 140, was discussed at length by the Competition Appeal Tribunal in *Tesco v OFT* [2012] CAT 31. At stage (i) it is not sufficient to show that retailer A knew supplier B 'might' pass on the information: para 78; and the Tribunal expressed doubts as to whether anything short of intention or actual foresight that supplier B will pass on the information will suffice: paras 350–354.

On 4 February 2015 the Commission issued a decision that an undertaking which provides broker services infringed Article 101 by facilitating the infringements by various banks in respect of the benchmark for trading yen interest rate derivatives: COMP/39861 *Yen Interest Rate Derivatives ('YIRD')*, decision of 4 February 2015.

2.069 **Concerted practices in vertical relationships.** The Commission's decisions in COMP/39847 *E-Books*, decisions of 12 December 2012 (OJ 2012 C283/7) and of 25 July 2013 (OJ 2013 C378/25), illustrate that as well as a supplier entering into a concerted practice with one or more of its customers, a concerted practice can also arise between multiple suppliers and a single distributor. The Commission accepted commitments from five publishing companies and Apple in respect of their arrangements for the sale of electronically formatted books. The publishing companies had each entered into agreements with Apple (having also discussed the arrangements between themselves) under which Apple acted as their sales agent and the publishers agreed to particular pricing terms.

The Commission's preliminary assessment was that the publishers and Apple had engaged in a concerted practice of moving from a wholesale arrangement to an agency arrangement, with a view either to raising the retail price of e-books or to avoiding the emergence of lower prices (in particular, to eliminate price competition between Apple and Amazon). The Commission has opened a similar investigation into the arrangements between Amazon and publishers: COMP/40153 *E-book MFNs*, and Press Release IP/15/5166 (11 June 2015).

Duration of a concerted practice. In Case T-540/08 *Esso v Commission*, **2.070**
EU:T:2014:630, [2014] 5 CMLR 507, at paras 83–85, the General Court held that even if representatives of an undertaking did not participate in certain unlawful meetings nonetheless the undertaking could be presumed throughout the period preceding those meetings to have taken account of information already exchanged with its competitors in determining its conduct on the market. It therefore upheld the Commission's findings as to the duration of the cartel.

Fn 326 The Court of Justice dismissed the undertakings' further appeals in Joined Cases C-239/11P, etc, *Siemens v Commission (Gas Insulated Switchgear)*, EU:C:2013:866, [2014] 4 CMLR 606. The Commission's appeal was upheld: see the update to paragraph 2.024, above.

Fn 329 The Court of Justice dismissed the undertakings' further appeals, on other grounds, in Joined Cases C-231/11P, etc, *Commission v Siemens and others*, EU:C:2014:256, [2014] 5 CMLR 7. The Commission's appeal was upheld: see the update to paragraph 2.024, above.

(c) Single continuous infringement

Concept of a single continuous infringement. **2.071**
Fn 330 On the application of the concept of a single and continuous infringement to cases under Article 102, the Court of Justice has dismissed the appeals, on other grounds, in Case C-457/10P *AstraZeneca v Commission*, EU:C:2012:770, [2013] 4 CMLR 233; and the General Court dismissed the appeals in Case T-286/09 *Intel v Commission*, EU:T:2014:547, [2014] 5 CMLR 270, at paras 1561–1563 (on further appeal, Case C-413/14P, not yet decided).

Fn 331 The appeal in Case T-426/10 *Moreda-Riviere Trefilerias*, against the Commission's decision in COMP/38344 *Pre-stressing Steel*, decision of 30 June 2010, was dismissed as inadmissible: Order of 25 November 2014. On further appeal, Case C-53/15P, not yet decided.

Fn 334 The Court of Justice in Case C-441/11P *Commission v Verhuizingen Coppens*, EU:C:2012:778, [2013] 4 CMLR 312 reversed the General Court's judgment annulling the Commission's decision in COMP/38543 *International Removals Services*, decision of 11 March 2008. It held that even though Coppens did not participate in the single and continuous infringement found by the

Commission, the General Court erred in annulling the decision entirely. It was to be annulled only in respect of the infringing behaviour in which Coppens had not engaged, and in respect of the attribution of a single and continuous infringement.

2.073 **Single continuous infringement: requisite elements.** The characterisation of an infringement as single and continuous does not relieve the Commission of the obligation to demonstrate that the various agreements and concerted practices constituting that single and continuous infringement themselves restricted competition: Case T-380/10 *Wabco Europe v Commission (Bathroom Fittings)*, EU:T:2013:449, [2014] 4 CMLR 138, para 92.

Fn 341 The Court of Justice dismissed the further appeal in Case C-444/11P *Team Relocations v Commission*, EU:C:2013:464, [2013] 5 CMLR 1335.

2.074 **Overall plan.** The Court of Justice in Joined Cases C-239/11P, etc, *Siemens v Commission (Gas Insulated Switchgear)*, EU:C:2013:866, [2014] 4 CMLR 606, at paras 241 et seq, dismissed an argument that the Commission must establish that the infringing conduct is complementary, as well as that it pursues a single objective, in order to find a single and continuous infringement.

The General Court upheld the Commission's conclusion in COMP/39181 *Candle Waxes*, decision of 1 October 2008, that there was a single and continuous infringement across two different product markets, where those product markets were vertically related. Slack wax is the raw material used in the manufacture of paraffin wax, and the anti-competitive agreement in respect of the upstream product was intended to strengthen the agreement in respect of the downstream product: Case T-566/08 *Total Raffinage Marketing*, EU:T:2013:423, paras 270–273 (fine reduced on grounds of duration) (on further appeal, Case C-597/13P, not yet decided). The General Court dismissed the other appeals, on other grounds, against the Commission's findings of infringement but reduced the fine imposed on five of the undertakings.

The General Court also upheld the Commission's conclusion in COMP/39092 *Bathroom Fittings*, decision of 23 June 2010, that there was a single and continuous infringement across three different product markets where those product markets were for complementary products: Case T-378/10 *Masco and others v Commission*, EU:T:2013:469, [2014] 4 CMLR 34, paras 56 et seq, and 115–116. The General Court noted in particular that the products were sold to a common customer base within the same distribution system, that the undertakings concerned belonged to umbrella associations and cross-product associations, and that the unlawful practices were implemented using the same methods, at the same time, in each of the three markets. On further appeal, Case C-614/13P, not yet decided.

Fn 345 The Court of Justice dismissed the further appeal in Case C-444/11P *Team Relocations v Commission*, EU:C:2013:464, [2013] 5 CMLR 1335.

Intentional contribution to the overall plan.   **2.075**

Fn 350 See, however, the General Court's judgments in Case T-380/10 *Wabco Europe v Commission (Bathroom Fittings)*, EU:T:2013:449, [2014] 4 CMLR 138; and Joined Cases T-379&381/10 *Keramag Keramische Werke and Others (Bathroom Fittings) v Commission*, EU:T:2013:457 (on further appeal, Case C-613/13P, not yet decided). Where the alleged cartel includes an exchange of commercially sensitive information, it is necessary that the recipient of the information be active on the cartelised market, such that there is potential for that recipient to modify its behaviour as a result of receiving the information, in order for the exchange to infringe Article 101. The Court emphasised at para 79 of *Wabco* that:

> 'it cannot be presumed that an agreement or a concerted practice whereby undertakings exchange information which is commercially sensitive but which relates to a product sold on a market on which they are not competitors has an anticompetitive object or effect on that market. A practice whereby an undertaking which is active on two distinct product markets provides to its competitors – which are present on one market – commercially sensitive information which relates to a second market – on which those competitors are not present – is not capable, in principle, of having an impact on competition on the second market.'

The Court held that its judgment in Joined Cases T-456&457/05 *Gütermann and Zwicky v Commission* [2010] ECR II-1443, relied upon by the Commission, would apply to a disclosure of commercially sensitive information with a view to restricting competition in the market on which the recipient of the information is active, by a disclosing party that is not itself active on that market; whereas in the decision under appeal, COMP/39092 *Bathroom Fittings*, decision of 23 June 2010, the Commission had (as the Court held, wrongly) found that the purpose of the disclosure was to restrict competition in a market on which the disclosing party was active but the recipient was not: see paras 98–99. See also Joined Cases T-379&381/10 *Keramag Keramische Werke and Others (Bathroom Fittings) v Commission*, EU:T:2013:457, paras 92 and 221 (on further appeal, Case C-613/13P, not yet decided).

Fn 351 See also Case C-444/11P *Team Relocations v Commission*, EU:C:2013:464, [2013] 5 CMLR 1335, para 52.

Fn 353 The Court of Justice in Case C-441/11P *Commission v Verhuizingen Coppens*, EU:C:2012:778, [2013] 4 CMLR 312 reversed the General Court's judgment annulling the Commission's decision in COMP/38543 *International Removals Services*, decision of 11 March 2008. It held that even though Coppens did not participate in the single and continuous infringement found by the Commission, the General Court erred in annulling the decision entirely. It was to be annulled only in respect of the infringing behaviour in which Coppens had not engaged, and in respect of the attribution of a single and continous infringement. In contrast, in Case C-444/11P *Team Relocations v Commission*, EU:C:2013:464, [2013] 5 CMLR 1335, the Court of Justice dismissed the appeal against the finding of a single and continuous infringement in the *International Removals Services* decision as against Team Relocations, because the General Court had found on the facts of that case that Team Relocations was aware of the infringing behaviour in which it did not participate.

Fn 354 The General Court upheld the Commission's conclusion in COMP/39181 *Candle Waxes*, decision of 1 October 2008, that there was a single and continuous infringement across two different product markets, where those product markets were vertically related. Slack wax is the raw material used in the manufacture of paraffin wax, and the anti-competitive agreement in respect of the upstream product was intended to strengthen the agreement in respect of the downstream product: Case T-566/08 *Total Raffinage Marketing*, EU:T:2013:423, paras 270–273 (fine reduced on grounds of duration (on further appeal, Case C-597/13P, not yet decided)). The General Court dismissed the other appeals, on other grounds, against the Commission's findings of infringement but reduced the fine imposed on five of the undertakings.

2.076 **Awareness.** In Joined Cases C-239/11P, etc, *Siemens v Commission (Gas Insulated Switchgear)*, EU:C:2013:866, [2014] 4 CMLR 606, at paras 250–253, the Court of Justice upheld the General Court's conclusion that the existence of an information exchange mechanism, whereby Japanese manufacturers were notified of the allocation of certain projects within the EEA, was sufficient that the Japanese manufacturers could reasonably have envisaged that the allocation of those projects was the result of collusive activity.

In Case T-378/10 *Masco and others v Commission*, EU:T:2013:469, [2014] 4 CMLR 34, paras 61–62 and 82, the General Court upheld the Commission's conclusion in COMP/39092 *Bathroom Fittings*, decision of 23 June 2010, that where undertakings are members of umbrella associations, or cross-product associations, they must be considered to have been aware of the infringing behaviour taking place in the product markets in which they were not themselves active. On further appeal, Case C-614/13P, not yet decided.

The Commission's decision in COMP/39188 *Bananas*, decision of 15 October 2008, has been upheld. On awareness, see in particular Joined Cases C-293&294/13P *Fresh Del Monte Produce*, EU:C:2015:416, [2015] 5 CMLR 513, para 160. The Commission's conclusion at para 252 of the decision, noted in footnote 359 of the main text, had been upheld by the General Court in Case T-587/08 *Fresh Del Monte Produce v Commission*, EU:T:2013:129, [2013] 4 CMLR 1091, at paras 586 et seq. On the facts, although the decision found the producer Chiquita was aware of the bilateral discussions between the other producers Dole and Weichert, it had found that there was not sufficient evidence to conclude Weichert was aware of discussions between Chiquita and Dole (Commission decision paras 254–258). The decision could not be interpreted therefore as attributing responsibility to Weichert for the infringement as a whole: para 646. The Court of Justice upheld that conclusion. Weichert's lack of awareness did not alter the finding that there was a single and continuous infringement even though liability could not be attributed to it for all aspects of the infringement.

In Case T-418/10 *Voestalpine v Commission*, EU:T:2015:516 the General Court considered the requirement to establish awareness in the context of agency. It held that the acts of the agent, who participates in anti-competitive conduct of which his principal is not aware, can be imputed to the principal just as those of an employee may be imputed to an employer in such circumstances: para 175. That imputation extends to finding the principal liable for participating in a single and continuous infringement, on the basis that it is considered to have been aware, through its agent, of the conduct of the other undertakings in pursuit of the same overall plan: paras 389 et seq.

Fn 362 In addition, see Case T-68/09 *Soliver v Commission* (*'Carglass'*), EU:T:2014:867, [2014] 5 CMLR 1168. The undertaking had engaged in anti-competitive contacts with its competitors in respect of a specific supply contract, but it was a small player in the market and it had not attended the bilateral and trilateral cartel meetings between the larger players at which the overall cartel, and its objectives, was discussed. The General Court held that there was insufficient evidence to establish that the undertaking knew, or should have known, that the contacts in which it engaged were part of a cartel covering the entire EEA market with a particular *modus operandi*. As the Commission's decision, COMP/39125 *Carglass*, decision of 11 February 2009, was not severable, it was annulled in its entirety as against that undertaking.

In respect of the cases noted in the footnote, the Court of Justice, disagreeing with Advocate General Mengozzi's Opinion of 28 February 2013, dismissed the Commission's appeal in Case C-287/11P *Aalberts Industries v Commission* (*'Copper Fittings'*) EU:C:2013:445, [2013] 5 CMLR 867, paras 37–45. It also dismissed the further appeal in Case C-70/12P *Quinn Barlo v Commission* (*'Methacrylates'*), EU:C:2013:351, [2013] 5 CMLR 637.

In addition, the Court of Justice in Case C-441/11P *Commission v Verhuizingen Coppens*, EU:C:2012:778, [2013] 4 CMLR 312 reversed the General Court's judgment annulling the Commission's decision in COMP/38543 *International Removals Services*, decision of 11 March 2008. It held that even though Coppens did not participate in the single and continuous infringement found by the Commission, the General Court erred in annulling the decision entirely. It was to be annulled only in respect of the infringing behaviour in which Coppens had not engaged, and in respect of the attribution of a single and continuous infringement. In contrast, in Case C-444/11P *Team Relocations v Commission*, EU:C:2013:464, [2013] 5 CMLR 1335, the Court of Justice dismissed the appeal against the finding of a single and continuous infringement in the *International Removals Services* decision as against Team Relocations, as the General Court had found on the facts of that case that Team Relocations was aware of the infringing behaviour in which it did not participate.

2.077 **Evidence of participation.**
Fn 364 The Court of Justice dismissed the undertakings' further appeals in Joined Cases C-239/11P, etc, *Siemens v Commission (Gas Insulated Switchgear)*, EU:C:2013:866, [2014] 4 CMLR 606. The Commission's appeal was upheld: see the update to paragraph 2.024, above.

Fn 365 The Court of Justice dismissed the further appeal in Case C-70/12P *Quinn Barlo v Commission* ('*Methacrylates*'), EU:C:2013:351, [2013] 5 CMLR 637. See also the update to paragraph 2.075, above, regarding the need to establish that the undertaking's conduct was infringing.

Fn 367 The Court of Justice dismissed the undertakings' further appeals in Joined Cases C-239/11P, etc, *Siemens v Commission (Gas Insulated Switchgear)*, EU:C:2013:866, [2014] 4 CMLR 606. The Commission's appeal was upheld: see the update to paragraph 2.024, above.

2.078 **Continuity and duration of participation.**
Fn 372 The Court of Justice dismissed the further appeal in Case C-290/11P *Comap v Comission (Copper Fittings)*, EU:C:2012:271. See also Case T-72/09 *Pilkington v Commission (Carglass)*, EU:T:2014:1094, in which the General Court confirmed that a 'roll-out' period, by which the cartel manifests itself progressively, is not incompatible with a finding that an overall plan existed: paras 124 et seq. On further appeal, on other grounds, in Case C-101/15P, not yet decided.

Fn 373 See also the General Court's judgment in Joined Cases T-147&148/09 *Trelleborg v Commission*, EU:T:2013:259, [2013] 5 CMLR 754, partially annulling the decision in COMP/39406 *Marine Hoses*, decision of 28 January 2009, as regards the duration of the infringement by two of the participants (see the update to footnote 374, below).

Fn 374 The Court of Justice dismissed the undertakings' further appeals in Joined Cases C-239/11P, etc, *Siemens v Commission (Gas Insulated Switchgear)*, EU:C:2013:866, [2014] 4 CMLR 606. The Commission's appeal was upheld: see the update to paragraph 2.024, above.

The appeal against the Commission's decision finding a single and continuous infringement in COMP/39406 *Marine Hoses*, decision of 28 January 2009, was upheld in Joined Cases T-147&148/09 *Trelleborg v Commission (Marine Hoses)*, EU:T:2013:259, [2013] 5 CMLR 754. Similarly to, and following, its findings in Case T-18/05 *IMI v Commission* [2010] ECR II-1769 referred to in the main text, the General Court found that the Commission had not demonstrated that Trelleborg's conduct continued uninterrupted. There was no evidence of its ongoing participation during one particular period, or that it was aware of the ongoing contacts between the other undertakings, and the Commission was not therefore entitled to rely on the fact that it had not publicly distanced itself from the cartel as sufficient basis for establishing its ongoing involvement: paras 66–68. However, as Trelleborg accepted that the cartel it rejoined was the same as that which it had left the infringement was to be treated as a single repeated infringement: paras 72 et seq. The duration of the infringement was reduced accordingly.

(d) Public distancing

Passive participation.   **2.079**

Fn 376 See also Case T-154/09 *Manuli Rubber Industries v Commission (Marine Hoses)*, EU:T:2013:260, paras 182 et seq, in which the General Court rejected a contention that the undertaking maintained contact with the other cartelists in order to give the impression that it had an interest in re-launching the cartel, and to protect itself against reprisals.

Publicly distancing oneself from an infringement.   If an infringement is ongo-   **2.080**
ing, and there is no evidence of an undertaking's actual participation in ongoing contacts or that it was aware of them, the Commission cannot rely on the under-taking's failure to distance itself publicly as a basis for establishing ongoing par-ticipation: Joined Cases T-147&148/09 *Trelleborg v Commission (Marine Hoses)*, EU:T:2013:259, [2013] 5 CMLR 754 (see the update to footnote 374, above). If there is evidence of an undertaking being left off the invitee list for meetings, that may be sufficient to establish that it has publicly distanced itself from the in-fringement: Case T-566/08 *Total Raffinage Marketing*, EU:T:2013:423, para 387 (fine reduced on grounds of duration) (on further appeal, Case C-634/13P, not yet decided). However, evidence of an undertaking being left off the circulation list for letters about price increases did not indicate the undertaking had publicly distanced itself from the cartel in circumstances where the infringing behaviour also included exchanges of commercially sensitive information, and customer and market allocations: Case T-540/08 *Esso v Commission*, EU:T:2014:630, [2014] 5 CMLR 507, para 51.

Fn 382 The Court of Justice dismissed the further appeal in Case C-290/11P *Comap v Comission (Copper Fittings)*, EU:C:2012:271. The complaint regarding the General Court's findings on public distancing was dismissed as inadmissible: para 78.

Fn 384 The Court of Justice dismissed the appeal in Case C-286/11P *Commission v Tomkins*, EU:C:2013:29, [2013] 4 CMLR 466. It held, disagreeing with Advocate General Mengozzi, that the General Court did not err in law by giving Tomkins the benefit of its subsidiary's appeal. In circumstances where the liability of a parent company is wholly derived from that of its subsidiary, and where both companies have brought actions before the European Courts seeking a reduction in their fines on the same basis (in this case, on the basis of the duration of the infringement), then it is not necessary for the scope of their actions, or the arguments deployed, to be identical in order for the General Court to recalculate the fine imposed on the parent company on account of the outcome of the appeal by the subsidiary.

Fn 386 The General Court dismissed the appeal against the Commission's decision in COMP/38344 *Pre-stressing Steel*, decision of 30 June 2010, in Case T-393/10 *Westfälische Drahtindustrie v Commission*, EU:T:2015:515, paras 196 et seq. It held that WDI's statement could not be regarded as a clear and unequivocal manifestation of an intention by WDI to distance itself from the agreement, because read in context the statement was in fact an endorsement by WDI of a proposal to establish a new quota system rather than persist with the existing system (on further appeal, Case C-523/15P, not yet decided).

Fn 388 See also Case T-462/07 *Galp Energía España v Commission*, EU:T:2013:459, [2014] 4 CMLR 272, para 475.

(e) Decisions by associations of undertakings

2.082 **Examples of associations.** The Court of Justice dismissed the further appeal against the Commission's decision in COMP/34579 *MasterCard*, decision of 19 December 2007, in Case C-382/12P *MasterCard v Commission*, EU:C:2014:2201, [2014] 5 CMLR 1062. It upheld the General Court's conclusion that MasterCard continued to operate, after its listing on the stock exchange, as 'an institutionalised form of coordination of the conduct of the banks'. The General Court's findings of fact that, first, the banks continued collectively to exercise decision-making powers in respect of the essential aspects of the operation of the organisation, and, secondly, that the MIFs reflected the aligned interests of MasterCard, its shareholders and the banks, were both relevant and sufficient for the purposes of assessing whether MasterCard could still be considered an 'association of undertakings': paras 68–72. The Court confirmed that commonality of interests between undertakings is not the exclusive criterion for determining whether a body is an association of undertakings: para 73.

Fn 393 For a further example of a professional regulatory body, see Case C-1/12 *Ordem dos Técnicos Oficiais de Contas v Autoridade da Concorrência*, EU:C:2013:127, [2013] 4 CMLR 651 regarding a body which regulates chartered accountants. See also *Competition Authority v Irish Medical Association*, Record No. 2013/7333P, in relation to the settlement of a case concerning the collective withdrawal of GP services in protest at proposed Government cuts to fees paid to GPs.

Fn 401 The Commission's decision in COMP/39510 *Ordre National des Pharmaciens en France (ONP)*, decision of 8 December 2010, was upheld as to liability in Case T-90/11 *ONP v Commission*, EU:T:2014:1049. See in particular para 321.

Decisions.   **2.083**

Fn 406 The Commission's decision in COMP/38698 *CISAC Agreements*, decision of 16 July 2008, has been partially annulled by the General Court: Cases T-392, 398, 401, 410, 411, 413–422, 425, 428, 432–434, 442/08, judgments of 12 April 2013. See the update to paragraph 2.065, above.

Fn 407 The Court of Justice dismissed the further appeal against the Commission's decision in COMP/34579 *MasterCard*, decision of 19 December 2007, in Case C-382/12P *MasterCard v Commission*, EU:C:2014:2201, [2014] 5 CMLR 1062. See the update to paragraph 2.082, above.

4. The Prevention, Restriction or Distortion of Competition

(a) Generally

Competition.   **2.086**

Fn 418 See also the General Court's observations in Case T-587/08 *Fresh Del Monte Produce v Commission*, EU:T:2013:129, [2013] 4 CMLR 1091, paras 459–460 (further appeal, on other grounds, dismissed in Joined Cases C-293&294/13P *Fresh Del Monte Produce*, EU:C:2015:416, [2015] 5 CMLR 513); and of the General Court and Court of Justice in Case T-588/08 *Dole Food Company v Commission*, EU:T:2013:130, para 65; and Case C-286/13P *Dole Food Company v Commission*, EU:C:2015:184, [2015] 4 CMLR 967, para 125.

On 21 March 2014 the Commission adopted Regulation 316/2014 on the application of Article 101(3) of the Treaty on the Functioning of the European Union to categories of technology transfer agreements, OJ 2014 L93/17. It entered into force on 1 May 2014, and replaces Regulation 772/2004 which expired on 30 April 2014. At the same time the Commission issued revised Guidelines on the application of Article 101 of the Treaty on the Functioning of the European Union to technology transfer agreements, OJ 2014 C89/3.

Restrictions must be assessed in context.   **2.089**

Fn 427 See also the Court of Justice's judgment in Case C-67/13P *Groupement des cartes bancaires v Commission*, EU:C:2014:2202, discussed in the update to paragraph 2.113, below, regarding the need to take account of the legal and economic context of the agreement in determining whether it can be characterised as a restriction by object; and its judgment in Case C-382/12P *MasterCard v Commission*, EU:C:2014:2201, [2014] 5 CMLR 1062 discussed in the updates to paragraphs 2.101 and 2.124, below, regarding the need to use a counterfactual that reflects the actual context of the agreement in determining whether that agreement has restrictive effects.

Restrictions of competition and restrictions of commercial freedom.   **2.091**

Fn 436 The Commission's decision in COMP/38606 *Groupement des Cartes Bancaires*, decision of 17 October 2007, was upheld by the General Court in Case

Article 101(1)

T-491/07 *CB v Commission*, EU:T:2012:633 and the Court of Justice overturned that judgment in Case C-67/13P *Groupement des cartes bancaires v Commission*, EU:C:2014:2202, discussed in the update to paragraph 2.113, below. The case has been referred back to the General Court.

The appeal in Case T-27/10 *AC-Treuhand*, EU:T:2014:59, was dismissed. The General Court followed its earlier judgment in Case T-99/04 *AC-Treuhand* [2008] ECR II-1501, [2008] 5 CMLR 962 and held that the undertaking which has participated in collusive conduct can be held liable for an infringement of Article 101 even if it is not active on the market affected by the restriction of competition. See in particular paras 36–47. On further appeal, Case C-194/14P, not yet decided.

2.093 **Restrictions of competition and detriment to consumers.**
Fn 441 Followed in Case T-587/08 *Del Monte Fresh Produce v Commission*, EU:T:2013:129, [2013] 4 CMLR 1091, paras 459–460 (further appeal, on other grounds, dismissed in Joined Cases C-293&294/13P *Fresh Del Monte Produce*, EU:C:2015:416, [2015] 5 CMLR 513); in Case T-588/08 *Dole Food Company v Commission*, EU:T:2013:130, para 65; and Case C-286/13P *Dole Food Company v Commission*, EU:C:2015:184, [2015] 4 CMLR 967, para 123; and in Case T-655/11 *FSL (Exotic fruit) v Commission*, EU:T:2015:383, para 537 (on further appeal, Case C-469/15P, not yet decided).

Fn 442 See also the General Court's observations in Case T-587/08 *Del Monte Fresh Produce v Commission*, EU:T:2013:129, [2013] 4 CMLR 1091, paras 459–460 (further appeal, on other grounds, dismissed in Joined Cases C-293&294/13P *Fresh Del Monte Produce*, EU:C:2015:416, [2015] 5 CMLR 513); and of the General Court and Court of Justice in Case T-588/08 *Dole Food Company v Commission*, EU:T:2013:130, para 65; and Case C-286/13P *Dole Food Company v Commission*, EU:C:2015:184, [2015] 4 CMLR 967, para 125.

(b) **Some basic concepts**

2.096 **Aspects of competition.**
Fn 452 On 21 March 2014 the Commission adopted Regulation 316/2014 on the application of Article 101(3) of the Treaty on the Functioning of the European Union to categories of technology transfer agreements, OJ 2014 L93/17. It entered into force on 1 May 2014, and replaces Regulation 772/2004 which expired on 30 April 2014. At the same time the Commission issued revised Guidelines on the application of Article 101 of the Treaty on the Functioning of the European Union to technology transfer agreements, OJ 2014 C89/3. The reference to paras 11–12 of the previous guidelines (OJ 2004 C101/2) should be read as paras 11–12 of the Revised Technology Transfer Guidelines.

2.097 **Actual and potential competition.** On 'potential' competition, see the Court of Justice's judgment in Joined Cases C-239/11P, etc, *Siemens v Commission (Gas*

Insulated Switchgear), EU:C:2013:866, [2014] 4 CMLR 606, in which it considered that the existence of an information exchange mechanism between Japanese and European manufacturers supported the General Court's conclusion that the Japanese manufacturers were 'potential competitors' on the European markets, as it showed they were perceived to be credible potential competitors by the European manufacturers: para 114. It also held that, because the Commission had established evidence of the existence of a concerted practice, it was not necessary to examine whether there was an alternative plausible explanation for the undertakings' conduct in refraining from entering each other's territories, such as the existence of alleged technical and economic barriers to entry into the European markets: paras 219 et seq. Similarly, see Case T-519/09 *Toshiba v Commission (Power Transformers)*, EU:T:2014:263, [2014] 5 CMLR 219, at paras 229–235 (on further appeal, Case C-373/14P, not yet decided).

Fn 460 The Commission has issued revised Guidelines on the application of Article 101 of the Treaty on the Functioning of the European Union to technology transfer agreements, OJ 2014 C89/3 ('Revised Technology Transfer Guidelines'), to accompany Regulation 316/2014 on the application of Article 101(3) of the Treaty on the Functioning of the European Union to categories of technology transfer agreements, OJ 2014 L93/17. Regulation 316/2014 entered into force on 1 May 2014, and replaces Regulation 772/2004 which expired on 30 April 2014. The Revised Technology Transfer Guidelines continue to indicate that entry has to be likely to occur within a period of one to two years in order to constitute a realistic competitive constraint: para 34 of the Revised Technology Transfer Guidelines.

Inter-brand and intra-brand competition. See also, in the UK's Competition **2.098** Appeal Tribunal, *Skyscanner v CMA* [2014] CAT 16, paras 100 and 159 in which the Tribunal quashed and remitted the Office of Fair Trading's decision in *Hotel online booking: decision to accept commitments to remove certain discounting restrictions for Online Travel Agents*, decision of 31 January 2014. The decision accepted commitments which the OFT concluded would encourage intra-brand competition, by allowing online travel agents to offer discounted hotel room prices to a closed group of consumers; however, the Tribunal held that the OFT had failed to consider the impact that the commitments would have on price transparency and on inter-brand competition between different hotels, by limiting the ability of meta-search websites to access those discounted prices. The Competition and Markets Authority subsequently closed the case.

Fn 462 The Commission's decision in COMP/38606 *Groupement des Cartes Bancaires*, decision of 17 October 2007, was upheld by the General Court in Case T-491/07 *CB v Commission*, EU:T:2012:633 on the basis that the arrangements were a restriction by object, and it was therefore not necessary to go on to consider their effects. The Court of Justice overturned that judgment in Case C-67/13P

Groupement des cartes bancaires v Commission, EU:C:2014:2202, discussed in the update to paragraph 2.113, below. The case has been referred back to the General Court for a consideration of the arrangements' effects.

2.099 **Inter-technology and intra-technology competition.** On 21 March 2014 the Commission adopted Regulation 316/2014 on the application of Article 101(3) of the Treaty on the Functioning of the European Union to categories of technology transfer agreements, OJ 2014 L93/17. It entered into force on 1 May 2014, and replaces Regulation 772/2004 which expired on 30 April 2014. The new Regulation does not contain an exception for restraints on passive sales by licensees into a territory or customer group which is supplied by another licensee: Article 4(2)(b)(ii) of Regulation 772/2004, not replicated in Regulation 316/2014.

Fn 466 The reference in the footnote of the main text to Article 4(2)(6)(ii) of Regulation 772/2004 should be to Article 4(2)(b)(ii) of Regulation 772/2004. The exception is not replicated in Regulation 316/2014.

2.101 **The counterfactual.** The Court of Justice in Case C-382/12P *MasterCard v Commission*, EU:C:2014:2201, [2014] 5 CMLR 1062 at para 108 held:

> '… irrespective of the context or aim in relation to which a counterfactual hypothesis is used, it is important that that hypothesis is appropriate to the issue it is supposed to clarify and that the assumption on which it is based is not unrealistic.'

The Court underlined that the same counterfactual is not necessarily appropriate to conceptually distinct issues, and concluded that the particular counterfactual relied upon in that case was appropriate for the purpose of determining whether the agreement in question was an objectively necessary ancillary restraint (see, further, the update to paragraph 2.149, below) but not for the purpose of determining whether it had the effect of restricting competition in the market (see, further, the update to paragraph 2.124, below).

2.104 **Per se and rule of reason.**
Fn 490 See also *Federal Trade Commission v Actavis and others*, of 17 June 2013, 570 U.S. (2013), in which the Supreme Court clarified that in the United States the rule of reason approach is to be applied to antitrust scrutiny of patent settlement agreements.

2.105 **No per se rules under Article 101(1).** The Court of Justice held in Case C-226/11 *Expedia Inc*, EU:C:2012:795, [2013] 4 CMLR 439, at paras 36–37, that an agreement that may affect trade between Member States and that has an anti-competitive object constitutes, by its nature and independently of any concrete effects that it may have, an appreciable restriction on competition. On 30 August 2014 the Commission adopted a revised *De Minimis* Notice to take account of this judgment: OJ 2014 C291/1 (see the update to paragraphs 2.164 et seq, below).

Objective necessity. 2.107
Fn 505 The Commission's decision in COMP/39510 *Ordre National des Pharmaciens en France (ONP)*, decision of 8 December 2010, was upheld as to liability in Case T-90/11 *ONP v Commission*, EU:T:2014:1049. See in particular para 327.

'Unfair competition' not deserving protection. An agreement intended to 2.109
exclude a competitor that had been operating illegally on the relevant market has also been held to infringe Article 101: Case C-68/12 *Protimonopolný úradv Slovenská sporitel'ňa*, EU:C:2013:71, [2013] 4 CMLR 491, paras 19–21. The Supreme Court of the Slovak Republic subsequently upheld the infringement decision of the Antimonopoly Office on 22 May 2013: ECN Brief 03/2013, p13.

Restrictions must be appreciable. The Court of Justice held in Case C-226/11 2.110
Expedia Inc, EU:C:2012:795, [2013] 4 CMLR 439, at paras 36–37, that an agreement that may affect trade between Member States and that has an anti-competitive object constitutes, by its nature and independently of any concrete effects that it may have, an appreciable restriction on competition. On 30 August 2014 the Commission adopted a revised *De Minimis* Notice to take account of this judgment: OJ 2014 C291/1 (see paragraphs 2.164 et seq of the main text, and the updates thereto, below).

(c) The 'object or effect' of anticompetitive conduct

In general. 2.111
Fn 525 The Court of Justice dismissed the further appeal against the Commission's decision in COMP/34579 *MasterCard*, decision of 19 December 2007, on other grounds in Case C-382/12P *MasterCard v Commission*, EU:C:2014:2201, [2014] 5 CMLR 1062.

Two stage examination. 2.112
Fn 527 In practice, it may be advisable nonetheless to examine the effects of an agreement on a precautionary basis: see, eg the appeals against the Commission's decision in COMP/38606 *Groupement des Cartes Bancaires*, decision of 17 October 2007. The General Court in Case T-491/07 *CB v Commission*, EU:T:2012:633 upheld the Commission's decision on the basis that the measures in question had as their object the restriction of competition, and it did not go on to consider their effects. The Court of Justice overturned that judgment in Case C-67/13P *Groupement des cartes bancaires v Commission*, EU:C:2014:2202, discussed in the update to paragraph 2.113, below. The case has therefore been referred back to the General Court to consider the Commission's findings as to the effects of the measures.

(d) Restriction of competition by object

2.113 **Ascertaining object: analysis of the agreement in its context.** The Court of Justice in Case C-67/13P *Groupement des cartes bancaires v Commission*, EU:C:2014:2202 at para 57 held:

> '... the essential legal criterion for ascertaining whether coordination between undertakings involves such a restriction of competition "by object" is the finding that such coordination reveals in itself a sufficient degree of harm to competition.'

It confirmed that the concept of a restriction by object must be interpreted restrictively: para 58; and that in considering all relevant aspects of the economic and legal context of the agreement it is immaterial whether those aspects relate to the relevant market or to other markets, particularly in a case concerning related markets and the more so in a case concerning a two-sided system: paras 78–79. In that particular case, the Court overturned the General Court's judgment that there was infringement by object, as it had not explained in what respect the restriction of competition revealed a sufficient degree of harm to be characterised as an object infringement: paras 55 et seq. In view of the General Court's findings of fact, first, that in a two-sided card payment system the issuing and acquisition activities are essential to one another and to the operation of the system, and, secondly, that the agreements in question sought to maintain a certain ratio between the issuing and acquiring activities of the group's members, the most that could be inferred from the terms of the agreements was that they had as their object the combatting of 'free-riding'. That objective is legitimate, and not harmful to the proper functioning of competition: paras 72–75.

In Case C-32/11 *Allianz Hungária Bistozitó*, EU:C:2013:160, [2013] 4 CMLR 863, the Court of Justice considered whether vertical agreements between car insurance companies and car repair shops had the object of restricting competition. It held that as the agreements were likely to affect two markets, their object must be determined by reference to both markets: para 42, and it was relevant to consider that the insurance companies aimed to maintain or increase their market share by entering the agreements: para 44. The Court also provided detailed guidance on the legal and economic factors that were relevant, in that case, to determining the object of the agreements.

Where the agreement or concerted practice consists of exchanging commercially sensitive information, one aspect of the context of the agreement that requires consideration is whether the recipient of the information is active in the cartelised market: see Case T-380/10 *Wabco Europe v Commission (Bathroom Fittings)*, EU:T:2013:449, [2014] 4 CMLR 138, in particular at para 79, discussed in the update to paragraph 2.075, above.

Fn 535 See also Case C-172/14 *ING Pensii*, EU:C:2015:484, [2015] 5 CMLR 820, para 33.

Object even if not implemented.   The General Court upheld the Commission's **2.115**
decision in COMP/38698 *CISAC Agreements*, decision of 16 July 2008, insofar
as it found the membership clause infringed Article 101: Cases T-392, 401, 422,
432/08 judgments of 12 April 2013. It partially annulled the decision on other
grounds in Cases T-392, 398, 401, 410, 411, 413–422, 425, 428, 432–434, 442/08,
judgments of 12 April 2013.

Object means no need to prove actual effects.   The General Court upheld **2.116**
the Commission's decision in COMP/39188 *Bananas*, decision of 15 October
2008, discussed in the main text in Case T-587/08 *Fresh Del Monte Produce
v Commission*, EU:T:2013:129, [2013] 4 CMLR 1091 (further appeal, on other
grounds, dismissed in Joined Cases C-293&294/13P *Fresh Del Monte Produce*,
EU:C:2015:416, [2015] 5 CMLR 513); and Case T-588/08 *Dole Food Company v
Commission*, EU:T:2013:130 (further appeal dismissed in Case C-286/13P *Dole
Food Company v Commission*, EU:C:2015:184, [2015] 4 CMLR 967).

In practice, it may be advisable to examine the effects of an agreement on a precautionary basis: see, eg the appeals against the Commission's decision in COMP/
38606 *Groupement des Cartes Bancaires*, decision of 17 October 2007. The
General Court in Case T-491/07 *CB v Commission*, EU:T:2012:633 upheld the
Commission's decision on the basis that the measures in question had as their
object the restriction of competition, and it did not go on to consider their effects.
The Court of Justice overturned that judgment in Case C-67/13P *Groupement des
cartes bancaires v Commission*, EU:C:2014:2202, discussed in the update to paragraph 2.113, above. The case has therefore been referred back to the General Court
to consider the Commission's findings as to the effects of the measures.

Fn 554 On this aspect of the Commission's decision in particular, see Case
T-587/08 *Fresh Del Monte Produce v Commission*, EU:T:2013:129, [2013] 4 CMLR
1091, paras 427–440 (further appeal, on other grounds, dismissed in Joined Cases
C-293&294/13P *Fresh Del Monte Produce*, EU:C:2015:416, [2015] 5 CMLR 513);
and Case T-588/08 *Dole Food Company v Commission*, EU:T:2013:130, paras
332–354 (further appeal dismissed in Case C-286/13P *Dole Food Company v
Commission*, EU:C:2015:184, [2015] 4 CMLR 967, paras 111 et seq).

Fn 556 On this aspect of the Commission's decision in particular, see Case
T-587/08 *Fresh Del Monte Produce v Commission*, EU:T:2013:129, [2013] 4 CMLR
1091, paras 304–308 (further appeal, on other grounds, dismissed in Joined Cases
C-293&294/13P *Fresh Del Monte Produce*, EU:C:2015:416, [2015] 5 CMLR 513);
and Case T-588/08 *Dole Food Company v Commission*, EU:T:2013:130, paras 69–71
(further appeal dismissed in Case C-286/13P *Dole Food Company v Commission*,
EU:C:2015:184, [2015] 4 CMLR 967, paras 111 et seq).

Fn 557 On this aspect of the Commission's decision in particular, see Case
T-587/08 *Fresh Del Monte Produce v Commission*, EU:T:2013:129, [2013] 4 CMLR

1091, para 427–440 (further appeal, on other grounds, dismissed in Joined Cases C-293&294/13P *Fresh Del Monte Produce*, EU:C:2015:416, [2015] 5 CMLR 513); and Case T-588/08 *Dole Food Company v Commission*, EU:T:2013:130, paras 332–354 (further appeal dismissed in Case C-286/13P *Dole Food Company v Commission*, EU:C:2015:184, [2015] 4 CMLR 967, paras 111 et seq).

2.117 **Object does not remove the need for some effects analysis.** The Court of Justice held in Case C-226/11 *Expedia Inc*, EU:C:2012:795, [2013] 4 CMLR 439, at paras 36–37, that an agreement that may affect trade between Member States and that has an anti-competitive object constitutes, by its nature and independently of any concrete effects that it may have, an appreciable restriction on competition. On 30 August 2014 the Commission adopted a revised *De Minimis* Notice to take account of this judgment: OJ 2014 C291/1 (see paragraphs 2.164 et seq of the main text, and the updates thereto, below). In practice, future decisions which find a restriction of competition by object will not need to go on to analyse concrete effects for the purposes of determining whether the agreement appreciably restricts competition.

2.118 **Market definition in object cases.** The Court of Justice held in Case C-226/11 *Expedia Inc*, EU:C:2012:795, [2013] 4 CMLR 439, at paras 36–37, that an agreement that may affect trade between Member States and that has an anti-competitive object constitutes, by its nature and independently of any concrete effects that it may have, an appreciable restriction on competition. On 30 August 2014 the Commission adopted a revised *De Minimis* Notice to take account of this judgment: OJ 2014 C291/1 (see paragraphs 2.164 et seq of the main text, and the updates thereto, below).

Fn 565 The Court of Justice dismissed the appeal in Case C-439/11P *Ziegler v Commission*, EU:C:2013:513, [2013] 5 CMLR. It confirmed that it is necessary to define the relevant market in order to determine whether there was an appreciable effect on trade between Member States in that market: para 63.

Fn 566 The Court of Justice dismissed the further appeal in Case C-444/11P *Team Relocations v Commission*, EU:C:2013:464, [2013] 5 CMLR 1335.

2.121 **Examples of horizontal object restrictions.** The Court of Justice held in Case C-68/12 *Protimonopolný úrad v Slovenská sporitel'ňa*, EU:C:2013:71, [2013] 4 CMLR 491, paras 19–21, that an agreement that is intended to exclude a competitor from the relevant market is a restriction by object, and it is not relevant that that competitor had been operating on the market illegally. The Supreme Court of the Slovak Republic subsequently upheld the infringement decision of the Antimonopoly Office on 22 May 2013: ECN Brief 03/2013, p13.

Fn 574 The Commission's decision in COMP/39510 *Ordre National des Pharmaciens en France (ONP)*, decision of 8 December 2010, was upheld as to liability in Case T-90/11 *ONP v Commission* EU:T:2014:1049. See in particular para 321.

Examples of vertical object restrictions.   **2.122**

Fn 581 For a further example see Case C-32/11 *Allianz Hungária Bistozitó*, EU:C:2013:160, [2013] 4 CMLR 863, paras 49–50, where the Court of Justice considered whether vertical agreements between car insurance companies and car repair shops had the object of restricting competition. It held that it was relevant to consider, *inter alia*, the fact that the terms of the agreements were based on a framework agreement, negotiated by the repair shops' trade association with the insurers, which contained recommended prices that insurers should pay to repairers for their work. There would be a restriction by object if the trade association had decided on recommended prices with the intention of harmonising prices, and the insurance companies confirmed those decisions in the framework agreement.

(e) Restriction of competition by effect

Effect. The Court of Justice in Case C-382/12P *MasterCard v Commission*, **2.124** EU:C:2014:2201, [2014] 5 CMLR 1062 confirmed that, for the purpose of assessing effects, it is necessary to consider as a counterfactual what would actually have happened in the absence of the agreement: paras 164 et seq. The General Court in that case had erred by assessing the effects of MasterCard's multilateral interchange fees against a counterfactual in which the MasterCard system was operated using a prohibition on *ex post* pricing (in which issuing banks would be prohibited from setting the amount of the interchange fee after the cardholder has already made its purchase from the merchant) without considering how realistic that counterfactual was. That counterfactual was appropriate in the context of assessing whether the agreement was an objectively necessary ancillary restraint (see the update to paragraph 2.149, below), but assessing the impact of the agreement on competition requires an assessment of the competition in question within the actual context in which it would occur in the absence of the agreement. On the facts of that case, however, the Court went on to find that it had not been contended before the General Court that the MasterCard system would have collapsed without the MIFs, and the only alternative before the Court was the *ex post* pricing prohibition. This was therefore the only plausible and likely alternative to the MIFs before the General Court, and the judgment could be upheld on alternative grounds.

Legal and economic context.   See the Court of Justice judgment in Case **2.126** C-382/12P *MasterCard v Commission*, EU:C:2014:2201, [2014] 5 CMLR 1062 on the construction of a counterfactual for assessing the effects of an agreement: discussed in the update to paragraph 2.124, above.

Effect on parties.   **2.131**

Fn 621 The Commission's decision in COMP/38606 *Groupement des Cartes Bancaires*, decision of 17 October 2007, was upheld by the General Court in Case T-491/07 *CB v Commission*, EU:T:2012:633 on the basis that the measures in question had as their object the restriction of competition, and it was not necessary to go on to consider their effects. The Court of Justice overturned that judgment in Case C-67/13P *Groupement des cartes bancaires v Commission*, EU:C:2014:2202, discussed in the update to paragraph 2.113, above. The Court of Justice has therefore referred the case back to the General Court to consider the Commission's findings as to the effects of the measures.

2.136 **Restrictions in licences of intellectual property rights.**
Fn 637 There have been a number of significant developments recently in the field of licensing intellectual property rights, which are discussed in the updates to paragraphs 9.072 et seq, below.

On 21 March 2014 the Commission adopted Regulation 316/2014 on the application of Article 101(3) of the Treaty on the Functioning of the European Union to categories of technology transfer agreements, OJ 2014 L93/17. It entered into force on 1 May 2014, and replaces Regulation 772/2004 which expired on 30 April 2014.

2.137 **Restrictions on remedies.**
Fn 638 See also the updates to paragraphs 9.124 and 9.171, below.

Fn 641 See also the update to paragraph 2.050, above.

(f) Restraints which typically fall outside Article 101(1)

2.140 **Licence of intellectual property rights.**
Fn 646 See also the updates to paragraphs 9.093 et seq, below.

(g) Ancillary restraints

2.147 **Ancillary restraints.**
Fn 663 For a further example, see COMP/39839 *Telefónica and Portugal Telecom*, decision of 23 January 2013, discussed in the update to paragraph 2.148, below (on appeal Cases T-208/13 *Portugal Telecom v Commission*; and T-216/13 *Telefónica v Commission*, not yet decided).

Fn 665 The Court of Justice dismissed the further appeal against the Commission's decision in COMP/34579 *MasterCard*, decision of 19 December 2007, in Case C-382/12P *MasterCard v Commission*, EU:C:2014:2201, [2014] 5 CMLR 1062. See the updates to paragraphs 2.149 and 2.150, below.

2.148 **Directly related.** In COMP/39839 *Telefónica and Portugal Telecom*, decision of 23 January 2013, paras 367 et seq, the Commission held that a clause by which the parties agreed not to compete in the Iberian pensinsula was not directly related to (or necessary for) the acquisition by Telefónica of the Brazilian mobile operator, Vivo, which until then had been jointly owned by Telefónica and Portugal Telecom (on appeal Cases T-208/13 *Portugal Telecom v Commission*; and T-216/13 *Telefónica v Commission*, not yet decided).

Objectively necessary. The Court of Justice in Case C-382/12P *MasterCard v* **2.149**
Commission, EU:C:2014:2201, [2014] 5 CMLR 1062 at para 91 held that in considering whether a restriction is an objectively necessary ancillary restraint the relevant question is whether the operation or activity would be impossible to carry out
without it, not whether it would have been more difficult to carry out in its absence,
or less profitable. For this purpose, the Commission is entitled to consider as a
counterfactual any realistic situation that might arise in the absence of the restriction, and does not have to confine itself to considering what would actually happen
in the absence of the restriction: para 111. In that case, the Commission was entitled to conclude that multilateral interchange fees were not objectively necessary by
reference to a counterfactual in which the MasterCard system was operated using
a prohibition on *ex post* pricing (in which issuing banks would be prohibited from
setting the amount of the interchange fee after the cardholder has already made its
purchase from the merchant). The counterfactual used for this purpose contrasts
with that required for the purposes of establishing the effects of the agreement: see
the update to paragraphs 2.101 and 2.124, above.

See also the Commission's decision in COMP/39839 *Telefónica and Portugal Telecom*,
decision of 23 January 2013, discussed in the update to paragraph 2.148, above.

Fn 675 The Commission's decision in COMP/38606 *Groupement des Cartes*
Bancaires, decision of 17 October 2007, was upheld by the General Court in Case
T-491/07 *CB v Commission*, EU:T:2012:633 on the basis that the measures in question had as their object the restriction of competition, and it was not necessary to
go on to consider their effects. The Court of Justice overturned that judgment in
Case C-67/13P *Groupement des cartes bancaires v Commission*, EU:C:2014:2202,
discussed in the update to paragraph 2.113, above. The Court of Justice has therefore referred the case back to the General Court to consider the Commission's
findings as to the effects of the measures.

Ancillary restraints are separate from the application of Article 101(3). The Court **2.150**
of Justice dismissed the further appeal against the Commission's decision in COMP/
34579 *MasterCard*, decision of 19 December 2007, in Case C-382/12P *MasterCard*
v Commission, EU:C:2014:2201, [2014] 5 CMLR 1062. In particular, it confirmed
that the General Court correctly focused on the benefits of multilateral interchange
fees ('MIFs') rather than of the MasterCard system as a whole in assessing the agreement under Article 101(3). The MIFs are not an objectively necessary ancillary restraint, which would have necessitated a consideration of the agreement together with
the main operation to which it is ancillary, and they were therefore to be analysed
separately from the main operation of the MasterCard system: paras 230–232.

(h) Regulatory rules

Professional rules. In Case C-1/12 *Ordem dos Técnicos Oficiais de Contas v* **2.153**
Autoridade da Concorrência, EU:C:2013:127, [2013] 4 CMLR 651, paras 96–100,

the Court of Justice held that a requirement for chartered accountants to obtain compulsory training through their professional association, or through training providers approved by it, was neither necessary nor proportionate to ensuring the quality of accountancy services.

2.154 **Sporting rules.**
Fn 692 The Court of Justice dismissed the further appeal in Case C-269/12P *Cañas v Commission*, EU:C:2013:415, regarding the alleged anti-competitiveness of certain anti-doping rules.

2.155 **Other regulatory rules.** In Case T-451/08 *Föreningen SvenskaTonsättares Internationella Musikbyrå v Commission*, EU:T:2013:189, [2013] 5 CMLR 577, paras 86 et seq, the General Court rejected the argument that the restriction of competition brought about by the concerted practice found by the Commission in COMP/38698 *CISAC Agreements*, decision of 16 July 2008, [2009] 4 CMLR 577, was inherent in, and proportional to, cultural objectives.

The High Court of Ireland in *Hyland v Dundalk Racing* [2014] IEHC 60 considered the compatibility of the Irish 'Pitch Rules', which govern the allocation of pitches in the bookmakers' ring at a racecourse, with Article 101 and the Irish Competition Act 2002. The Court noted that if the Pitch Rules had not allowed allotted pitches to be traded there would have been a clear breach of competition law. However, as they did allow such trade, the Court held that they regulated and promoted effective competition between bookmakers on racecourse sites, and they were pro-competitive. It drew upon the judgment of Brandeis J in *Board of Trade of Chicago v United States* 246 US 231 (1918), at 238–239, distinguishing rules that promote the operation of an orderly and transparent market, and those that suppress or destroy competition.

Fn 696 The Commission's decision in COMP/39510 *Ordre National des Pharmaciens en France (ONP)*, decision of 8 December 2010, was upheld as to liability in Case T-90/11 *ONP v Commission*, EU:T:2014:1049. See in particular para 327.

5. Appreciable Effect on Competition

2.156 **Generally.** The Court of Justice held in Case C-226/11 *Expedia Inc*, EU:C:2012: 795, [2013] 4 CMLR 439, paras 36–37, that an agreement that may affect trade between Member States and that has an anti-competitive object constitutes, by its nature and independently of any concrete effects that it may have, an appreciable restriction on competition. On 30 August 2014 the Commission adopted a revised *De Minimis* Notice to take account of this judgment: OJ 2014 C291/1. The revised Notice does not cover agreements which have as their object the prevention, restriction or distortion of competition within the internal market: para 2. The Commission has issued Guidance on restrictions of competition 'by object' for the purpose of defining which agreements may benefit from the *De Minimis* Notice (SWD(2014) 198 final).

(a) Jurisprudence of the EU Courts

Market structure. 2.160
Fn 712 The Court of Justice dismissed the further appeal against the Commission's decision in COMP/34579 *MasterCard*, decision of 19 December 2007, on other grounds, in Case C-382/12P *MasterCard v Commission*, EU:C: 2014:2201, [2014] 5 CMLR 1062.

(b) Commission *De Minimis* Notice

In general. On 30 August 2014 the Commission adopted a revised *De Minimis* 2.164
Notice to take account of the Court of Justice's judgment in Case C-226/11 *Expedia Inc*, EU:C:2012:795, [2013] 4 CMLR 439. The Court held in paras 36–37 that an agreement that may affect trade between Member States and that has an anti-competitive object constitutes, by its nature and independently of any concrete effect that it may have, an appreciable restriction on competition. The revised Notice (OJ 2014 C291/1) does not cover agreements which have as their object the prevention, restriction or distortion of competition within the internal market: para 2. The Commission has issued Guidance on restrictions of competition 'by object' for the purpose of defining which agreements may benefit from the *De Minimis* Notice (SWD(2014) 198 final).

De Minimis **Notice.** On 30 August 2014 the Commission adopted a revised 2.165
De Minimis Notice to take account of the Court of Justice's judgment in Case C-226/11 *Expedia Inc*, EU:C:2012:795, [2013] 4 CMLR 439. The Court held in paras 36–37 that an agreement that may affect trade between Member States and that has an anti-competitive object constitutes, by its nature and independently of any concrete effect that it may have, an appreciable restriction on competition. The revised Notice (OJ 2014 C291/1) does not cover agreements which have as their object the prevention, restriction or distortion of competition within the internal market: para 2. The Commission has issued Guidance on restrictions of competition 'by object' for the purpose of defining which agreements may benefit from the *De Minimis* Notice (SWD(2014) 198 final).

Status of the *De Minimis* Notice in Member States. The Court of Justice has 2.166
confirmed, in the reference for a preliminary ruling from the French Cour de Cassation, that although NCAs may take account of the market share thresholds set by the Commission's *De Minimis* Notice when determining whether an agreement has an appreciable effect on competition, they are not required to do so: Case C-226/11 *Expedia Inc*, EU:C:2012:795, [2013] 4 CMLR 439, para 31.

Fn 743 The Court of Justice held in Case C-681/11 *Schenker*, EU:C:2013:404, [2013] 5 CMLR 831 (disagreeing with Advocate General Kokott's Opinion of 28 February 2013) that reliance by an undertaking on legal advice or a previous NCA decision that its conduct was not contrary to EU competition law as it was *de minimis*, is not sufficient to show that an infringement was not committed intentionally or negligently, and thereby to escape a fine.

3

ARTICLE 101(3)

1. Introduction

Guidelines on the application of Article 101(3) to particular agreements.   **3.005**
Fn 11 On 21 March 2014 the Commission adopted Regulation 316/2014 on the application of Article 101(3) of the Treaty on the Functioning of the European Union to categories of technology transfer agreements, OJ 2014 L93/17. It entered into force on 1 May 2014, and replaces Regulation 772/2004 which expired on 30 April 2014. At the same time the Commission issued revised Guidelines on the application of Article 101 of the Treaty on the Functioning of the European Union to technology transfer agreements, OJ 2014 C89/3 ('Revised Technology Transfer Guidelines'). The reference to paras 146 et seq of the previous guidelines (OJ 2004 C101/2) should be read as paras 156 et seq of the Revised Technology Transfer Guidelines.

Fn 12 On 21 March 2014 the Commission adopted Regulation 316/2014 on the application of Article 101(3) of the Treaty on the Functioning of the European Union to categories of technology transfer agreements, OJ 2014 L93/17. It entered into force on 1 May 2014, and replaces Regulation 772/2004, which expired on 30 April 2014. The changes in Regulation 316/2014 are discussed in the updates to Chapter 9, below.

Fn 19 The Maritime Transport Guidelines, OJ 2008 C245/2: Vol II, App E20, expired on 26 September 2013, and the Commission has not renewed them: Press Release IP/13/122 (19 February 2013).

Power of the Commission to adopt decisions applying Article 101(3).   **3.007**
Fn 25 In respect of decisions applying Article 101(3) by NCAs, Directive 2014/104 on certain rules governing actions for damages under national law for infringements of the competition law provisions of the Member States and of the European Union, OJ 2014 L349/1, includes provision that where a NCA has taken a decision finding that either EU or national competition laws have been infringed, the national courts of that Member State are bound not to take a decision running counter to the NCA decision. The provision is, however, confined to 'infringement

decisions': Articles 2(11) and 9. The deadline for national implementation is 27 December 2016.

3.008 Application of Article 101(3) by NCAs.   Directive 2014/104 on certain rules governing actions for damages under national law for infringements of the competition law provisions of the Member States and of the European Union, OJ 2014 L349/1, includes provision that where a NCA has taken a decision finding that either EU or national competition laws have been infringed, the national courts of that Member State are bound not to take a decision running counter to the NCA decision. The provision is, however, confined to 'infringement decisions': Articles 2(11) and 9. The deadline for national implementation is 27 December 2016.

3.010 Review by the EU Courts of Commission decisions applying Article 101(3).   The Court of Justice dismissed the appeal in Case C-382/12P *MasterCard v Commission*, EU:C:2014:2201, [2014] 5 CMLR 1062. The judgment is discussed in the updates to paragraphs 3.024 et seq, below.

2. Application in Individual Cases

(a) Generally

3.011 Any agreement may benefit from Article 101(3).
Fn 37 The Court of Justice dismissed the appeal in Case C-382/12P *MasterCard v Commission*, EU:C:2014:2201, [2014] 5 CMLR 1062. The judgment is discussed in the updates to paragraphs 3.024 et seq, below

Fn 38 On 21 March 2014 the Commission adopted Regulation 316/2014 on the application of Article 101(3) of the Treaty on the Functioning of the European Union to categories of technology transfer agreements, OJ 2014 L93/17. It entered into force on 1 May 2014, and replaces Regulation 772/2004 which expired on 30 April 2014. At the same time the Commission issued revised Guidelines on the application of Article 101 of the Treaty on the Functioning of the European Union to technology transfer agreements, OJ 2014 C89/3 ('Revised Technology Transfer Guidelines'). The reference to p12 of the previous guidelines (OJ 2004 C101/2) should now be read as paras 18 and 95 of the Revised Technology Transfer Guidelines.

3.013 Agreements must satisfy all of the conditions in Article 101(3).
Fn 45 The Commission's decision in COMP/38606 *Groupement des Cartes Bancaires*, decision of 17 October 2007, was upheld by the General Court in Case T-491/07 *CB v Commission*, EU:T:2012:633. On the cumulative nature of the Article 101(3) conditions, see para 377. The Court of Justice overturned the judgment in Case C-67/13P *Groupement des cartes bancaires v Commission*,

EU:C:2014:2202, as the General Court erred in upholding the Commission's conclusion that the agreement was a restriction by object: see the update to paragraph 2.113, above. The case has therefore been referred back to the General Court.

Standard of proof.   The Court of Justice dismissed the appeal in Case **3.015** C-382/12P *MasterCard v Commission*, EU:C:2014:2201, [2014] 5 CMLR 1062. On the standard of proof to be applied in Article 101(3) cases, the Court held that the complaint by Bank of Scotland and Lloyds TSB Bank that the General Court should have adopted a balance of probabilities standard was inadmissible: paras 215–219. The other aspects of the judgment are discussed in the updates to paragraphs 3.024 et seq, below.

(b) The first condition: benefits of an agreement

(i) Generally

Benefits must be objective.   **3.022**
Fn 75 The Court of Justice dismissed the further appeal against the Commission's decision in COMP/34579 *MasterCard*, decision of 19 December 2007, in Case C-382/12P *MasterCard v Commission*, EU:C:2014:2201, [2014] 5 CMLR 1062.

Benefits in various markets.   The Court of Justice dismissed the appeal in Case **3.024** C-382/12P *MasterCard v Commission*, EU:C:2014:2201, [2014] 5 CMLR 1062. It confirmed that, in the case of a two-sided system, to determine whether an agreement meets the first condition of Article 101(3) it is necessary to take into account all the objective advantages flowing from it. That includes not only the advantages on the market on which the restriction is established but also on the other market where there is another group of consumers associated with the system. This is particularly important where there is interaction between the two sides of the system: para 237. However, the Court also confirmed that where the restrictive effects are felt only on one of the markets, the first condition of Article 101(3) can only be satisfied where some of the benefits are enjoyed by consumers on the market on which the restrictive effects are felt; if the benefits are entirely in the separate but connected market then they cannot, in themselves, compensate for the disadvantages of the agreement in the relevant market. It therefore upheld the General Court's conclusion that even if the MIFs lead to some benefit to cardholders, the absence of any benefits to merchants is sufficient to preclude the application of Article 101(3): paras 237 et seq.

Benefits must result from the agreement.   The Court of Justice dismissed the **3.026** appeal in Case C-382/12P *MasterCard v Commission*, EU:C:2014:2201, [2014] 5 CMLR 1062. It confirmed that the General Court correctly focused on the benefits of the MIFs rather than of the MasterCard system as a whole. The MIFs are not an objectively necessary ancillary restraint, and they must therefore be analysed separately from the main operation of the MasterCard system: paras 230–232.

3.030 Commission's current approach.

Fn 95 The Commission's decision in COMP/38698 *CISAC Agreements*, decision of 16 July 2008, [2009] 4 CMLR 577, has been partially annulled by the General Court, as the Commission had not established the existence of a concerted practice: Cases T-392, 398, 401, 410, 411, 413–422, 425, 428, 432–434, 442/08, judgments of 12 April 2013. However, in Case T-451/08 *Föreningen Svenska Tonsättares Internationella Musikbyrå v Commission*, EU:T:2013:189, [2013] 5 CMLR 577, the appellant did not contest the existence of a concerted practice, and the General Court went on to consider the practice's effects, and the potential application of Article 101(3) to it. The General Court dismissed the appeal, as a concerted practice limiting the territorial scope of licences was not indispensible for the maintenance of the national 'one-stop shops': see para 107. As the third condition was not met, the General Court did not consider the potential application of the other conditions.

Fn 99 The General Court dismissed the appeals against the Commission's findings of infringement in COMP/39181 *Candle Waxes*, decision of 1 October 2008, but reduced the fine imposed on five of the undertakings. On the application of Article 101(3), see Case T-544/08 *Hansen & Rosenthal and H&R Wax Company Vertrieb v Commission*, EU:T:2014:1075, paras 263 et seq (on further appeal, Case C-90/15P, not yet decided).

The General Court upheld the Commission's decision in COMP/39188 *Bananas*, decision of 15 October 2008, in Case T-587/08 *Fresh Del Monte Produce v Commission*, EU:T:2013:129, [2013] 4 CMLR 1091 (further appeal dismissed in Joined Cases C-293&294/13P *Fresh Del Monte Produce*, EU:C:2015:416, [2015] 5 CMLR 513); and Case T-588/08 *Dole Food Company v Commission*, EU:T:2013:130 (further appeal dismissed in Case C-286/13P *Dole Food Company v Commission*, EU:C:2015:184, [2015] 4 CMLR 967).

Fn 100 A more recent example is COMP/39398 *Visa MIF*, decision of 26 February 2014; see the update to paragraph 3.046, below.

3.031 Proving that efficiencies will result from an agreement. The Court of Justice dismissed the appeal in Case C-382/12P *MasterCard v Commission*, EU:C:2014:2201, [2014] 5 CMLR 1062. It was not claimed that the General Court had distorted the evidence in concluding that there were no objective benefits to the group of consumers on the relevant market, namely the merchants: para 243. In these circumstances, the Court of Justice rejected the argument that the benefits to consumers in separate but connected markets, the cardholders, could satisfy the requirements of Article 101(3): see the update to paragraphs 3.024 and 3.026, above.

Fn 103 The Commission's decision in COMP/38606 *Groupement des Cartes Bancaires*, decision of 17 October 2007, was upheld by the General Court in Case

T-491/07 *CB v Commission*, EU:T:2012:633 on the basis that the measures in question had as their object the restriction of competition, and it was not necessary to go on to consider their effects. On the interpretation of the economic evidence, the General Court agreed that the Commission had erred in certain respects but rejected the complaint that that error was sufficient to indicate bias. It also upheld the decision in respect of the alleged benefits of the agreement: para 374. The Court of Justice overturned the judgment in Case C-67/13P *Groupement des cartes bancaires v Commission*, EU:C:2014:2202, as the General Court erred in upholding the Commission's conclusion that the agreement was a restriction by object: see the update to paragraph 2.113, above. The case has therefore been referred back to the General Court to consider the Commission's findings as to the effects of the measures.

(ii) Cost efficiencies

Improvements to the structure of production.   3.033

Fn 109 The Court of Justice dismissed the further appeal against the Commission's decision in COMP/34579 *MasterCard*, decision of 19 December 2007, in Case C-382/12P *MasterCard v Commission*, EU:C:2014:2201, [2014] 5 CMLR 1062.

Stability and flexibility of supply.   3.034

Fn 115 The General Court dismissed the appeals against the Commission's findings of infringement in COMP/39181 *Candle Waxes*, decision of 1 October 2008, but reduced the fine imposed on five of the undertakings. On the application of Article 101(3), see Case T-544/08 *Hansen & Rosenthal and H&R Wax Company Vertrieb v Commission*, EU:T:2014:1075, paras 263 et seq (on further appeal, Case C-90/15P, not yet decided).

(iii) Qualitative efficiencies

Improved distribution.   3.039

Fn 144 The General Court upheld the Commission's decision in COMP/39188 *Bananas*, decision of 15 October 2008, in Case T-587/08 *Fresh Del Monte Produce v Commission*, EU:T:2013:129, [2013] 4 CMLR 1091 (further appeal dismissed in Joined Cases C-293&294/13P *Fresh Del Monte Produce*, EU:C:2015:416, [2015] 5 CMLR 513); and Case T-588/08 *Dole Food Company v Commission*, EU:T:2013:130 (further appeal dismissed in Case C-286/13P *Dole Food Company v Commission* EU:C:2015:184, [2015] 4 CMLR 967).

Fn 154 The Commission's decision in COMP/38698 *CISAC Agreements*, decision of 16 July 2008, [2009] 4 CMLR 577, has been partially annulled by the General Court, as the Commission had not established the existence of a concerted practice: Cases T-392, 398, 401, 410, 411, 413–422, 425, 428, 432–434, 442/08, judgments of 12 April 2013. However, in Case T-451/08 *Föreningen Svenska Tonsättares Internationella Musikbyrå v Commission*, EU:T:2013:189, [2013] 5 CMLR 577, the appellant did not contest the existence of a concerted practice, and the General Court went on to consider the practice's effects, and the application of Article 101(3) to it. The General Court dismissed the appeal, concluding that a concerted practice limiting the territorial scope of licences was not indispensible for the maintenance of the national 'one-stop shops': para 107. As the third condition was not met, the General Court did not consider the potential application of the other conditions.

3.040 Standardisation.
Fn 155 On 21 March 2014 the Commission adopted Regulation 316/2014 on the application of Article 101(3) of the Treaty on the Functioning of the European Union to categories of technology transfer agreements, OJ 2014 L93/17. It entered into force on 1 May 2014, and replaces Regulation 772/2004 which expired on 30 April 2014. At the same time it issued revised Guidelines on the application of Article 101 of the Treaty on the Functioning of the European Union to technology transfer agreements, OJ 2014 C89/3 ('Revised Technology Transfer Guidelines'). The reference to paras 210–235 of the previous guidelines (OJ 2004 C101/2) should be read as paras 244–273 of the Revised Technology Transfer Guidelines. The revised provisions on patent pools are discussed in the updates to paragraphs 9.066 et seq, below.

(iv) Improvements to market dynamics

3.046 Payment systems.   The Court of Justice considered the appeals in two cases concerning payment systems: Case C-382/12P *MasterCard v Commission*, EU:C:2014:2201, [2014] 5 CMLR 1062 and Case C-67/13P *Groupement des cartes bancaires v Commission*, EU:C:2014:2204.

In *MasterCard*, upholding the General Court's judgment, the Court confirmed that in the case of a two-sided system, to determine whether an agreement meets the first condition of Article 101(3) it is necessary to take into account all the objective advantages flowing from it. That includes not only the advantages on the market on which the restriction is established but also on the other market where there is another group of consumers associated with the system. This is particularly important where there is interaction between the two sides of the system: para 237. However, where the restrictive effects are felt only on one of the markets, Article 101(3) can only be satisfied where some of the benefits are enjoyed by consumers on the market on which the restrictive effects are felt; if the benefits are entirely in the separate but connected market then they cannot, in themselves, compensate for the disadvantages of the agreement in the relevant market. It therefore upheld the General Court's conclusion that even if the MIFs lead to some benefit to cardholders, the absence of any benefits to merchants is sufficient to preclude the application of Article 101(3): paras 237 et seq. It was not claimed that the General Court had distorted the evidence in concluding that there were no objective benefits to merchants: para 243.

In *Groupement des Cartes Bancaires*, the Court overturned the General Court's conclusion that the measures could be characterised as infringing Article 101(1) by object: see further the update to paragraph 2.113, above. As the General Court had not gone on to consider the Commission's findings of an infringement by effect, the Court of Justice has referred the case back to it for further consideration.

In addition, see the Commission's decision in COMP/39398 *Visa MIF*, decision of 26 February 2014, accepting commitments in particular to cap Visa Europe's credit card MIFs at 0.3 per cent for all consumer credit card transactions in the EEA where Visa Europe sets the rate. The Commission's preliminary assessment was that these MIFs did not meet the requirements for an exception under Article 101(3).

At the time of writing, the Commission's proceedings are ongoing in respect of the international inter-bank fees applied to transactions by card holders from outside the EEA at merchants within the EEA by Visa Inc (see COMP/39398 *Visa MIF*) and in respect of the rules on cross-border acquiring, and international inter-bank fees applied to transactions by card holders from outside the EEA at merchants within the EEA, by MasterCard (see COMP/40049 *MasterCard II*; a statement of objections was sent on 9 July 2015: Press Release IP/15/5323 (9 July 2015)).

(vi) Absence of benefit

No benefit from duplication of action by public authorities. In Case C-68/12 **3.053** *Protimonopolný úrad v Slovenská sporitel'ňa*, EU:C:2013:71, [2013] 4 CMLR 491, the Court of Justice held that an agreement between undertakings to eliminate a competitor from a market on which it had been operating illegally could not fall within Article 101(3) as it could not meet in particular the indispensability criteria. The Court held that the undertakings could have reported the illegal activity to the competent authorities. The Supreme Court of the Slovak Republic subsequently upheld the infringement decision of the Antimonopoly Office, on 22 May 2013: ECN Brief 03/2013, p13.

(c) The second condition: fair share of benefits for consumers

'Consumers' includes all users. **3.056**
Fn 214 The Commission's decision in COMP/38698 *CISAC Agreements*, decision of 16 July 2008, [2009] 4 CMLR 577, has been partially annulled by the General Court, as the Commission had not established the existence of a concerted practice: Cases T-392, 398, 401, 410, 411, 413–422, 425, 428, 432–434, 442/08, judgments of 12 April 2013. However, in Case T-451/08 *Föreningen Svenska Tonsättares Internationella Musikbyrå v Commission*, EU:T:2013:189, [2013] 5 CMLR 577, the appellant did not contest the existence of a concerted practice, and the General Court went on to consider the practice's effects, and the application of Article 101(3) to it. The General Court dismissed the appeal, concluding that a concerted practice limiting the territorial scope of licences was not indispensible for the maintenance of the national 'one-stop shops': see para 107. As the third

condition was not met, the General Court did not consider the potential application of the other conditions.

See also the Commission's decision in COMP/39839 *Telefónica/Portugal Telecom*,
decision of 23 January 2013, in which the Commission rejected the argument
that the agreement in question would not harm consumers as it was directed at
the corporate sector: see para 445 (on appeal, Cases T-208/13 *Portugal Telecom v
Commission*; and T-216/13 *Telefónica v Commission*, not yet decided).

3.057 **Carrying out the assessment of a fair share.**
Fn 215 The Court of Justice dismissed the appeal in Case C-382/12P *MasterCard v
Commission*, EU:C:2014:2201, [2014] 5 CMLR 1062. It confirmed that, in the case
of a two-sided system, to determine whether an agreement meets the first condition
of Article 101(3) it is necessary to take into account all the objective advantages
flowing from it. That includes not only the advantages on the market on which the
restriction is established but also on the other market where there is another group
of consumers associated with the system. This is particularly important where there
is interaction between the two sides of the system: para 237. However, where the
restrictive effects are felt only on one of the markets, Article 101(3) can only be satisfied where some of the benefits are enjoyed by consumers on the market on which
the restrictive effects are felt; if the benefits are entirely in the separate but connected
market then they cannot, in themselves, compensate for the disadvantages of the
agreement in the relevant market. It therefore upheld the General Court's conclusion that even if the MIFs lead to some benefit to cardholders, the absence of any
benefits to merchants is sufficient to preclude the application of Article 101(3): paras
237 et seq. It was not claimed that the General Court had distorted the evidence in
concluding that there were no objective benefits to merchants: para 243.

3.060 **Disadvantages for consumers.**
Fn 237 The Commission's decision in COMP/38698 *CISAC Agreements*, decision of 16 July 2008, [2009] 4 CMLR 577, has been partially annulled by the
General Court on appeal, as the Commission had not established the existence of
a concerted practice: Cases T-392, 398, 401, 410, 411, 413–422, 425, 428, 432–
434, 442/08, judgments of 12 April 2013. However, in Case T-451/08 *Föreningen
Svenska Tonsättares Internationella Musikbyrå v Commission*, EU:T:2013:189,
[2013] 5 CMLR 577, the appellant did not contest the existence of a concerted
practice, and the General Court went on to consider the practice's effects, and the
application of Article 101(3) to it. The General Court dismissed the appeal, concluding that a concerted practice limiting the territorial scope of licences was not
indispensable for the maintenance of the national 'one-stop shops': see para 107. As
the third condition was not met, the General Court did not consider the potential
application of the other conditions.

Fn 240 The Commission's decision in COMP/38606 *Groupement des Cartes
Bancaires*, decision of 17 October 2007, was upheld by the General Court in Case

T-491/07 *CB v Commission*, EU:T:2012:633. The Court of Justice overturned the judgment, in Case C-67/13P *Groupement des cartes bancaires v Commission*, EU:C:2014:2202, as the General Court erred in upholding the Commission's conclusion that the agreement was a restriction by object: see the update to paragraph 2.113, above. The case has therefore been referred back to the General Court.

Fn 244 See, however, Case C-382/12P *MasterCard v Commission*, EU:C: 2014:2201, [2014] 5 CMLR 1062 discussed in the update to paragraph 3.024, above. In the case of a two-sided system, where the restrictive effects are felt only on one of the markets, Article 101(3) can only be satisfied where some of the benefits are enjoyed by consumers on the market on which the restrictive effects are felt; if the benefits are entirely in the separate but connected market then they cannot, in themselves, compensate for the disadvantages of the agreement in the relevant market.

(d) The third condition: indispensability of restrictions

Generally.   3.062
Fn 248 The Court of Justice dismissed the further appeal against the Commission's decision in COMP/34579 *MasterCard*, decision of 19 December 2007, in Case C-382/12P *MasterCard v Commission*, EU:C:2014:2201, [2014] 5 CMLR 1062.

Indispensability of individual restrictions.   3.064
Fn 254 The Court of Justice dismissed the further appeal against the Commission's decision in COMP/34579 *MasterCard*, decision of 19 December 2007, in Case C-382/12P *MasterCard v Commission*, EU:C:2014:2201, [2014] 5 CMLR 1062.

Fn 257 The Commission's decision in COMP/38606 *Groupement des Cartes Bancaires*, decision of 17 October 2007, was upheld by the General Court in Case T-491/07 *CB v Commission*, EU:T:2012:633. The Court of Justice overturned the judgment, in Case C-67/13P *Groupement des cartes bancaires v Commission*, EU:C:2014:2202, as the General Court erred in upholding the Commission's conclusion that the agreement was a restriction by object: see the update to paragraph 2.113, above. The case has therefore been referred back to the General Court.

Hardcore restrictions.   A further example of a Commission decision conclud-   3.065
ing that the requirement of indispensability could not be met in respect of a hardcore restriction is COMP/39839 *Telefónica/Portugal Telecom*, decision of 23 January 2013, in which the Commission found that an agreement not to compete on the Iberian telecommunications market breached Article 101. It rejected Telefónica's argument that unless it accepted a non-compete clause, the agreement (by which Telefónica acquired the Brazilian mobile operator, Vivo, which until then had been jointly owned by Telefónica and Portugal Telecom) would not have been concluded. The Commission recalled that the requirement of indispensability relates to efficiencies, not to the agreement itself: para 444 (on

appeal, Cases T-208/13 *Portugal Telecom v Commission*; and T-216/13 *Telefónica v Commission*, not yet decided).

Fn 262 The Commission's decision in COMP/38698 *CISAC Agreements*, decision of 16 July 2008, [2009] 4 CMLR 577, has been partially annulled by the General Court, as the Commission had not established the existence of a concerted practice: Cases T-392, 398, 401, 410, 411, 413–422, 425, 428, 432–434, 442/08, judgments of 12 April 2013. However, in Case T-451/08 *Föreningen Svenska Tonsättares Internationella Musikbyrå v Commission*, EU:T:2013:189, [2013] 5 CMLR 577, the appellant did not contest the existence of a concerted practice, and the General Court went on to consider the practice's effects, and the application of Article 101(3) to it. The General Court dismissed the appeal, concluding that a concerted practice limiting the territorial scope of licences was not indispensible for the maintenance of the national 'one-stop shops': para 107.

(e) The fourth condition: no elimination of competition

3.067 Generally.

Fn 269 The Commission's decision in COMP/38698 *CISAC Agreements*, decision of 16 July 2008, [2009] 4 CMLR 577, has been partially annulled by the General Court, as the Commission had not established the existence of a concerted practice: Cases T-392, 398, 401, 410, 411, 413–422, 425, 428, 432–434, 442/08, judgments of 12 April 2013. However, in Case T-451/08 *Föreningen Svenska Tonsättares Internationella Musikbyrå v Commission*, EU:T:2013:189, [2013] 5 CMLR 577, the appellant did not contest the existence of a concerted practice, and the General Court went on to consider the practice's effects, and the application of Article 101(3) to it. The General Court dismissed the appeal, concluding that a concerted practice limiting the territorial scope of licences was not indispensible for the maintenance of the national 'one-stop shops': para 107. As the third condition was not met, the General Court did not consider the potential application of the other conditions.

3.068 Framework for analysis.

Fn 271 The Commission's decision in COMP/38698 *CISAC Agreements*, decision of 16 July 2008, [2009] 4 CMLR 577, has been partially annulled by the General Court, as the Commission had not established the existence of a concerted practice: Cases T-392, 398, 401, 410, 411, 413–422, 425, 428, 432–434, 442/08, judgments of 12 April 2013. However, in Case T-451/08 *Föreningen Svenska Tonsättares Internationella Musikbyrå v Commission*, EU:T:2013:189, [2013] 5 CMLR 577, the appellant did not contest the existence of a concerted practice, and the General Court went on to consider the practice's effects, and the application of Article 101(3) to it. The General Court dismissed the appeal, concluding that a concerted practice limiting the territorial scope of licences was not indispensible for the maintenance of the national 'one-stop shops': para 107. As the third condition was not met, the General Court did not consider the potential application of the other conditions.

Actual and potential competition.   On the meaning of 'potential' competition, **3.070** see the Court of Justice's judgment in Joined Cases C-239/11P, etc, *Siemens v Commission (Gas Insulated Switchgear)*, EU:C:2013:866, [2014] 4 CMLR 606, in which it considered that the existence of an information exchange mechanism between Japanese and European manufacturers supported the General Court's conclusion that the Japanese manufacturers were 'potential competitors' on the European markets, as it showed they were perceived to be credible potential competitors by the European manufacturers: para 114. It also held that, because the Commission had established evidence of the existence of a concerted practice, it was not necessary to examine whether there was an alternative plausible explanation for the undertakings' conduct in refraining from entering each other's territories, such as the existence of alleged technical and economic barriers to entry into the European markets: paras 219 et seq.

Channels of distribution.   **3.071**
Fn 292 The Commission's decision in COMP/38698 *CISAC Agreements*, decision of 16 July 2008, [2009] 4 CMLR 577, has been partially annulled by the General Court on appeal, as the Commission had not established the existence of a concerted practice: Cases T-392, 398, 401, 410, 411, 413–422, 425, 428, 432–434, 442/08, judgments of 12 April 2013. However, in Case T-451/08 *Föreningen Svenska Tonsättares Internationella Musikbyrå v Commission*, EU:T:2013:189, [2013] 5 CMLR 577, the appellant did not contest the existence of a concerted practice, and the General Court went on to consider the practice's effects, and the application of Article 101(3). The General Court dismissed the appeal, concluding that a concerted practice limiting the territorial scope of licences was not indispensible for the maintenance of the national 'one-stop shops': para 107. It upheld the Commission's decision in this regard, and against this appellant.

3. Block Exemption

(a) Generally

Individual agreements outside a block exemption may benefit from Article 101(3).   **3.074**
Fn 301 On 21 March 2014 the Commission adopted Regulation 316/2014 on the application of Article 101(3) of the Treaty on the Functioning of the European Union to categories of technology transfer agreements, OJ 2014 L93/17. It entered into force on 1 May 2014, and replaces Regulation 772/2004 which expired on 30 April 2014. At the same time the Commission issued revised Guidelines on the application of Article 101 of the Treaty on the Functioning of the European Union

to technology transfer agreements, OJ 2014 C89/3 ('Revised Technology Transfer Guidelines'). The reference to para 37 of the previous guidelines (OJ 2004 C101/2) should be read as para 43 of the Revised Technology Transfer Guidelines.

(b) Current block exemption regulations

3.084 **Technology transfer agreements.** On 21 March 2014 the Commission adopted Regulation 316/2014 on the application of Article 101(3) of the Treaty on the Functioning of the European Union to categories of technology transfer agreements, OJ 2014 L93/17. It entered into force on 1 May 2014, and replaces Regulation 772/2004 which expired on 30 April 2014.

Fn 336 The reference to Article 1(1)(b) of Regulation 772/2004 should be read as Article 1(1)(c) in Regulation 316/2014, and the reference to Article 2 of Regulation 772/2004 should be read as Article 2 of Regulation 316/2014.

Fn 337 The reference to Articles 4 and 3 of Regulation 772/2004 should be read as Articles 4 and 3, respectively, in Regulation 316/2014.

3.087 **Maritime transport services.**

Fn 350 The Commission has extended the maritime consortia block exemption regulation (Regulation 906/2009 (OJ 2009 L256/31)), which will expire on 25 April 2015, for a further five years to April 2020: Press Release IP/14/717 (24 June 2014).

Fn 353 The Commission has not renewed the Maritime Transport Guidelines, OJ 2008 C245/2, which expired on 26 September 2013: Press Release IP/13/122 (19 February 2013).

(c) Withdrawal and disapplication

3.092 **Disapplication of block exemption in respect of networks of agreements.** On 21 March 2014 the Commission adopted Regulation 316/2014 on the application of Article 101(3) of the Treaty on the Functioning of the European Union to categories of technology transfer agreements, OJ 2014 L93/17. It entered into force on 1 May 2014, and replaces Regulation 772/2004 which expired on 30 April 2014.

Fn 364 The reference to Article 7 of Regulation 772/2004 should be read as Article 7 of Regulation 316/2014.

4. Article 53(3) of the EEA Agreement

3.096 **Current block exemptions.** On 21 March 2014 the Commission adopted Regulation 316/2014 on the application of Article 101(3) of the Treaty on the

Functioning of the European Union to categories of technology transfer agreements, OJ 2014 L93/17. It entered into force on 1 May 2014, and replaces Regulation 772/2004, which expired on 30 April 2014. At the time of writing, the new block exemption has not been reflected in Annex XIV of the EEA Agreement.

4

MARKET DEFINITION

1. Introduction and Overview

(b) The concept of the relevant market

Meaning of a 'relevant market'.   4.003
Fn 9 The Court of Justice dismissed the further appeals in Case C-457/10P
AstraZeneca v Commission, EU:C:2012:770, [2013] 4 CMLR 233.

Fn 12 For extensive consideration of whether products were complements or
substitutes, see M.6166 *Deutsche Börse/NYSE Euronext* (1 February 2012), paras
305–367. The decision was upheld on appeal in Case T-175/12 *Deutsche Börse v
Commission*, EU:T:2015:148, [2015] 4 CMLR 1187, paras 71 et seq.

Leaving the relevant market open.   4.005
Fn 18 See also Case T-79/12 *Cisco Systems & Messagenet v Commission*,
EU:T:2013:635, paras 66 et seq, in which the General Court noted that the
Commission in M.6281 *Microsoft/Skype* (7 October 2011) had not adopted a position on whether it was necessary to determine the existence of narrower product
markets, and it upheld the Commission's analysis that in that case very high market
shares, and a high degree of market concentration on the Herfindahl-Hirschman
Index (see paragraph 8.213 of the main text), were not indicative of competition
concerns on any view of the relevant market.

(c) Relevance of market definition in EU competition law

Anti-competitive object under Article 101(1). The Court of Justice held in   4.006
Case C-226/11 *Expedia Inc*, EU:C:2012:795, [2013] 4 CMLR 439, paras 36–37,
that an agreement that may affect trade between Member States and that has
an anti-competitive object constitutes, by its nature and independently of any
concrete effect that it may have, an appreciable restriction on competition. On
30 August 2014 the Commission adopted a revised *De Minimis* Notice to take
account of this judgment: OJ 2014 C291/1. The revised Notice is discussed in the
updates to paragraphs 2.164 et seq, above.

The General Court's judgments in the appeals against the Commission's decision in COMP/39092 *Bathroom Fittings and Fixtures*, decision of 23 June 2010, highlight that market definition may be important in determining both the object and effect of an alleged infringement, where the behaviour in question consists of information exchange: the Court observed in Case T-380/10 *Wabco Europe v Commission (Bathroom Fittings)*, EU:T:2013:449, [2014] 4 CMLR 138, para 79:

> 'it cannot be presumed that an agreement or a concerted practice whereby undertakings exchange information which is commercially sensitive but which relates to a product sold on a market on which they are not competitors has an anti-competitive object or effect on that market. A practice whereby an undertaking which is active on two distinct product markets provides to its competitors – which are present on one market – commercially sensitive information which relates to a second market – on which those competitors are not present – is not capable, in principle, of having an impact on competition on the second market.'

See also Joined Cases T-379&381/10 *Keramag Keramische Werke and Others v Commission ('Bathroom Fittings')*, EU:T:2013:457, paras 92 and 221 (on further appeal, Case C-613/13P, not yet decided).

Fn 20 The Court of Justice dismissed the further appeal in Case C-439/11P *Ziegler v Commission*, EU:C:2013:513, [2013] 5 CMLR 1217. It confirmed that it is necessary to define the relevant market in order to apply a market share criterion (in that case, to determine whether there was an appreciable effect on trade between Member States in that market): para 63, but held that the Commission had in fact provided a sufficiently detailed description of the services with which its decision was concerned to constitute a definition of the market for these purposes: paras 67–73. See also Case T-82/08 *Guardian Industries Corp v Commission*, EU:T:2012:494, [2012] 5 CMLR 1234, at para 90 (on further appeal, Case C-580/12P, not yet decided).

Fn 23 The Court of Justice dismissed the further appeal, on other grounds, in Case C-510/11P *Kone v Commission ('Elevators and Escalators')*, EU:C:2013:696, [2014] 4 CMLR 371.

Fn 28 The General Court upheld the Commission's conclusion in COMP/39181 *Candle Waxes*, decision of 1 October 2008, that there was a single and continuous infringement across two different product markets, where those product markets were vertically related. Slack wax is the raw material used in the manufacture of paraffin wax, and the anti-competitive agreement in respect of the upstream product was intended to strengthen the agreement in respect of the downstream product: Case T-566/08 *Total Raffinage Marketing*, EU:T:2013:423, paras 270–273 (fine reduced on grounds of duration) (on further appeal, Case C-597/13P, not yet decided). The General Court dismissed the other appeals, on other grounds, against the Commission's findings of infringement but reduced the fine imposed on five of the undertakings.

See also Case T-135/09 *Nexans France v Commission*, EU:T:2012:596, [2013] 4 CMLR 195, paras 89–91 (Commission did not have reasonable grounds for ordering an inspection covering markets for which it had no evidence justifying an inspection). The further appeal, on other grounds, was dismissed in Case C-37/13P *Nexans v Commission*, EU:C:2014:2030, [2014] 5 CMLR 642.

Anti-competitive effect under Article 101(1).   **4.007**
Fn 29 The General Court's judgments in the appeals against the Commission's decision in COMP/39092 *Bathroom Fittings and Fixtures*, decision of 23 June 2010, highlight that market definition may be important in determining both the object and effect of an alleged infringement, where the behaviour in question consists of information exchange: the Court observed in Case T-380/10 *Wabco Europe v Commission (Bathroom Fittings)*, EU:T:2013:449, [2014] 4 CMLR 138, para 79:

> 'it cannot be presumed that an agreement or a concerted practice whereby undertakings exchange information which is commercially sensitive but which relates to a product sold on a market on which they are not competitors has an anti-competitive object or effect on that market. A practice whereby an undertaking which is active on two distinct product markets provides to its competitors – which are present on one market – commercially sensitive information which relates to a second market – on which those competitors are not present – is not capable, in principle, of having an impact on competition on the second market.'

See also Joined Cases T-379&381/10 *Keramag Keramische Werke and Others v Commission ('Bathroom Fittings')*, EU:T:2013:457, paras 92 and 221 (on further appeal, Case C-613/13P, not yet decided).

Fn 33 The Court of Justice dismissed the appeal in Case C-439/11P *Ziegler v Commission*, EU:C:2013:513, [2013] 5 CMLR 1217. It confirmed that it is necessary to define the relevant market in order to apply a market share criterion (in that case, to determine whether there was an appreciable effect on trade between Member States in that market): para 63, but held that the Commission had in fact provided a sufficiently detailed description of the services with which its decision was concerned to constitute a definition of the market for these purposes: paras 67–73.

(c) Methodology for defining the relevant market

(i) Jurisprudence and guidelines

Quantitative and qualitative approaches to market definition.   **4.011**
Fn 50 The Court of Justice dismissed the further appeals in Case C-457/10P *AstraZeneca v Commission*, EU:C:2012:770, [2013] 4 CMLR 233.

(ii) Factors relevant to defining relevant markets

Market definitions are contextual.   **4.014**
Fn 62 The Commission's decision in COMP/38606 *Groupement des Cartes Bancaires*, decision of 17 October 2007, was upheld by the General Court in Case

T-491/07 *CB v Commission*, EU:T:2012:633. On the relevant market being one on which the infringing undertaking is not active, see paras 83 and 104. The Court of Justice overturned the judgment, in Case C-67/13P *Groupement des cartes bancaires v Commission*, EU:C:2014:2202, discussed in the update to paragraph 2.113, above, and has referred the case back to the General Court.

Fn 63 See also Case T-556/08 *Slovenská pošta v Commission*, EU:T:2015:189, [2015] 4 CMLR 1024, paras 126 et seq. The General Court upheld the Commission's conclusion that hybrid mail services in Slovakia was a separate product market from traditional postal services, given there was demand and supply in Slovakia for integrated hybrid mail services. It specifically rejected the applicant's comparisons with the Commission's market definitions in previous decisions on the basis that 'the analysis carried out in those decisions is not necessarily applicable to other geographical markets, since the competition conditions in the various Member States may be fundamentally different': para 198. On further appeal, Case C-293/15P, not yet decided.

Fn 64 The General Court upheld the Commission's conclusion in COMP/39181 *Candle Waxes*, decision of 1 October 2008, that there was a single and continuous infringement across two different product markets, where those product markets were vertically related. Slack wax is the raw material used in the manufacture of paraffin wax, and the anti-competitive agreement in respect of the upstream product was intended to strengthen the agreement in respect of the downstream product: Case T-566/08 *Total Raffinage Marketing*, EU:T:2013:423, paras 270–273 (fine reduced on grounds of duration) (on further appeal, Case C-597/13P, not yet decided). The General Court dismissed the other appeals, on other grounds, against the Commission's findings of infringement but reduced the fine imposed on five of the undertakings.

Fn 66 See M.6266 *Johnson & Johnson/Synthes* (18 April 2012), para 23, for a discussion of possible bundled markets (rejected for lack of evidence).

Fn 68 See also M.6663 *Ryanair/Aer Lingus III* (27 February 2013), paras 69–73, in which the Commission treated as 'important factual elements which it takes into account in its assessment' its analyses of markets affected by an earlier proposal by Ryanair to acquire control over Aer Lingus, which had been upheld by the General Court (M.4439 *Ryanair/Aer Lingus* (27 June 2007); upheld in Case T-342/07 *Ryanair Holdings plc v European Commission* [2010] ECR II-03457). The Commission sought to ascertain whether there had been 'any significant changes in the market circumstances such as to warrant a different conclusion than the one reached in the 2007 Decision', but concluded that there had not. The appeal, in Case T-260/13 *Ryanair v Commission*, was withdrawn: Order of 28 October 2015.

4.015 'One-way' markets.

Fn 71 The Court of Justice dismissed the appeals in Case C-457/10P *AstraZeneca v Commission*, EU:C:2012:770, [2013] 4 CMLR 233. In particular, see paras 46–51, and the Court's finding at para 48 that 'the gradual nature of the increase in sales of a new product being substituted for an existing product does not necessarily mean that that latter product exercised on the former a significant competitive constraint'. The General Court was entitled to hold that it cannot be assumed there is a causal link between the gradual increase in sales of the new PPI product and a competitive constraint being exercised by the existing H2 blocker product.

Market definitions are not static.   4.016
Fn 72 See, however, M.7231 *Vodafone/ONO* (2 July 2014), para 16, in which the Commission dismissed a suggestion that there might be separate markets for broadband and ultrafast broadband, and considered that 'the increase in speeds is a sign of evolution of the market, rather than the creation of a new separate market'. See also M.7421 *Orange/Jazztel* (19 May 2015), paras 72 et seq, in which the Commission ultimately did not need to decide the relevant market definition but considered arguments that in Spain consumer demand for fixed voice telephony, internet and mobile telecommunications services, and to an extent pay-TV services, are converging as the price of purchasing these services in bundles tends to be lower than the price of purchasing them individually.

Fn 74 See also M.7231 *Vodafone/ONO* (2 July 2014), para 17, in which the Commission did not consider that mobile broadband services and fixed internet services were yet substitutable, but noted that 'it is possible that in the future the two services may converge'.

(iii) The SSNIP test

SSNIP test.   4.018
Fn 80 The General Court held in Case T-175/12 *Deutsche Börse v Commission*, EU:T:2015:148, [2015] 4 CMLR 1187, at para 84, that in circumstances where a customer cannot separate the various components of the price of a product then the 'price' used for the purposes of the SSNIP test can be the overall cost of trading.

(iv) Limitations on the SSNIP test

The 'cellophane fallacy'.   4.025
Fn 107 The Court of Justice dismissed the further appeal against the Commission's decision in COMP/34579 *MasterCard*, decision of 19 December 2007, in Case C-382/12P *Mastercard v Commission*, EU:C:2014:2201, [2014] 5 CMLR 1062.

2. Relevant Product Market

(a) Demand-side substitution

Product characteristics and functional interchangeability.   4.029
Fn 115 See also M.6458 *Universal Music Group/EMI Music* (21 September 2012), eg para 127, in which the Commission considers the different characteristics of recorded music in physical and digital formats.

4.030 **Switching data.** The Court of Justice dismissed the further appeals in Case C-457/10P *AstraZeneca v Commission*, EU:C:2012:770, [2013] 4 CMLR 233: see, in particular, paras 46–51. The Court held, at para 48, that 'the gradual nature of the increase in sales of a new product being substituted for an existing product does not necessarily mean that that latter product exercised on the former a significant competitive constraint'. The General Court was entitled to hold that it cannot be assumed there is a causal link between the gradual increase in sales of the new PPI product and a competitive constraint being exercised by the existing H2 blocker product.

4.033 **Switching costs and other barriers.**

Fn 135 For an example of a decision considering high switching costs and other barriers, see COMP/39230 *Rio Tinto Alcan*, decision of 20 December 2012, para 23.

Fn 136 For examples of additional barriers to switching, see M.6944 *Thermo Fisher Scientific/Life Technologies* (26 November 2013), para 256, in which the Commission found that there was unlikely to be switching in a market characterised by established commercial relationships and long-term contracts; and M.7265 *Zimmer/Biomet* (30 March 2015) in which it found that there were significant barriers to customer switching between orthopaedic implant products in circumstances where a track record of reliable product development is required, and surgeons are reluctant to switch suppliers because this may require retraining and may materially affect their success rates.

4.037 **Different absolute price levels.**

Fn 144 In M.5830 *Olympic/Aegean Airlines* (26 January 2011), the Commission stated at para 259 that 'Difference in price, in a differentiated products environment, provides a proxy of the distance in the product space between the two products. The larger this difference, the lower the likelihood that these two products are considered substitutable by a significant proportion of customers.' The appeal against the decision in Case T-202/11 *Aeroporia Aigaiou Aeroporiki and Marfin Investment Group Symmetochon v Commission*, was withdrawn on 10 September 2013.

See also, for example, M.6203 *Western Digital Ireland/Viviti Technologies* (23 November 2011), paras 150–151, 199–200 and 341, in which the Commission concluded that two products formed separate markets because, although there was scope to switch between them, the price differences meant that it would not be economic to do so; and M.6266 *Johnson & Johnson/Synthes* (18 April 2012), paras 76–77.

Fn 147 The Court of Justice dismissed the further appeals in Case C-457/10P *AstraZeneca v Commission*, EU:C:2012:770, [2013] 4 CMLR 233.

Fn 148 The Court of Justice dismissed the further appeals in Case C-457/10P *AstraZeneca v Commission*, EU:C:2012:770, [2013] 4 CMLR 233.

Critical loss analysis.   **4.039**

Fn 159 In M.5830 *Olympic/Aegean Airlines* (26 January 2011), para 249 the
Commission found that 'Critical Loss Analysis is not an appropriate tool for the
evaluation of the SSNIP test for the airline industry in view of the extent of price
discrimination and the difficulties in evaluating appropriately gross margins'. The
appeal against the decision in Case T-202/11 *Aeroporia Aigaiou Aeroporiki and Marfin
Investment Group Symmetochon v Commission*, was withdrawn on 10 September 2013.

In M.6166 *Deutsche Börse/NYSE Euronext* (1 February 2012) the limitations
of critical loss analysis are described at paras 344–349 (appeal dismissed, Case
T-175/12 *Deutsche Börse v Commission*, EU:T:2015:148, [2015] 4 CMLR 1187).

See also the UK OFT's decision in *Bunker fuel cards: investigation into alleged abuse
of dominance by bunker fuel card firm C H Jones*, CE/9278/10, in which the OFT
was persuaded that the critical loss analysis set out in its statement of objections
could not be relied upon in that case.

Price correlations.   **4.040**

Fn 163 See also M.6663 *Ryanair/Aer Lingus III* (27 February 2013), section 7.3.3
and Annex 1 (appeal, in Case T-260/13 *Ryanair v Commission*, withdrawn: Order
of 28 October 2015).

Fn 165 See, eg M.7061 *Huntsman/Rockwood* (10 September 2014), paras 141 et seq
in which the Commission conducted a price correlation analysis, but concluded
that the difficulties in controlling for demand shocks and in adequately controlling
for common cost shocks meant that the analysis could not be relied upon.

Trade relationships.   **4.042**

Fn 174 The appeal against the Commission's decision in Case M.6281 *Microsoft/
Skype* (7 October 2011) was dismissed in Case T-79/12 *Cisco Systems and Messagenet
v Commission*, EU:T:2013:635, [2014] 4 CMLR 709. The appeal, on other grounds,
against the Commission's decision in COMP/37990 *Intel*, decision of 13 May
2009, was dismissed in Case T-286/09 *Intel v Commission*, EU:T:2014:547, [2014]
5 CMLR 270 (on further appeal, Case C-413/14P, not yet decided).

Evidence of the views of customers and competitors.   **4.044**

Fn 176 For a further example, see M.6690 *Syniverse/Mach* (29 May 2013) in which
the Commission considered a proposed merger between the largest and second
largest operators in a number of markets for roaming technology services provided
to telecommunications companies, and sent around 240 requests for information
under Article 11 of the Merger Regulation (140 at Phase I, 100 at Phase II) to
MNOs, MVNOs, roaming hubs, actual competitors and potential competitors.

Fn 180 The Court of Justice dismissed the further appeal against the Commission's
decision in COMP/34579 *MasterCard*, decision of 19 December 2007, in Case
C-382/12P *Mastercard v Commission*, EU:C:2014:2201, [2014] 5 CMLR 1062.

4.045 Evidence from internal company documents.
Fn 181 The decision in M.6166 *Deutsche Börse/NYSE Euronext* (1 February 2012) was upheld on appeal in Case T-175/12 *Deutsche Börse v Commission*, EU:T:2015:148, [2015] 4 CMLR 1187, paras 71 et seq.

Fn 184 The Court of Justice dismissed the further appeal against the Commission's decision in COMP/34579 *MasterCard*, decision of 19 December 2007, in Case C-382/12P *Mastercard v Commission*, EU:C:2014:2201, [2014] 5 CMLR 1062.

(b) Supply-side substitution

4.047 Use of supply-side substitution in practice.   For a more recent example, see M.7435 *Merck/Sigma-Aldrich* (15 June 2015), paras 91 et seq, in which the Commission cleared a proposed concentration between undertakings active *inter alia* in the supply of laboratory chemicals. Particular chemicals have specific compositions and specific uses, and so are not substitutable on the demand side. However, on the supply side, a competitor active in a particular category of laboratory chemicals (solvents, inorganics, organics and other laboratory chemicals) would be capable of supplying any product within that category, switching production to the relevant products, and marketing them in the short term without incurring significant additional costs or risks.

4.048 Conditions for consideration of supply-side substitution.
Fn 192 In respect of suppliers being able to switch 'without incurring significant additional costs or risks', see M.6101 *UPM/Myllykoski and Rhein Paper* (13 July 2011), para 61.

4.050 Supply-side substitution evidence: switching costs.
Fn 203 The appeal, on other grounds, against the Commission's decision in COMP/37990 *Intel*, decision of 13 May 2009, was dismissed in Case T-286/09 *Intel v Commission*, EU:T:2014:547, [2014] 5 CMLR 270 (on further appeal, Case C-413/14P, not yet decided).

For a further example of a finding that switching costs would prevent supply-side substitution, see the UK CMA decision *Western Isles Road Fuels*, decision of 24 June 2014, in which the CMA considered that the need for access to marine terminals or similar facilities was critical to supplying road fuels to filling stations in the Western Isles, and the fact that one undertaking had exclusive access to the available terminals meant a substantial sunk investment would be required for a competitor to enter the road fuels wholesale market.

4.051 Supply-side substitution evidence: other barriers to switching.
Fn 205 See also M.6944 *Thermo Fisher Scientific/Life Technologies* (26 November 2013), paras 243 et seq, in which the Commission found that there was unlikely to be new market entry, and supply-side substitution, in the light of one of the parties holding patents for the relevant products, and the existence of pending patent

litigation; and M.7115 *Kuraray/GLSV Business* (29 April 2014), para 31, in which the Commission found that there was unlikely to be supply-side substitution between two different customer segments for PVB film products, in circumstances where developing a product for one of those customer segments required years of expertise.

(c) Particular issues in determining the relevant product market

(i) Connected markets

Connected markets.   4.054

Fn 208 See also Case COMP/39839 *Telefónica/Portugal Telecom*, decision of 23 January 2013, para 191, in which the Commission described the retail mobile market as including a 'cluster' of services.

Interaction between connected markets.   The Court of Justice dismissed the   4.055
further appeal in Case C-56/12P *European Federation of Ink and Ink Cartridge Manufacturers (EFIM) v Commission*, EU:C:2013:575. The Court confirmed the General Court's, and Commission's, approach of considering whether the markets for printers and cartridges were closely related, such that competition in the primary market for printers could exercise an effective discipline on the market for printer cartridges, by reference to the criteria set out in the main text: see paras 36 et seq.

See also M.7292 *DEMB/Mondelez/Charger Opco* (5 May 2015). The Commission found that there were separate, related markets for single-serve coffee machines and for the specific format consumables produced for each of those machines (coffee filter pads; N-capsules for Nespresso machines; other), and that it was therefore necessary to assess the impact that a concentration between two manufacturers of the consumables would have on the market for the machines: para 76. It concluded that the merger would not lead to a significant impediment to effective competition in the market for machines, *inter alia* as the merging parties cooperated closely with machine manufacturers, who would act as a constraint on the conduct of the JV: para 291, and as the JV would have an ongoing incentive not to hinder the position of the machine manufacturers given that sales of consumables depend on the machines with which they are compatible retaining market presence: paras 313 et seq.

System markets.   See also M.7292 *DEMB/Mondelez/Charger Opco* (5 May   4.056
2015). The Commission found that there were separate, related markets for single-serve coffee machines and for the specific format consumables produced for each of those machines (coffee filter pads; N-capsules for Nespresso machines; other), and that it was necessary to assess the impact that a concentration between two manufacturers of *inter alia* the consumables would have on the market for the machines: para 76. It was therefore not necessary to define a distinct relevant market for single-serve systems: paras 124–129.

4.059 **Separate markets for different stages of the production and distribution chain.**
Fn 227 The General Court judgment annulling the Commission's decision in
COMP/38700 *Greek Lignite and Electricity Generation*, decision of 5 March 2008,
was overturned by the Court of Justice in Case C-553/12P *Commission v DEI*,
EU:C:2014:2083, [2014] 5 CMLR 945.

4.060 **Market definition in two-sided markets.** The Court of Justice dismissed the
further appeal against the Commission's decision in COMP/34579 *MasterCard*,
decision of 19 December 2007, on other grounds, in Case C-382/12P *Mastercard
v Commission*, EU:C:2014:2201, [2014] 5 CMLR 1062.

Fn 233 The Commission's decision in COMP/38606 *Groupement des Cartes
Bancaires*, decision of 17 October 2007, was upheld by the General Court in Case
T-491/07 *CB v Commission*, EU:T:2012:633. On the two-sided nature of the system,
see para 104. The Court of Justice overturned the judgment, in Case C-67/13P
Groupement des cartes bancaires v Commission, EU:C:2014:2202, discussed in the
update to paragraph 2.113, above, and has referred the case back to the General Court.

(iii) Continuous chains of substitution

4.063 **Continuous chains of substitution.**
Fn 252 The appeal, on other grounds, against the Commission's decision in
COMP/37990 *Intel*, decision of 13 May 2009, was dismissed in Case T-286/09
Intel v Commission, EU:T:2014:547, [2014] 5 CMLR 270 (on further appeal, Case
C-413/14P, not yet decided).

(iv) Procurement markets

4.064 **Supply and procurement markets.**
Fn 256 See also, eg M.7120 *Ecom Agroindustrial/Armajaro Trading* (23 May 2014),
considering the procurement and supply of cocoa beans and products, and coffee beans.

4.065 **Technology markets.** On 21 March 2014, the Commission adopted Regulation
316/2014 on the application of Article 101(3) of the Treaty on the Functioning
of the European Union to categories of technology transfer agreements, OJ 2014
L93/17, to replace Regulation 772/2004 which expired on 30 April 2014. At the
same time, it issued revised accompanying Guidelines on the application of Article
101 of the Treaty on the Functioning of the European Union to technology transfer agreements, OJ 2014 C89/3 ('Revised Technology Transfer Guidelines').

Fn 260 The reference to para 2 of the previous guidelines (OJ 2004 C101/2)
should be a reference to para 22 of those guidelines, and it should now be read as
para 22 of the Revised Technology Transfer Guidelines.

Fn 262 The reference to Article 3(3) of Regulation 772/2004 should be read as
Article 8(d) in Regulation 316/2014, together with Article 1(1)(m) which defines
'relevant market' as including both a product market and a technology market.

Innovation markets.   **4.066**

Fn 265 See, more recently, M.7275 *Novartis/Glaxosmithkline Oncology Business* (28 January 2015), paras 89 et seq.

Fn 266 On 21 March 2014, the Commission adopted Regulation 316/2014 on the application of Article 101(3) of the Treaty on the Functioning of the European Union to categories of technology transfer agreements, OJ 2014 L93/17, to replace Regulation 772/2004 which expired on 30 April 2014. At the same time, it issued revised accompanying Guidelines on the application of Article 101 of the Treaty on the Functioning of the European Union to technology transfer agreements, OJ 2014 C89/3 ('Revised Technology Transfer Guidelines'). The reference to para 25 of the previous guidelines (OJ 2004 C101/2) should be read as para 26 of the Revised Technology Transfer Guidelines.

3. Relevant Geographic Market

(a) Overview

Definition of the relevant geographic market. On 16 March 2015 the **4.068**
Commission issued 'Market definition in a globalised world' (2015) 12 EU Competition Policy Brief, analysing the evolution of market definition in the Commission's decisions over the last decade.

Geographic market definition in the context of the removal of barriers to trade. **4.070**
Fn 278 The General Court judgment annulling the Commission's decision in COMP/38700 *Greek Lignite and Electricity Generation*, decision of 5 March 2008, was overturned by the Court of Justice in Case C-553/12P *Commission v DEI*, EU:C:2014:2083, [2014] 5 CMLR 945.

(b) Demand-side substitution

Transport costs.   **4.071**
Fn 280 See also M.7009 *Holcim/Cemex West* (5 June 2014), paras 63 et seq, in which the Commission concluded that the relevant geographic markets were the circular areas around individual cement plants, reflecting the distance at which suppliers could economically sell cement, those areas not being limited by national borders.

Geographic purchasing patterns and trade flows. See also, eg M.7120 *Ecom* **4.075**
Agroindustrial/Armajaro Trading (23 May 2014), paras 52 et seq, in which the Commission concluded that the relevant geographic market was global in scope taking into account *inter alia* the fact that the products in question, cocoa beans, were traded on futures markets accessible worldwide.

4.079 **Demand-side substitution evidence: internal company documents.**
Fn 311 For a further instance of the use by the Commission of internal company documents in the context of defining the geographic market, see M.6203 *Western Digital Ireland/Viviti Technologies* (23 November 2011), paras 394 et seq.

4.080 **Demand-side substitution evidence: views of customers and competitors.** In M.6690 *Syniverse/Mach* (29 May 2013), para 164, the Commission considered a proposed merger between the largest and second largest operators in a number of markets for roaming technology services provided to telecommunications companies, and received evidence from customers that they require '24/7' technical and customer care support in Europe and that EU data protection rules were important in their choice of service provider.

(c) Supply-side substitution

4.082 **Conditions for supply-side substitution.**
Fn 317 For a further example, see the UK CMA decision '*Western Isles Road Fuels*', decision of 24 June 2014, in which the CMA considered that the need for access to marine terminals or similar facilities was critical to supplying road fuels to filling stations in the Western Isles, and the fact that one undertaking had exclusive access to the available terminals meant a substantial sunk investment would be required for a competitor to enter the road fuels wholesale market.

4.084 **Legislative requirements or other barriers to switching by suppliers.** See also M.6541 *Glencor/Xstrata* (22 November 2012), paras 129 et seq, in which the Commission considered that the duty on importing zinc metal into the EEA from third countries was a significant constraint on imports, as it represented a significant share of the gross margin that could be realised by zinc metal smelters in the EEA.

Fn 325 The Commission's decision in COMP/38698 *CISAC Agreements*, decision of 16 July 2008, [2009] 4 CMLR 577, has been partially annulled by the General Court, on other grounds: Cases T-392, 398, 401, 410, 411, 413–422, 425, 428, 432–434, 442/08, judgments of 12 April 2013. In M.6800 *PRSfM/STIM/GEMA/JV* (16 June 2015), para 125, the Commission considered that the market for multi-territorial, multi-repertoire licensing of online performance rights was EEA-wide.

(d) Particular issues in determining the geographic market

4.086 **Markets for transport services.**
Fn 333 See also M.5830 *Olympic/Aegean Airlines* (26 January 2011) in which, on one route, air services and ferry services were found to be part of the same product market as regards time sensitive passengers: para 269. The appeal in Case T-202/11 *Aeroporia Aigaiou Aeroporiki and Marfin Investment Group Symmetochon v Commission* was withdrawn on 10 September 2013.

See also COMP/39595 *Continental/United/Lufthansa/Air Canada*, decision of 23 May 2013, paras 17–19; and M.6663 *Ryanair/Aer Lingus III* (27 February 2013), section 7.2 (appeal, in Case T-260/13 *Ryanair v Commission*, withdrawn: Order of 28 October 2015).

4. Temporal Market

Existence of a temporal dimension.   **4.087**

Fn 339 See also Case COMP/39654 *Reuters Instrument Codes*, decision of 20 December 2012, paras 28–30, identifying a market for certain types of 'real-time datafeeds'.

5

CARTELS

1. An Overview

Cartels are an enforcement priority.   **5.001**

Fn 1 In 2015 the Commission took five decisions, involving 21 undertakings or associations of undertakings, and imposed fines totalling €365m. The highest fine to date is that which was imposed on the participants in COMP/39437 *TV and computer monitor tubes*, decision of 5 December 2012, of €1.47 billion: Press Release IP/12/1317 (5 December 2012). The highest fine imposed on an undertaking for participation in a cartel remains COMP/39125 *Carglass*, decision of 12 November 2008, where Saint Gobain was fined €715,000,000. The General Court reduced the fine on appeal in Joined Cases T-56&73/09 *Saint Gobain (Carglass)*, EU:T:2014:160 (see the update to paragraph 14.042, below).

(a) The typical subject-matter of cartel activity

Restrictions ancillary to the cartel agreements.   **5.006**

Fn 8 The Court of Justice dismissed the further appeal in Case C-266/06P *Degussa v Commission* [2008] ECR I-81.

Fn 9 The General Court dismissed the appeals against the Commission's decision in COMP/39180 *Aluminium Fluoride*, decision of 25 June 2008, in Case T-404/08 *Fluorsid and Minmet v Commission*, EU:T:2013:321, [2013] 5 CMLR 902; and Case T-406/08 *Industries chimiques du fluor v Commission*, EU:T:2013:322 (further appeal, on other grounds, dismissed in Case C-467/13P, *Industries chimiques du fluor v Commission*, EU:C:2014:2274).

Fn 10 The Court of Justice dismissed the undertakings' further appeals against the decision in COMP/38899 *Gas Insulated Switchgear*, decision of 24 January 2007, in Joined Cases C-239/11P, etc, *Siemens v Commission (Gas Insulated Switchgear)*, EU:C:2013:866, [2014] 4 CMLR 606; and the appeal, on other grounds, in Case C-247/11P *Areva v Commission*, EU:C:2014:257, [2014] 4 CMLR 31. The Commission's appeal in Joined Cases C-239/11P, etc, *Siemens v Commission (Gas*

Insulated Switchgear), EU:C:2013:866, [2014] 4 CMLR 606 was upheld: see the update to paragraph 2.024, above.

Fn 14 The Court of Justice dismissed the further appeals against the decision in COMP/37766 *Netherlands Beer Market*, decision of 18 April 2007, in Case C-452/11P *Heineken Nederland and Heineken v Commission*, EU:C:2012:829; and C-445/11P *Bavaria v Commission*, EU:C:2012:828.

(b) How cartels operate

5.007 **The structure of cartels.** On the concepts of agreement and concerted practices, see also the updates to paragraphs 2.032 et seq, above.

5.008 **Single continuous infringement.** The General Court's approach in Case T-204&208/12 *Team Relocations v Commission (International Removal Services)* [2011] ECR II-3569, [2011] 5 CMLR 889 was upheld by the Court of Justice in Case C-444/11P *Team Relocations v Commission*, EU:C:2013:464, [2013] 5 CMLR 1335, at paras 51 et seq.

See also the updates to paragraphs 2.071 et seq, above.

5.009 **Participation in a cartel.** On participation, and the circumstances in which an undertaking will be treated as having distanced itself from a cartel, see also the updates to paragraphs 2.079 et seq, above.

5.010 **Liability of undertaking for the overall cartel.** On liability for cartel activities in which the undertaking did not directly participate, see also the updates to paragraphs 2.076 et seq, above.

Fn 27 The Court of Justice dismissed the further appeal on liability in Case C-70/12P *Quinn Barlo v Commission* ('*Methacrylates*'), EU:C:2013:351, [2013] 5 CMLR 637.

Fn 28 The Courts have ruled on the appeals against the Commission decisions noted in the footnote.

The decision in COMP/39396 *Calcium carbide and magnesium based reagents*, decision of 22 July 2009, was largely upheld on appeal: the appeals were dismissed in Cases T-352/09 *Novácke chemické závody v Commission*, EU:T:2012:673, [2013] 4 CMLR 734; T-392/09 *1. garantovana v Commission*, EU:T:2012:674 (further appeal dismissed, Case C-90/13P *1. garantovana v Commission*, EU:C:2014:326, [2014] 5 CMLR 79); T-400/09 *Ecka Granulate v Commission*, EU:T:2012:675; T-410/09 *Almamet v Commission*, EU:T:2012:676, [2013] 4 CMLR 788; Case T-399/09 *HSE v Commission*, EU:T:2013:647, [2014] CMLR 738; and Case T-384/09, T-384/09, *SKW v Commission* ECLI:EU:T:2014:27 (on further appeal, Case C-154/14P, not yet decided). The fines were reduced, but the appeals otherwise dismissed in Cases T-391/09 *Evonik Degussa v Commission*, EU:T:2014:22 (on further appeal, Case C-155/14, not yet decided); T-395/09 *Gigaset v Commission*, ECLI:EU:T:2014:23 and T-406/09 *Donau Chemie v Commission*, EU:T:2014:254.

The Commission's findings of infringement in decision COMP/39406 *Marine Hoses*, decision of 28 January 2009, were upheld in Cases T-146/09, etc, *Parker ITR and Parker-Hannifin v Commission (Marine Hoses)*, EU:T:2013:258, [2013] 5 CMLR 712 (the General Court's judgment was partially annulled, on different grounds on further appeal, in Case C-434/13P *Commission v Parker Hannifin Manufacturing and Parker-Hannifin*, EU:C:2014:2456, [2015] 4 CMLR 179).

The appeals against the Commission's decision in COMP/39180 *Aluminium Fluoride*, decision of 25 June 2008, were dismissed in Cases T-404/08 *Fluorsid and Minmet v Commission*, EU:T:2013:321, [2013] 5 CMLR 902; and Case T-406/08 *Industries chimiques du fluor v Commission*, EU:T:2013:322 (further appeal, on other grounds, dismissed in Case C-467/13P, *Industries chimiques du fluor v Commission*, EU:C:2014:2274).

Cartel 'consultancy'.   5.011
Fn 30 The appeal in Case T-27/10 *AC-Treuhand*, EU:T:2014:59 was dismissed. The General Court followed its earlier judgment in Case T-99/04 *AC-Treuhand*, EU:T:2008:256, [2008] ECR II-1501, [2008] 5 CMLR 962, and held that the undertaking which has participated in collusive conduct can be held liable for an infringement of Article 101 even if it is not active on the market affected by the restriction of competition. See in particular paras 36–47. On further appeal, Case C-194/14P, not yet decided.

In addition, on 4 February 2015 the Commission issued a decision that an undertaking which provides broker services infringed Article 101 by facilitating the infringements by various banks in respect of the benchmark for trading yen interest rate derivatives: COMP/39861 *Yen Interest Rate Derivatives ('YIRD')*, decision of 4 February 2015.

Fn 31 The Commission's findings of infringement in decision COMP/39406 *Marine Hoses*, decision of 28 January 2009, were upheld in Cases T-146/09, etc, *Parker ITR and Parker-Hannifin v Commission (Marine Hoses)*, EU:T:2013:258, [2013] 5 CMLR 712 (the General Court's judgment was partially annulled, on different grounds on further appeal, in Case C-434/13P *Commission v Parker Hannifin Manufacturing and Parker-Hannifin*, EU:C:2014:2456, [2015] 4 CMLR 179).

The General Court dismissed the appeals against the Commission's findings of infringement in COMP/39181 *Candle Waxes*, decision of 1 October 2008, but reduced the fine imposed on five of the undertakings. The appeals were dismissed in: Case T-548/08 *Total v Commission*, EU:T:2013:434 (on further appeal, Case C-597/13P, not yet decided); Case T-551/08 *H&R ChemPharm v Commission*, EU:T:2014:1081 (on further appeal, Case C-95/15P, not yet decided); Case T-550/08 *Tudapetrol Mineralölerzeugnisse Nils Hansen v Commission*, EU:T:2014:1079 (on further appeal, Case C-94/15P, not yet decided); Case T-562/08 *Repsol YPF Lubricantes y especialidades*, EU:T:2014:1078; and Case T-544/08 *Hansen & Rosenthal and H&R Wax Company Vertrieb v Commission*, EU:T:2014:1075 (on further appeal, Case C-90/15P, not yet decided). The fines were reduced, but the appeals otherwise dismissed, in: Case T-566/08 *Total Raffinage Marketing*, EU:T:2013:423 (fine reduced on grounds of duration) (on further appeal, Case C-634/13P, not yet decided); Case T-540/08 *Esso v Commission*, EU:T:2014:630, [2014] 5 CMLR 507 (fine reduced on grounds of duration of involvement of entities that merged during the infringement period); Case T-541/08 *Sasol v Commission*, EU:T:2014:628, [2014] 5 CMLR 729 (fine reduced on grounds of incorrect attribution of conduct by a joint venture); and Case T-543/08 *RWE v Commission*, EU:T:2014:627 (fine reduced on grounds of incorrect attribution of conduct by a joint venture); and Case T-558/08 *Eni v Commission*, EU:T:2014:1080 (fine reduced on grounds of incorrect application of an uplift for recidivism).

5.012 **Measures of concealment.**   On the EU Courts' approach to proving cartel-related infringements, see also the updates to Chapter 13, below.

Fn 33 The Court of Justice dismissed the undertakings' further appeals in Joined Cases C-239/11P, etc, *Siemens v Commission (Gas Insulated Switchgear)*, EU:C:2013:866, [2014] 4 CMLR 606; and the appeal, on other grounds, in Case C-247/11P *Areva v Commission*, EU:C:2014:257, [2014] 4 CMLR 31. The Commission's appeal in Joined Cases C-239/11P, etc, *Siemens v Commission (Gas Insulated Switchgear)*, EU:C:2013:866, [2014] 4 CMLR 606 was upheld: see the update to paragraph 2.024, above.

(c) Arguments typically used to justify cartels

5.013 No effects.
   Fn 36 In the appeals against the Commission's decision in COMP/38456 *Dutch Bitumen*, decision of 13 September 2006, the General Court reduced the fine imposed on Shell in Case T-343/06 *Shell Petroleum v Commission*, EU:T:2012:478, [2012] 5 CMLR 1064 (further appeal, in Case C-585/12P, withdrawn: Order of 11 April 2013), and dismissed the other appeals, on other grounds, in Cases T-344/06, etc, EU:T:2013:258 (further appeal by Kuwait Petroleum in C-581/12P dismissed in part as manifestly unfounded and in part as inadmissible: Order of 21 November 2013).

   Fn 37 The General Court upheld the Commission's decision in COMP/39188 *Bananas*, decision of 15 October 2008, in Case T-587/08 *Fresh Del Monte Produce v Commission*, EU:T:2013:129, [2013] 4 CMLR 1091 paras 305–308 (further appeal, on other grounds, dismissed in Joined Cases C-293&294/13P *Fresh Del Monte Produce*, EU:C:2015:416, [2015] 5 CMLR 513); and Case T-588/08 *Dole Food Company v Commission*, EU:T:2013:130, paras 67–71 (further appeal, on other grounds, dismissed in Case C-286/13P *Dole Food Company v Commission*, EU:C:2015:184, [2015] 4 CMLR 967).

In Case T-404/08 *Fluorsid and Minmet v Commission*, EU:T:2013:321, [2013] 5 CMLR 902, para 96, the General Court rejected an argument that implementation of an agreement, found by the Commission to have an anticompetitive object in COMP/39810 *Aluminium Fluoride*, decision of 25 June 2008, was 'impossible'.

No interest in or benefit from the cartel.   5.014

Fn 39 The Court of Justice dismissed the undertakings' further appeals against the decision in COMP/38899 *Gas Insulated Switchgear*, decision of 24 January 2007, in Joined Cases C-239/11P, etc, *Siemens v Commission (Gas Insulated Switchgear)*, EU:C:2013:866, [2014] 4 CMLR 606; and the appeal, on other grounds, in Case C-247/11P *Areva v Commission*, EU:C:2014:257, [2014] 4 CMLR 31. The Commission's appeal in Joined Cases C-239/11P, etc, *Siemens v Commission (Gas Insulated Switchgear)*, EU:C:2013:866, [2014] 4 CMLR 606 was upheld: see the update to paragraph 2.024, above.

Fn 40 The General Court upheld the Commission's decision in COMP/39188 *Bananas*, decision of 15 October 2008, in Case T-587/08 *Fresh Del Monte Produce v Commission*, EU:T:2013:129, [2013] 4 CMLR 1091 (further appeal, on other grounds, dismissed in Joined Cases C-293&294/13P *Fresh Del Monte Produce*, EU:C:2015:416, [2015] 5 CMLR 513); and Case T-588/08 *Dole Food Company v Commission*, EU:T:2013:130 (further appeal, on other grounds, dismissed in Case C-286/13P *Dole Food Company v Commission*, EU:C:2015:184, [2015] 4 CMLR 967).

Fn 42 The General Court dismissed the appeals against the Commission's decision in COMP/39810 *Aluminium Fluoride*, decision of 25 June 2008, in Case T-404/08 *Fluorsid and Minmet v Commission*, EU:T:2013:321, [2013] 5 CMLR 902; and Case T-406/08 *Industries chimiques du fluor v Commission*, EU:T:2013:322 (further appeal, on other grounds, dismissed in Case C-467/13P, *Industries chimiques du fluor v Commission*, EU:C:2014:2274). In *Fluorsid and Minment*, at para 96, the General Court rejected an argument that implementation of an agreement found by the Commission to have an anti-competitive object was 'impossible', as it was not necessary to examine the effects of the agreement once its anti-competitive object had been established.

Fn 43 The Commission's decision in *Bananas* was upheld on other grounds: see the update to footnote 40 above.

Participation under compulsion.   5.015

Fn 44 See also Case T-154/09 *Manuli Rubber Industries v Commission (Marine Hoses)*, EU:T:2013:260, paras 182 et seq, in which the General Court rejected a contention that the undertaking maintained contact with the other cartelists in order to give the impression that it had an interest in re-launching the cartel, and to protect itself against reprisals. See also paras 233 et seq, in which it rejected a contention that this could bear upon the gravity of the infringement for the purpose of determining the percentage of relevant sales on which to set the fine, and paras 285 et seq in which it rejected the contention that the Commission should have considered this a factor mitigating the fine.

Fn 45 The Court of Justice dismissed the further appeal in Case C-447/11P *Caffaro v Commission (Hydrogen peroxide and perborate)*, EU:C:2013:797. See, in particular, paras 30–31. See also T-406/09 *Donau Chemie v Commission (Calcium Carbide)*, EU:T:2014:254, at para 110.

Fn 46 See also Case T-154/09 *Manuli Rubber Industries v Commission (Marine Hoses)*, EU:T:2013:260, discussed in the update to footnote 44, above.

5.016 Not active on the cartelised market. The General Court distinguished its judgment in *Industrial Thread*, discussed in the main text (Joined Cases T-456&457/05 *Gütermann and Zwicky v Commission* [2010] ECR II-1443) in Case T-380/10 *Wabco Europe v Commission (Bathroom Fittings)*, EU:T:2013:449, [2014] 4 CMLR 138. Where the alleged cartel includes an exchange of commercially sensitive information, it is necessary that the recipient of the information be active on the cartelised market, such that there is potential for that recipient to modify its behaviour as a result of receiving the information, in order for the exchange to infringe Article 101. The Court emphasised at para 79 that:

> 'it cannot be presumed that an agreement or a concerted practice whereby undertakings exchange information which is commercially sensitive but which relates to a product sold on a market on which they are not competitors has an anticompetitive object or effect on that market. A practice whereby an undertaking which is active on two distinct product markets provides to its competitors – which are present on one market – commercially sensitive information which relates to a second market – on which those competitors are not present – is not capable, in principle, of having an impact on competition on the second market.'

The Court held that its judgment in Joined Cases T-456&457/05 *Gütermann and Zwicky v Commission* [2010] ECR II-1443, relied upon by the Commission, would apply to a disclosure of commercially sensitive information with a view to restricting competition in the market on which the recipient of the information is active, by a disclosing party that is not itself active on that market; whereas in the decision under appeal, COMP/39092 *Bathroom Fittings*, decision of 23 June 2010, the Commission had (as the Court held, wrongly) found that the purpose of the disclosure was to restrict competition in a market on which the disclosing party was active but the recipient was not: see paras 98–99. See also Joined Cases T-379&381/10 *Keramag Keramische Werke and Others (Bathroom Fittings) v Commission*, EU:T:2013:457, paras 92 and 221 (on further appeal, Case C-613/13P, not yet decided).

Fn 47 The appeal in Case C-537/10P *Deltafina v Commission*, was withdrawn by Order of 12 July 2011.

Industry crisis.　　　　　　　　　　　　　　　　　　　　**5.017**

Fn 49 In Case T-404/08 *Fluorsid and Minmet v Commission*, EU:T:2013:321, [2013] 5 CMLR 902, para 96; and Case T-406/08 *Industries chimiques du fluor v Commission*, EU:T:2013:322 para 90, the General Court confirmed that the Commission did not need to prove the effects of the cartel found in COMP/ 39810 *Aluminium Fluoride*, decision of 25 June 2008 (further appeal, on other grounds, dismissed in Case C-467/13P, *Industries chimiques du fluor v Commission*, EU:C:2014:2274). In *Fluorsid and Minmet* it rejected an argument that implementation of the agreement, found by the Commission to have an anti-competitive object, was 'impossible', as it was not necessary to examine the effects of the agreement once its anti-competitive object had been established.

Response to anti-competitive behaviour by other firms. The Court of　**5.018** Justice confirmed in Case C-68/12 *Protimonopolný úrad v Slovenská sporitel'ňa*, EU:C:2013:71, [2013] 4 CMLR 491, paras 19–21, that if an agreement is intended to exclude a competitor from the relevant market, it is not relevant that that competitor had been operating on the market illegally. The Supreme Court of the Slovak Republic subsequently upheld the infringement decision of the Antimonopoly Office on 22 May 2013: ECN Brief 03/2013, p13.

Government connivance. See also Case C-444/11P *Team Relocations v*　**5.019** *Commission*, EU:C:2013:464, [2013] 5 CMLR 1335, paras 148–150, in which the Court of Justice dismissed a complaint that the Commission had itself sought out cover prices from the cartelists.

Fn 52 The General Court dismissed the appeals against the Commission's findings of infringement in COMP/39181 *Candle Waxes*, decision of 1 October 2008, but reduced the fine imposed on five of the undertakings. The appeals were dismissed in: Case T-548/08 *Total v Commission*, EU:T:2013:434 (on further appeal, Case C-597/13P, not yet decided); Case T-551/08 *H&R ChemPharm v Commission*, EU:T:2014:1081 (on further appeal, Case C-95/15P, not yet decided); Case T-550/08 *Tudapetrol Mineralölerzeugnisse Nils Hansen v Commission*, EU:T:2014:1079 (on further appeal, Case C-94/15P, not yet decided); Case T-562/08 *Repsol YPF Lubricantes y especialidades*, EU:T:2014:1078; and Case T-544/08 *Hansen & Rosenthal and H&R Wax Company Vertrieb v Commission*, EU:T:2014:1075 (on further appeal, Case C-90/15P, not yet decided). The fines were reduced, but the appeals otherwise dismissed, in: Case T-566/08 *Total Raffinage Marketing*, EU:T:2013:423 (fine reduced on grounds of duration) (on further appeal, Case C-634/13P, not yet decided); Case T-540/08 *Esso v Commission*, EU:T:2014:630, [2014] 5 CMLR 507 (fine reduced on grounds of duration of involvement of entities that merged during the infringement period); Case T-541/08 *Sasol v Commission*, EU:T:2014:628, [2014] 5 CMLR 729 (fine reduced on grounds of incorrect attribution of conduct by a joint venture); and Case T-543/08 *RWE v Commission*, EU:T:2014:627 (fine reduced on grounds of incorrect attribution of conduct by a joint venture); and Case T-558/08 *Eni v Commission*, EU:T:2014:1080 (fine reduced on grounds of incorrect application of an uplift for recidivism).

Fn 53 See the update to footnote 52, above.

(d) Investigation and enforcement

5.021 **Information requests and inspections.** On the Commission's powers to gather information and to conduct inspections, see also the updates to paragraphs 13.011 et seq, below.

5.022 **The Leniency Notice.** A revised Model Leniency Programme was issued by the ECN in November 2012, and is available on DG Comp's website. The main changes are that all undertakings applying to the Commission for leniency in cases concerning more than three Member States will be able to submit a summary application to national competition authorities, where previously only the first applicant, ie the immunity applicant, was entitled to use summary applications under the model leniency programme; and the ECN has agreed on a standard template for summary applications, which can be used in all Member States. On the conditions for the grant of immunity under the Leniency Notice and the procedure for making an application, see also the updates to paragraphs 14.109 et seq, below.

Fn 59 The Court of Justice dismissed the further appeal in Case C-578/11P *Deltafina v Commission*, EU:C:2014:1460, [2014] 5 CMLR 599.

Fn 61 The ability of third parties to access leniency information from the Commission or from ECN members will be circumscribed by Directive 2014/104 on certain rules governing actions for damages under national law for infringements of the competition law provisions of the Member States and of the European Union, OJ 2014 L349/1. In particular, its provisions include:

(a) a complete prohibition on disclosure of leniency statements and settlement submissions, together with a requirement that such information shall be inadmissible in a damages action before the national court where a party has obtained it through access to the file (or otherwise be given equivalent protection to ensure the effectiveness of the prohibition on disclosure): Articles 6(6) and 7(1);

(b) a temporary prohibition on disclosure of *inter alia* information prepared specifically for the proceedings before a competition authority, until after the proceedings are closed; together with a requirement that such information shall be inadmissible in a damages action before the national court, where a party has obtained it through access to the file, until after the proceedings before the competition authority are closed (or otherwise be given equivalent protection to ensure the effectiveness of the temporary prohibition on disclosure): Article 6(5) and 7(2).

The prohibitions apply to documents/information relating to investigations by the Commission, as well as to investigations by national competition authorities. The deadline for national implementation is 27 December 2016.

Cartel settlement.   5.023

Fn 65 See also COMP/39748 *Automotive Wire Harnesses*, settlement decision of 10 July 2013; COMP/39801 *Polyurethane Foam*, decision of 29 January 2014; COMP/39952 *Power Exchanges*, decision of 5 March 2014; COMP/39922 *Automotive Bearings*, decision of 19 March 2014; COMP/39792 *Steel Abrasives*, decision of 2 April 2014; COMP/39965 *Mushrooms*, decision of 25 June 2014; COMP/39780 *Envelopes*, decision of 10 December 2014; and COMP/40055 *Parking Heaters*, decision of 17 June 2015.

Fn 66 See also COMP/39861 *Yen Interest Rate Derivatives ('YIRD')*, settlement decision of 4 December 2013, and COMP/39924 *Swiss Franc interest rate derivatives*, settlement decision of 21 October 2014.

Proving the infringement.   5.024

Fn 68 The Court of Justice dismissed the further appeal against the decision in COMP/37766 *Netherlands Beer Market*, decision of 18 April 2007, in Cases C-452/11P *Heineken Nederland and Heineken v Commission*, EU:C:2012:829; and C-445/11P *Bavaria v Commission*, EU:C:2012:828.

Fn 71 The General Court dismissed the appeals against the Commission's findings of infringement in COMP/39181 *Candle Waxes*, decision of 1 October 2008, but reduced the fine imposed on five of the undertakings. The appeals were dismissed in: Case T-548/08 *Total v Commission*, EU:T:2013:434 (on further appeal, Case C-597/13P, not yet decided); Case T-551/08 *H&R ChemPharm v Commission*, EU:T:2014:1081 (on further appeal, Case C-95/15P, not yet decided); Case T-550/08 *Tudapetrol Mineralölerzeugnisse Nils Hansen v Commission*, EU:T:2014:1079 (on further appeal, Case C-94/15P, not yet decided); Case T-562/08 *Repsol YPF Lubricantes y especialidades*, EU:T:2014:1078; and Case T-544/08 *Hansen & Rosenthal and H&R Wax Company Vertrieb v Commission*, EU:T:2014:1075 (on further appeal, Case C-90/15P, not yet decided). The fines were reduced, but the appeals otherwise dismissed, in: Case T-566/08 *Total Raffinage Marketing*, EU:T:2013:423 (fine reduced on grounds of duration) (on further appeal, Case C-634/13P, not yet decided); Case T-540/08 *Esso v Commission*, EU:T:2014:630, [2014] 5 CMLR 507 (fine reduced on grounds of duration of involvement of entities that merged during the infringement period); Case T-541/08 *Sasol v Commission*, EU:T:2014:628, [2014] 5 CMLR 729 (fine reduced on grounds of incorrect attribution of conduct by a joint venture); and Case T-543/08 *RWE v Commission*, EU:T:2014:627 (fine reduced on grounds of incorrect attribution of conduct by a joint venture); and Case T-558/08 *Eni v Commission*, EU:T:2014:1080 (fine reduced on grounds of incorrect application of an uplift for recidivism).

5.025 **Admissibility and probative value of evidence.** The Court of Justice dismissed the undertakings' further appeals in Joined Cases C-239/11P, etc, *Siemens v Commission (Gas Insulated Switchgear)*, EU:C:2013:866, [2014] 4 CMLR 606, discussed in the updates to paragraphs 5.027 and 5.028, below.

In Case T-286/09 *Intel v Commission*, EU:T:2014:547, [2014] 5 CMLR 270 the General Court held that a response to a request under Article 18 of Regulation 1/2003 from a third party undertaking that was a customer of the addressee of the decision (in that case, a dominant undertaking rather than a cartelist) is particularly reliable, in view of the risk of retaliatory measures that it faces from its supplier if it wrongly accuses it of anti-competitive conduct: see, eg paras 680 et seq. On further appeal, Case C-413/14P, not yet decided.

5.026 **Contemporaneous documents.**
Fn 80 The Court of Justice dismissed the further appeals against the decision in COMP/37766 *Netherlands Beer Market*, decision of 18 April 2007, in Cases C-452/11P *Heineken Nederland and Heineken v Commission*, EU:C:2012:829; and C-445/11P *Bavaria v Commission*, EU:C:2012:828.

5.027 **Documents from one cartel participant incriminating another undertaking.** In Joined Cases C-239/11P, etc, *Siemens v Commission (Gas Insulated Switchgear)*, EU:C:2013:866, [2014] 4 CMLR 606, the Court of Justice upheld the General Court's conclusion that the leniency applicant's evidence was credible and that the other cartelists' evidence was less so as they had sought to deny the existence of the common understanding and therefore were not acting against their own interests: see para 145 of the judgment, and the update to paragraph 5.028, below. The Court dismissed the argument that evidence corroborating the contents of a leniency statement has to be contemporaneous documentation and cannot comprise other statements made with a view to obtaining leniency. The principle of unfettered evaluation of evidence precludes any such rule: paras 191–192.

5.028 **Credibility of statements made by a leniency applicant.** In Joined Cases C-239/11P, etc, *Siemens v Commission (Gas Insulated Switchgear)*, EU:C:2013:866, [2014] 4 CMLR 606, the Court of Justice dismissed as inadmissible a complaint that the General Court should not have relied upon the witness evidence of the leniency applicant because of 'established knowledge relating to the functioning of the memory and the psychology of witnesses', and the possibility that an individual may have had an interest in maximising the unlawful conduct of competitors and minimising their own liability. The Court's powers to review findings of fact (discussed in paragraph 13.171 of the main text and the update thereto) do not extend to a review on this basis. The Court also upheld the General Court's conclusion that the leniency applicant's evidence was credible, in particular as its representative would have been aware of the potential negative consequences of submitting inaccurate information, and the applicant itself had acted against its own interests in applying for leniency because of the risk of damages actions being brought against it in national courts: paras 138 and 141. The Court also upheld the conclusion that evidence corroborating the contents of a leniency statement does not have to be contemporaneous documentation but can comprise other statements made with a view to obtaining leniency: para 191.

Fn 89 The General Court dismissed the appeals against the Commission's findings of infringement in COMP/39181 *Candle Waxes*, decision of 1 October 2008, but reduced the fine imposed on five of the undertakings. On the probative value of the leniency corporate statements relied upon by the Commission, see eg Case T-566/08 *Total Raffinage Marketing*, EU:T:2013:423, paras 69–71 (on further appeal, Case C-597/13P, not yet decided); and Case T-558/08 *Eni v Commission*, EU:T:2014:1080, paras 86 et seq.

On the economic benefits of submitting a leniency application, and the impact that it has on the credibility of the applicant that it obtains an economic benefit from securing leniency, see the discussion in the General Court's judgment in Case T-588/08 *Dole Food Company v Commission*, EU:T:2013:130, paras 86 et seq (further appeal, on other grounds, dismissed in Case C-286/13P *Dole Food Company v Commission*, EU:C:2015:184, [2015] 4 CMLR 967). Dole argued that the leniency application had been made in order to secure the completion of an acquisition by the leniency applicant of another company: the banks that had been asked to finance the acquisition had expressed concerns about the leniency applicant's operations, and had only agreed to provide the financing once immunity had been granted. The General Court rejected the argument that this undermined the leniency applicant's credibility. It held that 'the existence of a personal interest in reporting the existence of a concerted practice does not necessarily mean that the person doing so is unreliable': para 92. The existence of the banks' concerns reinforced the credibility of the evidence that the cartel existed, and any economic benefits that the leniency applicant obtained as a result of being granted immunity had to be balanced against the exposure to third party damages actions that would arise as a result of its admissions: paras 93–94.

Fn 90 In Case T-462/07 *Galp Energía España v Commission*, EU:T:2013:459, [2014] 4 CMLR 272, paras 129 et seq the General Court dismissed a complaint that two leniency applicants appeared to have coordinated their leniency applications.

Fn 91 The Court of Justice dismissed the further appeal in Case C-70/12P *Quinn Barlo v Commission* ('*Methacrylates*'), EU:C:2013:351, [2013] 5 CMLR 637. See also the General Court's judgment in Case T-588/08 *Dole Food Company v Commission*, EU:T:2013:130, at para 91 (further appeal, on other grounds, dismissed in Case C-286/13P *Dole Food Company v Commission*, EU:C:2015:184, [2015] 4 CMLR 967).

Fn 92 The Court of Justice dismissed the further appeal in Case C-70/12P *Quinn Barlo v Commission* ('*Methacrylates*'), EU:C:2013:351, [2013] 5 CMLR 637.

5.030 **Proof of duration of the cartel.** See, however, Case T-540/08 *Esso v Commission*, EU:T:2014:630, [2014] 5 CMLR 507, at paras 83–85, in which the General Court held that even if representatives of an undertaking did not participate in certain unlawful meetings nonetheless the undertaking could presumed throughout the period preceding those meetings to have taken account of information already exchanged with its competitors in determining its conduct on the market. It therefore upheld the Commission's findings as to the duration of the cartel.

(e) Sanctions and redress

5.031 **The harm caused by cartels.**
Fn 100 In the appeals against the Commission's decisions referred to in the footnote:

COMP/39188 *Bananas*, decision of 15 October 2008, was upheld. In particular, on the impact of the infringement on prices to consumers, see the Court of Justice's observations in Case C-286/13P *Dole Food Company v Commission*, EU:C:2015:184, [2015] 4 CMLR 967, paras 123–125. See also Case T-587/08 *Fresh Del Monte Produce v Commission*, EU:T:2013:129, [2013] 4 CMLR 1091 (further appeal, on other grounds, dismissed in Joined Cases C-293&294/13P *Fresh Del Monte Produce*, EU:C:2015:416, [2015] 5 CMLR 513).

COMP/39125 *Carglass*, decision of 12 November 2008, was partially upheld. In Case T-68/09 *Soliver v Commission* ('*Carglass*'), EU:T:2014:867, [2014] 5 CMLR 1168 it was annulled in respect of Soliver, as the Court held there was insufficient evidence to establish its participation in a single and continuous infringement and the decision was not severable; see the update to paragraph 2.076, above. The findings of infringement were upheld in Joined Cases T-56&73/09 *Saint Gobain (Carglass)*, EU:T:2014:160 (fine reduced on grounds of incorrect uplift for recidivism); and the appeal was dismissed in its entirety in Case T-72/09 *Pilkington v Commission*, EU:T:2014:1094 (on further appeal, Case C-101/15P, not yet decided).

5.032 **Fines—overview.** The approach of the General Court in the appeals against the Commission's decision in COMP/38543 *International Removals Services*, decision of 11 March 2008, was upheld by the Court of Justice in Case C-444/11P *Team Relocations v Commission*, EU:C:2013:464, [2013] 5 CMLR 1335, paras 139–141.

Following the judgment in Case C-226/11 *Expedia Inc*, EU:C:2012: 795, [2013] 4 CMLR 439, paras 36–37, in which the Court of Justice held that an agreement that may affect trade between Member States and that has an anti-competitive object constitutes, by its nature and independently of any concrete effect that it may have, an appreciable restriction on competition, the Commission has adopted a revised

De Minimis Notice: OJ 2014 C291/1. The revised Notice does not cover agreements which have as their object the prevention, restriction or distortion of competition within the internal market: para 2. The Commission has issued Guidance on restrictions of competition 'by object' for the purpose of defining which agreements may benefit from the *De Minimis* Notice (SWD(2014) 198 final).

See also the updates to Chapter 14, below.

Deterrence.   On the uplift of fines for deterrence, see also the update to paragraph 14.071, below.   **5.033**

Repeat infringements and other aggravating factors.   On recidivism and other aggravating factors, see also the updates to paragraphs 14.040 et seq, below.   **5.034**

Fn 110 In Case C-508/11P *Commission v Eni*, EU:C:2013:289, [2013] 5 CMLR 607, the Court of Justice dismissed the Commission's appeal against the General Court's judgment in Case T-39/07 *ENI v Commission*, [2011] ECR II-4457. The Commission issued a second statement of objections to Eni and Versalis on 1 March 2013, providing the explanation held by the General Court to have been absent from the decision in COMP/38638 *Butadeine Rubber and Emulsion Styrene Butadeine Rubber*, decision of 29 November 2006, [2009] 4 CMLR 421 (namely of the capacity in which, or extent to which, the undertaking was considered to have participated in a previous infringement) and reaching the provisional conclusion that an uplift should be imposed for recidivism: COMP/40032 *BR/ESBR Recidivism*, Press Release IP/13/179 (1 March 2013). The decision to initiate the procedure in COMP/40032 is on appeal in Case T-210/13 *Versalis v Commission*, and Case T-211/13 *Eni v Commission*, not yet decided.

Joint and several liability for payment of the fine.   In Joined Cases C-231/11P,   **5.035**
etc, *Commission v Siemens and others*, EU:C:2014:256, [2014] 5 CMLR 7, at paras 55 et seq the Court of Justice overturned the General Court's judgment that the Commission's powers to determine the fine to be imposed on different infringing undertakings, under Article 23(2) of Regulation 1/2003, includes the power exclusively to determine the proportions that particular legal entities within an undertaking should contribute towards payment of that fine. The Court held that although the Commission must necessarily address its decision to particular legal entities, its powers do not extend to determining the shares to be paid by different legal entities within an undertaking. It stated at para 58:

> 'While it follows from Article 23(2) of Regulation No 1/2003 that the Commission is entitled to hold a number of companies jointly and severally liable for payment of a fine, since they formed part of the same undertaking, it is not possible to conclude on the basis of either the wording of that provision or the objective of the joint and several liability mechanism that that power to impose penalties extends, beyond the determination of joint and several liability from an external perspective, to the power to determine the shares to be paid by those held jointly and severally liable from the perspective of their internal relationship.'

This determination is a matter for the national courts, applying national law to the dispute in a manner consistent with EU law.

On joint and several liability, see also the updates to paragraphs 14.086, below.

5.036 **Criminal sanctions.** The Enterprise and Regulatory Reform Act 2013 entered into force in April 2014. Section 47 amends s 188 of the Enterprise Act 2002 to remove the dishonesty requirement from the cartel offence, and adds ss 188A and 188B to clarify the circumstances in which the offence is committed. These provide:

(a) Under s 188A, parties to an arrangement that would otherwise be within the scope of the offence may bring the arrangement outside the scope, if they satisfy certain notification requirements. These are: (a) the notification exclusion (under the terms of the arrangement customers would be given relevant information about the arrangements before they enter into agreements for the supply to them of the product or service affected); (b) the bid-rigging notification exclusion (the person requesting bids would be given relevant information about the arrangements at or before the time when a bid is made); or (c) the publication exclusion (relevant information about the arrangement would be published, before the arrangements are implemented, in the manner specified at the time of the making of the agreement in an order made by the Secretary of State). 'Relevant information' for the purpose of these exclusions is defined as the names of the undertakings to which the arrangements relate; a description of the nature of the arrangements which is sufficient to show why they are or might be arrangements which fall within the scope of the offence; the products or services to which they relate; and any other information as may be specified in an order made by the Secretary of State.

(b) Under s 188B, three statutory defences are created. These are: (a) where the arrangements would affect supply in the UK, the individual did not intend that the nature of the arrangements would be concealed from customers before they enter into agreements for the supply to them of the product or service; (b) the individual did not intend that the nature of the arrangements would be concealed from the Competition and Markets Authority; (c) before making the agreement, the individual took reasonable steps to ensure that the nature of the arrangements would be disclosed to professional legal advisers, for the purpose of obtaining advice about them before they were made or implemented.

5.037 **Private actions for damages arising from cartel activity.** On 10 November 2014, Directive 2014/104 on certain rules governing actions for damages under national law for infringements of the competition law provisions of the Member States and of the European Union, OJ 2014 L349/1, was formally adopted. The deadline for national implementation is 27 December 2016. The detailed proposals are discussed in the updates to Chapter 16, below.

In respect of the issue of identifying potential defendants, noted in sub-paragraph (a) of the main text, see also the updates to paragraphs 16.023 et seq, below.

In respect of the issue of quantification of loss, noted in sub-paragraph (b) of the main text, the Commission has adopted a Communication on quantifying harm in actions for damages based on breaches of Article 101 or 102 TFEU (COM(2013) 3440, OJ 2013 C167/19), and an accompanying Practical Guide (SWD(2013) 205) ('Quantification Guide'). The details of the guidance are discussed in the updates to paragraph 16.077 et seq, below.

In respect of the issue of 'passing-on', noted in sub-paragraph (c) of the main text, see also the updates to paragraphs 16.087 et seq, below.

2. Prices and Pricing Restrictions

Effect of price-fixing on prices.   **5.040**
Fn 126 The Commission's decision in COMP/39188 *Bananas*, decision of 15 October 2008, was upheld. On the application of the approach laid down in Case C-8/08 *T-Mobile v Netherlands* [2009] ECR I-4529, see in particular Case C-286/13P *Dole Food Company v Commission*, EU:C:2015:184, [2015] 4 CMLR 967, paras 119 et seq. See also Case T-587/08 *Fresh Del Monte Produce v Commission*, EU:T:2013:129, [2013] 4 CMLR 1091, paras 459–460 (further appeal, on other grounds, dismissed in Joined Cases C-293&294/13P *Fresh Del Monte Produce*, EU:C:2015:416, [2015] 5 CMLR 513).

Fn 131 On this aspect of the Commission's decision in particular, see Case C-286/13P *Dole Food Company v Commission*, EU:C:2015:184, [2015] 4 CMLR 967, para 134; and Case T-587/08 *Fresh Del Monte Produce v Commission*, EU:T:2013:129, [2013] 4 CMLR 1091, paras 305–308 (further appeal, on other grounds, dismissed in Joined Cases C-293&294/13P *Fresh Del Monte Produce*, EU:C:2015:416, [2015] 5 CMLR 513).

Price-fixing. The Commission's findings of infringement in decision COMP/ **5.041**
39406 *Marine Hoses*, decision of 28 January 2009, discussed in the main text, were upheld in Cases T-146/09, etc, *Parker ITR and Parker-Hannifin v Commission (Marine Hoses)*, EU:T:2013:258, [2013] 5 CMLR 712 (the General Court's judgment was partially annulled, on different grounds on further appeal, in Case C-434/13P *Commission v Parker Hannifin Manufacturing and Parker-Hannifin*, EU:C:2014:2456, [2015] 4 CMLR 179).

Fn 135 The Commission's decision in COMP/39510 *Ordre national des pharmaciens en France (ONP)*, decision of 8 December 2010, was upheld on appeal in Case T-90/11 *Ordre national des pharmaciens en France (ONP) v Commission*, EU:T:2014:1049. See in particular para 321.

The OFT's decision in *Dairy Retail Prices Initiative*, of 26 July 2011, was partially annulled on appeal by the Competition Appeal Tribunal, in *Tesco v OFT* [2012] CAT 31.

Fn 141 See also Joined Cases T-379&381/10 *Keramag Keramische Werke and Others v Commission ('Bathroom Fittings')*, EU:T:2013:457, paras 59 et seq (on further appeal, Case C-613/13P, not yet decided). The General Court confirmed that the coordination of indicative list prices is an object infringement.

Fn 144 See also *BA/Virgin*, OFT decision of 19 April 2012, where the parties notified each other of their intentions to increase fuel surcharges, prior to those increases being announced publicly.

5.042 **Agreement to fix recommended or maximum prices.** As well as the forms of 'recommended' prices noted in the main text, coordination of indicative list prices is an infringement by object, as list prices serve as a starting point for subsequent price negotiations: Joined Cases T-379&381/10 *Keramag Keramische Werke and Others v Commission ('Bathroom Fittings')*, EU:T:2013:457, paras 59 et seq (on further appeal, Case C-613/13P, not yet decided).

5.043 **Elements added to price.**
Fn 158 The Commission's findings of infringement in decision COMP/39406 *Marine Hoses*, decision of 28 January 2009, were upheld in Cases T-146/09, etc, *Parker ITR and Parker-Hannifin v Commission (Marine Hoses)*, EU:T:2013:258, [2013] 5 CMLR 712 (the General Court's judgment was partially annulled, on different grounds on further appeal, in Case C-434/13P *Commission v Parker Hannifin Manufacturing and Parker-Hannifin*, EU:C:2014:2456, [2015] 4 CMLR 179).

5.044 **Common approaches to prices and structures.** Coordination of indicative list prices is an infringement by object, as list prices serve as a starting point for subsequent price negotiations: Joined Cases T-379&381/10 *Keramag Keramische Werke and Others v Commission ('Bathroom Fittings')*, EU:T:2013:457, paras 59 et seq (on further appeal, Case C-613/13P, not yet decided).

5.045 **Other contractual provisions related to pricing.**
Fn 162 The Commission's decisions in COMP/39847 *E-books*, decision of 12 December 2012 (OJ 2012 C283/7), and of 25 July 2013 (OJ 2013 C378/25) accepted commitments from five publishing companies, and Apple, *inter alia* not to enter into most favoured nation clauses for five years. The UK's OFT, and the German Bundeskartellamt, have closed their investigations into Amazon's pricing clauses, after Amazon agreed to remove these clauses from its contracts (ECN Brief 05/2013, p30). The Bundeskartellamt has found that most favoured nation pricing clauses in contracts between a hotel booking platform and hotels breach Article 101 and national competition law (on appeal to the Düsseldorf Higher Regional Court): ECN Brief 01/2014, p6.

See also M.6458 *Universal Music Group/EMI Music* (21 September 2012), in which the Commission cleared a merger upon Universal committing *inter alia* not to include most favoured national clauses in its licensing agreements with digital music services in the EEA for five years.

Price transparency.   The Commission's decision in COMP/39188 *Bananas*, decision of 15 October 2008, that the information exchanges were a concerted practice with an anti-competitive object, was upheld in Case C-286/13P *Dole Food Company v Commission*, EU:C:2015:184, [2015] 4 CMLR 967, para 134. See also Case T-587/08 *Fresh Del Monte Produce v Commission*, EU:T:2013:129, [2013] 4 CMLR 1091 (further appeal, on other grounds, dismissed in Joined Cases C-293&294/13P *Fresh Del Monte Produce*, EU:C:2015:416, [2015] 5 CMLR 513). In Case C-455/11P *Solvay v Commission*, EU:C:2013:796, [2014] 4 CMLR 581, at paras 39 et seq, the Court of Justice held that in a highly concentrated oligopolistic market the exchange of commercial information between competitors will itself allow operators to know the market positions and strategies of their competitors, and the exchange of such information in preparation for an anti-competitive agreement therefore suffices to prove the existence of a concerted practice. It is not necessary to establish that the competitors formally undertook to adopt a particular course of conduct, or that the competitors colluded over their future conduct on the market.

Fn 168   See also *BA/Virgin*, OFT decision of 19 April 2012.

Price agreements among distributors.

Fn 174   The test laid down by the Court of Appeal in *Argos & Littlewoods and JJB Sports v Office of Fair Trading* [2006] EWCA Civ 1318 was applied by the Competition Appeal Tribunal in *Tesco v OFT* [2012] CAT 31, which discusses in detail the state of mind required to satisfy the test.

See also the decisions of the Hungarian Competition Authority in Case Vj-115/2010 *W&H Dentalwerk Bürmoos*, and of the Romanian Competition Council, finding breaches of Article 101 by the manufacturers of dental equipment and their distributors, where the resale price charged by distributors was monitored by the manufacturer, and selling below the recommended retail price led to distributors being excluded from the distribution network: Hungarian Competition Authority decision, see ECN Brief 01/2014, p6; Romanian Competition Council decision, see ECN Brief 02/2014, p5.

Fixing of purchase prices.

Fn 191   The further appeal against Case T-38/05 *Agroexpansion* [2011] ECR II-7005 was dismissed by the Court of Justice in Case C-668/11P *Alliance One International v Commission*, EU:C:2013:614. The further appeal against Case T-41/05 *Dimons* [2011] ECR II-7101 was dismissed in Case C-679/11P *Alliance One International v Commission*, EU:C:2013:606, [2014] 4 CMLR 249.

5.046

5.047

5.052

Fn 192 The Court of Justice dismissed the further appeal in Case C-578/11P *Deltafina v Commission*, EU:C:2014:1460, [2014] 5 CMLR 599; and the further appeal in Case C-593/11P *Alliance One International* was dismissed as manifestly unfounded in part, and inadmissible in part, by Order of 13 December 2012. The Court of Justice upheld the appeal in Case C-652/11P *Mindo*, EU:C:2013:229, [2013] 4 CMLR 1, and has referred the case back to the General Court (remitted case not yet decided). The further appeal in Case C-654/11P *Transcatab* was dismissed by Order of 13 December 2012.

5.054   Resale price maintenance for books.
Fn 200 The Commission's decisions in COMP/39847 *E-books*, decision of 12 December 2012 (OJ 2012 C283/7), and of 25 July 2013 (OJ 2013 C378/25), accepted commitments from five publishing companies, and Apple, under which the undertakings agreed to terminate their agency agreements, to allow retailers full discretion to set their e-book prices for at least two years, and not to enter into most favoured nation clauses for five years. The UK's OFT, and the German Bundeskartellamt, have closed their investigations into Amazon's pricing clauses, after Amazon agreed to remove these clauses from its contracts (ECN Brief 05/ 2013, p30).

5.057   Price-fixing and Article 101(3).   The General Court has ruled on appeals against the two Commission decisions referred to in the main text.

The General Court dismissed the appeals against the Commission's findings of infringement in COMP/39181 *Candle Waxes*, decision of 1 October 2008, but reduced the fine imposed on five of the undertakings. On the application of Article 101(3), see Case T-544/08 *Hansen & Rosenthal and H&R Wax Company Vertrieb v Commission*, EU:T:2014:1075, paras 263 et seq (on further appeal, Case C-90/15P, not yet decided).

In respect of COMP/39188 *Bananas*, decision of 15 October 2008, the appeals on liability, on other grounds, were dismissed in Case T-587/08 *Fresh Del Monte Produce v Commission*, EU:T:2013:129, [2013] 4 CMLR 1091 (further appeal, on other grounds, dismissed in Joined Cases C-293&294/13P *Fresh Del Monte Produce*, EU:C:2015:416, [2015] 5 CMLR 513); and Case T-588/08 *Dole Food Company v Commission*, EU:T:2013:130 (further appeal, on other grounds, dismissed in Case C-286/13P *Dole Food Company v Commission*, EU:C:2015:184, [2015] 4 CMLR 967).

Fn 206 The Court of Justice dismissed the further appeal in Case C-382/12P *MasterCard v Commission*, EU:C:2014:2201, [2014] 5 CMLR 1062.

Fn 208 In the appeals, on other grounds, against COMP/39125 *Carglass*, decision of 12 November 2008, the decision was partially upheld. In Case T-68/09 *Soliver v Commission ('Carglass')*, EU:T:2014:867, [2014] 5 CMLR

1168 it was annulled in respect of Soliver, as the Court held there was insufficient evidence to establish its participation in a single and continuous infringement and the decision was not severable; see the update to paragraph 2.076, above. The findings of infringement were upheld in Joined Cases T-56&73/09 *Saint Gobain (Carglass)*, EU:T:2014:160 (fine reduced on grounds of incorrect uplift for recidivism); and the appeal was dismissed in its entirety in Case T-72/09 *Pilkington v Commission*, EU:T:2014:1094 (on further appeal, Case C-101/15P, not yet decided).

Relevance of legislative price controls.   **5.059**
Fn 219 The General Court dismissed the appeals against the Commission's findings of infringement in COMP/39181 *Candle Waxes*, decision of 1 October 2008, but reduced the fine imposed on five of the undertakings. MOL, the undertaking to whom the Commission's findings in this regard were addressed, did not appeal the decision.

3. Output Restrictions

Limitation of output and production.   **5.060**
Fn 221 The Court of Justice dismissed the undertakings' further appeals against the decision in COMP/38899 *Gas Insulated Switchgear*, decision of 24 January 2007, in Joined Cases C-239/11P, etc, *Siemens v Commission (Gas Insulated Switchgear)*, EU:C:2013:866, [2014] 4 CMLR 606; and the appeal, on other grounds, in Case C-247/11P *Areva v Commission*, EU:C:2014:257, [2014] 4 CMLR 31. The Commission's appeal in Joined Cases C-239/11P, etc, *Siemens v Commission (Gas Insulated Switchgear)*, EU:C:2013:866, [2014] 4 CMLR 606 was upheld: see the update to paragraph 2.024, above.

Fn 223 The decision in COMP/39396 *Calcium carbide and magnesium based reagents*, decision of 22 July 2009, was largely upheld on appeal: the appeals were dismissed in Cases T-352/09 *Novácke chemické závody v Commission*, EU:T:2012:673, [2013] 4 CMLR 734; T-392/09 *1. garantovana v Commission*, EU:T:2012:674 (further appeal dismissed, Case C-90/13P *1. garantovana v Commission*, EU:C:2014:326, [2014] 5 CMLR 79); T-400/09 *Ecka Granulate v Commission*, EU:T:2012:675; T-410/09 *Almamet v Commission*, EU:T:2012:676, [2013] 4 CMLR 788; T-399/09 *HSE v Commission*, EU:T:2013:647, [2014] CMLR 738; and T-384/09 *SKW v Commission* ECLI:EU:T:2014:27 (on further appeal, Case C-154/14P, not yet decided). The fines were reduced, but the appeals otherwise dismissed in Cases T-391/09 *Evonik Degussa v Commission*, EU:T:2014:22 (on further appeal, Case C-155/14, not yet decided); T-395/09 *Gigaset v Commission*, ECLI:EU:T:2014:23; and T-406/09 *Donau Chemie v Commission*, EU:T:2014:254.

4. Market-sharing and Customer Allocation

(a) Generally

5.065 Market-sharing.

Fn 238 The Court of Justice dismissed the undertakings' further appeals against the decision in COMP/38899 *Gas Insulated Switchgear*, decision of 24 January 2007, in Joined Cases C-239/11P, etc, *Siemens v Commission (Gas Insulated Switchgear)*, EU:C:2013:866, [2014] 4 CMLR 606; and the appeal, on other grounds, in Case C-247/11P *Areva v Commission*, EU:C:2014:257, [2014] 4 CMLR 31. The Commission's appeal in Joined Cases C-239/11P, etc, *Siemens v Commission (Gas Insulated Switchgear)*, EU:C:2013:866, [2014] 4 CMLR 606 was upheld: see the update to paragraph 2.024, above.

Fn 241 The Commission's findings of infringement in decision COMP/39406 *Marine Hoses*, decision of 28 January 2009, discussed in the main text were upheld in Cases T-146/09, etc, *Parker ITR and Parker-Hannifin v Commission (Marine Hoses)*, EU:T:2013:258, [2013] 5 CMLR 712 (the General Court's judgment was partially annulled, on different grounds on further appeal, in Case C-434/13P *Commission v Parker Hannifin Manufacturing and Parker-Hannifin*, EU:C:2014:2456, [2015] 4 CMLR 179).

In the appeals against COMP/39125 *Carglass*, decision of 12 November 2008, the decision was partially upheld. In Case T-68/09 *Soliver v Commission ('Carglass')*, EU:T:2014:867, [2014] 5 CMLR 1168 it was annulled in respect of Soliver, as the Court held there was insufficient evidence to establish its participation in a single and continuous infringement and the decision was not severable; see the update to paragraph 2.076, above. The findings of infringement were upheld in Joined Cases T-56&73/09 *Saint Gobain (Carglass)*, EU:T:2014:160 (fine reduced on grounds of incorrect uplift for recidivism); and the appeal was dismissed in its entirety in Case T-72/09 *Pilkington v Commission*, EU:T:2014:1094 (on further appeal, Case C-101/15P, not yet decided).

5.066 Market-sharing between producers.

Fn 242 See also COMP/39839 *Telefónica and Portugal Telecom*, decision of 23 January 2013, concerning an agreement under which the parties agreed not to compete in the Iberian pensinsula, following the acquisition by Telefónica of the Brazilian mobile operator, Vivo, which until then had been jointly owned by Telefónica and Portugal Telecom (on appeal, Case T-208/13 *Portugal Telecom v Commission*; and Case T-216/13 *Telefónica v Commission*, not yet decided).

Fn 244 See also COMP/39839 *Telefónica and Portugal Telecom*, decision of 23 January 2013, referred to in the update to footnote 242, above.

The Court of Justice dismissed the undertakings' further appeals against the decision in COMP/38899 *Gas Insulated Switchgear*, decision of 24 January 2007, in

Joined Cases C-239/11P, etc, *Siemens v Commission (Gas Insulated Switchgear)*, EU:C:2013:866, [2014] 4 CMLR 606; and the appeal, on other grounds, in Case C-247/11P *Areva v Commission*, EU:C:2014:257, [2014] 4 CMLR 31. The Commission's appeal in Joined Cases C-239/11P, etc, *Siemens v Commission (Gas Insulated Switchgear)*, EU:C:2013:866, [2014] 4 CMLR 606 was upheld: see the update to paragraph 2.024, above.

The General Court dismissed the appeals against the Commission's findings of infringement in COMP/39181 *Candle Waxes*, decision of 1 October 2008, but reduced the fine imposed on five of the undertakings. The appeals were dismissed in: Case T-548/08 *Total v Commission*, EU:T:2013:434 (on further appeal, Case C-597/13P, not yet decided); Case T-551/08 *H&R ChemPharm v Commission*, EU:T:2014:1081 (on further appeal, Case C-95/15P, not yet decided); Case T-550/08 *Tudapetrol Mineralölerzeugnisse Nils Hansen v Commission*, EU:T:2014:1079 (on further appeal, Case C-94/15P, not yet decided); Case T-562/08 *Repsol YPF Lubricantes y especialidades*, EU:T:2014:1078; and Case T-544/08 *Hansen & Rosenthal and H&R Wax Company Vertrieb v Commission*, EU:T:2014:1075 (on further appeal, Case C-90/15P, not yet decided). The fines were reduced, but the appeals otherwise dismissed, in: Case T-566/08 *Total Raffinage Marketing*, EU:T:2013:423 (fine reduced on grounds of duration) (on further appeal, Case C-634/13P, not yet decided); Case T-540/08 *Esso v Commission*, EU:T:2014:630, [2014] 5 CMLR 507 (fine reduced on grounds of duration of involvement of entities that merged during the infringement period); Case T-541/08 *Sasol v Commission*, EU:T:2014:628, [2014] 5 CMLR 729 (fine reduced on grounds of incorrect attribution of conduct by a joint venture); and Case T-543/08 *RWE v Commission*, EU:T:2014:627 (fine reduced on grounds of incorrect attribution of conduct by a joint venture); and Case T-558/08 *Eni v Commission*, EU:T:2014:1080 (fine reduced on grounds of incorrect application of an uplift for recidivism).

The findings of infringement in COMP/39406 *Marine Hoses*, decision of 28 January 2009, were also upheld in Cases T-146/09, etc, *Parker ITR and Parker-Hannifin v Commission (Marine Hoses)*, EU:T:2013:258, [2013] 5 CMLR 712 (the General Court's judgment was partially annulled, on different grounds on further appeal, in Case C-434/13P *Commission v Parker Hannifin Manufacturing and Parker-Hannifin*, EU:C:2014:2456, [2015] 4 CMLR 179).

The Commission's finding of infringement in COMP/39129 *Power Transformers*, decision of 7 October 2009, was upheld in Case T-519/09 *Toshiba v Commission*, EU:T:2014:263, [2014] 5 CMLR 219 (on further appeal, Case C-373/14P, not yet decided).

Fn 245 The decision in COMP/39396 *Calcium carbide and magnesium based reagents*, decision of 22 July 2009, was largely upheld on appeal: the appeals were dismissed in Cases T-352/09 *Nováccke chemické závody v Commission*, EU:T:2012:673, [2013] 4 CMLR 734; T-392/09 *1. garantovaná v Commission*, EU:T:2012:674

(further appeal dismissed, Case C-90/13P *1. garantovana v Commission*, EU:C:2014:326, [2014] 5 CMLR 79); T-400/09 *Ecka Granulate v Commission*, EU:T:2012:675; T-410/09 *Almamet v Commission*, EU:T:2012:676, [2013] 4 CMLR 788; T-399/09 *HSE v Commission*, EU:T:2013:647, [2014] CMLR 738; and T-384/09 *SKW v Commission* ECLI:EU:T:2014:27 (on further appeal, Case C-154/14P, not yet decided). The fines were reduced, but the appeals otherwise dismissed in Cases T-391/09 *Evonik Degussa v Commission*, EU:T:2014:22 (on further appeal, Case C-155/14, not yet decided); T-395/09 *Gigaset v Commission*, ECLI:EU:T:2014:23; and T-406/09 *Donau Chemie v Commission*, EU:T:2014:254.

Fn 247 The Commission's finding of infringement in COMP/39129 *Power Transformers*, decision of 7 October 2009, was upheld in Case T-519/09 *Toshiba v Commission*, EU:T:2014:263, [2014] 5 CMLR 219 (on further appeal, Case C-373/14P, not yet decided).

5.068 Market-sharing between purchasers.
Fn 249 The further appeal against Case T-38/05 *Agroexpansion* [2011] ECR II-7005 was dismissed by the Court of Justice in Case C-668/11P *Alliance One International v Commission*, EU:C:2013:614. The further appeal from the General Court's judgment in Case T-41/05 *Dimons* [2011] ECR II-7101 was dismissed in Case C-679/11P *Alliance One International v Commission*, EU:C:2013:606, [2014] 4 CMLR 249.

Fn 250 The Court of Justice dismissed the further appeal in Case C-578/11P *Deltafina v Commission*, EU:C:2014:1460, [2014] 5 CMLR 599.

5.072 Market-sharing and trade with third countries. The Court of Justice dismissed the undertakings' further appeals against the decision in COMP/38899 *Gas Insulated Switchgear*, decision of 24 January 2007, in Joined Cases C-239/11P, etc, *Siemens v Commission (Gas Insulated Switchgear)*, EU:C:2013:866, [2014] 4 CMLR 606; and the appeal, on other grounds, in Case C-247/11P *Areva v Commission*, EU:C:2014:257, [2014] 4 CMLR 31. The Commission's appeal in Joined Cases C-239/11P, etc, *Siemens v Commission (Gas Insulated Switchgear)*, EU:C:2013:866, [2014] 4 CMLR 606 was upheld: see the update to paragraph 2.024, above.

See also the General Court's judgment in Case T-519/09 *Toshiba v Commission*, EU:T:2014:263, [2014] 5 CMLR 219, against the Commission's decision in COMP/39129 *Power Transformers*, decision of 7 October 2009 (on further appeal, Case C-373/14P, not yet decided).

5.073 Market-sharing under Article 101(3).
Fn 266 The appeal, on other grounds, in Case T-519/09 *Toshiba v Commission (Power Transformers)*, EU:T:2014:263, [2014] 5 CMLR 219 against the decision in COMP/39129 *Power Transformers*, decision of 7 October 2009, was dismissed (on further appeal, Case C-373/14P, not yet decided).

The General Court dismissed the appeals against the Commission's findings of infringement in COMP/39181 *Candle Waxes*, decision of 1 October 2008, but reduced the fine imposed on five of the undertakings. On the application of Article 101(3), see Case T-544/08 *Hansen & Rosenthal and H&R Wax Company Vertrieb v Commission*, EU:T:2014:1075, paras 263 et seq (on further appeal, Case C-90/15P, not yet decided).

(c) Vertical arrangements between competitors

Market division by intellectual property rights. On 21 March 2014 the **5.081** Commission adopted Regulation 316/2014 on the application of Article 101(3) of the Treaty on the Functioning of the European Union to categories of technology transfer agreements, OJ 2014 L93/17. It entered into force on 1 May 2014, and replaces Regulation 772/2004 which expired on 30 April 2014. The new Regulation is discussed in the updates to Chapter 9, below.

(d) Customer allocation

Customer allocation. **5.083**
Fn 292 The General Court has ruled on appeals against a number of the decisions referred to in the footnote:

The General Court dismissed the appeals against the Commission's findings of infringement in COMP/39181 *Candle Waxes*, decision of 1 October 2008, but reduced the fine imposed on five of the undertakings. The appeals were dismissed in: Case T-548/08 *Total v Commission*, EU:T:2013:434 (on further appeal, Case C-597/13P, not yet decided); Case T-551/08 *H&R ChemPharm v Commission*, EU:T:2014:1081 (on further appeal, Case C-95/15P, not yet decided); Case T-550/08 *Tudapetrol Mineralölerzeugnisse Nils Hansen v Commission*, EU:T:2014:1079 (on further appeal, Case C-94/15P, not yet decided); Case T-562/08 *Repsol YPF Lubricantes y especialidades*, EU:T:2014:1078; and Case T-544/08 *Hansen & Rosenthal and H&R Wax Company Vertrieb v Commission*, EU:T:2014:1075 (on further appeal, Case C-90/15P, not yet decided). The fines were reduced, but the appeals otherwise dismissed, in: Case T-566/08 *Total Raffinage Marketing*, EU:T:2013:423 (fine reduced on grounds of duration) (on further appeal, Case C-634/13P, not yet decided); Case T-540/08 *Esso v Commission*, EU:T:2014:630, [2014] 5 CMLR 507 (fine reduced on grounds of duration of involvement of entities that merged during the infringement period); Case T-541/08 *Sasol v Commission*, EU:T:2014:628, [2014] 5 CMLR 729 (fine reduced on grounds of incorrect attribution of conduct by a joint venture); and Case T-543/08 *RWE v Commission*, EU:T:2014:627 (fine reduced on grounds of incorrect attribution of conduct by a joint venture); and Case T-558/08 *Eni v Commission*, EU:T:2014:1080 (fine reduced on grounds of incorrect application of an uplift for recidivism).

The decision in COMP/39396 *Calcium carbide and magnesium based reagents*, decision of 22 July 2009, was largely upheld on appeal: the appeals were dismissed in Cases T-352/09 *Novácke chemické závody v Commission*, EU:T:2012:673, [2013] 4 CMLR 734; T-392/09 *1. garantovana v Commission*, EU:T:2012:674 (further appeal dismissed, Case C-90/13P *1. garantovana v Commission*, EU:C:2014:326, [2014] 5 CMLR 79); T-400/09 *Ecka Granulate v Commission*, EU:T:2012:675; T-410/09 *Almamet v Commission*, EU:T:2012:676, [2013] 4 CMLR 788; T-399/09 *HSE v Commission*, EU:T:2013:647, [2014] CMLR 738; and T-384/09 *SKW v Commission* ECLI:EU:T:2014:27 (on further appeal, Case C-154/14P, not yet decided). The fines were reduced, but the appeals otherwise dismissed in Cases T-391/09 *Evonik Degussa v Commission*, EU:T:2014:22 (on further appeal, Case C-155/14, not yet decided); T-395/09 *Gigaset v Commission*, ECLI:EU:T:2014:23 and T-406/09 *Donau Chemie v Commission*, EU:T:2014:254.

5. Information Exchange

5.085 **Information exchange ancillary to a cartel.** The General Court has ruled on a number of appeals against the decisions referred to in the main text.

In respect of COMP/39406 *Marine Hoses*, decision of 28 January 2009, the General Court upheld the Commission's findings of infringement in Cases T-146/09, etc, *Parker ITR and Parker-Hannifin v Commission (Marine Hoses)*, EU:T:2013:258, [2013] 5 CMLR 712 (the General Court's judgment was partially annulled, on other grounds on further appeal, in Case C-434/13P *Commission v Parker Hannifin Manufacturing and Parker-Hannifin*, EU:C:2014:2456, [2015] 4 CMLR 179).

In respect of COMP/39188 *Bananas*, decision of 15 October 2008, the Commission's finding that the information exchanges were a concerted practice with an anti-competitive object, was upheld in Case C-286/13P *Dole Food Company v Commission*, EU:C:2015:184, [2015] 4 CMLR 967, para 134. In the General Court the particular distinction which the Commission had drawn between infringements by object and effect, based on whether the information was exchanged before or after transaction prices were set, was upheld: Case T-588/08 *Dole Food Company v Commission*, EU:T:2013:130. See also Case T-587/08 *Fresh Del Monte Produce v Commission*, EU:T:2013:129, [2013] 4 CMLR 1091 (further appeal, on other grounds, dismissed in Joined Cases C-293&294/13P *Fresh Del Monte Produce*, EU:C:2015:416, [2015] 5 CMLR 513).

The General Court has emphasised that in order for the exchange of sensitive information to constitute a breach of Article 101, the undertakings concerned must be competitors in the relevant product market, such that there is potential for the recipient of the information to modify its conduct as a result of having received that information. In appeals against the Commission's decision in COMP/39092 *Bathroom*

Fittings, decision of 23 June 2010, which concerned a single and continuous infringement across three separate product markets, the General Court held that:

> 'it cannot be presumed that an agreement or a concerted practice whereby undertakings exchange information which is commercially sensitive but which relates to a product sold on a market on which they are not competitors has an anti-competitive object or effect on that market. A practice whereby an undertaking which is active on two distinct product markets provides to its competitors – which are present on one market – commercially sensitive information which relates to a second market – on which those competitors are not present – is not capable, in principle, of having an impact on competition on the second market.'

See Case T-380/10 *Wabco Europe v Commission (Bathroom Fittings)*, EU:T:2013:449, [2014] 4 CMLR 138, paras 78 et seq; and Joined Cases T-379&381/10 *Keramag Keramische Werke and Others (Bathroom Fittings) v Commission*, EU:T:2013:457, paras 92 and 221 (on further appeal, Case C-613/13P, not yet decided).

Fn 295 In Case T-404/08 *Fluorsid and Minmet v Commission*, EU:T:2013:321, [2013] 5 CMLR 902, para 94; and Case T-406/08 *Industries chimiques du fluor v Commission*, EU:T:2013:322, paras 88 and 106, the General Court upheld the Commission's decision in COMP/39810 *Aluminium Fluoride*, decision of 25 June 2008, in respect of the exchange of information (further appeal, on other grounds, dismissed in Case C-467/13P, *Industries chimiques du fluor v Commission*, EU:C:2014:2274).

6. Collective Exclusive Dealing

(b) Joint tendering and bid-rigging

Generally.   **5.090**
Fn 312 See also COMP/39748 *Automotive Wire Harnesses*, decision of 10 July 2013, Press Release IP/13/673 (10 July 2013).

The Commission's findings of infringement in COMP/39406 *Marine Hoses*, decision of 28 January 2009, were upheld in Case T-146/09 *Parker ITR and Parker-Hannifin v Commission (Marine Hoses)*, EU:T:2013:258, [2013] 5 CMLR 712 (the General Court's judgment was partially annulled, on different grounds on further appeal, in Case C-434/13P *Commission v Parker Hannifin Manufacturing and Parker-Hannifin*, EU:C:2014:2456, [2015] 4 CMLR 179).

The Court of Justice dismissed the undertakings' further appeals against the decision in COMP/38899 *Gas Insulated Switchgear*, decision of 24 January 2007, in Joined Cases C-239/11P, etc, *Siemens v Commission (Gas Insulated Switchgear)*, EU:C:2013:866, [2014] 4 CMLR 606; and the appeal, on other grounds, in Case C-247/11P *Areva v Commission*, EU:C:2014:257, [2014] 4 CMLR 31. The Commission's appeal in Joined Cases C-239/11P, etc, *Siemens v Commission (Gas*

Insulated Switchgear), EU:C:2013:866, [2014] 4 CMLR 606 was upheld: see the update to paragraph 2.024, above.

The further appeal against COMP/38823 *Elevators and Escalators*, decision of 21 February 2007, in Case C-493/11P, etc, *United Technologies*, was dismissed as partly inadmissible, and partly clearly unfounded, by Order of 15 June 2012.

In the further appeals against the Commission's decision in COMP/38543 *International Removals Services*, decision of 11 March 2008, the Court of Justice in Case C-441/11P *Commission v Verhuizingen Coppens*, EU:C:2012:778, [2013] 4 CMLR 312 reversed the General Court's judgment, holding that it had erred in annulling the decision in its entirety. The Court instead upheld the Commission's decision in respect of Coppens' participation in cover pricing, and annulled it partially. The Court dismissed the further appeals in Case C-439/11P *Ziegler v Commission*, EU:C:2013:513, [2013] 5 CMLR 1217; and Case C-444/11P *Team Relocations v Commission*, EU:C:2013:464, [2013] 5 CMLR 1335.

5.091 **Bid-rigging.** The Commission's findings of infringement in decision COMP/39406 *Marine Hoses*, decision of 28 January 2009, were upheld in Cases T-146/09, etc, *Parker ITR and Parker-Hannifin v Commission (Marine Hoses)*, EU:T:2013:258, [2013] 5 CMLR 712 (the General Court's judgment was partially overturned, on different grounds on further appeal, in Case C-434/13P *Commission v Parker Hannifin Manufacturing and Parker-Hannifin*, EU:C:2014:2456, [2015] 4 CMLR 179).

Fn 318 On 26 February 2014, three new directives on public procurement were adopted: Directive 2014/24 on public procurement and repealing Directive 2004/18/EC (OJ 2014 L94/65); Directive 2014/25 on procurement by entities operating in the water, energy, transport and postal services sectors and repealing Directive 2004/17/EC (OJ 2014 L94/243); and Directive 2014/23 on the award of concession contracts (OJ 2014 L94/1). They entered into force on 17 April 2014.

Fn 319 The Danish Competition and Consumer Authority published guidelines on fighting bid rigging in public procurement 29 November 2012: ECN Brief 01/2013, p22.

5.093 **Cover pricing.**
Fn 323 The Court of Justice in Case C-441/11P *Commission v Verhuizingen Coppens*, EU:C:2012:778, [2013] CMLR 312, set aside the General Court's judgment, and instead annulled the Commission decision only in respect of Verhuizingen Coppens' participation in the cartel activities beyond cover pricing, and the attribution to it of a single and continuous infringement.

6

NON-COVERT HORIZONTAL
COOPERATION

1. Introduction

(b) Joint ventures: the Merger Regulation and the application of Article 101

Scrutiny of an existing JV under Article 101. The Court of Justice in Case **6.010**
C-179/12P *Dow Chemical Company v Commission*, EU:C:2013:605, [2014]
4 CMLR 220; and Case C-172/12P *El du Pont de Nemours v Commission*,
EU:C:2013:601, [2014] 4 CMLR 236 confirmed that, provided the factual evidence demonstrates the actual exercise of decisive influence, there is no error of
law in holding two parent companies and the joint venture in which they each
have a 50 per cent shareholding to be a single undertaking for the purposes (and
only for the purposes) of establishing liability for participation in an infringement of competition law: see in particular *Dow*, para 58 and *du Pont*, para 47.

In Case T-541/08 *Sasol v Commission (Candle Waxes)* EU:T:2014:628, [2014] 5
CMLR 729, at paras 40 et seq, the General Court considered the circumstances
in which the conduct of a joint venture can be imputed to one parent company
alone. The Commission had attributed liability to Sasol, which owned two-thirds
of the shares in the joint venture, using evidence of its ability to exercise decisive
influence without finding that it had actually exercised decisive influence. The
Court held that the Commission can establish actual decisive influence by way
of an abstract analysis of the documents signed before a joint venture began to
operate, along the lines of the analysis conducted under Regulation 139/2004 (the
Merger Regulation) to determine whether the company is able to 'control' the
joint venture, in as much as the Commission may presume that the legislation and
provisions of agreements relating to the operation of that undertaking, in particular the joint venture's articles of association and the shareholder and voting rights
agreement, have been implemented and complied with: para 49. However, it is
open to the Commission and the undertaking concerned to adduce evidence that
the joint venture's commercial decisions were taken by procedures other than those
apparent from the mere abstract examination of the agreements, and in particular

that they were taken by several or all of the parent companies unanimously: para 50. In that case, the General Court held that the Commission had made an error of assessment in dismissing the evidence that the other parent company of the joint venture exercised decisive influence jointly with the one to which liability had been attributed. See also Case T-543/08 *RWE v Commission (Candle Waxes)* EU:T:2014:627, at paras 99 et seq, in which the General Court considered the joint attribution of liability to both parents of a joint venture on the basis of ability to exercise decisive influence.

Fn 27 The Court of Justice dismissed the further appeal in Case C-382/12P *MasterCard v Commission*, EU:C:2014:2201, [2014] 5 CMLR 1062 and confirmed that the multilateral interchange fees ('MIFs') used in the MasterCard system were to be characterised as a decision of an association of undertakings. The General Court's findings of fact that, first, the banks continued collectively to exercise decision-making powers in respect of the essential aspects of the operation of the organisation, and, secondly, that the MIFs reflected the aligned interests of MasterCard, its shareholders and the banks, were both relevant and sufficient for the purposes of assessing whether MasterCard could still be considered an 'association of undertakings' within Article 101: paras 68 et seq. The other aspects of the Court's conclusions are discussed in the update to paragraph 6.107, below.

(c) Sources of law and general principles for assessment

6.012 *De minimis* **and safe harbours.**
Fn 34 On 30 August 2014 the Commission adopted a revised *De Minimis* Notice to take account of the Court of Justice's judgment in Case C-226/11 *Expedia Inc*, EU:C:2012:795, [2013] 4 CMLR 439: OJ 2014 C291/1. The Court held in paras 36–37 of its judgment that an agreement that may affect trade between Member States and that has an anti-competitive object constitutes, by its nature and independently of any concrete effects that it may have, an appreciable restriction on competition. The revised Notice makes clear that it applies only to agreements which have the effect of preventing, restricting or distorting competition.

6.013 Centre of gravity of cooperation.
Fn 39 The General Court upheld the Commission's decision in COMP/38698 *CISAC Agreements*, decision of 16 July 2008, insofar as it found that the exclusivity clause (Cases T-401/08 *Säveltäjäin Tekijänoikeustoimisto Teosto v Commission*, EU:T:2013:170, [2013] 5 CMLR 15) and membership clause (Cases T-392, 401, 422, 432/08, judgments of 12 April 2013, [2013] 5 CMLR 15) in the agreements infringed Article 101. It partially annulled the decision, in respect of the Commission's conclusions as to the existence of a concerted practice, in Cases T-392, 398, 401, 410, 411, 413–422, 425, 428, 432–434, 442/08, judgments of 12 April 2013.

6.016 Ancillary restraints. In Case C-382/12/P *MasterCard v Commission*, EU:C:2014:2201, [2014] 5 CMLR 1062 at para 91 the Court of Justice held that in considering whether a restriction is an objectively necessary ancillary restraint the relevant question is whether the joint venture would be impossible to carry out without it, not whether it would have been more difficult to carry out in its absence, or less profitable.

Fn 62 See also the Commission's decision in COMP/39839 *Telefónica/Portugal Telecom*, decision of 23 January 2013, paras 367 et seq, concerning a clause in which the parties agreed not to compete in the Iberian pensinsula following the acquisition by Telefónica of the Brazilian mobile operator, Vivo, which until then had been jointly owned by Telefónica and Portugal Telecom (on appeal, Cases T-208/13 *Portugal Telecom v Commission*; and T-216/13 *Telefónica v Commission*, not yet decided).

2. Information Exchange

(a) Introduction

Stand-alone information exchanges. In C-455/11P *Solvay v Commission*, EU:C:2013:796, [2014] 4 CMLR 581, at paras 39 et seq, the Court of Justice held that in a highly concentrated oligopolistic market the exchange of commercial information between competitors will itself allow operators to know the market positions and strategies of their competitors, and the exchange of such information in preparation for an anti-competitive agreement therefore suffices to prove the existence of a concerted practice. It is not necessary to establish that the competitors formally undertook to adopt a particular course of conduct, or that the competitors colluded over their future conduct on the market.   **6.019**

(b) Information exchange amounting to an agreement, concerted practice or decision by an association of undertakings

Direct or indirect sharing of data. In order for the exchange of information to constitute a breach of Article 101 the undertakings concerned must be competitors in the relevant product market, such that there is potential for the recipient of the information to modify its conduct as a result of having received that information. The General Court emphasised in Case T-380/10 *Wabco Europe v Commission (Bathroom Fittings)*, EU:T:2013:449, [2014] 4 CMLR 138, paras 78 et seq that: **6.020**

> 'it cannot be presumed that an agreement or a concerted practice whereby undertakings exchange information which is commercially sensitive but which relates to a product sold on a market on which they are not competitors has an anti-competitive object or effect on that market. A practice whereby an undertaking which is active on two distinct product markets provides to its competitors – which are present on one market – commercially sensitive information which relates to a second market – on which those competitors are not present – is not capable,

105

in principle, of having an impact on competition on the second market.': see in particular para 79.

The Court distinguished its earlier case law in Joined Cases T-456&457/05 *Gütermann and Zwicky v Commission* [2010] ECR II-1443, relied upon by the Commission, on the basis that that judgment would apply to a disclosure of commercially sensitive information with a view to restricting competition in the market on which the recipient of the information is active, by a disclosing party that is not itself active on that market, whereas in the decision under appeal, COMP/39092 *Bathroom Fittings*, decision of 23 June 2010, the Commission had (as the Court held, wrongly) found that the purpose of the disclosure was to restrict competition in a market on which the disclosing party was active but the recipient was not: see paras 98–99. See also Joined Cases T-379&381/10 *Keramag Keramische Werke and Others (Bathroom Fittings) v Commission*, EU:T:2013:457, paras 92 and 221 (on further appeal, Case C-613/13P, not yet decided).

6.022 **Dissemination of information by an association of undertakings.** There is also a risk, where an undertaking is a member of an umbrella association, or cross-product association, that it will be considered to be aware of the anti-competitive behaviour of the other members: see Case T-378/10 *Masco and others v Commission*, EU:T:2013:469, [2014] 4 CMLR 34, paras 61–62 and 82, in which the General Court upheld the Commission's conclusion in COMP/ 39092 *Bathroom Fittings*, decision of 23 June 2010, finding that the undertaking concerned must have been aware of the anti-competitive behaviour of the other members, for the purposes of finding a single and continuous infringement (see paragraphs 2.076 et seq, and the updates thereto). On further appeal, Case C-614/13P, not yet decided.

6.023 **'Hub and spoke' or 'ABC' collusion.** On 4 February 2015 the Commission issued a decision that an undertaking which provides broker services infringed Article 101 by facilitating the infringements by various banks in respect of the benchmark for trading yen interest rate derivatives: COMP/39861 *Yen Interest Rate Derivatives ('YIRD')*, decision of 4 February 2015.

The Supreme Court of Lithuania has referred to the Court of Justice for a preliminary ruling questions concerning participation in a common computerised information system, and whether the participating undertakings agree to a restriction on price discounts when the system includes a notice stating that discounting is restricted and there are technical restrictions on discounting: Case C-74/14 *UAB Eturas*, not yet decided. The undertakings have been fined by the Competition Council for a concerted practice in their online sales.

Fn 86 The Commission's preliminary assessment in its commitments decision in COMP/39847 *E-Books*, decision of 12 December 2012 (OJ 2012 C283/7), was that the publishing companies had each entered into agreements with Apple, having also discussed the arrangements between themselves: paras 29 and 34.

Hub and spoke agreements in national enforcement.   **6.024**
Fn 87 The OFT's *Dairy Retail Prices Initiative* decision was partially annulled on
appeal by the Competition Appeal Tribunal, in *Tesco v OFT* [2012] CAT 31.

Fn 88 The state of mind required to satisfy the test laid down by the Court of
Appeal in *Argos & Littlewoods and JJB Sports v OFT* [2006] EWCA Civ 1318, para
141 was discussed at length by the Competition Appeal Tribunal in *Tesco v OFT*
[2012] CAT 31. At stage (i) it is not sufficient to show retailer A knew supplier B
'might' pass on the information: para 78, and the Tribunal expressed doubts as to
whether anything short of intention or actual foresight that supplier B will pass on
the information will suffice: paras 350–354.

(c) Analysis of the competitive effects of information exchanges

Object restrictions: practices facilitating the fixing of purchase or selling   **6.027**
prices.   See also the General Court judgments in Case T-380/10 *Wabco Europe
v Commission (Bathroom Fittings)*, EU:T:2013:449, [2014] 4 CMLR 138, paras
78–79; and Joined Cases T-379&381/10 *Keramag Keramische Werke and Others
(Bathroom Fittings) v Commission*, EU:T:2013:457, paras 92 and 221 (on further
appeal, Case C-613/13P, not yet decided), discussed in the update to paragraph
6.020, above.

Pre-pricing communications and exchange of quotation prices. The   **6.028**
Commission's decision in COMP/39188 *Bananas*, decision of 15 October
2008, that the information exchanges were a concerted practice with an anti-
competitive object, was upheld in Case C-286/13P *Dole Food Company v
Commission*, EU:C:2015:184, [2015] 4 CMLR 967, para 134. See also Case
T-587/08 *Fresh Del Monte Produce v Commission*, EU:T:2013:129, [2013] 4
CMLR 1091 (further appeal, on other grounds, dismissed in Joined Cases
C-293&294/13P *Fresh Del Monte Produce*, EU:C:2015:416, [2015] 5 CMLR 513).
Similarly, the Commission's decision in COMP/39482 *Exotic fruit (Bananas)*,
decision of 12 October 2011, was upheld in Case T-655/11 *FSL (Exotic fruit) v
Commission*, EU:T:2015:383. The General Court dismissed an argument that the
communication in question related only to market trends: paras 465 et seq. On
further appeal, Case C-469/15P, not yet decided.

See also Case T-558/08 *Eni v Commission*, EU:T:2014:1080, paras 152–155, in
which the General Court upheld the Commission's decision that there had been
an unlawful information exchange, going beyond the undertakings exchanging information already available to them from the public domain, in circumstances where the information exchanged included proposed price increases on a
producer-by-producer basis and the date on which those increases were proposed
to be implemented, whereas the publicly available information was an industry
average.

Fn 101 Although the appeal by Weichert was dismissed as inadmissible, it intervened in the appeal by its parent company, Del Monte. Its attempt to bring a separate appeal against the General Court's judgment in those proceedings was also held to be inadmissible, although it was permitted to make submissions in Del Monte's appeal: Joined Cases C-293&294/13P *Fresh Del Monte Produce*, EU:C:2015:416, [2015] 5 CMLR 513, paras 47 and 63.

Fn 102 On this aspect of the appeal, see Case T-588/08 *Dole v Commission*, EU:T:2013:130, paras 53 et seq, where the General Court dismisses the argument. Further appeal dismissed in Case C-286/13P *Dole Food Company v Commission*, EU:C:2015:184, [2015] 4 CMLR 967, at paras 112 et seq.

6.029 **Horizontal Cooperation Guidelines.**
Fn 106 See also, eg C-455/11P *Solvay v Commission*, EU:C:2013:796, [2014] 4 CMLR 581, at paras 39 et seq, in which the Court of Justice held that in a highly concentrated oligopolistic market the exchange of commercial information between competitors will itself allow operators to know the market positions and strategies of their competitors, and the exchange of such information in preparation for an anti-competitive agreement therefore suffices to prove the existence of a concerted practice. It is not necessary to establish that the competitors formally undertook to adopt a particular course of conduct, or that the competitors colluded over their future conduct on the market.

6.030 **Disclosure of pricing information: cases at the national level.**   The OFT decision in *BA/Virgin*, decision of 19 April 2012, is a further example of a NCA decision finding that exchanges of information are an object infringement. The OFT condemned the sharing of confidential future pricing information by one airline with another regarding increases in fuel surcharges.

Fn 111 The OFT's *Dairy Retail Prices Initiative* decision was partially annulled on appeal by the Competition Appeal Tribunal, in *Tesco v OFT* [2012] CAT 31.

6.031 **Article 101(1): restrictive by effect.**   Subject to proof to the contrary, which the undertaking concerned must adduce, it is presumed that undertakings taking part in a concerted action and remaining active on the relevant market take account of the information exchanged with their competitors in determining their conduct on that market: see Case C-8/08 *T-Mobile Netherlands and Others* [2009] ECR I-4529, at para 51. In C-455/11P *Solvay v Commission*, EU:C:2013:796, [2014] 4 CMLR 581, at paras 39 et seq, the Court of Justice dismissed Solvay's appeal against the General Court's conclusion that it had not rebutted the presumption that it had acted on the information it had received. The Court held that data illustrating the competitive nature of the market and decreases in market prices is not sufficient to rebut the presumption because it does not show that the undertaking determined its conduct without reference to the information it had received, or that uncertainties regarding its conduct in the market had not been eliminated by the receipt of that information.

The nature and economic conditions of the relevant market and the nature **6.032**
of the product. See also C-455/11P *Solvay v Commission*, EU:C:2013:796,
[2014] 4 CMLR 581, at paras 39 et seq, in which the Court of Justice held that
in a highly concentrated oligopolistic market the exchange of commercial information between competitors will itself allow operators to know the market positions and strategies of their competitors, and the exchange of such information
in preparation for an anti-competitive agreement therefore suffices to prove the
existence of a concerted practice. It is not necessary to establish that the competitors formally undertook to adopt a particular course of conduct, or that the competitors colluded over their future conduct on the market. In that case the Court
dismissed Solvay's appeal against the General Court's conclusion that it had not
rebutted the presumption that it had acted on the information it had received.
The Court held that data illustrating the competitive nature of the market and
decreases in market prices is not sufficient to rebut the presumption because it
does not show that the undertaking determined its conduct without reference to
the information it had received, or that uncertainties regarding its conduct in the
market had not been eliminated by the receipt of that information.

3. Cooperation in Research and Development

Technology transfer agreements. On 21 March 2014 the Commission **6.044**
adopted Regulation 316/2014 on the application of Article 101(3) of the Treaty
on the Functioning of the European Union to categories of technology transfer
agreements, OJ 2014 L93/17. It entered into force on 1 May 2014, and replaces
Regulation 772/2004 which expired on 30 April 2014.

Fn 166 The reference to Article 1(1)(b) of Regulation 772/2004 should be read as
Article 1(1)(c) in Regulation 316/2014.

Fn 167 The reference to Article 3(1) of Regulation 772/2004 should be read as
Article 3(1) in Regulation 316/2014.

Fn 168 The reference to Article 4(1)(d) of Regulation 772/2004 should be read as
Article 4(1)(d) in Regulation 316/2014.

5. Joint Purchasing Agreements

Competition concerns. **6.067**
Fn 301 The Court of Justice dismissed the further appeal in Case C-578/11P
Deltafina v Commission, EU:C:2014:1460, [2014] 5 CMLR 599. The further
appeal in Case C-593/11P *Alliance One International* was dismissed as manifestly
unfounded in part, and inadmissible in part, by Order of 13 December 2012. The

Court of Justice upheld the appeal in Case C-652/11P *Mindo*, EU:C:2013:229, [2013] 4 CMLR 1381, and has referred the case back to the General Court (remitted case not yet decided). The further appeal in Case C-654/11P *Transcatab* was dismissed by Order of 13 December 2012.

(a) Assessment under Article 101(1)

6.071 Effect restrictions.
Fn 319 The Maritime Transport Guidelines, OJ 2008 C245/2: Vol II, App E20, expired on 26 September 2013, and the Commission has not renewed them: Press Release IP/13/122 (19 February 2013).

7. Standardisation Agreements and Agreements on Standard Terms

6.080 Standardisation agreements.
Fn 369 The Commission's decision in COMP/39510 *Ordre National des Pharmaciens en France (ONP)*, decision of 8 December 2010, was upheld as to liability in Case T-90/11 *ONP v Commission*, EU:T:2014:1049.

6.081 Agreements as to standard terms.
Fn 373 The Court of Justice has handed down a number of significant judgments on standard terms used in the banking sector: see the updates to paragraphs 6.102 et seq, below.

6.082 Relevant markets.
Fn 377 In Case C-327/12 *SOA Nazionale Costruttori*, EU:C:2013:827, at paras 27 et seq, the Court of Justice held that private bodies providing certification services under a statutory certification scheme are engaged in an economic activity.

(a) Assessment under Article 101(1)

6.085 Restrictions by object.
Fn 390 For a further example, see the decision of the Belgian Competition Council finding that three Belgian cement producers, their trade association, and the National Centre for Technical and Scientific Research for the cement industry had all colluded, in breach of Article 101, with the aim of delaying the adoption of a licence, and of the standards, that would make it possible to use a particular alternative component in ready-mix concrete in Belgium. Sales of cement as a component in ready-mix concrete were secured by the delay: ECN Brief 04/2013, p5.

6.086 Restrictive effects of standardisation agreements.
Fn 393 On access to intellectual property rights necessary to comply with the standard, see also the updates to paragraph 6.087, below.

FRAND commitments.   **6.087**

Fn 402 The appeals by Hynix Semiconductor (now trading as SK Hynix Inc) in Joined Cases T-148&149/10 against COMP/38636 *Rambus*, decision of 9 December 2009, were withdrawn on 5 July 2013.

The Court of Justice in Case C-170/13 *Huawei v ZTE*, EU:C:2015:477 confirmed that a refusal by the proprietor of a standard essential patent ('SEP') to grant a licence on fair, reasonable and non-discriminatory ('FRAND') terms, in circumstances where the patent has acquired SEP status as a result of the proprietor having irrevocably undertaken to the standard-setting body that it will license on FRAND terms, may also in principle be contrary to Article 102: para 53. The proprietor's undertaking does not, however, deprive it of its right to bring an action before the courts of a Member State to enforce its patent, so long as it complies with specific requirements when it does so. These are to notify the alleged infringer of the SEP and its breach; to make a specific, written offer of a licence on FRAND terms specifying the royalty and the way in which it has been calculated. The alleged infringer must respond in good faith, and without delay. If it does not accept the offer, it must promptly make a written counter-offer that corresponds to FRAND terms, and if its counter-offer is rejected and it is using the teachings of the SEP then from the point of rejection it must provide appropriate security. The parties may agree to submit the determination of the amount of the royalty to a third party. If the proprietor has complied with the requirements incumbent upon it, or if the alleged infringer has failed to comply with the requirements incumbent upon it, then it is not an abuse of the proprietor's dominant position for it to commence litigation to enforce its patent.

In the Commission's investigation into alleged abusive conduct in relation to IPR used in international telecoms standards, in COMP/39985 *Motorola – enforcement of ETSI standards essential patents*, decision of 29 April 2014, the Commission found Motorola had breached Article 102 by seeking an injunction in Germany against Apple for breach of its standard essential patents (which were essential to meeting the European Telecommunications Standardisation Institute's (ETSI) GPRS standard, part of the GSM standard, which is a key industry standard for mobile and wireless communications), in circumstances where it had committed to license on FRAND terms, and where Apple was willing to enter into a licence agreement and to be bound by a determination by the German Court of the FRAND terms. However, in view of the novelty of the infringement finding, no fine has been imposed.

The Commission accepted commitments from Samsung in COMP/39939 *Samsung – enforcement of ETSI standards essential patents*, decision of 29 April 2014. In its preliminary assessment, the Commission considered that Samsung infringed Article 102 by seeking injunctions against Apple in several Member

States to enforce its patents that were essential to complying with ETSI's 3G UMTS standard (a key standard for mobile and wireless communications), and that Samsung had committed to license on FRAND terms. The Commission accepted commitments under which Samsung agrees, in essence, for a period of five years not to seek an injunction before any court or tribunal in the EEA for infringement of its standard essential patents implemented in mobile devices against a potential licensee that agrees to, and complies with, a particular framework set out in the commitments decision for determining the terms of a licence.

See also *Unwired Planet International v Huawei* [2015] EWHC 2097 (Pat) on the application of Article 101 to an agreement transferring SEP rights. The High Court struck out a defence to an infringement action in which it had been contended that the agreement to transfer the SEPs to Unwired Planet, a 'patent assertion entity', was void under Article 101 for failing fully and effectively to confer on potential licensees the right to obtain from the transferee a licence on FRAND terms; or for failing to transfer the FRAND obligation previously undertaken by the transferor, as opposed to requiring the transferee to offer a new FRAND undertaking (meaning, in particular, that the transferee would not need to have regard to the terms on which the transferor had hitherto licensed commercial parties under those patents, as part of the obligation to offer terms that are non-discriminatory). The Court refused to strike out two further defences. Under the first, Samsung argued that the agreement to transfer the SEPs was void under Article 101 as it permitted the transferor to retain a substantial share in the licensing revenue generated by the transferee and to achieve higher royalties. Under the second, the agreement was alleged to be unlawful and void as it contained payment terms encouraging or requiring the transferee to charge higher royalties. The decision to strike out the first defence is on appeal to the Court of Appeal, not yet decided.

8. Trade Associations

(a) Membership rules

6.096 **Restrictions on ceasing membership or membership of competing organisations.** See also the Commission's findings in respect of the membership clause in the model contract drawn up by CISAC for use by its members, in COMP/38698 *CISAC Agreements*, decision of 16 July 2008, [2009] 4 CMLR 577. The General Court dismissed the appeals against this aspect of the Commission's decision: Cases T-392, 401, 422, 432/08, EU:T:2013:170, [2013] 5 CMLR 15. The decision was partially annulled on other grounds: Cases T-392, 398, 401, 410, 411, 413–422, 425, 428, 432–434, 442/08, judgments of 12 April 2013.

9. Horizontal Cooperation Agreements—Illustrations from Specific Sectors

(a) Airlines

Collaborative arrangements.   **6.100**
Fn 449 See also COMP/39595 *Continental/United/Lufthansa/Air Canada*, decision of 23 May 2013 accepting commitments under Article 9 of Regulation 1/
2003; and COMP/39964 *Air France/KLM/Alitalia/Delta*, decision of 12 May 2015
accepting commitments *inter alia* to make slots available to competing airlines.

(b) Banking and payment services

Generally.   See also the Report on Competition Policy (2012). The Commission   **6.102**
observes that 'a viable, transparent and competitive banking system providing
finance to the real economy is a necessary precondition to restore sustainable
growth' (p2).

Competition, the single market and regulation of financial services.   Regulation   **6.103**
924/2009 was amended by Regulation 260/2012 establishing technical and business requirements for credit transfers and direct debits in euro and amending
Regulation 924/2009, OJ 2012 L94/22, which was adopted on 12 March 2012.
This obliges all users to move to the new Single Euro Payment Area systems
established by the European Payments Council. Following the Green Paper
'Towards an integrated European market for card, internet and mobile payments'
COM/2011/0941 final (11 January 2012), the EU adopted Directive 2015/2366
on Payment Services, OJ 2015 L337/35; and Regulation 2015/751 on Interchange
Fees for Card-Based Payment Transactions, OJ 2015 L123/1, which includes a
cap on interchange fees, and which entered into force on 8 June 2015.

Price-fixing in the banking sector.   The Commission's decision in COMP/   **6.105**
38606 *Groupement des Cartes Bancaires*, decision of 17 October 2007, was upheld
by the General Court in Case T-491/07 *CB v Commission*, EU:T:2012:633 on the
basis that the measures in question had as their object the restriction of competition, and it was not necessary to go on to consider their effects. The Court of
Justice overturned that judgment in Case C-67/13P *Groupement des cartes bancaires v Commission*, EU:C:2014:2202. It held that the General Court had not
explained in what respect the restriction of competition revealed a sufficient degree
of harm to be characterised as an object infringement: paras 55 et seq. In view
of the General Court's findings of fact, first, that in a two-sided card payment
system the issuing and acquisition activities are essential to one another and to the
operation of the system, and, secondly, that the agreements in question sought to
maintain a certain ratio between the issuing and acquiring activities of the group's
members, the most that could be inferred from the terms of the agreements was

that they had as their object the combatting of 'free-riding'. That objective is legitimate, and not harmful to the proper functioning of competition: paras 72–75. The Court of Justice therefore referred the case back to the General Court to consider the Commission's findings as to the effects of the measures.

The Commission has taken steps to address the manipulation by various banks of the benchmark used in derivatives trading. On 12 June 2014, Regulation 596/2014 on market abuse (OJ 2014 L173/1), and Directive 2014/57 on criminal sanctions for market abuse (OJ 2014 L173/179), were adopted which include provisions making the manipulation of benchmarks a criminal offence: see Articles 2(2)(c), 12 and 15 of Regulation 596/2014, and Articles 1(4)(c) and 5 of Directive 2014/57. In respect of the benchmark for trading yen interest rate derivatives, the Commission settled with eight undertakings for their participation in cartels and imposed fines totalling €1.71 billion; COMP/39861 *Yen Interest Rate Derivatives ('YIRD')*, decision of 4 December 2013. On 4 February 2015 it issued a decision that another undertaking, which provides broker services, had facilitated six of the seven infringements: COMP/39861 *Yen Interest Rate Derivatives ('YIRD')*, decision of 4 February 2015. In respect of the manipulation of Swiss franc interest rates, it settled with two undertakings in COMP/39924 *Swiss Franc Interest Rate Derivatives (CHF LIBOR)*, decision of 21 October 2014, and with four undertakings in COMP/39924 *Swiss Franc Interest Rate Derivatives (Bid Ask Spread Infringement)*, decision of 21 October 2014. On 20 May 2014 it also sent a statement of objections to three undertakings for their alleged participation in cartels in the markets for interest rate derivative trading: COMP/39914 *Euro Interest Rate Derivatives*.

6.106 **Exclusion of competitors from horizontal arrangements.** In Case C-68/12 *Protimonopolný úrad v Slovenská sporiteľňa*, EU:C:2013:71, [2013] 4 CMLR 491, the Court of Justice considered the compatibility of an agreement between undertakings to eliminate a competitor from a market on which it had been operating illegally, with Article 101. The Court held that such an agreement could not fall within Article 101(3) as it could not meet in particular the indispensability criteria. The undertakings could have reported the illegal activity to the competent authorities. The Supreme Court of the Slovak Republic subsequently upheld the infringement decision of the Antimonopoly Office, on 22 May 2013: ECN Brief 03/2013, p13.

The Commission has issued a statement of objections in COMP/39745 *CDS – Information Market*, regarding agreements between thirteen investment banks, the International Swaps and Derivatives Association and a data service provider, by which they prevented two exchanges from entering the credit derivatives market. The ISDA and data service provider were instructed by the investment banks which controlled them not to grant licences for data and index benchmarks to two exchanges that sought to enter the market: see Press Release IP/613/630 (1 July 2013). The investigation in COMP/39730 *CDS – Clearing* is ongoing.

Fn 481 Regulation 924/2009 was amended by Regulation 260/2012 establishing technical and business requirements for credit transfers and direct debits in euro and amending Regulation (EC) No 924/2009, which was adopted on 12 March 2012. This obliges all users to move to the new Single Euro Payment Area systems established by the European Payments Council.

Multilateral Interchange Fees. The Court of Justice dismissed the further **6.107** appeal in Case C-382/12P *MasterCard v Commission*, EU:C:2014:2201, [2014] 5 CMLR 1062 and upheld the General Court's conclusions discussed in the main text. In particular:

(a) in considering whether the MIFs were objectively necessary ancillary restraints, the General Court correctly asked whether the MasterCard system would be impossible to carry out without the MIFs, rather than whether it would simply have been more difficult or less profitable in their absence: para 91. For this purpose, it was entitled to consider as a counterfactual any realistic situation that might arise in the absence of the MIFs: para 111. See, further, the update to paragraph 2.149, above;

(b) in considering whether the MIFs had a restrictive effect, the General Court did err in assessing the MIFs against a counterfactual in which the MasterCard system was operated using a prohibition on *ex post* pricing (in which issuing banks would be prohibited from setting the amount of the interchange fee after the cardholder has already made its purchase from the merchant) without considering how realistic that counterfactual was. For the purpose of assessing effects, it is necessary to consider as a counterfactual what would actually have happened in the absence of the agreement: paras 164 et seq. However, on the facts of that case, it had not been contended before the General Court that the MasterCard system would have collapsed without the MIFs, and the only alternative before the Court was the *ex post* pricing prohibition. This was therefore the only plausible and likely alternative to the MIFs. The judgment could be upheld on alternative grounds. See, further, the update to paragraph 2.124, above;

(c) in considering whether the MIFs were within Article 101(3), the General Court correctly focused on the benefits of the MIFs rather than of the MasterCard system as a whole: paras 230–232. The Court of Justice upheld the conclusion that the benefits of the MIFs did not outweigh their restrictive effects. In the case of a two-sided system, where the restrictive effects are felt only on one of the markets, the first condition of Article 101(3) can only be satisfied where some of the benefits are enjoyed by consumers on the market on which the restrictive effects are felt; if the benefits are entirely in the separate but connected market then they cannot, in themselves, compensate for the disadvantages of the agreement in the relevant market. Therefore even if the MIFs lead to some benefit to cardholders, the absence of any benefits to merchants was sufficient to preclude the application of Article 101(3): paras 237 et seq. See, further, the updates to Chapter 3, above.

Regulation 2015/751 on interchange fees for card-based payment transactions OJ 2015 L123/1, which includes a cap on interchange fees, entered into force on 8 June 2015.

Fn 482 Following the Commission's investigation of Visa Europe's MIFs for transactions with consumer credit cards, it has accepted commitments in particular to cap Visa Europe's credit card MIFs at 0.3 per cent for all consumer credit card transactions in the EEA where Visa Europe sets the rate: COMP/39398 *Visa MIF*, decision of 26 February 2014. This follows its earlier decision on 8 December 2010 accepting commitments in respect of Visa Europe's MIFs on consumer debit card transactions. The level of 0.3 per cent is the same as that to which MasterCard undertook to reduce its fees, pending its appeal against the decision in COMP/34579 *MasterCard*, decision of 19 December 2007. It represents a reduction of 40–60 per cent of Visa Europe's MIFs.

At the time of writing, the Commission's proceedings are ongoing in respect of the international inter-bank fees applied to transactions by card holders from outside the EEA at merchants within the EEA by Visa Inc (see COMP/39398 *Visa MIF*); and in respect of the rules on cross-border acquiring, and international inter-bank fees applied to transactions by card holders from outside the EEA at merchants within the EEA, by MasterCard (see COMP/40049 *MasterCard II*; a statement of objections was sent on 9 July 2015: see Press Release IP/15/5323 (9 July 2015)).

6.108 **MIFs: Scrutiny by Member States and the Commission.** In Poland, the Court of Competition and Consumer Protection upheld a decision that the Visa and MasterCard systems breach national and EU competition law: ECN Brief 05/2013, p13. The French Autorité de la Concurrence accepted commitments by both Visa and MasterCard to reduce the level of their fees in France on payments/withdrawals on their Visa and MasterCard 'only' cards (ie those outside the Cartes Bancaires system): Decision 13-D-17 of 20 September 2013 (MasterCard), and Decision 13-D-18 of 20 September 2013 (Visa); also ECN Brief 05/2013, p7.

(c) Professional services

(i) Measures adopted by a professional association

6.110 **Decisions by associations of undertakings.**
Fn 498 The Commission's decision in COMP/39510 *Ordre National des Pharmaciens en France (ONP)*, decision of 8 December 2010, was upheld as to liability in Case T-90/11 *ONP v Commission* EU:T:2014:1049.

Fn 499 See also Case C-1/12 *Ordem dos Técnicos Oficiais de Contas v Autoridade da Concorrência*, EU:C:2013:127, [2013] 4 CMLR 651, para 48; and *Competition Authority v Irish Medical Association*, Record No. 2013/7333P, in relation to the settlement of a case concerning the collective withdrawal of GP services in protest at proposed Government cuts to fees paid to GPs.

Fn 501 In Case C-327/12 *SOA Nazionale Costruttori*, EU:C:2013:827, at paras 27 et seq, the Court of Justice held that private bodies providing certification services under a statutory certification scheme are engaged in an economic activity. The Court noted in particular that the bodies did not perform any standardisation tasks, or make decisions connected with the exercise of public powers.

(ii) Analysing the competitive effects of professional rules

Fee scales and pricing practices.   The Commission's decision in COMP/39510   **6.111** *Ordre National des Pharmaciens en France (ONP)*, decision of 8 December 2010, was upheld as to liability in Case T-90/11 *ONP v Commission* EU:T:2014:1049. See in particular para 321.

Fn 507 See also *Competition Authority v Irish Medical Association*, Record No. 2013/7333P, in relation to the settlement of a case concerning the collective withdrawal of GP services in protest at proposed Government cuts to fees paid to GPs.

Other professional rules.   The Court of Justice confirmed in Case C-1/12 *Ordem*   **6.113** *dos Técnicos Oficiais de Contas v Autoridade da Concorrência*, EU:C:2013:127, [2013] 4 CMLR 651, that Article 101 applies to the rules of a professional association for chartered accountants requiring them to obtain compulsory ongoing professional training through the association itself, or undertakings approved by it.

Fn 516 See also Case C-1/12 *Ordem dos Técnicos Oficiais de Contas v Autoridade da Concorrência*, EU:C:2013:127, [2013] 4 CMLR 651, which was a preliminary reference arising from appeal proceedings following an infringement decision by the Autoridade da Concorrência (the Portuguese NCA), against the Order of Chartered Accountants in respect of their rules on compulsory ongoing professional training.

The Italian Competition Authority issued an infringement decision on 23 April 2013 against five Bar Associations for imposing additional registration requirements on non-Italian lawyers: ECN Brief 03/2013, p10.

(d) Sporting bodies and competitions

Scope of Article 101(1) in relation to sporting events.   The High Court of   **6.116** Ireland in *Hyland v Dundalk Racing* [2014] IEHC 60 considered the compatibility of the Irish 'Pitch Rules', which govern the allocation of pitches in the bookmakers' ring at a racecourse, with Article 101 and the Irish Competition Act 2002. The Court noted that if the Pitch Rules had not allowed allotted pitches to be traded there would have been a clear breach of competition law. However, as they did allow such trade, the Court held that they regulated and promoted effective competition between bookmakers on racecourse sites, and they were pro-competitive. It drew upon the judgment of Brandeis J in *Board of Trade of Chicago v United States* 246 US 231 (1918), at 238–239, distinguishing rules that promote the operation of an orderly and transparent market, and those that suppress or destroy competition.

6.117 *Meca-Medina* **and 'sporting rules'.**
Fn 531 The Court of Justice dismissed the further appeal in Case C-269/12P *Cañas v Commission*, EU:C:2013:415, regarding the alleged anti-competitiveness of certain anti-doping rules.

(f) E-commerce platforms

6.124 **E-commerce platforms: generally.**   On 6 May 2015 the Commission launched an inquiry into the e-commerce sector: see Press Release IP/15/4921 (6 May 2015). A preliminary report is expected in mid-2016, and the final report in the first quarter of 2017.

On the need for platforms to access information, see, in the UK's Competition Appeal Tribunal, *Skyscanner v CMA* [2014] CAT 16, paras 100 and 159, in which the Tribunal quashed and remitted the Office of Fair Trading's decision in *Hotel online booking: decision to accept commitments to remove certain discounting restrictions for Online Travel Agents*, decision of 31 January 2014. The decision accepted commitments which the OFT concluded would encourage intra-brand competition, by allowing online travel agents to offer discounted hotel room prices to a closed group of consumers; however, the Tribunal held that the OFT had failed to consider the impact that the commitments would have on price transparency and on inter-brand competition between different hotels, by limiting the ability of meta-search websites to access those discounted prices. The Competition and Markets Authority subsequently closed the case.

Fn 553 See also M.6314 *Telefónica UK/Vodafone UK/EE/JV* (4 September 2012), in which the Commission considered a full-function JV established by three of the leading UK MNOs to operate in the nascent 'mCommerce' sector (mobile commerce sector) which encompasses mobile payments, mobile advertising and data analytics, and which has developed with the rapid emergence and market penetration of smartphone technology; and equivalent decisions clearing JVs intended to operate in Spain, M.6956 *Telefónica/Caixabank/Banco Santander/JV* (14 August 2013); and Belgium, M.6967 *BNP Paribas Fortis/Belgacom/Belgian MobileWallet JV* (11 October 2013).

6.125 **E-commerce platforms: basic analysis.**   On 6 May 2015 the Commission launched an inquiry into the e-commerce sector: see Press Release IP/15/4921 (6 May 2015). A preliminary report is expected in mid-2016, and the final report in the first quarter of 2017.

Fn 556 For an example of a decision in which the Commission considered the creation of an e-commerce joint venture, see M.6314 *Telefónica UK/Vodafone UK/EE/ JV* (4 September 2012), in which the Commission considered a full-function joint venture established by three of the leading UK MNOs to operate in the nascent 'mCommerce' sector (or mobile commerce sector) which encompasses mobile payments, mobile advertising and data analytics, and which has developed with the rapid emergence and market penetration of smartphone technology; and equivalent decisions clearing joint ventures intended to operate in Spain, M.6956 *Telefónica/Caixabank/Banco Santander/JV* (14 August 2013); and Belgium, M.6967 *BNP Paribas Fortis/Belgacom/Belgian MobileWallet JV* (11 October 2013).

E-commerce platforms: Article 101(1).   On 6 May 2015 the Commission   **6.126** launched an inquiry into the e-commerce sector: see Press Release IP/15/4921 (6 May 2015). A preliminary report is expected in mid-2016, and the final report in the first quarter of 2017.

The Supreme Court of Lithuania has referred to the Court of Justice for a preliminary ruling questions concerning participation in a common computerised information system, and whether the participating undertakings agree to a restriction on price discounts when the system includes a notice stating that discounting is restricted and there are technical restrictions on discounting: Case C-74/14 *UAB Eturas*, not yet decided. The undertakings have been fined by the Competition Council for a concerted practice in their online sales.

In Germany, the Bundeskartellamt has found that most favoured nation pricing clauses in contracts between a hotel booking platform and hotels breach Article 101 and national competition law (on appeal to the Düsseldorf Higher Regional Court): ECN Brief 01/2014, p6. In the UK, the Office of Fair Trading's decision in *Hotel online booking: decision to accept commitments to remove certain discounting restrictions for Online Travel Agents*, decision of 31 January 2014, was quashed and remitted in *Skyscanner v CMA* [2014] CAT 16, paras 100 and 159. The decision focused on the availability of discounted prices, and did not find that the most favoured nation clauses were a restriction of competition. It accepted commitments that would encourage intra-brand competition, by allowing online travel agents to offer discounted hotel room prices to a closed group of consumers, but the Tribunal found the OFT had failed to consider the impact that the commitments would have on price transparency and on inter-brand competition between different hotels, by limiting the ability of meta-search websites to access those discounted prices.

7

VERTICAL AGREEMENTS AFFECTING DISTRIBUTION OR SUPPLY

2. Vertical Agreements: General Principles

(c) Approach to the application of Article 101

Anti-competitive object. 7.016

Fn 38 See also Case C-32/11 *Allianz Hungária Bistozitó*, EU:C:2013:160, [2013] 4 CMLR 863, in which the Court of Justice was asked to consider whether vertical agreements between car insurance companies and car repair shops had the object of restricting competition. It held that it was relevant to consider, *inter alia*, the fact that the terms of the agreements were based on a framework agreement, negotiated by the repair shops' trade association with the insurers, which contained recommended prices that insurers should pay to repairers for their work. There would be a restriction by object if the trade association had decided on recommended prices with the intention of harmonising prices, and the insurance companies confirmed those decisions in the framework agreement.

Vertical restraints of minor importance. The Court of Justice held in Case 7.020 C-226/11 *Expedia Inc*, EU:C:2012:795, [2013] 4 CMLR 439, paras 36–37, that an agreement that may affect trade between Member States and that has an anti-competitive object constitutes, by its nature and independently of any concrete effect that it may have, an appreciable restriction on competition. On 30 August 2014 the Commission adopted a revised *De Minimis* Notice to take account of this judgment: OJ 2014 C291/1. The revised Notice does not cover agreements which have as their object the prevention, restriction or distortion of competition within the internal market: para 2. The Commission has issued Guidance on restrictions of competition 'by object' for the purpose of defining which agreements may benefit from the *De Minimis* Notice (SWD(2014) 198 final).

3. Regulation 330/2010

(a) Scope

7.029 **Retailers' associations.**

Fn 80 For an illustration, see Case C-32/11 *Allianz Hungária Bistozitó*, EU:C:2013:160, [2013] 4 CMLR 863, in which the Court of Justice was asked to consider whether vertical agreements between car insurance companies and car repair shops had the object of restricting competition. It held that it was relevant to consider, *inter alia*, the fact that the terms of the agreements were based on a framework agreement, negotiated by the repair shops' trade association with the insurers, which contained recommended prices that insurers should pay to repairers for their work. There would be a restriction by object if the trade association had decided on recommended prices with the intention of harmonising prices, and the insurance companies confirmed those decisions in the framework agreement.

(c) Hardcore restrictions

(i) Resale price maintenance

7.039 **RPM can be achieved through indirect means.**

Fn 112 On most-favoured nation clauses, see also the Commission's decisions in COMP/39847 *E-books*, decisions of 12 December 2012 (OJ 2012 C283/7) and of 25 July 2013 (OJ 2013 C378/25) accepting commitments from five publishing companies, and Apple. The Commission has opened a similar investigation into the arrangements between Amazon and publishers: COMP/40153 *E-book MFNs*, and Press Release IP/15/5166 (11 June 2015). In Germany, the Bundeskartellamt has found that most favoured nation pricing clauses in contracts between a hotel booking platform and hotels breach Article 101 and national competition law (on appeal to the Düsseldorf Higher Regional Court): ECN Brief 01/2014, p6.

7.040 **RPM is a restriction by object under Article 101(1).**

Fn 114 See also the Commission's decisions in COMP/39847 *E-books*, decisions of 12 December 2012 (OJ 2012 C283/7) and of 25 July 2013 (OJ 2013 C378/25) accepting commitments from five publishing companies, and Apple. The Commission has opened a similar investigation into the arrangements between Amazon and publishers: COMP/40153 *E-book MFNs*, and Press Release IP/15/5166 (11 June 2015).

7.041 **RPM can be *de minimis*.** The Court of Justice held in Case C-226/11 *Expedia Inc*, EU:C:2012:795, [2013] 4 CMLR 439, at paras 36–37, that an agreement that may affect trade between Member States and that has an anti-competitive object constitutes, by its nature and independently of any concrete effects that it may have, an appreciable restriction on competition. As RPM is a restriction by object (see paragraph 7.040 of the main text), it will therefore not be considered *de minimis* where it may affect trade between Member States.

Recommended resale prices.   **7.043**
Fn 123 See also the decisions of the Hungarian Competition Authority in Case Vj-115/2010 *W&H Dentalwerk Bürmoos*, and of the Romanian Competition Council, both finding breaches of Article 101 TFEU by manufacturers of dental equipment and their distributors. In both cases the resale prices charged by distributors were monitored by the manufacturers, and selling below the recommended retail price led to distributors being excluded from the distribution networks: Hungarian Competition Authority decision, see ECN Brief 01/2014, p6; Romanian Competition Council decision, see ECN Brief 02/2014, p5.

4. Exclusive Distribution and Supply Agreements

(b) Restrictions on sales outside the exclusive grant

'Active' and 'passive' sales. The Irish High Court held in *SRI Apparel v* **7.069**
Revolution Workwear and others [2013] IEHC 289, para 61, that the use by a distributor (in that case, a distributor in a selective distribution agreement) of the website Amazon was active selling rather than passive, and that an agreement to restrict such activity was therefore within the scope of Article 4(b)(i) of Regulation 330/2010 (the Vertical Block Exemption).

Sales over the internet. See, however, *SRI Apparel v Revolution Workwear and* **7.070**
others [2013] IEHC 289, para 61, in which the Irish High Court held that the use by a distributor (in that case, a distributor in a selective distribution agreement) of the website Amazon was active selling rather than passive, and that an agreement to restrict such activity was therefore within the scope of Article 4(b)(i) of Regulation 330/2010 (the Vertical Block Exemption).

(d) Other common clauses in exclusive agreements

Exchange of information between supplier and distributor.   **7.087**
Fn 280 The test laid down by the Court of Appeal in *Argos & Littlewoods and JJB Sports v Office of Fair Trading* [2006] EWCA Civ 1318 was applied by the Competition Appeal Tribunal in *Tesco v OFT* [2012] CAT 31, which discusses in detail the state of mind required to satisfy the test.

5. Selective Distribution Systems

(b) The principles established by the EU Courts

7.101 **Limits on internet sales by authorised resellers.** The Irish High Court held in *SRI Apparel v Revolution Workwear and others* [2013] IEHC 289, para 61, that the use by a distributor of the website Amazon was active selling rather than passive, and that an agreement to restrict such activity was within the scope of Article 4(b)(i) of Regulation 330/2010 (the Vertical Block Exemption).

See also the OFT's decision CE/9578-12 '*Roma-branded mobility scooters: prohibitions on online sales and online price advertising*', decision of 5 August 2013, in which the OFT found that an agreement or concerted practice in which a manufacturer prevented the distributors in its selective distribution system from selling its products online, or advertising their prices online, was a restriction of competition by object. The Austrian Cartel Court in *Pioneer Electronics Deutschland*, 27 Kt 20/14, upheld the fines imposed on manufacturers of electronic equipment for agreements which, *inter alia*, restricted online sales of several high-end products sold under a selective distribution system.

(c) The application of the block exemption

7.108 **Hardcore restrictions: resale to end-users or other authorised distributors.** **Fn 392** On restriction of sales by a selective distributor via the internet, see *SRI Apparel v Revolution Workwear and others* [2013] IEHC 289, at para 61, in which the Irish High Court held that the use by a distributor of the website Amazon was active selling rather than passive, and that an agreement to restrict such activity was within the scope of Article 4(b)(i) of Regulation 330/2010 (the Vertical Block Exemption).

See also the OFT's decision CE/9578-12 '*Roma-branded mobility scooters: prohibitions on online sales and online price advertising*', decision of 5 August 2013, in which the OFT found that an agreement or concerted practice in which a manufacturer prevented the distributors in its selective distribution system from selling its products online, or advertising their prices online, was a restriction of competition by object. The Austrian Cartel Court in *Pioneer Electronics Deutschland*, 27 Kt 20/14, upheld the fines imposed on manufacturers of electronic equipment for agreements which, *inter alia*, restricted online sales of several high-end products sold under a selective distribution system.

8. Franchising Agreements

(c) Regulation 330/2010 and franchise agreements

Non-compete obligations.   7.179

Fn 634 On 21 March 2014 the Commission adopted Regulation 316/2014 on the application of Article 101(3) of the Treaty on the Functioning of the European Union to categories of technology transfer agreements, OJ 2014 L93/17. It entered into force on 1 May 2014, and replaces Regulation 772/2004 which expired on 30 April 2014. The reference to Article 1(1)(i) of Regulation 772/2004 should be read as Article 1(1)(i) in Regulation 316/2014.

9. Agency Agreements

Agent acting for more than one principal.   See also the Commission's decisions   7.184
in COMP/39847 *E-Books*, decisions of 12 December 2012 (OJ 2012 C283/7) and of 25 July 2013 (OJ 2013 C378/25). The Commission's preliminary assessment was that five publishing companies had engaged in a concerted practice by all moving the sales of their electronically formatted books to Apple from a wholesale model to an agency model, employing the same terms in the agency agreements, and discussing among themselves their intention to move to that model. It accepted commitments from the five publishing companies and Apple. The Commission has opened a similar investigation into the arrangements between Amazon and publishers: COMP/40153 *E-book MFNs*, and Press Release IP/15/5166 (11 June 2015).

Market for the distribution of the principal's products.   7.185
Fn 650 See also Case T-418/10 *Voestalpine v Commission*, EU:T:2015:516, discussed in the updates to paragraphs 2.030 and 2.038, above.

11. Waste Packaging Recycling Arrangements

Generally.   7.201
Fn 693 For an example of a hardcore restriction, see the decision of the Romanian Competition Council finding various manufacturers of electronic household appliances engaged in a concerted practice to fix the level of discounts given to customers when they acquired new equipment and returned their old equipment. All were members of an association established to manage waste electrical and electronic equipment. See ECN Brief 01/2014, p11.

7.204 **Licence fees for the use of the Green Dot logo.** The Supreme Court of the Slovak Republic held in *Železničná spoločnosť Cargo Slovakia*, on 23 May 2013, that ENVI-PAK, which held the licence to the Green Dot mark in Slovakia, had abused its dominant position by setting the fees for sub-licensing the use of the dot in such a way that it was payable only where the companies used the waste collection, recovery and recycling services of its competitors, and not where they used ENVI-PAK's own services: ECN Brief 03/2013, p14. The Commission submitted written observations to the Supreme Court pursuant to Article 15(3) of Regulation 1/2003 (see paragraph 15.051 of the main text on Article 15(3) of Regulation 1/2003), which are available on the 'Cooperation with national courts' section of the DG Comp website (at the time of writing, not yet available in English).

8

MERGER CONTROL

1. Introduction

(b) Commission guidance

Implementing Regulation and Notices.   As part of its simplification of pro-   **8.007**
cedures under the Merger Regulation, on 5 December 2013 the Commission
adopted Regulation 1269/2013, amending Regulation 802/2004 implementing
Council Regulation 139/2004 on the control of concentrations between undertakings: OJ 2013 L336/1 ('the Amended Implementation Regulation'). The
Amended Implementation Regulation includes revised annexes, including a revised Form CO, Form RS and Short Form. It entered into force on 1 January
2014. At the same time, the Commission adopted a Notice on a simplified procedure for treatment of certain concentrations under Regulation 139/2004: OJ
2013 L366/5 ('Revised Simplified Procedure Notice').

(c) Case law and statistics

Statistics.   The statistics in the main text can be updated, as follows, for the   **8.010**
period 1 August 2012–31 December 2015:

(a) Total number of notifications and referrals by year

Year	Notifications to Commission	Referrals from Member States to Commission		Referrals from Commission to Member States	
		Pre notification (Art 4(5))	Post- notification (Art 22)	Pre notification (Art 4(4))	Post- notification (Art 9)
2012	283	22	2	12	2
2013	277	11	1	9	0
2014	303	19	1	14	0
2015	337	19	1	12	1
Total	3376	287	22	110	30

(b) Different Phase I outcomes by year

Year	Clearance decisions				Referred to Phase II		Notifications withdrawn during Phase I	
	Unconditional		Conditional					
2012	254	(92%)	9	(3%)	10	(4%)	4	(1%)
2013	252	(93%)	11	(4%)	6	(2%)	1	(1%)
2014	280	(92%)	12	(4%)	8	(2%)	6	(2%)
2015	297	(91%)	13	(4%)	11	(3%)	6	(2%)
Total	3354	(91%)	154	(4%)	108	(3%)	64	(2%)

(c) Different Phase II outcomes by year

Year	Clearance decisions				Prohibition decisions		Notifications withdrawn during Phase II	
	Unconditional		Conditional					
2012	1	(11%)	6	(67%)	1	(11%)	1	(11%)
2013	2	(33%)	2	(33%)	2	(33%)	0	(0%)
2014	2	(29%)	5	(71%)	0	(0%)	0	(0%)
2015	1	(10%)	7	(70%)	0	(0%)	2	(20%)
Total	33	(31%)	48	(46%)	6	(6%)	18	(17%)

2. Jurisdictional Scope of the Merger Regulation

(b) Concentrations

(i) In general

8.017 **State-controlled undertakings.**
Fn 43 See also M.6801 *Rosneft/TNK-BP* (8 March 2013), taking into account the other entities owned by the Russian state in the oil and gas sector.

(iv) Sole control

8.028 **Acquisition of sole control.**
Fn 71 On the reference by the OFT to the Competition Commission of Ryanair's acquisition of a minority shareholding in Aer Lingus, the Competition Commission concluded in *Ryanair Holdings and Aer Lingus Group*, decision of 28 August 2013, that the acquisition of a minority shareholding in Aer Lingus has led, or may be expected to lead, to a substantial lessening of competition in the markets for air passenger services between Great Britain and the Republic of Ireland, and it ordered partial divestiture. The Competition Appeal Tribunal, in *Ryanair Holdings v Competition and Markets Authority* [2014] CAT 3, upheld the Competition Commission's decision, and dismissed the argument that it breached the duty of sincere cooperation under Article 4(3) TEU to order divestiture while Ryanair's

appeal to the General Court was pending. The Tribunal held that as the divestiture order concerned Ryanair's existing minority shareholding, rather than the proposed acquisition that was under consideration by the European Commission and is currently before the General Court, there was no breach of the duty.

Sole control through minority shareholding.   The General Court dismissed **8.029** the appeal in Case T-332/09 *Electrabel v Commission*, EU:T:2012:672. It upheld the Commission's approach of basing its analysis of whether or not sole control exists on the evidence of the presence of shareholders at shareholder meetings in previous years, and rejected the argument that it is necessary to look at the situation at general meetings for several years *after* the increase in capital likely to give rise to sole control, in order to confirm whether such control does in fact exist: paras 45 et seq, in particular para 48. The Court of Justice dismissed the further appeal on other grounds in Case C-84/13P *Electrabel v Commission*, EU:C:2014:2040. On the appeal, and further appeal, against the fine imposed, see the update to paragraph 8.188, below.

Other factors leading to *de facto* control.   **8.032**
Fn 85 The appeal against the Commission's decision in M.6447 *IAG/bmi* (30 March 2012) in Case T-344/12 *Virgin Atlantic Airways v Commission* was withdrawn: Order of 15 July 2014.

(v) Joint control

Concept of joint control.   **8.033**
Fn 86 See, for example, M.6439 *AGRANA/RWA/JV* (4 April 2012), para 14: the Commission considered joint control arose because the business plan for the first five years of the JV had to be adopted by mutual consent of the parent companies; and M.7270 *Ceské Aeroholding/Travel Service/Ceské Aerolinie* (18 December 2014), para 6: joint control arose where the shareholders agreed always to vote together on resolutions regarding the business plan, fleet composition and the appointment of directors.

(vii) Interrelated transactions

'Warehousing' arrangements.   **8.049**
Fn 129 The Court of Justice dismissed the further appeal in Case C-551/10P *Éditions Odile Jacob v Commission*, EU:C:2012:681, [2013] 4 CMLR 11. It held that even if the General Court had erred in its conclusion that the transactions did not enable Lagardère to acquire control, or joint control, of the target assets, that had no consequences other than that the notification of the concentration might be found to have been made late, or that the concentration might be found to have been implemented prematurely. That may expose the parties to penalties, but it does not lead to the Commission decision being annulled as it does not bear upon whether the concentration is compatible with the common market: see paras 37–38.

(viii) Specific operations that are not concentrations

8.051 **Article 3(5)(a) in practice.** The Court of Justice dismissed the further appeal in Case C-551/10P *Éditions Odile Jacob v Commission*, EU:C:2012:681, [2013] 4 CMLR 11. It held that even if the General Court had erred in its conclusion that the transactions did not enable Lagardère to acquire control, or joint control, of the target assets, that had no consequences other than that the notification of the concentration might be found to have been made late, or that the concentration might be found to have been implemented prematurely. That may expose the parties to penalties, but it does not lead to the Commission decision being annulled as it does not bear upon whether the concentration is compatible with the common market: see paras 37–38.

(d) EU dimension

(i) Turnover thresholds

8.061 **Worldwide and EU-wide turnover.** In M.7217 *Facebook/Whatsapp* (3 October 2014), para 9, the Commission found that it did not have jurisdiction to consider the merger, notwithstanding Facebook acquired Whatsapp for USD19 billion, because Whatsapp (which provides a free service in most Member States and does not sell advertising space) had a turnover that did not reach the €100 million threshold. It was able to consider the transaction only by virtue of the parties requesting a referral under Article 4(5) of Merger Regulation (see paragraphs 8.085 et seq of the main text).

(iii) Undertakings concerned

8.075 **Acquisitions by State-controlled companies.**
Fn 208 See also M.6801 *Rosneft/TNK-BP* (8 March 2013), in which the Commission considered, though ultimately did not need to decide, whether Rosneft has decision-making powers independently from the Russian state.

(iv) Identification of a 'group' for the purpose of calculating turnover

8.076 **Group turnover for the purposes of Article 5(4).**
Fn 212 The appeal against the Commission's decision in M.6447 *IAG/bmi* (30 March 2012) in Case T-344/12 *Virgin Atlantic Airways v Commission* was withdrawn: Order of 15 July 2014.

(e) Pre-notification reallocation of jurisdiction

(i) Article 4(4) referrals from Commission to NCAs

8.082 **Voluntary procedure.** As part of its simplification of procedures under the Merger Regulation, on 5 December 2013 the Commission adopted Regulation 1269/2013, amending Regulation 802/2004 implementing Council Regulation 139/2004 on the control of concentrations between undertakings: OJ 2013 L336/1 ('the Amended Implementation Regulation'). The Amended Implementation

Regulation includes revised annexes including a revised Form CO, Form RS and Short Form. It entered into force on 1 January 2014.

Consequences of Article 4(4) referral.   **8.084**
Fn 230 At the time of writing, the Commission has made three further partial referrals, in addition to those noted in the footnote: M.6753 *Orkla/Rieber & Son* (25 January 2013), in which the Commission agreed to a request to refer the Norwegian aspects of the case to the Norwegian competition authority and retained jurisdiction over the rest of the transaction; M.6982 *Altor Fund III/Tryghedsgruppen/Elixia/HFN Group* (23 October 2013); and M.7677 *Obi/Baumax Certain Assets* (4 August 2015).

(ii) Article 4(5) referrals to Commission

Suitable cases for Article 4(5) referral. In M.7217 *Facebook/Whatsapp* **8.085**
(3 October 2014), para 9 the Commission found that it did not have jurisdiction to consider the merger, notwithstanding Facebook acquired Whatsapp for USD19 billion, because Whatsapp (which provides a free service in most Member States and does not sell advertising space) had a turnover that did not reach the €100 million threshold (see paragraphs 8.061 of the main text). It was able to consider the transaction only by virtue of the parties requesting a referral under Article 4(5) of Merger Regulation.

Voluntary procedure. As part of its simplification of procedures under the Merger **8.086**
Regulation, on 5 December 2013 the Commission adopted Regulation 1269/2013, amending Regulation 802/2004 implementing Council Regulation 139/2004 on the control of concentrations between undertakings: OJ 2013 L336/1 ('the Amended Implementation Regulation'). The Amended Implementation Regulation includes revised annexes including a revised Form RS. It entered into force on 1 January 2014.

(iii) Formalities and review

Form RS.   **8.089**
Fn 239 As part of its simplification of procedures under the Merger Regulation, on 5 December 2013 the Commission adopted Regulation 1269/2013, amending Regulation 802/2004 implementing Council Regulation 139/2004 on the control of concentrations between undertakings: OJ 2013 L336/1 ('the Amending Implementation Regulation'). Article 1(2) of the Amending Implementation Regulation amends Article 3(2) of the Implementing Regulation, to clarify that the number of copies to be provided, and their format, is that specified by the Commission from time to time in the Official Journal. It entered into force on 1 January 2014.

Croatia's joining the EU, on 1 July 2013, has not affected the number of copies of Form RS that must be submitted.

Review of pre-notification referral procedures. As part of its simplification of **8.090**
procedures under the Merger Regulation, on 5 December 2013 the Commission adopted Regulation 1269/2013, amending Regulation 802/2004 implementing

Council Regulation 139/2004 on the control of concentrations between undertakings: OJ 2013 L336/1 ('the Amended Implementation Regulation'). The Amended Implementation Regulation includes revised annexes including a revised Form RS. It entered into force on 1 January 2014.

(f) Post-notification reallocation of jurisdiction

(i) Article 9 referrals from Commission to NCAs

8.091 **Legal requirements under Article 9.**
Fn 244 Recent examples are M.6321 *Buitenfood/AD Van Geloven Holding/JV (Article 9(3) decision)* (13 January 2012): partial referral at the request of the Dutch competition authority, as the concentration would significantly affect competition in the market for frozen snacks in the Netherlands; and M.7565 *Danish Crown/Tican (Article 9(3) decision)* (17 July 2015): partial referral at the request of the Danish competition authority.

8.092 **Commission's discretion under Article 9(2)(a).**
Fn 248 The appeal against the Commission's decision in M.5960 *Credit Agricole/Cassa di Risparmio della Spezia/Agences Intesa San Paolo* (10 November 2010) in Case T-45/11 *Italy v Commission* was withdrawn: Order of 27 May 2013.

Fn 250 See also M.7018 *Telefonica Deutschland/E-Plus* (30 January 2014), rejecting a request for referral in the mobile telecommunications sector. Although the conditions in Article 9(2) of the Merger Regulation were satisfied the Commission was best placed to review the concentration in light of the need to ensure consistency in the application of merger control rules in the mobile telecommunications sector, and given the Commission's experience in assessing cases in this sector. Similarly, see M.7499 *Altice/PT Portugal* (20 April 2015), rejecting a request for referral in the fixed telecommunications sector.

Fn 251 See, for example, M.6321 *Buitenfood/AD Van Geloven Holding/JV* (13 January 2012): partial referral at the request of the Dutch competition authority, as the concentration would significantly affect competition in the market for frozen snacks in the Netherlands, and a decision taken the same day clearing the aspects of the concentration not related to the Netherlands.

3. Procedure

(a) In general

(ii) Pre-notification contacts

8.109 **Initial contact.**
Fn 309 As part of its simplification of procedures under the Merger Regulation, on 5 December 2013 the Commission adopted Regulation 1269/2013,

amending Regulation 802/2004 implementing Council Regulation 139/2004 on the control of concentrations between undertakings: OJ 2013 L336/1 ('the Amended Implementation Regulation'). The Amended Implementation Regulation includes revised annexes including a revised Form CO. It entered into force on 1 January 2014.

(iii) Obligation to notify

Waivers regarding provision of information. As part of its simplification of procedures under the Merger Regulation, on 5 December 2013 the Commission adopted Regulation 1269/2013, amending Regulation 802/2004 implementing Council Regulation 139/2004 on the control of concentrations between undertakings: OJ 2013 L336/1 ('the Amended Implementation Regulation'). The Amended Implementation Regulation includes revised annexes including a revised Form CO. It entered into force on 1 January 2014. The revised Form CO specifies the particular types of information that, in the Commission's experience, are not necessary in a significant number of cases and which parties are particularly invited to consider requesting be waived: para 1.4(g). **8.114**

Supply of incorrect or misleading information. **8.115**
Fn 331 The Commission closed an investigation into Ahlstrom, Munksjö Oyj and Munksjö AB, regarding the information they provided as to the relevant market in which a concentration was proposed, following the parties' explanations in response to a statement of objections: M.7191 *Munksjö/Ahlstrom*, Press Release IP/14/1222 (29 October 2014).

(iv) Formalities

Form CO. As part of its simplification of procedures under the Merger Regulation, on 5 December 2013 the Commission adopted Regulation 1269/2013, amending Regulation 802/2004 implementing Council Regulation 139/2004 on the control of concentrations between undertakings: OJ 2013 L336/1 ('the Amended Implementation Regulation'). The Amended Implementation Regulation includes revised annexes including a revised Form CO. It entered into force on 1 January 2014. The revised Form CO: **8.117**

(a) redefines what is to be considered an 'affected market': Revised Form CO, section 6.3 (see the update to paragraph 8.194, below);
(b) encourages parties voluntarily to submit a description of the data that each of the undertakings collects and holds (including the type(s) of data, the level of disaggregation, the time period covered, and the format in which it is held) in cases where a quantitative economic analysis of the affected markets is likely to be useful: Revised Form CO, question 1.8;
(c) encourages parties voluntarily to facilitate international cooperation between the Commission and the competition authorities of non-EEA countries that are also reviewing the concentration, by submitting a list of which non-EEA competition authorities are reviewing the concentration: Revised Form CO, question 1.10.

8.118 **Submission of notification and supporting documentation.**

Fn 338 As part of its simplification of procedures under the Merger Regulation, on 5 December 2013 the Commission adopted Regulation 1269/2013, amending Regulation 802/2004 implementing Council Regulation 139/2004 on the control of concentrations between undertakings: OJ 2013 L336/1 ('the Amending Implementation Regulation'). Article 1(2) of the Amending Implementation Regulation amends Article 3(2) of the Implementing Regulation, to clarify that the number of copies to be provided, and their format, is that specified by the Commission from time to time in the Official Journal. It entered into force on 1 January 2014.

Fn 340 See the update to footnote 338, above. Croatia's joining the EU, on 1 July 2013, has not affected the number of copies of Form CO that must be submitted.

Fn 342 See the update to paragraph 8.117, above, on the Commission's amendment to Form CO to encourage parties to take steps to facilitate co-operation between the Commission and the competition authorities of non-EEA countries.

(v) Simplified procedure

8.122 **Generally.** As part of its simplification of procedures under the Merger Regulation, on 5 December 2013 the Commission adopted Regulation 1269/2013, amending Regulation 802/2004 implementing Council Regulation 139/2004 on the control of concentrations between undertakings: OJ 2013 L336/1 ('the Amended Implementation Regulation'). The Amended Implementation Regulation includes revised annexes including a revised Short Form, and Recital (3) states that a larger number of concentrations should be notified using the Short Form. It entered into force on 1 January 2014. At the same time, the Commission adopted a Notice on a simplified procedure for treatment of certain concentrations under Regulation 139/2004: OJ 2013 L366/5 ('Revised Simplified Procedure Notice'). The detailed proposals are discussed in the update to paragraph 8.123, below.

8.123 **Eligible cases.** As part of its simplification of procedures under the Merger Regulation, on 5 December 2013 the Commission adopted Regulation 1269/2013, amending Regulation 802/2004 implementing Council Regulation 139/2004 on the control of concentrations between undertakings: OJ 2013 L336/1 ('the Amended Implementation Regulation'). The Amended Implementation Regulation includes revised annexes including a revised Short Form, and Recital (3) states that a larger number of concentrations should be notified using the Short Form. It entered into force on 1 January 2014. At the same time, the Commission adopted a Notice on a simplified procedure for treatment of certain concentrations under Regulation 139/2004: OJ 2013 L366/5 ('Revised

Simplified Procedure Notice'). The Revised Simplified Procedures Notice revises the categories of cases in which the simplified procedure is available:

(a) the combined market share threshold for parties in a horizontal relationship is increased from 15 per cent to 20 per cent;
(b) the market share threshold for parties in a vertical relationship is increased from 25 per cent to 30 per cent; and
(c) it is now available in cases where on all plausible market definitions the combined market share of parties in a horizontal relationship is below 50 per cent, and the increment ('delta') of the Herfindahl-Hirschman Index ('HHI') resulting from the concentration is below 150 (for the HHI, and calculation of the delta, see paragraph 8.213 and footnote 663 in the main text).

Short Form.   As part of its simplification of procedures under the Merger   **8.124**
Regulation, on 5 December 2013 the Commission adopted Regulation 1269/ 2013, amending Regulation 802/2004 implementing Council Regulation 139/ 2004 on the control of concentrations between undertakings: OJ 2013 L336/1 ('the Amending Implementation Regulation'). The Amended Implementation Regulation includes revised annexes including a revised Short Form. Article 1(2) of the Amending Implementation Regulation amends Article 3(2) of the Implementing Regulation, to clarify that the number of copies to be provided, and their format, is that specified by the Commission from time to time in the Official Journal. It entered into force on 1 January 2014.

Croatia's joining the EU, on 1 July 2013, has not affected the number of copies of the Short Form that must be submitted.

Exceptions.   **8.125**
Fn 361 As part of its simplification of procedures under the Merger Regulation, on 5 December 2013 the Commission adopted Regulation 1269/2013, amending Regulation 802/2004 implementing Council Regulation 139/2004 on the control of concentrations between undertakings: OJ 2013 L336/1 ('the Amended Implementation Regulation'). The Amended Implementation Regulation includes revised annexes including a revised Short Form. It entered into force on 1 January 2014. At the same time, the Commission adopted a Notice on a simplified procedure for treatment of certain concentrations under Regulation 139/2004: OJ 2013 L366/5 ('Revised Simplified Procedure Notice'). The references to paras 6– 11 of the Simplified Procedure Notice should be read as paras 8–17 of the Revised Simplified Procedure Notice.

(vi) Suspension of concentrations

Completion in breach.   **8.130**
Fn 372 The General Court dismissed the appeal in Case T-332/09 *Electrabel v Commission*, EU:T:2012:672, and the Court of Justice dismissed the further appeal in Case C-84/13P *Electrabel v Commission*, EU:C:2014:2040. On the appeal,

and further appeal, against the fine imposed, see the update to paragraph 8.188, below. See also M.6850 *Marine Harvest/Morpol* (23 July 2014), imposing a fine of €20 million on Marine Harvest, in similar circumstances to *Electrabel*. Marine Harvest failed to notify the Commission of its acquisition of *de facto* control over a competitor undertaking, through its acquisition of a 48.5 per cent shareholding, until eight months after completion. Following *Electrabel*, the Commission found that Marine Harvest should have been aware of its obligation to notify and await clearance, and that this was a serious infringement: M.6850 *Marine Harvest/ Morpol* (23 July 2014).

(c) In-depth Phase II investigation

(i) Phase II process

8.149 **Notifying parties' access to file and key documents.**
Fn 438. As part of its simplification of procedures under the Merger Regulation, on 5 December 2013 the Commission adopted Regulation 1269/2013, amending Regulation 802/2004 implementing Council Regulation 139/2004 on the control of concentrations between undertakings: OJ 2013 L336/1 ('the Amending Implementation Regulation'). Article 1(7) of the Amending Implementation Regulation amends Article 17(3) of the Implementing Regulation, to include correspondence between the Commission and the competition authorities of non-EEA countries.

(iv) Possible outcomes at Phase II

8.159 **Decisions following a Phase II investigation.**
Fn 478 At the time of writing, there have been 24 prohibition decisions: see the update to table (c) at paragraph 8.010, above. Recent prohibition decisions are M.6570 *UPS/TNT Express* (30 January 2013) (on appeal, Case T-194/13 *United Parcel Service v Commission*, not yet decided); and M.6663 *Ryanair/Aer Lingus III* (27 February 2013) (appeal in Case T-260/13 *Ryanair v Commission*, withdrawn: Order of 28 October 2015). The appeal in Case T-202/11 *Aeroporia Aigaiou Aeroporiki and Marfin Investment Group Symmetochon v Commission* was withdrawn on 10 September 2013.

The decision in M.6166 *Deutsche Börse/NYSE Euronext* (1 February 2012) was upheld in Case T-175/12 *Deutsche Börse v Commission*, EU:T:2015:148, [2015] 4 CMLR 1187.

(d) Commitments to enable clearance

(i) Commitments at Phase I or Phase II

8.165 **In general.**
Fn 495 See also Case T-471/11 *Éditions Odile Jacob v Commission*, EU:T:2014:739, paras 74 et seq.

Phase I commitments.   **8.168**
Fn 501 See also M.6503 *LaPoste/Swiss Post/JV* (4 July 2012) and M.7252 *Holcim/Lafarge* (15 December 2014).

Phase II commitments.   **8.169**
Fn 507 As part of its simplification of procedures under the Merger Regulation, on 5 December 2013 the Commission adopted Regulation 1269/2013, amending Regulation 802/2004 implementing Council Regulation 139/2004 on the control of concentrations between undertakings: OJ 2013 L336/1 ('the Amended Implementation Regulation'). It entered into force on 1 January 2014. Article 1(8) of the Amended Implementation Regulation amends Article 19(2) of the Implementing Regulation to clarify that where offered commitments are modified on day 55 or thereafter, the modified commitments are deemed to be new commitments for the purposes of the second sentence of Article 10(3) of the Merger Regulation, such that the time limit is extended to 105 working days.

Common principles   **8.170**
Fn 514 For an example of the Commission rejecting commitments initially proposed in part on the basis that non-compliance would be difficult to monitor, and of the parties formulating alternative proposals that did not require active ongoing monitoring, see M.6541 *Glencore/Xstrata* (22 November 2014), paras 502, and 526–531.

(ii) Scope of commitments

Structural and behavioural commitments.   **8.171**
Fn 516 See also M.6459 *Sony/Mubadala Development/EMI Music Publishing* (19 April 2012) (divestment of certain rights in works and future works, and non-solicitation agreement).

Fn 517 For an example in the telecommunications sector, see M.6497 *Hutchinson 3G Austria/Orange Austria* (12 December 2012) in which the Commission granted clearance at Phase II, subject to two conditions: that Hutchinson divest itself of spectrum frequency bands, and that it enter into network access agreements to grant mobile virtual network operators (MVNOs) wholesale access to up to 30 per cent of its network capacity in the coming 10-year period.

Fn 518 See also M.6455 *SCA/Georgia–Pacific Europe* (5 July 2012), paras 288–297.

Fn 523 In M.6992 *Hutchinson 3G UK/Telefonica Ireland* (28 May 2014) the Commission granted clearance at Phase II, subject to conditions similar to those imposed in M.6497 *Hutchinson 3G Austria/Orange Austria* (12 December 2012) (see the update to footnote 517, above) but in addition required that the merged entity continue to offer a network sharing agreement to Eircom, one of its competitors, on improved terms, in order to ensure that Eircom should remain an effective and viable competitor.

Fn 525 In addition to supplying products or services to third parties, the Commission may also accept a commitment to supply to the newly created divested business, in order to ensure it is a viable competitor in the market: M.7115 *Kuraray/GLSV Business* (29 April 2014), paras 141–142, in which the Commission accepted a divestiture commitment together with a commitment to enter into a long-term supply agreement with the divestiture business for the supply of raw materials to it, at a price to be determined by an independent expert (whose appointment would be agreed with the monitoring trustee) on a fair and competitive 'cost plus' basis.

Fn 527 See also M.6564 *ARM/Giesecke & Devrient/Gemalto/JV* (7 November 2012): upstream undertaking to provide interoperability information on the same terms to the JV and to its competitors.

8.172 **Divestiture.** On 5 December 2013 the Commission published model texts on divestiture commitments and on trustee mandates, together with Best Practice Guidelines: The Commission's Model Texts for Divestiture Commitments and the Trustee Mandate under the Merger Regulation; all are available under 'Legislation' in the Mergers section of the DG Comp website.

Fn 533 For recent examples of this approach in practice, see M.7115 *Kuraray/ GLSV Business* (29 April 2014), paras 141–142, in which the Commission accepted a divestiture commitment together with a commitment to enter into a long-term supply agreement with the divestiture business for the supply of raw materials to it, in order to ensure that it is a viable competitor in the market. The price for the raw materials is to be determined by an independent expert (whose appointment would be agreed with the monitoring trustee) on a fair and competitive 'cost plus' basis. Similarly, in M.7421 *Orange/Jazztel* (19 May 2015), paras 903 et seq, in which the Commission accepted a divestiture commitment together with a commitment to allow the divestiture business wholesale access to Jazztel's network, at prices that replicate the parties' current variable costs, for up to 8 years in order to ensure that it is a viable competitor in the market.

In M.7435 *Merck/Sigma-Aldrich* (15 June 2015), paras 91 et seq, the Commission cleared a proposed concentration between undertakings active *inter alia* in the supply of laboratory chemicals subject to a divestiture commitment that covered the entire value chain, including: manufacturing assets; certain brands and trademark rights; transfer of know-how and associated intellectual property rights; transfer of all product descriptions and product specific information displayed on Sigma's e-commerce platform, a transitional support agreement to assist the purchaser of the divestment business in developing its e-commerce platform, and in the meantime an obligation to grant access to Sigma's e-commerce platform; and temporary access for the divestment business to an order entry and distribution service.

In M.7061 *Huntsman/Rockwood* (10 September 2014), as the main barrier to entry into the EEA market was access to technology and know-how, and there was over-capacity in the market, the Commission concluded that a competitor provided with the adequate technology would have the ability to compete effectively on the market using its existing production equipment, and it accepted a commitment to divest technology and know-how.

See M.7275 *Novartis/Glaxosmithkline Oncology Business* (28 January 2015), paras 285 et seq, for an example of a structural remedy accommodating third party contractual rights. The divestment assets consisted primarily of two of Novartis' pipeline pharmaceutical products, one of which was owned by a third party, Array, and was being developed by Novartis under an exclusive licence. Novartis committed to return the licence to Array; to divest the other product also to it; and to oblige Array to negotiate an agreement with a fourth party, to be approved by the Commission, for the development and commercialisation of the products failing which a licence to develop and commercialise the products would be assigned to a divestiture trustee for sale. In parallel, Novartis and Array entered into a contractual agreement mirroring the commitments.

Fn 536 For an example of the General Court dismissing a challenge to the Commission's approval of a purchaser, see Case T-471/11 *Éditions Odile Jacob v Commission*, EU:T:2014:739. For an example of the Commission approving a purchaser, and simultaneously approving the purchaser's acquisition of the divestment business under the Merger Regulation, see M.7584 *International Chemical Investors/INEOS Chlorovinyls Business* (9 June 2015) (business divested pursuant to the commitments provided in M.6905 *INEOS/Solvay/JV* (8 May 2014)), and Press Release IP/15/5147 (9 June 2015).

In M.7252 *Holcim/Lafarge* (15 December 2014), in view of the scale of the business to be divested, the Commission accepted that divestiture could take place either by selling the divestiture business to an approved purchaser in the conventional manner, or by selling at least 50 per cent of the shares in the business to an approved purchaser with the balance being sold through capital markets. The core shareholders in the existing businesses provided an undertaking that they would not re-acquire shares in the divested business via the capital market flotation: paras 492 and 567(iii).

Upfront buyer, alternative and 'crown jewel' divestiture remedies.   **8.173**
Fn 537 In M.6570 *UPS/TNT Express* (30 January 2013) the Commission prohibited the concentration as an upfront buyer commitment had not been offered, and the attempt to sign a binding agreement with a suitable purchaser before the end of the Commission's investigation did not materialise. On appeal, Case T-194/13 *United Parcel Service v Commission*, not yet decided. For more recent examples, see also M.6690 *Syniverse/Mach* (29 May 2013), paras 750 et seq, in which Mach gave

commitments to divest itself of a significant part of its assets in the EEA, including its entire EEA data clearing services and EEA near trade roaming data exchange services, and strict purchaser criteria together with an upfront buyer commitment, in order to obtain clearance at Phase II; M.7104 *Crown Holdings/Mivisa* (14 March 2014), paras 216 and 226; and M.7265 *Zimmer/Biomet* (30 March 2015), paras 1963 et seq.

(iii) Implementation of commitments

8.175   **Role of trustees.**   On 5 December 2013 the Commission published model texts on divestiture commitments and on trustee mandates, together with Best Practice Guidelines: The Commission's Model Texts for Divestiture Commitments and the Trustee Mandate under the Merger Regulation; all are available under 'Legislation' in the Mergers section of the DG Comp website.

Fn 547 The Court of Justice in Cases C-553&554/10P *Commission v Éditions Odile Jacob*, EU:C:2012:682, [2013] 4 CMLR 55, disagreed with Advocate General Mazák's Opinion of 27 March 2012 and upheld the General Court's judgment in Case T-452/04 *Éditions Odile Jacob v Commission* [2010] ECR II-4713. The Court of Justice held that the trustee in that case was not independent of the parties, as required by their commitments, and the General Court was correct in concluding that that alone was sufficient basis for annulling the decision approving the purchaser. The Court of Justice rejected the argument that it was necessary to establish that the lack of independence had actually affected the trustee's choice of purchaser: para 52. The parallel appeal in Case C-551/10P *Éditions Odile Jacob*, EU:C:2012:681, [2013] 4 CMLR 11 (against the General Court judgment in Case T-279/04 *Éditions Odile Jacob v Commission* [2010] ECR II-0185, upholding the Commission's decision to clear the concentration) was dismissed, as was the appeal against the Commission's subsequent approval of the purchaser: Case T-471/11 *Éditions Odile Jacob v Commission*, EU:T:2014:739.

8.176   **Failure to comply with commitments.**
Fn 549   See also Case T-471/11 *Éditions Odile Jacob v Commission*, EU:T:2014:739, paras 74 et seq.

(e) Commission's powers of investigation

(iii) Confidentiality and business secrets

8.184   **Public access to documents.**   The General Court has confirmed that, in addition to the exceptions from disclosure provided for in Article 4(2) of Regulation 1049/2001, discussed in the main text, the Commission's internal documents prepared in the course of merger control proceedings may also fall within the exception in Article 4(3) of Regulation 1049/2001. That exception will apply where the Commission's decision-making process may be prejudiced by disclosure of the document, and in particular in circumstances where its investigation has closed but its decision is under appeal and the possibility remains that it will be required to re-open its proceedings: Case T-561/12 *Beninca v Commission*, EU:T:2013:558, [2014] 4 CMLR 549, paras 28 et seq, in particular para 36 (request for disclosure of an internal Commission memorandum which related to M.6166 *NYSE Euronext/ Deutsche Börse* (1 February 2012), at the time of the request under appeal in Case T-175/12 *Deutsche Börse v Commission*, EU:T:2015:148, [2015] 4 CMLR 1187).

(f) Commission's powers of sanction

(i) *In general*

Measures following a prohibition decision.   8.185
Fn 581 No further decisions imposing remedies under Article 8(4) were issued between 1 August 2012 and 31 September 2014. The total number of decisions remains four.

(ii) *Fines and penalty payments*

Fines for procedural infringements.   8.187
Fn 587 The Commission closed an investigation into Ahlstrom, Munksjö Oyj and Munksjö AB, regarding the information they provided as to the relevant market in which a concentration was proposed, following the parties' explanations in response to a statement of objections: M.7191 *Munksjö/Ahlstrom*, Press Release IP/14/1222 (29 October 2014).

Fines for substantive infringements.   In Case T-332/09 *Electrabel v Commission*,   8.188
EU:T:2012:672, the General Court upheld the Commission's conclusion that Electrabel had acquired control in December 2003 (on the acquisition of control, see the update to paragraph 8.029, above), and rejected a complaint that the fine was disproportionate. It observed that €20 million represented only 0.42 per cent of the legal maximum that the Commission could have imposed: paras 225–226, 283, and 303. It held *inter alia* that:

(a) the Commission correctly concluded that a failure to notify is a serious infringement: para 235;
(b) it is not relevant that the question of whether control has been acquired is complex, because Electrabel should have erred on the side of caution and contacted the Commission in those circumstances: paras 248–255; and
(c) the overall proportionality of a fine cannot usefully be assessed by reference to earlier Commission decisions which are distinguishable on their facts (paras 284–286); or to the fines imposed in cartel cases which pursue particular objectives linked to the secret nature of cartels (para 292); or to decisions taken by NCAs (para 301).

The Court of Justice dismissed the further appeal in Case C-84/13P *Electrabel v Commission*, EU:C:2014:2040, as partly inadmissible and partly unfounded.

The Commission has imposed a fine of €20 million on Marine Harvest, in similar circumstances to *Electrabel*. Marine Harvest failed to notify the Commission of its acquisition of *de facto* control over a competitor undertaking, through its acquisition of a 48.5 per cent shareholding, until eight months after completion. Following *Electrabel*, the Commission found that Marine Harvest should have been aware of its obligation to notify and await clearance, and that this was a serious infringement: M.6850 *Marine Harvest/Morpol* (23 July 2014).

4. Substantive Appraisal of Concentrations

(b) Market definition

(i) Affected markets for Form CO purposes

8.194 **Market definition and relevant markets.** As part of its simplification of procedures under the Merger Regulation, on 5 December 2013 the Commission adopted Regulation 1269/2013, amending Regulation 802/2004 implementing Council Regulation 139/2004 on the control of concentrations between undertakings: OJ 2013 L336/1 ('the Amended Implementation Regulation'). The Amended Implementation Regulation includes revised annexes including a revised Form CO. It entered into force on 1 January 2014. The revised Form CO increases the market share thresholds discussed in the main text:

(a) *horizontally affected markets:* the combined market share threshold is increased from 15 per cent to 20 per cent; and

(b) *vertically affected markets:* the market share threshold for parties in a vertical relationship is increased from 25 per cent to 30 per cent. It also clarifies that the market share thresholds are to be applied to all plausible market definitions. See Form CO, question 6.3(b).

(iii) Geographic market

8.198 **Relevant geographic market.**
Fn 615 See also Case T-405/08 *SPAR Österreichische Warenhandel v Commission*, EU:T:2013:306, paras 115 et seq, in which the General Court upheld the Commission's decision in M.5047 *REWE/ADEG* (29 April 2011), finding the relevant geographic market to be national but analysing competitive effects also at the subnational level of political districts.

(c) SIEC test

(ii) Relationship with concept of dominance

8.203 **Dominance remains a relevant consideration.** In M.7047 *Microsoft/Nokia* (4 December 2013), the Commission considered concerns expressed by certain respondents that Nokia divesting itself of a part of its business, which would be acquired by Microsoft, would lead to the removal of various competitive constraints to which Nokia had previously been subject on its exploitation of its patent portfolio. The Commission concluded that these concerns were outside the scope of the Merger Regulation, as the regime only covers the likely post-transaction conduct of the merged entity, or the merged entity together with third parties: paras 222 et seq. The concerns expressed about Nokia would be addressed by Article 102. The Commission noted its position on the obligations of holders of standard essential patents to license on fair, reasonable and non-discriminatory ('FRAND') terms, and on the application of Article 102 to an undertaking seeking injunctions in circumstances where FRAND terms have not been agreed (see the discussion in paragraph 9.060 of the main text, and the update thereto).

Fn 628 In M.6503 *LaPoste/Swiss Post/JV* (4 July 2012) the Commission noted the 'very strong position' of La Poste, as the incumbent operator on a market which had been liberalised fairly recently and in which 'no entrants are to be expected in the medium term': para 85. It considered the JV would strengthen that position, and cleared the merger after accepting divestiture commitments at Phase I. In M.6690 *Syniverse/Mach* (29 May 2013) the Commission considered a proposed merger between the largest and second largest operators in a number of markets for roaming technology services provided to telecommunications companies, such as data clearing and financial settlement, that would have created a dominant player with virtual monopoly market shares: see paras 202 et seq. It cleared the concentration after accepting commitments at Phase II to divest a significant part of Mach's assets in the EEA. In M.7047 *Microsoft/Nokia* (4 December 2013), the Commission considered the likely effects of the concentration in the light of the fact that the parties held various patents including standard essential patents, as defined by the European Telecommunication Standard Institute (ETSI). It concluded that the concentration would not strengthen Microsoft's upstream position with respect to its patent portfolio for smart mobile devices, as the patents it would acquire from Nokia were not standard essential patents, and its exposure to third party intellectual property rights would be increased through its need to renew Nokia's existing licensing agreements on their expiry: para 94.

Dominance is no longer a pre-requisite.   In respect of the note in the main **8.204** text that there may be a significant impediment to effective competition if the concentration involves the elimination of important competitive constraints that the merging parties exerted upon each other, see M.7047 *Microsoft/Nokia* (4 December 2013), discussed in the update to paragraph 8.203, above.

(iv) General content of assessment

Counterfactual.   **8.208**
Fn 630 The appeal against the Commission's decision in M.6447 *IAG/bmi* (30 March 2012) in Case T-344/12 *Virgin Atlantic Airways v Commission* was withdrawn: Order of 15 July 2014.

8.211 Priority principle for contemporaneous transactions.
Fn 656 Western Digital's challenges to the lawfulness of the Commission's priority rule in Cases T-452/11 and T-60/12 were withdrawn: Orders of 20 September 2012.

(d) Unilateral effects

(i) In general

8.213 Relevance of market shares and concentration levels. The Commission is entitled to leave open the question of market definition if the concentration does not give rise to competition concerns on any plausible market definition, and in circumstances where the Commission does not reach a definitive view about market definition, market shares and market concentration levels cannot be used as indica of competition concerns: Case T-79/12 *Cisco Systems & Messagenet v Commission*, EU:T:2013:635, at paras 65 et seq. The General Court went on to uphold the Commission's analysis in M.6281 *Microsoft/Skype* (7 October 2011) that in that case very high market shares, and a high degree of market concentration on the Herfindahl-Hirschman Index, were not indicative of competition concerns on any view of the relevant market. The Court accepted the Commission's evidence that there were significant fluctuations in market shares; the sector was characterised by short innovation cycles; there was an increase in demand for the services in question via different platforms and the merged entity would not be able to respond to that particular demand; there was an effective competitor for the merged entity; and the merged entity would be severely restricted in its ability to price freely as consumers of the services in question expect to receive it free of charge.

In M.7217 *Facebook/Whatsapp* (3 October 2014), paras 97 et seq the Commission expressed some difficulty in finding a metric with which to measure market shares. It accepted the parties' suggestion of reach data as a 'best available proxy', and following Case T-79/12 *Cisco Systems & Messagenet v Commission*, EU:T:2013:635, para 69 noted that the market had similar features—fast-growing, frequent market entry and short innovation cycles—such that high market shares would not necessarily be indicative of market power in any event.

Fn 662 See, eg, M.7479 *Kingspan/Steel Partners* (16 March 2015), paras 66 et seq.

Fn 663 Although the Commission may consider the HHI, it is not obliged to do so: Case T-405/08 *SPAR Österreichische Warenhandel v Commission*, EU:T:2013:306, paras 66–69. For an example of the Commission using the HHI, see M.6541 *Glencore/Xstrata* (22 November 2012). Contrast paras 169 and 175 (the merged entity's market share in the supply of zinc metal would be above 40 per cent, and the post-merger HHI above 2000 with a delta of up to 900, so there was a serious risk that the merged entity would have significant market power, and the concentration presented a serious risk of non-coordinated effects in the zinc supply markets), and paras 282–286 (the merged entity's market share in copper concentrate and secondary copper products remained below 10–20 per cent, and the post-merger HHI 'well below 2000', so the concentration was not likely to give rise to competition concerns in the copper markets).

Fn 665 In M.6690 *Syniverse/Mach* (29 May 2013) the Commission considered detailed arguments from the parties that the relevant markets were characterised by contestable 'Bertrand' competition, such that the presence of only two players in the market did not lead to coordination and higher prices, and market shares and concentration levels should not be relied upon: paras 211 et seq. The Commission did not agree that the markets were in fact contestable, and in particular concluded that the barriers to expansion that would be faced by smaller competitors in a post-merger situation were such that they would not be credible threats to the merged entity. It went on to clear the concentration after accepting commitments at Phase II to divest a significant part of Mach's assets in the EEA.

For a further example of other relevant factors, see Case T-79/12 *Cisco Systems & Messagenet v Commission*, EU:T:2013:635, at paras 65 et seq, discussed in the update to the main paragraph, above.

(ii) Relevant considerations

Relevant factors. 8.216
Fn 672 See, eg M.7387 *BP/Statoil Fuel and Retail Aviation* (15 December 2014), para 58 in which the Commission considered a diversion ratio showing that between 70–80 per cent of the business lost by one of the parties in the previous three years had been lost to the other party.

Fn 677 See also M.7387 *BP/Statoil Fuel and Retail Aviation* (15 December 2014), eg para 127, considering the position of purchasers who engage in 'multi-sourcing' in circumstances where, post-merger, neither of the two suppliers used would face competition in respect of the demand that they were covering.

In M.7292 *DEMB/Mondelez/Charger Opco* (5 May 2015), paras 374 and 396–398, the Commission found that one of the parties to the concentration had 'must-have' brands, and the other party was a close competitor. This reduced any countervailing buyer power that some purchasers would otherwise have had.

Fn 686 In M.6690 *Syniverse/Mach* (29 May 2013) the Commission considered a proposed merger between the largest and second largest operators in a number of markets for roaming technology services provided to telecommunications companies, such as data clearing and financial settlement, that would have created a dominant player with virtual monopoly market shares. The parties argued that the relevant markets were characterised by contestable 'Bertrand' competition, such that the presence of only two players in the market did not lead to coordination and higher prices, and market shares and concentration levels should not be relied upon: paras 211 et seq. The Commission did not agree that the markets were in fact contestable, and in particular concluded that the barriers to expansion that would be faced by smaller competitors in a post-merger situation were such that they would not be credible threats to the merged entity. It went on to clear the concentration after accepting commitments at Phase II to divest a significant part of Mach's assets in the EEA.

For an example of a finding that a concentration would hinder the expansion of competition by reducing the incentive of one of the parties to bring pipeline products onto the market, thus reducing potential competition, see M.7275 *Novartis/ Glaxosmithkline Oncology Business* (28 January 2015), paras 57–59.

Fn 687 See also M.7421 *Orange/Jazztel* (19 May 2015), paras 310 et seq, in which the Commission examined the parties' 'gross add shares' (the number of new customers gained by each party) as a measure of their success in attracting new customers and of their ability to act as a competitive constraint on other market players, rather than their static market shares.

As to the significance of innovative new products, see, eg M.7326 *Medtronic/ Covidien* (28 November 2014), in which the Commission considered the concentration would remove the competitive constraint exercised by a product currently in development: paras 243 et seq, and cleared the merger at Phase II subject to a commitment to divest that particular product: paras 408 et seq.

8.217 **Application of unilateral effects analysis in practice.** In M.6905 *INEOS/ Solvay/JV* (8 May 2014), paras 702 et seq and Annex A, the Commission was able to analyse likely effects, *ex ante*, by considering the effects which previous mergers in the same sector had had *ex post* (using transaction data and costs and margins data the Commission conducted a differences-in-differences analysis of INEOS' prices following two previous mergers in which it had participated, and concluded that INEOS had been able to increase its prices to a greater extent than its competitors following the second of those mergers).

(e) Coordinated effects

(i) In general

8.219 **Opportunities for tacit collusion.** In M.7009 *Holcim/Cemex West* (5 June 2014), the Commission concluded that it could not exclude there being a degree of coordination in the markets, but that the particular concentration under consideration would not itself have the effect of facilitating that coordination, or of making it more stable or more effective.

Fn 696 See M.7009 *Holcim/Cemex West* (5 June 2014), paras 167 et seq, for an example of the Commission considering the potential for tacit collusion in the form of customer allocation.

Characterising a market as oligopolistic.   **8.220**
Fn 697 In M.7009 *Holcim/Cemex West* (5 June 2014), para 165 the Commission
concluded that past cartel behaviour can 'provide a useful insight as to possible
mechanisms of coordination'.

(ii) Relevant considerations

Reaching terms of coordination.   **8.221**
Fn 699 For example, see M.7009 *Holcim/Cemex West* (5 June 2014), paras 210
et seq, in which the Commission concluded that it was easier to reach terms of
coordination in circumstances where there was a stable economic environment, a
small number of competitors, a homogeneous product, inelasticity of demand and
a relative symmetry of competitors.

(f) Vertical and conglomerate effects

(i) Vertical effects

Degree of market power. As part of its simplification of procedures under the   **8.230**
Merger Regulation, on 5 December 2013 the Commission adopted Regulation
1269/2013, amending Regulation 802/2004 implementing Council Regulation
139/2004 on the control of concentrations between undertakings: OJ 2013 L336/1
('the Amended Implementation Regulation'). The Amended Implementation
Regulation includes revised annexes including a revised Form CO. It entered
into force on 1 January 2014. The revised Form CO increases the market share
threshold on closely related markets from 25 per cent to 30 per cent, and requires
it to be applied to all plausible market definitions: Form CO, question 6.3(b).

Fn 721 See, eg M.6910 *Gazprom/Wintershall/Target Companies* (3 December
2013), para 57.

Input foreclosure. In M.6314 *Telefónica UK/Vodafone UK/EE/JV* (4 September   **8.231**
2012) the Commission sought the assistance of an industry regulator, OFCOM,
to understand whether the parties had the ability to engage in input foreclosure,
including whether the regulatory system was such that their incentives to do so
were affected: paras 294 et seq.

Fn 726 See also M.6568 *Cisco Systems/NDS Group* (23 July 2012), paras 113–115;
M.6560 *EQT VI/BSN Medical* (7 August 2012); and M.7337 *IMS Health/Cegedim
Business* (19 December 2014), paras 239 et seq.

Customer foreclosure. In respect of the incentive to foreclose, see, eg M.7270
Ceské Aeroholding/Travel Service/Ceské Aerolinie (18 December 2014), paras
121–123.   **8.232**

Fn 728 For a further example, see M.6944 *Thermo Fisher Scientific/Life Technologies*
(26 November 2013), paras 362 et seq.

Fn 730 See, for example, M.6314 *Telefónica UK/Vodafone UK/EE/JV* (4 September 2012) para 249.

(ii) Conglomerate effects

8.234 **Conglomerate effects.**
Fn 733 See, eg M.7337 *IMS Health/Cegedim Business* (19 December 2014), paras 262 et seq.

8.235 **Anti-competitive foreclosure.** For a recent example of the Commission investigating potential conglomerate effects on closely related markets, see M.7292 *DEMB/Mondelez/Charger Opco* (5 May 2015), paras 618 et seq. The Commission found that the JV would own a number of 'must-have' brands across various different coffee markets, and considered whether it would be able to impose weaker brands on retailers by bundling. In that case it found that the merged entity would not be likely to be able to engage in such foreclosure, as its competitors also owned a portfolio of products and many retailers' practice was to negotiate separately for each type of coffee product.

The Commission may also investigate potential conglomerate effects where the parties have market power in geographically neighbouring markets. In M.7332 *BSkyB/Sky Deutschland/Sky Italia* (11 September 2014), paras 130 et seq, it considered whether the concentration of parties with significant market power in the UK and Ireland, Germany and Austria, and Italy, respectively, could increase BSkyB's negotiating power in relation to licensors of audio-visual content and TV channel suppliers, by combining negotiations and contracts in different EEA territories; or could result in other distributors being *de facto* cut out of the negotiation process for key content.

On whether the merged entity would have the economic incentive to foreclose, see for example M.6671 *LBO France/Aviapartner* (30 November 2012), paras 152 et seq; and M.6584 *Vodafone/Cable & Wireless Worldwide* (3 July 2012), para 109.

Fn 736 As part of its simplification of procedures under the Merger Regulation, on 5 December 2013 the Commission adopted Regulation 1269/2013, amending Regulation 802/2004 implementing Council Regulation 139/2004 on the control of concentrations between undertakings: OJ 2013 L336/1 ('the Amended Implementation Regulation'). The Amended Implementation Regulation includes revised annexes including a revised Form CO. It entered into force on 1 January 2014. The revised Form CO increases the market share threshold on closely related markets from 25 per cent to 30 per cent, and requires it to be applied to all plausible market definitions: Form CO, question 6.3(b).

Fn 738 See also M.6671 *LBO France/Aviapartner* (30 November 2012), paras 152 et seq.

Portfolios of consumer goods. For a recent example, see M.7292 *DEMB/* **8.236**
Mondelez/Charger Opco (5 May 2015), paras 618 et seq. The Commission found
that the JV would own a number of 'must-have' brands across various different
coffee markets, and considered whether it would be able to impose weaker brands
on retailers by bundling. In that case it found that the merged entity would not
be likely to be able to engage in such foreclosure, as its competitors also owned a
portfolio of products and many retailers' practice was to negotiate separately for
each type of coffee product.

Tying or bundling of related products. **8.237**
Fn 746 See also M.6568 *Cisco Systems/NDS Group* (23 July 2012), paras 97–103
and 110–112.

Concerns regarding interoperability. The Commission's decision in M.6281 **8.238**
Microsoft/Skype (7 October 2011), discussed in the main text, was upheld by
the General Court in Case T-79/12 *Cisco Systems & Messagenet v Commission*,
EU:T:2013: 635. The Court held that the concerns identified by the appellants,
which centred on the merged entity creating an integrated product with preferential interoperability (as between Skype and 'Lync', Microsoft's communications
software program aimed at undertakings) were too uncertain to be considered a
direct and immediate effect of the concentration. They depended on a series of
factors which were not all certain to occur in the sufficiently near future: paras
121–122. The Court also held that there were no tangible factors to support the
conclusion that the merged entity would have the ability and incentive to implement a foreclosure strategy, for example as there was no tangible evidence of the
existence, scale or development of demand for such a product; there was sufficient
time for the entity's competitors to develop commercial strategies to meet any
foreclosure strategy that might be adopted; and in the absence of evidence of
demand for such a product it was difficult to assess whether a foreclosure strategy
would be profitable for the new entity: paras 123 et seq.

In M.6564 *ARM/Giesecke & Devrient/ Gemalto/JV* (7 November 2012) the
Commission considered that ARM had the necessary market power in the
market upstream from the JV, and an incentive, to degrade the interoperability of its product with the downstream products of the JV's competitors. The
Commission accepted commitments to make interoperability information available on the same terms to the JV and its competitors, and granted Phase I clearance. In M.6490 *EADS/Israel Aerospace Industries/JV* (16 July 2012), para 28, the
Commission considered that where a joint venture was established to develop
a new product for towing aircraft, a key part of its commercial strategy was to
ensure the product's interoperability with different types of aircraft. There was
no incentive to restrict interoperability, as that would reduce demand for the new
product.

(g) Other considerations relevant to substantive appraisal

(i) Buyer power

8.240 **Increased buyer power for the merged entity.** See also M.7000 *Ziggo/Liberty Global* (10 October 2014). The Commission granted Phase II clearance to the merger of two operators of cable networks in the Netherlands, subject to commitments. Although the parties' networks did not overlap, they acquired the same content from TV broadcasters for inclusion in their pay-TV services. The Commission considered that the concentration would increase Liberty's buyer power as against TV channel broadcasters, and thereby allow it to hinder innovation in the delivery of audio-visual content over the internet: paras 362 et seq. Liberty therefore committed to divestment of its premium pay-TV channel, to terminate the clauses in its channel carriage agreements that limited broadcasters' ability to offer their channels and content over the internet, and to refrain from including such clauses in its future agreements for eight years.

8.241 **Customers' countervailing buyer power.**
Fn 755 See also M.6843 *Siemens/Invensys Rail* (18 April 2013), paras 52–53, in which the Commission concluded that customers' sophisticated tendering procedures gave them significant countervailing buyer power; and M.6789 *Bertalsman/ Pearson/Penguin Random House* (5 April 2013), paras 245–246, in which it concluded that there was countervailing buyer power in circumstances where the largest five customers accounted for more than 50 per cent of sales in the UK, and more than 75 per cent of sales in Ireland, and the majority of the competitors who responded to the Commission's investigation considered that those customers typically exercise their bargaining power during negotiations.

Fn 758 See also M.6535 *Glory/Talaris Topco* (3 July 2012), paras 47–49; and M.7023 *Publicis/Omnicom* (9 January 2014), in which the Commission approved the merger at Phase I, in particular in view of the bidding nature of the markets which would facilitate switching if the merged entity were to increase its prices or to decrease the quality of its services.

Fn 759 See also M.6611 *Arla Foods/Milk Link* (27 September 2012), paras 114–118.

(ii) Efficiencies

8.242 **Efficiencies.** In M.6490 *EADS/Israel Aerospace Industries/JV* (16 July 2012), paras 20 et seq, the Commission considered that a JV set up to develop and produce an entirely new product 'is *a priori* unlikely to have negative effects on final consumers'.

8.243 **Proving efficiencies.**
Fn 764 The decision in M.6166 *Deutsche Börse/NYSE Euronext* (1 February 2012) was upheld in Case T-175/12 *Deutsche Börse v Commission*, EU:T:2015:148, [2015] 4 CMLR 1187, paras 267 et seq. The General Court in particular upheld the

Commission's approach of considering not only what efficiencies might arise from the proposed concentration, but also whether the merged entity would claw those efficiencies back from customers: para 273.

In the recently published M.6905 *INEOS/Solvay/JV* (8 May 2014), paras 1090 et seq the Commission accepted that some of the claimed efficiencies would result from the concentration, but concluded that there was doubt as to the time at which those efficiencies would be achieved; whether the expected benefits would be passed through to consumers; and the magnitude, merger specificity, verifiability, timeliness and pass-on of efficiencies in a scenario in which the remedies proposed in the commitments were implemented.

For other examples, see M.6497 *Hutchinson 3G Austria/Orange Austria* (12 December 2012), paras 403 et seq (the efficiencies claimed were not sufficiently verifiable); M.6690 *Syniverse/Mach* (29 May 2013), paras 652–654 (the efficiencies claimed were not verified, and also given the extremely high market share that the merged entity would hold it was very doubtful that any efficiencies would be passed through to consumers); and M.7421 *Orange/Jazztel* (19 May 2015), para 747 (some of the claimed efficiencies would result from the concentration, but they were not sufficient to outweigh the anti-competitive effects of the merger).

(iii) *Failing firm defence*

Criteria of failing firm defence.   In two recent decisions, the Commission **8.244** has concluded that the criteria of the failing firm defence are met. In M.6360 *Nynas/Shell/Harburg* (2 September 2013) it accepted that the operator of the Harburg refinery for napthenic base and process oils was economically unsustainable and would exit the market if the concentration did not proceed. As there were no alternative buyers for the assets, the most likely alternative scenario to the proposed transaction would be the closure of the refinery, such that the reduction of the number of competitors in the market would occur anyway and would not be caused by the acquisition itself. Moreover, the closure of the refinery would lead to EEA demand being met by imports and consequently higher prices for consumers due to import costs. In M.6796 *Aegean/Olympic II* (9 October 2013) the Commission approved the merger it had previously prohibited in M.5830 *Olympic/Aegean Airlines* (26 January 2011). It was satisfied that Olympic was likely to go out of business if the concentration did not proceed, as its sole shareholder had indicated an intention to withdraw its financial support and there were no alternative buyers for the assets. The decision contrasts with that in M.6447 *IAG/bmi* (30 March 2012) section VII (appeal in Case T-344/12 *Virgin Atlantic Airways v Commission* withdrawn: Order of 15 July 2014), where the Commission considered that the failing firm defence was not met as the assets of bmi consisted primarily in slot pairs at Heathrow airport, and these assets were not likely to exit the market.

Fn 766 The appeal against the Commission's decision in M.6447 *IAG/bmi* (30 March 2012) in Case T-344/12 *Virgin Atlantic Airways v Commission* was withdrawn: Order of 15 July 2014. See also the update to the main text, above, on M.6796 *Aegean / Olympic II* (9 October 2013).

(h) Coordinative aspects of certain full-function joint ventures

(i) In general

8.245 **Spill-over effects.** In M.6477 *BP/Chevron/ENI/Sonangol/Total/JV* (16 May 2012), paras 30–31, the Commission noted that the JV agreements included a mechanism to prevent the parents acquiring commercially sensitive information, and that the market was not sufficiently transparent to facilitate coordination. In M.6800 *PRSfM/STIM/GEMA/JV* (16 June 2015), para 299, the Commission found that on the widest possible market definition the parents and the JV were active in the same market; however, as they would serve different customers and offer different licences (the JV offering multi-territorial licences only, and for different repertoire) the concentration was unlikely to lead to coordination.

Fn 770 See also M.6485 *Euler Hermes/Mapfre/Mapfre CC* (20 September 2012), para 23; and M.6314 *Telefónica UK/Vodafone UK/EE/JV* (4 September 2012), para 585.

(ii) Concentrations with an EU dimension

8.246 **Article 2(4) of the Merger Regulation.**
Fn 772 For a recent example, see M.6905 *INEOS/Solvay/JV* (8 May 2014).

5. Judicial Review by the EU Courts

(c) Persons entitled to appeal

8.253 **Competitors and customers.**
Fn 807 See also Case T-79/12 *Cisco Systems & Messagenet v Commission*, EU:T:2013:635, at paras 33 et seq.

(d) Scope of judicial review

(i) Application of the law

8.260 **Substantive issues.** The General Court confirmed in Case T-79/12 *Cisco Systems & Messagenet v Commission*, EU:T:2013:635, at para 46, that the standard of proof it will apply in reviewing decisions adopted under Article 6 of the Merger Regulation is the same as that which it applies when reviewing decisions adopted under Article 8.

(iii) Economic issues

Standard of review   8.263

Fn 833 See also Case T-471/11 *Éditions Odile Jacob v Commission*, EU:T:2014:739, paras 137 and 146.

(e) Standard of proof

Borderline cases.   The General Court confirmed in Case T-79/12 *Cisco Systems* 8.266
& Messagenet v Commission, EU:T:2013:635, at para 46, that the standard of proof it will apply in reviewing decisions adopted under Article 6 of the Merger Regulation is the same as that which it applies when reviewing decisions adopted under Article 8, namely the balance of probabilities as to the most likely economic outcome. It dismissed an argument that in an Article 6 decision the Commission must show beyond reasonable doubt that the concentration does not give rise to competition concerns.

6. Application of Articles 101 and 102 in Field of Mergers and Acquisitions

(a) Background

Application of Article 102 to acquisitions.   In M.7047 *Microsoft/Nokia* 8.269
(4 December 2013), the Commission considered concerns expressed by certain respondents that Nokia divesting itself of a part of its business, which would be acquired by Microsoft, would lead to the removal of various competitive constraints to which Nokia had previously been subject on its exploitation of its patent portfolio. The Commission concluded that these concerns were outside the scope of the Merger Regulation, as the regime only covers the likely post-transaction conduct of the merged entity, or the merged entity together with third parties: paras 222 et seq. The concerns expressed would be addressed by Article 102. The Commission noted its position on the obligations of holders of standard essential patents to licence on fair, reasonable and non-discriminatory ('FRAND') terms, and on the application of Article 102 to an undertaking seeking injunctions in circumstances where FRAND terms have not been agreed (see the discussion in paragraph 9.060 of the main text, and the update thereto).

7. National Merger Control and International Cooperation

(a) National merger control regimes within EEA

National control where application of the Merger Regulation is contested. 8.289
The European Commission has prohibited the concentration notified in M.6663

Ryanair/Aer Lingus III (27 February 2013) (appeal, in Case T-260/13 *Ryanair v Commission*, withdrawn: Order of 28 October 2015). The Competition Commission subsequently concluded in *Ryanair Holdings and Aer Lingus Group*, decision of 28 August 2013, that Ryanair's acquisition of a minority shareholding in Aer Lingus has led, or may be expected to lead, to a substantial lessening of competition in the markets for air passenger services between Great Britain and the Republic of Ireland, and ordered partial divestiture. The Competition Appeal Tribunal, in *Ryanair Holdings v Competition and Markets Authority* [2014] CAT 3, upheld the Competition Commission's decision, and dismissed the argument that it breached the duty of sincere cooperation under Article 4(3) TEU to order divestiture while Ryanair's appeal to the General Court was pending. The Tribunal held that as the divestiture order concerned Ryanair's existing minority shareholding, rather than the proposed acquisition that was under consideration by the European Commission and is currently before the General Court, there was no breach of the duty.

8.291 **Outline of national merger control rules in the EEA.** As at 31 August 2014, the following entries should be substituted at the appropriate place in the table:

Belgium	(a) combined turnover in Belgium in excess of €100m; and (b) at least two parties each have turnover in Belgium in excess of €40m	Mandatory prior notification to Belgian Competition Authority
Italy	(a) combined turnover in Italy of €489m; or (b) target has turnover in Italy of €49m *(These thresholds are revised annually to take account of inflation; above figures were revised in March 2014.)*	Mandatory prior notification to the Autorità Garante della Concorrenza e del Mercato (Competition Authority)
Germany	(a) combined worldwide turnover of €500m; and (b) at least one party has turnover in Germany of €25m; and (c) at least one other party has turnover in Germany of €5m Exceptionally notification may not be necessary if there is an independent (non-affiliated) undertaking, merging with another undertaking, which has worldwide turnover of not more than €10m; *(NB: If the only relevant market is a minor market where goods/services have been offered for at least five years and total annual turnover was less than €15m in the last calendar year, the transaction must be notified. However, such transaction will not be prohibited.)*	Mandatory prior notification to Bundeskartellamt (Federal Cartel Office or BKartA)

Netherlands	(a) combined worldwide turnover of €113.45m; and (b) at least two parties each have turnover in the Netherlands of €30m	Mandatory prior notification to the Autoriteit Consument en Market (Authority for Consumers and Markets)
Spain	(a) combined turnover in Spain of €240m; and (b) at least two parties each have turnover in Spain of €60m OR (c) creation or strengthening of combined market share in Spain of 30%, or acquisition of target which has 30% market share (even if no overlap). (This threshold does not apply if target's turnover in Spain was under €10m in the last financial year, provided that the parties' individual or combined market share is under 50%)	Mandatory prior notification to Comisión Nacional de los Mercados y la Competencia (National Commission on Markets and Competition)
United Kingdom	(a) target has turnover in the UK of £70m (c.€82.42m); or (b) as a result of the transaction, parties have a share of supply of goods or services of any description of 25% or more in the UK (or a substantial part of the UK)	Voluntary notification to the Competition and Markets Authority

(c) Cooperation with countries outside the EEA

Canada, Japan and Korea and Switzerland.   The EU has signed a cooperation **8.297** agreement on competition matters with the Swiss Confederation, subject to ratification: see Press Release IP/13/444 (17 May 2013).

In addition, a memorandum to increase cooperation between DG Competition and the Competition Commission of India was signed on 21 November 2013: see Press Release IP/13/1143 (21 November 2013).

Multilateral international cooperation.   As part of its simplification of pro- **8.298** cedures under the Merger Regulation, on 5 December 2013 the Commission adopted Regulation 1269/2013, amending Regulation 802/2004 implementing Council Regulation 139/2004 on the control of concentrations between undertakings: OJ 2013 L336/1 ('the Amended Implementation Regulation'). The Amended Implementation Regulation includes revised annexes including a revised Form CO. It entered into force on 1 January 2014. The revised Form CO encourages parties voluntarily to facilitate international cooperation between the Commission and the competition authorities of non-EEA countries that are also reviewing the concentration, by submitting a list of which non-EEA competition authorities are reviewing the concentration: Revised Form CO, question 1.10.

An example of multilateral international cooperation is M.6944 *Thermo Fisher Scientific/Life Technologies* (26 November 2013), where the Commission cooperated during the pre-notification and Phase I stages in particular with the US Federal Trade Commission and the Australian Competition and Consumer Commission in the mutual exchange of evidence; and also cooperated with the Ministry of Commerce of China, the Japan Fair Trade Commission, the Competition Bureau of Canada and the Commerce Commission of New Zealand (see also Press Release IP/13/1167 (26 November 2013)).

9

INTELLECTUAL PROPERTY RIGHTS

1. Introduction

Licensing of the rights.   On 21 March 2014 the Commission adopted Regulation   **9.004**
316/2014 on the application of Article 101(3) of the Treaty on the Functioning
of the European Union to categories of technology transfer agreements, OJ 2014
L93/17. It entered into force on 1 May 2014, and replaces Regulation 772/2004,
which expired on 30 April 2014. The individual changes are noted in the relevant
paragraph updates, below.

2. Free Movement and Intellectual Property Rights

Generally.   The Court of Justice upheld the legality of the Council's decision   **9.008**
authorising the use of the enhanced cooperation procedure under Article 20
TEU in the area of the creation of a unitary patent (Council Decision 2011/167/
EU of 10 March 2011): see Joined Cases C-274&295/11 *Spain & Italy v Council*,
EU:C:2013:240, [2013] 3 CMLR 623.

(b) The right of production or reproduction

Trade marks.   In Case C-561/11 *Fédération Cynologique Internationale v*   **9.014**
Federación Canina Internacional de Perros de Pura Raza, EU:C:2013:91, the
Court of Justice held that a 'third party', whom a trade mark proprietor would
be justified under Article 36 in suing for infringement of his mark, includes
a third-party proprietor of a later registered Community trade mark. The later
registered trade mark does not have to be declared invalid before the proprietor
of the earlier trade mark can enforce his rights. In Case C-661/11 *Martin Y Paz
v David Depuydt*, EU:C:2013:577, paras 57 et seq, the Court confirmed that a
trade mark proprietor who has previously consented to shared use of his trade
mark is entitled to withdraw that consent and regain exclusive use.

(c) The right of distribution

(ii) Conditions for the exhaustion of the distribution right

9.026 **Goods in transit through Union territory.**
Fn 67 See also Regulation 608/2013 concerning customs enforcement of intellectual property rights and repealing Regulation 1383/2003, adopted on 12 June 2013: OJ 2013 L181/15.

9.027 **Markets in which intellectual property protection is not available.** In Case C-98/13 *Blomqvist v Rolex*, EU:C:2014:55, the Court of Justice considered the position of the holder of an intellectual property right where counterfeit goods are put on the market in an EU Member State in which intellectual property protection is available, by a seller located outside the EEA in a third country where such protection is not. A Danish national purchased a watch from a seller located in Hong Kong, using the seller's website, and the watch was subsequently seised by the Danish customs authority as a counterfeit 'Rolex'. The Court held that the sale of goods to a customer in a Member State, via a website, is a 'distribution to the public' of copyright-protected goods, under Article 4 of the Copyright Directive, or a 'use in the course of trade' of a trademark, under Article 5 of the Trademark Directive. The fact that the sale was made from a third country does not deprive the intellectual property right holder of its protection where the sale was made to a customer within the EU.

Similarly, in Case C-516/13 *Dimensione Direct Sales v Knoll International*, EU:C:2015:315, paras 26 et seq, the Court of Justice held that there is also an infringement of the right of exclusive distribution where a trader who does not hold the copyright engages in a commercial act, such as offering for sale or advertising, in the territory of the Member State in which works are protected. Dimensione had advertised furniture for sale, in particular designs in which Knoll owned the copyright, on its website and in newspapers and magazines in Germany. The Court confirmed that it is not necessary that there should be a transfer of ownership to a purchaser on the basis of an offer for sale in order for the rights holder's rights to be infringed.

(e) The exclusive right to provide services

9.040 **Public performance.** In Case C-283/10 *Circul Globus Bucureşti*, EU:C:2011:772, [2011] ECR I-12031, para 41, the Court of Justice clarified that the concept of 'communication to the public' in Article 3(1) of Directive 2001/29 (the Copyright Directive) is limited to situations where the public is not present at the place where the performance or direct presentation takes place. It does not include, therefore, a communication which is carried out directly in a place open to the public, such as a circus.

9.042 **Exhaustion of rights: Coditel (No. 1).** In Case C-607/11 *ITV Broadcasting and others*, EU:C:2013:147, [2013] 3 CMLR 1 the Court of Justice considered the position under Directive 2001/29 (the Copyright Directive) in connection with a company that captures television broadcasts and retransmits them via the internet in real time. It held that the original broadcast does not exhaust the right to communicate to the public, and the retransmission via the internet constitutes a 'communication to the public' within Article 3(1) that the copyright holder is entitled to prohibit. The Court of Justice held that it was immaterial whether the retransmitting company could be considered a competitor of the broadcasters: para 47. The Court has also confirmed in Case C-466/12 *Svensson v Retriever Sverige*, EU:C:2014:76, [2014] 3 CMLR 73, that providing hyperlinks to another website which contains protected works is an act of 'communication' within the scope of the Directive; however, if that other website can be accessed without restriction by members of the public, then the provision of a hyperlink is not a new communication of the protected works that the rights holder is entitled to prohibit. The person providing the hyperlink is a member of the public to whom the works have already been communicated by the first website.

Exhaustion of rights: Football Association Premier League.   The Outer House   **9.043** of the Scottish Court of Sessions has followed the Court of Justice's judgment in Cases C-403&429/08 *Football Association Premier League v QC Leisure/Murphy v Media Protection Services*, EU:C:2011:631, [2011] ECR I-9083, [2012] 1 CMLR 769, in *Scottish Premier League v Lisini Pub Management Company* [2013] CSOH 48.

The Commission has launched an investigation into whether the licensing arrangements between several US film studios and European pay-TV broadcasters are in breach of Article 101, on a similar basis to the arrangements found to be infringing in *Football Association Premier League*: COMP/40023 *Cross-border access to pay-TV content;* and has issued a statement of objections: IP/15/5432 (23 July 2015).

Fn 122   In Case C-351/12 *OSA*, EU:C:2014:110, [2014] 4 CMLR 671, at paras 72 et seq, the Court of Justice considered that preventing a user of protected works from accessing the services of collecting societies located in other Member States did not go beyond what was necessary to protect intellectual property rights. The territorial protection, and monitoring, of rights is the most effective means of achieving that protection.

3. Articles 101 and 102 and the Enforcement of Intellectual Property Rights

(b) Other abusive conduct

Acquisition of competing technology.   In COMP/39612 *Perindopril (Servier)*,   **9.058** decision of 9 July 2013, the Commission found that by holding a number of secondary patents for the ACE inhibitor drug perindopril and acquiring the most advanced source of non-protected technology, and then by entering into reverse payment settlement agreements with the five generics companies that sought to enter the market, Servier had abused its dominant position in the market, contrary to Article 102. On appeal, Case T-691/14, not yet decided.

9.059   Abuse of regulatory process.   The Court of Justice dismissed the appeals in Case C-457/10P *AstraZeneca v Commission*, EU:C:2012:770, [2013] 4 CMLR 233. It was argued that deliberate fraud or deceit should be required in order to find an abuse in the context of alleged misrepresentations to public authorities for the purposes of acquiring exclusive rights: para 71. The Court of Justice did not directly rule on the point, but held that AstraZeneca had, on the facts of that case, deliberately misled the relevant patent offices, and that a consideration of whether a dominant undertaking has misled the authorities 'may' vary according to the circumstances of each case: paras 74 et seq. It suggested, however, that not every objectively wrong representation will be an abuse, where it was made unintentionally and immediately rectified: para 99.

9.060   Patent ambushes.   The Court of Justice in Case C-170/13 *Huawei v ZTE*, EU:C:2015:477 confirmed that a refusal by the proprietor of a standard essential patent ('SEP') to grant a licence on fair, reasonable and non-discriminatory ('FRAND') terms, in circumstances where the patent has acquired SEP status as a result of the proprietor having irrevocably undertaken to the standard-setting body that it will license on FRAND terms, may also in principle be contrary to Article 102: para 53. The proprietor's undertaking does not, however, deprive it of its right to bring an action before the courts of a Member State to enforce its patent, so long as it complies with specific requirements when it does so. These are to notify the alleged infringer of the SEP and its breach; to make a specific, written offer of a licence on FRAND terms specifying the royalty and the way in which it has been calculated. The alleged infringer must respond in good faith, and without delay. If it does not accept the offer, it must promptly make a written counter-offer that corresponds to FRAND terms, and if its counter-offer is rejected and it is using the teachings of the SEP then from the point of rejection it must provide appropriate security. The parties may agree to submit the determination of the amount of the royalty to a third party. If the proprietor has complied with the requirements incumbent upon it, or if the alleged infringer has failed to comply with the requirements incumbent upon it, then it is not an abuse of the proprietor's dominant position for it to commence litigation to enforce its patent.

See also the Commission's investigation into alleged abusive conduct in relation to IPR used in international telecoms standards. In COMP/39985 *Motorola – enforcement of ETSI standards essential patents*, decision of 29 April 2014, the Commission found that Motorola breached Article 102 by seeking an injunction in Germany against Apple for breach of its SEPs (which were essential to meeting the

European Telecommunications Standardisation Institute's (ETSI) GPRS standard, part of the GSM standard, which is a key industry standard for mobile and wireless communications), in circumstances where it had committed to license on FRAND terms, and where Apple was willing to enter into a licence agreement and to be bound by a determination by the German Court of the FRAND terms. However, in view of the novelty of the infringement finding, no fine has been imposed. The Commission accepted commitments from Samsung in COMP/39939 *Samsung – enforcement of ETSI standards essential patents*, decision of 29 April 2014. In its preliminary assessment, the Commission considered that Samsung had infringed Article 102 by seeking injunctions against Apple in several Member States to enforce its SEPs that were essential to complying with ETSI's 3G UMTS standard (a key standard for mobile and wireless communications), and that Samsung had committed to license on FRAND terms. The Commission accepted commitments under which Samsung agrees, in essence, for a period of five years not to seek an injunction before any court or tribunal in the EEA for infringement of its SEPs implemented in mobile devices against a potential licensee that agrees to, and complies with, a particular framework set out in the commitments decision for determining the terms of a licence.

Fn 183 The appeals by Hynix Semiconductor (now trading as SK Hynix Inc) in Joined Cases T-148&149/10 against COMP/38636 *Rambus*, decision of 9 December 2009, were withdrawn on 5 July 2013.

On the Commission's investigation into alleged abusive conduct in relation to IPR used in international telecoms standards, see the update to the main paragraph, above.

The pharmaceutical sector inquiry report. The Commission has continued to **9.061** monitor patent settlements between originator and generics companies, and its Reports are also available on the DG Comp website: First Report of 5 July 2010, in respect of the period mid-2008 to end 2009; Second Report of 6 July 2011, in respect of the period January to December 2010; Third Report of 25 July 2012, in respect of the period January to December 2011; Fourth Report of 9 December 2013, in respect of the period January to December 2012; and Fifth Report of 5 December 2014, in respect of the period January to December 2013.

Following the sector inquiry report, the Commission has taken enforcement action against several originator companies and the generic companies with which they entered into patent settlement agreements. Lundbeck and four groups of generics companies have been fined for infringing Article 101 by entering into 'reverse payment' settlement agreements, in respect of the antidepressant drug citalopram: COMP/39226 *Lundbeck*, decision of 19 June 2013. The decision is under appeal: Cases T-460/13, etc, not yet decided. In COMP/39685 *Johnson & Johnson and Novartis*, decision of 10 December 2013, the Commission found that a 'co-promotion' agreement under which Novartis' Dutch subsidiary,

Sandoz, had strong financial incentives to refrain from entering the Netherlands market for the analgesic drug fentanyl infringed Article 101. In COMP/39612 *Perindopril (Servier)*, decision of 9 July 2013, as well as finding that reverse settlement agreements between Servier and five generics companies breached Article 101, the Commission found that Servier's conduct infringed Article 102. It considered that by holding a number of secondary patents for the ACE inhibitor drug perindopril and acquiring the most advanced source of non-protected technology, and then by entering into reverse payment settlement agreements with the five generics companies that sought to enter the market, Servier had abused its dominant position in the market. On appeal, Case T-691/14, not yet decided.

Similar concerns regarding patent settlements have arisen in the United States, and the US Supreme Court judgment in *Federal Trade Commission v Actavis and others*, of 17 June 2013, 570 U.S. (2013) clarified that in the United States a 'rule of reason' approach is to be applied to antitrust scrutiny of such agreements, that is, the courts will consider in the light of all the relevant facts and circumstances whether a particular agreement has overall pro-competitive or anti-competitive effects on the relevant market (see further paragraphs 2.104 et seq of the main text).

In France, the Autorité de la concurrence has taken a number of decisions against originator companies for adopting strategies of unjustifiedly denigrating their generic competitors. On 14 May 2013 it fined Sanofi-Aventis €40.6 million for abuse of dominance by denigrating the generic versions of clopidogrel, an anti-platelet medication used to prevent relapses of serious cardiovascular diseases: Decision 13-D-11 of 14 May 2013. Sanofi-Aventis had adopted a strategy of questioning, with doctors and pharmacists, the efficacy and safety of the generics' products, and intimating that the doctors/pharmacists could be held liable for any problems they caused, in order to limit generic entry and protect the market position of its branded clopidogrel 'Plavix', and its own generic 'Clopidogrel Winthrop'. The Autorité found Sanofi-Aventis' communications were based on unsubstantiated assertion. See also ECN Brief 03/2013, p8. The appeal to the Cour d'Appel de Paris was dismissed, by decision of 18 December 2014. On 19 December 2013 the Autorité fined Schering-Plough €15.3 million for abuse of dominance by unjustifiedly denigrating the generic version of buprenorphine, used to treat opiate addiction: Decision 13-D-21 of December 2013; appeal to the Cour d'Appel de Paris, dismissed on 26 May 2015. See also ECN Brief 01/2014, p5. The Autorité is still investigating a possible breach in respect of the analgesic fentanyl.

9.062 **Abusive defence of patent litigation.** See also the Court of Justice in Case C-170/13 *Huawei v ZTE*, EU:C:2015:477, regarding the abusive commencement of patent litigation. A dominant undertaking brought proceedings before a Member State court to enforce a standard essential patent ('SEP'), in circumstances where the patent had acquired SEP status as a result of the proprietor having irrevocably undertaken to the standard-setting body that it will license on fair, reasonable and non-discriminatory ('FRAND') terms. The Court held that to bring such proceedings may in principle be contrary to Article 102. The proprietor's undertaking to the standard setting body does not deprive it of its right to bring an action before the courts of a Member State to enforce its patent, but it must comply with specific requirements when it does so. These are to notify the alleged infringer of the SEP and its breach; to make a specific, written offer of a licence on FRAND terms specifying the royalty and the way in which it has been calculated. The alleged infringer must respond in good faith, and without delay. If it does not accept the offer, it must promptly make a written counter-offer that corresponds to FRAND terms, and if its counter-offer is rejected and it is using the teachings of the SEP then from the point of rejection it must provide appropriate security. The parties may agree to submit the determination of the amount of the royalty to a third party. If the proprietor has complied with the requirements incumbent upon it, or if the alleged infringer has failed to comply with the requirements incumbent upon it, then it is not an abuse of the proprietor's dominant position for it to commence litigation to enforce its patent.

Unfair prices.   See also Case C-351/12 *OSA*, EU:C:2014:110, [2014] 4 CMLR   **9.063**
671. The Court of Justice held that if a collecting society charges fees that are appreciably higher than those charged by collecting societies in other Member States, without the difference being objectively justified by the different conditions in those other Member States, those fees may infringe Article 102.

4. Collective Licensing of Intellectual Property Rights

Generally.   On the application of Article 101 to an agreement transferring   **9.065**
standard essential patent ('SEP') rights, see *Unwired Planet International v Huawei and others* [2015] EWHC 2097 (Pat). The High Court struck out a defence to an infringement action in which it had been contended that the agreement to transfer the SEPs to Unwired Planet, a 'patent assertion entity', was void under Article 101 for failing fully and effectively to confer on potential licensees the right to obtain from the transferee a licence on FRAND terms; or for failing to transfer the FRAND obligation previously undertaken by the transferor, as opposed to requiring the transferee to offer a new FRAND undertaking (meaning, in particular, that the transferee would not need to have regard to the terms on which the transferor had hitherto licensed commercial parties under those patents, as part of the obligation to offer terms that are non-discriminatory). The Court refused to strike out two further defences. Under the first, Samsung argued that the agreement to transfer the SEPs was void under Article 101 as it permitted the transferor to retain a substantial share in the licensing revenue

generated by the transferee and to achieve higher royalties. Under the second, the agreement was alleged to be unlawful and void as it contained payment terms encouraging or requiring the transferee to charge higher royalties. The decision to strike out the first defence is on appeal to the Court of Appeal, not yet decided.

Fn 200 The Commission has issued revised Guidelines on the application of Article 101 of the Treaty on the Functioning of the European Union to technology transfer agreements, OJ 2014 C89/3 ('Revised Technology Transfer Guidelines'), to accompany Regulation 316/2014 on the application of Article 101(3) of the Treaty on the Functioning of the European Union to categories of technology transfer agreements, OJ 2014 L93/17, replacing Regulation 772/2004 which expired on 30 April 2014.

(a) Patent pools

9.066 Pooling protected technologies. The Commission has issued revised Guidelines on the application of Article 101 of the Treaty on the Functioning of the European Union to technology transfer agreements, OJ 2014 C89/3 ('Revised Technology Transfer Guidelines'), to accompany Regulation 316/2014 on the application of Article 101(3) of the Treaty on the Functioning of the European Union to categories of technology transfer agreements, OJ 2014 L93/17, replacing Regulation 772/2004 which expired on 30 April 2014. The Revised Technology Transfer Guidelines clarify that a technology is 'essential' either where it is essential to produce a particular product or to carry out a particular process to which the pooled technologies relate, or where it is essential to produce such a product or carry out such a process in accordance with a standard which includes the pooled technologies: para 252 of the Revised Technology Transfer Guidelines.

9.067 Competition risk: price-fixing and market-sharing.
Fn 202 The Commission has issued revised Guidelines on the application of Article 101 of the Treaty on the Functioning of the European Union to technology transfer agreements, OJ 2014 C89/3 ('Revised Technology Transfer Guidelines'), to accompany Regulation 316/2014 on the application of Article 101(3) of the Treaty on the Functioning of the European Union to categories of technology transfer agreements, OJ 2014 L93/17, replacing Regulation 772/2004 which expired on 30 April 2014. The reference to para 219 of the previous guidelines (OJ 2004 C101/2) should be read as para 255 of the Revised Technology Transfer Guidelines.

9.068 Competition risk: foreclosure of competing technologies.
Fn 205 The Commission has issued revised Guidelines on the application of Article 101 of the Treaty on the Functioning of the European Union to technology transfer agreements, OJ 2014 C89/3 ('Revised Technology Transfer Guidelines'), to accompany Regulation 316/2014 on the application of Article 101(3) of the Treaty on the Functioning of the European Union to categories of technology

transfer agreements, OJ 2014 L93/17, replacing Regulation 772/2004 which expired on 30 April 2014. The reference to paras 221 and 222 of the previous guidelines (OJ 2004 C101/2) should be read as paras 262–264 of the Revised Technology Transfer Guidelines.

Access to the pooled work or technology. On 21 March 2014 the **9.069** Commission adopted Regulation 316/2014 on the application of Article 101(3) of the Treaty on the Functioning of the European Union to categories of technology transfer agreements, OJ 2014 L93/17. It entered into force on 1 May 2014, and replaces Regulation 772/2004, which expired on 30 April 2014. At the same time, it issued revised Guidelines on the application of Article 101 of the Treaty on the Functioning of the European Union to technology transfer agreements, OJ 2014 C89/3 ('Revised Technology Transfer Guidelines'). The Revised Technology Transfer Guidelines clarify that licensing out from the patent pool is generally a multiparty agreement, taking into account that the contributors commonly determine the conditions for such licensing out, and it is therefore not covered by the block exemption: para 247 of the Revised Technology Transfer Guidelines. Individual licences granted to third parties will therefore fall to be considered individually under Article 101, at least where they are concluded on the basis of common conditions, rather than under Regulation 316/2014.

(b) Copyright collecting societies

Pooling protected works. The General Court has upheld the Commission's **9.070** decision in COMP/38698 *CISAC Agreements*, decision of 16 July 2008, [2009] 4 CMLR 577, regarding the clause in the collecting societies' agreement that prevented them from adding to their rights pools the rights of persons having nationality of one of the countries in which a competing society operates (referred to in the General Court's judgments as the 'membership clause'): Cases T-392, 401, 422, 432/08, judgments of 12 April 2013, [2013] 5 CMLR 15. It partially annulled the decision on other grounds in Cases T-392, 398, 401, 410, 411, 413–422, 425, 428, 432–434, 442/08, judgments of 12 April 2013.

On 26 February 2014, Directive 2014/26 on collective management of copyright and related rights and multi-territorial licensing of rights in musical works for online use in the internal market, was adopted: OJ 2014 L84/72.

Following the *CISAC* decision, and the collecting societies' subsequent move towards granting multi-territorial licences, in M.6800 *PRSfM/STIM/GEMA/JV* (16 June 2015), the Commission cleared a JV between three collecting societies that will undertake multi-territorial, multi-repertoire licensing of online performance rights, subject to commitments. The Commission did not consider that the concentration would be likely to lead to increased bargaining power and more onerous licensing terms, but it noted that the additional aggregation of any further repertoire, as a result of the JV entering into agreements with other collecting societies or certain publishers, would fall to be considered under Article 101: paras 302–303.

The Netherlands NCA has accepted commitments from the Dutch copyright collecting society to allow composers and songwriters more choice as to the rights they transfer to the society, after commencing an investigation into whether the society had abused a dominant position by requiring all rights be transferred to it, if a copyright holder wished to join the society, including the right to collect royalties for performances on the internet where the copyright holders would have the technical means to collect the royalties themselves, if they wished. See ECN Brief 03/2014, p6.

5. Licensing Intellectual Property Rights

(a) Introduction

9.072 Generally.   On 21 March 2014 the Commission adopted Regulation 316/2014 on the application of Article 101(3) of the Treaty on the Functioning of the European Union to categories of technology transfer agreements, OJ 2014 L93/17. It entered into force on 1 May 2014, and replaces Regulation 772/2004, which expired on 30 April 2014. At the same time, it issued revised Guidelines on the application of Article 101 of the Treaty on the Functioning of the European Union to technology transfer agreements, OJ 2014 C89/3 ('Revised Technology Transfer Guidelines').

9.075 Technology Transfer Guidelines.   The Commission has issued revised Guidelines on the application of Article 101 of the Treaty on the Functioning of the European Union to technology transfer agreements, OJ 2014 C89/3 ('Revised Technology Transfer Guidelines'), to accompany Regulation 316/2014 on the application of Article 101(3) of the Treaty on the Functioning of the European Union to categories of technology transfer agreements, OJ 2014 L93/17, replacing Regulation 772/2004 which expired on 30 April 2014.

Fn 236 The reference to para 131 of the previous guidelines (OJ 2004 C101/2) should be read as para 157 of the Revised Technology Transfer Guidelines.

Fn 238 The reference to paras 8, 9, 17 and 36 of the previous guidelines (OJ 2004 C101/2) should be read as paras 8, 9, 17 and 42 of the Revised Technology Transfer Guidelines.

9.076 Safe harbour.

Fn 239 The Commission has issued revised Guidelines on the application of Article 101 of the Treaty on the Functioning of the European Union to technology transfer agreements, OJ 2014 C89/3 ('Revised Technology Transfer Guidelines'), to accompany Regulation 316/2014 on the application of Article 101(3) of the Treaty on the Functioning of the European Union to categories of technology transfer agreements, OJ 2014 L93/17, replacing Regulation 772/2004 which expired on 30 April 2014. The reference to para 131 of the previous guidelines (OJ 2004 C101/2) should be read as para 157 of the Revised Technology Transfer Guidelines.

Factors relevant to the application of Article 101.   **9.077**
Fn 240 The Commission has issued revised Guidelines on the application of Article 101 of the Treaty on the Functioning of the European Union to technology transfer agreements, OJ 2014 C89/3 ('Revised Technology Transfer Guidelines'), to accompany Regulation 316/2014 on the application of Article 101(3) of the Treaty on the Functioning of the European Union to categories of technology transfer agreements, OJ 2014 L93/17, replacing Regulation 772/2004 which expired on 30 April 2014. The reference to para 11 of the previous guidelines (OJ 2004 C101/2) should be read as para 11 of the Revised Technology Transfer Guidelines.

Fn 241 The reference to paras 132 et seq of the previous guidelines (OJ 2004 C101/2) should be read as paras 159 et seq of the Revised Technology Transfer Guidelines.

Fn 242 The reference to para 140 of the previous guidelines (OJ 2004 C101/2) should be read as para 168 of the Revised Technology Transfer Guidelines.

Intra-technology and inter-technology competition.   **9.078**
Fn 243 The Commission has issued revised Guidelines on the application of Article 101 of the Treaty on the Functioning of the European Union to technology transfer agreements, OJ 2014 C89/3 ('Revised Technology Transfer Guidelines'), to accompany Regulation 316/2014 on the application of Article 101(3) of the Treaty on the Functioning of the European Union to categories of technology transfer agreements, OJ 2014 L93/17, replacing Regulation 772/2004 which expired on 30 April 2014. The reference to paras 12 and 142 et seq of the previous guidelines (OJ 2004 C101/2) should be read as paras 12 and 170 et seq of the Revised Technology Transfer Guidelines.

Fn 244 The reference to paras 11 and 12 of the previous guidelines (OJ 2004 C101/2) should be read as paras 11 and 12 of the Revised Technology Transfer Guidelines.

Fn 245 The reference to paras 12 and 145 of the previous guidelines (OJ 2004 C101/2) should be read as paras 12 and 172 of the Revised Technology Transfer Guidelines.

Competing and non-competing undertakings.   **9.079**
Fn 247 On 21 March 2014 the Commission adopted Regulation 316/2014 on the application of Article 101(3) of the Treaty on the Functioning of the European

Union to categories of technology transfer agreements, OJ 2014 L93/17. It entered into force on 1 May 2014, and replaces Regulation 772/2004, which expired on 30 April 2014. The reference to Article 1(1)(j) of Regulation 772/2004 should be read as Article 1(1)(n) of Regulation 316/2014.

Fn 248 At the same time as Regulation 316/2014 was published, the Commission issued revised Guidelines on the application of Article 101 of the Treaty on the Functioning of the European Union to technology transfer agreements, OJ 2014 C89/3 ('Revised Technology Transfer Guidelines'). The reference to para 29 of the previous guidelines (OJ 2004 C101/2) should be read as para 36 of the Revised Technology Transfer Guidelines.

Fn 249 The reference to Article 1(1)(j) of Regulation 772/2004 should be read as Article 1(1)(n) of Regulation 316/2014. The reference to para 22 of the previous guidelines (OJ 2004 C101/2) should be read as para 21 of the Revised Technology Transfer Guidelines.

Fn 250 The reference to paras 30 and 66 of the previous guidelines (OJ 2004 C101/2) should be read as paras 36 and 83 of the Revised Technology Transfer Guidelines.

9.080 **Determining the competitive relationship.**
Fn 251 The Commission has issued revised Guidelines on the application of Article 101 of the Treaty on the Functioning of the European Union to technology transfer agreements, OJ 2014 C89/3 ('Revised Technology Transfer Guidelines'), to accompany Regulation 316/2014 on the application of Article 101(3) of the Treaty on the Functioning of the European Union to categories of technology transfer agreements, OJ 2014 L93/17, replacing Regulation 772/2004 which expired on 30 April 2014. The reference to para 32 of the previous guidelines (OJ 2004 C101/2) should be read as para 33 of the Revised Technology Transfer Guidelines.

9.081 **Development of competition after conclusion of the agreement.**
Fn 252 The Commission has issued revised Guidelines on the application of Article 101 of the Treaty on the Functioning of the European Union to technology transfer agreements, OJ 2014 C89/3 ('Revised Technology Transfer Guidelines'), to accompany Regulation 316/2014 on the application of Article 101(3) of the Treaty on the Functioning of the European Union to categories of technology transfer agreements, OJ 2014 L93/17, replacing Regulation 772/2004 which expired on 30 April 2014. The reference to para 31 of the previous guidelines (OJ 2004 C101/2) should be read as para 38 of the Revised Technology Transfer Guidelines. The reference to Article 4(3) of Regulation 772/2004 should be read as Article 4(3) of Regulation 316/2014.

Fn 253 The reference to para 31 of the previous guidelines (OJ 2004 C101/2) should be read as para 37 of the Revised Technology Transfer Guidelines.

Reciprocal and non-reciprocal licences. On 21 March 2014 the Commission **9.082** adopted Regulation 316/2014 on the application of Article 101(3) of the Treaty on the Functioning of the European Union to categories of technology transfer agreements, OJ 2014 L93/17. It entered into force on 1 May 2014, and replaces Regulation 772/2004, which expired on 30 April 2014. The reference to Articles 1(1)(c) and 1(1)(d) of Regulation 772/2004 should be read as Articles 1(1)(d) and 1(1)(e) of Regulation 316/2014.

Fn 254 The reference to Article 1(1)(e) of Regulation 772/2004 should be read as Article 1(1)(f) of Regulation 316/2014.

Fn 255 The reference to Article 1(1)(d) of Regulation 772/2004 should be read as Article 1(1)(e) of Regulation 316/2014.

Fn 256 On 21 March 2014, at the same time as the Commission published Regulation 316/2014, it issued revised Guidelines on the application of Article 101 of the Treaty on the Functioning of the European Union to technology transfer agreements, OJ 2014 C89/3 ('Revised Technology Transfer Guidelines'). The reference to para 78 of the previous guidelines (OJ 2004 C101/2) should be read as para 98 of the Revised Technology Transfer Guidelines.

Licensing different types of intellectual property right. On 21 March 2014 the **9.083** Commission adopted Regulation 316/2014 on the application of Article 101(3) of the Treaty on the Functioning of the European Union to categories of technology transfer agreements, OJ 2014 L93/17. It entered into force on 1 May 2014, and replaces Regulation 772/2004, which expired on 30 April 2014.

Fn 258 See also Article 1(1)(b)(vi) of Regulation 316/2014, which provides expressly that plant breeders' certificates are 'technology rights' for the purposes of the Regulation.

(b) Typical clauses in licensing agreements

(i) Clauses concerning royalties

Royalties generally. In *Unwired Planet International v Huawei and others* [2015] **9.085** EWHC 2097 (Pat) the High Court refused to strike out a defence to an infringement action in which it is contended that the transfer of standard essential patent rights to Unwired Planet is void under Article 101, as it contains payment terms encouraging or requiring the transferee to charge higher royalties. On appeal to the Court of Appeal, on other grounds, not yet decided.

Fn 263 On 21 March 2014, at the same time as the Commission published Regulation 316/2014, it issued revised Guidelines on the application of Article 101 of the Treaty on the Functioning of the European Union to technology transfer agreements, OJ 2014 C89/3 ('Revised Technology Transfer Guidelines'). The reference to para 156 of the previous guidelines (OJ 2004 C101/2) should be read as para 184 of the Revised Technology Transfer Guidelines.

Fn 264 The reference to para 156 of the previous guidelines (OJ 2004 C101/2) should be read as para 184 of the Revised Technology Transfer Guidelines.

9.086 **Minimum royalties.** In *Unwired Planet International v Huawei and others* [2015] EWHC 2097 (Pat) the High Court refused to strike out a defence to an infringement action in which it is contended that the transfer of standard essential patent rights to Unwired Planet is void under Article 101, as it contains payment terms encouraging or requiring the transferee to charge higher royalties. On appeal to the Court of Appeal, on other grounds, not yet decided.

Fn 267 On 21 March 2014, at the same time as the Commission published Regulation 316/2014, it issued revised Guidelines on the application of Article 101 of the Treaty on the Functioning of the European Union to technology transfer agreements, OJ 2014 C89/3 ('Revised Technology Transfer Guidelines'). The reference to para 155(e) of the previous guidelines (OJ 2004 C101/2) should be read as para 183(e) of the Revised Technology Transfer Guidelines.

Fn 268 The reference to paras 80, 157 and 207 of the previous guidelines (OJ 2004 C101/2) should be read as paras 100, 185 and 240 of the Revised Technology Transfer Guidelines.

Fn 269 The reference to para 79 of the previous guidelines (OJ 2004 C101/2) should be read as para 99 of the Revised Technology Transfer Guidelines.

9.087 **Duration of royalty obligations**
Fn 271 On 21 March 2014, at the same time as the Commission published Regulation 316/2014, it issued revised Guidelines on the application of Article 101 of the Treaty on the Functioning of the European Union to technology transfer agreements, OJ 2014 C89/3 ('Revised Technology Transfer Guidelines'). The reference to para 159 of the previous guidelines (OJ 2004 C101/2) should be read as para 187 of the Revised Technology Transfer Guidelines.

Fn 273 The reference to Article 2 of Regulation 772/2004 should be read as Article 2 of Regulation 316/2014, and the reference to para 54 of the previous guidelines (OJ 2004 C101/2) should be read as para 67 of the Revised Technology Transfer Guidelines.

9.090 **Royalties on products not using the patent**
Fn 277 On 21 March 2014, at the same time as the Commission published Regulation 316/2014, it issued revised Guidelines on the application of Article 101 of the Treaty on the Functioning of the European Union to technology transfer agreements, OJ 2014 C89/3 ('Revised Technology Transfer Guidelines'). The reference to para 157 of the previous guidelines (OJ 2004 C101/2) should be read as para 185 of the Revised Technology Transfer Guidelines.

Fn 281 Regulation 316/2014 does not refer explicitly to clauses that require a licensee to pay royalties when it manufactures products which are the subject-matter of the agreement without making use of the licensor's work or technology. However, para 188 of the Revised Technology Transfer Guidelines now reflects the Commission's position as set out in its decisions and statements noted in footnotes 277–280 of the main text.

Royalty clauses in agreements between competitors.   9.091

Fn 283 On 21 March 2014, at the same time as the Commission published Regulation 316/2014, it issued revised Guidelines on the application of Article 101 of the Treaty on the Functioning of the European Union to technology transfer agreements, OJ 2014 C89/3 ('Revised Technology Transfer Guidelines'). The reference to paras 80 and 157 of the previous guidelines (OJ 2004 C101/2) should be read as paras 100 and 185 of the Revised Technology Transfer Guidelines.

Fn 284 The reference to para 158 of the previous guidelines (OJ 2004 C101/2) should be read as para 103 of the Revised Technology Transfer Guidelines.

Abusive royalties.   In respect of the Green Dot scheme, the Supreme Court   9.092
of the Slovak Republic held in *Železničná spoločnosť Cargo Slovakia*, on 23 May 2013, that ENVI-PAK, which held the licence to the Green Dot mark in Slovakia, had abused its dominant position by setting the fees for sub-licensing the use of the dot in such a way that it was payable only where the companies used the waste collection, recovery and recycling services of its competitors, and not where they used ENVI-PAK's own services: ECN Brief 03/2013, p14. The Commission submitted written observations to the Supreme Court pursuant to Article 15(3) of Regulation 1/2003 (see paragraph 15.051 of the main text on Article 15(3) of Regulation 1/2003), which are available on the 'Cooperation with national courts' section of the DG Comp website (not available in English).

See also Case C-351/12 *OSA*, EU:C:2014:110, [2014] 4 CMLR 671. The Court of Justice held that if a collecting society charges fees that are appreciably higher than those charged by collecting societies in other Member States, without the difference being objectively justified by the different conditions in those other Member States, those fees may infringe Article 102.

On the obligation of a dominant undertaking to license on fair, reasonable and non-discriminatory ('FRAND') terms, see also the recent cases concerning the licensing of standards essential patents ('SEPs') used in international telecoms standards. The Court of Justice in Case C-170/13 *Huawei v ZTE*, EU:C:2015:477 held that a refusal by the proprietor of a SEP to grant a licence on FRAND terms, in circumstances where the patent has acquired SEP status as a result of the proprietor having irrevocably undertaken to the standard-setting body that it will license on FRAND terms, may in principle be contrary to Article 102: para 53. The proprietor's undertaking does not, however, deprive it of its right to bring an action before the courts of a Member State to enforce its patent, so long as it complies with specific requirements when it does so. These are to notify the alleged infringer of the SEP and its breach; to make a specific, written offer of a licence on FRAND terms specifying the royalty and the way in which it has been calculated. The alleged infringer must respond in good faith, and without delay. If it does not accept the offer, it must promptly make a written counter-offer that corresponds to FRAND terms, and if its counter-offer is rejected and it is using the teachings of the SEP then from the point of rejection it must provide appropriate security. The parties may agree to submit the determination of the amount of the royalty to a third party. If the proprietor has complied with the requirements incumbent upon it, or if the alleged infringer has failed to comply with the requirements incumbent upon it, then it is not an abuse of the proprietor's dominant position for it to commence litigation to enforce its patent.

In COMP/39985 *Motorola – enforcement of ETSI standards essential patents*, decision of 29 April 2014, the Commission found that Motorola breached Article 102 by seeking an injunction in Germany against Apple for breach of its standard essential patents (which were essential to meeting the European Telecommunications Standardisation Institute's (ETSI) GPRS standard, part of the GSM standard, which is a key industry standard for mobile and wireless communications), in circumstances where it had committed to license on FRAND terms, and where Apple was willing to enter into a licence agreement and to be bound by a determination by the German Court of the FRAND terms. However, in view of the novelty of the infringement finding, no fine has been imposed.

The Commission accepted commitments from Samsung in COMP/39939 *Samsung – enforcement of ETSI standards essential patents*, decision of 29 April 2014. In its preliminary assessment, the Commission considered that Samsung had infringed Article 102 by seeking injunctions against Apple in several Member States to enforce its patents that were essential to complying with ETSI's 3G UMTS standard (a key standard for mobile and wireless communications), and that Samsung had committed to license on FRAND terms. The Commission accepted commitments under which Samsung agrees, in essence, for a period of five years not to seek an injunction before any court or tribunal in the EEA for infringement of its standard essential patents implemented in mobile devices against a potential licensee that agrees to, and complies with, a particular framework set out in the commitments decision for determining the terms of a licence.

(ii) Clauses concerning the grant of exclusive territories

9.093 **Types of licences.**
Fn 293 On 21 March 2014, at the same time as the Commission published Regulation 316/2014, it issued revised Guidelines on the application of Article 101 of the Treaty on the Functioning of the European Union to technology transfer

agreements, OJ 2014 C89/3 ('Revised Technology Transfer Guidelines'). The reference to paras 162–167 of the previous guidelines (OJ 2004 C101/2) should be read as paras 190–196 of the Revised Technology Transfer Guidelines.

Exclusive grant to non-competitors: open exclusivity.   **9.094**
Fn 294 On 21 March 2014, at the same time as the Commission published Regulation 316/2014, it issued revised Guidelines on the application of Article 101 of the Treaty on the Functioning of the European Union to technology transfer agreements, OJ 2014 C89/3 ('Revised Technology Transfer Guidelines'). The reference to para 166 of the previous guidelines (OJ 2004 C101/2) should be read as para 195 of the Revised Technology Transfer Guidelines.

Fn 301   The reference to Article 4(1)(c)(ii) of Regulation 772/2004 should be read as Article 4(1)(c)(i) of Regulation 316/2014.

Fn 304   The reference to Regulation 772/2004 should be read as Regulation 316/2014. The reference to para 164 of the previous guidelines (OJ 2004 C101/2) should be read as para 193 of the Revised Technology Transfer Guidelines.

Reciprocal exclusive licensing between competitors.   On 21 March 2014 the   **9.096**
Commission adopted Regulation 316/2014 on the application of Article 101(3) of the Treaty on the Functioning of the European Union to categories of technology transfer agreements, OJ 2014 L93/17. It entered into force on 1 May 2014, and replaces Regulation 772/2004, which expired on 30 April 2014.

Fn 317   The reference to Article 4(1)(c) of Regulation 772/2004 should be read as Article 4(1)(c) of Regulation 316/2014.

Fn 318   At the same time as the Commission published Regulation 316/2014 it issued revised Guidelines on the application of Article 101 of the Treaty on the Functioning of the European Union to technology transfer agreements, OJ 2014 C89/3 ('Revised Technology Transfer Guidelines'). The reference to para 163 of the previous guidelines (OJ 2004 C101/2) should be read as para 192 of the Revised Technology Transfer Guidelines.

Sales restrictions on the licensor.   On 21 March 2014, at the same time as   **9.097**
the Commission published Regulation 316/2014, it issued revised Guidelines on the application of Article 101 of the Treaty on the Functioning of the European Union to technology transfer agreements, OJ 2014 C89/3 ('Revised Technology Transfer Guidelines').

Fn 319   The reference to para 173 of the previous guidelines (OJ 2004 C101/2) should be read as para 202 of the Revised Technology Transfer Guidelines.

Exploitation by licensee in the territory of the licensor.   **9.098**
Fn 320 On 21 March 2014, at the same time as the Commission published Regulation 316/2014, it issued revised Guidelines on the application of Article 101

of the Treaty on the Functioning of the European Union to technology transfer agreements, OJ 2014 C89/3 ('Revised Technology Transfer Guidelines'). The reference to para 172 of the previous guidelines (OJ 2004 C101/2) should be read as para 201 of the Revised Technology Transfer Guidelines: the Commission has revised the wording to 'In the absence of such restrictions the licensor would risk facing active competition in its main area of activity'.

Fn 321 The reference to para 169 of the previous guidelines (OJ 2004 C101/2) should be read as para 198 of the Revised Technology Transfer Guidelines.

9.100 **Restrictions on direct sales by licensee into territory of another licensee.** On 21 March 2014 the Commission adopted Regulation 316/2014 on the application of Article 101(3) of the Treaty on the Functioning of the European Union to categories of technology transfer agreements, OJ 2014 L93/17. It entered into force on 1 May 2014, and replaces Regulation 772/2004, which expired on 30 April 2014. Regulation 316/2014 makes clear that restrictions of passive sales by the licensee into the territory of another licensee will not benefit from the block exemption. It does not contain an exception for restraints on passive sales by licensees into a territory or to a customer group which is supplied by another licensee: Article 4(2)(b)(ii) of Regulation 772/2004 is not replicated in Regulation 316/2014.

Fn 327 Regulation 316/2014 does not contain an exception for restraints on passive sales by licensees into a territory or to a customer group which is supplied by another licensee: Article 4(2)(b)(ii) of Regulation 772/2004 is not replicated in Regulation 316/2014.

Fn 328 At the same time as the Commission published Regulation 316/2014 it issued revised Guidelines on the application of Article 101 of the Treaty on the Functioning of the European Union to technology transfer agreements, OJ 2014 C89/3 ('Revised Technology Transfer Guidelines'). The reference to para 171 of the previous guidelines (OJ 2004 C101/2) should be read as para 200 of the Revised Technology Transfer Guidelines.

Fn 329 The reference to para 174 of the previous guidelines (OJ 2004 C101/2) should be read as para 203 of the Revised Technology Transfer Guidelines.

9.101 **Parallel traders.** On 21 March 2014 the Commission adopted Regulation 316/2014 on the application of Article 101(3) of the Treaty on the Functioning of the European Union to categories of technology transfer agreements, OJ 2014 L93/17. It entered into force on 1 May 2014, and replaces Regulation 772/2004, which expired on 30 April 2014.

9.102 **Customer restrictions.**
Fn 331 On 21 March 2014, at the same time as the Commission published Regulation 316/2014, it issued revised Guidelines on the application of Article 101 of the Treaty on the Functioning of the European Union to technology transfer

agreements, OJ 2014 C89/3 ('Revised Technology Transfer Guidelines'). The reference to para 180 of the previous guidelines (OJ 2004 C101/2) should be read as para 209 of the Revised Technology Transfer Guidelines.

Fn 332 The reference to paras 162–174 of the previous guidelines (OJ 2004 C101/2) should be read as paras 190–196 of the Revised Technology Transfer Guidelines.

(iii) Restrictions concerning the licensee's production of goods

Restrictions on output in licence.   9.103

Fn 333 On 21 March 2014, at the same time as the Commission published Regulation 316/2014, it issued revised Guidelines on the application of Article 101 of the Treaty on the Functioning of the European Union to technology transfer agreements, OJ 2014 C89/3 ('Revised Technology Transfer Guidelines'). The reference to para 178 of the previous guidelines (OJ 2004 C101/2) should be read as para 207 of the Revised Technology Transfer Guidelines.

Fn 335 The reference to paras 177–178 of the previous guidelines (OJ 2004 C101/2) should be read as paras 206–207 of the Revised Technology Transfer Guidelines.

Fn 336 The reference to para 175 of the previous guidelines (OJ 2004 C101/2) should be read as para 204 of the Revised Technology Transfer Guidelines.

Fn 337 The reference to para 175 of the previous guidelines (OJ 2004 C101/2) should be read as para 204 of the Revised Technology Transfer Guidelines.

Captive use restrictions in licence between competitors.   9.104

Fn 338 On 21 March 2014, at the same time as the Commission published Regulation 316/2014, it issued revised Guidelines on the application of Article 101 of the Treaty on the Functioning of the European Union to technology transfer agreements, OJ 2014 C89/3 ('Revised Technology Transfer Guidelines'). The reference to para 186 of the previous guidelines (OJ 2004 C101/2) should be read as para 216 of the Revised Technology Transfer Guidelines.

Fn 339 The reference to para 187 of the previous guidelines (OJ 2004 C101/2) should be read as para 217 of the Revised Technology Transfer Guidelines.

Fn 340 The reference to para 187 of the previous guidelines (OJ 2004 C101/2) should be read as para 217 of the Revised Technology Transfer Guidelines.

Captive use restrictions in licence between non-competitors.   9.105

Fn 341 On 21 March 2014, at the same time as the Commission published Regulation 316/2014, it issued revised Guidelines on the application of Article 101 of the Treaty on the Functioning of the European Union to technology transfer agreements, OJ 2014 C89/3 ('Revised Technology Transfer Guidelines'). The reference to para 186 of the previous guidelines (OJ 2004 C101/2) should be read as para 216 of the Revised Technology Transfer Guidelines.

Fn 342 The reference to paras 188 and 190 of the previous guidelines (OJ 2004 C101/2) should be read as paras 218 and 220 of the Revised Technology Transfer Guidelines.

9.106 **Field of use or restrictions in licence between competitors.** On 21 March 2014 the Commission adopted Regulation 316/2014 on the application of Article 101(3) of the Treaty on the Functioning of the European Union to categories of technology transfer agreements, OJ 2014 L93/17. It entered into force on 1 May 2014, and replaces Regulation 772/2004, which expired on 30 April 2014. The reference to Article 4(1)(c) of Regulation 772/2004 should be read as Article 4(1)(c) of Regulation 316/2014.

Fn 343 On 21 March 2014, at the same time as the Commission published Regulation 316/2014, it issued revised Guidelines on the application of Article 101 of the Treaty on the Functioning of the European Union to technology transfer agreements, OJ 2014 C89/3 ('Revised Technology Transfer Guidelines'). The reference to paras 179 and 181 of the previous guidelines (OJ 2004 C101/2) should be read as paras 208 and 211 of the Revised Technology Transfer Guidelines.

Fn 344 The reference to para 181 of the previous guidelines (OJ 2004 C101/2) should be read as para 211 of the Revised Technology Transfer Guidelines.

Fn 345 The reference to para 183 of the previous guidelines (OJ 2004 C101/2) should be read as para 213 of the Revised Technology Transfer Guidelines.

Fn 346 The reference to paras 181 and 163 of the previous guidelines (OJ 2004 C101/2) should be read as paras 211 and 192 of the Revised Technology Transfer Guidelines.

Fn 347 The reference to para 183 of the previous guidelines (OJ 2004 C101/2) should be read as para 213 of the Revised Technology Transfer Guidelines.

Fn 349 The reference to Article 4(1)(c)(ii) of Regulation 772/2004 should be read as Article 4(1)(c)(i) of Regulation 316/2014.

9.107 **Field of use or product market restrictions in licence between non-competitors.** **Fn 350** On 21 March 2014, at the same time as the Commission published Regulation 316/2014, it issued revised Guidelines on the application of Article 101 of the Treaty on the Functioning of the European Union to technology transfer agreements, OJ 2014 C89/3 ('Revised Technology Transfer Guidelines'). The reference to para 180 of the previous guidelines (OJ 2004 C101/2) should be read as para 209 of the Revised Technology Transfer Guidelines.

Fn 351 The reference to para 184 of the previous guidelines (OJ 2004 C101/2) should be read as para 214 of the Revised Technology Transfer Guidelines.

Fn 352 The reference to para 185 of the previous guidelines (OJ 2004 C101/2) should be read as para 215 of the Revised Technology Transfer Guidelines.

Minimum quality.   **9.108**
Fn 354 On 21 March 2014, at the same time as the Commission published Regulation 316/2014, it issued revised Guidelines on the application of Article 101 of the Treaty on the Functioning of the European Union to technology transfer agreements, OJ 2014 C89/3 ('Revised Technology Transfer Guidelines'). The reference to para 194 of the previous guidelines (OJ 2004 C101/2) should be read as para 224 of the Revised Technology Transfer Guidelines.

Fn 356 The reference to para 94 of the previous guidelines (OJ 2004 C101/2) should be read as para 115 of the Revised Technology Transfer Guidelines.

Minimum quantities.   On 21 March 2014 the Commission adopted Regulation   **9.109**
316/2014 on the application of Article 101(3) of the Treaty on the Functioning of the European Union to categories of technology transfer agreements, OJ 2014 L93/17. It entered into force on 1 May 2014, and replaces Regulation 772/2004, which expired on 30 April 2014.

Fn 359 On 21 March 2014, at the same time as the Commission published Regulation 316/2014, it issued revised Guidelines on the application of Article 101 of the Treaty on the Functioning of the European Union to technology transfer agreements, OJ 2014 C89/3 ('Revised Technology Transfer Guidelines'). The reference to para 155(e) of the previous guidelines (OJ 2004 C101/2) should be read as para 183(e) of the Revised Technology Transfer Guidelines.

Fn 361 The reference to Article 4(2)(a) of Regulation 772/2004 should be read as Article 4(2)(a) of Regulation 316/2014.

Handling competing products or technologies.   On 21 March 2014 the   **9.110**
Commission adopted Regulation 316/2014 on the application of Article 101(3) of the Treaty on the Functioning of the European Union to categories of technology transfer agreements, OJ 2014 L93/17. It entered into force on 1 May 2014, and replaces Regulation 772/2004, which expired on 30 April 2014. At the same time it issued revised Guidelines on the application of Article 101 of the Treaty on the Functioning of the European Union to technology transfer agreements, OJ 2014 C89/3 ('Revised Technology Transfer Guidelines').

Fn 362 The reference to paras 196–203 of the previous guidelines (OJ 2004 C101/2) should be read as paras 226–233 of the Revised Technology Transfer Guidelines.

Fn 363 The reference to Article 4(1) of Regulation 772/2004 should be read as Article 4(1) of Regulation 316/2014.

Prices.   On 21 March 2014 the Commission adopted Regulation 316/2014   **9.111**
on the application of Article 101(3) of the Treaty on the Functioning of the European Union to categories of technology transfer agreements, OJ 2014 L93/17. It entered into force on 1 May 2014, and replaces Regulation 772/2004, which expired on 30 April 2014. At the same time it issued revised Guidelines on

the application of Article 101 of the Treaty on the Functioning of the European Union to technology transfer agreements, OJ 2014 C89/3 ('Revised Technology Transfer Guidelines').

Fn 364 The reference to Articles 4(1)(a) and 4(2)(a) of Regulation 772/2004 should be read as Articles 4(1)(a) and 4(2)(a) of Regulation 316/2014.

Fn 366 The reference to Articles 4(1)(a) and 4(2)(a) of Regulation 772/2004 should be read as Articles 4(1)(a) and 4(2)(a) of Regulation 316/2014. The reference to paras 79 and 97 of the previous guidelines (OJ 2004 C101/2) should be read as paras 99 and 118 of the Revised Technology Transfer Guidelines.

9.112 **Obligation on licensee to use licensor's get-up.** On 21 March 2014 the Commission adopted Regulation 316/2014 on the application of Article 101(3) of the Treaty on the Functioning of the European Union to categories of technology transfer agreements, OJ 2014 L93/17. It entered into force on 1 May 2014, and replaces Regulation 772/2004, which expired on 30 April 2014. At the same time it issued revised Guidelines on the application of Article 101 of the Treaty on the Functioning of the European Union to technology transfer agreements, OJ 2014 C89/3 ('Revised Technology Transfer Guidelines').

Fn 367 The reference to para 155(f) of the previous guidelines (OJ 2004 C101/2) should be read as para 183(f) of the Revised Technology Transfer Guidelines.

Fn 368 The reference to Article 1(1)(b) of Regulation 772/2004 should be read as Article 2(3) of Regulation 316/2014. The reference to paras 79 and 97 of the previous guidelines (OJ 2004 C101/2) should be read as paras 99 and 118 of the Revised Technology Transfer Guidelines.

(iv) Restrictions concerning the licensee's provision of services

9.113 **Territorial allocation: mere grant of an exclusive licence.**
Fn 373 The Commission's decision in COMP/38698 *CISAC Agreements*, decision of 16 July 2008, [2009] 4 CMLR 577, was partially annulled by the General Court, on other grounds: Cases T-392, 398, 401, 410, 411, 413–422, 425, 428, 432–434, 442/08, judgments of 12 April 2013.

9.114 **Territorial protection: open exclusivity.** On 21 March 2014 the Commission adopted Regulation 316/2014 on the application of Article 101(3) of the Treaty on the Functioning of the European Union to categories of technology transfer agreements, OJ 2014 L93/17. It entered into force on 1 May 2014, and replaces Regulation 772/2004, which expired on 30 April 2014. The new Regulation makes clear that restrictions of passive sales by the licensee into the territory of another licensee will not benefit from the block exemption.

The Commission has launched an investigation into whether the licensing arrangements between several US film studios and European pay-TV broadcasters are in breach of Article 101, on a similar basis to the arrangements found to be infringing in Joined Cases C-403&429/08 *Football Association Premier League v QC Leisure/Murphy v Media Protection Services*, EU:2011:631, [2011] ECR I-9083, [2012] 1 CMLR 769: COMP/40023 *Cross-border access to pay-TV content*; and has issued a statement of objections: IP/15/5432 (23 July 2015).

Fn 377 The reference to Article 4(2)(b)(i) and (ii) of Regulation 772/2004 should be read as Articles 4(2)(b)(i) of Regulation 316/2014. Article 4(2)(b)(ii) of Regulation 772/2004 is not replicated in Regulation 316/2014.

Market-sharing as opposed to territorial allocation. The Commission's deci- **9.115** sion in COMP/38698 *CISAC Agreements*, decision of 16 July 2008, was partially annulled by the General Court: Cases T-392, 398, 401, 410, 411, 413–422, 425, 428, 432–434, 442/08, judgments of 12 April 2013. The Court held that the Commission did not have sufficient evidence to establish the existence of a concerted practice, and that the need for the societies to monitor rights uses did provide a plausible explanation for their parallel behaviour.

Market-sharing: justification. The Commission's decision in COMP/38698 **9.116** *CISAC Agreements*, decision of 16 July 2008, [2009] 4 CMLR 577, has been partially annulled by the General Court: Cases T-392, 398, 401, 410, 411, 413–422, 425, 428, 432–434, 442/08, judgments of 12 April 2013. The Court held that the Commission did not have sufficient evidence to establish the existence of a concerted practice, and that the need for the societies to monitor rights uses did provide a plausible explanation for their parallel behaviour. However, in Case T-451/08 *Föreningen Svenska Tonsättares Internationella Musikbyrå v Commission*, EU:T:2013:189, [2013] 5 CMLR 577, the appellant did not contest the existence of a concerted practice, and the General Court went on to consider the practice's effects, and the potential application of Article 101(3) to it. The General Court dismissed the appeal, as a concerted practice limiting the territorial scope of licences was not indispensable for the maintenance of the national 'one-stop shops': see para 107. As the third condition was not met, the General Court did not consider the potential application of the other conditions.

(v) Other restrictions on the licensee

Improvements. On 21 March 2014 the Commission adopted Regulation 316/ **9.119** 2014 on the application of Article 101(3) of the Treaty on the Functioning of the European Union to categories of technology transfer agreements, OJ 2014 L93/17. It entered into force on 1 May 2014, and replaces Regulation 772/2004, which expired on 30 April 2014. At the same time it issued revised Guidelines on the application of Article 101 of the Treaty on the Functioning of the European Union to technology transfer agreements, OJ 2014 C89/3 ('Revised Technology Transfer Guidelines'). The new Regulation no longer distinguishes 'severable' improvements, and refers simply to the licensor's own improvements to, or own new applications of, the licensed technology: Article 5(1)(a) of Regulation 316/2014. Moreover, the Commission no longer states that exclusive grant backs and assignments of non-severable improvements fall outside Article 101(1), but rather observes that individual assessment will be required: para 128 of the Revised Technology Transfer Guidelines.

9.120 **Tying and bundling obligations.**   In COMP/39230 *Rio Tinto Alcan*, decision of 20 December 2012, the Commission accepted commitments from Rio Tinto to amend its technology transfer agreements for its aluminium smelting technology, which had required licensees to purchase speciality cranes used in aluminium smelters from Rio Tinto's subsidiary.

Fn 396 On 21 March 2014, at the same time as the Commission published Regulation 316/2014, it issued revised Guidelines on the application of Article 101 of the Treaty on the Functioning of the European Union to technology transfer agreements, OJ 2014 C89/3 ('Revised Technology Transfer Guidelines'). The reference to para 194 of the previous guidelines (OJ 2004 C101/2) should be read as para 224 of the Revised Technology Transfer Guidelines.

Fn 397 The reference to para 193 of the previous guidelines (OJ 2004 C101/2) should be read as para 223 of the Revised Technology Transfer Guidelines.

9.122 **Dealing with infringers.**

Fn 399 On 21 March 2014, at the same time as the Commission published Regulation 316/2014, it issued revised Guidelines on the application of Article 101 of the Treaty on the Functioning of the European Union to technology transfer agreements, OJ 2014 C89/3 ('Revised Technology Transfer Guidelines'). The reference to para 155(d) of the previous guidelines (OJ 2004 C101/2) should be read as para 183(d) of the Revised Technology Transfer Guidelines.

9.123 **'Most favoured licensee' clause.**

Fn 400 On 21 March 2014, at the same time as the Commission published Regulation 316/2014, it issued revised Guidelines on the application of Article 101 of the Treaty on the Functioning of the European Union to technology transfer agreements, OJ 2014 C89/3 ('Revised Technology Transfer Guidelines'). The reference to para 97 of the previous guidelines (OJ 2004 C101/2) should be read as para 118 of the Revised Technology Transfer Guidelines.

9.124 **'No-challenge' clause.**   On 21 March 2014 the Commission adopted Regulation 316/2014 on the application of Article 101(3) of the Treaty on the Functioning of the European Union to categories of technology transfer agreements, OJ 2014 L93/17. It entered into force on 1 May 2014, and replaces Regulation 772/2004, which expired on 30 April 2014. At the same time it issued revised Guidelines on the application of Article 101 of the Treaty on the Functioning of the European Union to technology transfer agreements, OJ 2014 C89/3 ('Revised Technology Transfer Guidelines'). Under the new Regulation, a term which prevents the licensee from challenging the validity of the rights continues to be an excluded restriction; in addition, it will no longer be permissible to provide for the termination of the licence agreement in the event of a challenge by the licensee, if the licence agreement is non-exclusive: Article 5(1)(b) of Regulation 316/2014. Termination clauses in exclusive agreements will continue to benefit from the exemption.

Fn 404 The reference to Article 5(1)(c) of Regulation 772/2004 should be read as Article 5(1)(b) of Regulation 316/2014. The reference to para 112 of the previous guidelines (OJ 2004 C101/2) should be read as paras 134–140 of the Revised Technology Transfer Guidelines.

(vi) Obligations extending after expiry of the licence or of the rights

Confidentiality of know-how. 9.125

Fn 405 On 21 March 2014, at the same time as the Commission published Regulation 316/2014, it issued revised Guidelines on the application of Article 101 of the Treaty on the Functioning of the European Union to technology transfer agreements, OJ 2014 C89/3 ('Revised Technology Transfer Guidelines'). The reference to para 155 of the previous guidelines (OJ 2004 C101/2) should be read as para 183 of the Revised Technology Transfer Guidelines.

Non-exploitation after termination. 9.127

Fn 410 On 21 March 2014, at the same time as the Commission published Regulation 316/2014, it issued revised Guidelines on the application of Article 101 of the Treaty on the Functioning of the European Union to technology transfer agreements, OJ 2014 C89/3 ('Revised Technology Transfer Guidelines'). The reference to para 155 of the previous guidelines (OJ 2004 C101/2) should be read as para 183 of the Revised Technology Transfer Guidelines.

Settlement of litigation or disputes. The Commission has issued a decision 9.129 in COMP/39226 *Lundbeck*, decision of 19 June 2013. It found that agreements between Lundbeck and several groups of generics companies to settle patent litigation in respect of the drug citalopram, on terms that included the generics refraining from entering the market independently, Lundbeck paying significant sums to the generics, and Lundbeck guaranteeing the generics a profit margin on a distribution agreement, breached Article 101. The decision is under appeal: Cases T-460/13, etc, not yet decided. In COMP/39612 *Perindopril (Servier)*, decision of 9 July 2013, as well as finding that reverse payment settlement agreements between Servier and five generics companies breached Article 101, the Commission found that Servier's conduct infringed Article 102. It considered that by holding a number of secondary patents for the drug perindopril and acquiring the most advanced source of non-protected technology, and then by entering into reverse payment settlement agreements with the five generics companies that sought to enter the market, Servier had abused its dominant position in the market. On appeal, Case T-691/14, not yet decided.

On 21 March 2014, at the same time as the Commission published Regulation 316/
2014, it issued revised Guidelines on the application of Article 101 of the Treaty
on the Functioning of the European Union to technology transfer agreements, OJ
2014 C89/3 ('Revised Technology Transfer Guidelines'). The Revised Technology
Transfer Guidelines contain new guidance on the settlement of disputes concerning intellectual property rights: paras 234–243 of the Revised Technology Transfer
Guidelines. The guidance clarifies, in particular that:

(a) agreements that include value transfers for a limitation on entry, or licensing
     of technology rights leading to a delay or limitation on entry, may be caught
     by Article 101(1);
(b) agreements that include cross licensing, and impose restrictions on the use of
     the technology licensed, may be caught by Article 101(1);
(c) agreements that include non-challenge clauses are generally outside
     Article 101(1), as the purpose of the agreement is to settle existing disputes
     and avoid future disputes. Such clauses may fall within Article 101(1), how-
     ever, in individual cases, for example if the agreement was concluded follow-
     ing the provision of misleading information.

6. The Block Exemption for Technology Transfer Agreements

(a) Introduction

9.130 **The move to a more economics-based approach.** On 21 March 2014 the
Commission adopted Regulation 316/2014 on the application of Article 101(3) of
the Treaty on the Functioning of the European Union to categories of technology
transfer agreements, OJ 2014 L93/17. It entered into force on 1 May 2014, and replaces Regulation 772/2004, which expired on 30 April 2014. The new Regulation
makes only incremental changes to the approach set out in Regulation 772/2004,
as the Commission's review confirmed that the overall structure had worked well.
The individual changes are noted in the relevant paragraph updates, below.

9.131 **Interpretation by the Commission's Guidelines.** On 21 March 2014, at the
same time as the Commission published Regulation 316/2014 (see update to paragraph 9.130, above), it issued revised Guidelines on the application of Article 101
of the Treaty on the Functioning of the European Union to technology transfer
agreements, OJ 2014 C89/3 ('Revised Technology Transfer Guidelines').

Fn 422 The reference to para 65 of the previous guidelines (OJ 2004 C101/2)
should be read as para 79 of the Revised Technology Transfer Guidelines, and the
reference to Recital (12) of Regulation 772/2004 should be read as Recital (13) of
Regulation 316/2014.

(b) Relationship between Regulation 772/2004 and other block exemptions

Other relevant block exemptions. On 21 March 2014 the Commission **9.133** adopted Regulation 316/2014 on the application of Article 101(3) of the Treaty on the Functioning of the European Union to categories of technology transfer agreements, OJ 2014 L93/17. It entered into force on 1 May 2014, and replaces Regulation 772/2004, which expired on 30 April 2014. The new Regulation clarifies the relationship between the technology transfer block exemption, and two other potentially applicable block exemption Regulations: Regulation 1217/2010 on the application of Article 101(3) of the Treaty on the Functioning of the European Union to certain categories of research and development agreements, OJ 2010 L335/36, and Regulation 1218/2010 on the application of Article 101(3) of the Treaty on the Functioning of the European Union to certain categories of specialisation agreements, OJ 2010 L335/43. Regulation 316/2014 makes clear that it does not apply to licensing arrangements in research and development agreements within the scope of Regulation 1217/2010, or to specialisation agreements within the scope of Regulation 1218/2010: Article 9 of Regulation 316/2014.

Research and development and specialisation agreements. On 21 March **9.135** 2014 the Commission adopted Regulation 316/2014 on the application of Article 101(3) of the Treaty on the Functioning of the European Union to categories of technology transfer agreements, OJ 2014 L93/17. It entered into force on 1 May 2014, and replaces Regulation 772/2004, which expired on 30 April 2014. The new Regulation clarifies the relationship between the technology transfer block exemption, and two other potentially applicable block exemption Regulations: Regulation 1217/2010 on the application of Article 101(3) of the Treaty on the Functioning of the European Union to certain categories of research and development agreements, OJ 2010 L335/36, and Regulation 1218/2010 on the application of Article 101(3) of the Treaty on the Functioning of the European Union to certain categories of specialisation agreements, OJ 2010 L335/43. Regulation 316/2014 makes clear that it does not apply to licensing arrangements in research and development agreements within the scope of Regulation 1217/2010, or to specialisation agreements within the scope of Regulation 1218/2010: Article 9 of Regulation 316/2014.

(c) The scope of Regulation 772/2004

Agreements falling within the scope of Regulation 772/2004. On 21 March **9.136** 2014 the Commission adopted Regulation 316/2014 on the application of Article 101(3) of the Treaty on the Functioning of the European Union to categories of technology transfer agreements, OJ 2014 L93/17. It entered into force on 1 May 2014, and replaces Regulation 772/2004, which expired on 30 April 2014. The scope of the new Regulation has not changed. To identify the kinds of agreements that benefit from the block exemption, Article 2 of Regulation 316/2014 should be read in conjunction with the definitions in Article 1.

9.137 **Technology transfer agreements.** On 21 March 2014 the Commission adopted Regulation 316/2014 on the application of Article 101(3) of the Treaty on the Functioning of the European Union to categories of technology transfer agreements, OJ 2014 L93/17. It entered into force on 1 May 2014, and replaces Regulation 772/2004, which expired on 30 April 2014. The definition of 'technology transfer agreement' is contained in Article 1(1)(c) of Regulation 316/2014. It covers technology rights licensing agreements, and certain assignments of technology rights (see the update to paragraph 9.140, below). The definition of an 'agreement' remains unchanged: Article 1(1)(a). 'Technology rights' means 'know-how', and patents; utility models; design rights; topographies of semiconductor products; supplementary protection certificates for medicinal products or other products for which such supplementary protection certificates may be obtained; plant breeders' certificates; and software copyrights: Article 1(1)(b). The definition of 'know-how' remains unchanged: Article 1(1)(i).

Fn 434 On 21 March 2014, at the same time as the Commission published Regulation 316/2014, it issued revised Guidelines on the application of Article 101 of the Treaty on the Functioning of the European Union to technology transfer agreements, OJ 2014 C89/3 ('Revised Technology Transfer Guidelines'). The reference to paras 46 et seq of the previous guidelines (OJ 2004 C101/2) should be read as paras 44 et seq of the Revised Technology Transfer Guidelines.

Fn 435 The references should be read as per the update to the main paragraph, above.

Fn 436 The reference to para 48 of the previous guidelines (OJ 2004 C101/2) should be read as para 51 of the Revised Technology Transfer Guidelines.

9.138 **Supplementary sale and purchase of goods.** On 21 March 2014 the Commission adopted Regulation 316/2014 on the application of Article 101(3) of the Treaty on the Functioning of the European Union to categories of technology transfer agreements, OJ 2014 L93/17. It entered into force on 1 May 2014, and replaces Regulation 772/2004, which expired on 30 April 2014. The new Regulation removes the test set out in Article 1(1)(b) of Regulation 772/2004 of whether the sale and purchase provisions in a technology transfer agreement constitute the 'primary object' of the agreement. The exemption will now be available in respect of sale and purchase provisions if, and to the extent that, those provisions are directly related to the production or sale of the contract products: Article 2(3) of Regulation 316/2014.

Fn 438 The reference to Article 1(1)(b) of Regulation 772/2004 should be read as Article 2(3) of Regulation 316/2014. On 21 March 2014, at the same time as the Commission published Regulation 316/2014, it issued revised Guidelines on the application of Article 101 of the Treaty on the Functioning of the European Union to technology transfer agreements, OJ 2014 C89/3 ('Revised Technology Transfer Guidelines'). The reference to para 49 of the previous guidelines (OJ 2004 C101/2) should be read as para 46 of the Revised Technology Transfer Guidelines.

Fn 439 The reference to the definition of 'contract goods' in Article 1(1)(f) of Regulation 772/2004 should be read as the definition of 'contract products' in Article 1(1)(g) of Regulation 316/2014. The reference to para 49 of the previous guidelines (OJ 2004 C101/2) should be read as para 46 of the Revised Technology Transfer Guidelines.

Fn 440 The reference to para 49 of the previous guidelines (OJ 2004 C101/2) should be read as para 46 of the Revised Technology Transfer Guidelines.

Supplementary licence of other intellectual property rights. On 21 March 2014 the Commission adopted Regulation 316/2014 on the application of Article 101(3) of the Treaty on the Functioning of the European Union to categories of technology transfer agreements, OJ 2014 L93/17. It entered into force on 1 May 2014, and replaces Regulation 772/2004, which expired on 30 April 2014. The new Regulation applies to agreements which license other rights, if, and to the extent that, those provisions are directly related to the production or sale of the contract products: Article 2(3) of Regulation 316/2014. It is no longer a re-quirement that the licensing of the other rights should not be the primary object of the agreement. **9.139**

Fn 441 Regulation 316/2014 applies to agreements which license other rights by virtue of the scope of the exemption in Article 2(3), rather than by virtue of the definition of a technology transfer agreement.

Fn 442 At the same time as the Commission published Regulation 316/2014 it issued revised Guidelines on the application of Article 101 of the Treaty on the Functioning of the European Union to technology transfer agreements, OJ 2014 C89/3 ('Revised Technology Transfer Guidelines'). The reference to para 50 of the previous guidelines (OJ 2004 C101/2) should be read as para 47 of the Revised Technology Transfer Guidelines.

Fn 443 The reference to paras 51–53 of the previous guidelines (OJ 2004 C101/2) should be read as paras 47–50 of the Revised Technology Transfer Guidelines.

Assignments. On 21 March 2014 the Commission adopted Regulation 316/2014 on the application of Article 101(3) of the Treaty on the Functioning of the European Union to categories of technology transfer agreements, OJ 2014 L93/17. It entered into force on 1 May 2014, and replaces Regulation 772/2004, which expired on 30 April 2014. The new Regulation defines 'technology trans-fer agreements' as including assignments of technology rights for the purpose of the production of contract products, where part of the risk associated with the **9.140**

exploitation of the technology remains with the assignor: Article 1(1)(c)(ii) of Regulation 316/2014.

9.141 **Agreement between two undertakings.**   On 21 March 2014 the Commission adopted Regulation 316/2014 on the application of Article 101(3) of the Treaty on the Functioning of the European Union to categories of technology transfer agreements, OJ 2014 L93/17. It entered into force on 1 May 2014, and replaces Regulation 772/2004, which expired on 30 April 2014. The new Regulation will continue to apply only to technology transfer agreements between two undertakings: Article 1(1)(c) of Regulation 316/2014. The term 'undertaking', as well as the terms 'licensor' and 'licensee', includes connected undertakings: Article 1(2).

Fn 446 On 21 March 2014, at the same time as the Commission published Regulation 316/2014, it issued revised Guidelines on the application of Article 101 of the Treaty on the Functioning of the European Union to technology transfer agreements, OJ 2014 C89/3 ('Revised Technology Transfer Guidelines'). The reference to paras 49 and 40 of the previous guidelines (OJ 2004 C101/2) should be read as paras 54–57 of the Revised Technology Transfer Guidelines.

9.142 **Product of the contract products.**
Fn 447 On 21 March 2014 the Commission adopted Regulation 316/2014 on the application of Article 101(3) of the Treaty on the Functioning of the European Union to categories of technology transfer agreements, OJ 2014 L93/17. It entered into force on 1 May 2014, and replaces Regulation 772/2004, which expired on 30 April 2014. In the new Regulation, the definition of 'technology transfer agreement' includes a requirement that the agreement must be entered into for the purpose of the production of contract products by the licensee and/or its sub-contractor: Article 1(1)(c)(i) of Regulation 316/2014. At the same time as the Commission published Regulation 316/2014 it issued revised Guidelines on the application of Article 101 of the Treaty on the Functioning of the European Union to technology transfer agreements, OJ 2014 C89/3 ('Revised Technology Transfer Guidelines'). The reference to paras 41–46 and 49 of the previous guidelines (OJ 2004 C101/2) should be read as paras 58–66 of the Revised Technology Transfer Guidelines.

Fn 448 The reference to para 42 of the previous guidelines (OJ 2004 C101/2) should be read as para 60 of the Revised Technology Transfer Guidelines.

Fn 449 The reference to para 44 of the previous guidelines (OJ 2004 C101/2) should be read as para 64 of the Revised Technology Transfer Guidelines.

9.143 **Duration of protection.**   On 21 March 2014 the Commission adopted Regulation 316/2014 on the application of Article 101(3) of the Treaty on the Functioning of the European Union to categories of technology transfer agreements, OJ 2014 L93/17. It entered into force on 1 May 2014, and replaces Regulation 772/2004, which expired on 30 April 2014. The new Regulation will continue to apply for as long as the intellectual property right in the licensed technology has not expired, lapsed, or been declared invalid: Article 2(2) of Regulation 316/2014.

Fn 450 On 21 March 2014, at the same time as the Commission published Regulation 316/2014, it issued revised Guidelines on the application of Article 101 of the Treaty on the Functioning of the European Union to technology transfer agreements, OJ 2014 C89/3 ('Revised Technology Transfer Guidelines'). The reference to para 55 of the previous guidelines (OJ 2004 C101/2) should be read as para 68 of the Revised Technology Transfer Guidelines.

(d) Market share thresholds

Likelihood of harm to competitors.   9.144
Fn 451 On 21 March 2014 the Commission adopted Regulation 316/2014 on the application of Article 101(3) of the Treaty on the Functioning of the European Union to categories of technology transfer agreements, OJ 2014 L93/17. It entered into force on 1 May 2014, and replaces Regulation 772/2004, which expired on 30 April 2014. The reference to Recital (12) of Regulation 772/2004 should be read as Recital (13) of Regulation 316/2014. At the same time, it issued revised Guidelines on the application of Article 101 of the Treaty on the Functioning of the European Union to technology transfer agreements, OJ 2014 C89/3 ('Revised Technology Transfer Guidelines'). The reference to para 65 of the previous guidelines (OJ 2004 C101/2) should be read as para 79 of the Revised Technology Transfer Guidelines.

Market definition.   9.145
Fn 452 On 21 March 2014 the Commission adopted Regulation 316/2014 on the application of Article 101(3) of the Treaty on the Functioning of the European Union to categories of technology transfer agreements, OJ 2014 L93/17. It entered into force on 1 May 2014, and replaces Regulation 772/2004, which expired on 30 April 2014. At the same time, it issued revised Guidelines on the application of Article 101 of the Treaty on the Functioning of the European Union to technology transfer agreements, OJ 2014 C89/3 ('Revised Technology Transfer Guidelines'). The reference to paras 19–25 of the previous guidelines (OJ 2004 C101/2) should be read as paras 19–26 of the Revised Technology Transfer Guidelines.

Fn 454 The reference to paras 19–25 of the previous guidelines (OJ 2004 C101/2) should be read as paras 19–26 of the Revised Technology Transfer Guidelines.

Fn 455 The reference to para 20 of the previous guidelines (OJ 2004 C101/2) should be read as para 20 of the Revised Technology Transfer Guidelines.

The product market.   9.146
Fn 456 On 21 March 2014 the Commission adopted Regulation 316/2014 on the application of Article 101(3) of the Treaty on the Functioning of the European Union to categories of technology transfer agreements, OJ 2014 L93/17. It entered

into force on 1 May 2014, and replaces Regulation 772/2004, which expired on 30 April 2014. At the same time, it issued revised Guidelines on the application of Article 101 of the Treaty on the Functioning of the European Union to technology transfer agreements, OJ 2014 C89/3 ('Revised Technology Transfer Guidelines'). The reference to para 21 of the previous guidelines (OJ 2004 C101/2) should be read as para 21 of the Revised Technology Transfer Guidelines.

Fn 457 The reference to para 21 of the previous guidelines (OJ 2004 C101/2) should be read as para 21 of the Revised Technology Transfer Guidelines.

Fn 459 The Court of Justice dismissed the appeals in Case C-457/10P *AstraZeneca v Commission*, EU:C:2012:770, [2013] 4 CMLR 233.

9.147 **The technology market.**
Fn 462 On 21 March 2014 the Commission adopted Regulation 316/2014 on the application of Article 101(3) of the Treaty on the Functioning of the European Union to categories of technology transfer agreements, OJ 2014 L93/17. It entered into force on 1 May 2014, and replaces Regulation 772/2004, which expired on 30 April 2014. At the same time, it issued revised Guidelines on the application of Article 101 of the Treaty on the Functioning of the European Union to technology transfer agreements, OJ 2014 C89/3 ('Revised Technology Transfer Guidelines'). The reference to para 22 of the previous guidelines (OJ 2004 C101/2) should be read as para 22 of the Revised Technology Transfer Guidelines.

Fn 464 The reference to para 22 of the previous guidelines (OJ 2004 C101/2) should be read as para 22 of the Revised Technology Transfer Guidelines.

9.148 **Geographic market.**
Fn 465 The General Court dismissed the appeal in Case T-286/09 *Intel v Commission*, EU:T:2014:547 (on further appeal, Case C-413/14P, not yet decided).

9.149 **Shares of technology and product markets.**
Fn 468 On 21 March 2014 the Commission adopted Regulation 316/2014 on the application of Article 101(3) of the Treaty on the Functioning of the European Union to categories of technology transfer agreements, OJ 2014 L93/17. It entered into force on 1 May 2014, and replaces Regulation 772/2004, which expired on 30 April 2014. At the same time, it issued revised Guidelines on the application of Article 101 of the Treaty on the Functioning of the European Union to technology transfer agreements, OJ 2014 C89/3 ('Revised Technology Transfer Guidelines'). The reference to para 73 of the previous guidelines (OJ 2004 C101/2) should be read as para 93 of the Revised Technology Transfer Guidelines.

9.150 **Market share thresholds for competing and non-competing undertakings.** On 21 March 2014 the Commission adopted Regulation 316/2014 on the application of Article 101(3) of the Treaty on the Functioning of the European Union to categories of technology transfer agreements, OJ 2014 L93/17. It entered into force on 1 May 2014, and replaces Regulation 772/2004, which expired on 30 April 2014. The market share thresholds remain the same as under Regulation 772/2004, and as stated in the main text: Article 3 of Regulation 316/2014.

Fn 469 The reference to Article 3(1) of Regulation 772/2004 should be read as Article 3(1) of Regulation 316/2014. The definition of competing undertakings is in Article 1(1)(n) of Regulation 316/2014.

Fn 470 The reference to Article 3(2) of Regulation 772/2004 should be read as Article 3(2) of Regulation 316/2014.

Fn 471 The reference to Article 8(1) of Regulation 772/2004 should be read as Article 8(1) of Regulation 316/2014.

Fn 472 On 21 March 2014, at the same time as the Commission published Regulation 316/2014, it issued revised Guidelines on the application of Article 101 of the Treaty on the Functioning of the European Union to technology transfer agreements, OJ 2014 C89/3 ('Revised Technology Transfer Guidelines'). The reference to para 73 of the previous guidelines (OJ 2004 C101/2) should be read as para 93 of the Revised Technology Transfer Guidelines.

(e) Hardcore restrictions

Hardcore restrictions: competing and non-competing undertakings. On **9.151** 21 March 2014 the Commission adopted Regulation 316/2014 on the application of Article 101(3) of the Treaty on the Functioning of the European Union to categories of technology transfer agreements, OJ 2014 L93/17. It entered into force on 1 May 2014, and replaces Regulation 772/2004, which expired on 30 April 2014. The hardcore restrictions in agreements between competing undertakings are set out in Article 4(1); those in agreements between non-competing undertakings are set out in Article 4(2). Article 4(3) continues to provide that non-competing undertakings which become competitors following the conclusion of the agreement will be subject to the restrictions in Article 4(2).

Hardcore restrictions and competing undertakings. **9.152**
Fn 475 On 21 March 2014, at the same time as the Commission published Regulation 316/2014, it issued revised Guidelines on the application of Article 101 of the Treaty on the Functioning of the European Union to technology transfer agreements, OJ 2014 C89/3 ('Revised Technology Transfer Guidelines'). The reference to section 4.2 of the previous guidelines (OJ 2004 C101/2) should be read as section 3.4.2 of the Revised Technology Transfer Guidelines.

Restrictions on price setting between competing undertakings. **9.153**
Fn 476 On 21 March 2014 the Commission adopted Regulation 316/2014 on the application of Article 101(3) of the Treaty on the Functioning of the European

Union to categories of technology transfer agreements, OJ 2014 L93/17. It entered into force on 1 May 2014, and replaces Regulation 772/2004, which expired on 30 April 2014. The reference to Article 4(1)(a) of Regulation 772/2004 should be read as Article 4(1)(a) of Regulation 316/2014.

Fn 477 On 21 March 2014, at the same time as the Commission published Regulation 316/2014, it issued revised Guidelines on the application of Article 101 of the Treaty on the Functioning of the European Union to technology transfer agreements, OJ 2014 C89/3 ('Revised Technology Transfer Guidelines'). The reference to para 79 of the previous guidelines (OJ 2004 C101/2) should be read as para 99 of the Revised Technology Transfer Guidelines.

Fn 479 The reference to para 81 of the previous guidelines (OJ 2004 C101/2) should be read as para 101 of the Revised Technology Transfer Guidelines.

9.154 **Price-fixing in cross-licences.** On 21 March 2014 the Commission adopted Regulation 316/2014 on the application of Article 101(3) of the Treaty on the Functioning of the European Union to categories of technology transfer agreements, OJ 2014 L93/17, to replace Regulation 772/2004 which expired on 30 April 2014. At the same time, it issued revised Guidelines on the application of Article 101 of the Treaty on the Functioning of the European Union to technology transfer agreements, OJ 2014 C89/3 ('Revised Technology Transfer Guidelines'). The reference to para 80 of the previous guidelines (OJ 2004 C101/2) should be read as para 100 of the Revised Technology Transfer Guidelines.

9.155 **Output limitations: reciprocal and non-reciprocal agreements between competing undertakings.**
Fn 481 On 21 March 2014 the Commission adopted Regulation 316/2014 on the application of Article 101(3) of the Treaty on the Functioning of the European Union to categories of technology transfer agreements, OJ 2014 L93/17. It entered into force on 1 May 2014, and replaces Regulation 772/2004, which expired on 30 April 2014. The reference to Article 4(1)(b) of Regulation 772/2004 should be read as Article 4(1)(b) of Regulation 316/2014.

Fn 482 On 21 March 2014, at the same time as the Commission published Regulation 316/2014, it issued revised Guidelines on the application of Article 101 of the Treaty on the Functioning of the European Union to technology transfer agreements, OJ 2014 C89/3 ('Revised Technology Transfer Guidelines'). The reference to paras 82–83 of the previous guidelines (OJ 2004 C101/2) should be read as paras 103–104 of the Revised Technology Transfer Guidelines.

9.156 **Market allocation and competing undertakings.**
Fn 483 On 21 March 2014 the Commission adopted Regulation 316/2014 on the application of Article 101(3) of the Treaty on the Functioning of the European Union to categories of technology transfer agreements, OJ 2014 L93/17. It entered into force on 1 May 2014, and replaces Regulation 772/2004, which expired on

30 April 2014. The reference to Article 4(1)(c) of Regulation 772/2004 should be read as Article 4(1)(c) of Regulation 316/2014.

Field of use restrictions between competing undertakings. On 21 March **9.157** 2014 the Commission adopted Regulation 316/2014 on the application of Article 101(3) of the Treaty on the Functioning of the European Union to categories of technology transfer agreements, OJ 2014 L93/17. It entered into force on 1 May 2014, and replaces Regulation 772/2004, which expired on 30 April 2014. Although the list of hardcore restrictions in agreements between competing undertakings has not changed in substance, Article 4(1)(c) of the new Regulation contains a shorter list of hardcore restrictions in agreements between competing undertakings than did Article 4(1)(c) of Regulation 772/2004. The Commission has stated that its intention is to simplify the drafting, but not to change the list as a matter of substance: see Commission MEMO/14/208 of 21 March 2014.

Fn 484 On 21 March 2014, at the same time as the Commission published Regulation 316/2014, it issued revised Guidelines on the application of Article 101 of the Treaty on the Functioning of the European Union to technology transfer agreements, OJ 2014 C89/3 ('Revised Technology Transfer Guidelines'). The reference to paras 179–183 of the previous guidelines (OJ 2004 C101/2) should be read as paras 208–215 of the Revised Technology Transfer Guidelines.

Fn 485 Article 4(1)(c)(i) of Regulation 772/2004 has not been replicated in Regulation 316/2014. The Commission considers that restrictions of this nature do not have as their object the allocation of markets or customers: para 113 of the Revised Technology Transfer Guidelines.

Fn 486 The reference to para 180 of the previous guidelines (OJ 2004 C101/2) should be read as para 209 of the Revised Technology Transfer Guidelines.

Fn 487 The reference to para 90 of the previous guidelines (OJ 2004 C101/2) should be read as para 113 of the Revised Technology Transfer Guidelines.

Territorial restrictions between competing undertakings. On 21 March 2014 **9.158** the Commission adopted Regulation 316/2014 on the application of Article 101(3) of the Treaty on the Functioning of the European Union to categories of technology transfer agreements, OJ 2014 L93/17. It entered into force on 1 May 2014, and replaces Regulation 772/2004, which expired on 30 April 2014. Although the list of hardcore restrictions in agreements between competing undertakings has not changed in substance, Article 4(1)(c) of the new Regulation contains a shorter list of hardcore restrictions in agreements between competing undertakings than did Article 4(1)(c) of Regulation 772/2004. The Commission has stated that its intention is to simplify the drafting, but not to change the list as a matter of substance: see Commission MEMO/14/208 of 21 March 2014. As respects the exception to the prohibition on territorial restrictions set out in paragraph 9.158(b) of the main text, Article 4(c)(iii) of Regulation 772/2004 has not been replicated in Regulation 316/2014. The Commission considers that the appointment of a sole licensee in a particular territory does not constitute a hardcore restriction: see para 109 of the revised Guidelines on the application of Article 101 of the Treaty on the Functioning of the European Union to technology transfer agreements, OJ 2014 C89/3 ('Revised Technology Transfer Guidelines').

Fn 490 The reference to Article 4(1)(c)(ii) of Regulation 772/2004 should be read as Article 4(1)(c)(i) of Regulation 316/2014.

Fn 491 See the update to the main paragraph, above.

Fn 492 The reference to Article 4(1)(c)(iv) of Regulation 772/2004 should be read as Article 4(1)(c)(i) of Regulation 316/2014.

Fn 493 The reference to Article 4(1)(c)(v) of Regulation 772/2004 should be read as Article 4(1)(c)(ii) of Regulation 316/2014.

9.159 **Customer group restrictions between competing undertakings.**
Fn 494 On 21 March 2014 the Commission adopted Regulation 316/2014 on the application of Article 101(3) of the Treaty on the Functioning of the European Union to categories of technology transfer agreements, OJ 2014 L93/17. It entered into force on 1 May 2014, and replaces Regulation 772/2004, which expired on 30 April 2014. The reference to Article 4(1)(c)(iv) of Regulation 772/2004 should be read as Article 4(1)(c)(i) of Regulation 316/2014.

Fn 495 The reference to Article 4(1)(c)(v) of Regulation 772/2004 should be read as Article 4(1)(c)(ii) of Regulation 316/2014. On 21 March 2014, at the same time as the Commission published Regulation 316/2014, it issued revised Guidelines on the application of Article 101 of the Treaty on the Functioning of the European Union to technology transfer agreements, OJ 2014 C89/3 ('Revised Technology Transfer Guidelines'). The reference to para 89 of the previous guidelines (OJ 2004 C101/2) should be read as para 110 of the Revised Technology Transfer Guidelines.

Fn 496 The reference to Article 4(1)(c)(vi) of Regulation 772/2004 should be read as Article 4(1)(c)(iii) of Regulation 316/2014, and the reference to paras 92 and 186–190 of the previous guidelines (OJ 2004 C101/2) should be read as paras 111 and 216–220 of the Revised Technology Transfer Guidelines.

Fn 498 The reference to Article 4(1)(c)(vii) of Regulation 772/2004 should be read as Article 4(1)(c)(iv) of Regulation 316/2014.

9.160 **Restrictions on use and development of technology between competing undertakings.** On 21 March 2014 the Commission adopted Regulation 316/2014 on the application of Article 101(3) of the Treaty on the Functioning of the European Union to categories of technology transfer agreements, OJ 2014 L93/17. It entered into force on 1 May 2014, and replaces Regulation 772/2004, which expired on 30 April 2014. The reference to Article 4(1)(d) of Regulation 772/2004 should be read as Article 4(1)(d) of Regulation 316/2014.

Fn 499 On 21 March 2014, at the same time as the Commission published Regulation 316/2014, it issued revised Guidelines on the application of Article 101 of the Treaty on the Functioning of the European Union to technology transfer agreements, OJ 2014 C89/3 ('Revised Technology Transfer Guidelines'). The reference to para 95 of the previous guidelines (OJ 2004 C101/2) should be read as para 116 of the Revised Technology Transfer Guidelines.

Fn 500 The reference to para 94 of the previous guidelines (OJ 2004 C101/2) should be read as para 115 of the Revised Technology Transfer Guidelines.

Fn 501 The reference to para 94 of the previous guidelines (OJ 2004 C101/2) should be read as para 115 of the Revised Technology Transfer Guidelines.

Hardcore restrictions and non-competing undertakings.   On 21 March 2014 **9.161** the Commission adopted Regulation 316/2014 on the application of Article 101(3) of the Treaty on the Functioning of the European Union to categories of technology transfer agreements, OJ 2014 L93/17, to replace Regulation 772/2004 which expired on 30 April 2014. The reference to Article 4(2) of Regulation 772/2004 should be read as Article 4(2) of Regulation 316/2014.

Fn 502 The reference to Article 4(3) of Regulation 772/2004 should be read as Article 4(3) of Regulation 316/2014.

Price restrictions between non-competing undertakings.   **9.162**
Fn 503 On 21 March 2014 the Commission adopted Regulation 316/2014 on the application of Article 101(3) of the Treaty on the Functioning of the European Union to categories of technology transfer agreements, OJ 2014 L93/17. It entered into force on 1 May 2014, and replaces Regulation 772/2004, which expired on 30 April 2014. The reference to Article 4(2) of Regulation 772/2004 should be read as Article 4(2) of Regulation 316/2014.

Fn 504 On 21 March 2014, at the same time as the Commission published Regulation 316/2014, it issued revised Guidelines on the application of Article 101 of the Treaty on the Functioning of the European Union to technology transfer agreements, OJ 2014 C89/3 ('Revised Technology Transfer Guidelines'). The reference to para 97 of the previous guidelines (OJ 2004 C101/2) should be read as para 118 of the Revised Technology Transfer Guidelines.

Restrictions on sales by licensor in agreement between non-competing parties. **9.163**
Fn 505 On 21 March 2014 the Commission adopted Regulation 316/2014 on the application of Article 101(3) of the Treaty on the Functioning of the European Union to categories of technology transfer agreements, OJ 2014 L93/17. It entered into force on 1 May 2014, and replaces Regulation 772/2004, which expired on 30 April 2014. At the same time it issued revised Guidelines on the application of

Article 101 of the Treaty on the Functioning of the European Union to technology transfer agreements, OJ 2014 C89/3 ('Revised Technology Transfer Guidelines'). The reference to para 99 of the previous guidelines (OJ 2004 C101/2) should be read as para 120 of the Revised Technology Transfer Guidelines.

9.164 **Restriction on active sales by non-competing licensee.** On 21 March 2014 the Commission adopted Regulation 316/2014 on the application of Article 101(3) of the Treaty on the Functioning of the European Union to categories of technology transfer agreements, OJ 2014 L93/17. It entered into force on 1 May 2014, and replaces Regulation 772/2004, which expired on 30 April 2014. The new Regulation does not contain an exception for restraints on passive sales by licensees into a territory or customer group which is supplied by another licensee: Article 4(2)(b)(ii) of Regulation 772/2004, not replicated in Regulation 316/2014.

Fn 506 The reference to Article 4(2)(b)(i) of Regulation 772/2004 should be read as Article 4(2)(b)(i) of Regulation 316/2014. Article 4(2)(b)(ii) of Regulation 772/2014 has not been replicated (see update to main paragraph, above).

Fn 507 The reference to Article 4(2)(c) of Regulation 772/2004 should be read as Article 4(2)(c) of Regulation 316/2014.

Fn 508 The reference to Article 4(2)(c) of Regulation 772/2004 should be read as Article 4(2)(c) of Regulation 316/2014.

Fn 509 On 21 March 2014, at the same time as the Commission published Regulation 316/2014, it issued revised Guidelines on the application of Article 101 of the Treaty on the Functioning of the European Union to technology transfer agreements, OJ 2014 C89/3 ('Revised Technology Transfer Guidelines'). The reference to para 99 of the previous guidelines (OJ 2004 C101/2) should be read as para 120 of the Revised Technology Transfer Guidelines.

9.165 **Restriction on passive sales by non-competing licensee.** On 21 March 2014 the Commission adopted Regulation 316/2014 on the application of Article 101(3) of the Treaty on the Functioning of the European Union to categories of technology transfer agreements, OJ 2014 L93/17. It entered into force on 1 May 2014, and replaces Regulation 772/2004, which expired on 30 April 2014. The reference to Article 4(2)(b) of Regulation 772/2004 should be read as Article 4(2)(b) of Regulation 316/2014. The new Regulation does not contain an exception for restraints on passive sales by licensees into a territory or to a customer group which is supplied by another licensee: Article 4(2)(b)(ii) of Regulation 772/2004, not replicated in Regulation 316/2014. The final sentence of paragraph 9.165 in the main text is therefore no longer applicable.

Fn 510 On 21 March 2014, at the same time as the Commission published Regulation 316/2014, it issued revised Guidelines on the application of Article 101 of the Treaty on the Functioning of the European Union to technology transfer agreements, OJ 2014 C89/3 ('Revised Technology Transfer Guidelines'). The reference to para 98 of the previous guidelines (OJ 2004 C101/2) should be read as para 119 of the Revised Technology Transfer Guidelines.

Fn 511 The reference to para 100 of the previous guidelines (OJ 2004 C101/2) should be read as para 121 of the Revised Technology Transfer Guidelines.

Fn 512 See update to main paragraph, above.

Captive use restrictions between non-competing undertakings.   **9.166**
Fn 513 On 21 March 2014 the Commission adopted Regulation 316/2014 on the application of Article 101(3) of the Treaty on the Functioning of the European Union to categories of technology transfer agreements, OJ 2014 L93/17. It entered into force on 1 May 2014, and replaces Regulation 772/2004, which expired on 30 April 2014. The reference to Article 4(2)(b)(iii) of Regulation 772/2004 should be read as Article 4(2)(b)(ii) of Regulation 316/2014. At the same time, the Commission issued revised Guidelines on the application of Article 101 of the Treaty on the Functioning of the European Union to technology transfer agreements, OJ 2014 C89/3 ('Revised Technology Transfer Guidelines'). The reference to paras 102 and 186–190 of the previous guidelines (OJ 2004 C101/2) should be read as paras 122 and 216–220 of the Revised Technology Transfer Guidelines.

Fn 514 The reference to Article 4(2)(b)(iv) of Regulation 772/2004 should be read as Article 4(2)(b)(iii) of Regulation 316/2014. The reference to para 103 of the previous guidelines (OJ 2004 C101/2) should be read as para 123 of the Revised Technology Transfer Guidelines.

Restriction on sales to end-users between non-competing parties.   **9.167**
Fn 515 On 21 March 2014 the Commission adopted Regulation 316/2014 on the application of Article 101(3) of the Treaty on the Functioning of the European Union to categories of technology transfer agreements, OJ 2014 L93/17. It entered into force on 1 May 2014, and replaces Regulation 772/2004, which expired on 30 April 2014. The reference to Article 4(2)(b)(v) of Regulation 772/2004 should be read as Article 4(2)(b)(iv) of Regulation 316/2014. At the same time, the Commission issued revised Guidelines on the application of Article 101 of the Treaty on the Functioning of the European Union to technology transfer agreements, OJ 2014 C89/3 ('Revised Technology Transfer Guidelines'). The reference to para 104 of the previous guidelines (OJ 2004 C101/2) should be read as para 124 of the Revised Technology Transfer Guidelines.

Restrictions in a selective distribution network.   **9.168**
Fn 516 On 21 March 2014 the Commission adopted Regulation 316/2014 on the application of Article 101(3) of the Treaty on the Functioning of the European Union to categories of technology transfer agreements, OJ 2014 L93/17. It entered into force on 1 May 2014, and replaces Regulation 772/2004, which expired on

30 April 2014. The reference to Article 4(2)(b)(vi) of Regulation 772/2004 should be read as Article 4(2)(b)(v) of Regulation 316/2014.

Fn 517 The reference to Article 4(2)(c) of Regulation 772/2004 should be read as Article 4(2)(c) of Regulation 316/2014. At the same time, the Commission issued revised Guidelines on the application of Article 101 of the Treaty on the Functioning of the European Union to technology transfer agreements, OJ 2014 C89/3 ('Revised Technology Transfer Guidelines'). The reference to para 104 of the previous guidelines (OJ 2004 C101/2) should be read as para 125 of the Revised Technology Transfer Guidelines.

(f) Excluded restrictions

9.169 **Excluded restrictions.** On 21 March 2014 the Commission adopted Regulation 316/2014 on the application of Article 101(3) of the Treaty on the Functioning of the European Union to categories of technology transfer agreements, OJ 2014 L93/17. It entered into force on 1 May 2014, and replaces Regulation 772/2004, which expired on 30 April 2014. The reference to Article 5 of Regulation 772/2004 should be read as Article 5 of Regulation 316/2014.

9.170 **Assignment or licensing of severable improvements.** On 21 March 2014 the Commission adopted Regulation 316/2014 on the application of Article 101(3) of the Treaty on the Functioning of the European Union to categories of technology transfer agreements, OJ 2014 L93/17. It entered into force on 1 May 2014, and replaces Regulation 772/2004, which expired on 30 April 2014. The reference to Article 5(1)(a) of Regulation 772/2004 should be read as Article 5(1)(a) of Regulation 316/2014. The new Regulation no longer distinguishes 'severable' improvements, and refers simply to the licensor's own improvements to, or own new applications of, the licensed technology: Article 5(1)(a) of Regulation 316/2014. Thus, all exclusive grant-back obligations are now excluded from the exemption.

On 21 March 2014, at the same time as the Commission published Regulation 316/2014, it issued revised Guidelines on the application of Article 101 of the Treaty on the Functioning of the European Union to technology transfer agreements, OJ 2014 C89/3 ('Revised Technology Transfer Guidelines'). The Commission no longer states that exclusive grant backs and assignments of non-severable improvements fall outside Article 101(1), but rather observes that individual assessment will be required: para 128 of the Revised Technology Transfer Guidelines.

Fn 518 The reference to Article 5(1)(a) of Regulation 772/2004 should be read as Article 5(1)(a) of Regulation 316/2014.

Fn 519 The reference to Article 5(1)(b) of Regulation 772/2004 should be read as Article 5(1)(a) of Regulation 316/2014.

Fn 520 The reference to Article 1(1)(n) of Regulation 772/2004 is no longer applicable, as the distinction between 'severable' and non-severable improvements has been removed: see update to main paragraph, above.

Fn 521 See the update to the main paragraph, above. The Revised Technology Transfer Guidelines state that individual assessment will be required.

Fn 522 The reference to para 109 of the previous guidelines (OJ 2004 C101/2) should be read as para 131 of the Revised Technology Transfer Guidelines.

Fn 523 The reference to para 110 of the previous guidelines (OJ 2004 C101/2) should be read as para 130 of the Revised Technology Transfer Guidelines.

'No challenge' clauses.   On 21 March 2014 the Commission adopted Regulation **9.171** 316/2014 on the application of Article 101(3) of the Treaty on the Functioning of the European Union to categories of technology transfer agreements, OJ 2014 L93/17. It entered into force on 1 May 2014, and replaces Regulation 772/2004, which expired on 30 April 2014. The reference to Article 5(1)(c) of Regulation 772/2004 should be read as Article 5(1)(b) of Regulation 316/2014. Under the new Regulation, a term which prevents the licensee from challenging the validity of the rights continues to be an excluded restriction; in addition, it will no longer be permissible to provide for the termination of the licence agreement in the event of a challenge by the licensee, if the licence agreement is non-exclusive: Article 5(1)(b) of Regulation 316/2014. Termination clauses in exclusive agreements will continue to benefit from the exemption.

Fn 524 The reference to Article 5(1)(c) of Regulation 772/2004 should be read as Article 5(1)(b) of Regulation 316/2014. On 21 March 2014, at the same time as the Commission published Regulation 316/2014, it issued revised Guidelines on the application of Article 101 of the Treaty on the Functioning of the European Union to technology transfer agreements, OJ 2014 C89/3 ('Revised Technology Transfer Guidelines'). The reference to para 112 of the previous guidelines (OJ 2004 C101/2) should be read as paras 133–135 of the Revised Technology Transfer Guidelines.

Fn 525 The reference to Article 5(1)(c) of Regulation 772/2004 should be read as Article 5(1)(b) of Regulation 316/2014.

Exploitation of licensee's own technology.   **9.172**
Fn 527 On 21 March 2014 the Commission adopted Regulation 316/2014 on the application of Article 101(3) of the Treaty on the Functioning of the European Union to categories of technology transfer agreements, OJ 2014 L93/17. It entered into force on 1 May 2014, and replaces Regulation 772/2004, which expired on 30 April 2014. The reference to Article 5(2) of Regulation 772/2004 should be read as Article 5(2) of Regulation 316/2014, and reference to Article 4(1)(d) of Regulation 772/2004 should be read as Article 4(1)(d) of Regulation 316/2014.

Fn 528 The reference to Article 5(2) of Regulation 772/2004 should be read as Article 5(2) of Regulation 316/2014. On 21 March 2014, at the same time as the Commission published Regulation 316/2014, it issued revised Guidelines on the application of Article 101 of the Treaty on the Functioning of the European Union to technology transfer agreements, OJ 2014 C89/3 ('Revised Technology Transfer Guidelines'). The reference to paras 114–116 of the previous guidelines (OJ 2004 C101/2) should be read as paras 141–143 of the Revised Technology Transfer Guidelines.

(g) Withdrawal of the block exemption

9.173 Withdrawal in individual cases. On 21 March 2014 the Commission adopted Regulation 316/2014 on the application of Article 101(3) of the Treaty on the Functioning of the European Union to categories of technology transfer agreements, OJ 2014 L93/17. It entered into force on 1 May 2014, and replaces Regulation 772/2004, which expired on 30 April 2014. The reference to Article 6 of Regulation 772/2004 should be read as Article 6 of Regulation 316/2014. The Commission will no longer be able to withdraw the benefit of the block exemption in circumstances where the parties do not exploit the licensed technology: Regulation 316/2014 does not replicate Article 6(1)(c) of Regulation 772/2004.

Fn 529 On 21 March 2014, at the same time as the Commission published Regulation 316/2014, it issued revised Guidelines on the application of Article 101 of the Treaty on the Functioning of the European Union to technology transfer agreements, OJ 2014 C89/3 ('Revised Technology Transfer Guidelines'). The reference to para 119 of the previous guidelines (OJ 2004 C101/2) should be read as para 146 of the Revised Technology Transfer Guidelines.

Fn 530 The reference to Article 6(1)(a) of Regulation 772/2004 should be read as Article 6(1)(a) of Regulation 316/2014.

Fn 531 The reference to Article 6(1)(b) of Regulation 772/2004 should be read as Article 6(1)(b) of Regulation 316/2014.

Fn 532 Article 6(1)(c) of Regulation 772/2004 has not been replicated in Regulation 316/2014.

Fn 533 The reference to Article 6(2) of Regulation 772/2004 should be read as Article 6(2) of Regulation 316/2014.

9.174 Disapplication to parallel networks of licences.
Fn 534 On 21 March 2014 the Commission adopted Regulation 316/2014 on the application of Article 101(3) of the Treaty on the Functioning of the European Union to categories of technology transfer agreements, OJ 2014 L93/17. It entered into force on 1 May 2014, and replaces Regulation 772/2004, which expired on

30 April 2014. The reference to Article 7(1) of Regulation 772/2004 should be read as Article 7(1) of Regulation 316/2014. At the same time, it issued revised Guidelines on the application of Article 101 of the Treaty on the Functioning of the European Union to technology transfer agreements, OJ 2014 C89/3 ('Revised Technology Transfer Guidelines'). The reference to para 127 of the previous guidelines (OJ 2004 C101/2) should be read as para 153 of the Revised Technology Transfer Guidelines.

(h) Review of Regulation 772/2004

Review of block exemption.   On 21 March 2014 the Commission adopted **9.175** Regulation 316/2014 on the application of Article 101(3) TFEU to categories of technology transfer agreement (OJ 2014 L93/17), and replacement guidelines (OJ 2014 C89/3), which will apply from 1 May 2014. The changes made by those provisions is discussed in the updates to the relevant paragraphs of the main text, above.

10

ARTICLE 102

1. Introduction

(a) Generally

The Commission's Guidance on its enforcement priorities in relation to ex-   **10.004**
clusionary conduct by dominant undertakings. The General Court in Case
T-286/09 *Intel v Commission*, EU:T:2014:547, [2014] 5 CMLR 270, held that the
Guidance on the Commission's enforcement priorities in applying Article 82 of
the EC Treaty to abusive exclusionary conduct by dominant undertakings, OJ
2009 C45/7, sets priorities for the Commission's future enforcement activities; it
does not apply to proceedings that had already been initiated before it was published, even if it was published prior to the adoption of the Commission's decision
in those proceedings. The Guidance therefore did not affect the General Court's
conclusion that it was not necessary for the Commission to conduct an 'as efficient competitor' test to determine whether Intel's rebate arrangements were
abusive: paras 154–156. On further appeal, Case C-413/14P, not yet decided. The
significance of the Guidance for future cases remains undecided.

Fn 19 The General Court dismissed the challenge, on other grounds, in Case
T-201/11 *Si.mobil v Commission*, EU:T:2014:1096. See the update to paragraph
15.015, below.

Link between dominant position and abuse.   **10.009**
Fn 38 The Court of Justice dismissed the appeals in Case C-457/10P *AstraZeneca
v Commission*, EU:C:2012:770, [2013] 4 CMLR 233.

Fn 44 The Court of Justice dismissed the appeals in Case C-457/10P *AstraZeneca
v Commission*, EU:C:2012:770, [2013] 4 CMLR 233.

(b) Relationship between Article 102 and other competition rules

Circumstances where both Articles 101 and 102 may apply. A recent example   **10.011**
is the Commission's decision in COMP/39612 *Perindopril (Servier)*, decision of

9 July 2014, in which the Commission found that Servier's conduct infringed Article 102, as well as finding that the reverse payment settlement agreements it entered into with five generics companies breached Article 101. The Commission considered that by holding a number of secondary patents for the drug perindopril and acquiring the most advanced source of non-protected technology, and then by entering into reverse payment settlement agreements with the five generics companies that sought to enter the market, Servier had abused its dominant position in the market. See Press Release IP/14/799 (9 July 2014). On appeal, Case T-691/14, not yet decided.

2. Dominant Position

(a) Generally

10.020 **Indicators of dominance.**
Fn 81 The Court of Justice dismissed the appeals in Case C-457/10P *AstraZeneca v Commission*, EU:C:2012:770, [2013] 4 CMLR 233. In dismissing the cross-appeal by the European Federation of Pharmaceutical Industries and Associations, the Court upheld the General Court's conclusions on market power. It rejected the argument that insufficient weight had been attached to the powers of the State as a monopsonist purchaser and as price regulator, both as inadmissible and as unfounded: paras 175–181. The complaint that the General Court erred in taking into account AstraZeneca's first-mover status and financial resources was held to be inadmissible, and the complaint that it erred in taking into account AstraZeneca's intellectual property rights was dismissed: paras 185–188.

(b) The market position of the undertaking itself and its competitors

10.022 **Caution about market shares.**
Fn 86 The General Court dismissed the appeal, on other grounds, against the Commission decision in COMP/37990 *Intel*, decision of 13 May 2009, in Case T-286/09 *Intel v Commission*, EU:T:2014:547, [2014] 5 CMLR 270 (on further appeal, Case C-413/14P, not yet decided).

Fn 89 The Court of Justice dismissed the appeals in Case C-457/10P *AstraZeneca v Commission*, EU:C:2012:770, [2013] 4 CMLR 233. On this point, see in particular para 177.

10.024 **Market share levels.**
Fn 101 The General Court dismissed the appeal, on other grounds, against the Commission decision in COMP/37990 *Intel*, decision of 13 May 2009, in Case T-286/09 *Intel v Commission*, EU:T:2014:547, [2014] 5 CMLR 270 (on further appeal, Case C-413/14P, not yet decided). The Court of Justice dismissed the

appeals in Case C-457/10P *AstraZeneca v Commission*, EU:C:2012:770, [2013] 4 CMLR 233.

Fn 102 The Court of Justice dismissed the appeals in Case C-457/10P *AstraZeneca v Commission*, EU:C:2012:770, [2013] 4 CMLR 233. On this point, see in particular para 188.

Market shares of competitors.   **10.025**
Fn 108 The Court of Justice dismissed the appeals in Case C-457/10P *AstraZeneca v Commission*, EU:C:2012:770, [2013] 4 CMLR 233.

Stability of market shares.   **10.026**
Fn 111 The Court of Justice has dismissed the further appeal in Case C-295/12P *Telefónica de España v Commission*, EU:C:2014:2062.

Overall size and strength.   **10.029**
Fn 117 The Court of Justice dismissed the appeals in Case C-457/10P *AstraZeneca v Commission*, EU:C:2012:770, [2013] 4 CMLR 233. In dismissing the cross-appeal by the European Federation of Pharmaceutical Industries and Associations, the Court held to be inadmissible the complaint that the General Court erred in taking into account AstraZeneca's first-mover status and financial resources, and it dismissed the complaint that the General Court erred in taking into account AstraZeneca's intellectual property rights: paras 185–188.

Incumbency and 'first mover advantage'.   **10.030**
Fn 121 The Court of Justice dismissed the appeals in Case C-457/10P *AstraZeneca v Commission*, EU:C:2012:770, [2013] 4 CMLR 233. The cross-appeal by the European Federation of Pharmaceutical Industries and Associations against the General Court having taken into account AstraZeneca's first-mover status was dismissed as inadmissible: para 185.

(c) Barriers to entry and expansion

Economies of scale and fixed costs.   **10.033**
Fn 126 The General Court dismissed the appeal, on other grounds, against the Commission decision in COMP/37990 *Intel*, decision of 13 May 2009, in Case T-286/09 *Intel v Commission*, EU:T:2014:547, [2014] 5 CMLR 270 (on further appeal, Case C-413/14P, not yet decided).

Technical barriers.   **10.034**
Fn 133 The Court of Justice dismissed the appeals, on other grounds, in Case C-457/10P *AstraZeneca v Commission*, EU:C:2012:770, [2013] 4 CMLR 233.

Fn 134 The appeals by Hynix Semiconductor (now trading as SK Hynix Inc) in Joined Cases T-148&149/10 against the Commission's decision in COMP/38636 *Rambus*, decision of 9 December 2009, were withdrawn on 5 July 2013.

10.036 Structural barriers: vertical integration.
Fn 143 The Court of Justice dismissed the appeals in Case C-457/10P *AstraZeneca v Commission*, EU:C:2012:770, [2013] 4 CMLR 233. On this point, see in particular para 188.

Fn 145 The Court of Justice has dismissed the further appeal in Case C-295/12P *Telefónica de España v Commission*, EU:C:2014:2062.

10.038 Strategic barriers: conduct as evidence of dominance.   The Court of Justice dismissed the appeals in Case C-457/10P *AstraZeneca v Commission*, EU:C:2012:770, [2013] 4 CMLR 233. On this point, see in particular para 185.

10.039 Advertising and reputational effects.
Fn 156 The General Court dismissed the appeal, on other grounds, against the Commission decision in COMP/37990 *Intel*, decision of 13 May 2009, in Case T-286/09 *Intel v Commission*, EU:T:2014:547, [2014] 5 CMLR 270 (on further appeal, Case C-413/14P, not yet decided).

(d) Countervailing market power

10.041 Countervailing buyer power.
Fn 164 The Court of Justice dismissed the appeals in Case C-457/10P *AstraZeneca v Commission*, EU:C:2012:770, [2013] 4 CMLR 233. The cross-appeal by the European Federation of Pharmaceutical Industries and Associations, in which it was contended that the General Court had attached insufficient weight to the powers of the State as a monopsonist purchaser and as price regulator, was dismissed both as inadmissible and as unfounded: paras 175–181.

Fn 165 The General Court dismissed the appeal, on other grounds, against the Commission decision in COMP/37990 *Intel*, decision of 13 May 2009, in Case T-286/09 *Intel v Commission*, EU:T:2014:547, [2014] 5 CMLR 270 (on further appeal, Case C-413/14P, not yet decided).

(e) Appraisal of market power in more complex cases

10.046 Separate market for spare parts and ancillary services.   The Danish Competition Council on 12 June 2013 found that Deutz, a German engine manufacturer, had abused its dominant position by preventing the supply of spare parts for its engines (which were used in trains owned and operated by the Danish State Railway) outside of its exclusive dealership network. The Competition Council also found that the agreement between Deutz and its Danish distributor infringed Article 101 as it prevented parallel imports: see ECN Brief 03/2013, p5.

Fn 172 In Case C-56/12P *European Federation of Ink and Ink Cartridge Manufacturers (EFIM) v Commission*, EU:C:2013:575, the Court of Justice dismissed the appeal against the General Court's conclusion that there were separate markets for printers and ink-jet cartridges, and upheld its rejection of the complaint alleging abuse of dominance in the market for the supply of ink cartridges. The case is discussed in paragraph 4.055 of the main text, and the update thereto.

3. Abuse of a Dominant Position

(a) Introduction

Relevant factors for finding abuse.   In respect of the evidence required to sub-   **10.056**
stantiate an infringement, in Case T-286/09 *Intel v Commission*, EU:T:2014:547, [2014] 5 CMLR 270 the General Court held that a response to a request under Article 18 of Regulation 1/2003 from a third party undertaking that was a customer of the dominant undertaking is particularly reliable, in view of the risk of retaliatory measures that it faces if it wrongly accuses the dominant undertaking of anti-competitive conduct: eg paras 680 et seq. Moreover, the Court held that it is not necessary to require corroborative evidence to support such a response, in the same way as under Article 101 where one cartelist admits participation in an infringement and the other cartelist(s) contests its accuracy. The third party Article 18 response could, on its own, suffice to prove the facts constituting an infringement of Article 102: paras 717 et seq. On further appeal, Case C-413/14P, not yet decided.

(b) Some basic concepts

Anti-competitive intent.   **10.058**
Fn 231 In C-457/10P *AstraZeneca v Commission*, EU:C:2012:770, [2013] 4 CMLR 233, it was argued that deliberate fraud or deceit should be required in order to find an abuse in the context of alleged misrepresentations to public authorities for the purposes of acquiring exclusive rights: para 71. The Court of Justice did not directly rule on the point, but held that AstraZeneca had, on the facts of that case, deliberately misled the relevant patent offices, and that a consideration of whether a dominant undertaking has misled the authorities 'may' vary according to the circumstances of each case: paras 74 et seq. It suggested, however, that not every objectively wrong representation will be an abuse, where it was made unintentionally and immediately rectified: para 99.

Fn 236 The Court of Justice dismissed the appeals in Case C-457/10P *AstraZeneca v Commission*, EU:C:2012:770, [2013] 4 CMLR 233. On this point, see in particular para 129.

Anti-competitive effects. In Case T-286/09 *Intel v Commission*,   **10.059**
EU:T:2014:547, [2014] 5 CMLR 270 the General Court held that in the case of 'exclusivity rebates' (see the updates to paragraphs 10.091 et seq, below) it is

not necessary to establish anti-competitive effects, as these rebates are by their very nature capable of restricting competition. The case law requires a consideration of the effects of a rebate only where it is non-exclusive but may nonetheless have a loyalty-inducing effect: paras 80 et seq. The General Court further dismissed the complaints regarding the Commission's application of the 'as efficient competitor' or 'AEC' test. It held that even if it were necessary to consider the effects of the rebates in question, it would still not be necessary to do so by means of an AEC test. An AEC test would establish whether access to the market had been made impossible by the conduct in question, but it would not rule out the possibility that it had been made more difficult and it would not therefore rule out that there had been a foreclosure effect: paras 142 et seq. The Court distinguished the case law requiring an analysis of the circumstances of the case, and the application of an AEC test, as being concerned with pricing practices: paras 99 and 152 respectively. It also held that the Guidance on the Commission's enforcement priorities in applying Article 82 of the EC Treaty to abusive exclusionary conduct by dominant undertakings, OJ 2009 C45/7, sets priorities for the Commission's future enforcement activities; it does not apply to proceedings that had already been initiated before it was published, even if it was published prior to the adoption of the contested decision in those proceedings. The Guidance therefore did not affect its conclusion that it was not necessary for the Commission to conduct an AEC test: paras 154–156. On further appeal, Case C-413/14P, not yet decided.

Fn 238 See also C-457/10P *AstraZeneca v Commission*, EU:C:2012:770, [2013] 4 CMLR 233, para 112.

Fn 241 The Court of Justice dismissed the appeals in Case C-457/10P *AstraZeneca v Commission*, EU:C:2012:770, [2013] 4 CMLR 233. On this point, see in particular para 112: 'it is sufficient to demonstrate that there is a potential anti-competitive effect'. It also dismissed the further appeal in Case C-295/12P *Telefónica de España v Commission*, EU:C:2014:2062.

10.062 **Proportionality.**
Fn 249 The Court of Justice dismissed the appeals, on other grounds, in Case C-457/10P *AstraZeneca v Commission*, EU:C:2012:770, [2013] 4 CMLR 233.

10.080 **Alignment of prices with the competition.**
Fn 295 See also the decision of the French Autorité de la concurrence, fining the owners of a daily sports newspaper for having launched a product to compete with a new entrant, using the same format, price, and date of launch as the new entrant's product, at a cost to it that included sacrificing some of its sales of its traditional product in favour of the new product: Decision 14-D-02 of 20 February 2014, on appeal to the Cour d'Appel de Paris, not yet decided; see also ECN Brief 02/2014, p7.

(c) Own market abuses

(iii) Fidelity and loyalty rebates

Fidelity rebates, discounts and similar practices. In Case T-286/09 *Intel v* **10.091**
Commission, EU:T:2014:547, [2014] 5 CMLR 270 the General Court distinguished three types of rebates, all of which it held require different analyses under
Article 102:

(a) Quantity rebates: rebates linked solely to the volume of purchases made from
the dominant undertaking. These are presumed to be linked to efficiencies
and economies of scale and are generally considered not to have foreclosure
effects: para 75, following Case T-203/01 *Michelin v Commission* [2003] ECR
II-4071, para 58.

(b) Exclusivity rebates: rebates which are conditional upon the purchaser obtaining all, or most, of its requirements from the dominant undertaking. These
are designed to prevent customers from obtaining their supplies from competing producers and are by their very nature capable of restricting competition. It is not necessary to consider the individual circumstances of the case
to determine whether they have a foreclosure effect: paras 76 et seq, following
Case 85/76 *Hoffmann-La Roche v Commission* [1979] ECR 461, paras 89–90.
It is also not necessary to consider whether there might be other reasons for
the purchaser obtaining all, or most, of its requirements from the dominant undertaking; the relevant question is whether the level of the rebates
is conditional upon exclusivity: eg paras 539 et seq. The Court's judgment
regarding the need to assess effects is discussed in the update to paragraph
10.059, above.

(c) Non-exclusive rebates, which may nonetheless have loyalty-inducing effects: rebates which are granted on a basis other than volume of purchases,
or exclusivity. An example of such a rebate would be one that depends on the
attainment of non-exclusive sales objectives. These require a consideration
of all the circumstances, in particular the criteria for determining whether
the rebate is granted, to analyse whether they tend to remove or restrict the
buyer's freedom to choose his supplier, to bar competitors from accessing the
market, or to strengthen the supplier's dominant position: paras 78 et seq; following *Michelin* para 74; and Case C-95/04 P *British Airways v Commission*
[2007] ECR I-2331.

On further appeal, Case C-413/14P, not yet decided.

Two stages of analysis. In Case T-286/09 *Intel v Commission*, EU:T:2014:547, **10.092**
[2014] 5 CMLR 270, the General Court has distinguished three types of rebates,
all of which require different analysis under Article 102: see the update to paragraph 10.091, above. The first stage of the analysis described in the main text is
only necessary in the case of non-exclusive rebates that may nonetheless have

loyalty-inducing effects. As to the requirement to show that the rebates result in below cost pricing, the General Court dismissed the complaints regarding the Commission's application of the 'as efficient competitor' or 'AEC' test, as it was not necessary to conduct such a test: see the update to paragraph 10.059, above. On further appeal, Case C-413/14P, not yet decided.

10.093 **Exclusionary effect of loyalty rebates.** In Case T-286/09 *Intel v Commission*, EU:T:2014:547, [2014] 5 CMLR 270, the General Court has distinguished three types of rebates, all of which require different analysis under Article 102: see the update to paragraph 10.091, above. An analysis of the exclusionary effects of the rebates is only necessary in the case of non-exclusive rebates that may nonetheless have loyalty-inducing effects. On further appeal, Case C-413/14P, not yet decided.

10.094 **Exclusionary effect of turnover-related discounts.** In Case T-286/09 *Intel v Commission*, EU:T:2014:547, [2014] 5 CMLR 270, the General Court has distinguished three types of rebates, all of which require different analysis under Article 102: see the update to paragraph 10.091, above. An analysis of the exclusionary effects of the rebates is only necessary in the case of non-exclusive rebates that may nonetheless have loyalty-inducing effects. Turnover-related discounts would fall within this category, on the General Court's analysis. On further appeal, Case C-413/14P, not yet decided.

10.095 **Exclusionary effect of stepped discount arrangements.** In Case T-286/09 *Intel v Commission*, EU:T:2014:547, [2014] 5 CMLR 270, the General Court has distinguished three types of rebates, all of which require different analysis under Article 102: see the update to paragraph 10.091, above. An analysis of the exclusionary effects of the rebates is only necessary in the case of non-exclusive rebates that may nonetheless have loyalty-inducing effects. Stepped discounts would fall within this category, on the General Court's analysis. On further appeal, Case C-413/14P, not yet decided.

10.096 **Criticism of the case law.** In Case T-286/09 *Intel v Commission*, EU:T:2014:547, [2014] 5 CMLR 270, the General Court has distinguished three types of rebates, all of which require different analysis under Article 102: see the update to paragraph 10.091, above. An analysis of the exclusionary effects of the rebates is only necessary in the case of non-exclusive rebates that may nonetheless have loyalty-inducing effects. As the Court considered that Intel's rebates fell within its second category of exclusive rebates, which are by their very nature capable of restricting competition, it held that no effects analysis was necessary. It did not consider the question whether the Commission should be required to establish likely, as opposed to possible, exclusionary effects in those cases where an effects analysis is required. On further appeal, Case C-413/14P, not yet decided.

10.097 **Discounts dependent on the dominant firm's discretion.** In Case T-286/09 *Intel v Commission*, EU:T:2014:547, [2014] 5 CMLR 270, the General Court has distinguished three types of rebates, all of which require different analysis under Article 102: see the update to paragraph 10.091, above. An analysis of the exclusionary effects of the rebates is only necessary in the case of non-exclusive rebates that may nonetheless have loyalty-inducing effects. Discretionary discounts would fall within this category, on the General Court's analysis. On further appeal, Case C-413/14P, not yet decided.

Bundled rebates.   In Case T-286/09 *Intel v Commission*, EU:T:2014:547, [2014] **10.098**
5 CMLR 270, the General Court has distinguished three types of rebates, all of which require different analysis under Article 102: see the update to paragraph 10.091, above. An analysis of the exclusionary effects of the rebates is only necessary in the case of non-exclusive rebates that may nonetheless have loyalty-inducing effects. Bundled rebates would fall within this category, on the General Court's analysis. On further appeal, Case C-413/14P, not yet decided.

(iv) Exclusive dealing and long-term contracts

Exclusive dealing.   In Case T-286/09 *Intel v Commission*, EU:T:2014:547, [2014] **10.101**
5 CMLR 270, at paras 167 et seq, the General Court upheld the Commission's conclusion that payments by a dominant undertaking to a distributor for exclusive purchase of the dominant undertaking's products were to be considered equivalent to the rebates granted to the dominant undertaking's direct customers. Both types of payments entailed the dominant undertaking using its power on the non-contestable part of the market as leverage in the contestable part, to make it more difficult for its competitor to access the contestable part. The only difference between the payments was the level of the supply chain at which the recipients operated. The General Court also held that it is not necessary, in the context of Article 102, to analyse the cumulative effect of a network of exclusive relationship as in the context of Article 101: para 170. On further appeal, Case C-413/14P, not yet decided.

Fn 381 See also the decision of the Danish Competition Council of 12 June 2013 finding an abuse of dominance by Deutz, a German engine manufacturer, in preventing the supply of spare parts for its engines (which were used in trains owned and operated by the Danish State Railway) outside of its exclusive dealership network. The Competition Council also found that the agreement between Deutz and its Danish distributor infringed Article 101 as it prevented parallel imports: ECN Brief 03/2013, p5.

Fn 382 See also, for example, the UK CMA decision *'Western Isles Road Fuels'*, decision of 24 June 2014, in which the CMA accepted commitments to amend or terminate contracts which contained five-year exclusive purchasing obligations.

Long-term agreements.   **10.102**
Fn 385 See also, for example, the UK CMA decision *'Western Isles Road Fuels'*, decision of 24 June 2014, in which the CMA accepted commitments to amend or terminate contracts which contained five-year exclusive purchasing obligations.

10.105 Product swaps.

Fn 394 The Commission decision in COMP/37990 *Intel*, decision of 13 May 2009, was upheld on appeal in Case T-286/09 *Intel v Commission*, EU:T:2014:547, [2014] 5 CMLR 270 (on further appeal, Case C-413/14P, not yet decided). The General Court confirmed that Intel's payments to its customers to delay the launch of products that incorporated its competitor's central processing units were abusive, and it upheld the Commission's reliance on Case T-228/97 *Irish Sugar v Commission* [1999] ECR II-2969 in that regard: see paras 198 et seq.

(v) Excessive pricing

10.110 Royalties for intellectual property rights. In Case C-351/12 *OSA*, EU:C:2014:110, [2014] 4 CMLR 671 the Court of Justice held that if a collecting society charges fees that are appreciably higher than those charged by collecting societies in other Member States, without the difference being objectively justified by the different conditions in those other Member States, those fees may infringe Article 102. Similarly, the Competition Council of Latvia has fined the Latvian collective copyright management association, which has exclusive rights to license public use of musical works in Latvia, for abusing its dominant position by imposing excessive royalty tariffs. The Competition Council compared the level of tariffs imposed across Europe, and in particular in neighbouring Lithuania and Estonia, with those in Latvia and found that the tariffs in Latvia were 50–100 per cent higher than in other Member States: ECN Brief 02/2013, p8.

10.111 Benchmark comparators. In Case C-351/12 *OSA*, EU:C:2014:110, [2014] 4 CMLR 671 the Court of Justice held that if a collecting society charges fees that are appreciably higher than those charged by collecting societies in other Member States, without the difference being objectively justified by the different conditions in those other Member States, those fees may infringe Article 102.

(d) Related market abuses

(ii) Margin squeeze

10.114 Margin squeezing is a distinct abuse.

Fn 434 The finding of abuse of dominance against TeliaSonera was upheld by the Swedish Market Court, although the fine imposed on it by the City Court was reduced: ECN Brief 02/2013, p13.

Fn 436 The Court of Justice dismissed the further appeal in Case C-295/12P *Telefónica de España v Commission*, EU:C:2014:2062.

Fn 437 The Court of Justice dismissed the further appeal in Case C-295/12P *Telefónica de España v Commission*, EU:C:2014:2062.

10.115 Margin squeeze: the applicable costs test. The Court of Justice dismissed the further appeal in Case C-295/12P *Telefónica de España v Commission*, EU:C:2014:2062.

Need to prove anti-competitive effects.   See also the Court of Justice's judg-   **10.116**
ment in Case C-295/12P *Telefónica de España v Commission*, EU:C:2014:2062, at
para 124, in which the Court held:

> '… in order to establish that a practice such as a margin squeeze is abusive, that
> practice must have an anti-competitive effect on the market, although the effect
> does not necessarily have to be concrete, it being sufficient to demonstrate that
> there is a potential anti-competitive effect which may exclude competitors who are
> at least as efficient as the dominant undertaking …'

Margin squeezing: remedies.   **10.120**
Fn 466 In *Albion Water v Dŵr Cymru Cyfyngedig* [2013] CAT 6, the Competition
Appeal Tribunal rejected Dŵr Cymru's argument that for the purposes of quantifying the damage that Albion had suffered as a result of the margin squeeze
it had to determine what price could lawfully have been charged. It held that
where a dominant undertaking could have charged a range of prices, absent its
unlawful conduct, the counterfactual should be constructed using a figure in the
middle of the range of lawful prices, not the highest that could lawfully have been
charged: paras 69–71.

Cross-subsidisation as a distinct form of abuse?   See also the decision of the   **10.121**
French Autorité de la concurrence accepting commitments from the monopoly
provider of horse race betting at physical outlets in France that it will keep bets
placed at its physical outlets separate from those placed with it online. This
was not a case in which the dominant undertaking used cross-subsidisation to
cover losses in the related market, but rather where the revenues generated in
one market were used to enhance the product offered in the related market,
resulting in an advantage that commercial rivals could not match. The Autorité
accepted commitments in response to a complaint from one of the dominant
undertaking's competitors in the provision on online betting services that the
practice of pooling bets meant the dominant undertaking was able to offer
much larger prizes, which undertakings providing online betting services only
could not compete with: Decision 14-D-04 of 25 February 2014; see also ECN
Brief 02/2014, p8.

(iv) Tying and bundling

Two distinct products must be tied.   **10.124**
Fn 479 The Commission exercised its power under Article 23(2)(c) of Regulation
1/2003 for the first time in COMP/39530 *Microsoft – Tying*, decision of 6 March
2013, when Microsoft failed to comply with the commitments decision of
16 December 2009. It imposed a fine of €561 million.

The General Court dismissed the appeal in Case T-74/11 *Omnis Group v
Commission*, EU:T:2013:283, as there was not sufficient evidence to establish that
there was or might be an abuse.

10.127 **Tying of other ancillary services.**
Fn 491 The Commission has accepted commitments offered by Rio Tinto Alcan to address concerns relating to the tying of its aluminium smelting technology to the supply of its aluminium smelter equipment: COMP/39230 *Rio Tinto Alcan*, decision of 20 December 2012.

10.128 **Objective justification of tying practices.** In COMP/39230 *Rio Tinto Alcan*, decision of 20 December 2012, paras 86 et seq. the putatively dominant undertaking wished to rely on alleged efficiencies, and the Commission's preliminary assessment was that it could not do so as it did not meet the four criteria outlined in para 30 of its Guidance on the Commission's enforcement priorities in applying Article 82 of the EC Treaty to abusive exclusionary conduct by dominant undertakings, OJ 2009 C45/7. Moreover, it considered that 'any efficiency enhancing tying must be driven by customer preferences for joint consumption': para 89.

(v) Refusal to supply

10.131 **Constructive refusal to supply.**
Fn 505 See also the decision of the Italian Competition Authority of 9 May 2013 finding Telecom Italia, the incumbent in telecommunications markets in Italy, had constructively refused to supply access to its network by rejecting a large proportion of competitors' wholesale orders. The Competition Authority found that the orders were rejected as a result of the different delivery processes Telecom Italia used to provide wholesale services as compared with those it used internally, and that Telecom Italia could have adjusted the delivery processes to reduce the level of rejections of wholesale orders by competitors: ECN Brief 03/2013, p6.

10.133 **Exclusion of downstream competition.**
Fn 516 See also, for example, the decision of the Slovakian Antimonopoly Office finding an abusive refusal to supply electric locomotives to the dominant company's competitors in the freight rail transport market, who were only able to access less efficient and more costly diesel locomotives: ECN Brief 04/2013, p9. Decision on appeal, not yet decided.

10.139 **Dominant undertaking's presence in downstream market.** In *Arriva the Shires v London Luton Airport* [2014] EWHC 64 (Ch), the High Court held that a refusal to supply can be an abuse even in circumstances where the dominant undertaking is neither present in the downstream market, nor restricting the ability of its upstream competitors to access a downstream market. The General Court judgment in Case T-128/98 *Aéroports de Paris v Commission* [2000] ECR II-3929 at para 173 establishes that it is not necessary for a dominant undertaking to obtain a commercial benefit from its conduct in order for that conduct to be considered abusive, and that case is not confined to discriminatory pricing complaints. In the alternative, the Court held that if it did have to be shown that the dominant undertaking obtained a commercial benefit, that benefit need not be obtained as a result of the dominant undertaking being present on the downstream market. It could be obtained from the dominant undertaking having an interest in the downstream market, such as, in that case, by it receiving revenues from the grant of an exclusive right to downstream operators. The Court concluded that, in that case, granting an exclusive right to access the Luton airport bus station, in order to operate coach journeys between Luton Airport and London, for a period of seven years was anti-competitive and distorted competition between coach operators. The grant of that right was analogous to the grant considered by the European Commission in Case COMP/38173 *Joint selling of the media rights for the FA Premier League*, decision of 22 March 2006.

Refusal to satisfy demand generated by parallel trade. In *Chemistree Homecare*   **10.141**
v Abbvie [2013] EWHC 264 (Ch), paras 43–44, the High Court held that where a dominant undertaking has chosen to distribute its product by supplying only to retailers, and has a policy of not supplying wholesalers, then orders placed by a customer for the undisclosed purpose of reselling the product on the wholesale market are not ordinary (upheld, on other grounds, in *Chemistree Homecare v Abbvie* [2013] EWCA Civ 1338, where the Court of Appeal agreed that dominance could not be established).

(e) Other forms of abuse

Generally.   **10.142**
Fn 555 In France, the Autorité de la concurrence has taken a number of decisions against originator pharmaceutical companies for abusing their dominant positions by adopting strategies of unjustifiedly denigrating their generic competitors. On 14 May 2013 it fined Sanofi-Aventis €40.6 million for abuse of dominance by denigrating the generic versions of clopidogrel, an anti-platelet medication used to prevent relapses of serious cardiovascular diseases: Decision 13-D-11 of 14 May 2013. Sanofi-Aventis had adopted a strategy of questioning, with doctors and pharmacists, the efficacy and safety of the generics' products, and intimating that the doctors/pharmacists could be held liable for any problems they caused, in order to limit generic entry and protect the market position of its branded clopidogrel 'Plavix', and its own generic 'Clopidogrel Winthrop'. The Autorité found Sanofi-Aventis' communications were based on unsubstantiated assertion. The appeal to the Cour d'Appel de Paris was dismissed, by decision of 18 December 2014. See also ECN Brief 03/2013, p8. On 19 December 2013 the Autorité fined Schering-Plough €15.3 million for abuse of dominance by unjustifiedly denigrating the generic version of buprenorphine, used to treat opiate addiction: Decision 13-D-21 of December 2013; appeal to the Cour d'Appel de Paris, dismissed on 26 May 2015.

See also ECN Brief 01/2014, p5. The Autorité is still investigating a possible breach in respect of fentanyl, an analgesic.

In addition, the French Autorité de la concurrence has fined the electricity provider EDF for abuse of dominance by allowing one of its subsidiaries, operating in the emerging market for photovoltaic solar power, to market its services under the EDF brand (including using a similar logo and trademark to EDF) and using the EDF customer database to access customers for marketing purposes. Competitors were adversely affected, because consumers confused the subsidiary with EDF itself, and competitors could not replicate the advantages that the subsidiary enjoyed. Decision 13-D-20 of 17 December 2013, appeal to the the Cour d'Appel de Paris dismissed, 9 April 2014. See also ECN Brief 01/2014, p7.

10.143 **Unfair trading conditions.**
Fn 556 More recently, see COMP/39523 *Slovak Telekom*, decision of 15 October 2014, in which the Commission found Slovak Telekom and its parent company, Deutsche Telekom, infringed Article 102 by setting unfair terms and conditions for unbundled access to its local loop and imposing a margin squeeze. On appeal, Case T-851/14 *Slovak Telekom v Commission*, and T-827/14 *Deutsche Telekom v Commission*, not yet decided.

10.145 **Unfair trading conditions imposed by a collective agreement or as standard industry practice.** The Netherlands NCA has accepted commitments from the Dutch copyright collecting society to undertake to allow composers and songwriters more choice as to the rights they transfer to the society, after commencing an investigation into whether the society had abused a dominant position by requiring all rights be transferred to it, if a copyright holder wished to join the society, including the right to collect royalties for performances on the internet where the copyright holders would have the technical means to collect the royalties themselves, if they wished. See ECN Brief 03/2014, p6.

10.146 **Abuse by sporting bodies.**
Fn 573 The Court of Justice dismissed the further appeal in Case C-269/12P *Cañas v Commission*, EU:C:2013:415, regarding the alleged anti-competitiveness of certain anti-doping rules.

10.151 **Abusive use of litigation.** The Court of Justice in Case C-170/13 *Huawei v ZTE* EU:C:2015:477 considered whether it was contrary to Article 102 for a dominant undertaking to bring proceedings before a Member State court to enforce a standard essential patent ('SEP'), in circumstances where the patent has acquired SEP status as a result of the proprietor having irrevocably undertaken to the standard-setting body that it will license on fair, reasonable and non-discriminatory ('FRAND') terms. The Court held that to bring such proceedings may in principle be contrary to Article 102. The proprietor's undertaking to the standard setting body does not deprive it of its right to bring an action before the courts of a Member State to enforce its patent, but it must comply with specific requirements when it does so. These are to notify the alleged infringer of the SEP and its breach; to make a specific, written offer of a licence on FRAND terms specifying the royalty and the way in which it has been calculated. The alleged infringer must respond in good faith, and without delay. If it does not accept the offer, it must promptly make a written counter-offer that corresponds to FRAND terms, and if its counter-offer is rejected and it is using the teachings of the SEP then from the point of rejection it must provide appropriate security. The parties may agree to submit the determination of the amount of the royalty to a third party. If the proprietor has complied with the requirements incumbent upon it, or if the alleged infringer has failed to comply with the requirements incumbent upon it, then it is not an abuse of the proprietor's dominant position for it to commence litigation to enforce its patent.

Following its investigation into alleged abusive conduct in relation to intellectual property rights used in international telecoms standards, in COMP/39985 *Motorola – enforcement of ETSI standards essential patents*, decision of 29 April 2014, the Commission has found Motorola breached Article 102 by seeking an injunction in Germany against Apple for breach of standard essential patents (which were essential to meeting the European Telecommunications Standardisation Institute's (ETSI) GPRS standard, part of the GSM standard, which is a key industry standard for mobile and wireless communications), in circumstances where it had committed to license on FRAND terms, and where Apple was willing to enter into a licence agreement and to be bound by a determination by the German Court of the FRAND terms. However, in view of the novelty of the infringement finding, no fine has been imposed.

The Commission accepted commitments from Samsung in COMP/39939 *Samsung – enforcement of ETSI standards essential patents*, decision of 29 April 2014. In its preliminary assessment, the Commission considered that Samsung had infringed Article 102 by seeking injunctions against Apple in several Member States to enforce SEPs that were essential to complying with ETSI's 3G UMTS standard (a key standard for mobile and wireless communications), and that Samsung had committed to license on FRAND terms. The Commission has accepted commitments under which Samsung agrees, in essence, for a period of five years not to seek an injunction before any court or tribunal in the EEA for infringement of its SEPs implemented in mobile devices against a potential licensee that agrees to, and complies with, a particular framework set out in the commitments decision for determining the terms of a licence.

In COMP/39612 *Perindopril (Servier)*, decision of 9 July 2013, the Commission found that Servier had infringed Article 102 by entering into agreements with five generics companies in the settlement of litigation, which included 'reverse payments' by Servier to those companies, together with an agreement to purchase the most advanced non-protected technology. On appeal, Case T-691/14, not yet decided.

Fn 592 The Court of Justice dismissed the appeals, on other grounds, in Case C-457/10P *AstraZeneca v Commission*, EU:C:2012:770, [2013] 4 CMLR 233.

11

THE COMPETITION RULES AND
THE ACTS OF MEMBER STATES

2. State Compulsion

Scope for residual competition. **11.006**
Fn 19 The Court of Justice dismissed the further appeal in Case C-181/11P
Compañía española de tabaco en rama v Commission, EU:C:2012:455.

3. The Application and Enforcement of the Prohibition
in Article 106(1)

Public undertakings. **11.011**
Fn 41 The General Court judgment annulling the Commission's decision in
COMP/38700 *Greek Lignite and Electricity Generation*, decision of 5 March 2008,
was overturned by the Court of Justice in Case C-553/12P *Commission v DEI*,
EU:C:2014:2083, [2014] 5 CMLR 945. See the update to paragraph 11.021, below.

Undertakings granted special or exclusive rights. Similarly to the au- **11.012**
thors' rights society case considered in the main text, in Case T-55/08 *UEFA v
Commission*, EU:T:2011:43 [2011] ECR II-0271, at paras 165–171, the General
Court held that broadcasters that benefited from being able to broadcast events
designated by a Member State as events of major importance for society within
that Member State (under Directive Article 3a(1) of Council Directive 89/552/
EEC of 3 October 1989 on the coordination of certain provisions laid down by
law, regulation or administrative action in Member States concerning the pursuit
of television broadcasting activities (OJ 1989 L 298, p23)) are not within the
scope of Article 106(1), because it was open to all broadcasters to acquire the right
to broadcast such events. The fact that in practice certain broadcasters would not
be interested in acquiring the right, because they were only interested in exclusive
broadcasting, was not sufficient to render the rights granted 'exclusive' within
Article 106(1). The Court upheld the Commission's decision that the designation

by the UK of the European Football Championship as an event of major importance for UK society was compatible with EU law. The Court of Justice dismissed the further appeal in Cases C-201, 204, 205/11P *UEFA and FIFA v Commission*, EU:C:2013:519, [2014] 1 CMLR 471, paras 78–79.

Fn 43 The General Court judgment annulling the Commission's decision in COMP/38700 *Greek Lignite and Electricity Generation*, decision of 5 March 2008, was overturned by the Court of Justice in Case C-553/12P *Commission v DEI*, EU:C:2014:2083, [2014] 5 CMLR 945. See the update to paragraph 11.021, below.

11.013 **Special and exclusive rights.**
Fn 52 In Case C-327/12 *SOA Nazionale Costruttori*, EU:C:2013:827, at paras 41– 42, the Court of Justice held that special and exclusive rights were not granted in circumstances where a limited number of undertakings were entrusted with the task of providing certification services under a statutory certification scheme, as the scheme permitted additional undertakings to be authorised to provide the services if they met the statutory conditions for doing so.

11.014 **Measures of the Member State.**   The General Court upheld the Commission's decision in COMP/39562 *Slovakian postal legislation relating to hybrid mail services*, decision of 7 October 2008, discussed in the main text, in Case T-556/08 *Slovenská pošta v Commission*, EU:T:2015:189, [2015] 4 CMLR 1024. On further appeal, Case C-293/15P, not yet decided.

11.016 **Link between the measure and the breach by the undertaking.**   The Court of Justice in Case C-553/12P *Commission v DEI*, EU:C:2014:2083, [2014] 5 CMLR 945, at para 42 followed Case C-49/07 *MOTOE*, EU:C:2008:376, [2008] ECR I-4863, [2008] 5 CMLR 790 and confirmed that there will be a breach of Article 106 in conjunction with Article 102 where a measure imputable to a Member State gives rise to a risk of an abuse of a dominant position. It overturned the General Court judgment discussed in paragraph 11.021 of the main text (see the update thereto, below).

11.017 **Inability to satisfy demand.**   The General Court upheld the Commission's decision in COMP/39562 *Slovakian postal legislation relating to hybrid mail services*, decision of 7 October 2008, discussed in the main text, in Case T-556/08 *Slovenská pošta v Commission*, EU:T:2015:189, [2015] 4 CMLR 1024. The General Court in particular upheld the Commission's conclusion that the delivery of hybrid mail was accompanied by demand for specific additional services which Slovenská pošta was not able to satisfy: para 350. On further appeal, Case C-293/15P, not yet decided.

11.018 **Extension of dominance into neighbouring markets.**   The Court of Justice in Case C-553/12P *Commission v DEI*, EU:C:2014:2083, [2014] 5 CMLR 945, at paras 58–59 dismissed the argument that an extension of dominance into neighbouring markets will not infringe Article 106 in conjunction with Article 102 unless the State measure at issue grants or enhances special or exclusive rights. It is sufficient that the State measure at issue creates a situation in which a public undertaking, or an undertaking which has been granted special or exclusive rights, is led to abuse its dominant position. The Court also confirmed that it is an infringement of Article 106 in conjunction with Article 102 'as such' to extend a dominant position into a neighbouring market without objective justification, where the extension results from a State measure. It dismissed the argument that it was necessary to show in every case that the undertaking enjoys a legal or *de facto* monopoly; that the State measure at issue grants exclusive or special rights over the market into which dominance has been extended; that the undertaking in question has any regulatory powers; or that there is an impact on consumers: paras 66–68.

Fn 68 The General Court upheld the Commission's decision in COMP/39562 *Slovakian postal legislation relating to hybrid mail services*, decision of 7 October 2008, in Case T-556/08 *Slovenská pošta v Commission*, EU:T:2015:189, [2015] 4 CMLR 1024.

Fee tariffs. In *Shannon LNG and another v Commission for Energy Regulation* **11.020** *and others* [2013] IEHC 568, the High Court of Ireland dismissed a complaint that the methodology adopted by the regulator for setting the tariff for access to and use of the gas transmission system and pipeline network would lead to the transmission operator abusing its dominant position contrary to Article 102, and would constitute an unlawful state measure contrary to Article 106. No actual tariffs had yet been determined, so it could not be said that the regulator's methodology would necessarily bring about either abusive conduct or an advantage to the transmission operator.

Distortion of competition in the market not enough. The Court of Justice in **11.021** Case C-553/12P *Commission v DEI*, EU:C:2014:2083, [2014] 5 CMLR 945, has overturned the General Court judgment discussed in the main text. In order to establish an infringement of Article 106 in conjunction with Article 102 it is not necessary for the Commission to show that a former monopolistic undertaking, which continues to hold a dominant position, has in fact abused that dominant position. An infringement will arise where inequality of opportunity between operators, and thus distorted competition, is the result of a State measure. The Court held at paragraph 46 that:

> '... infringement of [Article 106] in conjunction with [Article 102] may be established irrespective of whether any abuse actually exists. All that is necessary is for the Commission to identify a potential or actual anti-competitive consequence liable to result from the State measure at issue. Such an infringement may thus be established where the State measures at issue allowing the public undertaking or the undertaking which was granted special or exclusive rights to maintain (for example, by hindering new entrants to the market), strengthen or extend its dominant position over another market, thereby restricting competition, without it being necessary to prove the existence of actual abuse.'

6. Derogations under Articles 106(2) and 346

(a) Article 106(2) TFEU: services of general interest

11.046 **In general.** To satisfy Article 106(2), the Member State must also establish that the rights granted to the undertaking are proportionate, and in particular do not go beyond what is necessary effectively to achieve the objective pursued: see the update to paragraph 11.058, below.

11.048 **Article 106(2) and State aids.**
Fn 165 The Commission issued a Staff Working Document, in April 2013 (SWD(2013) 53/final 2, *'Guide to the application of the European Union rules on state aid, public procurement and the internal market to services of general economic interest, and in particular to social services of general interest'.*

11.049 **The act of entrustment.** The Commission issued a Staff Working Document, in April 2013 (SWD(2013) 53/final 2, *'Guide to the application of the European Union rules on state aid, public procurement and the internal market to services of general economic interest, and in particular to social services of general interest'.* It contains the same indication as to the requirements of an 'act of entrustment': see section 3.2.2, in particular para 55.

11.051 **Member States' discretion in defining SGEIs.** The Commission issued a Staff Working Document, in April 2013 (SWD(2013) 53/final 2, *'Guide to the application of the European Union rules on state aid, public procurement and the internal market to services of general economic interest, and in particular to social services of general interest'.* On the definition of SGEIs, see section 2, in particular para 5.

Fn 177 See also Case T-57/11 *Castelnou Energía v Commission*, EU:T:2014:1021, para 136. The General Court further held, at para 190, that if a measure falls within Article 106(2), and does not pursue environmental protection objectives, the Commission does not have to assess the compatibility of the measure with EU environmental rules, because if it were to do so would it encroach on the Member States' discretion to identify the services they will regard as SGEIs.

11.053 **Activities which are SGEIs.**
Fn 185 See also Case T-57/11 *Castelnou Energía v Commission*, EU:T:2014:1021, paras 136 et seq.

Fn 186 For a more recent example, see SA.38788 *Compensation to Post Office Limited for costs incurred in providing SGEIs 2015–2018*, decision of 19 March 2015.

11.054 **Activities which are not SGEIs.** In Case C-1/12 *Ordem dos Técnicos Oficiais de Contas v Autoridade da Concorrência*, EU:C:2013:127, [2013] 4 CMLR 651, para 105, the Court of Justice expressed doubts as to whether the provision of compulsory training to chartered accountants is within the scope of Article 106(2).

Fn 194 The Commission's decision in COMP/38698 *CISAC Agreements*, decision of 16 July 2008, was partially annulled by the General Court on other grounds: Cases T-392, 398, 401, 410, 411, 413–422, 425, 428, 432–434, 442/08, judgments of 12 April 2013, [2013] 5 CMLR 536.

Fn 197 The Commission issued a Staff Working Document, in April 2013 (SWD(2013) 53/final 2, *'Guide to the application of the European Union rules on state aid, public procurement and the internal market to services of general economic interest, and in particular to social services of general interest'*. On activities consisting in advertising, e-commerce, the use of premium-rate telephone numbers in prize games, sponsorship and merchandising, see para 7.

Fn 198 In the revised Staff Working Document, see para 10.

Obstructing the performance of the tasks. To satisfy Article 106(2), the Member State must establish that the rights granted to the undertaking are proportionate, and in particular do not go beyond what is necessary effectively to achieve the objective pursued: see the update to paragraph 11.058, below.   **11.056**

Fn 200 See also Case T-137/10 *Coordination bruxelloise d'Institutions sociales et de santé ('CBI') v Commission*, EU:T:2012:584, in which the General Court annulled the Commission's decision in Case NN54/2009 approving aid to public hospitals in Belgium, as the Commission did not have sufficient information to approve a State aid under Article 106(2) without opening a formal investigation.

Fn 203 See also Case T-57/11 *Castelnou Energía v Commission*, EU:T:2014:1021, paras 170–171.

Fn 204 See also Case T-57/11 *Castelnou Energía v Commission*, EU:T:2014:1021, paras 170–171.

The 'tailpiece': adverse development of trade. The 'tailpiece' of Article 106(2) has been interpreted by the General Court as requiring an assessment of the proportionality of the rights granted to the undertaking. The rights granted will fall outside Article 106(2) if they 'affect trade and competition significantly and to an extent which is manifestly disproportionate to the objectives pursued by the Member States': Joined Cases T-533/10&151/11 *DTS and Telfónica v Commission*, EU:T:2014:629 (on further appeal, Case C-449/14P, not yet decided). See also Case T-57/11 *Castelnou Energía v Commission*, EU:T:2014:1021, paras 147 et seq. Where Article 106(2) is relied on in respect of a measure which is State aid, the measure will by definition give rise to distortions, and it can only be considered to fall outside of Article 106(2) therefore where the distortions in question are 'substantially and manifestly disproportionate': Case T-57/11 *Castelnou Energía v Commission*, EU:T:2014:1021, paras 163–164.   **11.058**

12

SECTORAL REGIMES

2. Electronic Communications

(a) Regulatory framework

Revised regulatory framework.   **12.006**

Fn 13 The infraction proceedings brought by the Commission have been withdrawn: C-325/12 *Commission v Portugal* by Order of 5 November 2012; Case C-330/12 *Commission v Poland* by Order of 27 March 2013; and C-407/12 *Commission v Slovenia* by Order of 27 March 2013.

(i) Framework Directive

Obligations on NRAs.   **12.009**

Fn 37 On the role of the NRA in resolving disputes where it has not imposed *ex ante* regulation, see *British Telecommunications v Telefónica O2 UK* [2014] UKSC 42. Where the measure which the NRA proposes to adopt in order to resolve a dispute pursuant to Article 20 may affect trade between Member States, it must follow the procedure in Article 7(3) of the Framework Directive: Case C-3/14 *Prezes Urzędu Komunikacji Elektronicznej v T-Mobile Polska*, EU:C:2015:232, para 42.

Fn 38 The Court of Justice held in Case C-282/13 *T-Mobile Austria v Telefon-Kontrol-Kommission*, EU:C:2015:24 that an undertaking is 'affected' for the purposes of Article 4(1) of the Framework Directive in circumstances where it provides electronic communications networks or services; is a competitor of the undertaking which is party to a procedure for the authorisation of a transfer of rights to use radio frequencies (under Article 5(6) of the Authorisation Directive) and the addressee of the decision of the NRA; and its position in the market is likely to be impacted by the NRA's decision.

Exclusion of content regulation.   In Case C-518/11 *UPC Nederland v Gemeente*   **12.011** *Hilversum*, EU:C:2013:709, at para 47, the Court of Justice held that the definition of 'electronic communications services' in Article 2(c) of the Framework Directive includes the service of supplying a basic cable package, notwithstanding that the charge for that package includes the cost of payments to broadcasters and copyright collecting societies in connection with the transmission of programme content, as well as the cost of transmission.

12.013 **Imposition of regulatory obligations on undertakings.** In Case C-518/11 *UPC Nederland v Gemeente Hilversum*, EU:C:2013:709, the Court of Justice held that the common regulatory framework precludes a public authority that has not been designated as a NRA from intervening directly in a communication service provider's retail tariffs. The public authority had entered into a contractual arrangement with the provider of basic cable services, at the time the latter was privatised, which included a clause stipulating that the tariff for the service would increase annually only in accordance with the consumer price index. The Court confirmed that the common regulatory framework precludes a public authority from relying upon such a clause.

(ii) Access Directive

12.026 **Powers and responsibilities of NRAs.**
Fn 129 See also Case C-556/12 *TDC v Teleklagenaevnet*, EU:C:2014:2009.

(iii) Authorisation Directive

12.027 **General authorisation regime.**
Fn 137 In *Recall Support Services and others v Secretary of State for Culture, Media and Sport* [2013] EWHC 3091 (Ch), the High Court of England and Wales held that the UK's decision to impose a specific licence requirement, going beyond a general authorisation, on the commercial provision of communications services to multiple users through GSM gateway devices was justified on grounds of public security under Article 5 of the Authorisation Directive. The High Court did not accept that a licensing requirement was justified in relation to the commercial provision of communications services to a single user through a GSM gateway device.

Fn 144 Article 13 of the Authorisation Directive does not preclude operators providing electronic communications networks or services being subject to a general tax on establishments, on account of the presence on public or private property of the masts, pylons or antennae which are necessary for their activity, where the event that gives rise to the tax liability is not linked to the granting of rights of use for radio frequencies or rights to install facilities within the scope of Article 13 but is imposed on all legal entities established in the taxable region: Joined Cases C-256&264/13 *Provincie Antwerpen v Belgacom & Mobistar*, EU:C:2014:2149.

Questions have been referred to the Court of Justice for a preliminary ruling on whether Articles 12 and 13 of the Authorisation Directive preclude Member States from imposing a tax on telecommunications infrastructure: see Cases C-346/13 *Ville de Mons v KPM Group Belgium*, not yet decided; and C-454/13 *Belgacom v Commune d-Etterbeek*, not yet decided.

Fn 145 In Case C-375/11 *Belgacom v Belgium*, EU:C:2013:185, [2013] 3 CMLR 185, three Belgian mobile operators challenged spectrum renewal fees imposed under Belgian national law as incompatible with Article 12 of the Authorisation Directive. The Court of Justice held that a renewal fee for rights to use the spectrum falls under Article 13 of the Authorisation Directive: paras 37–39. Therefore, provided such a fee complies with the requirements of Article 13, it is not precluded by Articles 12 and 13: para 48.

The infraction proceedings against Hungary for its 'telecoms tax', referred to in the main text, is Case C-462/12 *Commission v Hungary*. The proceedings were withdrawn by Order on 22 November 2013.

(iv) Universal Service Directive

Designation and financing of undertakings. 12.032
Fn 170 The infraction proceedings against Portugal for its failure to designate a universal services provider, referred to in the main text, is Case C-325/12 *Commission v Portugal*. The proceedings were withdrawn by Order of 5 November 2012.

(v) Directive on competition in the market for ECNs and ECSs

Abolition of special and exclusive rights. In infraction proceedings against 12.033
Bulgaria, the Court of Justice held that a national scheme for the allocation of radio frequencies used for digital terrestrial broadcasting, which excluded television content providers whose programmes were not broadcast in Bulgaria and operators of telecommunications networks; and which provided for allocations to be made to only two providers in circumstances where the spectrum available would have allowed allocations to be made to five, was disproportionate and in breach of the requirements of Directive 2002/77 (the Telecommunications Competition Directive): see Case C-376/13 *Commission v Bulgaria* EU:C:2015:266.

(b) Application of competition law

(ii) Relationship of competition rules and sector-specific regulation

Parallel application of sectoral regulation and competition law. See also the 12.044
Court of Justice's judgment in Case C-295/12P *Telefónica de España v Commission*, EU:C:2014:2062, which confirms that the application of Article 102 is not restricted by the existence of an *ex ante* regulatory framework, and that compliance by an undertaking with the regulatory framework does not mean that its conduct complies with Article 102: paras 128 and 133, respectively.

More recently, in COMP/39523 *Slovak Telekom*, decision of 15 October 2014, the Commission has found Slovak Telekom and its parent company, Deutsche Telekom, infringed Article 102 by setting unfair terms and conditions for unbundled access to its local loop and imposing a margin squeeze. On appeal, Case T-851/14 *Slovak Telekom v Commission*, and T-827/14 *Deutsche Telekom v Commission*, not yet decided.

(iii) Application of Article 101

12.047 **Prevalence of agreements.** In COMP/39839 *Telefónica and Portugal Telecom*, decision of 23 January 2013, the Commission concluded that the agreement between Telefónica and Portugal Telecom not to compete on the Iberian telecommunications market for a period of time following the acquisition by Telefónica of sole control over the Brazilian mobile operator, Vivo, which had previously been owned by both parties (as noted in footnote 241 of the main text) breached Article 101, and it fined the parties €79 million. On appeal, Cases T-208/13 *Portugal Telecom v Commission*; and T-216/13 *Telefónica v Commission*, not yet decided.

12.049 **Price agreements.**
Fn 248 The Commission issued decisions in COMP/39847 *E-books*, decisions of 12 December 2012 (OJ 2012 C283/7) and of 25 July 2013 (OJ 2013 C378/25) accepting commitments from five publishing companies and Apple, to abandon the most favoured nation clauses.

12.054 **Interplay between agreements on standards and intellectual property rights.**
Fn 258 The appeals by Hynix Semiconductor (now trading as SK Hynix Inc) in Joined Cases T-148&149/10 against COMP/38636 *Rambus*, decision of 9 December 2009, were withdrawn on 5 July 2013.

In the Commission's investigation into alleged abusive conduct in relation to IPR used in international telecoms standards, in COMP/39985 *Motorola – enforcement of ETSI standards essential patents*, decision of 29 April 2014, the Commission found that Motorola breached Article 102 by seeking an injunction in Germany against Apple for breach of its standard essential patents (which were essential to meeting the European Telecommunications Standardisation Institute's (ETSI) GPRS standard, part of the GSM standard, which is a key industry standard for mobile and wireless communications), in circumstances where it had committed to license on fair, reasonable, and non-discriminatory terms ('FRAND' terms), and where Apple was willing to enter into a licence agreement and to be bound by a determination by the German Court of the FRAND terms. However, in view of the novelty of the infringement finding, no fine was imposed. The Commission accepted commitments from Samsung in COMP/39939 *Samsung – enforcement of ETSI standards essential patents*, decision of 29 April 2014. In its preliminary assessment, the Commission considered that Samsung had infringed Article 102 by seeking injunctions against Apple in several Member States to enforce patents that were essential to complying with ETSI's 3G UMTS standard (a key standard for mobile and wireless communications), and that Samsung had committed to license on FRAND terms. The Commission has accepted commitments under which Samsung agrees, in essence, for a period of five years not to seek an injunction before any court or tribunal in the EEA for infringement of its standard essential patents implemented in mobile devices against a potential licensee that agrees to, and complies with, a particular framework set out in the commitments decision for determining the terms of a licence.

(iv) Joint ventures and mergers

Mergers and full-function joint ventures.   **12.066**
Fn 289 See also M.6314 *Telefónica UK/Vodafone UK/EE/JV* (4 September 2012) (a full-function JV created to operate in the nascent 'mCommerce' sector, which consists of mobile payment applications, mobile advertising, and data analytics services); and equivalent decisions clearing JVs intended to operate in Spain M.6956 *Telefónica/Caixabank/Banco Santander/JV* (14 August 2013); and in Belgium, M.6967 *BNP Paribas Fortis/Belgacom/Belgian MobileWallet JV* (11 October 2013).

Mergers in the fixed communications sector.   In M.7000 *Ziggo/Liberty Global* **12.067** (10 October 2014) the Commission granted Phase II clearance to the merger of two operators of cable networks in the Netherlands, subject to commitments. Although the parties' networks did not overlap, they acquired the same content from TV broadcasters for inclusion in their pay-TV services. The Commission considered that the concentration would increase Liberty's buyer power as against TV channel broadcasters, and thereby allow it to hinder innovation in the delivery of audio-visual content over the internet: paras 362 et seq. Liberty therefore committed to divestment of its premium pay-TV channel, to terminate the clauses in its channel carriage agreements that limited broadcasters' ability to offer their channels and content over the internet, and to refrain from including such clauses in its future agreements for eight years. In M.7499 *Altice/PT Portugal* (20 April 2015) the Commission granted Phase II clearance subject to commitments. The parties' activities overlapped on the markets in Portugal for the retail supply of fixed voice services; the retail supply of fixed internet access services; the retail supply of pay-TV services; the retail supply of multiple play services; B2B telecommunication services; the wholesale supply of leased lines; the wholesale market for call origination services at a fixed location; and the wholesale market for call transit services at a fixed location. The merger was cleared subject to Altice committing to divest itself of its two subsidiaries through which it currently operates in Portugal.

The Commission has also considered a number of proposed mergers between undertakings in the fixed and mobile communications sectors. For example, in M.6990 *Vodafone/Kabel Deutschland* (20 September 2013) the Commission granted unconditional Phase I clearance to the acquisition by Vodafone (primarily active in the mobile telephony sector) of Kabel Deutschland (primarily active in cable TV, fixed line telephony and internet access services), as it considered that the parties' economic activities are largely complementary, and the incremental increase in their market shares in those markets where they do overlap would not appreciably alter competition. In M.7421 *Orange/Jazztel* (19 May 2015) the Commission cleared the acquisition by Orange (primarily active in the mobile telephony sector) of Jazztel (primarily active in cable TV, fixed line telephony and internet access services) at Phase II after accepting a divestiture commitment together with a commitment to allow the divestiture business wholesale access to Jazztel's network, at prices that replicate the parties' current variable costs, for up to eight years in order to ensure that it is a viable competitor in the market: paras 903 et seq.

12.068 **Mergers in the mobile communications sector.** In M.6497 *Hutchinson 3G Austria/Orange Austria* (12 December 2012) the Commission granted clearance at Phase II, subject to two conditions: that Hutchinson divest itself of spectrum frequency bands, and that it enter into network access agreements to grant mobile virtual network operators (MVNOs) wholesale access to up to 30 per cent of its network capacity in the coming 10-year period. In M.6992 *Hutchinson 3G UK/Telefonica Ireland* (28 May 2014) the Commission granted clearance at Phase II, subject to conditions similar to those imposed in M.6497 *Hutchinson 3G Austria/Orange Austria* (12 December 2012) but in addition required that the merged entity continue to offer a network sharing agreement to Eircom, one of its competitors, on improved terms, in order to ensure that Eircom should remain an effective and viable competitor.

The Commission has also considered a number of proposed mergers between undertakings in the fixed and mobile communications sectors. For example, in M.6990 *Vodafone/Kabel Deutschland* (20 September 2013) the Commission granted unconditional Phase I clearance to the acquisition by Vodafone (primarily active in the mobile telephony sector) of Kabel Deutschland (primarily active in cable TV, fixed line telephony and internet access services), as it considered that the parties' economic activities are largely complementary, and the incremental increase in their market shares in those markets where they do overlap will not appreciably alter competition. In M.7421 *Orange/Jazztel* (19 May 2015) the Commission cleared the acquisition by Orange (primarily active in the mobile telephony sector) of Jazztel (primarily active in cable TV, fixed line telephony and internet access services) at Phase II after accepting a divestiture commitment together with a commitment to allow the divestiture business wholesale access to Jazztel's network, at prices that replicate the parties' current variable costs, for up to eight years in order to ensure that it is a viable competitor in the market: paras 903 et seq.

(v) Application of Article 102

Restricting activities of competitors.   More recently, in COMP/39523 *Slovak*   **12.074**
Telekom, decision of 15 October 2014, the Commission found Slovak Telekom
and its parent company, Deutsche Telekom, infringed Article 102 by setting unfair terms and conditions for unbundled access to its local loop, which
amounted to a refusal to supply, and imposing a margin squeeze. On appeal,
Case T-851/14 *Slovak Telekom v Commission*, and T-827/14 *Deutsche Telekom v
Commission*, not yet decided.

Excessive pricing.   A further example is the decision of the French Autorité de la   **12.081**
concurrence fining the telecoms company SRR, which operates on La Réunion,
for charging excessive and discriminatory prices for calls terminating on competitors' networks, as compared with the prices for calls terminating on its own
network. The Autorité found the difference in prices was more than three times
higher than the differences in costs: Decision 14-D-05 of 13 June 2014; see also
ECN Brief 03/2014, p10.

Examples of margin squeeze.   More recently, see COMP/39523 *Slovak Telekom*,   **12.083**
decision of 15 October 2014, in which the Commission found Slovak Telekom
and its parent company, Deutsche Telekom, infringed Article 102 by setting
unfair terms and conditions for unbundled access to its local loop and imposing
a margin squeeze. On appeal, Case T-851/14 *Slovak Telekom v Commission*, and
T-827/14 *Deutsche Telekom v Commission*, not yet decided.

Fn 338 The Court of Justice has dismissed the further appeal in Case C-295/12P
Telefónica de España v Commission, EU:C:2014:2062.

Fn 339 The General Court dismissed the appeal in Case T-201/11 *Si.mobil v
Commission*, EU:T:2014:1096. It held that provided two conditions are met—the
NCA is 'dealing with the case' and the complaint before the Commission relates to
the same agreement/decision of an association/concerted practice as is being dealt
with by the NCA—then that is sufficient basis for the Commission to reject a complaint, without it being necessary to consider further whether there is an EU interest in the Commission investigating: paras 33 et seq. In any event, the Network
Notice does not create rights for individuals to have complaints dealt with by any
particular authority, and even if the Commission were to have been 'best placed'
to deal with the case the applicant would not have had a right to have its complaint
dealt with by the Commission: para 40. The General Court also held that to be
satisfied that a NCA is 'dealing with the case' the Commission must ascertain that
the NCA is actually investigating it, as opposed merely to having received a complaint or having opened a case of its own initiative, but the Commission does not
have assess whether the NCA is taking a well-founded approach to the case, or that
it has the institutional, financial and technical means available to it to accomplish
the tasks entrusted to it: paras 47 et seq.

3. Energy

(a) Introduction

12.091 **Energy 2020.**
Fn 358 Croatia also joined the EU, on 1 July 2013.

(c) Electricity

(i) Generally

12.102 **Definition of retail markets.**
Fn 394 The General Court judgment annulling the Commission's decision in COMP/38700 *Greek Lignite and Electricity Generation*, decision of 5 March 2008, was overturned by the Court of Justice in Case C-553/12P *Commission v DEI*, EU:C:2014:2083, [2014] 5 CMLR 945.

(ii) Long-term arrangements and exclusivity

12.104 **Capacity withholding.**
Fn 398 In COMP/39727 *CEZ* the Commission accepted commitments that include CEZ divesting itself of generation capacity, decision of 10 April 2013.

(iii) Imports and exports

12.106 **Discrimination and the internal market.** The Commission has taken two infringement decisions against national power exchanges: in COMP/39984 *OPCOM/Romanian Power Exchange*, decision of 5 March 2014, it fined the Romanian power exchange, OPCOM, for breaching Article 102 by requiring electricity traders to be VAT registered in Romania in order to participate in the Exchange. The Commission considered that this created an artificial barrier to entry for non-Romanian EU traders, and reduced liquidity on the Romanian wholesale electricity market. In COMP/39952 *Power Exchanges*, decision of 5 March 2014, it fined two European spot power exchanges, EPEX Spot and Nord Pool Spot, for breaching Article 101 by entering into a market allocation agreement along the lines of national boundaries.

The Commission has also sent a statement of objections in COMP/39767 *BEH*, as it considers it a breach of Article 102 for Bulgarian Energy Holding, BEH, to prescribe in its electricity supply contracts the territory into which its electricity may be resold (either restricting it to Bulgaria, or restricting it to export): see Press Release IP/14/922 (12 August 2014). It has also sent a statement of objections to Gazprom, the Russian producer and supplier of natural gas, concerning alleged infringements of Article 102 in the upstream supply markets in Central and Eastern

Europe: COMP/39816 *Upstream gas supplies in Central and Eastern Europe*, Press
Release IP/15/4828 (22 April 2015).

Fn 405 In COMP/39727 *CEZ* the Commission accepted commitments that include CEZ divesting itself of generation capacity, decision of 10 April 2013.

Article 106. The Court of Justice in Case C-553/12P *Commission v DEI*,   **12.108**
EU:C:2014:2083, [2014] 5 CMLR 945 has overturned the General Court judgment discussed in the main text. In order to establish an infringement of Article
106 in conjunction with Article 102 it is not necessary for the Commission to
show that a former monopolistic undertaking, which continues to hold a dominant position, has in fact abused that dominant position. An infringement will
arise where inequality of opportunity between operators, and thus distorted competition, is the result of a State measure. The Court held at para 46 that:

> '... infringement of [Article 106] in conjunction with [Article 102] may be estab-
> lished irrespective of whether any abuse actually exists. All that is necessary is for
> the Commission to identify a potential or actual anti-competitive consequence
> liable to result from the State measure at issue. Such an infringement may thus
> be established where the State measures at issue allowing the public undertak-
> ing or the undertaking which was granted special or exclusive rights to maintain
> (for example, by hindering new entrants to the market), strengthen or extend its
> dominant position over another market, thereby restricting competition, without
> it being necessary to prove the existence of actual abuse.'

(d) Gas

(ii) Application of the competition rules

Capacity management issues leading to divestment. The Commission has   **12.113**
sent a statement of objections in COMP/39849 *BEH gas* to the Bulgarian gas
supplier and transmission asset owner, as it considers it has breached Article 102
by hindering third party access to its infrastructure: see Press Release IP/15/4651
(23 March 2015).

Similarly to the decision in COMP/39402 *RWE Gas Foreclosure*, decision of 18 March
2009, discussed in the main text see also the decision of the Greek competition authority, of 30 April 2013, fining the Hellenic Gas Transmission System Operator,
which is a wholly owned subsidiary of DEPA, the incumbent supplier of natural gas
in Greece, for having denied access to the gas transmission network to an undertaking that is a customer and potential competitor of DEPA: ECN Brief 03/2013, p9.

Margin squeeze. In *Shannon LNG and another v Commission for Energy*   **12.115**
Regulation and others [2013] IEHC 568, the High Court of Ireland rejected a complaint that the methodology adopted by the regulator for calculating tariffs for the
use of, and access to, the transmission system and pipeline network would lead to

the transmission operator abusing its dominant position contrary to Article 102, and would constitute an unlawful state measure contrary to Article 106. The High Court held that as no actual tariffs had yet been set, it could not be said that the regulator's methodology would necessarily bring about either abusive conduct or an advantage to the transmission operator. It also considered the requirements of the Third Gas Directive as respects tariff setting, and held that it does not require that an 'interconnector' be treated separately from the transmission pipeline for tariff-setting purposes; nor does Article 13 of that Directive (which states that tariffs must 'reflect actual costs incurred') require that a tariff be set by reference to specific parts of the infrastructure, rather than by reference to the revenue required to maintain, operate and develop the transmission system as a whole.

12.116 **Territorial restrictions.**
Fn 435 The Commission has sent a statement of objections to the Russian gas producer and supplier Gazprom, concerning alleged infringements of Article 102: COMP/39816 *Upstream gas supplies in Central and Eastern Europe*; see Press Release IP/15/4828 (22 April 2015).

12.117 **Mergers.**
Fn 437 Recent examples of decisions clearing mergers in the gas and oil sector include M.6081 *Rosneft/TNK-BP* (8 March 2013), in which the Commission concluded that the acquisition of sole control by Rosneft of TNK-BP would not give rise to competition concerns in view of the constraints that the merged entity would continue to face from other strong competitors; M.6910 *Gazprom/Wintershall/ Target Companies* (3 December 2013), in which Gazprom's acquisition of German and Dutch gas supply and storage joint ventures would not give rise to competition concerns, as the overlaps in the parties' activities in the upstream market were largely pre-existing, and there were sufficient competitors in the market to ensure that supplies in the downstream market could not be restricted; and M.7631 *Royal Dutch Shell/BG Group* (2 September 2015), in which Shell's acquisition of the BG Group would not give rise to competition concerns as the merged entity would continue to face constraints from imports and from new facilities coming online in the near future; and as its conduct would be constrained by the downstream wholesalers who are shareholders in its facilities and by existing long-term supply contract.

4. Insurance

12.122 **Insurance block exemption.** At the time of writing, the Commission is consulting on the functioning of the block exemption, and whether to renew it when it expires in March 2017.

12.133 **Insurance intermediaries.** In Case C-32/11 *Allianz HungáriaBistozító*, EU:C:2013:160, [2013] 4 CMLR 863, paras 46–48, the Court of Justice held that vertical agreements between insurers and car dealers which made the dealers' remuneration for their car repair services dependent on the number of insurance policies they sold on the insurers' behalves may be an object infringement of Article 101, in particular where national law requires that intermediaries and brokers should be independent of insurers.

The Italian competition authority accepted commitments from several large national insurance companies in Italy, to amend their vertical agreements with insurance brokers which had *de facto* prevented brokers from dealing with more than one insurance company. The insurers have committed to remove references to exclusivity, and to remove all provisions which discourage brokers from dealing with more than one insurance company. ECN Brief 03/2014, p5.

5. Postal Services

(b) Liberalisation

Reservation of services. The General Court upheld the Commission's decision **12.139** in COMP/39562 *Slovakian postal legislation relating to hybrid mail services*, decision of 7 October 2008, discussed in the main text, in Case T-556/08 *Slovenská pošta v Commission*, EU:T:2015:189, [2015] 4 CMLR 1024. It confirmed the Commission's conclusion that hybrid mail services in Slovakia was a separate product market from traditional postal services, and that the calculations put forward for the costs of providing a universal service in Slovakia did not justify the re-monopolisation of the hybrid mail services. On further appeal, Case C-293/15P, not yet decided.

Universal service. As respects financing the provision of the universal **12.140** service, an example of a Member State being found to have allowed compensation that confers an unfair advantage on the USP is the Commission's decision in SA.17653 *Deutsche Post*, decision of 12 September 2007. This found the pension subsidies that Deutsche Post received from the State, and the high regulated letter prices allowed to cover its pension costs, to be an incompatible state aid (on appeal, Cases T-143/12 and T-152/12, not yet decided). The Commission referred Germany to the Court of Justice for failing to recover the sums in question from Deutsche Post: Case C-674/13 *Commission v Germany*, EU:C:2015:302. See also Case T-556/08 *Slovenská pošta v Commission*, EU:T:2015:189, [2015] 4 CMLR 1024, in which the General Court upheld the Commission's conclusion that the costs of providing the universal service did not justify the re-monopolisation of a hybrid mail postal service, as competition for that service would not put Slovenská pošta at risk of being unable to perform its universal service obligation.

(c) **Application of the competition rules**

12.143 **Jurisprudence of the EU Courts and the Commission.** Recent developments in the postal sector have also been subject to scrutiny under the merger regime. In particular, in M.6570 *UPS/TNT Express* (30 January 2013) the Commission prohibited a proposed acquisition by UPS of TNT Express, which would have reduced the number of companies operating on the markets for international express deliveries of small packages in the EEA from four to three or two. Although the parties offered divestiture commitments, the Commission considered these insufficient in the absence of an upfront buyer commitment: see Press Release IP/13/68 (30 January 2013). On appeal, Case T-194/13 *United Parcel Service v Commission*, not yet decided. In M.6503 *LaPoste/Swiss Post/JV* (4 July 2012) the Commission cleared a joint venture between LaPoste and Swiss Post to carry out their international mail deliveries, subject to divestiture commitments. The Commission considered in particular the 'very strong position' of La Poste, as the incumbent operator on a market which had been liberalised fairly recently, and in which 'no entrants are to be expected in the medium term': para 85. It considered the JV would strengthen that position. The merger was cleared on condition that Swiss Post divest itself of its French subsidiary.

Fn 503 See also Case T-556/08 *Slovenská pošta v Commission*, EU:T:2015:189, [2015] 4 CMLR 1024, discussed in the update to paragraph 12.139, above. The General Court held, in particular, that the Postal Sector Competition Notice provisions in respect of market definition set out general guidance, and it is still necessary to consider individual products in the particular circumstances of each case when defining the relevant market: para 120. In that case, it confirmed the Commission's conclusion that hybrid mail services in Slovakia was a separate product market from traditional postal services. On further appeal, Case C-293/15P, not yet decided.

6. Agriculture

(b) **Application of the competition rules**

12.153 **Regulation 1184/2006 and the Single CMO Regulation.** On 17 December 2013, the Parliament and Council adopted Regulation 1308/2013 establishing a common organisation of the markets in agricultural products, OJ 2013 L347/671, replacing Regulation 1234/2007 ('the Revised Single CMO Regulation').

At the time of writing, the Commission is consulting on draft guidelines on the joint selling of olive oil, beef and veal livestock, and arable crops: Press Release IP/15/3322 (15 January 2015).

12.154 **Application of competition rules.** On 17 December 2013, the Parliament and Council adopted Regulation 1308/2013 establishing a common organisation of the markets in agricultural products, OJ 2013 L347/671, replacing Regulation

1234/2007 ('the Revised Single CMO Regulation'). Under Article 206 of the Revised Single CMO Regulation, Articles 101–106 TFEU and any implementing provisions shall apply to all agreements, decisions and practices referred to Article 101(1) and 102 which relate to the production of, or trade in, agricultural products, save that:

(a) the 'relevant market' for the purposes of the application of those provisions is to be determined according to Article 207 of the Revised Single CMO Regulation;

(b) a 'dominant position' for the purposes of the application of those provisions is to be determined according to Article 208 of the Revised Single CMO Regulation;

(c) Article 101 shall not apply to agreements, decisions or practices necessary for the attainment of the objectives in Article 39 TFEU; or to agreements, decisions or practices of farmers, farmers' associations, or associations of such associations, or producer organisations recognised under Article 152 of the Revised Single CMO Regulation, or associations of producer organisations recognised under Article 156 of the Revised Single CMO Regulation, which concern the production or sale of agricultural products or the use of joint facilities for the storage, treatment or processing of agricultural products, unless the objectives of Article 39 TFEU are jeopardised: Article 209 of the Revised Single CMO Regulation;

(d) Article 101 shall not apply to agreements, decisions or practices of inter-branch organisations recognised under Article 157 of the Revised Single CMO Regulation, provided that they have been notified to the Commission and found to be compatible with the Union rules: Article 210 of the Revised Single CMO Regulation.

The Revised Single CMO Regulation does not restrict the application of Articles 101–106 to particular agricultural products as did the Single CMO Regulation.

The Commission has commenced infraction proceedings against Hungary, sending it a reasoned opinion under Article 258 TFEU, after it adopted a law that prevents its national competition authority from sanctioning cartels on agricultural products.

The first exception: national market organisations. On 17 December 2013, the **12.155** Parliament and Council adopted Regulation 1308/2013 establishing a common organisation of the markets in agricultural products, OJ 2013 L347/671, replacing Regulation 1234/2007 ('the Revised Single CMO Regulation'): see the update to paragraph 12.154, above. The exception for agreements, decisions and practices which form an integral part of a national market organisation has not been replicated.

The second exception: necessary under Article 39. On 17 December 2013, the **12.156** Parliament and Council adopted Regulation 1308/2013 establishing a common organisation of the markets in agricultural products, OJ 2013 L347/671, replacing Regulation 1234/2007 ('the Revised Single CMO Regulation'): see the update to paragraph 12.154, above. The exception for agreements, decisions and practices which are necessary for the attainment of the objectives of Article 39 TFEU is now contained in Article 209(1) of the Revised Single CMO Regulation.

12.157 **The third exception: farmers' associations.** On 17 December 2013, the Parliament and Council adopted Regulation 1308/2013 establishing a common organisation of the markets in agricultural products, OJ 2013 L347/671, replacing Regulation 1234/2007 ('the Revised Single CMO Regulation'): see the update to paragraph 12.154, above. The exception for farmers associations is now contained in Article 209(1) of the Revised Single CMO Regulation.

12.158 **Procedure.** On 17 December 2013, the Parliament and Council adopted Regulation 1308/2013 establishing a common organisation of the markets in agricultural products, OJ 2013 L347/671, replacing Regulation 1234/2007 ('the Revised Single CMO Regulation'): see the update to paragraph 12.154, above. Under the Revised Single CMO Regulation, agreements, decisions and concerted practices falling within the exception in Article 209(1) (see the update to paragraph 12.154, above) are outside the scope of Article 101 TFEU and no prior decision to that effect is required: Article 209(2) of the Revised Single CMO Regulation. A decision by the Commission is required only in respect of the application of the exception in Article 210 (see the update to paragraph 12.154, above): Article 210(2) of the Revised Single CMO Regulation.

12.159 **Article 101(3).** On 17 December 2013, the Parliament and Council adopted Regulation 1308/2013 establishing a common organisation of the markets in agricultural products, OJ 2013 L347/671, replacing Regulation 1234/2007 ('the Revised Single CMO Regulation'): see the update to paragraph 12.154, above.

The ECN has published a report on the activities of competition authorities in the food sector, which summarises the actions taken by the Commission and the Member States' national competition authorities in this area, '*ECN Report on competition law enforcement and market monitoring activities by European competition authorities in the food sector*', of 24 May 2012: the Report is available on the ECN section of the DG Comp website.

7. Transport

(b) Rail, road and inland waterway transport

(i) Application of the competition rules

12.169 **Article 102.** The Commission accepted commitments from Deutsche Bahn in COMP/39678 *Deutsche Bahn I*, decision of 18 December 2013, regarding the pricing structure adopted by companies in its group for supplying traction current, used to power locomotives, which the Commission considered may have restricted access to the markets for the provision of rail freight and long-distance passenger transport services in Germany by imposing a margin squeeze. Deutsche Bahn is the sole owner of the specific electricity grid required to distribute the traction current, and operates downstream rail services. It agreed to alter its pricing structure, so that the discounts it offers can in practice be obtained by companies other than its own downstream entities.

The Commission has sent a statement of objections to the Lithuanian railway incumbent concerning the removal of railway track connecting Latvia and Lithuania, which the Commission considers may have prevented rail freight customers from using other rail operators: COMP/39813 *Baltic Rail Transport*; see Press Release IP/15/2940 (5 January 2015).

(ii) Liberalisation measures in the railway sector

First railway package.   **12.171**
Fn 590 The Court of Justice has ruled on the proceedings brought by the Commission for failure to implement: see Case C-557/10 *Commission v Portugal*, EU:C:2012:662; C-528/10 *Commission v Greece*, EU:C:2012:690; and Cases C-473/10, etc, *Commission v Hungary*, EU:C:2013:113.

Second and third railway packages.   On 30 January 2013, the Commission **12.172** published proposals for a Fourth Railway Package. The proposals are available on the DG TRANS website, at http://ec.europa.eu/transport/modes/rail/packages/ 2013_en.htm.

Single European Railway Area.   On 21 November 2012, Directive 2012/34 **12.173** establishing a single European railway area, was adopted: OJ 2012 L343/32. The deadline for transposition is 16 June 2015: Article 64 of Directive 2012/34.

(c) Maritime transport

(i) Application of the competition rules

Application of Regulation 1/2003.   The Commission did not renew the **12.174** Maritime Transport Guidelines, OJ 2008 C245/2: Vol II, App E20, which expired on 26 September 2013: see Press Release IP/13/122 (19 February 2013).

Scope of the Maritime Transport Guidelines.   The Commission did not **12.175** renew the Maritime Transport Guidelines, OJ 2008 C245/2: Vol II, App E20, which expired on 26 September 2013: see Press Release IP/13/122 (19 February 2013).

Product market definition.   The Commission did not renew the Maritime **12.176** Transport Guidelines, OJ 2008 C245/2: Vol II, App E20, which expired on 26 September 2013: see Press Release IP/13/122 (19 February 2013).

12.177 Geographic market definition. The Commission did not renew the Maritime Transport Guidelines, OJ 2008 C245/2: Vol II, App E20, which expired on 26 September 2013: see Press Release IP/13/122 (19 February 2013).

12.178 Market shares. The Commission did not renew the Maritime Transport Guidelines, OJ 2008 C245/2: Vol II, App E20, which expired on 26 September 2013: see Press Release IP/13/122 (19 February 2013).

12.179 Technical agreements.

Fn 618 The Commission did not renew the Maritime Transport Guidelines, OJ 2008 C245/2: Vol II, App E20, which expired on 26 September 2013: see Press Release IP/13/122 (19 February 2013).

Fn 619 ibid.

12.180 Other horizontal agreements. The Commission did not renew the Maritime Transport Guidelines, OJ 2008 C245/2: Vol II, App E20, which expired on 26 September 2013: see Press Release IP/13/122 (19 February 2013).

(ii) Block exemption for consortia

12.181 Generally. The Commission has extended the maritime consortia block exemption regulation (Regulation 906/2009 (OJ 2009 L256/31)), which expired on 25 April 2015, for a further 5 years to April 2020: Press Release IP/14/717 (24 June 2014).

(d) Air transport

(iii) Particular issues

12.195 Airline alliances.

Fn 662 See also COMP/39595 *Continental/United/Lufthansa/Air Canada*, decision of 23 May 2013, accepting commitments under Article 9 of Regulation 1/2003 in respect of a revenue sharing joint venture between Star Alliance members Air Canada, United and Lufthansa, and COMP/39964 *Air France/KLM/Alitalia/Delta*, decision of 12 May 2015 accepting commitments *inter alia* to make slots available to competing airlines.

12.198 Groundhandling services. In Case C-288/11P *Mitteldeutsche Flughafen and Flughafen Leipzig-Halle v Commission*, EU:C:2012:821, [2013] 2 CMLR 483, at paras 46 et seq, the Court of Justice confirmed that the construction of airport infrastructure is a part of the economic activity of operating an airport. The construction of an additional runway at an existing airport could not be divorced from the economic activity of operating a passenger airport, but was to be treated as part of the costs that an airport operator would normally have to bear itself for the purpose of carrying out that activity.

13

ENFORCEMENT AND PROCEDURE

1. Introduction

The Commission's priorities.   **13.005**
Fn 17 In Case T-286/09 *Intel v Commission*, EU:T:2014:547, [2014] 5 CMLR 270, the General Court held that the Guidance on the Commission's enforcement priorities in applying Article 82 of the EC Treaty to abusive exclusionary conduct by dominant undertakings, OJ 2009 C45/7, sets priorities for the Commission's future enforcement activities, and does not apply to proceedings that had already been initiated before it was published, even if it was published prior to the adoption of the Commission's decision in those proceedings. The Guidance therefore did not affect the General Court's conclusion that it was not necessary for the Commission to conduct an 'as efficient competitor' test to determine whether Intel's rebate arrangements were abusive: paras 154–156. On further appeal, Case C-413/14P, not yet decided.

2. Fundamental Rights and the Commission's Powers of Enforcement

Relevant rights.   **13.007**
Fn 25 The General Court in Case T-135/09 *Nexans France v Commission*, EU:T:2012:596, [2013] CMLR 4 195, at paras 119 et seq held that the challenge to the Commission's action in copying the whole hard drive of a laptop seized during a dawn raid was inadmissible: see the update to paragraph 13.030, below. The further appeal, on other grounds, was dismissed in Case C-37/13P *Nexans v Commission*, EU:C:2014:2030, [2014] 5 CMLR 642.

Fn 36 The Court of Justice held in Case C-439/11P *Ziegler v Commission*, EU:C:2013:513, [2013] 5 CMLR 1217, para 154, that it is the principle of good administration in Article 41 of the Charter of Fundamental Rights that applies to administrative proceedings before the Commission, rather than Article 47. Article 41 provides for a right to have one's affairs handled impartially by the EU institutions. That requirement of impartiality encompasses subjective impartiality (the member of the institution concerned who is responsible for the matter may not show bias or personal prejudice) and objective impartiality (there must be sufficient guarantees to exclude any legitimate doubt as to bias). In respect of the complaint that the appellant's rights had been breached by the Commission investigating an alleged infringement of competition law where it was also itself a victim of that alleged infringement, the Court held that the Commission's objective impartiality is secured in these circumstances by ensuring that the part of the Commission bringing the infringement action is not the same part as that which suffered the damage, and by the addressees' right to appeal the Commission's decision in the European Courts under Article 263 TFEU, which provides the guarantees required by the Charter: paras 157–160.

In Case T-286/09 *Intel v Commission*, EU:T:2014:547, [2014] 5 CMLR 270, the General Court considered the application of Article 41 of the Charter of Fundamental Rights to the Commission's decisions as to the documents it will obtain during the course of its investigation, and to its recording of interviews conducted on a voluntary basis. See the updates to paragraphs 13.011 and 13.019, below.

Fn 38 The Court of Justice confirmed in Case C-439/11P *Ziegler v Commission*, EU:C:2013:513, [2013] 5 CMLR 1217, para 154, that it is the principle of good administration in Article 41 of the Charter that applies to administrative proceedings before the Commission, rather than Article 47. Article 41 provides for a right to have one's affairs handled impartially by the EU institutions. That requirement of impartiality encompasses subjective impartiality (the member of the institution concerned who is responsible for the matter may not show bias or personal prejudice) and objective impartiality (there must be sufficient guarantees to exclude any legitimate doubt as to bias). In respect of the complaint that the appellant's rights had been breached by the Commission investigating an alleged infringement of competition law where it was also itself a victim of that alleged infringement, the Court held that the Commission's objective impartiality is secured in these circumstances by ensuring that the part of the Commission bringing the infringement action is not the same part as that which suffered the damage, and by the addressees' right to appeal the Commission's decision in the European Courts under Article 263 TFEU, which provides the guarantees required by the Charter: paras 157–160.

See also Case C-199/11 *Europese Gemeenschap v Otis*, EU:C:2012:684, [2013] 4 CMLR 141, in which the Court of Justice was asked whether it was compatible with Article 47 of the Charter of Fundamental Rights for the Commission to bring a civil action in a Member State to seek to recover the damages it has suffered as a result of an infringement of competition law, where it would be relying on its own infringement decision to establish liability, and Article 16(1) of Regulation 1/2003 would prevent the defendant from contesting the decision. The Court confirmed that the Commission is not precluded from bringing such a civil action in a Member State, and in these circumstances the defendant's rights under Article 47 of the Charter are adequately protected by its right to appeal the Commission's decision in the European Courts under Article 263 TFEU, and its right to contest causation and damage in the Member State court.

Right to a fair trial.   The Court of Justice held in Case C-439/11P *Ziegler v*   **13.008**
Commission, EU:C:2013:513, [2013] 5 CMLR 1217, para 154, that it is the principle of good administration in Article 41 of the Charter of Fundamental Rights that applies to administrative proceedings before the Commission, rather than Article 47.

Criminal charge'.   In Case C-501/11P *Schindler v Commission (Elevators and*   **13.009**
Escalators), EU:C:2013:522, [2013] 5 CMLR 1387, paras 33–38, the Court of Justice rejected an argument that the imposition of fines by the Commission, rather than by a court, is contrary to Article 6 ECHR and Article 47 of the Charter of Fundamental Rights. The power of review by the General Court under Article 263 TFEU, together with the unlimited jurisdiction to review the fine under Article 261 TFEU and Article 31 of Regulation 1/2003, is sufficient to comply with the requirements of effective judicial protection. See also Case T-406/10 *Emesa v Commission*, EU:T:2015:499, paras 123 et seq.

Article 8 of the Convention: respect for private and family life.   The General   **13.010**
Court in Joined Cases T-289/11, etc, *Deutsche Bahn and others v Commission*, EU:T:2013:404, confirmed that the exercise of the Commission's powers of inspection under Article 20(4) of Regulation 1/2003 is a 'clear interference' with the right to respect for private and family life under Article 8 of the ECHR/ Article 7 of the Charter of Fundamental Rights. However, it dismissed a complaint that the absence of a requirement for prior judicial authorisation renders the inspection a disproportionate interference as there are sufficient safeguards in place to ensure that rights are protected: paras 65 et seq. Further appeal on this ground dismissed, Case C-583/13 *Deutsche Bahn v Commission*, EU:C:2015:404, [2015] 5 CMLR 341, para 25.

3. The Commission's Powers of Investigation

(a) Power to obtain information

Information from undertakings.   The General Court in Case T-286/09 *Intel v*   **13.011**
Commission, EU:T:2014:547, [2014] 5 CMLR 270, at paras 340 et seq considered in detail the implications of Article 41 of the Charter on Fundamental Rights for the Commission's decisions as to the information it gathers from undertakings

during the course of its investigation. Intel complained that the Commission had failed to obtain documents from the complainant that Intel maintained would have been exculpatory, and which Intel was aware existed as a result of those documents having been disclosed to it in proceedings in the State of Delaware. The General Court held that, in principle, it is for the Commission to decide how it wishes to conduct an investigation, what documents it must collect in order to have a sufficiently complete picture of the case, and when the documents it has gathered are sufficient. It is not appropriate to impose on the Commission an obligation to obtain as many documents as possible in order to ensure that it obtains all potentially exculpatory material. If an undertaking requests that the Commission obtain additional documents, the Commission has a margin of discretion in deciding whether to accede to it. However, Article 41 of the Charter entails a duty to examine carefully and impartially all aspects of the case. The General Court held that the Commission will be obliged to obtain documents at an undertaking's request in exceptional circumstances, where four cumulative conditions are met:

(a) it is impossible for the undertaking to obtain the documents itself. This will require the undertaking to show that it took all steps to obtain the documents itself;
(b) the documents must be identified as precisely as the undertaking is able;
(c) the documents must probably be of considerable importance to the undertaking's defence. The Commission has a margin of discretion in deciding whether the significance of the alleged exculpatory evidence justifies it obtaining that evidence;
(d) the volume of documents must be proportionate to their importance to the case. The Commission may take into consideration the delay that would be occasioned by obtaining and analysing the documents as requested.

On further appeal, Case C-413/14P, not yet decided.

Fn 58 On the choice between making a simple request, and taking a decision, see the update to paragraph 13.013, below.

13.013 **Decision requiring information.** On the choice between making a simple request, and taking a decision, see the General Court's judgments in the appeals against the Commission's decision to require information in Case COMP/39520 *Cement and related products*, decision of 30 March 2011, under Article 18(3) of Regulation 1/2003. In Case T-306/11 *Schwenk Zement v Commission*, EU:T:2014:123, at para 49, the General Court confirmed that the decision to require information by adopting a decision under Article 18(3), rather than by making a request under Article 18(2), must be proportionate. In that case it held that the use of Article 18(3) was proportionate (on further appeal, Case C-248/14P, not yet decided). In Case T-296/11 *Cementos Portland Valderrivas v Commission*, EU:T:2014:121, at the applicant's request the General Court adopted measures of inquiry and reviewed the evidence in the Commission's possession on which it had based its decision to conduct an investigation. The Court held that the Commission must be in possession of sufficiently serious evidence, consistent with the suspicion of an infringement, to justify adopting a decision under Article 18(3), and if an applicant puts forward factors that cast doubt on the sufficiently serious nature of the evidence then the General Court will examine the evidence on review: paras 40 et seq. On the facts of that case, the Court held that the Commission's evidence was consistent with a reasonable suspicion of infringement, and upheld the decision. On further appeal, Case C-248/14P, not yet decided.

In respect of the time limit set for complying with the decision, the General Court held in Case T-306/11 *Schwenk Zement v Commission*, EU:T:2014:123, at para 73 that the time limit that the Commission imposes for compliance with a decision under Article 18(3) must be adequate to allow the undertaking to ensure that the information it provides is accurate, complete and not misleading. In that case, a time limit of two weeks for a response to a certain set of questions was disproportionately short, and the decision was annulled to that extent. On further appeal, Case C-248/14P, not yet decided.

'Necessity' for information requested.   The General Court in Case T-286/09 **13.016** *Intel v Commission*, EU:T:2014:547, [2014] 5 CMLR 270, at paras 340 et seq considered in detail the implications of Article 41 of the Charter on Fundamental Rights for the Commission's decisions as to the information it gathers from undertakings during the course of its investigation, and in particular a complaint that the Commission had failed to obtain certain documents during the course of its investigation: see update to paragraph 13.011, above. On further appeal, Case C-413/14P, not yet decided.

See also Case T-296/11 *Cementos Portland Valderrivas v Commission*, EU:T:2014:121, on review by the General Court of the evidence in the Commission's possession on which the decision under Article 18(3) of Regulation 1/2003 is based: update to paragraph 13.013, above.

Penalties in respect of information.   In view of the Commission's powers to **13.017** impose financial penalties, the time limit set for complying with a decision under Article 18(3) must be adequate to allow the undertaking to ensure that the information it provides is accurate, complete, and not misleading: Case T-306/11 *Schwenk Zement v Commission*, EU:T:2014:123, para 73. In that case, a time limit of two weeks for a response to a certain set of questions was disproportionately short, and the decision was annulled to that extent. On further appeal, Case C-248/14P, not yet decided.

Voluntary interviews.   In Case T-286/09 *Intel v Commission*, EU:T:2014:547, **13.019** [2014] 5 CMLR 270, at paras 612 et seq, the General Court analysed the procedural requirements to which the Commission is subject in conducting voluntary interviews. It dismissed a complaint that the Commission had failed adequately to record meetings and telephone conversations that took place during the course of its investigation, and one meeting in particular where the note on the file allegedly indicated that the interviewee was likely to have given exculpatory evidence. The Court held that the Commission has a discretion whether it conducts interviews on a voluntary basis, or under Article 19 of Regulation 1/2003, and where it decides to conduct an interview on a voluntary basis the requirements of Article 3 of Regulation 773/2004 do not apply: paras 615 and 618. Article 41 of the Charter of Fundamental Rights imposes on the Commission a duty to examine carefully and impartially all the relevant aspects of the individual case, but the existence, nature and extent of a duty to record the information the Commission receives during meetings or telephone conversations depends on the content of that information. It must establish adequate documentation, in the file to which the undertakings concerned have access, on the essential aspects of the investigation including all information 'of a certain importance and which bears an objective link with the subject-matter of an investigation, irrespective of whether it is incriminating or exculpatory': para 620. The General Court held the Commission failed to comply with this requirement by failing to place in the file at least a succinct note containing, subject to any requests for confidentiality, the name of the participants and a brief summary of the subjects addressed, where it had conducted a voluntary interview lasting five hours with a senior executive of Intel's largest customer, on matters with an objective link to the substance of the investigation: para 621. However, the breach was subsequently remedied, and the administrative procedure was therefore not vitiated by an irregularity. The General Court also held that if there had been an irregularity, in the circumstances of the case the criteria for determining whether the undertaking's rights of defence had been affected were the same as those for determining whether an applicant's rights of defence are affected by non-disclosure of documents on the file. Thus the applicant must adduce *prima facie* evidence that the Commission failed to record exculpatory evidence, which was at variance with the thrust of the documentary evidence on which the Commission relied or, at least which sheds different light on it: paras 626–629. On further appeal, Case C-413/14P, not yet decided.

13.021 **Information gathering for sectoral inquiries.**   On 22 July 2013, the Council adopted Regulation 734/2013, amending Regulation 659/99 (the Procedural Regulation), OJ 2013 L204/15, as a result of which the Commission now has power also to conduct general inquiries into any economic sector, or type of aid instrument, to consider their compatibility with the EU rules on State aid, Articles 107 and 108 TFEU: see Article 20a of Regulation 659/99 as amended.

(b) Powers of inspection

Powers of inspection of business premises.   On the Commission's discretion to   **13.022**
determine the need for an inspection, see the General Court's judgment in Case
T-402/13 *Orange v Commission*, EU:T:2014:991. The Commission adopted an
inspection decision under Article 20(4) of Regulation 1/2003, after the French
NCA had accepted commitments to address a complaint about Orange abusing a dominant position contrary to Article 102. The General Court held that a
NCA decision accepting commitments does not preclude the Commission from
investigating the conduct in question, as the Commission is not bound by the
NCA's decision: paras 27 et seq. The fact that the Commission did not exercise
its discretion under Article 11(6) of Regulation 1/2003 to relieve the NCA of its
jurisdiction to apply Articles 101 and 102 does not render an inspection decision
inappropriate: paras 32 et seq (see paragraphs 15.017 et seq of the main text regarding Article 11(6) of Regulation 1/2003). It was 'at the very least unfortunate'
that the Commission adopted an inspection decision without first examining the
documents on the NCA's file, but that failure did not render the inspection decision disproportionate because the NCA had not itself conducted an inspection
but had considered only such documents as Orange had provided to it voluntarily: para 56. The General Court also held that although it will determine whether
a decision to conduct an inspection is arbitrary in circumstances where an undertaking puts forward arguments liable to cast doubt on the reasonableness of
grounds relied upon by the Commission, it can also conduct a review by examining the statement of reasons set out in the inspection decision and conclude that
the decision was not arbitrary on the sole basis of those reasons: para 93.

Inspection of undertakings pursuant to decision.   The General Court in Joined   **13.025**
Cases T-289/11, etc, *Deutsche Bahn and others v Commission*, EU:T:2013:404,
rejected a challenge to a Commission inspection decision under Article 20(4)
of Regulation 1/2003 based on the absence of a requirement for prior judicial
authorisation of the inspection. The General Court accepted that the exercise of
the Commission's powers of inspection under Article 20(4) is a 'clear interference'
with the right to respect for private and family life under Article 8 of the ECHR/
Article 7 of the Charter of Fundamental Rights, but held that the absence of a
requirement for prior judicial authorisation does not render it a disproportionate
interference as there are sufficient safeguards in place to ensure that rights are
protected: see paras 65 et seq. Further appeal on this ground dismissed, Case
C-583/13, *Deutsche Bahn v Commission*, EU:C:2015:404, [2015] 5 CMLR 341,
para 25.

Fn 122 See also Case T-272/12 *Energetický a průmyslový v Commission*,
EU:T:2014:995, in which the General Court confirmed that if the inspection decision is correctly notified, there is no requirement for the inspectors to inform the
persons concerned during the inspection that a failure to comply with the decision

could lead to the imposition of a fine. The undertaking's rights of defence are safe-guarded by the terms of the inspection decision making this clear: para 71.

Fn 123 On the Commission's obligation to specify the subject-matter of the inspection, in the light of the fact that it is not required to set out any precise legal analysis, see Case C-37/13P *Nexans v Commission*, EU:C:2014:2030, [2014] 5 CMLR 642, in which the Court of Justice dismissed a complaint that the Commission had not specified adequately the subject-matter of the decision by stating that the infringement was 'probably' global in geographical scope. It upheld the General Court's judgment, in which it had found that the Commission complies with its duty to specify the subject-matter of its investigation where its decision is sufficient to enable the undertaking to assess the scope of its duty to cooperate. The Commission had done so adequately, even though the General Court accepted that the decision 'could have been less ambiguous' (Case T-135/09 *Nexans and Nexans France v Commission*, EU:T:2012:596, [2013] 4 CMLR 195, at paras 53 et seq).

See also Case T-410/09 *Almamet v Commission*, EU:T:2012:676, [2013] 4 CMLR 788 at paras 34 et seq, in which the General Court considered a complaint about the Commission having based an infringement decision on evidence that was gathered unlawfully, as it was outside the scope of the inspection decision. The General Court held that any addressee can challenge an infringement decision on the basis that the underlying evidence was gathered without using the procedures laid down for gathering it lawfully, such as those in Article 20 of Regulation 1/2003; however, where the complaint is about procedural irregularities in how the process was conducted, that complaint can only be made by the party from whom the evidence was gathered. In that case, Almamet challenged COMP/39396 *Calcium carbide and magnesium based reagents*, decision of 22 July 2009, [2010] 5 CMLR 1368, on the basis that the Commission had gathered evidence from the premises of another undertaking, Ecka, that related to subject-matter outside the scope of the inspection decision. The General Court held that:

> 'where, as in this case, a party other than the party that submitted to an inspection conducted by the Commission under Article 20 of Regulation No 1/2003 invokes an infringement, during that inspection, of safeguards designed to ensure respect for fundamental rights, the Court must confine itself to checking that the Commission did in fact use the procedure laid down to that effect, without going into the details of the conduct of that procedure unless the party in question invokes a procedural irregularity likely to concern it directly.'

See also Case T-272/12 *Energetický a průmyslový v Commission*, EU:T:2014:995, in which the General Court observed that the purpose of the statement of reasons on which an inspection decision is based is to show that the inspection is justified. The statement of reasons must therefore state the suppositions and presumptions that the Commission wishes to investigate: para 65.

Inspections and the right to privacy.   The General Court in Joined Cases   **13.028**
T-289/11, etc, *Deutsche Bahn and others v Commission*, EU:T:2013:404, confirmed
that the exercise of the Commission's powers of inspection under Article 20(4) of
Regulation 1/2003 is a 'clear interference' with the right to respect for private and
family life under Article 8 of the ECHR/Article 7 of the Charter of Fundamental
Rights. However, it dismissed a complaint that the absence of a requirement for
prior judicial authorisation renders the inspection a disproportionate interference,
as there are sufficient safeguards in place to ensure that rights are protected: paras
65 et seq. Further appeal on this ground dismissed, Case C-583/13 *Deutsche Bahn
v Commission*, EU:C:2015:404, [2015] 5 CMLR 341, para 25.

Powers that can be exercised during an inspection.   The General Court in   **13.030**
Case T-135/09 *Nexans France v Commission*, EU:T:2012:596, [2013] CMLR
4 195, paras 119 et seq, held that the challenge to the Commission's action in
copying the whole hard drive of a laptop seized during a dawn raid was inadmissible. The General Court considered that the Commission's action was a measure implementing the decision under which the inspection was ordered, and it
was not itself a decision that could be annulled by the Court. Its legality could
only be examined in the context of an appeal against any infringement decision the Commission may issue under Article 101, or an appeal against a decision imposing a penalty under Article 23 of Regulation 1/2003 for refusing to
cooperate with the inspection. The General Court has therefore not considered
directly the question of whether Article 20(2)(c) of Regulation 1/2003 includes a
power for the Commission to take a copy of the whole of a computer hard drive
and review the contents at its premises in Brussels at a later date. The further
appeal, on other grounds, was dismissed in Case C-37/13P *Nexans v Commission*,
EU:C:2014:2030, [2014] 5 CMLR 642.

The conduct of the inspection.   The Commission has published a demonstra-   **13.031**
tion of its methodology for extracting, encrypting and storing electronic data
during antitrust inspections. The demonstration is available on the DG Comp
website.

Penalties in respect of non-compliance.   **13.032**
Fn 166 On refusal to submit to inspections ordered by decision, or producing
the required records of a business in incomplete form, the General Court in Case
T-272/12 *Energetický a průmyslový v Commission*, EU:T:2014:995 upheld the
Commission's decision imposing a fine of €2.5 million on two Czech companies for
negligently allowing an individual to access his email account after the Commission
had requested it be blocked, and for intentionally diverting incoming emails to a
server, during the course of the Commission's inspection. In respect of the finding that the undertakings had negligently allowed access to an email account, the
General Court held that the mere fact that the undertaking had failed to obtain
exclusive access to email accounts as requested was sufficient for the incident to be

properly characterised as a refusal to submit to the inspection: para 38. It was not necessary to show that the contents of the accounts were deleted or manipulated, or that a back-up to the server had not taken place such that the contents of the account could not be verified: paras 39 et seq. The finding of negligence was upheld, as it was incumbent upon the undertaking to take all necessary measures to implement the inspectors' instructions and the inspectors could not be required to inform each person within the undertaking of their duties in the circumstances of the case: para 45. In respect of the intentional diversion of incoming emails to a server, the General Court held that it was not necessary to show that the emails were not available on the server: paras 50–51. The General Court also confirmed that if the inspection decision is correctly notified, there is no requirement for the inspectors to inform the persons concerned during the inspection that a failure to comply with the decision could lead to the imposition of a fine. The undertaking's rights of defence are safeguarded by the terms of the decision making this clear: para 71. Nor is there a requirement to notify individuals within the undertaking that access to their emails will be blocked, as inspectors are entitled to assume that the undertaking will take the necessary steps to implement their instructions, once they have been given: para 78. Finally, the Court upheld the amount of the fine. It upheld the Commission's finding that a failure to render email accounts completely inaccessible to account holders is by its very nature a serious infringement of an undertaking's procedural obligations during an inspection. It is necessary to take into consideration the need to ensure a sufficient deterrent effect, and the deterrent effect is all the more important in respect of electronic files as they are much easier and quicker to manipulate, and inspectors do not know whether the electronic data to which they have access is complete and intact: para 108.

13.033 **Limits on the Commission's use of information acquired.** The Court of Justice confirmed in Case C-583/13P *Deutsche Bahn v Commission*, EU:C:2015:404, [2015] 5 CMLR 341 that it is lawful for the Commission to use documents which it happened to obtain during the course of an inspection as a basis upon which to decide under Article 20(4) of Regulation 1/2003 to conduct further inspections, if the information in the documents indicates that there is an infringement of competition law and an inquiry is needed to verify or supplement that information: para 59. See also Directive 2014/104 on certain rules governing actions for damages under national law for infringements of the competition law provisions of the Member States and of the European Union, OJ 2014 L349/1, which will protect leniency statements and settlement submissions from disclosure in national proceedings, and certain other information from disclosure before a competition authority has closed its proceedings: Articles 6 and 7. The deadline for national implementation is 27 December 2016. The Commission's willingness to transmit such documents to national courts, under Article 15 of Regulation 1/2003, for the purposes of national proceedings is likely to be impacted by the provisions.

Cooperation between the Commission and national courts. See, however, **13.034**
Directive 2014/104 on certain rules governing actions for damages under national law for infringements of the competition law provisions of the Member
States and of the European Union OJ 2014 L349/1, which will protect leniency
statements and settlement submissions from disclosure in national proceedings,
and certain other information from disclosure before a competition authority has
closed its proceedings: Articles 6 and 7. The deadline for national implementation
is 27 December 2016. The Commission's willingness to transmit such documents
to national courts, under Article 15 of Regulation 1/2003, for the purposes of
national proceedings is likely to be impacted by the provisions.

Confidential information passed to NCAs. In Case T-655/11 *FSL (Exotic* **13.035**
fruit) v Commission, EU:T:2015:383, paras 71 et seq, the General Court dismissed
an argument that the protections afforded to an undertaking by Article 12 of
Regulation 1/2003 should apply, by analogy, to information gathered by the
Commission from national regulatory authorities other than the relevant NCA.
In COMP/39482 *Exotic fruit (Bananas)*, decision of 12 October 2011, the
Commission had relied upon evidence transmitted to it by the Italian tax authority. The appellants contended that Article 12 should be interpreted extending to
such a situation, in order to prevent the Commission from effectively circumventing the procedural safeguards and limitations laid down in Regulation 1/2003.
The General Court held that Article 12 could not be interpreted as extending that
far, and that if it were to be so interpreted it would moreover impose too great
a burden on the Commission in proving infringements of Articles 101 and 102.
The question of whether it is lawful for national regulatory authorities other than
the NCA to transmit information to the Commission is governed by national
law. On further appeal, Case C-469/15P, not yet decided.

(c) Privilege

Foreign law prohibitions. See also the judgment of the Court of Appeal in **13.040**
England and Wales in *National Grid Electricity Transmission v ABB* [2013]
EWCA Civ 1234, confirming that the English High Court has power to order
disclosure of documents notwithstanding the French law prohibition on them
being provided directly (without recourse to the special procedures for the taking
of evidence abroad laid down in Regulation 1206/2001).

4. Complaints

Procedure: second stage. **13.047**
Fn 262 The General Court will only review a refusal to grant an extension of
the period for responding to the Article 7(1) letter where there has been a manifest failure to have regard to the circumstances of the case, likely to compromise

the applicant's right to be associated closely with the procedure: Joined Cases T-104/07&339/08 *Belgische Vereniging van handelaars in- en uitvoerdersgeslependiamant (BVGD) and Diamanthandel A. Spira v Commission*, EU:T:2013:366, [2013] 5 CMLR 1055, para 144.

Fn 266 See also Joined Cases T-104/07&339/08 *Belgische Vereniging van handelaars in- en uitvoerdersgeslependiamant (BVGD) and Diamanthandel A. Spira v Commission*, EU:T:2013:366, [2013] 5 CMLR 1055, paras 90 et seq.

13.048 **Procedure: third stage.**   For an example of significant new evidence emerging, and the Commission re-opening a matter once a decision rejecting a complaint has already been taken, see the Commission's decision in COMP/39221 *De Beers/ DTC Supplier of Choice*, decision of 5 June 2008, in which the Commission re-considered its decision of 26 January 2007 rejecting a complaint, following the General Court judgment in Case T-170/06 *Alrosa v Commission* [2006] ECR II-2601. The Commission's reconsidered decision was upheld in Joined Cases T-104/07&339/08 *Belgische Vereniging van handelaars in- en uitvoerdersgeslependiamant (BVGD) and Diamanthandel A. Spira v Commission*, EU:T:2013:366, [2013] 5 CMLR 1055. The General Court confirmed that the Commission's power to reconsider its previous decisions arises under the general principle of the right of an authority to re-examine, amend and withdraw its decisions, rather than under Article 7 of Regulation 773/2004: see paras 58 et seq.

13.050 **Lack of Union interest.**   In addition to the criteria outlined in the Complaints Notice, and discussed in the main text, for assessing Union interest the Commission may also have regard to measures taken by national authorities: T-432/10 *Vivendi v Commission (France Télécom)*, EU:T:2013:538, paras 26 and 42 et seq.

Fn 284 The Court of Justice dismissed the further appeal in Case C-56/12P *European Federation of Ink and Ink Cartridge Manufacturers (EFIM) v Commission*, EU:C:2013:575. The case is discussed in paragraph 4.055 of the main text, and the update thereto above.

Fn 289 See also Joined Cases T-104/07&339/08 *Belgische Vereniging van handelaars in- en uitvoerdersgeslependiamant (BVGD) and Diamanthandel A. Spira v Commission*, EU:T:2013:366, [2013] 5 CMLR 1055, paras 189 et seq.

Fn 302 The General Court dismissed the appeal in Case T-201/11 *Si.mobil v Commission*, EU:T:2014:1096. It held that provided two conditions were met—the NCA was 'dealing with the case' and the case related to the same agreement/decision of an association/concerted practice—then that was sufficient basis for the Commission to reject a complaint, without it being necessary to consider further whether there was an EU interest in the Commission investigating: paras 33 et seq. In any event, the Network Notice does not create rights for individuals to have complaints dealt with by any particular authority, and even if the Commission were to be 'best placed' to deal with the case the applicant would not have had a right to have its complaint dealt with by the Commission: para 40. The General Court also held that to be satisfied that a NCA is 'dealing with the case' the Commission must ascertain that the NCA is actually investigating it, as opposed merely to having received a complaint or having opened a case of its own initiative, but the Commission does not have to assess whether the NCA is taking a well-founded approach to the case, or that it has the institutional, financial and technical means available to it to accomplish the tasks entrusted to it: paras 47 et seq.

Complainant's rights after initiation of procedure.   **13.051**
Fn 303 See also Joined Cases T-104/07&339/08 *Belgische Vereniging van handelaars in- en uitvoerdersgeslependiamant (BVGD) and Diamanthandel A. Spira v Commission*, EU:T:2013:366, [2013] 5 CMLR 1055, para 168.

5. Formal Procedure Prior to an Adverse Decision

(a) The nature of Commission proceedings

An 'administrative' procedure.   In Case C-501/11P *Schindler v Commission* **13.052**
(Elevators and Escalators), EU:C:2013:522, [2013] 5 CMLR 1387, the Court of Justice followed the approach of the European Court of Human Rights in App 43509/08 *Menarini Diagnostics v Italy*, judgment of 27 September 2011 (referred to in footnote 319 of the main text), and rejected an argument that the imposition of fines by the Commission, rather than by a court, was contrary to Article 6 of the ECHR and Article 47 of the Charter of Fundamental Rights. It held that the power of review by the Court under Article 263 TFEU, together with the un-limited jurisdiction to review the fine under Article 261 TFEU and Article 31 of Regulation 1/2003, is sufficient to comply with the requirements of effective judicial protection. In Case C-439/11P *Ziegler v Commission*, EU:C:2013:513, [2013] 5 CMLR 1217, para 154, the Court confirmed that it is the principle of good administration in Article 41 of the Charter of Fundamental Rights that applies to administrative proceedings before the Commission, rather than Article 47.

Fn 317 The General Court dismissed the complaint regarding the compatibility of the administrative procedure with Article 6(1) of the ECHR: Joined Cases T-56&73/09 *Saint Gobain (Carglass)*, EU:T:2014:160 (fine reduced on the basis that the uplift for recidivism was incorrectly applied; see the update to paragraph 14.042, below).

Fn 321 The General Court in Case T-286/09 *Intel v Commission*, EU:T:2014:547, [2014] 5 CMLR 270, paras 612 et seq, analysed the procedural requirements to which the Commission is subject in conducting voluntary interviews during the course of its investigation, and in particular the obligation imposed by Article 41 of the Charter on Fundamental Rights adequately to record those interviews: see the update to paragraph 13.019, above. On further appeal, Case C-413/14P, not yet decided.

13.053 **Hearing by 'an independent and impartial tribunal'.** In Case C-501/11P *Schindler v Commission (Elevators and Escalators)*, EU:C:2013:522, [2013] 5 CMLR 1387, the Court of Justice followed the approach of the European Court of Human Rights in App 43509/08 *Menarini Diagnostics v Italy*, judgment of 27 September 2011 (referred to in footnote 319 of the main text), and rejected an argument that the imposition of fines by the Commission, rather than by a court, was contrary to Article 6 of the ECHR and Article 47 of the Charter of Fundamental Rights. It held that the power of review by the Court under Article 263 TFEU, together with the unlimited jurisdiction to review the fine under Article 261 TFEU and Article 31 of Regulation 1/2003, is sufficient to comply with the requirements of effective judicial protection. In Case C-439/11P *Ziegler v Commission*, EU:C:2013:513, [2013] 5 CMLR 1217, para 154, the Court confirmed that it is the principle of good administration in Article 41 of the Charter of Fundamental Rights that applies to administrative proceedings before the Commission, rather than Article 47.

13.054 **Presumption of innocence and burden of proof.** The General Court in Case T-286/09 *Intel v Commission*, EU:T:2014:547, [2014] 5 CMLR 270 at paras 64–67 held that the principle that it is for the Commission to produce a body of evidence which, viewed as a whole, is sufficiently precise and consistent to support the firm conviction that the alleged infringement took place, without it being necessary for every individual item of evidence to meet that requirement in relation to every aspect of the infringement, applies in cases under Article 102 as well as Article 101. On further appeal, Case C-413/14P, not yet decided. On the review by the General Court of such evidence, see the update to paragraph 13.144, below.

Fn 327 The Court of Justice dismissed the appeals in Case C-457/10P *AstraZeneca v Commission*, EU:C:2012:770, [2013] 4 CMLR 233; and the undertakings' further appeals in Joined Cases C-239/11P, etc, *Siemens v Commission (Gas Insulated Switchgear)*, EU:C:2013:866, [2014] 4 CMLR 606. The Commission's appeal in Joined Cases C-239/11P, etc, *Siemens v Commission (Gas Insulated Switchgear)*, EU:C:2013:866, [2014] 4 CMLR 606 was upheld: see the update to paragraph 2.024, above.

13.055 **The right to be heard.** In Case T-286/09 *Intel v Commission*, EU:T:2014:547, [2014] 5 CMLR 270, the General Court dismissed a complaint that the Commission breached the undertaking's right to be heard by refusing to hold a second hearing in relation to a supplementary statement of objections, even though it raised new allegations not contained in the statement of objections, because the undertaking had not made a request for such a hearing within the time-frame stipulated by the Commission in accordance with Articles 10(2) and 12

of Regulation 773/2004: paras 325–326. It also dismissed a complaint in relation to a letter of facts, which set out additional items of evidence on which
the Commission intended to rely in a potential final decision, as the right to
a hearing under Article 12 of Regulation 773/2004 arises only in respect of a
statement of objections: para 327. On further appeal, Case C-413/14P, not yet
decided.

Delay.   In Case C-50/12P *Kendrion v Commission*, EU:C:2013:771, [2014] 4   **13.056**
CMLR 454, at paras 91 et seq, the Court ruled that the sanction for a breach
by the Court of its obligation under Article 47 of the Charter on Fundamental
Rights to adjudicate on cases within a reasonable time is a claim for damages
against the EU under Article 268 TFEU and the second paragraph of Article 340
TFEU. This is an effective remedy. The approach taken by the Court in Case
C-185/95P *Baustahlgewebe v Commission* [1998] ECR I-8417, [1999] 4 CMLR
1203, of reducing the fine was not to be followed. On the facts of *Kendrion*, the
proceedings before the General Court had taken five years and nine months,
which the Court of Justice considered breached Article 47 of the Charter, and to
be a sufficiently serious breach of a rule of law intended to confer rights on individuals to sound in damages. However, a separate action before the General Court was
required to recover those damages. This approach has been followed in subsequent
cases, see, eg Case C-578/11P *Deltafina v Commission*, EU:C:2014:1460, [2014]
5 CMLR 599 at paras 80 et seq; and Case C-243/12P *FLS Plast v Commission*,
EU:C:2014:2006 [2014] 5 CMLR 675 at paras 130 et seq.

The General Court in Case T-286/09 *Intel v Commission*, EU:T:2014:547, [2014]
5 CMLR 270, at paras 1639 et seq dismissed as inadmissible a complaint that
the fine should be reduced on account of the administrative procedure before the
Commission having taken nine years. On further appeal, Case C-413/14P, not yet
decided.

In Case T-47/10 *GEA Group v Commission*, EU:T:2015:506, [2015] 5 CMLR 617,
paras 309 et seq the General Court dismissed a complaint that the undertaking's
rights of defence had been breached by the six year delay to the administrative
proceedings which resulted from the dispute between it and the Commission over
the seizure of documents (discussed in paragraphs 13.037 and 13.038 of the main
text). It did, however, find that the Commission had breached the principle of
equal treatment by reducing the fine imposed on all the undertakings except the
applicant. The Commission argued that as the applicant had been responsible for
the dispute which occasioned the delay in the administrative proceedings, it was
in an objectively different situation to the other undertakings. The General Court
held that that argument was not compatible with the principle of effective judicial protection, and would deter undertakings from exercising their right to bring judicial proceedings while they were involved in an investigation by the Commission.
On further appeal, Case C-515/15P, not yet decided.

(b) Initiation of proceedings and the statement of objections

13.057 **Initiation of proceedings.**
Fn 356 The reference in the footnote should be to Article 10 of Regulation 1/2003, rather than to Article 10 of Regulation 773/2004.

Fn 364 In Case T-27/10 *AC-Treuhand*, EU:T:2014:59, at paras 170 et seq, the General Court held that an undertaking should be notified at the preliminary investigation stage of the object and purpose of the Commission's investigation, in order to ensure that its ability to exercise its rights of defence at the *inter partes* stage is not compromised by the passage of time between the two stages. AC-Treuhand complained that it had not been notified of the Commission's investigation into its role until a few weeks before the statement of objections was issued, by which time its witnesses' memories were fainter than they would have been at the preliminary investigation stage, and they were therefore less credible than they would have been at that stage. The Court considered that even though AC-Treuhand had not been notified that a finding against it was in contemplation, it had received adequate notification of the object and purpose of the Commission's investigation at the preliminary investigation stage through receiving an information request under Article 18 of Regulation 1/2003. On further appeal, Case C-194/14P, not yet decided. In a separate appeal against the same decision, the General Court dismissed a complaint that the Commission notifying different undertakings of its investigation at different stages of the investigation breaches the principle of equal treatment: Case T-46/10 *Faci v Commission*, EU:T:2014:138, [2014] 4 CMLR 930, at para 148 (further appeal dismissed as in part manifestly unfounded, and in part inadmissible: Order of 11 June 2015).

13.059 **Closure of the investigation.**
Fn 368 For a recent example, see the decision to close the investigation into the practices of telecoms operators in the internet connectivity market: see Press Release IP/14/1089 (3 October 2014).

13.062 **Statement of objections where fines proposed.**
Fn 389 See also Case C-612/12P *Ballast Nedam (Dutch Bitumen)* EU:C:2014:193, [2014] 4 CMLR 921.

13.063 **Obligation to supply relevant documents.** In Case T-404/08 *Fluorsid and Minmet v Commission*, EU:T:2013:321, [2013] 5 CMLR 902, paras 120 et seq; and Case T-406/08 *Industries chimiques du fluor v Commission*, EU:T:2013:322, paras 136 et seq, the General Court held that where a statement of objections does not expressly refer to particular documents on which the Commission subsequently relies in an infringement decision, but those documents were included in the administrative file and the statement of objections sets out provisional findings of a single and continuous infringement, based on ongoing bilateral and multilateral contacts, that is sufficient to alert the undertaking to the fact that the

Commission could use those documents as incriminating evidence against the undertaking. Further appeal dismissed in Case C-467/13P, *Industries chimiques du fluor v Commission*, EU:C:2014:2274, paras 23 et seq.

Fn 398 See, however, Case T-404/08 *Fluorsid and Minmet v Commission*, EU:T:2013:321, [2013] 5 CMLR 902, paras 120 et seq; and Case T-406/08 *Industries chimiques du fluor v Commission*, EU:T:2013:322, paras 136 et seq, discussed in the update to the main paragraph, above.

Supplementary statement of objections and 'letters of facts'.   In Case T-286/09   **13.066**
Intel v Commission, EU:T:2014:547, [2014] 5 CMLR 270, the General Court dismissed a complaint that the Commission breached the undertaking's right to be heard by refusing to hold a second hearing in relation to a supplementary statement of objections, even though it raised new allegations not contained in the statement of objections, because the undertaking had not made a request for such a hearing within the timeframe stipulated by the Commission in accordance with Articles 10(2) and 12 of Regulation 773/2004: paras 325–326. It also dismissed a complaint in relation to a letter of facts, which set out additional items of evidence on which the Commission intended to rely in a potential final decision, as the right to a hearing under Article 12 of Regulation 773/2004 arises only in respect of a statement of objections: para 327. On further appeal, Case C-413/14P, not yet decided.

(c) Access to the file

Access to the file.   The General Court in Case T-286/09 *Intel v Commission*,   **13.067**
EU:T:2014:547, [2014] 5 CMLR 270, at paras 349 et seq dismissed an argument that the case law on failure to grant an undertaking access to exculpatory documents in the file applies *a fortiori* to exculpatory documents that the Commission has failed to gather. The General Court's judgment is discussed in the update to paragraph 13.011, above, in respect of the Commission's obligation to obtain documents at an undertaking's request. The General Court also considered a complaint that the Commission had failed adequately to record a voluntary meeting conducted during the course of the investigation: see the update to paragraph 13.019, above. On further appeal, Case C-413/14P, not yet decided.

The Commission's Access to the File Notice.   The Access to the File Notice was   **13.068**
amended on 5 August 2015, to take account of Directive 2014/104 on certain rules governing actions for damages under national law for infringements of the competition law provisions of the Member States and of the European Union, OJ 2014 L349/1. See: OJ 2015 C256/3.

Effect of lack of access on validity of decision.   The failure to provide access to   **13.069**
inculpatory documents will also lead to those documents being excluded from the evidence upon which the Commission may rely in its decision: see Joined Cases T-379&381/10 *Keramag Keramische Werke and Others v Commission* ('*Bathroom*

Fittings'), EU:T:2013:457, paras 115–116 and 264, in which the General Court held to be inadmissible a document relied on by the Commission in its decision which had not been disclosed to the undertaking concerned, and it reviewed the sufficiency of the Commission's evidence finding an infringement in the absence of that document. On further appeal, Case C-613/13P, not yet decided.

13.070 **Exculpatory and incriminating documents.** In respect of exculpatory documents, the Court of Justice in Joined Cases C-239/11P, etc, *Siemens v Commission (Gas Insulated Switchgear)*, EU:C:2013:866, [2014] 4 CMLR 606, at paras 363 et seq, confirmed that an undertaking does not have to show that the content of the Commission's decision would have been different if it had been granted access to the documents in question. The undertaking's rights of defence are infringed if a document 'could have been useful for its defence': para 367. The Court went on to hold that documents are not exculpatory evidence to which access must be granted where the undertaking is already familiar with their content through other documents to which it has access, and another undertaking's response to a statement of objections is not exculpatory where the argument it contains is identical in substance to the undertaking's own: para 377.

Fn 435 See also Joined Cases T-379&381/10 *Keramag Keramische Werke and Others v Commission ('Bathroom Fittings')*, EU:T:2013:457, paras 115–116 and 264. The General Court held to be inadmissible a document relied on by the Commission in its decision which had not been disclosed to the undertaking concerned, when reviewing the sufficiency of the Commission's evidence finding an infringement. On further appeal, Case C-613/13P, not yet decided.

Fn 436 The fact that one undertaking puts forward substantially the same arguments as another undertaking involved in the Commission's investigation does not constitute exculpatory evidence: eg Case T-47/10 *Akzo Nobel v Commission*, EU:T:2015:506, [2015] 5 CMLR 617, para 350.

13.071 **When the right of access to the file arises.**
Fn 445 In Case T-343/06 *Shell Petroleum v Commission*, EU:T:2012:478, [2012] 5 CMLR 1064, paras 84–94, the General Court held that where other parties' replies contain incriminating or exculpatory material the Commission's obligation to grant access to those replies is confined to those passages which contain such incriminating or exculpatory material, placed in context if that is necessary to understand them. It does not extend to the whole document. The further appeal, in Case C-585/12P, was withdrawn: Order of 11 April 2013.

In Joined Cases C-239/11P, etc, *Siemens v Commission (Gas Insulated Switchgear)*, EU:C:2013:866, [2014] 4 CMLR 606, at para 377, the Court of Justice held that another undertaking's response to a statement of objections is not exculpatory evidence to which access must be granted where the argument it contains is identical in substance to the undertaking's own.

The documents to which access is granted. **13.072**

Fn 449 The Court of Justice dismissed the further appeal, on other grounds, in Case C-449/11P *Solvay Solexis v Commission (Hydrogen peroxide and perborate)*, EU:C:2013:802.

In Case T-343/06 *Shell Petroleum v Commission*, EU:T:2012:478, [2012] 5 CMLR 1064, paras 84–94, the General Court held that the Commission's obligation to grant access to other parties' replies is confined to those passages which contain the incriminating or exculpatory material, placed in context if that is necessary to understand them. It does not extend to the whole document. The further appeal, in Case C-585/12P, was withdrawn: Order of 11 April 2013.

In Joined Cases C-239/11P, etc, *Siemens v Commission (Gas Insulated Switchgear)*, EU:C:2013:866, [2014] 4 CMLR 606, at para 377, the Court of Justice held that another undertaking's response to a statement of objections is not exculpatory evidence to which access must be granted where the argument it contains is identical in substance to the undertaking's own.

Internal Commission documents. **13.073**

Fn 462 The Court of Justice in Case C-365/12P *Commission v EnBW Energie Baden-Württemberg ('EnBW')*, EU:C:2014:112, [2014] 4 CMLR 30, at paras 79 et seq, held that by analogy with the approach taken in respect of requests for documents on merger proceedings (Case C-404/10 P *Commission v Éditions Odile Jacob*, EU:C:2013:808, [2013] 4 CMLR 11; and Case C-477/10 P *Commission v Agrofert Holding*, EU:C:2012:394, [2012] 5 CMLR 510, discussed in paragraph 8.184 of the main text), and on State aid proceedings (Case C-139/07P *Commission v Technische Glaswerke Ilmenau*, EU:C:2010:376, [2010] ECR I-5885, discussed in paragraphs 16.046 et seq of the main text), the Commission is entitled to apply a general presumption that disclosure of documents on its file in an antitrust investigation would undermine the protection of the commercial interests of the undertakings involved in those proceedings, as well as the protection of the purpose of investigations relating to such proceedings, within the meaning of the first and third indents of Article 4(2) of Regulation 1049/2001. Otherwise, the restrictive rules on access to the file in Regulation 1/2003 and Regulation 773/2004 could be undermined: paras 88–90. It is not necessary to examine each document individually and determine the application of the exceptions to each: para 93. The Commission is also entitled to apply a presumption that disclosure of its internal documents (such as background notes on the evidence, correspondence with other competition authorities, and consultations with other departments in the Commission) would seriously undermine the Commission's decision-making process, within the meaning of the second paragraph of Article 4(3) of Regulation 1049/2001, in circumstances where an appeal against the Commission's decision is still ongoing, and the possibility remains that it may be called upon to re-open its investigation: para 114. The presumption can be rebutted if there is evidence that it would be in the public interest to disclose the documents, but a general statement that disclosure is required for the purposes of bringing a claim for compensation in the national courts will not suffice: a requestor has to establish that particular documents are necessary for that purpose in order for its rights to compensation to constitute an overriding public interest in disclosure: paras 107 and 132. See, further, the update to paragraph 16.046, below.

See also Case T-561/12 *Beninca v Commission*, EU:T:2013:558, [2014] 4 CMLR 549, regarding a request under Regulation 1049/2001 for internal Commission documents prepared in the context of the merger control regime. The General Court confirmed that the Commission's internal documents prepared in the course of merger control proceedings may fall within the exception in Article 4(3) of Regulation 1049/2001. That exception will apply where the Commission's decision-making process may be prejudiced by disclosure of the document, and in particular in circumstances where its investigation has closed but its decision is under appeal and the possibility remains that it will be required to re-open its proceedings. The request was for disclosure of an internal Commission memorandum which related to M.6166 *NYSE Euronext/Deutsche Börse* (1 February 2012), at the time of the request under appeal in Case T-175/12 *Deutsche Börse v Commission*, EU:T:2015:148, [2015] 4 CMLR 1187. Similarly, in Case T-456/13 *Sea Handling v Commission*, EU:T:2015:185, para 63, the General Court confirmed that the Commission is entitled to apply a general presumption that disclosure of documents on its file in a State aid investigation would undermine the protection of the purpose of investigations relating to such proceedings, within the meaning of the third indent of Article 4(2) of Regulation 1049/2001.

13.077 **Disclosure of non-accessible documents.** In Case T-286/09 *Intel v Commission*, EU:T:2014:547, [2014] 5 CMLR 270, at para 1458, the General Court held:

> '... it may not be necessary that the undertaking concerned is put in a position to have access to a document used by the Commission as inculpatory evidence in its entirety. Where a third party has an interest in confidential treatment, the Commission may replace certain passages of a document containing inculpatory evidence by non-confidential summaries or may delete them, on condition that it does not rely on the passages that it treats as confidential and that the context of the passages on which it relies remains sufficiently comprehensible to enable the undertaking concerned to make effective use of its rights of defence.'

On further appeal, Case C-413/14P, not yet decided.

In Case T-655/11 *FSL (Exotic fruit) v Commission*, EU:T:2015:383, para 403, the General Court dismissed a complaint that the Commission had not granted access to confidential parts of the responses by third parties to information requests. It upheld the Commission's argument that it was legitimate to refuse access in circumstances where the addressee of the decision was in a position to place economic or commercial pressure on those parties, being a competitor, trading partner, customer or supplier. On further appeal, Case C-469/15P, not yet decided.

Obligation to identify confidential information when submitted. The **13.078**
Commission has issued an informal guidance paper on confidentiality claims
(March 2012), which is available on the 'Practical Information' section of the
DG Comp website.

Provision of documents from the file to third parties. See also Joined Cases **13.081**
T-104/07&339/08 *Belgische Vereniging van handelaars in- en uitvoerdersgeslependiamant (BVGD) and Diamanthandel A. Spira v Commission*, EU:T:2013:366,
[2013] 5 CMLR 1055, paras 90 et seq.

(d) The hearing and subsequently

Hearings. **13.082**
Fn 505 The request for an oral hearing must, however, be made within the timeframe stipulated by the Commission in accordance with Articles 10(2) and 12 of
Regulation 773/2004 for filing written submissions and for making a request for
an oral hearing. There is no breach of the undertaking's right to be heard if the
Commission refuses to hold a hearing having not received a request within that
timeframe: Case T-286/09 *Intel v Commission*, EU:T:2014:547, [2014] 5 CMLR
270, paras 325–326. The right to be heard under Article 12 of Regulation 773/
2004 does not arise in relation to a letter of facts: Case T-286/09 *Intel v Commission*,
EU:T:2014:547, [2014] 5 CMLR 270, para 327. On further appeal, Case C-413/14P,
not yet decided.

Conduct of the hearing. **13.084**
Fn 522 See also Case T-384/09 *SKW v Commission*, EU:T:2014:27, at paras 58–
59, upholding the Hearing Officer's refusal to hold a part of the hearing *in camera*,
because the matters which the applicant wished to canvass without the other parties present were matters engaging another undertaking's rights of defence and
were not essential to the applicant's defence.

Fn 528 The Court of Justice dismissed the undertakings' further appeals in
Joined Cases C-231/11P, etc, *Commission v Siemens and others*, EU:C:2014:256,
[2014] 5 CMLR 7. It upheld the Commission's appeal: see the update to paragraph
14.080, below.

Developments during the course of the procedure. In Case C-485/11 *Akzo* **13.087**
Nobel v Commission, EU:T:2015:517, [2015] 5 CMLR 671 the General Court
annulled a decision in which the Commission attempted to amend the decision
in COMP/38859 *Heat Stabilisers*, decision of 11 November 2009, in the light of
the Court of Justice's judgment in Case C-201/09P *ArcelorMittal Luxembourg v
Commission*, EU:C:2011:190. The General Court considered that it was sufficient
for the Commission to write to the applicant and afford it an opportunity to
comment, without it being necessary to issue a further statement of objections;
however, it found that the three or four working days which the Commission

had provided the applicant in which to respond to its communications was inadequate and breached the undertaking's rights of defence.

13.090   Rules of Procedure on adoption of decisions.
Fn 563 The Court of Justice dismissed the further appeals, on other grounds, in Joined Cases C-239/11P, etc, *Siemens v Commission (Gas Insulated Switchgear)*, EU:C:2013:866, [2014] 4 CMLR 606.

13.091   Readoption of decision following annulment.
Fn 564 The Court of Justice dismissed the further appeal against the readopted decision in COMP/36212 *Carbonless Paper*, decision of 23 June 2010, in Case C-414/12P *Bolloré v Commission*, E:C:2014:301. In particular, it dismissed a complaint that the lapse of time since the infringement breached Bolloré's rights of defence: paras 61 et seq.

See, also, eg COMP/40032 *BR/ESBR Recidivism*, in which the Commission has issued a second statement of objections to Eni and Versalis, providing an explanation (held to have been absent from COMP/38638 *Butadiene Rubber*, decision of 29 November 2006, by the Court of Justice in Case C-508/11P *Eni v Commission*, EU:C:2013:289, [2013] 5 CMLR 607, at paras 129–133; and Case C-511/11P *Versalis v Commission*, EU:C:2013:386, [2013] 5 CMLR 797, at paras 142–146) of why the fines imposed on Eni and Versalis should be uplifted for recidivism: Press Release IP/13/179 (1 March 2013). The decision to initiate the procedure in COMP/40032 is on appeal in Case T-210/13 *Versalis v Commission*, and Case T-211/13 *Eni v Commission*, not yet decided.

13.092   Relationship between the decision and the statement of objections.
Fn 569 See, however, Case T-404/08 *Fluorsid and Minmet v Commission*, EU:T:2013:321, [2013] 5 CMLR 902, paras 120 et seq; and Case T-406/08 *Industries chimiques du fluor v Commission*, EU:T:2013:322, paras 136 et seq, in which the General Court held that where a statement of objections does not expressly refer to particular documents which the Commission subsequently relies on in an infringement decision, but those documents were included in the administrative file and the statement of objections sets out provisional findings of a single and continuous infringement, based on ongoing bilateral and multilateral contacts, that is sufficient to alert the undertaking to the fact that the Commission could use those documents as incriminating evidence against the undertaking. Further appeal dismissed in Case C-467/13P, *Industries chimiques du fluor v Commission*, EU:C:2014:2274, paras 23 et seq.

13.093   Legal status of the decision.
Fn 573 See also the General Court judgment in Case T-462/07 *Galp Energía España v Commission*, EU:T:2013:459, [2014] 4 CMLR 272, paras 89-91, where the Court refused to consider an application to annul a Commission decision in its entirety and not only in respect of the particular applicants (on further appeal,

on other grounds, in Case C-603/13P, not yet decided). This, and Case C-310/97P *Commission v AssiDomän*, EU:C:1999:407, [1999] ECR I-5363, were considered by the UK Supreme Court in *Deutsche Bahn v Morgan Crucible Company* [2014] UKSC 24, overturning the Court of Appeal judgment cited in the main text. The Supreme Court held that the relevant 'decision', for the purposes of bringing a monetary claim before the Competition Appeal Tribunal under section 47A of the Competition Act 1998, is the individual decision taken against the individual addressee. The Commission submitted observations to the Court, pursuant to Article 15(3) of Regulation 1/2003 (discussed in paragraph 15.051 of the main text), which are available on the *Amicus Curiae* section of the DG Comp website.

Fn 577 On the ability of undertakings that are not addressees of an infringement decision to bring a challenge, see also the General Court's judgment in Case T-442/08 *International Confederation of Societies of Authors and Composers (CISAC) v Commission*, EU:T:2013:188, [2013] 5 CMLR 536, paras 63 et seq, discussed in the update to paragraph 13.132, below.

Publication of decisions. Disputes as to whether information should be re- **13.094**
dacted from a decision before it is published, as comprising a business secret or otherwise being confidential (for example, under the principles outlined in Case T-474/04 *Pergan Hilfsstoffe für industrielle Prozesse v Commission* [2007] ECR II-4225), are determined by the Hearing Officer. If the Commission accepts an undertaking's request for confidentiality, the Hearing Officer does not have power to reject it: Case T-462/15 *Pilkington v Commission*, EU:T:2015:508, para 31.

The General Court confirmed in Case T-341/12 *Evonika Degussa v Commission*, EU:T:2015:51 that the Hearing Officer is not competent to hear objections to publication based on the principles of legitimate expectations or equal treatment: para 44. It also considered the balance to be struck between the Commission's obligation to publish decisions, and its obligation to protect business secrets and other confidential information, in the context of a decision to publish parts of a decision which set out the facts constituting an infringement and which the applicant considered amounted to the publication of leniency material. The Court held that the publication of a decision should not be conflated with the publication of information under Regulation 1049/2001, and that the Commission publishing the parts of its decision which set out the facts constituting an infringement would not result in the communication to third parties of requests for leniency submitted by the applicant to the Commission, of minutes recording oral statements made by the applicant pursuant to the leniency programme, or of documents which the applicant voluntarily submitted to the Commission during the investigation. The Commission is entitled to publish such parts of its decision, unless the three cumulative criteria are met for establishing that the information is covered by professional secrecy (discussed in paragraph 15.029 of the main text). In that case, the information met the first two criteria, as it was known only to a limited number of persons; and its disclosure would be likely to cause serious harm to the person who provided it as it would cause reputational damage and would expose the undertaking to damages actions. The third criterion was not, however, met in particular because of the public interest in knowing as fully as possible the reasons behind any Commission action; the interests of economic operators in knowing the sort of behaviour for which they are liable to be penalised; and the interest of persons harmed by the infringement in being informed of the details so that they can assert their right to compensation: para 107. On further appeal, Case C-162/51P, not yet decided.

See also Case T-465/12 *AGC Glass Europe v Commission*, EU:T:2015:505; and Case T-462/15 *Pilkington v Commission*, EU:T:2015:508, in which the General Court dismissed similar appeals against Hearing Officers' decisions. In particular, the General Court rejected the argument that information identifying the infringing undertakings' customers was a business secret or otherwise confidential, in circumstances where the undertakings themselves supplied each other with the identities of their customers as part of the infringement; where the market under consideration was characterised by a degree of transparency; and where that information was included in the decision as part of the narrative account of the infringement: *AGC Glass* paras 36 et seq. and *Pilkington* paras 56 et seq. It also rejected an argument that information regarding the undertakings' pricing information, quantities of sales, and quota allocations was a business secret or otherwise confidential, in circumstances where the undertakings themselves supplied each other with this information as part of the infringement: *Pilkington* paras 60 et seq. *AGC Glass* is on further appeal, Case C-517/15P, not yet decided.

In Case T-534/11 *Schenker v Commission*, EU:T:2014:854 the General Court considered the application of Regulation 1049/2001 to a request for disclosure of a Commission decision. The Commission's obligation to respond to the request within a mandatory timeframe under Article 8 of Regulation 1049/2001 must be reconciled with its obligation not to disclose information covered by professional secrecy: this means that the Commission must endeavour to complete a non-confidential version of the decision in the shortest possible timeframe and in any event within a reasonable timeframe, established on the basis of the specific circumstances of each case: paras 129–130; and, within the mandatory timeframe, the Commission must disclose all parts of its decision in respect of which requests for confidential treatment are not still outstanding: paras 137–138.

The Commission has published Guidance on the preparation of public versions of Commission Decisions adopted under Articles 7–10, 23 and 24 of Regulation 1/2003, which sets out the kinds of information the Commission will redact, and the procedures to be followed in requesting redactions. The guidance is available on the DG Comp website.

6. Commitments and Settlement

(a) Cartel settlement

The procedure and settlement notice.   The Settlement Notice was amended on   **13.096**
5 August 2015, to take account of Directive 2014/104 on certain rules governing
actions for damages under national law for infringements of the competition law
provisions of the Member States and of the European Union, OJ 2014 L349/1.
See: OJ 2015 C256/2.

Cartel settlement: other procedural aspects.   The General Court held in Case   **13.099**
T-456/10 *Timab Industries*, EU:T:2015:296, [2015] 5 CMLR 7 that if a settlement involves some, but not all, of the participants in an infringement (either
because one or more parties have withdrawn from the settlement discussions, or
because the Commission terminates the discussions with one or more parties)
then the Commission must observe the principle of equal treatment as between
addressees of the decision taken under the settlement procedure and the addressees of the decision taken under the Regulation 773/2004 procedure. This means
that, in determining the amount of the fine, there cannot be any discrimination
between the addressees with respect to the information and calculation methods used which are not affected by the specific features of the settlement procedure: paras 71 et seq. However, an indication given during settlement discussions
of the range of fines does not bind the Commission if a party withdraws from
those discussions: para 105. The Commission will thereafter apply the Fining
Guidelines in determining the amount of the fine, taking into account the evidence that is available to it. In this particular case, the fact that the Commission
could no longer rely on the withdrawing party's settlement submissions meant
that the duration of the infringement was shorter, but that the average annual
value of sales and additional amount were higher and the reductions for cooperation outside the Leniency Notice and for settlement were no longer available,
meaning the fine was therefore higher. On further appeal, Case C-411/15P, not
yet decided.

Fn 596 The Settlement Notice was amended on 5 August 2015, to take account of
Directive 2014/104 on certain rules governing actions for damages under national
law for infringements of the competition law provisions of the Member States and
of the European Union, OJ 2014 L349/1. See: OJ 2015 C256/2. Paragraph 27 of
the Notice has been substituted.

Fn 597 The Settlement Notice was amended on 5 August 2015, to take account of
Directive 2014/104 on certain rules governing actions for damages under national
law for infringements of the competition law provisions of the Member States and
of the European Union, OJ 2014 L349/1. See: OJ 2015 C256/2. Paragraph 29 of
the Notice has been substituted.

Fn 600 The Settlement Notice was amended on 5 August 2015, to take account of Directive 2014/104 on certain rules governing actions for damages under national law for infringements of the competition law provisions of the Member States and of the European Union, OJ 2014 L349/1. See: OJ 2015 C256/2. Paragraph 39 of the Notice has been substituted.

(b) Commitments

13.100 **Article 9 of Regulation 1/2003.** On 5 March 2014 the Commission issued guidance 'To commit or not to commit? Deciding between prohibition and commitment' (2014) 3 EU Competition Policy Brief, outlining the relevant considerations and criteria that it will take into account in deciding whether it would be appropriate to deal with a case by way of a prohibition decision under Article 7 of Regulation 1/2003, or a commitments decision under Article 9.

Fn 602 More recent commitments decisions include COMP/39847 *E-Books*, decisions of 12 December 2012 and 25 July 2013; COMP/39230 *Rio Tinto Alcan*, decision of 20 December 2012; COMP/39654 *Reuters Instrument Codes (RICs)*, decision of 20 December 2012; COMP/39727 *ČEZ*, decision of 10 April 2013; COMP/39595 *Continental/United/Lufthansa/Air Canada*, decision of 23 May 2013; COMP/39678 *Deutsche Bahn I*, decision of 18 December 2013; COMP/39731 *Deutsche Bahn II*, decision of 18 December 2012; COMP/39398 *Visa MIF*, decision of 26 February 2014; and COMP/39939 *Samsung – Enforcement of UMTS standard essential patents*, decision of 29 April 2014.

The appeals, noted in the footnote, by Hynix Semiconductor (now trading as SK Hynix Inc) in Joined Cases T-148&149/10 against COMP/38636 *Rambus*, decision of 9 December 2009, were withdrawn on 5 July 2013.

13.103 **Enforcement and withdrawal.** In Case T-342/11 *Confederación Española de Empresarios de Estaciones de Servicio ('CEEES') v Commission*, EU:T:2014:60, the General Court set out the considerations which apply to the Commission's decision whether to re-open its investigation, or to impose a fine under Article 23(2)(c) of Regulation 1/2003, or to impose daily penalty payments under Article 24(1)(c), if an undertaking breaches its commitments. The Court confirmed that the Commission is not obliged to take any of these actions in response to non-compliance, but has a discretion in this regard: paras 47–49. In exercising that discretion, the Commission is required to have regard to the same factors as when it is considering whether to reject a complaint about an alleged breach of Articles 101 or 102, namely the significance of the alleged infringement for the functioning of the internal market, the probability of establishing the existence and extent of the infringement and the level of investigation that would be required in order to do so, and the significance of the Commission's task in monitoring compliance with competition law: paras 60–62. It may also take into account any steps taken by NCAs in respect of the undertaking's conduct: para 68. In that case, the Commission was entitled to reject a complaint by a third party about conduct by Repsol, on the basis that the Spanish NCA had issued a decision finding that Repsol had breached Article 101 and had adopted measures that were sufficient to ensure that Repsol refrained from the conduct complained of in future.

The Commission exercised its power under Article 23(2)(c) of Regulation 1/2003 for the first time in COMP/39530 *Microsoft – Tying*, decision of 6 March 2013, for Microsoft's failure to comply with the commitment decision of 16 December 2009. It imposed a fine of €561 million.

8. Findings of Inapplicability, Declarations of Infringement and Orders to Terminate

Power to order positive action.   **13.115**
Fn 675 The Court of Justice dismissed the further appeal, on other grounds, in Case C-382/12P *Mastercard v Commission*, EU:C:2014:2201, [2014] 5 CMLR 1062.

9. Review by the General Court

(a) Review of fines under Article 261 TFEU

Article 261 TFEU: unlimited jurisdiction regarding fines. The Court may   **13.123** also take into account evidence on which the Commission did not rely in its decision, and which is not admissible for the purposes of review under Article 263 TFEU: Case T-462/07 *Galp Energía España v Commission*, EU:T:2013:459, [2014] 4 CMLR 272. The General Court partially annulled a Commission decision because the evidence relied upon for a finding of a single and continuous infringement did not establish that the undertaking was aware of the infringing activities in which it did not participate. Although a subsequent statement from the undertaking confirmed that it had in fact been so aware, that evidence was not admissible on a review under Article 263 TFEU: see paras 288 et seq (see also paragraph 13.153, and the update thereto, below). However, the General Court held that it could take account of that evidence in the exercise of its unlimited jurisdiction regarding fines under Article 261 TFEU, and on that basis it considered that the starting point the Commission had used to determine the undertaking's fine should not be adjusted, notwithstanding that it took into account the infringing behaviours which, on review under Article 263 TFEU, the undertaking could not be held liable for: see paras 615 et seq. On further appeal, Case C-603/13P, not yet decided

Fn 705 See also Case C-501/11P *Schindler v Commission (Elevators and Escalators)*, EU:C:2013:522, [2013] 5 CMLR 1387, paras 33–38.

13.124 **The Commission's discretion and the Fining Guidelines.**

Fn 709 See also Case C-501/11P *Schindler v Commission (Elevators and Escalators)*, EU:C:2013:522, [2013] 5 CMLR 1387, paras 33–38 and 155–160. The Court of Justice will consider whether the General Court conducted an in-depth review in substance, even if the judgment under appeal states that it is according the Commission a considerable margin of discretion. In Case C-510/11P *Kone v Commission*, EU:C:2013:696, [2014] 4 CMLR 371, the Court of Justice considered whether the General Court conducted an in-depth review in substance, notwithstanding it had stated that the test it was applying was whether the Commission had 'manifestly [gone] beyond the bounds of that margin' of discretion: see paras 40 and 44 et seq.

Fn 713 The Court of Justice dismissed the further appeal in Case C-70/12P *Quinn Barlo v Commission* ('*Methacrylates*'), EU:C:2013:351, [2013] 5 CMLR 637.

Fn 715 See also Case C-70/12P *Quinn Barlo v Commission* ('*Methacrylates*'), EU:C:2013:351, [2013] 5 CMLR 637, para 46.

13.127 **Adjustment of fines in cases of unequal treatment.** See also Joined Cases T-147&148/09 *Trelleborg v Commission*, EU:T:2013:259, [2013] 5 CMLR 754, para 104, in which the General Court dismissed a complaint that the Commission had breached the principle of equal treatment in the manner in which it had applied the limitation period to different undertakings. The General Court held that even if the Commission had erred as respects its conclusion that proceedings against another undertaking were time-barred, it was not open to Trelleborg to rely on that illegality as a basis for claiming that proceedings against it should also have been treated as time-barred.

See, further, paragraph 14.081 of the main text, and the updates thereto, regarding the principle of equal treatment and the imposition of fines.

(b) Review of Commission decisions

(i) Reviewable acts of the Commission and standing to bring appeal

13.131 **Non-reviewable 'acts' of the Commission.** In addition to the acts which are listed in the main text as non-reviewable, measures taken by the Commission to implement an inspection decision are not reviewable by the General Court: Case T-135/09 *Nexans France v Commission*, EU:T:2012:596, [2013] CMLR 4 195, paras 119 et seq, discussed in the update to paragraph 13.030, above. The further appeal, on other grounds, was dismissed in Case C-37/13P *Nexans v Commission*, EU:C:2014:2030, [2014] 5 CMLR 642.

13.132 **Standing to bring appeal.** The General Court in Case T-442/08 *International Confederation of Societies of Authors and Composers (CISAC) v Commission*, EU:T:2013:188, [2013] 5 CMLR 536, paras 63 et seq, permitted CISAC to challenge the Commission's decision in COMP/38698 *CISAC Agreements*, decision of 16 July 2008, [2009] 4 CMLR 577. CISAC is a non-profit non-governmental organisation whose principal task is representing the entities that were addressed by the Commission decision, and facilitating cooperation between them. It had been an addressee of the statement of objections, but was not an addressee of the final decision. The General Court considered that the decision was of direct and individual concern to CISAC, as its activities would be relevant to assessing whether the addressees were bringing to an end the concerted practice found in the decision, and as the decision affected its role as a facilitator of cooperation (particularly in mediating between the societies on issues relating to the grant of multi-territorial licences).

Fn 757 The Court of Justice confirmed in C-583/11P *Inuit Tapiriit Kanatami v Parliament*, EU:C:2013:625, [2013] 3 CMLR 758, that legislation cannot be considered to be a 'regulatory act' within Article 263(4) TFEU.

Fn 762 The Court of Justice in C-452/10P *BNP Paribas v Commission*, EU:C:2012:366, [2012] 3 CMLR 723, upheld the appeal against the General Court's judgment, but gave final judgment rather than remit the appeal and dismissed the challenge to the Commission's decision.

(ii) The grounds of annulment

Procedural irregularities. A further example of a procedural irregularity which **13.134** was held not to vitiate the Commission's decision was (a) an initial refusal by the Commission to grant access to original recordings of an interview it had conducted with an employee of a leniency applicant; and (b) an incorrect transcription of the interview (which was revealed when the Commission subsequently granted partial access to the recording), omitting a statement by a Commission official that the witness should not worry about whether the answer to the question he had been asked was 'true or not'. The General Court held that as the undertaking had eventually been granted full access to the original recording, and the Commission had not relied on that particular witness' evidence in its statement of objections, the irregularity did not vitiate the Commission's decision: Case T-482/07 *Nynäs v Commission*, EU:C:2013:437, paras 104 et seq.

Failure to respect the rights of the defence. **13.135**
Fn 784 See also T-587/08 *Fresh Del Monte Produce*, EU:T:2013:129, [2013] 4 CMLR 1091, paras 704–713 (further appeal, on other grounds, dismissed in Joined Cases C-293&294/13P *Fresh Del Monte Produce*, EU:C:2015:416, [2015] 5 CMLR 513).

Adequacy of reasoning. **13.137**
Fn 794 The Court of Justice dismissed the appeals in Case C-457/10P *AstraZeneca v Commission*, EU:C:2012:770, [2013] 4 CMLR 233.

Fn 800 A further, recent example is the General Court's judgment in Case T-380/10 *Wabco Europe v Commission (Bathroom Fittings)*, EU:T:2013:449, [2014] 4 CMLR 138, paras 108–112.

13.139 **Breach of general principles of EU law.**
Fn 813 For a more recent example, see Case T-286/09 *Intel v Commission*, EU:T:2014:547, [2014] 5 CMLR 270, at paras 160–169. The General Court dismissed a complaint that Intel had a legitimate expectation that the Commission would apply an 'as efficient competitor' test, or 'AEC' test, in determining whether its rebate arrangements infringed Article 102. Although the Commission stated in the statement of objections that if it were necessary to establish that the rebates were capable of foreclosing competitors then it would rely on an AEC test, and the application of the test played an important role during the administrative procedure, Intel could not show a precise assurance had been given that the Commission would not rely on other evidence to establish foreclosure. On further appeal, Case C-413/14P, not yet decided.

(iii) The standard of review

13.143 **Errors of law.**
Fn 822 The Court of Justice in Case C-439/11P *Ziegler v Commission*, EU:C:2013:513, [2013] 5 CMLR 1217, held that it is necessary to define the relevant market in order to determine whether there was an appreciable effect on trade between Member States in that market: para 63. However, the Commission had provided a sufficiently detailed description of the services with which its decision was concerned to constitute a definition of the market for these purposes: paras 67–73.

13.144 **Errors of fact.** The General Court in Case T-286/09 *Intel v Commission*, EU:T:2014:547, [2014] 5 CMLR 270 at paras 64–67 held that the principle that it is for the Commission to produce a body of evidence which, viewed as a whole, is sufficiently precise and consistent to support the firm conviction that the alleged infringement took place, without it being necessary for every individual item of evidence to meet that requirement in relation to every aspect of the infringement, applies in cases under Article 102 as well as Article 101. Once the Commission has produced such evidence, the review by the General Court will fall into two categories:

(a) where the Commission finds an infringement on the basis that established facts cannot be explained other than by the existence of anti-competitive behaviour, the General Court will consider whether the undertaking has put forward arguments which cast the facts established by the Commission in a different light and thus allow another plausible explanation of the facts;
(b) where the Commission finds an infringement on the basis of evidence that demonstrates the existence of an infringement, the General Court will consider whether the undertaking has proved both the existence of any

circumstances which it alleges cast doubt on the probative value of that evidence, and also that those circumstances do cast doubt on the probative value of the evidence. The undertaking cannot adduce evidence of the existence of such circumstances, and then shift the burden of proof onto the Commission to establish that they do not affect the probative value of the evidence.

On further appeal, Case C-413/14P, not yet decided.

Decisions involving complex economic assessment. In addition to the decisions listed in the main text, in Case C-73/11 *Frucona Košice v Commission*, EU:C:2013:32, [2013] 2 CMLR 719, paras 74–75, the Court of Justice held that determining whether a measure amounts to a State aid because the public authority did not act in the same way as a private creditor involves the kind of complex economic assessment which may result in the European courts conducting a more limited review. **13.147**

Fn 836 A recent example of a judgment in respect of a clearance decision is Case T-405/08 *SPAR Österreiche Warenhandel v Commission*, EU:T:2013:306.

Exercise of the Commission's discretion. The case law referred to in the main text should be read in the light of the Court of Justice's judgment in Case C-510/11P *Kone v Commission*, EU:C:2013:696, [2014] 4 CMLR 371, at least insofar as the discretion exercised by the Commission pertains to fines. The appellant complained that by considering only whether the Commission had 'manifestly [gone] beyond the bounds of [its] margin' of discretion in assessing the cooperation of an undertaking under the Leniency Notice the General Court had failed to comply with Article 47 of the Charter on Fundamental Rights, and Article 6 of the ECHR. The Court of Justice accepted that the manifest error test does not meet the requirements of Article 47 Charter/Article 6 ECHR: para 44. The Court cannot use the Commission's margin of discretion as a basis for dispensing with the conduct of an in-depth review of the law and of the facts: see paragraph 13.124 of the main text, and the updates thereto, above. **13.149**

Fn 844 See also Joined Cases T-104/07&339/08 *Belgische Vereniging van handelaars in- en uitvoerdersgeslependiamant (BVGD) and Diamanthandel A. Spira v Commission*, EU:T:2013:366, [2013] 5 CMLR 1055, paras 219 et seq.

(iv) Procedural aspects

Whether decisions can be supported by new material. Although the Commission is not permitted to rely on evidence that is not contained in the decision for the purposes of review under Article 263 TFEU, the General Court may nonetheless take such evidence into account in the exercise of its unlimited jurisdiction regarding fines under Article 261 TFEU: Case T-462/07 *Galp Energía España v Commission*, EU:T:2013:459, [2014] 4 CMLR 272 (on further **13.153**

appeal, Case C-603/13P, not yet decided), discussed in the update to paragraph 13.123, above.

Fn 864 See also Case T-380/10 *Wabco Europe v Commission (Bathroom Fittings)*, EU:T:2013:449, [2014] 4 CMLR 138, paras 108–112, in which the General Court rejected the Commission's attempt to provide additional arguments in support of its decision, and partially annulled the decision on grounds of lack of reasons.

13.154 **Measures of organisation and inquiry.**   With respect to the General Court hearing oral evidence, the Court of Justice observed in Case C-501/11P *Schindler v Commission (Elevators and Escalators)*, EU:C:2013:522, [2013] 5 CMLR 1387, para 46, that it is for an applicant to apply for witnesses to be examined. It appears that the General Court cannot be criticised on appeal for not having heard witness evidence of its own motion. The Court of Justice in Joined Cases C-239/11P, etc, *Siemens v Commission (Gas Insulated Switchgear)*, EU:C:2013:866, [2014] 4 CMLR 606, at paras 319–325 confirmed that the Commission's, and the General Court's, discretion whether to require the attendance of a witness for examination is compatible with the right to a fair hearing under Article 6 of the ECHR.

Fn 874 See also Case T-296/11 *Cementos Portland Valderrivas v Commission*, EU:T:2014:121 (measures taken to request that the Commission produce the documents that underpinned its decision to request information under Article 18(3) of Regulation 1/2003; see the update to paragraph 13.103, above).

Fn 876 See also Case C-578/11P *Deltafina v Commission*, EU:C:2014:1460, [2014] 5 CMLR 599, at paras 60–62, in which the Court of Justice held that although the General Court follows a legitimate practice of questioning the parties' representatives on technical matters and complex facts during the oral hearing of an appeal, in that case it went beyond what may be carried out under that practice (as opposed to what may be carried out by summoning those individuals to appear as witnesses) by asking the parties' representatives for their understanding of what was agreed between the Commission and the undertaking during certain meetings/conversations that took place during the Commission's investigation. The Court went on to hold that that irregularity did not, however, infringe the undertaking's right to a fair hearing.

13.155 **Interveners.**
Fn 879 In respect of a plea of inadmissibility, however, the Court should still examine an objection raised by interveners (but not by the Commission) as a lack of legal interest is an absolute bar to bringing proceedings: Case T-471/11 *Éditions Odile Jacob v Commission*, EU:T:2014:739, para 38.

13.156 **Power of partial annulment.**   In Case C-441/11P *Commission v Verhuizingen Coppens*, EU:C:2012:778, [2013] 4 CMLR 312, the Court of Justice held that the General Court erred in annulling COMP/38543 *International Removal Service*, decision of 11 March 2008, entirely rather than partially. The General Court had annulled the decision in relation to Coppens on the basis that it had only engaged in one of the two infringing behaviours found by the Commission (it engaged in cover pricing, but had not entered into compensation agreements). The Court of Justice held that the decision should have been annulled only in respect of the infringing behaviour in which Coppens had not engaged, and in respect of the attribution of a single and continuous infringement. The Court of Justice held that the Commission's decision stood in respect of the infringing behaviour in which Coppens did engage. For an example of the General Court applying this judgment, see Case T-462/07 *Galp Energía España v Commission*, EU:T:2013:459, [2014] 4 CMLR 272, paras 535 et seq (on further appeal, on other grounds, in Case C-603/13P, not yet decided).

In Case C-287/11P *Commission v Aalberts (Fittings Cartel)*, EU:C:2013:445, [2013] 5 CMLR 867, the Court of Justice held that the General Court was correct to annul COMP/38121 *Fittings* (OJ 2007 L283/63) in its entirety, as the conduct in which the undertaking had engaged was not specified as an infringement in the decision, and as such it could not be severed from the remainder of the decision.

Consequences of successful appeal by some addressees of the decision. The **13.157** General Court's judgments in the 22 appeals brought against COMP/38698 *CISAC Agreements*, decision of 16 July 2008, [2009] 4 CMLR 577, illustrate the operation of this principle. The General Court annulled the Commission decision finding an anti-competitive concerted practice, as against 21 of the appellants (Cases T-392, 398, 401, 410, 411, 413–422, 425, 428, 432–434, 442/08, judgments of 12 April 2013). However, it dismissed the appeal against this finding brought on different grounds in Case T-451/08 *Föreningen Svenska Tonsättares Internationella Musikbyrå v Commission*, EU:T:2013:189 [2013] 5 CMLR 577. This appellant had not pleaded that the Commission had insufficient evidence to establish a concerted practice, which was the ground of appeal that succeeded in the 21 other appeals. The General Court held that its attempt to adopt the other appellants' submissions on this ground was inadmissible, and it therefore went on to consider the grounds of appeal that had been advanced. The appeal on these other grounds was dismissed.

Fn 887 In the UK, the High Court in *Lindum Construction and others v OFT* [2014] EWHC 1613 (Ch) dismissed a claim in restitution for repayment of the penalty paid by several addressees of an OFT decision, which they had not appealed but which other addressees had appealed successfully in *Imperial Tobacco Group and others v Office of Fair Trading* [2011] CAT 41. In *OFT v Somerfield Stores, and OFT v Gallaher Group* [2014] EWCA Civ 400, the Court of Appeal overturned a judgment of the Competition Appeal Tribunal in which it had granted other non-appealing addressees of the same OFT decision permission to appeal out of time, as successful appeals by other parties are not 'exceptional circumstances' for the purposes of extending time to appeal under the Tribunal's rules.

Fn 888 See also Cases T-496/07 *Repsol Lubricantes y Especialidades v Commission*, EU:T:2013:464, paras 444 et seq; and T-495/07 *PROAS v Commission*, EU:T:2013:452, paras 456 et seq. The General Court had partially annulled the Commission's decision as against two of the addressees, on the basis that the evidence of the leniency applicants, on which the Commission had relied, was not sufficient to establish those addressees' participation in certain aspects of the infringing conduct. In *Repsol* and *PROAS* the General Court refused the Commission's request that it should increase the fines imposed on the leniency applicants on account of the successful appeal by the other two addressees (on further appeal, Case C-617/13P *Repsol v Commission*, not yet decided; and Case C-616/13P *PROAS v Commission*, not yet decided). In Case T-462/07 *Galp Energía España v Commission*, EU:T:2013:459, [2014] 4 CMLR 272, paras 89–91, the Court refused to consider an application to annul a Commission decision in its entirety, and not only in respect of the particular applicants (on further appeal, on other grounds, in Case C-603/13P, not yet decided).

The treatment of a decision as a 'bundle of individual decisions', each applying to each of the addressees, has been considered also in a number of UK cases. In *Deutsche Bahn v Morgan Crucible Company* [2014] UKSC 24 the Supreme Court overturned the Court of Appeal, and held that the relevant 'decision', for the purposes of the limitation period for bringing a monetary claim before the Competition Appeal Tribunal under section 47A of the Competition Act 1998, is the individual decision taken against the individual addressee by the Commission. The judgments in Case C-310/97P *Commission v AssiDomän*, EU:C:1999:407, [1999] ECR I-5363 and Case T-462/07 *Galp Energía España v Commission*, EU:T:2013:459, [2014] 4 CMLR 272 confirm that a Commission decision is binding as against an addressee who does not appeal it, and the appeals (including successful appeals) by other addressees do not affect a non-appealing addressee's liability in damages for the infringement that was found against it in the Commission's decision. The Commission submitted observations to the Court, pursuant to Article 15(3) of Regulation 1/2003 (discussed in paragraph 15.051 of the main text), which are available on the *Amicus Curiae* section of the DG Comp website. In *Lindum Construction and others v OFT* [2014] EWHC 1613 (Ch) the High Court dismissed a claim in restitution for repayment of the penalty paid by the addressees of an OFT decision, which they had not appealed but which other addressees had appealed successfully in *Imperial Tobacco Group and others v Office of Fair Trading* [2011] CAT 41. In *OFT v Somerfield Stores, and OFT v Gallaher Group* [2014] EWCA Civ 400, the Court of Appeal overturned a judgment of the Competition Appeal Tribunal in which it had granted other non-appealing addressees of the same OFT decision permission to appeal out of time, as successful appeals by other parties are not 'exceptional circumstances' for the purposes of extending time to appeal under the Tribunal's rules.

Fn 889 The Court of Justice dismissed the appeal in Case C-286/11P *Commission v Tomkins*, EU:C:2013:29, [2013] 4 CMLR 466. It held, disagreeing with Advocate General Mengozzi, that the General Court did not err in law by giving Tomkins the benefit of its subsidiary's appeal. In circumstances where the liability of a parent company is wholly derived from that of its subsidiary, and where both companies have brought actions before the European Courts seeking a reduction in their fines on the same basis (in this case, on the basis of the duration of the infringement), then it is not necessary for the scope of their actions, or the arguments deployed, to be identical in order for the General Court to recalculate the fine imposed on the parent company on account of the outcome of the appeal by the subsidiary.

See also Case C-679/11P *Alliance One International v Commission*, EU:C:2013:606, [2014] 4 CMLR 249, paras 106–107. The Court of Justice dismissed a cross-appeal by the Commission against the General Court's judgment in Case T-41/05 *Dimons* [2011] ECR II-7101, in which the General Court had reduced the fine imposed on the parent company, Dimon, on account of the reduction of the fine imposed on its subsidiary in Case T-38/05 *Agroexpansion* [2011] ECR II-7005.

See also Joined Cases C-293&294/13P *Fresh Del Monte Produce*, EU:C:2015:416, [2015] 5 CMLR 513, para 52, in which the Court of Justice held that a subsidiary company which had not appealed the Commission's decision had an interest in making submissions in the parent company's appeal, because if the attribution of the fine to the parent company were to be annulled then the subsidiary would be responsible for the fine alone, not jointly and severally with the parent.

Costs and other orders.   **13.160**
Fn 906 See also C-452/10P *BNP Paribas v Commission*, EU:C:2012:366, [2012] 3 CMLR 723.

(d) Interim relief from the General Court

Generally.   **13.164**
Fn 931 See also Case T-164/12 *Alstom v Commission*, Order of the President of 29 November 2012, [2013] 4 CMLR 415, allowing an intervention by National Grid. The appeal concerned a decision by the Commission to transmit information to the High Court of England & Wales, under Article 15(1) of Regulation 1/2003 (see paragraphs 15.047 and 16.041 of the main text on Article 15(1) of Regulation 1/2003). National Grid was the claimant in the proceedings before the national court, and the request to the Commission under Article 15(1) was made at its application. It was allowed to intervene in the General Court proceedings, and to make representations on the application for interim measures.

13.169   **Interim measures to suspend a decision taken during an investigation.**
Fn 965   The General Court dismissed Intel's complaint regarding the Commission's alleged failure to obtain exculpatory documents: Case T-286/09 *Intel v Commission*, EU:T:2014:547, [2014] 5 CMLR 270, paras 340 et seq, discussed in the update to paragraph 13.011, above.

10. Appeals to the Court of Justice

13.170   **Appeal from judgments of the General Court.**
Fn 971   The procedure of the Court of Justice is now governed by Supplementary Rules, issued on 1 February 2014, as well as by the Statute of the Court of Justice and the Rules of Procedure: OJ 2014 L32/37.

13.171   **Review by the Court of Justice.**   In Joined Cases C-239/11P, etc, *Siemens v Commission (Gas Insulated Switchgear)*, EU:C:2013:866, [2014] 4 CMLR 606, at paras 38 et seq, the Court of Justice confirmed that its powers to review findings of fact include the power to review substantive inaccuracies, distortion of evidence, the legal characterisation of evidence, and questions of compliance with the rules on the taking of evidence and the burden of proof. They do not extend to alleged infringements of purported principles derived from experience. The Court therefore dismissed as inadmissible a complaint that the General Court should not have relied upon the witness evidence of the leniency applicant because of 'established knowledge relating to the functioning of the memory and the psychology of witnesses', and the possibility that an individual may have had an interest in maximising the unlawful conduct of competitors and minimising their own liability. A review of that nature requires a factual assessment which is fundamentally different from the marginal review which the Court carries out when an appellant complains, in a sufficiently detailed manner, that the General Court distorted the evidence. Such a distortion must be obvious from the documents in the Court's file, without there being any need to carry out a new assessment of the facts and the evidence.

13.176   **Exercise of the jurisdiction.**
Fn 987   In Case C-50/12P *Kendrion v Commission*, EU:C:2013:771, [2014] 4 CMLR 454, at paras 91 et seq, the Court ruled that the sanction for a breach by the Court of its obligation under Article 47 of the Charter on Fundamental Rights to adjudicate cases within a reasonable time is a claim for damages against the EU under Article 268 TFEU and the second paragraph of Article 340 TFEU. This is an effective remedy. The approach taken by the Court in Case C-185/95P *Baustahlgewebe v Commission* [1998] ECR I-8417, [1999] 4 CMLR 1203, of reducing the fine was not to be followed.

14

FINES FOR SUBSTANTIVE
INFRINGEMENTS

1. Introduction

(a) Jurisdiction and the Commission's discretion

The jurisdiction to fine.   **14.001**
Fn 1 In 2015 the Commission imposed fines totalling €365m (compared with
€1.69 billion in 2014, €1.88 billion in 2013, €1.88 billion in 2012, €614m in 2011
and €2.87 billion in 2010).

Legal certainty.   **14.004**
Fn 17 See also Case C-501/11P *Schindler v Commission (Elevators and Escalators)*,
EU:C:2013:522, [2013] 5 CMLR 1387, para 58.

Retroactive application of Fining Guidelines. The General Court held that   **14.005**
the retroactive application of the 2006 Fining Guidelines (OJ 2006 C210/2) is
compatible with the principle of legal certainty, with Article 7 of the ECHR
and with Article 49 of the Charter on Fundamental Rights; this applies *a fortiori* where those Guidelines are applied to a single infringement that ended
only after those Guidelines were adopted: Case T-286/09 *Intel v Commission*,
EU:T:2014:547, at paras 1596–1598 (on further appeal, Case C-413/14P, not yet
decided). See Joined Cases T-389&419/10 *SLM and Ori Martin v Commission*,
EU:T:2015:513, para 107, concerning an infringement which had concluded prior
to the 2006 Fining Guidelines being adopted (on further appeal, Cases 490/15P,
etc, not yet decided).

Fines and the European Convention on Human Rights. In Case C-501/11P   **14.006**
Schindler v Commission (Elevators and Escalators), EU:C:2013:522, [2013] 5
CMLR 1387, the Court of Justice followed the approach of the European Court
of Human Rights in App 43509/08 *Menarini Diagnostics v Italy*, judgment of
27 September 2011, and rejected an argument that the imposition of fines by the
Commission, rather than by a court, was contrary to Article 6 of the ECHR and
Article 47 of the Charter of Fundamental Rights. It held that the power of review

by the Court under Article 263 TFEU, together with the unlimited jurisdiction to review the fine under Article 261 TFEU and Article 31 of Regulation 1/2003, is sufficient to comply with the requirements of effective judicial protection.

Article 49 of the Charter of Fundamental Rights requires that the penalties must be proportionate to the infringement. For examples of the General Court concluding that a penalty is disproportionate, see Case T-418/10 *Voestalpine v Commission*, EU:T:2015:516, paras 442 et seq; and Joined Cases T-389&419/10 *SLM and Ori Martin v Commission*, EU:T:2015:513, para 326, (on further appeal, Cases 490/15P, etc, not yet decided) concerning the Commission's approach in COMP/38344 *Pre-stressing Steel*, decision of 30 June 2010.

14.008 **Method of calculating the fine.** The General Court held that the Commission may decide, in a case which concerns a cartel involving several smaller players on the market and one major player which has received immunity on account of its cooperation with the Commission, to reduce the fine to be imposed on the smaller players in order to avoid a situation in which those smaller players exit the market and the immunity applicant is left in a dominant or monopolistic position: Case T-392/09 *1. garantovaná v Commission*, EU:T:2012:674, [2014] 5 CMLR 132 at para 116, following the Opinion of Advocate General Geelhoed in Case C-289/04 P *Showa Denko v Commission* [2006] ECR I-5859, para 61. The further appeal on other grounds was dismissed in Case C-90/13P *1. garantovaná v Commission*, EU:C:2014:326, [2014] 5 CMLR 79.

Fn 24 A number of the appeals against the Commission's decision in COMP/ 38344 *Pre-stressing Steel*, decision of 30 June 2010, have been upheld: eg Case T-418/10 *Voestalpine v Commission*, EU:T:2015:516, paras 442 et seq; and Joined Cases T-389&419/10 *SLM and Ori Martin v Commission*, EU:T:2015:513, para 326, (on further appeal, Cases 490/15P, etc, not yet decided) in which the General Court held that the fine imposed was disproportionate. The Commission's decision in COMP/37990 *Intel*, decision of 13 May 2009, was upheld on appeal in Case T-286/09 *Intel v Commission*, EU:T:2014:547, [2014] 5 CMLR 270 (on further appeal, Case C-413/14P, not yet decided).

(b) Intentional or negligent infringement

14.009 **Generally.** It is not necessary to establish separately intentional or negligent conduct on the part of a parent company, where it is held liable for the conduct of its subsidiary as part of the same undertaking: Case C-501/11P *Schindler v Commission (Elevators and Escalators)*, EU:C:2013:522, [2013] 5 CMLR 1387, paras 90 and 101 et seq.

Fn 41 The Court of Justice confirmed in Case C-681/11 *Schenker*, EU:C:2013:404, [2013] 5 CMLR 831, that Article 5 of Regulation 1/2003 does not require Member States to establish conditions of intention or negligence for the imposition of a fine, but if they do so then those conditions must be at least as stringent as those in Article 23 of Regulation 1/2003: paras 35–36. Disagreeing with Advocate General Kokott's Opinion of 28 February 2013, the Court held that reliance by an undertaking on legal advice or a previous NCA decision that its conduct was not contrary to EU competition law is not sufficient to show that an infringement was not committed intentionally or negligently. To avoid a finding that an infringement was committed intentionally or negligently, an undertaking must show that it could not have been aware of the anti-competitive nature of its conduct. If an undertaking characterised its conduct wrongly in law, then it cannot show that it could not have been aware of the anti-competitive nature of its conduct: para 38.

Knowledge of the law is not a prerequisite to intention.   **14.011**
Fn 54 The Court of Justice dismissed the appeals in Case C-457/10P *AstraZeneca v Commission*, EU:C:2012:770, [2013] 4 CMLR 233, paras 74 et seq.

Rebutting intention or negligence.   The Court of Justice confirmed in Case   **14.014**
C-681/11 *Schenker*, EU:C:2013:404, [2013] 5 CMLR 831, that reliance by an undertaking on legal advice or a previous NCA decision that its conduct was not contrary to EU competition law is not sufficient to show that an infringement was not committed intentionally or negligently. To avoid a finding that an infringement was committed intentionally or negligently, an undertaking must show that it could not have been aware of the anti-competitive nature of its conduct. If an undertaking characterised its conduct wrongly in law, then it cannot show that it could not have been aware of the anti-competitive nature of its conduct: para 38.

2. The Basic Amount of the Fine

In general.   **14.016**
Fn 74 See the update to paragraph 14.027, below on the Court of Justice's judgment in Case C-444/11P *Team Relocations v Commission*, EU:C:2013:464, [2013] 5 CMLR 1335.

(a) Value of sales

(i) Applicable turnover

Sales in the relevant market.   The Court of Justice upheld the General Court's   **14.019**
approach of including all sales in the relevant market which could have been affected, rather than only the sales shown to have been affected, by the infringing conduct: Case C-444/11P *Team Relocations v Commission*, EU:C:2013:464, [2013] 5 CMLR 1335; see in particular paras 77 et seq. Following that approach, in Case C-286/13P *Dole Food Company v Commission*, EU:C:2015:184, [2015] 4 CMLR 967, para 150, the Court dismissed a complaint that this entailed bringing

into the calculation sales made in the relevant market by subsidiary companies which were not involved in the infringement.

See also Joined Cases T-379&381/10 *Keramag Keramische Werke and Others (Bathroom Fittings) v Commission*, EU:T:2013:457. paras 361–362, where the General Court rejected an argument that an undertaking's sales made in the same market, but through a separate distribution channel and with different rebate structures and prices and list prices, should be excluded from the value of sales for fining purposes as the infringement was likely to relate to these sales indirectly, within the meaning of the Fining Guidelines. On further appeal, Case C-613/13P, not yet decided.

In Case T-72/09 *Pilkington v Commission*, EU:T:2014:1094, [2015] 4 CMLR 227 at paras 217 et seq, the General Court dismissed a complaint that the Commission had erred in including sales in the value of sales calculation which had been made on the basis of contracts concluded prior to the commencement of the infringement and not renegotiated during the period of the infringement. On further appeal, Case C-101/15P, not yet decided.

Fn 77 On the inclusion of intra-group sales, see also Case C-231/14P *Innolux v Commission (Liquid Crystal Displays)*, EU:C:2015:451, discussed in the update to paragraph 14.020, below.

Fn 85 The Court of Justice dismissed the appeal in Case C-444/11P *Team Relocations v Commission*, EU:C:2013:464, [2013] 5 CMLR 1335; see in particular paras 77 et seq. It also dismissed the appeal in Case C-276/11P *Viega v Commission*, EU:C:2013:163.

14.020 **Direct and indirect sales.** The Commission's approach in its decision in COMP/39309 *Liquid Crystal Displays*, decision of 8 December 2010, discussed in the main text at paragraph 14.020 was upheld in Case C-231/14P *Innolux v Commission (Liquid Crystal Displays)*, EU:C:2015:451; and Case C-227/14P, *LG Display v Commission (Liquid Crystal Displays)*, EU:C:2015:258, [2015] 4 CMLR 1165. The Commission had calculated the undertakings' value of sales on the basis of direct sales of the cartelised LCD product into the EEA, and in addition a proportion of the value of the sales made by different companies within the same undertakings, into the EEA, of finished products into which the cartelised LCD product had been incorporated. The Court in particular dismissed a complaint that the latter should have been excluded on the basis that the Commission's findings of infringement did not extend to finished products incorporating LCDs. It held that although the finished products were sold onto a separate downstream market from the cartelised products, nonetheless sales of the finished products by a vertically integrated cartel participant were liable to affect competition in that downstream market, either because the cartelist would pass on the price increase on the cartelised product, or it would obtain a cost advantage by not doing so: *Innolux*, paras 56–57. Those sales were therefore properly considered to be related to the infringement, within para 13 of the Fining Guidelines. The Court also rejected the contention that the Commission's approach exceeded its territorial jurisdiction, in breach of the principles laid down in Joined Cases 89/85, etc, *Ahlström Osakeyhtiö and Others v Commission* [1988] ECR 5193, 'Wood Pulp I' (discussed in paragraph 1.115 of the main text) by effectively bringing into account sales that were made to subsidiary companies outside the EEA. Disagreeing with the Opinion of Advocate General Wathelet, EU:C:2015:292, the Court held that the Commission had jurisdiction to apply Article 101 to the cartel, because the cartelists made direct sales of the cartelised product into the EEA, and that the appropriate method for determining the fine to be imposed in respect of that cartel was a separate question to jurisdiction. The Commission was entitled to take the approach that it had done in order to determine the fine, as sales of finished products on the downstream market in the EEA were affected by the cartel: *Innolux*, paras 71 et seq.

Fn 86 The General Court in Joined Cases T-56&73/09 *Saint Gobain (Carglass)*, EU:T:2014:160, at paras 154 et seq, dismissed a complaint that the Commission had failed to give adequate reasons for its approach to determining the value of sales in COMP/39125 *Carglass*, decision of 12 November 2008 (fine reduced, on the basis that the uplift for recidivism was incorrectly applied; see the update to paragraph 14.042, below). In Case T-72/09 *Pilkington v Commission*, EU:T:2014:1094, [2015] 4 CMLR 227 at paras 213 et seq, it upheld the Commission's approach of calculating an annual weighted average value of sales for each undertaking, during the period of its participation in the infringement, using its value of sales during the 'roll-out' and 'decline' periods of the cartel on transactions for which there was direct evidence of collusion, and its value of sales on all transactions in the EEA during the remaining period. This reflected that the cartel in question had varied in intensity during the infringement period. On further appeal, on other grounds, in Case C-101/15P, not yet decided.

In respect of the judgment in Cases T-204&212/08 *Team Relocations v Commission (International Removal Services)* [2011] ECR II-3569, [2011] 5 CMLR 889, the Court of Justice dismissed the further appeal, on other grounds, in Case C-444/11P *Team Relocations v Commission*, EU:C:2013:464, [2013] 5 CMLR 1335.

Fn 87 The Commission decision in COMP/37990 *Intel*, decision of 13 May 2009, was upheld on appeal in Case T-286/09 *Intel v Commission*, EU:T:2014:547, [2014] 5 CMLR 270 (on further appeal, Case C-413/14P, not yet decided).

Captive sales. The Court of Justice in Case C-580/12P *Guardian Industries v Commission*, EU:C:2014:2363 confirmed that the principle of equal treatment requires that the Commission should take account of internal sales in identifying an undertaking's value of sales. It dismissed the Commission's argument that it has a discretion whether to include such sales, which the Commission **14.021**

can lawfully exercise by considering whether the infringement found relates to internal sales as well as to sales to third parties, and whether the vertically integrated undertaking derives a benefit in the downstream market from its participation in an infringement in the upstream market. The General Court's judgment (Case T-82/08 *Guardian Industries v Commission*, EU:T:2012:494, [2012] 5 CMLR 1234, paras 104–106) was set aside, and the Commission's decision in COMP/39165 *Flat Glass*, decision of 28 November 2007, partially annulled.

Fn 88 The appeals against the Commission's decision in COMP/39180 *Aluminium Fluoride*, decision of 25 June 2008, in Case T-404/08 *Fluorsid and Minmet v Commission*, EU:T:2013:321, [2013] 5 CMLR 902; and Case T-406/08 *Industries chimiques du fluor v Commission*, EU:T:2013:322 were dismissed (further appeal, on other grounds, dismissed in Case C-467/13P, *Industries chimiques du fluor v Commission*, EU:C:2014:2274).

Fn 89 The Commission's approach in its decision in COMP/39309 *Liquid Crystal Displays*, decision of 8 December 2010 was upheld in C-231/14P *Innolux v Commission (Liquid Crystal Displays)*, EU:C:2015:451; and Case C-227/14P, *LG Display v Commission (Liquid Crystal Displays)*, EU:C:2015:258, [2015] 4 CMLR 1165). See the update to paragraph 14.020, above.

14.023 **Calculating sales over time.** The Commission's approach in COMP/38866 *Animal Feed Phosphates*, decision of 20 July 2010, discussed in the main text, appears doubtful in view of the General Court judgment in Case T-286/09 *Intel v Commission*, EU:T:2014:547. The Court, at para 1577, dismissed an argument that the Commission is required to consider the value of sales in the EEA by reference to the Member States comprising the EEA at different stages of the infringement. In that case, Intel argued that 12 Member States had joined the EEA during the infringement period, and that, as these states were beyond the Commission's jurisdiction during the earlier part of the infringement, Intel's sales into those states during the earlier period had to be excluded from the value of sales calculation. The General Court held that the relevant year for determining the undertaking's value of sales is normally the last full business year of its infringement, and that the scope of the EEA is to be determined by reference to that year. As the 12 Member States were within the EEA in the last full business year of Intel's infringement, the Commission was entitled to take into account Intel's value of sales in those Member States. On further appeal, Case C-413/14P, not yet decided.

14.024 **Sales outside the EEA.** In order to determine the value of sales of undertakings within the EEA, to which their shares of sales in the relevant geographic area (wider than the EEA) should be applied, the Commission may consider the sales invoiced in the EEA by the undertaking, rather than the sales delivered by it in the EEA, provided that using sales invoiced in the EEA 'reflects the reality of the market, that is to say for it to be the best criterion for ascertaining the effects of the cartel on competition in the EEA'. That criterion will be met in circumstances where the end use location of the relevant product is outside Europe but some of the main original equipment manufacturers are based in the EEA: Case T-146/09 *Parker ITR and Parker-Hannifin v Commission (Marine Hoses)*, EU:T:2013:258, [2013] 5 CMLR 712, paras 208 et seq (partially annulled, on other grounds on further appeal, in Case C-434/13P *Commission v Parker Hannifin Manufacturing and Parker-Hannifin* EU:C:2014:2456, [2015] 4 CMLR 179; see the update to paragraph 14.101, below).

As regards the meaning of 'the EEA', the General Court in Case T-286/09 *Intel v Commission*, EU:T:2014:547, at para 1577, dismissed an argument that the Commission is required to consider the value of sales in the EEA by reference to the Member States comprising the EEA at different stages of the infringement. In that case, Intel argued that 12 Member States had joined the EEA during the infringement period, and that, as these states were beyond the Commission's jurisdiction during the earlier part of the infringement, Intel's sales into those states during the earlier period had to be excluded from the value of sales calculation. The General Court held that the relevant year for determining the undertaking's value of sales is normally the last full business year of its infringement, and that the scope of the EEA is to be determined by reference to that year. As the 12 Member States were within the EEA in the last full business year of Intel's infringement, the Commission was entitled to take into account Intel's value of sales in those Member States. On further appeal, Case C-413/14P, not yet decided.

Fn 94 The Commission's decision in COMP/39129 *Power Transformers*, decision of 7 October 2009, was upheld in Case T-519/09 *Toshiba v Commission*, EU:T:2014:263, [2014] 5 CMLR 219 at paras 270 et seq. The General Court dismissed a complaint that the Commission should have considered the value of sales in the EEA and Japan as representing the sales affected by the infringement, rather than worldwide sales. It held that the purpose of paragraph 18 of the Fining Guidelines is to determine the undertaking's notional sales in the EEA, and that for that purpose the Commission relies on the presumption that in the absence of the restriction of competition the producers would have achieved market shares in the EEA equivalent to their market shares worldwide. It is therefore relevant to look at the undertaking's worldwide sales. The Court also confirmed that the approach set out in paragraph 18 of the Fining Guidelines is not contrary to Article 49 of the Charter of Fundamental Rights. On further appeal, Case C-373/14P, not yet decided.

The General Court upheld the Commission's analysis of the geographic scope of the cartel in COMP/39180 *Aluminium Fluoride*, decision of 25 June 2008, in Case T-404/08 *Fluorsid and Minmet v Commission*, EU:T:2013:321, [2013] 5 CMLR 902, paras 158 et seq.

On the Commission's application of paragraph 18 of the Fining Guidelines in COMP/39406 *Marine Hoses*, decision of 28 January 2009, see Cases T-146/09, etc, *Parker ITR and Parker-Hannifin v Commission (Marine Hoses)*, EU:T:2013:258, [2013] 5 CMLR 712, discussed in the update to the main paragraph, above.

(ii) Year of turnover

14.025   **The last full business year.**   In Case T-391/09 *Evonik Degussa v Commission*, EU:T:2014:22, at para 131, where the period covered by the infringement was less than a full year, the General Court upheld the Commission's approach of determining the relevant value of sales by extrapolating the turnover achieved in the infringement period to a full year (on further appeal, Case C-155/14, not yet decided).

Fn 96 The Court of Justice dismissed the appeal against this part of the General Court's judgment in Joined Cases C-231/11P, etc, *Commission v Siemens and others*, EU:C:2014:256, [2014] 5 CMLR 7.

In the appeals against COMP/39181 *Candle Waxes*, decision of 1 October 2008, the General Court upheld the Commission's approach of using the last three years of sales, as the last year of the infringement was 2004 which was an exceptional year for the industry as the EU was enlarged, and in particular Hungary (where one of the participants was based) joined the EU: see, eg T-566/08 *Total Raffinage Marketing*, EU:T:2013:423, paras 415 et seq (fine reduced on grounds of duration) (on further appeal, Case C-634/13P, not yet decided). It upheld the complaint in Case T-540/08 *Esso v Commission*, EU:T:2014:630, [2014] 5 CMLR 507, that the Commission had failed to reflect the fact that before the merger between Exxon and Mobil, Exxon's paraffin wax business did not participate in the infringement (see also the update to paragraph 14.035, below).

14.026   **Use of a different year.**   In Case T-72/09 *Pilkington v Commission*, EU:T:2014:1094, [2015] 4 CMLR 227, at paras 213 et seq, the General Court upheld the Commission's approach in COMP/39125 *Carglass*, decision of 12 November 2008, in which the Commission had adopted a different approach to reflect the fact that the cartel in question had varied in intensity during the infringement period. The Commission calculated an annual weighted average value of sales for each undertaking, during the period of its participation in the infringement, using its value of sales during the 'roll-out' and 'decline' periods of the cartel on transactions for which there was direct evidence of collusion, and its value of sales on all transactions in the EEA during the remaining period. On further appeal, on other grounds, in Case C-101/15P, not yet decided.

The General Court dismissed the appeal, on other grounds, in Case T-655/11 *FSL v Commission*, EU:T:2015:383 against the Commission's approach in COMP/39482 *Exotic fruit (Bananas)*, decision of 12 October 2011, discussed in the main text. On further appeal, Case C-469/15P, not yet decided.

Fn 104 The Commission's decisions noted in the footnote were upheld in Case T-562/08 *Repsol YPF Lubricantes y especialidades (Candle Waxes)*, EU:T:2014:1078; and in Cases T-146/09, etc, *Parker ITR and Parker-Hannifin v Commission (Marine Hoses)*, EU:T:2013:258, [2013] 5 CMLR 712 (partially annulled, on a different ground on further appeal; in Case C-434/13P *Commission v Parker Hannifin Manufacturing and Parker-Hannifin*, EU:C:2014:2456, [2015] 4 CMLR 179; see the update to paragraph 14.101, below).

(b) Percentage of the value of sales to reflect gravity of infringement

The 1998 and 2006 Fining Guidelines compared.　In Cases C-444/11P *Team* **14.027** *Relocations v Commission*, EU:C:2013:464, [2013] 5 CMLR 1335 and C-439/11P *Ziegler v Commission*, EU:C:2013:513, [2013] 5 CMLR 1217, the Commission asked the Court of Justice to substitute different grounds for the General Court's judgment in Case T-204&212/08 *Team Relocations v Commission (International Removal Services)* [2011] ECR II-3569, [2011] 5 CMLR 889, insofar as the General Court held that the 2006 Guidelines impose a more onerous obligation on the Commission to state reasons for its fining decisions than did the 1998 Guidelines. The Court of Justice held that the General Court had erred in stating that the 2006 Guidelines impose a more onerous obligation on the Commission, although as this was not an error that bore upon its assessments of the merits of the appeal it refused to substitute the grounds requested: paras 94 and 116–117 in *Team Relocations* and paras 108 and 111–112 in *Ziegler*.

Fn 111 The Court of Justice dismissed the further appeal in Case C-444/11P *Team Relocations v Commission*, EU:C:2013:464, [2013] 5 CMLR 1335. On this point, see paras 124–126, in which the Court confirmed that the appellant had 'no right to receive a specific explanation regarding the choice to apply that percentage' given that the percentage chosen was at the lower end of the range. To the same effect, see Case C-439/11P *Zeigler v Commission*, EU:C:2013:513, [2013] 5 CMLR 1217, paras 122–125; and Case C-429/11P *Portielje and Gosselin v Commission*, EU:C:2013:463, paras 128–130.

In Case C-440/11P *Commission v Portielje and Gosselin*, EU:C:2013:514, [2013] 5 CMLR 1291, the Court of Justice upheld the Commission's appeal and over-turned the General Court judgment in Cases T-208&209/08 *Gosselin Group v Commission* [2011] ECR II-03639, [2013] 4 CMLR 671.

Fn 112 The Commission's decision in COMP/39406 *Marine Hoses*, decision of 28 January 2009, was upheld in respect of the gravity of the infringement, the seri-ousness of which was 'indisputable': see for example Case T-146/09 *Parker ITR and Parker-Hannifin v Commission (Marine Hoses)*, EU:T:2013:258, [2013] 5 CMLR 712, para 252 (partially annulled, on other grounds on further appeal, in Case C-434/13P *Commission v Parker Hannifin Manufacturing and Parker-Hannifin*, EU:C:2014:2456, [2015] 4 CMLR 179; see the update to paragraph 14.101, below).

14.028 **Factors influencing gravity of infringement.**
Fn 116 The General Court upheld the Commission's decision in COMP/39188 *Bananas*, decision of 15 October 2008, in Case T-587/08 *Fresh Del Monte Produce v Commission*, EU:T:2013:129, [2013] 4 CMLR 1091 (further appeal, on other grounds, dismissed in Joined Cases C-293&294/13P *Fresh Del Monte Produce*, EU:C:2015:416, [2015] 5 CMLR 513); and Case T-588/08 *Dole Food Company v Commission*, EU:T:2013:130 (further appeal, on other grounds, dismissed in Case C-286/13P *Dole Food Company v Commission*, EU:C:2015:184, [2015] 4 CMLR 967).

Fn 117 The General Court partially annulled the Commission's decision in COMP/39092 *Bathroom Fittings*, decision of 23 June 2010, in Case T-380/10 *Wabco Europe v Commission*, EU:T:2013:449, [2014] 4 CMLR 138; Joined Cases T-378&379/10 *Keramag v Commission*, EU:T:2013:457 (on further appeal, Case C-613/13P, not yet decided); Joined Cases T-373/10, etc, *Villeroy & Boch Austria v Commission*, EU:T:2013:455 (on further appeal, Case C-626/13P, not yet decided); Case T-364/10 *Duravit v Commission*, EU:T:2013:477 (on further appeal, Case C-609/13P, not yet decided); and Case T-412/10 *Roca v Commission*, EU:T:2013:444 (on further appeal, Case C-638/13P, not yet decided), and it reduced the fine in Case T-408/10 *Roca Sanitaro v Commission*, EU:T:2013:440 (on further appeal, Case C-636/13P, not yet decided). The remaining appeals, in Cases T-368/10, etc, *Rubinetteria Ciscal v Commission*, EU:T:2013:460, were dismissed.

14.029 **Differing percentages for participants.** The Court of Justice approved the Commission's and General Court's approach discussed in the main text in Cases C-429/11P *Portielje and Gosselin v Commission*, EU:C:2013:463, at paras 91 et seq; and Case C-444/11P *Team Relocations v Commission*, EU:C:2013:464, [2013] 5 CMLR 1335, at paras 101 et seq.

Fn 121 In respect of the Commission's decision in COMP/39181 *Candle Waxes*, decision of 1 October 2008, the General Court dismissed appeals regarding the multiplier set by the Commission: see in particular Case T-551/08 *H&R ChemPharm v Commission*, EU:T:2014:1081, paras 307 et seq, in which the Court held that the multiplier of 17 per cent applied to three of the undertakings was not disproportionate either in its own right, or relative to the multiplier set for the undertakings found to have engaged in market-sharing and customer allocation as well as price-fixing (on further appeal, Case C-95/15P, not yet decided).

In respect of the Commission's decision in COMP/38589 *Heat Stabilisers*, decision of 11 November 2009, see Case T-46/10 *Faci v Commission*, EU:T:2014:138, [2014] 4 CMLR 930, in particular at para 196 (further appeal dismissed as in part manifestly unfounded, and in part inadmissible: Order of 11 June 2015).

Fn 122 The Court of Justice dismissed the further appeal in Case C-444/11P *Team Relocations v Commission*, EU:C:2013:464, [2013] 5 CMLR 1335, paras 104–106. In addition, in Case T-352/09 *Nováćke chemické závody v Commission*,

EU:T:2012:673, [2013] 4 CMLR 734, para 58, the General Court rejected the argument that the Commission was obliged to consider the relative gravity of the undertakings' involvement when determining the gravity of the infringement. It held that this 'has to be examined in the context of the possible application of aggravating or mitigating circumstances'.

Actual effect of infringement. In Cases C-508/11P *Eni v Commission*, **14.030** EU:C:2013:289, [2013] 5 CMLR 607, paras 96–98; and C-511/11P *Versalis v Commission*, EU:C:2013:386, [2013] 5 CMLR 797, paras 82–84, the Court of Justice held that in the case of a horizontal pricing or market-sharing agreement it would be 'superfluous' to look at the effects of the agreement in order to determine the gravity of the infringement. Also, in Case C-457/10P *AstraZeneca v Commission*, EU:C:2012:770, [2013] 4 CMLR 233, para 165, the Court of Justice held that a lack of anti-competitive effects was not to be taken into account in circumstances where highly anti-competitive conduct, that was likely to have significant effects on competition, did not have the effects expected because of the intervention of a third party.

The General Court in Case T-286/09 *Intel v Commission*, EU:T:2014:547, at para 1625, held that although the 2006 Fining Guidelines (OJ 2006 C210/2) do not require the Commission to consider the actual effects of the infringement, they do not preclude it, and if the Commission elects to consider actual effects under the 2006 Guidelines, then the case law regarding paragraph 1A of the 1998 Fining Guidelines (discussed in paragraph 14.030 of the main text) will apply. On further appeal, Case C-413/14P, not yet decided.

Implementation of the infringement. The General Court in Case T-286/09 **14.031** *Intel v Commission*, EU:T:2014:547, at para 1625, held that although the 2006 Fining Guidelines (OJ 2006 C210/2) do not require the Commission to consider the actual effects of the infringement, they do not preclude it, and, if the Commission elects to consider actual effects under the 2006 Guidelines, then the case law regarding paragraph 1A of the 1998 Fining Guidelines (discussed in paragraph 14.030 of the main text) will apply. On further appeal, Case C-413/14P, not yet decided.

Fn 130 The General Court dismissed the appeals against the Commission's findings of infringement in COMP/39181 *Candle Waxes*, decision of 1 October 2008, but reduced the fine imposed on five of the undertakings. On the alleged failure to implement the cartel, as a mitigating circumstance, see Case T-558/08 *Eni v Commission*, EU:T:2014:1080, paras 234 et seq.

(c) **Duration of the infringement**

In general. In Case T-566/08 *Total Raffinage Marketing v Commission (Candle* **14.032** *Waxes)*, EU:T:2013:423, paras 549 et seq, the General Court held that a practice of rounding part years to the nearest whole number can breach the principle of equal treatment by treating the different situations of undertakings in the same way. For example, in that case Total had participated for seven months and 28 days, ExxonMobile for 11 months and 20 days, and both were held responsible for a whole year of participation. On further appeal, Case C-634/13P, not yet decided.

14.033 **Different multipliers.**

Fn 136 The General Court dismissed the appeals against the Commission's findings of infringement in COMP/39181 *Candle Waxes*, decision of 1 October 2008, but reduced the fine imposed on five of the undertakings. The appeals were dismissed in: Case T-548/08 *Total v Commission*, EU:T:2013:434 (on further appeal, Case C-597/13P, not yet decided); Case T-551/08 *H&R ChemPharm v Commission*, EU:T:2014:1081 (on further appeal, Case C-95/15P, not yet decided); Case T-550/08 *Tudapetrol Mineralölerzeugnisse Nils Hansen v Commission*, EU:T:2014:1079 (on further appeal, Case C-94/15P, not yet decided); Case T-562/08 *Repsol YPF Lubricantes y especialidades*, EU:T:2014:1078; and Case T-544/08 *Hansen & Rosenthal and H&R Wax Company Vertrieb v Commission*, EU:T:2014:1075 (on further appeal, Case C-90/15P, not yet decided). The fines were reduced, but the appeals otherwise dismissed, in: Case T-566/08 *Total Raffinage Marketing*, EU:T:2013:423 (fine reduced on grounds of duration) (on further appeal, Case C-634/13P, not yet decided); Case T-540/08 *Esso v Commission*, EU:T:2014:630, [2014] 5 CMLR 507 (fine reduced on grounds of duration of involvement of entities that merged during the infringement period); Case T-541/08 *Sasol v Commission*, EU:T:2014:628, [2014] 5 CMLR 729 (fine reduced on grounds of incorrect attribution of conduct by a joint venture); and Case T-543/08 *RWE v Commission*, EU:T:2014:627 (fine reduced on grounds of incorrect attribution of conduct by a joint venture); and Case T-558/08 *Eni v Commission*, EU:T:2014:1080 (fine reduced on grounds of incorrect application of an uplift for recidivism).

14.035 **Legal considerations affecting duration.** The Court of Justice in Case C-70/12P *Quinn Barlo v Commission* ('*Methacrylates*'), EU:C:2013:351, [2013] 5 CMLR 637, para 40, held that as Article 101 applies to the economic consequences of agreements or any comparable form of concertation or coordination, rather than their legal form, an infringement may be found throughout the period in which unlawful prices were applied by an undertaking, even though the unlawful contacts formally have come to an end. See also Case T-540/08 *Esso v Commission*, EU:T:2014:630, [2014] 5 CMLR 507, at paras 81–85, in which the General Court held that an infringement extended throughout a period in which the undertaking may be presumed to have taken account of information already exchanged with its competitors in determining its conduct on the market, even though the unlawful contacts had formally come to an end.

In Case T-566/08 *Total Raffinage Marketing v Commission (Candle Waxes)*, EU:T:2013:423, paras 549 et seq, the General Court held that the Commission must comply with the principle of equal treatment in determining the multiplier, and that a practice of rounding part years to the nearest whole number can breach the principle of equal treatment by treating the different situations of undertakings in the same way. For example, in that case Total had participated for seven months and 28 days, ExxonMobile for 11 months and 20 days, and both were held responsible for a whole year of participation. On further appeal, Case C-634/13P, not yet decided. See also Case T-540/08 *Esso v Commission*, EU:T:2014:630, [2014] 5 CMLR 507, at paras 102 et seq, in which the General Court held that the Commission breached the principle of equal treatment by imposing a fine which did not reflect the fact that prior to a merger between two entities only one of them had participated in the infringement. The Commission had applied a multiplier for the full duration of the cartel to the value of sales of the merged entity, ExxonMobil, even though before the merger Exxon's paraffin wax business did not participate in the infringement. The General Court held that this approach did not reflect the economic reality of the years preceding the merger.

Fn 138 The further appeal, on other grounds, in Case C-499/11P *Dow Chemical v Commission (Butadiene rubber)*, EU:C:2013:482, [2014] 4 CMLR 13, was dismissed.

Fn 140 See also Case T-147&148/09 *Trelleborg v Commission (Marine Hoses)*, EU:T:2013:259, [2013] 5 CMLR 754, considering the distinction between single and continuous, and single repeated, infringements. The Commission cannot rely on an undertaking's failure to distance itself publicly from an infringement as a basis for establishing that undertaking's ongoing participation in it, if the normal functioning of the cartel has been interrupted, there is no evidence of its actual participation in ongoing contacts, and nor is there evidence that it was aware of contacts between other undertakings with a view to re-starting the cartel: paras 68–69. In that case, however, the infringement was to be treated as a single repeated infringement as Trelleborg had rejoined the cartel and accepted that the cartel it rejoined was the same as that which it had left: paras 72 et seq. The duration of the infringement was reduced accordingly.

Fn 142 The Court of Justice dismissed the further appeal in Case C-70/12P *Quinn Barlo v Commission ('Methacrylates')*, EU:C:2013:351, [2013] 5 CMLR 637.

(d) Additional amount for cartel participants

Hardcore cartels. **14.036**

Fn 146 The Court of Justice dismissed the further appeal in Case C-444/11P *Team Relocations v Commission*, EU:C:2013:464, [2013] 5 CMLR 1335. On this point, see paras 124–126 in which the Court confirmed that the appellant had 'no right to receive a specific explanation regarding the choice to apply that percentage' given that the percentage chosen was at the lower end of the range. To the same effect, see Case C-439/11P *Zeigler v Commission* EU:C:2013:513, [2013] 5 CMLR 1217, paras 122–125; and Case C-429/11P *Portielje and Gosselinv Commission*, EU:C:2013:463, paras 128–130.

14.037   The additional amount or 'entry fee'.
Fn 147 The Court of Justice upheld the General Court's judgment in Case C-444/11P *Team Relocations v Commission*, EU:C:2013:464, [2013] 5 CMLR 1335, at paras 139–141.

3. Aggravating and Mitigating Circumstances

(a) Adjustment of the basic amount

14.038   In general.
Fn 152 The Court of Justice dismissed the appeal in C-429/11P *Portielje and Gosselin v Commission*, EU:C:2013:463, paras 91 et seq. See also the Court of Justice's judgment in Case C-440/11P *Commission v Portielje and Gosselin*, EU:C:2013:514, [2013] 5 CMLR 1291, paras 110 et seq.

(b) Aggravating circumstances

(i) Repeat infringements

14.041   The previous infringement(s).
Fn 162 The decision in COMP/39396 *Calcium Carbide and magnesium based reagents*, decision of 22 July 2009, was largely upheld on appeal. On the relevance of subsequently introduced compliance programmes, see, eg Case T-406/09 *Donau Chemie v Commission*, EU:T:2014:254.

14.042   The previous infringer. The Court of Justice in Cases C-508/11P *Eni v Commission*, EU:C:2013:289, [2013] 5 CMLR 607, paras 129–133; and C-511/11P *Versalis v Commission*, EU:C:2013:386, [2013] 5 CMLR 797, paras 142–146, confirms that the Commission must provide an adequate explanation of the capacity in which, and the extent to which, the allegedly recidivist undertaking is considered to have participated in a previous infringement. The Court of Justice agreed with the General Court that the Commission had failed to provide sufficient explanation in its decision in COMP/38638 *Butadiene Rubber*, decision of 29 November 2006, of why Eni and Versalis, which were not addressees of the decisions in *Polypropylene*, OJ 1986 L230/1; or *PVC II*, OJ 1994 L239/14, were considered to have been involved in those infringements, and in what capacity and to what extent. It upheld the General Court's judgments annulling the uplift for recidivism. The Commission issued a second statement of objections to Eni and Versalis on 1 March 2013, providing the explanation held by the General Court to have been absent from the decision and reaching the provisional conclusion that an uplift should be imposed for recidivism: COMP/40032 *BR/ESBR Recidivism*, Press Release IP/13/179 (1 March 2013). The decision to initiate the procedure in COMP/40032 is on appeal in Case T-210/13 *Versalis v Commission*, and Case T-211/13 *Eni v Commission*, not yet decided.

In Joined Cases C-93&123/13P *Commission v Eni & Versalis (Chloroprene rubber)*, EU:C:2015:150, [2015] 45 CMLR 727, at para 91 the Court confirmed that to impose an uplift for recidivism on a parent company it is not necessary for that parent company to have been the subject of an earlier decision, but only that it should have been part of the same undertaking as the infringing subsidiary at the time of the earlier infringement. The parent company's rights of defence are met by the opportunity afforded to it in the subsequent proceedings to dispute the allegation of recidivism.

The General Court has overturned the Commission's decision to uplift the fine for recidivism in a number of cases. In Case T-391/09 *Evonik Degussa v Commission*, EU:T:2014:22, at paras 153 et seq, it overturned an uplift imposed on a parent company where the subsidiary involved in the earlier infringement had not been a part of the same undertaking as the parent at the time of the earlier infringement, and so the parent had had no opportunity to challenge the earlier decision (on further appeal, Case C-155/14, not yet decided). In Joined Cases T-56&73/09 *Saint Gobain (Carglass)*, EU:T:2014:160, at paras 314 et seq, it reduced an uplift imposed on a parent company where, in the case of one of two earlier infringements, the subsidiary involved was different from that involved in the later infringement and although already owned by the parent at the time of the earlier infringement, the parent had not been made an addressee of the Commission's earlier decision. The General Court considered that the parent company had not had the opportunity, in response to the earlier decision, of disputing its liability for the subsidiary's conduct, and the passage of time since the earlier decision meant that it was difficult, if not impossible, for it to do so now. It therefore reduced the uplift applied on account of this earlier infringement. In Case T-558/08 *Eni v Commission*, EU:T:2014:1080, at paras 296 et seq, it reduced the uplift imposed by the Commission as Eni had not been an addressee of the decisions in *Polypropylene*, OJ 1986 L230/1; or *PVC II*, OJ 1994 L239/14. The latter two judgments appear doubtful following Joined Cases C-93&123/13P, discussed above.

Fn 167 The uplift for recidivism applied to Degussa in COMP/39396 *Calcium carbide and magnesium based reagents for the steel and gas industries*, decision of 22 July 2009, was overturned by the General Court. In Case T-391/09 *Evonik Degussa v Commission*, EU:T:2014:22, at paras 153 et seq, it held that the subsidiary involved in the earlier infringement had not been a part of the undertaking at the time of the earlier infringement, and so the parent had had no opportunity to challenge the earlier decision (on further appeal, Case C-155/14, not yet decided).

(ii) Refusal to cooperate with the Commission's investigation

14.045 **Provision of misleading information.**   In Case T-91/11 *Innolux v Commission (Liquid Crystal Displays)*, EU:T:2014:92, [2014] 4 CMLR 798, at para 172 the General Court adjusted the fine imposed on Innolux on account of an error that had been made in the data submitted to the Commission. A third party consultant had submitted sales data to the Commission on behalf of Innolux, and in error had included data on non-cartelised products. The Court held, in the exercise of its unlimited jurisdiction as to fines, that this should not be considered an aggravating circumstance for the purposes of setting the fine. Although Innolux had been negligent in the instructions it had given to its consultants, it had not sought to mislead the Commission, nor did it have any interest in doing so given that the inclusion of additional products in its sales data would only lead to an increase in the fine calculated by the Commission. Further appeal, on other grounds, dismissed: Case C-231/14P, *Innolux v Commission (Liquid Crystal Displays)*, EU:C:2015:451.

(iii) Instigators, 'ring leaders' and retaliatory measures

14.047 **Generally.**
Fn 180 The uplift of 50 per cent of Shell's fine as both an instigator and a leader in COMP/F/38456 *Bitumen (Netherlands)*, OJ 2007 L196/40, was overturned in Case T-343/06 *Shell Petroleum v Commission*, EU:T:2012:478, [2012] 5 CMLR 1064 (further appeal, in Case C-585/12P, withdrawn: Order of 11 April 2013). The appeal in Case C-537/10P *Deltafina v Commission* was withdrawn by Order of 12 July 2011.

14.049 **Leaders.**   Where the Commission finds a single and continuous infringement, it is not necessary that an undertaking's role as leader should extend to all parts of the infringement in order for it to be characterised as a leader for fining purposes: Case T-541/08 *Sasol v Commission (Candle Waxes)*, EU:T:2014:628, [2014] 5 CMLR 729, at para 394.

Fn 190 The Court of Justice dismissed the undertakings' further appeals, on other grounds, in Case C-247/11P *Areva v Commission (Gas Insulated Switchgear)*, EU:C:2014:257, [2014] 4 CMLR 31; and Joined Cases C-239/11P, etc, *Siemens v Commission (Gas Insulated Switchgear)*, EU:C:2013:866, [2014] 4 CMLR 606.

(c) **Mitigating circumstances**

14.051 **In general.**   The General Court upheld the Commission's decision in COMP/ 39188 *Bananas*, decision of 15 October 2008, in Case T-587/08 *Fresh Del Monte Produce v Commission*, EU:T:2013:129, [2013] 4 CMLR 1091 (further appeal, on other grounds, dismissed in Joined Cases C-293&294/13P *Fresh Del Monte Produce*, EU:C:2015:416, [2015] 5 CMLR 513); and Case T-588/08 *Dole Food Company v Commission*, EU:T:2013:130 (further appeal, on other grounds, dismissed in Case C-286/13P *Dole Food Company v Commission*, EU:C:2015:184, [2015] 4 CMLR 967).

Fn 197 The General Court dismissed the appeal against the Commission's finding that the circumstances in COMP/39482 *Exotic fruit (Bananas)*, decision of 12 October 2011, were not similar to those in COMP/39188 *Bananas*, decision of 15 October 2008, in Case T-655/11 *FSL v Commission* EU:T:2015:383, paras 547 et seq. On further appeal, Case C-469/15P, not yet decided.

(i) Factors arising from matters following the Commission's investigation

Prompt termination of an infringement.   14.052
Fn 206 The Court of Justice dismissed the further appeals, on other grounds, in Case C-439/11P *Zeigler v Commission*, EU:C:2013:513, [2013] 5 CMLR 1217.

Introduction of competition compliance programme. The Court of Justice in   14.053
Case C-501/11P *Schindler v Commission (Elevators and Escalators)*, EU:C:2013:522, [2013] 5 CMLR 1387, para 144, dismissed an appeal against the General Court's approach to the relevance of competition compliance programmes, holding that the appellant's compliance programme 'evidently had no positive effect and, on the contrary, made it more difficult to uncover the infringements at issue'.

Fn 210 The Court of Justice dismissed the further appeal in Case C-70/12P *Quinn Barlo v Commission ('Methacrylates')*, EU:C:2013:351, [2013] 5 CMLR 637.

Fn 211 The decision in COMP/39396 *Calcium Carbide and magnesium based reagents*, decision of 22 July 2009, was largely upheld on appeal. On the relevance of subsequently introduced compliance programmes see, eg Case T-406/09 *Donau Chemie v Commission*, EU:T:2014:254.

Non-contestation or admission of facts in the statement of objections.   14.056
Fn 226 The Court of Justice dismissed the further appeal, on other grounds, in Case C-510/11P *Kone v Commission ('Elevators and Escalators')*, EU:C:2013:696, [2014] 4 CMLR 371.

Reduction of fine for delay. In Case C-50/12P *Kendrion v Commission*,   14.061
EU:C:2013:771, [2014] 4 CMLR 454, at paras 91 et seq, the Court ruled that the sanction for a breach by the Court of its obligation under Article 47 of the Charter on Fundamental Rights to adjudicate on cases within a reasonable time is a claim for damages against the EU under Article 268 TFEU and the second paragraph of Article 340 TFEU. This is an effective remedy. The approach taken by the Court in Case C-185/95P *Baustahlgewebe v Commission* [1998] ECR I-8417, [1999] 4 CMLR 1203, of reducing the fine (noted in footnote 243 of the main text) was not to be followed. On the facts of *Kendrion*, the proceedings before the General Court had taken five years and nine months, which the Court of Justice considered breached Article 47 of the Charter, and to be a sufficiently serious breach of a rule of law intended to confer rights on individuals to sound in damages. However, a separate action before the General Court was required to recover those damages. This approach has been followed in subsequent

cases, see, eg Case C-578/11P *Deltafina v Commission*, EU:C:2014:1460, [2014] 5 CMLR 599, at paras 80 et seq; and Case C-243/12P *FLS Plast v Commission*, EU:C:2014:2006 [2014] 5 CMLR 675, at paras 130 et seq.

The General Court in Case T-286/09 *Intel v Commission*, EU:T:2014:547, [2014] 5 CMLR 270, at paras 1639 et seq, dismissed as inadmissible a complaint that the fine should be reduced on account of the administrative procedure before the Commission having taken nine years. On further appeal, Case C-413/14P, not yet decided.

In Case T-47/10 *Akzo Nobel v Commission*, EU:T:2015:506, [2015] 5 CMLR 617, paras 309 et seq the General Court considered the consequences of the six-year delay to the administrative proceedings which had resulted from the dispute between the applicant and the Commission over the seizure of documents (discussed in paragraphs 13.037 and 13.038 of the main text). The General Court dismissed a complaint that the undertaking's rights of defence had been breached by the delay, but reduced the fine as it found that the Commission had breached the principle of equal treatment by reducing the fine imposed on all the undertakings except the applicant. The Commission argued that as the applicant had been responsible for the dispute which occasioned the delay in the administrative proceedings, it was in an objectively different situation to the other undertakings. The General Court held that that argument was not compatible with the principle of effective judicial protection, and would deter undertakings from exercising their right to bring judicial proceedings while they were involved in an investigation by the Commission. On further appeal, Case C-515/15P, not yet decided.

Fn 241 The Court of Justice dismissed the further appeal against the readopted decision in COMP/36212 *Carbonless Paper*, decision of 23 June 2010, in Case C-414/12P *Bolloré v Commission*, EU:C:2014:301. In particular, it dismissed a complaint that the lapse of time since the infringement breached Bolloré's rights of defence: see paras 61 et seq.

Fn 244 The General Court dismissed an appeal against the Commission's approach in COMP/38344 *Pre-stressing Steel*, decision of 30 June 2010, in Case T-436/10 *HIT Groep*, EU:T:2015:514, paras 247 et seq (on further appeal, Case C-514/15P, not yet decided).

Fn 245 The Court of Justice dismissed the further appeals against the decision in COMP/37766 *Netherlands Beer Market*, decision of 18 April 2007, in Case C-452/11P *Heineken Nederland and Heineken v Commission*, EU:C:2012:829; and C-445/11P *Bavaria v Commission*, EU:C:2012:828.

(ii) Factors relating to the undertaking's culpability for the infringement

14.065 **Pressure from others.**
Fn 266 The Court of Justice dismissed the further appeals, on other grounds, in Cases C-439/11P *Zeigler v Commission*, EU:C:2013:513, [2013] 5 CMLR

1217; and C-444/11P *Team Relocations v Commission*, EU:C:2013:464, [2013] 5 CMLR 1335.

Encouragement or authorisation by a public authority.   The mere fact that an   **14.066**
infringing subsidiary was previously owned by the State, before the State decided to transfer its shareholding to a private entity, does not mean that the State
encouraged or authorised the subsidiary's subsequent unlawful conduct: Case
T-399/09 *HSE v Commission (Calcium Carbide Cartel)*, EU:T:2013:647, [2014]
CMLR 738, para 147.

Fn 267 The Court of Justice dismissed the further appeal in C-444/11P *Team
Relocations v Commission*, EU:C:2013:464, [2013] 5 CMLR 1335, paras 148–150.

Fn 273 The Court of Justice dismissed the further appeal in C-444/11P *Team
Relocations v Commission*, EU:C:2013:464, [2013] 5 CMLR 1335, paras 148–150.

(iii) Symbolic fines

Novelty of infringement.   A recent example of the Commission deciding not to   **14.069**
impose a fine is COMP/39985 *Motorola – enforcement of ETSI standards essential
patents*, decision of 29 April 2014. The decision follows the Commission's investigation into alleged abusive conduct in relation to the intellectual property rights
used in international telecoms standards. The Commission found that Motorola
had breached Article 102 by seeking an injunction in Germany against Apple
for infringement of its standard essential patents (which were essential to meeting the European Telecommunications Standardisation Institute's (ETSI) GPRS
standard, part of the GSM standard, which is a key industry standard for mobile
and wireless communications), in circumstances where it had committed to license on fair, reasonable and non-discriminatory terms ('FRAND' terms), and
where Apple was willing to enter into a licence agreement and to be bound by a
determination by the German Court of the FRAND terms. In view of the novelty of the infringement finding, the Commission decided not to impose a fine.

Fn 289 The General Court dismissed AC-Treuhand's appeal against the
Commission's decision in COMP/38589 *Heat Stabilisers*, decision of 11 November
2009, in Case T-27/10 *AC-Treuhand*, EU:T:2014:59. In particular, at paras 285
et seq, the General Court dismissed AC-Treuhand's complaint that, following
the Commission's decision only to impose a symbolic fine on it in COMP/37857
Organic Peroxides, OJ 2005 L110/44, [2005] 5 CMLR 579, the Commission was
obliged to impose only a symbolic fine on it in the *Heat Stabilisers* case. On further
appeal, Case C-194/14P, not yet decided.

The Court of Justice upheld the appeal in Case C-652/11P *Mindo v Commission*,
EU:C:213:229, [2013] 4 CMLR 1381, and referred the case back to the General
Court (remitted case not yet decided). The further appeal in Case C-654/11P
Transcatab was dismissed by Order of 13 December 2012.

Fn 291 The Court of Justice dismissed the appeals in Case C-457/10P *AstraZeneca v Commission*, EU:C:2012:770, [2013] 4 CMLR 233.

(iv) Other factors

14.070 In general.
Fn 296 The General Court dismissed an appeal against the Commission's refusal in COMP/39396 *Calcium carbide and magnesium based reagents for the steel and gas industries*, decision of 22 July 2009, to take into account the poor financial and economic state of the industry as a mitigating factor: Case T-391/09 *Evonik Degussa v Commission*, EU:T:2014:22, at paras 185–188 (on further appeal, Case C-155/14, not yet decided).

4. Deterrence, Disgorgement of Benefit and Inability to Pay

(a) Deterrence

14.071 In general. In Case T-352/09 *Nováčke chemické závody v Commission*, EU:T:2012:673, [2013] 4 CMLR 734, paras 62–64, the General Court emphasised that while the Commission has a power to increase a fine for deterrence, it has no obligation to do so.

14.072 Deterrence based on total turnover of the undertaking. The Court of Justice dismissed an argument that the multiplier applied for deterrence must be in strict accordance with the ratio of the undertakings' turnovers compared to each other, as the fines that would be imposed on the largest undertakings in the cartel might in those circumstances be disproportionate to the gravity of the infringement: Case C-499/11P *Dow Chemical v Commission (Butadiene rubber)*, EU:C:2013:482, [2014] 4 CMLR 13, paras 88–92. It also confirmed that the multiplier applied to the fine imposed on a parent company for deterrence is not affected by the fact that it is only attributed with liability for the conduct of its subsidiary for part of the period of the infringement. It is determined according to the undertaking's size and resources at the time of the Commission's decision: Case C-679/11P *Alliance One International v Commission*, EU:C:2013:606, [2014] 4 CMLR 249, para 75.

Fn 314 The case references in the footnote to the main text should read Cases T-144/07, etc, *ThyssenKrupp* and on further appeal, Cases C-504/11P, etc, withdrawn by Order of 8 May 2012.

(c) Inability to pay

14.075 The Fining Guidelines. The Court of Justice confirmed that the Commission has no obligation to take an undertaking's financial hardship into account if it does not receive a request from it, under paragraph 35 of the Fining Guidelines, before it issues the infringement decision: Case C-444/11P *Team Relocations v Commission*, EU:C:2013:464, [2013] 5 CMLR 1335, paras 184 et seq. The Court of Justice rejected a complaint that the Commission breaches the principle of equal treatment in circumstances where it refuses to reduce the fine imposed on an undertaking under paragraph 35 of the Fining Guidelines because that undertaking did not submit a request for such a reduction prior to the decision being issued. An undertaking that fails to submit a timely request, as required by paragraph 35 of the Fining Guidelines, is not in a comparable situation with an undertaking that did submit such a request.

The Court of Justice also confirmed that inability to pay may be taken into account under paragraph 37 of the Fining Guidelines, as well as under paragraph 35. In its decision in COMP/38543 *International Removals Services*, decision of 11 March 2008, the Commission had reduced the fine imposed on Interdean under paragraph 37 rather than paragraph 35. The Court of Justice in Case C-439/11P *Ziegler v Commission*, EU:C:2013:513, [2013] 5 CMLR 1217, held that an inability or reduced ability to pay under paragraph 35 cannot be sufficient alone to give rise to a reduction in the fine under paragraph 37, but that an inability to pay may be relevant to determining whether to make a reduction under paragraph 37: see paras 171–174.

Approach of the EU Courts. The General Court held that the Commission **14.076** may decide, in a case which concerns a cartel involving several smaller players on the market and one major player which has received immunity on account of its cooperation with the Commission, to reduce the fine to be imposed on the smaller players in order to avoid a situation in which those smaller players exit the market and the immunity applicant is left in a dominant or monopolistic position: Case T-392/09 *1. garantovaná v Commission*, EU:T:2012:674, [2014] 5 CMLR 132, at para 116, following the Opinion of Advocate General Geelhoed in Case C-289/04 P *Showa Denko v Commission* [2006] ECR I-5859, para 61. In that case, the Court held that the fact that several undertakings had submitted requests for their inability to pay to be taken into account did not indicate that a reduction should be made on this basis: para 129. Further appeal, on other grounds, dismissed in Case C-90/13P *1. garantovaná v Commission*, EU:C:2014:326, [2014] 5 CMLR 79.

Fn 328 The Court of Justice confirmed that the Commission has no obligation to take financial hardship into account if it does not receive a request from the undertaking, under paragraph 35 of the Fining Guidelines, before it issues the infringement decision: Case C-444/11P *Team Relocations v Commission*, EU:C:2013:464, [2013] 5 CMLR 1335, paras 184 et seq, discussed in the update to paragraph 14.075, above.

Fn 331 The Court of Justice dismissed the further appeal, on other grounds, in C-444/11P *Team Relocations v Commission*, EU:C:2013:464, [2013] 5 CMLR 1335.

See also Case T-352/09 *Novácke chemické závody v Commission*, EU:T:2012:673, [2013] 4 CMLR 734, paras 198–199, in which the General Court held that merely showing that an undertaking would be forced into bankruptcy by the imposition of a fine is not sufficient to meet this condition. The undertaking must also address the consequences of bankruptcy on its ongoing operations, and the possibility of its assets being transferred to another company.

14.077 **The Commission's approach.**   The appeals against the Commission's approach to applying paragraph 35 of the Fining Guidelines, in COMP/39396 *Calcium carbide and magnesium based reagents*, decision of 22 July 2009, discussed in the main text, have largely been dismissed. The General Court confirmed in Case T-392/09 *1. garantovaná v Commission*, EU:T:2012:674, [2014] 5 CMLR 132, at paras 144 et seq, that 'there can be no question of the "economic viability" of an undertaking that has itself decided to terminate its activities and to realise all its assets' and it upheld the decision not to reduce this undertaking's fine under paragraph 35 of the Fining Guidelines (further appeal dismissed in C-90/13P *1. garantovaná v Commission*, EU:C:2014:326, [2014] 5 CMLR 79). In Case T-410/09 *Almamet v Commission*, EU:T:2012:676, [2013] 4 CMLR 788, paras 265–269 the General Court rejected a complaint from the undertaking that had received a reduction under paragraph 35 of the Fining Guidelines that the fine was nonetheless disproportionate. In Case T-352/09 *Novácke chemické závody v Commission*, EU:T:2012:673, [2013] 4 CMLR 734; Case T-384/09 *SKW v Commission*, ECLI:EU:T:2014:27 (on further appeal, Case C-154/14P, not yet decided); and Case T-406/09 *Donau Chemie v Commission*, EU:T:2014:254 the General Court rejected complaints by other addressees of the decision, one of which had subsequently been declared bankrupt, that they too should have received a reduction in their fines on this basis. See also Case T-400/09 *Ecka Granulate v Commission*, EU:T:2012:675.

In respect of the Commission's decision in COMP/38543 *International Removals Services*, decision of 11 March 2008, reducing the fine imposed on Interdean under paragraph 37 of the Fining Guidelines, see the Court of Justice in Case C-439/11P *Ziegler v Commission*, EU:C:2013:513, [2013] 5 CMLR 1217, discussed in the update to paragraph 14.075, above.

(d) Cap on fines

14.078 **Maximum fine and consequential adjustment.**   In Case C-50/12P *Kendrion v Commission*, EU:C:2013:771, [2014] 4 CMLR 454, the Court of Justice held that the cap on fines, of 10 per cent of the undertaking's turnover, can be applied separately to the parent and the infringing subsidiary companies where those entities have ceased to form part of the same undertaking. In that case, the former subsidiary company had benefitted from the application of the cap, and the former parent company had been held liable for the full amount. The Court dismissed the argument that, because liability was imposed on a joint and several basis, Kendrion could not be held liable for a larger fine than its former subsidiary: para 57. It also held that Kendrion and its subsidiary ceasing to be part of the same undertaking was a factor that differentiated Kendrion from the other parent companies addressed by the Commission's decision, which justified Kendrion being fined for a larger amount than its subsidiary where the other parent company addressees had not been: paras 66 et seq.

The General Court confirmed that where the Commission finds two separate infringements and therefore imposes two separate fines, rather than a single and continuous infringement, the 10 per cent limit is applied separately to each of those fines even if the result is the two fines together exceeding 10 per cent of the undertaking's turnover in the previous business year: Case T-27/10 *AC-Treuhand*, EU:T:2014:59, at para 231 (on further appeal, Case C-194/14P, not yet decided).

The mere fact that the fine imposed on one undertaking is close to or equal to the cap in Article 23(2) of Regulation 1/2003, but the fine imposed on other addressees of the decision is not, is not relevant to the assessment of whether or not that fine is proportionate: Case T-72/09 *Pilkington v Commission*, EU:T:2014:1094, [2015] 4 CMLR 227 at para 281. On further appeal, Case C-101/15P, not yet decided.

Fn 338 In contrast with the position under Article 23(2) of Regulation 1/2003, the German Bundesgerichtshof has held that the 10 per cent limit in German competition law must be interpreted as the upper range of the 'frame' within which a judge can set a sanction for breach of competition law, in order to comply with the principle *nulla poena sin lege*. It cannot be interpreted as a cap to cut the fine imposed at a maximum level: ECN Brief 02/2013, p14.

Fn 340 See, however, Case T-541/08 *Sasol v Commission*, EU:T:2014:628, [2014] 5 CMLR 729, at para 452, in which the General Court held that it was appropriate to apply the cap separately to a subsidiary from its parent company for a particular period of the infringement, in circumstances where the subsidiary had not been a part of the same undertaking during that period of the infringement, and the Commission had breached the principle of equal treatment by failing to attribute responsibility to the former parent for the subsidiary's conduct during that period (see the update to paragraph 14.097, below).

Fn 342 See also Case C-408/12P *YKK v Commission*, EU:C:2014:2153, [2014] 5 CMLR 1223, paras 55 et seq.

Year of turnover for application of cap.   14.079
Fn 344 The Commission's approach in COMP/39396 *Calcium carbide and magnesium based reagents*, decision of 22 July 2009, was upheld by the General Court in Case T-392/09 *1. garantovaná v Commission*, EU:T:2012:674, at paras 62 et seq (further appeal dismissed, Case C-90/13P *1. garantovaná v Commission*, EU:C:2014:326, [2014] 5 CMLR 79). Its approach in COMP/38344 *Pre-stressing Steel*, decision of 30 June 2010, was upheld in Case T-436/10 *HIT Groep*

EU:T:2015:514, para 182 (on further appeal, Case C-514/15P, not yet decided); also in Case T-391/10 *Nedri Spanstaal*, EU:T:2015:509, para 97, in which the General Court held that the fact there had been an increase in raw material costs, such that an undertaking's turnover is significantly higher in the preceding business year than in previous years, does not prevent the Commission from using the preceding business year in determining the application of the cap.

Fn 345 See also Case C-50/12P *Kendrion v Commission*, EU:C:2013:771, [2014] 4 CMLR 454, in which the Court of Justice held that the cap on fines, of 10 per cent of the undertaking's turnover, can be applied separately to the parent and the infringing subsidiary companies where those entities have ceased to form part of the same undertaking. In that case, the former subsidiary company had benefited from the application of the cap, and the former parent company had been held liable for the full amount. The Court held that Kendrion and its subsidiary ceasing to be part of the same undertaking was a factor that differentiated Kendrion from the other parent companies addressed by the Commission's decision, and that justified Kendrion being fined for a larger amount than its subsidiary where the other parent company addressees had not been: paras 66 et seq.

5. Ancillary Matters of Law and Practice

(a) Determination of fines for different infringing parties

14.080 **In general.** The Court of Justice overturned the General Court's judgment that the Commission's powers to determine the fine to be imposed on different infringing undertakings, under Article 23(2) of Regulation 1/2003, includes the power exclusively to determine the proportions that particular legal entities within an undertaking should contribute towards payment of that fine: Joined Cases C-231/11P, etc, *Commission v Siemens and others*, EU:C:2014:256, [2014] 5 CMLR 7, at paras 55 et seq. The Court held that, although the Commission must necessarily address its decision to particular legal entities, its powers do not extend to determining the shares to be paid by different legal entities within an undertaking. It stated at para 58:

> 'While it follows from Article 23(2) of Regulation No 1/2003 that the Commission is entitled to hold a number of companies jointly and severally liable for payment of a fine, since they formed part of the same undertaking, it is not possible to conclude on the basis of either the wording of that provision or the objective of the joint and several liability mechanism that that power to impose penalties extends, beyond the determination of joint and several liability from an external perspective, to the power to determine the shares to be paid by those held jointly and severally liable from the perspective of their internal relationship.'

This determination is a matter for the national courts, applying national law to the dispute in a manner consistent with EU law.

The General Court also confirmed that the Commission may decide, in a case which concerns a cartel involving several smaller players on the market and one major player which has received immunity on account of its cooperation with the Commission, to reduce the fine to be imposed on the smaller players in order to avoid a situation in which those smaller players exit the market and the immunity applicant is left in a dominant or monopolistic position: Case T-392/09 *1. garantovaná v Commission*, EU:T:2012:674, [2014] 5 CMLR 132, at para 116, following the Opinion of Advocate General Geelhoed in Case C-289/04 P *Showa Denko v Commission* [2006] ECR I-5859, para 61 (further appeal, on other grounds, dismissed in Case C-90/13P *1. garantovaná v Commission*, EU:C:2014:326, [2014] 5 CMLR 79).

Principle of equal treatment.   The principle of equal treatment must also be rec-   **14.081**
onciled with the principle of legality. See, for example, Joined Cases C-239/11P, etc, *Siemens v Commission (Gas Insulated Switchgear)*, EU:C:2013:866, [2014] 4 CMLR 606, para 291, in which the Court of Justice dismissed a complaint that the Commission had breached the principle of equal treatment in selecting the reference year for determining the addressees' turnovers. Siemens contended that its fine should have been calculated by the same reference year as the Japanese manufacturers'. The Court noted that the General Court had already confirmed that the selection of the reference year for the Japanese manufacturers was illegal, and held that Siemens could not rely upon that selection to seek a variation of its fine according to that same reference year. See also Joined Cases T-147&148/09 *Trelleborg v Commission*, EU:T:2013:259, [2013] 5 CMLR 754, para 104, regarding the manner in which the Commission had applied the limitation period to different undertakings. The General Court held that even if the Commission had erred as respects its conclusion that proceedings against another undertaking were time-barred, it was not open to Trelleborg to rely on that illegality as a basis for claiming that proceedings against it should also have been treated as time-barred. Also Joined Cases T-379&381/10 *Keramag Keramische Werke and Others (Bathroom Fittings) v Commission*, EU:T:2013:457, paras 345–347 (on further appeal, Case C-613/13P, not yet decided); and Case T-655/11 *FSL (Exotic fruit) v Commission*, EU:T:2015:383, paras 555 et seq (on further appeal, Case C-469/15P, not yet decided) in which the General Court rejected complaints that the Commission had breached the principle of equal treatment by not investigating other undertakings which the appellants alleged were also involved in the infringements.

Where some, but not all, of the participants in an infringement settle with the Commission, the General Court held in Case T-456/10 *Timab Industries*, EU:T:2015:296, [2015] 5 CMLR 7 that the Commission must observe the principle of equal treatment as between addressees of the decision taken under the settlement procedure and the addressees of the decision taken under the Regulation 773/2004 procedure. This means that, in determining the amount of the fine, there cannot be any discrimination between the addressees with respect to the information and calculation methods used which are not affected by the specific features of the settlement procedure: paras 71 et seq. However, an indication given during settlement discussions of the range of fines does not bind the Commission if a party withdraws from those discussions: para 105. The Commission will thereafter apply the Fining Guidelines in determining the amount of the fine, taking into account the evidence that is available to it. In this particular case, the fact that the Commission could no longer rely on the withdrawing party's settlement submissions meant that the duration of the infringement was shorter, but that the average annual value of sales and additional amount were higher and the reductions for cooperation outside the Leniency Notice and for settlement were no longer available, meaning the fine was therefore higher. On further appeal, Case C-411/15P, not yet decided.

Fn 352 See also the General Court judgment in T-395/09 *Gigaset v Commission*, ECLI:EU:T:2014:23, at paras 170 et seq.

Fn 353 See also Case C-444/11P *Team Relocations v Commission*, EU:C:2013:464, [2013] 5 CMLR 1335, paras 66 and 150, in which the Court of Justice dismissed an argument that the General Court was required to explain the reasons for its judgment in the light of a previous judgment it had given in a separate appeal against the same Commission decision.

Fn 358 See also Case C-499/11P *Dow Chemical v Commission (Butadiene rubber)*, EU:C:2013:482, [2014] 4 CMLR 13, paras 88–92, in which the Court of Justice dismissed an argument that the multiplier applied for deterrence must be in strict accordance with the ratio of the undertakings' turnovers compared to each other, as the fines that would be imposed on the largest undertakings in the cartel might in those circumstances be disproportionate to the gravity of the infringement; and Case T-154/09 *Manuli Rubber Industries v Commission*, EU:T:2013:260, para 264, in which the General Court observed that there is no requirement for the fines imposed on small or medium-sized undertakings not to be higher, as a percentage of turnover, than the amount of the fines imposed on larger undertakings.

14.082 **Relevance of previous fining decisions.** On the explanation required where the Commission changes its approach, the Court of Justice's judgment in Case C-521/09P *Elf Aquitaine v Commission* [2011] ECR II-8947, paras 152–170, indicates that a detailed explanation will also be required where the Commission takes an approach to fining a particular undertaking that is different to the approach it has taken in a previous decision addressed to that same undertaking. The Court of Justice held that the Commission had not adequately explained why it had attributed the conduct of a subsidiary company, Atofina, to the parent company Elf Aquitaine in COMP/37773 *MCAA*, decision of 19 January 2005, but not in COMP/37857 *Organic Peroxides*, decision of 10 December 2003.

See also Case C-444/11P *Team Relocations v Commission*, EU:C:2013:464, [2013] 5 CMLR 1335, paras 66 and 150, in which the Court of Justice dismissed an argument that the General Court was required to explain the reasons for its judgment in the light of a previous judgment it had given in a separate appeal against the same Commission decision. In Case C-586/12P *Koninklijke Wegenbouw Stevin v Commission*, EU:C:2013:863, a similar complaint was dismissed as an inadmissible challenge to the General Court's assessment of the evidence.

Fn 369 See also Case T-286/09 *Intel v Commission*, EU:T:2014:547, at paras 1613–1619 (on further appeal, Case C-413/14P, not yet decided).

Professional bodies.   **14.084**

Fn 376 The Commission's decision in COMP/39510 *Ordre National des Pharmaciens en France (ONP)*, decision of 8 December 2010, was upheld as to liability in Case T-90/11 *ONP v Commission*, EU:T:2014:1049, but the General Court reduced the fine to take account of a mitigating circumstance. The Court dismissed the ONP's argument that because it was a non-profit organisation with a public service remit there should have been no fine at all, or only a symbolic fine. The Court held that this did not mean that it did not confer advantages on certain private interests when carrying out its remit: para 363.

(b) Fines on parent and successor companies

In general.   **14.085**

Fn 380 The Commission's powers to determine the fine to be imposed on different infringing undertakings, under Article 23(2) of Regulation 1/2003, and to determine which legal entities within the undertakings should be required to pay the fines imposed, does not include the power to determine the shares that the particular legal entities should contribute towards payment: Joined Cases C-231/11P, etc, *Commission v Siemens and others*, EU:C:2014:256, [2014] 5 CMLR 7, at paras 55 et seq. The Court held, overturning the General Court's judgment, at para 58:

> 'While it follows from Article 23(2) of Regulation No 1/2003 that the Commission is entitled to hold a number of companies jointly and severally liable for payment of a fine, since they formed part of the same undertaking, it is not possible to conclude on the basis of either the wording of that provision or the objective of the joint and several liability mechanism that that power to impose penalties extends, beyond the determination of joint and several liability from an external perspective, to the power to determine the shares to be paid by those held jointly and severally liable from the perspective of their internal relationship.'

This determination is a matter for the national courts, applying national law to the dispute in a manner consistent with EU law.

Effect of joint and several liability.   In Case C-247/11P *Areva v Commission*,   **14.086**
EU:C:2014:257, [2014] 4 CMLR 31, at paras 186–188, the Court of Justice dismissed a complaint by a parent company which had sold its infringing subsidiary

that the imposition of joint and several liability on it and the subsidiary breached its right to an effective legal remedy by restricting its freedom of choice as to whether to bring an appeal against the Commission's decision. The Court held that it was 'simply the unavoidable consequence' of joint and several liability that the parent company would be obliged to appeal if the subsidiary did, in order to avoid having to pay the fine imposed in full.

See also Case C-50/12P *Kendrion v Commission*, EU:C:2013:771, [2014] 4 CMLR 454, at para 57, in which the Court of Justice dismissed the argument that because liability was imposed on a joint and several basis, the parent could not be held liable for a larger fine than its former subsidiary. In that case, the cap on fines of 10 per cent of the undertaking's turnover was applied separately to the parent and the infringing subsidiary companies, as those entities had ceased to form part of the same undertaking, and only the former subsidiary company had benefitted from the application of the cap whereas the former parent company had been held liable for the full amount.

Fn 382 The Court of Justice dismissed the appeal against this part of the General Court's judgment, in Joined Cases C-231/11P, etc, *Commission v Siemens and others*, EU:C:2014:256, [2014] 5 CMLR 7, at paras 90 et seq.

Fn 383 The Court of Justice dismissed the appeal in Case C-286/11P *Commission v Tomkins*, EU:C:2013:29, [2013] 4 CMLR 466. Disagreeing with Advocate General Mengozzi, the Court held that in circumstances where the liability of a parent company is wholly derived from that of its subsidiary, and where both companies have brought actions before the European Courts seeking a reduction in their fines on the same basis (in this case, on the basis of the duration of the infringement), then it is not necessary for the scope of their actions, or the arguments deployed, to be identical in order for the General Court to recalculate the fine imposed on the parent company on account of the outcome of the appeal by the subsidiary.

See also Case C-679/11P *Alliance One International v Commission*, EU:C:2013:606, [2014] 4 CMLR 249, paras 106–107, in which the Court of Justice dismissed a cross-appeal by the Commission against the General Court's judgment in Case T-41/05 *Dimons* [2011] ECR II-7101, in which the General Court had reduced the fine imposed on the parent company, Dimon, on account of the reduction of the fine imposed on its subsidiary in Case T-38/05 *Agroexpansion* [2011] ECR II-7005.

(i) Parents and subsidiaries

14.087 **Undertakings as an economic entity.** In Case T-399/09 *HSE v Commission (Calcium Carbide Cartel)*, EU:T:2013:647, [2014] CMLR 738, the General Court observed that the case law on the concept of economic unity applies equally to companies which are owned, directly or indirectly, by the State: para 48. It also applies to holding companies, whose ownership of a subsidiary is only temporary: para 59.

Decisive influence.   **14.089**

Fn 398 The Court of Justice in Case C-440/11P *Commission v Portielje and Gosselin*, EU:C:2013:514, [2013] 5 CMLR 1291, upheld the Commission's appeal and overturned the General Court judgment in Joined Cases T-208&209/08 *Gosselin Group v Commission* [2011] ECR II-03639, [2013] 4 CMLR 671. The Court confirmed that if a company holds all the capital, or almost all the capital, in a subsidiary company that is sufficient basis for the application of the presumption of decisive influence, and it is not relevant to consider whether the parent company is also itself engaged in an economic activity and individually constitutes an undertaking, if it is part of the same undertaking as the subsidiary: paras 41–46. The Court also overturned the General Court's conclusion that Portielje had rebutted the presumption of decisive influence: paras 65–73. The appeal in Case C-429/11P *Portielje and Gosselin v Commission*, EU:C:2013:463, was dismissed.

Presumption when a parent owns all of the shares in a subsidiary. The General   **14.090**
Court held in Case C-343/06 *Shell Petroleum v Commission*, EU:T:2012:478, [2012] 5 CMLR 1064, paras 45–51, that the Commission is entitled to apply a presumption of decisive influence where two legal entities within the same undertaking together own all of the shares in a subsidiary, and are in a situation that is analogous to a single legal entity owning all those shares. The infringing subsidiary, Shell Nederland Verkoopmaatschappij ('SNV') was owned, indirectly, by Shell Transport and Trading ('STT'), and Koninklijke Nederlandsche Petroleum Maatschappij ('KNPM'), who held 40 per cent and 60 per cent shares respectively in the holding company that owned SNV. The General Court held that in the light of the structure of the Shell group the situation was analogous to SNV being held by a single parent company, and the Commission was entitled to rely on a presumption that the two companies STT and KNPM exercised a decisive influence over SNV's conduct. The further appeal, in Case C-585/12P, was withdrawn: Order of 11 April 2013.

Fn 406 The Court of Justice dismissed the appeals in Joined Cases C-628/10P&14/11P *Alliance One v Commission*, EU:C:2012:479, [2012] 5 CMLR 738. In particular, see paras 50 et seq, and the update to paragraph 14.095, below.

In the appeals against COMP/39181 *Candle Waxes*, decision of 1 October 2008, the General Court upheld the attribution of liability to Total in the absence of specific indica to corroborate the presumption that it did exercise decisive influence: Cases T-548/08 *Total v Commission*, EU:T:2013:434, paras 34–37 (on further appeal, Case C-597/13P, not yet decided); and T-566/08 *Total Raffinage Marketing*, EU:T:2013:423, paras 494 et seq (fine reduced on grounds of duration) (on further appeal, Case C-634/13P, not yet decided). However, it reduced the fine on three undertakings on grounds of incorrect attribution: Case T-540/08 *Esso v Commission*, EU:T:2014:630, [2014] 5 CMLR 507 (fine reduced on grounds of duration of involvement of entities that merged during the infringement period;

see the update to paragraph 14.035, above); Case T-541/08 *Sasol v Commission*, EU:T:2014:628, [2014] 5 CMLR 729 (fine reduced on grounds of incorrect attribution of conduct by a joint venture; see the update to paragraph 14.096, below); and Case T-543/08 *RWE v Commission*, EU:T:2014:627 (fine reduced on grounds of incorrect attribution of conduct by a joint venture; see the update to paragraph 14.096, below). The other appeals are still pending.

14.091 **Presumption when a parent owns virtually all of the shares in a subsidiary.** The Court of Justice in Case C-508/11P *Eni v Commission*, EU:C:2013:289, [2013] 5 CMLR 607, para 47, confirmed that the presumption of decisive influence arises where a parent company holds 'all or almost all' of the shares in a subsidiary.

Fn 408 The Court of Justice upheld the appeal, on other grounds, in Case C-521/09P *Elf Aquitaine v Commission*, [2011] ECR I-8947.

Fn 410 The Court of Justice dismissed the further appeal in Case C-289/11P *Legris Industries v Commission* (*Copper Fittings*), EU:C:2012:270.

14.092 **The presumption of decisive influence is rebuttable.**
Fn 411 The further appeal in Case C-494/11P *General Technic-Otis v Commission* was dismissed by Order of 15 June 2012.

14.093 **Evidence rebutting the presumption of decisive influence.** A further factor that has been held to be insufficient to rebut the presumption of decisive influence is the systematic refusal of an individual employee/consultant of the subsidiary to comply with the parent company's instructions and commercial policy, and his ignoring of the parent company's code of ethics: Case T-146/09 *Parker ITR and Parker-Hannifin v Commission (Marine Hoses)*, EU:T:2013:258, [2013] 5 CMLR 712, paras 185 et seq (partially annulled, on a different ground on further appeal, in Case C-434/13P *Commission v Parker Hannifin Manufacturing and Parker-Hannifin*, EU:C:2014:2456, [2015] 4 CMLR 179; see the update to paragraph 14.101, below).

In Case C-521/09P *Elf Aquitaine v Commission* [2011] ECR I-8497, the Court of Justice held that although the Commission is not obliged to make the same assessment of whether to impose liability on a parent company as in its previous decisions, it is required to explain its reasons if it makes a different assessment in respect of the same parent company in a subsequent case. The Court of Justice considered that the Commission had not adequately explained why it had attributed the conduct of a subsidiary company, Atofina, to the parent company Elf Aquitaine in COMP/37773 *MCAA*, decision of 19 January 2005, but not in COMP/37857 *Organic Peroxides*, decision of 10 December 2003.

In respect of the appeals against the Commission's decision in COMP/38543 *International Removals Services*, decision of 11 March 2008, referred to in the main text, the Court of Justice in Case C-440/11P *Commission v Portielje and Gosselin*,

EU:C:2013:514, [2013] 5 CMLR 1291, upheld the Commission's appeal and overturned the General Court judgment in Joined Cases T-208&209/08 *Gosselin Group v Commission* [2011] ECR II-03639, [2013] 4 CMLR 671. In respect of the points noted in footnote 429 of the main text, the Court confirmed that the mere fact that the holding entity did not adopt any management decisions in a manner consistent with the formal requirements of national company law is not sufficient to rebut the presumption of decisive influence: paras 66 and 83. The appeal in Case C-429/11P *Portielje and Gosselin v Commission*, EU:C:2013:463, was dismissed.

Fn 416 The Court of Justice dismissed the appeals in Joined Cases C-628/10P&14/11P *Alliance One v Commission*, EU:C:2012:479, [2012] 5 CMLR 738. The further appeal in Case C-495/11P *Total and Elf Aquitaine v Commission (Hydrogen Peroxide and Perborate)* was dismissed by Order of 13 September 2012.

Fn 418 The Court of Justice dismissed the further appeal in Case C-289/11P *Legris Industries v Commission (Copper Fittings)*, EU:C:2012:270, para 55, as inadmissible.

Fn 420 The Court of Justice dismissed the appeal, and the Commission's cross-appeal, in Case C-508/11P *Eni v Commission*, EU:C:2013:289, [2013] 5 CMLR 607, paras 64–69.

Fn 422 See also Case T-146/09 *Parker ITR and Parker-Hannifin v Commission (Marine Hoses)*, EU:T:2013:258, [2013] 5 CMLR 712, para 181 (partially annulled, on a different ground on further appeal, in Case C-434/13P *Commission v Parker Hannifin Manufacturing and Parker-Hannifin*, EU:C:2014:2456, [2015] 4 CMLR 179; see the update to paragraph 14.101, below).

Fn 427 See also the General Court judgment in Case T-392/09 *1. garantovaná v Commission*, EU:T:2012:674, [2014] 5 CMLR 132 para 56 (further appeal dismissed, Case C-90/13P *1. garantovaná v Commission*, EU:C:2014:326, [2014] 5 CMLR 79).

Fn 428 The Court of Justice dismissed the further appeal in Case C-499/11P *Dow Chemical v Commission (Butadiene rubber)*, EU:C:2013:482, [2014] 4 CMLR 13. See also the Court of Justice's judgments in Case C-521/09P *Elf Aquitaine v Commission* [2011] ECR II-8947 (discussed in the update to the main paragraph, above).

The Commission's treatment of rebuttal evidence. In Case C-247/11P *Areva* **14.094** *v Commission*, EU:C:2014:257, [2014] 4 CMLR 31, the Court of Justice held that if the Commission relies on a 'dual basis' method of attribution (see the update to paragraph 14.095, below), which assesses evidence of actual exercise of decisive influence as well as relying upon the presumption of decisive influence, the Commission fulfils its obligation to state reasons if it conducts a 'global assessment' of the arguments put forward by the parent company to rebut the evidence: para 42. In respect of its finding of actual decisive influence, the

Commission does not have to show that the parent company actually used the organisational, economic and legal links that characterise its relationship with the subsidiary by reference to particular actual conduct on the relevant market, as that would render the presumption of decisive influence ineffective: para 91.

For a recent example of the General Court overturning a Commission decision for failure to set out adequate reasons for rejecting rebuttal evidence, see Case T-517/09 *Alstom v Commission (Power Transformers)*, EU:T:2014:999.

14.095 **Decisive influence established on the facts.**   The Court of Justice confirmed in Joined Cases C-628/10P&14/11P *Alliance One v Commission*, EU:C:2012:479, [2012] 5 CMLR 738 that the Commission can lawfully rely on a 'dual basis' method of attribution, which assesses evidence of actual exercise of decisive influence as well as relying upon the presumption of decisive influence. However, it held that there would be a breach of the principle of equal treatment if the Commission relied on evidence of actual exercise of decisive influence in order to attribute responsibility to some parent companies, but sought to rely solely on the presumption of decisive influence as a basis for attribution in respect of others. In Case C-247/11P *Areva v Commission*, EU:C:2014:257, [2014] 4 CMLR 31, it further considered the requirements with which the Commission must comply if it relies on this 'dual basis' method. It held that the Commission fulfils its obligation to state reasons if it conducts a 'global assessment' of the arguments put forward by the parent company to rebut the evidence: para 42. In respect of a finding of actual exercise of decisive influence, the Commission does not have to show that the parent company actually used the organisational, economic and legal links that characterise its relationship with the subsidiary by reference to particular actual conduct on the relevant market, as that would render the presumption ineffective: para 91.

The General Court upheld the Commission's decision in COMP/39188 *Bananas*, decision of 15 October 2008, in Case T-587/08 *Fresh Del Monte Produce v Commission*, EU:T:2013:129, [2013] 4 CMLR 1091. The Court of Justice dismissed the further appeal in Joined Cases C-293&294/13P *Fresh Del Monte Produce*, EU:C:2015:416, [2015] 5 CMLR 513: paras 75 et seq.

14.096 **Decisive influence over the conduct of a joint venture.**   The Court of Justice upheld the Commission's approach to attributing responsibility to parent companies for the conduct of a joint venture in COMP/38629 *Chloroprene Rubber*, decision of 5 December 2007. In Cases C-179/12P *Dow Chemical Company v Commission*, EU:C:2013:605, [2014] 4 CMLR 220; and C-172/12P *El du Pont de Nemours v Commission*, EU:C:2013:601, [2014] 4 CMLR 236, the Court held that, provided the factual evidence demonstrates the actual exercise of decisive influence, there is no error of law in holding two parent companies and the joint venture in which they each have a 50 per cent shareholding to be a single undertaking for the purposes (and only for the purposes) of establishing liability for participation in an infringement of competition law: see in particular *Dow*, para 58 and *du Pont*, para 47.

In Case T-541/08 *Sasol v Commission*, EU:T:2014:628, [2014] 5 CMLR 729, at paras 40 et seq, the General Court considered the circumstances in which the conduct of a joint venture can be imputed to one parent company alone. The Commission had attributed conduct to Sasol, which owned two-thirds of the shares in the joint venture, using evidence of its ability to exercise decisive influence and without finding decisive influence had actually been exercised. The Court held that actual decisive influence can be established by an abstract analysis of the documents signed before the joint venture began to operate, along the lines of the analysis conducted under Regulation 139/2004 (the Merger Regulation) to determine whether the company is able to 'control' the undertaking, in as much as the Commission may presume that the legislation and provisions of agreements relating to the operation of that undertaking, in particular the joint venture's articles of association and the shareholder and voting rights agreement, have been implemented and complied with: para 49. However, it is open to the Commission and the undertaking concerned to adduce evidence that the joint venture's commercial decisions were taken by procedures other than those apparent from the mere abstract examination of the agreements, and in particular that they were taken by several or all of the parent companies unanimously: para 50. In that case, the General Court held that the Commission had made an error of assessment in dismissing the evidence that the other parent company exercised decisive influence jointly. See also Case T-543/08 *RWE v Commission*, EU:T:2014:627, at paras 99 et seq, regarding the joint attribution of liability to both parents of a joint venture on the basis of ability to exercise decisive influence.

Fn 440 On the compatibility of the Commission's approach with the Merger Regulation, see in particular *Dow*, paras 58 and 64–66, and *du Pont*, paras 47 and 51–53. See also the General Court's judgment in Case T-541/08 *Sasol v Commission*, EU:T:2014:628, [2014] 5 CMLR 729, discussed in the update to the main paragraph, above.

Equal treatment of parent companies. The Court of Justice confirmed in **14.097** Joined Cases C-628/10P&14/11P *Alliance One v Commission*, EU:C:2012:479, [2012] 5 CMLR 738 that the Commission can lawfully rely on a 'dual basis' method of attribution, which assesses evidence of actual exercise of decisive influence as well as relying upon the presumption of decisive influence, but that there would be a breach of the principle of equal treatment if the Commission relied on evidence of actual exercise of decisive influence in order to attribute responsibility to some parent companies, but sought to rely solely on the presumption of decisive influence as a basis for attribution in respect of others.

See also Case T-541/08 *Sasol v Commission*, EU:T:2014:628, [2014] 5 CMLR 729, at paras 185–188, in which the General Court held that there was a breach of equal treatment in circumstances where, during the infringement period, a majority shareholding in a subsidiary had been transferred and the subsidiary operated as a joint venture, and then the remaining shareholding was subsequently transferred to the majority shareholder, and the Commission had attributed liability to the new owner for the period following its acquisition of sole ownership without also attributing liability to the original owner for the period of its sole ownership.

Fn 441 The Court of Justice dismissed the appeals in Joined Cases C-628/10P&14/11P *Alliance One v Commission*, EU:C:2012:479, [2012] 5 CMLR 738. See the update to the main paragraph, above.

Fn 442 The Court of Justice dismissed the appeals in Joined Cases C-628/10P&14/11P *Alliance One v Commission*, EU:C:2012:479, [2012] 5 CMLR 738. See the update to the main paragraph, above.

14.099 **Responsibility of a principal for conduct of its agent.** The Commission's decision in COMP/3844 *Pre-stressing Steel*, decision of 30 June 2010, was upheld in Case T-418/10 *Voestalpine v Commission*, EU:T:2015:516. It is not relevant that the principal is unaware of the agent's participation in anti-competitive conduct. The acts of the agent can be imputed to the principal just as those of an employee may be imputed to an employer: para 175. An agent who acts on behalf of two principals, both of which participated in the cartel, could be considered to be part of the same undertaking as one of them. In such a situation, the relevant question is whether the agent acts as an independent trader free to determine his own business strategy, or whether the functions he carries out on behalf of the principal in question are an integral part of the latter's activities: paras 149 et seq.

(ii) Successor undertakings

14.100 **Liability of new parent company of infringing subsidiary.**
Fn 448 The Court of Justice upheld the appeal against the method used to determine the fine on the successive parent companies of the infringing subsidiary in Case C-247/11P *Areva v Commission*, EU:C:2014:257, [2014] 4 CMLR 31 at paras 129 et seq. See the update to paragraph 14.101, below.

14.101 **Subsidiary is sold by one parent to another and subsidiary continues as a legal entity.** In Case C-247/11P *Areva v Commission*, EU:C:2014:257, [2014] 4 CMLR 31 at paras 129 et seq the Court held that it is unlawful for the Commission to adopt a 'cascade' method of determining the fines to be imposed on successive parent companies for the infringing conduct of their subsidiaries. The Commission had imposed a fine on the successor parent, jointly and severally with the subsidiary, and had incorporated that fine in its entirety in the fine imposed on the original parent. The Court of Justice held that this approach breached the principle that penalties must be specific to the offender and the offence, and the principle of legal certainty, as it effectively imposed joint and several liability on the original and successor parents.

Fn 452 See also Case C-434/13P *Commission v Parker Hannifin Manufacturing and Parker-Hannifin*, EU:C:2014:2456, [2015] 4 CMLR 179, considering the operation of the principle of economic continuity and the ongoing liability of the subsidiary. The marine hoses business of Saiag had been transferred to Parker Hannifin in two stages: first it was transferred to an existing subsidiary of Saiag, and second Parker Hannifin had acquired from Saiag the shares in that subsidiary. The Commission in COMP/39406 *Marine Hoses*, decision of 28 January 2009, held the subsidiary liable for infringing conduct before, and after, the transfer, and attributed liability to Parker Hannifin for the infringing conduct following its acquisition of the shares from Saiag. The General Court annulled the decision, in Case T-146/09 *Parker ITR and Parker-Hannifin v Commission (Marine Hoses)*, EU:T:2013:258, [2013] 5 CMLR 712, paras 83 et seq, on the basis that the subsidiary had had no involvement in the marine hoses business prior to the first stage of the transfer (ie the marine hoses business being transferred into it by the Saiag parent company). The Court of Justice upheld the Commission's appeal against that judgment, on the basis that the General Court had failed to consider the relevance of the first stage of the transfer. It confirmed that the date on which economic continuity is to be assessed is the date of the transfer: para 50, and that the reasons why a transfer is made are not relevant: para 53. The case has been remitted to the General Court, to consider the structural links between Saiag and the subsidiary at the time the first stage of the transfer was effected.

Liability of new parent absorbing infringing subsidiary. 14.102

Fn 455 The Court of Justice dismissed the further appeal in Case C-448/11P *SNIA v Commission (Hydrogen peroxide and perborate)*, EU:C:2013:797. See, in particular, paras 26–28.

Fn 456 The Court of Justice upheld the appeal against the method used to determine the fine on the successive parent companies of the infringing subsidiary in Case C-247/11P *Areva v Commission*, EU:C:2014:257, [2014] 4 CMLR 31 at paras 129 et seq. See the update to paragraph 14.101, above.

Fn 459 The General Court dismissed the appeal against the Commission's approach in COMP/38344 *Pre-stressing Steel*, decision of 30 June 2010, on other grounds, in Case T-423/10 *Redaelli Tecna*, EU:T:2015:511.

Responsibility where original and new parents in same undertaking. See 14.103
also Case C-511/11P *Versalis v Commission*, EU:C:2013:386, [2013] 5 CMLR 797, paras 52–58. The strategic chemical business activities of EniChem, which included the activities in respect of which the Commission found an infringement in COMP/38638 *Butadiene Rubber*, decision of 29 November 2006, had been transferred to Versalis, a second subsidiary of the parent company Eni. The proceedings against EniChem were closed, and the Commission decision was addressed to Eni and Versalis. The Court of Justice upheld the attribution of

EniChem's conduct to Versalis as both entities were wholly owned subsidiaries of Eni, and part of the same undertaking.

(c) Limits on the ability to fine: double jeopardy and time limits

14.106 **Limitation period for imposition of fines.** The limitation period may be invoked separately by each of the legal persons subject to proceedings brought by the Commission, notwithstanding that Article 25(4) refers to 'undertakings'. Thus a subsidiary may benefit from the expiry of the limitation period, without the liability of the parent being affected: Case T-47/10 *GEA Group v Commission*, EU:T:2015:506, [2015] 5 CMLR 617, paras 126–128. On further appeal, Case C-515/15P, not yet decided.

6. The Leniency Notice

(a) The grant of immunity from fines

14.109 **The 2006 Leniency Notice.** The protection given to corporate statements made by companies in their application for leniency has been extended by Directive 2014/104 on certain rules governing actions for damages under national law for infringements of the competition law provisions of the Member States and of the European Union OJ 2014 L349/1. In particular, its provisions include a complete prohibition on disclosure of leniency statements, together with a requirement that such information shall be inadmissible in a damages action before the national court where a party has obtained it through access to the file (or otherwise be given equivalent protection to ensure the effectiveness of the prohibition on disclosure): Articles 6(6) and 7(1). The deadline for national implementation is 27 December 2016. The Leniency Notice was amended on 5 August 2015, to take account of the new Directive: OJ 2015 C256/1. Paragraph 34 of the Notice has been substituted, and a new paragraph 35a added.

Fn 499 The Court of Justice dismissed the further appeal, on other grounds, in Case C-501/11P *Schindler v Commission (Elevators and Escalators)*, EU:C:2013:522, [2013] 5 CMLR 1387.

14.112 **Paragraph 8(b) immunity.**
Fn 501 The General Court's judgment in Case T-151/07 *Kone Oyj*, EU:T:2011:365, [2011] 5 CMLR 1065, was upheld on further appeal: Case C-510/11P *Kone v Commission*, EU:C:2013:696, [2014] 4 CMLR 371. On the standard of review to be applied to the Commission's consideration of the extent of an undertaking's cooperation, see the update to paragraph 14.128, below.

Fn 504 The Court of Justice dismissed the further appeal in Case C-578/11P *Deltafina v Commission*, EU:C:2014:1460, [2014] 5 CMLR 599, against the

Commission's decision that Deltafina had failed to comply with its obligation to cooperate by breaching confidentiality. The further appeal in Case C-654/11P *Transcatab* was dismissed by Order of 13 December 2012.

Additional conditions. The General Court held in Case T-655/11 *FSL v* **14.113** *Commission*, EU:T:2015:383, para 149, that in circumstances where an immunity application reveals facts which the Commission considers constitute two separate infringements, such that the Commission conducts two separate investigations, the duty of cooperation requires the immunity applicant to cooperate in both investigations and to continue to do so even after securing final immunity with regard to one of the infringements covered by one of the investigations. In that case, the General Court dismissed a complaint that the Commission had mis-used its powers by requiring the immunity applicant to cooperate in its investigation in COMP/39482 *Exotic fruit (Bananas)*, decision of 12 October 2011. On further appeal, Case C-469/15P, not yet decided.

(b) Procedure for applications and securing a marker

Procedure for applications for immunity. The General Court held in Case **14.114** T-404/08 *Fluorsid and Minmet v Commission*, EU:T:2013:321, [2013] 5 CMLR 902, paras 135–136, that if the Commission does not intend to grant immunity it has no obligation to notify the applicant undertaking at the statement of objections stage.

Formal application and grant of conditional immunity. Articles 6(6) and 7(1) **14.116** of Directive 2014/104 on certain rules governing actions for damages under national law for infringements of the competition law provisions of the Member States and of the European Union OJ 2014 L349/1, provide that disclosure of leniency statements in civil litigation should be prohibited, and that they should be inadmissible in a damages action before the national court where a party has obtained them through access to the file (or otherwise be given equivalent protection to ensure the effectiveness of the prohibition on disclosure). The deadline for national implementation is 27 December 2016. In order to ensure that undertakings do not attempt to use the new protection for leniency statements as a vehicle for evading disclosure, the Commission has published a guidance document on 'Delivering Oral Statements at DG Comp', 8 October 2013, which makes clear that a description of the alleged cartel can be provided orally, but other information must be submitted in writing. The Commission may ask the undertaking to withdraw its statement, and resubmit it, if it does not comply with the guidance. The guidance is available in the Leniency section of the DG Comp website.

Joint applications and applications by parents and subsidiaries. In Case **14.117** C-238/12P *FLSmidth v Commission*, EU:C:2014:284, [2014] 4 CMLR 1164, at paras 83–87; and in Case C-243/12P *FLS Plast v Commission*, EU:C:2014:2006 [2014] 5 CMLR 675, at paras 85–87, the Court of Justice confirmed that a former parent company is not entitled to the benefit of a reduction in the fine on account of cooperation by its former subsidiary, as the former parent does not contribute to the detection of the infringement, nor does it exercise decisive influence over the subsidiary at the time of the cooperation being given. Conversely, in Case T-406/10 *Emesa v Commission*, EU:T:2015:499, at paras 161 et seq, the General Court held that a former subsidiary is not entitled to the benefit of a reduction in the fine on account of cooperation by its former parent, as it is not part of the undertaking which has cooperated with the Commission.

14.118 **Grant of final immunity.** The Court of Justice dismissed the further appeal in Case C-578/11P *Deltafina v Commission*, EU:C:2014:1460, [2014] 5 CMLR 599, against the Commission's decision that Deltafina had failed to comply with its obligation to cooperate by breaching confidentiality.

(c) Partial immunity and reductions

14.119 **In general.**
Fn 528 The Court of Justice dismissed the further appeal in C-455/11P *Solvay v Commission*, EU:C:2013:796, [2014] 4 CMLR 581.

14.120 **Percentage reductions.**
Fn 529 The Court of Justice dismissed the further appeal in Case C-70/12P *Quinn Barlo v Commission* ('*Methacrylates*'), EU:C:2013:351, [2013] 5 CMLR 637.

14.121 **Evidence adding significant added value.**
Fn 531 The Court of Justice dismissed the Commission's cross-appeal on this point in C-455/11P *Solvay v Commission*, EU:C:2013:796, [2014] 4 CMLR 581, at paras 89 et seq. For further examples of the General Court disagreeing with the Commission's exercise of its discretion in determining the reduction in an undertaking's fine, see Case T-154/09 *Manuli Rubber Industries v Commission*, EU:T:2013:260, paras 318 et seq; and Case T-406/09 *Donau Chemie v Commission*, EU:T:2014:254.

Fn 534 The further appeal in Case C-494/11P *Otis v Commission (Elevators and Escalators)* was dismissed by Order of 15 June 2012.

14.122 **Effective immunity.** The General Court dismissed an argument, in Case T-370/06 *Kuwait Petroleum v Commission*, EU:T:2012:493, [2012] 5 CMLR 1209, that effective immunity under paragraph 23(b) of the 2002 Leniency Notice should be available not only where the undertaking provides evidence of facts previously unknown to the Commission, but also where the undertaking provides evidence that enables the Commission to prove an infringement that it otherwise would not have had sufficient evidence to prove. The General Court held, at para 33, that the Commission's power under paragraph 23(b) of the 2002 Leniency Notice must be interpreted restrictively. Where an undertaking provides evidence that corroborates facts already known, the Commission is entitled to treat that as cooperation warranting a percentage reduction. The further appeal in Case C-581/12P was dismissed in part as manifestly unfounded and in part as inadmissible: Order of 21 November 2013.

See also Case T-380/10 *Wabco Europe v Commission (Bathroom Fittings)*, EU:T:2013:449, [2014] 4 CMLR 138, paras 133 et seq. The Commission had granted partial immunity under paragraph 23(b) of the 2002 Leniency Notice in respect of the infringements in which the undertaking had been involved in Belgium and France, and the General Court held that once it had done so the Commission was required to remove the value of the undertaking's sales in those geographic areas from its calculation of the basic amount of the fine. Similarly, in Case T-128/11 *LG Display v Commission (Liquid Crystal Displays)*, EU:T:2014:88, [2014] 4 CMLR 24, at paras 195–203, the General Court held that where an undertaking had been granted partial immunity under paragraph 23(b) of the 2002 Leniency Notice for having provided evidence of facts bearing upon the duration of the infringement, the Commission must not only adjust the multiplier on account of duration, but also the reference year used to determine the undertaking's relevant value of sales (further appeal, on other grounds, dismissed: Case C-227/14P *LG Display v Commission (Liquid Crystal Displays)*, EU:C:2015:258, [2015] 4 CMLR 1165).

(d) Interaction with national systems

ECN Model Leniency Programme. A revised Model Leniency Programme **14.125** was issued in November 2012. The main changes are that all undertakings applying to the Commission for leniency in cases concerning more than three Member States will be able to submit a summary application to national competition authorities, where previously only the first applicant, ie the immunity applicant, was entitled to use summary applications under the model leniency programme; and the ECN has agreed on a standard template for summary applications, which can be used in all Member States. The revised Model Programme is available in the ECN section of the DG Comp website.

Protection of corporate statements from disclosure. Articles 6(6) and 7(1) **14.126** of Directive 2014/104 on certain rules governing actions for damages under national law for infringements of the competition law provisions of the Member States and of the European Union OJ 2014 L349/1, provide that disclosure of leniency statements in civil litigation should be prohibited, and that they should be inadmissible in a damages action before the national court where a party has obtained them through access to the file (or otherwise be given equivalent protection to ensure the effectiveness of the prohibition on disclosure). The deadline for national implementation is 27 December 2016. The Leniency Notice was amended on 5 August 2015, to take account of the new Directive: OJ 2015 C256/1.

In order to ensure that undertakings do not attempt to use the new protection for leniency statements as a vehicle for evading disclosure, the Commission has published a guidance document on 'Delivering Oral Statements at DG Comp', 8 October 2013, which makes clear that a description of the alleged cartel can be provided orally, but other information must be submitted in writing. The Commission may ask the undertaking to withdraw its statement, and resubmit it, if it does not comply with the guidance. The guidance is available in the Leniency section of the DG Comp website.

(e) Review by the EU Courts of the application of the Leniency Notice

14.127 **In general.** See, however, Joined Cases C-293&294/13P *Fresh Del Monte Produce*, EU:C:2015:416, [2015] 5 CMLR 513, paras 180 et seq, in which the Court of Justice confirmed that the assistance provided by an undertaking may only be taken into account for the purposes of determining the fine where it has been provided without the Commission having asked for it. If information is provided in response to a request under Article 18(2) of Regulation 1/2003, then irrespective of the fact that the undertaking was not legally obliged to provide it (in contrast to a decision under Article 18(3) of Regulation 1/2003), it is not information provided voluntarily. The Court considered that the approach adopted by the General Court, which had granted a 10 per cent reduction (Case T-587/08 *Fresh Del Monte Produce*, EU:T:2013:129, [2013] 4 CMLR 1091, paras 885–886), would undermine the purpose of the leniency regime and the incentives it establishes, as it would make reductions more widely available and would encourage undertakings to delay their cooperation.

14.128 **Review of the Commission's discretion.** The case law referred to in the main text should now be read in the light of the Court of Justice's judgment in Case C-510/11P *Kone v Commission*, EU:C:2013:696, [2014] 4 CMLR 371. The appellant complained that by considering only whether the Commission had 'manifestly [gone] beyond the bounds of [its] margin' of discretion in assessing the cooperation of an undertaking under the Leniency Notice the General Court had failed to comply with Article 47 of the Charter on Fundamental Rights, and Article 6 of the ECHR. The Court of Justice accepted that the manifest error test does not meet the requirements of Article 47 Charter/Article 6 ECHR: para 44. The Court cannot use the Commission's margin of discretion as a basis for dispensing with the conduct of an in-depth review of the law and of the facts. The Court went on to hold that, notwithstanding the General Court appeared to apply an incorrect legal test, on the facts of the case the General Court had conducted an in-depth review of the fine in substance: see paragraph 13.124, and the updates thereto, above. The Court of Justice in C-455/11P *Solvay v Commission*, EU:C:2013:796, [2014] 4 CMLR 581, at para 69, held that in circumstances where the General Court has conducted an in-depth review in substance, the Court of Justice will not substitute its view for that of the General Court.

Fn 553 The Court of Justice dismissed the further appeal, on other grounds, in Joined Cases C-239/11P, etc, *Siemens v Commission (Gas Insulated Switchgear)*, EU:C:2013:866, [2014] 4 CMLR 606.

Fn 554 See also Case T-347/06 *Nynäs v Commission*, EU:T:2012:480, [2012] 5 CMLR 1139, para 62.

Legal status of the Leniency Notice.   **14.129**
Fn 557 The Court of Justice dismissed the further appeal in Case C-578/11P *Deltafina v Commission*, EU:C:2014:1460, [2014] 5 CMLR 599.

7. Settlement

Reduction in fine under the Settlement Notice. The General Court held in   **14.132**
Case T-456/10 *Timab Industries*, EU:T:2015:296, [2015] 5 CMLR 7 that if a settlement involves some, but not all, of the participants in an infringement (either because one or more parties have withdrawn from the settlement discussions, or because the Commission terminates the discussions with one or more parties) then the Commission must observe the principle of equal treatment as between addressees of the decision taken under the settlement procedure and the addressees of the decision taken under the Regulation 773/2004 procedure. This means that, in determining the amount of the fine, there cannot be any discrimination between the addressees with respect to the information and calculation methods used which are not affected by the specific features of the settlement procedure: paras 71 et seq. However, an indication given during settlement discussions of the range of fines does not bind the Commission if a party withdraws from those discussions: para 105. The Commission will thereafter apply the Fining Guidelines in determining the amount of the fine, taking into account the evidence that is available to it. In this particular case, the fact that the Commission could no longer rely on the withdrawing party's settlement submissions meant that the duration of the infringement was shorter, but that the average annual value of sales and additional amount were higher and the reductions for cooperation outside the Leniency Notice and for settlement were no longer available, meaning the fine was therefore higher. On further appeal, Case C-411/15P, not yet decided.

8. Periodic Penalty Payments

In general.   **14.133**
Fn 570 The Court of Justice dismissed the further appeal, on other grounds, in Case C-382/12P *Mastercard v Commission*, EU:C:2014:2201, [2014] 5 CMLR 1062.

15

THE ENFORCEMENT OF THE COMPETITION RULES BY NATIONAL COMPETITION AUTHORITIES

2. The European Competition Network ('ECN')

Generally. The ECN published a Report on Investigative Powers and a Report   **15.005**
on Decision-Making Powers, both of 31 October 2012, which contain comparative analyses of the enforcement powers conferred on NCAs in different Member
States, and identify areas of divergence. Subsequently, it has published a series of
Recommendations on key investigative and decision-making powers that it considers NCAs should have available in their competition toolbox. All are available
on the ECN section of the DG Comp website.

Fn 13 A revised Model Leniency Programme was issued by the ECN in November
2012, and is available on the ECN section of the DG Comp website.

Competence to adopt decisions. The Court of Justice confirmed in Case   **15.010**
C-681/11 *Schenker*, EU:C:2013:404, [2013] 5 CMLR 831 that Article 5 of
Regulation 1/2003 does not require Member States to establish conditions of
intention or negligence for the imposition of a fine on an undertaking by a NCA,
but that if a Member State does establish such conditions then they must be at
least as stringent as those in Article 23 of Regulation 1/2003 (ie the undertaking must be required to show that it could not have been aware of the anti-
competitive nature of its conduct): paras 35–36. The Court also confirmed that
although Article 5 does not expressly provide a power for NCAs to declare that
an infringement has occurred without imposing a fine, it does not exclude them
having that power. If an undertaking has participated in a leniency programme
then the NCA may confine its decision against that undertaking to a finding that
an infringement occurred, without imposing a fine.

In Case T-355/13 *easyJet v Commission*, EU:T:2015:36, at para 34, the General
Court held that a NCA has power pursuant to Article 5 of Regulation 1/2003 to
reject a case on grounds of administrative priorities.

3. Cooperation between Members of the ECN in the Application of the Competition Rules

(a) Avoidance of multiple proceedings

(i) Principles of case allocation

15.014 **Notification of proceedings.**
Fn 46 As at 31 December 2015, 1,769 investigations had been notified by NCAs through the ECN. The five leading NCAs in terms of numbers of cases notified remained as stated in the main text.

15.015 **Challenging decisions as to case allocation.** In Case T-201/11 *Si.mobil v Commission*, EU:T:2014:1096, [2015] 4 CMLR 329, the General Court dismissed a challenge to the Commission's decision to reject a complaint on the basis that a NCA was already investigating. The General Court held that provided two conditions are met—the NCA is 'dealing with the case' and the complaint before the Commission relates to the same agreement/decision of an association/concerted practice as is being dealt with by the NCA—then that is sufficient basis for the Commission to reject a complaint, without it being necessary to consider further whether there is an EU interest in the Commission investigating: paras 33 et seq. In any event, the Network Notice does not create rights for individuals to have complaints dealt with by any particular authority, and even if the Commission were to have been 'best placed' to deal with the case the applicant would not have had a right to have its complaint dealt with by the Commission: para 40. The General Court also held that to be satisfied that a NCA is 'dealing with the case' the Commission must ascertain that the NCA is actually investigating it, as opposed merely to having received a complaint or having opened a case of its own initiative, but the Commission does not have to assess whether the NCA is taking a well-founded approach to the case, or that it has the institutional, financial and technical means available to it to accomplish the tasks entrusted to it: paras 47 et seq.

Fn 47 The General Court dismissed the challenge in Case T-201/11 *Si.mobil v Commission*, EU:T:2014:1096, [2015] 4 CMLR 329; see the update to the main paragraph, above.

(iii) Re-allocation between NCAs and the Commission

15.017 **Cases dealt with by the Commission.**
Fn 56 See also the General Court's judgment Case T-402/13 *Orange v Commission*, EU:T:2014:991. The Commission adopted an inspection decision under Article 20(4) of Regulation 1/2003, after the French NCA had accepted commitments to address a complaint about Orange abusing a dominant position contrary to Article 102. The General Court held that a NCA decision accepting

commitments does not preclude the Commission from investigating the conduct in question, as the Commission is not bound by the NCA's decision: paras 27 et seq. The fact that the Commission did not exercise its discretion under Article 11(6) of Regulation 1/2003 to relieve the NCA of its jurisdiction to apply Articles 101 and 102 does not render an inspection decision inappropriate: paras 32 et seq.

Fn 59 In Case T-201/11 *Si.mobil v Commission*, EU:T:2014:1096, [2015] 4 CMLR 329, the General Court held that to be satisfied that a NCA is 'dealing with the case' the Commission must ascertain that the NCA is actually investigating it, as opposed merely to having received a complaint or having opened a case of its own initiative, but the Commission does not have to assess whether the NCA is taking a well-founded approach to the case, or that it has the institutional, financial and technical means available to it to accomplish the tasks entrusted to it: paras 47 et seq.

Effect of the Commission initiating proceedings on the competences of NCAs.　See also Case T-342/11 *Confederación Española de Empresarios de Estaciones de Servicio ('CEEES') v Commission*, EU:T:2014:60, at paras 67–68, in which the General Court held that if the Commission adopts a commitments decision under Article 9 of Regulation 1/2003 (see paragraphs 13.095 et seq of the main text), a NCA can subsequently take action against that undertaking. If the undertaking acts in breach of the commitments decision, the Commission will be entitled to have regard to any action taken by the NCA in deciding whether to take any action itself, and if so what, in response to a complaint. **15.019**

(iv) Parallel and multiple proceedings

Parallel investigations by NCAs.　**15.021**
Fn 68 The Court of Justice dismissed the further appeal in Case C-382/12P *MasterCard v Commission*, EU:C:2014:2201, [2014] 5 CMLR 1062.

Coordinated investigations by NCAs and the Commission.　For an example of cooperation between NCAs and the Commission, see Press Release IP/14/2661 (15 December 2014) in which the Commission announced the launch of market tests by the French, Swedish and Italian NCAs into commitments offered by Booking.com regarding the removal of parity pricing clauses in its contracts with hotels. The Commission is not investigating the conduct in question, but it is coordinating the national investigations of the three NCAs. **15.022**

Fn 70 The Commission's decisions in COMP/39847 *E-books*, decisions of 12 December 2012 (OJ 2012 C283/7) and of 25 July 2013 (OJ 2013 C378/25) accepting commitments from five publishing companies, and Apple, considered the sale of e-books *inter alia* in the UK.

Subsequent investigations by a different competition authority.　A complaint 'has already been dealt with' by another competition authority for the purposes **15.023**

of Article 13(2) of Regulation 1/2003 where it has been rejected on grounds of administrative priorities. The Commission is not required to accept a complaint that has been rejected by a NCA on priority grounds: Case T-355/13 *easyJet v Commission*, EU:T:2015:36, paras 25 et seq.

(c) Exchange of information

(i) Restrictions on the type of information exchanged

15.030 **Disclosure outside the ECN: the relevance of rights of defence to the scope of the 'professional secrecy' obligation.**
Fn 105 See also Case C-365/12P *Commission v EnBW Energie Baden-Württemberg ('EnBW')*, EU:C:2014:112, [2014] 4 CMLR 30, discussed in the update to paragraph 16.046, below. On the disclosure of information exchanged between ECN members specifically, the General Court held in Case T-623/13 *Unión de Almacenistas de Hierros de España v Commission*, EU:T:2015:268 that the Commission is entitled to apply a general presumption that documents submitted to it by a NCA under Article 11(4) of Regulation 1/2003 are within the scope of the exemptions from disclosure in Articles 4(2) first and third indent, of Regulation 1049/2001, as their disclosure would harm the commercial interests of third parties and the objectives on NCA investigations: para 64.

(ii) Restrictions on the use by ECN members of information exchanged

15.031 **Restrictions as to use of information exchanged.** In Case T-655/11 *FSL (Exotic fruit) v Commission*, EU:T:2015:383, paras 71 et seq, the General Court dismissed an argument that the protections afforded to an undertaking by Article 12 of Regulation 1/2003 should apply, by analogy, to information gathered by the Commission from national regulatory authorities other than the relevant NCA. In COMP/39482 *Exotic fruit (Bananas)*, decision of 12 October 2011, the Commission had relied upon evidence transmitted to it by the Italian tax authority. The appellants contended that Article 12 should be interpreted extending to such a situation, in order to prevent the Commission from effectively circumventing the procedural safeguards and limitations laid down in Regulation 1/2003. The General Court held that Article 12 could not be interpreted as extending that far, and that if it were to be so interpreted it would moreover impose too great a burden on the Commission in proving infringements of Articles 101 and 102. The question of whether it is lawful for national regulatory authorities other than the NCA to transmit information to the Commission is governed by national law. On further appeal, Case C-469/15P, not yet decided.

15.032 **'Subject-matter' and 'use in evidence' under Article 12.** On the interpretation of the scope of Article 12 of Regulation 1/2003, see also Case T-655/11 *FSL (Exotic fruit) v Commission*, EU:T:2015:383, paras 71 et seq, discussed in the update to paragraph 15.031 above.

(d) Exchange of information and leniency regimes of ECN members

Disclosure of leniency information to third parties.   The ability of third parties   **15.040**
to access leniency information from the Commission or from ECN members will
be circumscribed by Directive 2014/104 on certain rules governing actions for
damages under national law for infringements of the competition law provisions
of the Member States and of the European Union, OJ 2014 L349/1. In particular,
its provisions include:

(a) a complete prohibition on disclosure of leniency statements and settlement
    submissions, together with a requirement that such information shall be in-
    admissible in a damages action before the national court where a party has
    obtained it through access to the file (or otherwise be given equivalent pro-
    tection to ensure the effectiveness of the prohibition on disclosure): Articles
    6(6) and 7(1);
(b) a temporary prohibition on disclosure of *inter alia* information prepared spe-
    cifically for the proceedings before a competition authority, until after the
    proceedings are closed; together with a requirement that such information
    shall be inadmissible in a damages action before the national court, where a
    party has obtained it through access to the file, until after the proceedings
    before the competition authority are closed (or otherwise be given equivalent
    protection to ensure the effectiveness of the temporary prohibition on disclo-
    sure): Article 6(5) and 7(2).

The prohibitions apply to documents/information relating to investigations by the
Commission, as well as to investigations by NCAs. The deadline for national implementation is 27 December 2016.

(e) Ongoing liaison on policy and proceedings

Subsequent liaison in a case being dealt with by an NCA.   **15.041**
Fn 141 As of 31 December 2015, 907 envisaged NCA decisions had been notified
to the ECN. The leading NCAs in terms of numbers of cases dealt with remained
as stated in the main text.

4. Cooperation between the Commission and National Courts

Generally.   The National Courts Notice was amended on 5 August 2015, to   **15.043**
take account of Directive 2014/104 on certain rules governing actions for damages under national law for infringements of the competition law provisions of
the Member States and of the European Union, OJ 2014 L349/1. See: OJ 2015
C256/5, and the update to paragraph 15.049, below.

15.047 **Transmission of information by the Commission.** On 22 July 2013, the Council adopted Regulation 734/2013, amending Regulation 659/99 (the Procedural Regulation), OJ 2013 L204/15, as a result of which the Commission may now provide information in its possession, or its opinion, to national courts applying the EU rules on State aid, Articles 107 and 108 TFEU: see Article 23a of Regulation 659/99 as amended.

The Court of Appeal confirmed, in *National Grid Electricity Transmission v ABB* [2013] EWCA Civ 1234, that the English High Court has power to order disclosure of documents, notwithstanding the French law prohibition on them being provided directly (without recourse to the special procedures for the taking of evidence abroad laid down in Regulation 1206/2001). The High Court therefore withdrew its request to the Commission under Article 15(1) of Regulation 1/2003, discussed in the main text.

15.049 **Non-transmission of leniency and settlement procedure information.** The ability of third parties to access leniency and settlement procedure information from the Commission will be circumscribed by Directive 2014/104 on certain rules governing actions for damages under national law for infringements of the competition law provisions of the Member States and of the European Union OJ 2014 L349/1. In particular, its provisions include:

(a) a complete prohibition on disclosure of leniency statements and settlement submissions, together with a requirement that such information shall be inadmissible in a damages action before the national court where a party has obtained it through access to the file (or otherwise be given equivalent protection to ensure the effectiveness of the prohibition on disclosure): Articles 6(6) and 7(1);

(b) a temporary prohibition on disclosure of *inter alia* information prepared specifically for the proceedings before a competition authority, and settlement submissions that have been withdrawn, until after the proceedings are closed; together with a requirement that such information shall be inadmissible in a damages action before the national court, where a party has obtained it through access to the file, until after the proceedings before the competition authority are closed (or otherwise be given equivalent protection to ensure the effectiveness of the temporary prohibition on disclosure): Article 6(5) and 7(2).

The prohibitions apply to documents/information relating to investigations by the Commission, as well as to investigations by NCAs. The deadline for national implementation is 27 December 2016.

The National Courts Notice was amended on 5 August 2015, to take account of the new Directive: OJ 2015 C256/5.

15.051 **Submission of observations of an NCA and the Commission to the national court.** A recent example of the Commission submitting observations to the

United Kingdom courts is *Deutsche Bahn v Morgan Crucible Company* [2014] UKSC 24, in which the Commission submitted observations on the question of the legal status of a Commission infringement decision addressed to a party being sued in a civil claim for damages, in circumstances where the Commission decision had been the subject of successful appeals by other addressees to the European Courts (discussed in paragraph 13.093 of the main text, and the update thereto). The Commission's observations are available on the *Amicus Curiae* section of the DG Comp website.

Commission as a party to proceedings before a national court. In Case   **15.052** C-199/11 *Europese Gemeenschap v Otis*, EU:C:2012:684, [2013] 4 CMLR 141 the Court of Justice confirmed that the Commission can appear as a claimant in proceedings in a Member State court, in order to seek damages for losses the EU institutions have suffered as a result of a breach of competition law. The Court was asked whether it was compatible with Article 47 of the Charter of Fundamental Rights for the Commission to bring an action for damages in the courts of a Member State where it would be relying on its own infringement decision to establish liability, and Article 16(1) of Regulation 1/2003 would prevent the defendant from contesting the decision. It held that the Commission has authority to appear in Member State proceedings in these circumstances, and that the defendant's rights under Article 47 of the Charter are adequately protected by its right to appeal the Commission's decision in the European Courts under Article 263 TFEU, and its right to contest causation and damages in the Member State court.

Effect of a Commission investigation on a national court.   **15.053**
Fn 182 Recent examples of the High Court exercising its discretion whether to allow national proceedings to progress include *Secretary of State for Health v Servier* [2012] EWHC 2761 (Ch), staying proceedings until after the oral hearing before the Commission in COMP/39612 *Perindopril (Servier)*, but refusing to extend the stay until a decision was issued following the oral hearing; and *Infederation v Google* [2013] EWHC 2295 (Ch), refusing a stay other than on one issue, and otherwise ordering staged disclosure while the Commission investigation in COMP/39740 *Google* is ongoing.

5. Convergence and Consistency in the Application of the Competition Rules

(a) Parallel application of EU and national competition law

Generally. Directive 2014/104 on certain rules governing actions for damages   **15.055** under national law for infringements of the competition law provisions of the Member States and of the European Union, OJ 2014 L349/1, includes provision that where a NCA has taken a decision finding an infringement of either EU or national competition laws, the national courts of that Member State are bound not to take a decision running counter to it. This will make NCA infringement decisions binding upon national courts in the same way that Commission infringement decisions are binding under Article 16 of Regulation 1/2003. In addition, a final decision by a NCA in another Member State may, in accordance with national law, be presented before the national courts as at least *prima facie* evidence that an infringement of competition law has occurred and, as appropriate, may be assessed along with any other evidence adduced by the parties. See Articles 9(1) and 9(2). The deadline for national implementation is 27 December 2016.

15.056 General duties owed under the TFEU.

Fn 189 For an example of the duty of sincere cooperation under Article 4(3) TEU being considered in a Member State, see the Competition Appeal Tribunal judgment in *Ryanair Holdings v Competition and Markets Authority* [2014] CAT 3, upholding a decision of the Competition Commission to order divestiture of Ryanair's existing minority shareholding in Aer Lingus (*Ryanair Holdings and Aer Lingus Group*, decision of 28 August 2013), while an appeal by Ryanair to the General Court was pending (Case T-260/13 *Ryanair v Commission*, subsequently withdrawn: Order of 28 October 2015) against M.6663 *Ryanair/Aer Lingus III* (27 February 2013). The Tribunal dismissed the argument that the Competition Commission's decision breached the duty of sincere cooperation under Article 4(3) TEU, as it concerned Ryanair's existing minority shareholding rather than the proposed acquisition that was under consideration by the European Commission and is currently before the General Court.

(b) The convergence rule

15.058 The convergence rule and Article 101.

Fn 195 The Court of Justice in Case C-226/11 *Expedia Inc*, EU:C:2012:795, [2013] 4 CMLR 439, para 31, confirmed that although NCAs may take account of the market share thresholds set by the Commission's *De Minimis* Notice when determining whether an agreement has an appreciable effect on competition, they are not required to do so.

(c) Consistency with decisions of ECN members

15.063 Effect of prior Commission decisions: generally.

Fn 206 See, further, the Competition Appeal Tribunal judgment in *Ryanair Holdings v Competition and Markets Authority* [2014] CAT 3, upholding a decision of the Competition Commission to order divestiture of Ryanair's existing minority shareholding in Aer Lingus (*Ryanair Holdings and Aer Lingus Group*, decision of 28 August 2013), while an appeal by Ryanair to the General Court was pending (Case T-260/13 *Ryanair v Commission*, subsequently withdrawn: Order of

28 October 2015) against M.6663 *Ryanair/Aer Lingus III* (27 February 2013). The Tribunal dismissed the argument that the Competition Commission's decision breached the duty of sincere cooperation under Article 4(3) TEU, as it concerned Ryanair's existing minority shareholding rather than the proposed acquisition that was under consideration by the European Commission and is currently before the General Court.

The effect of an appeal against a Commission decision.   **15.064**
Fn 209 Further examples include: *WM Morrison Supermarkets v Mastercard and others* [2013] EWHC 1071 (Comm), applying *National Grid Electricity Transmission v ABB and others* [2009] EWHC 1326 and refusing to stay proceedings that were brought in reliance on the Commission decision on multilateral interchange fees (see footnote 68 in the main text); and *CDC Project 14 v Shell and others*, judgment of the District Court of the Hague of 1 May 2013, Case No C/09/414499/HA ZA 12-293, refusing to stay proceedings before pleadings had closed in a claim brought in reliance on COMP/39181 *Candle Wax*, decision of 1 October 2008.

Effect of an NCA's decision in another Member State.   Directive 2014/104 on   **15.076**
certain rules governing actions for damages under national law for infringements of the competition law provisions of the Member States and of the European Union OJ 2014 L349/1, includes provision that Member States shall ensure that a final decision by a NCA in another Member State may, in accordance with national law, be presented before the national courts as at least *prima facie* evidence that an infringement of competition law has occurred and, as appropriate, may be assessed along with any other evidence adduced by the parties: Article 9(2).

16

LITIGATING INFRINGEMENTS
IN THE NATIONAL COURTS

1. Introduction

Preliminary references to the Court of Justice.   **16.003**

Fn 10 See also *R (Air Transport Association of America) v Secretary of State for Climate Change* [2010] EWHC 1554 (Admin), in which parties were permitted to join the proceedings before the reference for a preliminary ruling was made, and *FAPL v QC Leisure* [2008] EWHC 2897 was distinguished: paras 20–21.

Limited jurisdiction over mergers and joint ventures.   **16.007**

Fn 28 See also the Competition Appeal Tribunal judgment in *Ryanair Holdings v Competition and Markets Authority* [2014] CAT 3, upholding a decision of the Competition Commission to order divestiture of Ryanair's existing minority shareholding in Aer Lingus (*Ryanair Holdings and Aer Lingus Group*, decision of 28 August 2013), while an appeal by Ryanair to the General Court was pending (Case T-260/13 *Ryanair v Commission*, subsequently withdrawn: Order of 28 October 2015) against M.6663 *Ryanair/Aer Lingus III* (27 February 2013). The Tribunal dismissed the argument that the Competition Commission's decision breached the duty of sincere cooperation under Article 4(3) TEU, as it concerned Ryanair's existing minority shareholding rather than the proposed acquisition that was under consideration by the European Commission and is currently before the General Court.

2. Effectiveness and Equivalence of National Procedures

Examples of lack of effectiveness of domestic procedures.   **16.011**

Fn 42 The Court of Justice held in Case C-536/11 *Bundeswettbewerbsbehörde v Donau Chemie*, EU:C:2013:366, [2013] 5 CMLR 658 that where a potential damages claimant seeks access to documents which form part of the file in public law proceedings concerning the application of Article 101, it is incompatible with

European law, in particular the principle of effectiveness, for such access to be made subject to the consent of the parties to those proceedings. A domestic rule to that effect would be liable to make it impossible or excessively difficult to protect the right to compensation conferred on parties adversely affected by an infringement of Article 101. It must be possible for a national court to balance the competing interests in each individual case, in order to determine whether access should be granted or not, in the same way as in respect of leniency materials following Case C-360/09 *Pfleiderer v Bundeskartellampt*, EU:C:2011:389, [2011] ECR I-5161. See further paragraph 16.043, and update thereto, below.

3. Forum and Applicable Law

(a) Brussels Regulation and Lugano Convention

16.014 Foreign jurisdiction.
Fn 50 The 15th Edition of Collins (ed), *Dicey, Morris and Collins on The Conflict of Laws* (2012) is now available.

16.015 The Brussels I Regulation. A recast 'Brussels II Regulation' (Regulation 1215/ 2012 on jurisdiction and the recognition and enforcement of judgments in civil and commercial matters (recast), OJ 2012 L351/1) was adopted on 20 December 2012, in order to develop further the European area of justice by removing the remaining obstacles to the free movement of judicial decisions in line with the principle of mutual recognition. It will apply to all of the EU Member States except for Denmark (Recital (41) Brussels II Regulation: the UK and Ireland have exercised their right to 'opt-in' to the measure, but Denmark has not). The main changes from the Brussels I Regulation are:

(a) a provision conferring priority on the courts of a Member State in whose favour the parties to the dispute have concluded a jurisdiction agreement: Articles 31(2) and 31(3) Brussels II Regulation;

(b) the extension of the rules on jurisdiction to disputes involving non-EU defendants, including to situations where the same issue is pending before a court inside and outside the EU: Articles 33 and 34 Brussels II Regulation.

Brussels II applies from 10 January 2015: Article 81 Brussels II Regulation. Where judgments are handed down prior to that date, or instruments are drawn up or settlements are approved or concluded prior to that date, they will continue to be governed by Brussels I Regulation: Article 66(2) Brussels II Regulation.

16.018 Scope of application.
Fn 57 More recently, in England, see *Deutsche Bahn v Morgan Crucible* [2013] CAT 18; affirmed on appeal at [2013] EWCA Civ 1484, discussed in the update to paragraph 16.021, below.

General jurisdiction. A recast 'Brussels II Regulation' (Regulation 1215/2012 **16.019** on jurisdiction and the recognition and enforcement of judgments in civil and commercial matters (recast), OJ 2012 L351/1) was adopted on 20 December 2012 and entered into force on 10 January 2015: see the update to paragraph 16.015, above. The reference to Article 2(1) of the Brussels I Regulation should be read as Article 4 of the Brussels II Regulation.

Special jurisdiction. A recast 'Brussels II Regulation' (Regulation 1215/2012 on **16.020** jurisdiction and the recognition and enforcement of judgments in civil and commercial matters (recast), OJ 2012 L351/1) was adopted on 20 December 2012 and entered into force on 10 January 2015: see the update to paragraph 16.015, above. The reference to Article 5(1) of the Brussels I Regulation should be read as Article 7(1) of the Brussels II Regulation; Article 5(3) of Brussels I as Article 7(3) of Brussels II; Article 5(5) of Brussels I as Article 7(5) of Brussels II; Article 15 of Brussels I as Article 17 of Brussels II; and Article 6(1) of Brussels I as Article 8(1) of Brussels II.

Matters relating to a contract or tort. A recast 'Brussels II Regulation' **16.021** (Regulation 1215/2012 on jurisdiction and the recognition and enforcement of judgments in civil and commercial matters (recast), OJ 2012 L351/1) was adopted on 20 December 2012 and entered into force on 10 January 2015: see the update to paragraph 16.015, above. The reference to Article 5(1) of the Brussels I Regulation should be read as Article 7(1) of the Brussels II Regulation, and the reference to Article 5(3) of Brussels I as Article 7(3) of Brussels II.

In a preliminary ruling on a number of questions referred to it by the Landgericht Dortmund, the Court of Justice in Case C-352/13 *Cartel Damage Claims Hydrogen Peroxide (CDC) v Evonik Degussa and others*, EU:C:2015:335, [2015] 5 CMLR 285 held that in the context of a follow-on damages action brought against defendants domiciled in different Member States, and relying upon a decision from the European Commission finding that those defendants participated in a single and continuous infringement of competition law, for the purposes of Article 5(3):

(a) the place of the event giving rise to damage is the place at which the cartel was concluded; or, if the cartel consisted of a number of collusive agreements and there was one particular agreement which was the sole cause of damage to the claimant, the place at which that agreement was concluded: para 50; and

(b) the place where the harmful event occurred, when the damage is an alleged overcharge, is in general the place at which the claimant's registered office is located: para 56.

The Court also confirmed that a valid jurisdiction or arbitration clause in a contract for the supply of goods is to be given effect if it excludes the jurisdiction that the court would otherwise have under Article 5(3) and/or Article 6; however, it is for the national court to determine whether the clause in question binds the parties to the proceedings before it, and whether the clause, properly interpreted, does in fact derogate from the court's jurisdiction. In particular, a clause which abstractly refers to all disputes arising from contractual relationships must be regarded as not extending to a dispute relating to the tortious liability that results from an infringement of competition law, and as not validly derogating from the court's jurisdiction, whereas a clause which does refer to disputes concerning liability that results from an infringement of competition law will constitute a valid derogation: paras 57 et seq.

Fn 66 For an example of these principles being applied in a national court, see *Ryanair v Esso Italiana* [2013] EWCA Civ 1450, discussed in the update to paragraph 16.022, below.

Fn 67 For an example of these principles being applied in a national court, see *Ryanair v Esso Italiana* [2013] EWCA Civ 1450, discussed in the update to paragraph 16.022, below.

Fn 69 The 15th Edition of Collins (ed), *Dicey, Morris and Collins on The Conflict of Laws* (2012) is now available. The relevant paragraphs in the new edition are 11-285 et seq.

Fn 70 In *Bord Na Mona Horticulture v British Industries* [2012] EWHC 3346 (Comm), paras 85–86, the High Court considered the case to be one where it was difficult to say where the harmful event occurred, and could not be satisfied that it took place in England. The claimants could proceed only on the basis that they suffered damage in England.

Fn 71 On the application of the principle laid down in Case C-220/88 *Dumez France v Hessiche Landesbank (Helaba)* [1990] ECR I-49, para 22, to competition damages claims, see *Deutsche Bahn v Morgan Crucible* [2013] CAT 18; affirmed on appeal at [2013] EWCA Civ 1484 (permission to appeal refused in a reasoned judgment by two Lords Justices). The UK Competition Appeal Tribunal rejected the non-UK domiciled defendants' contention that, since many of the claimants' purchases from the defendants were allegedly indirect, the damage sustained was incapable of founding jurisdiction under Article 5(3). The Court of Appeal confirmed that that judgment was correct. Article 5(3) does not require that, in order to be a relevant connecting factor between a defendant and the putative jurisdiction, the harmful event must be one of which the claimant is an immediate victim. That would involve a search for a connecting factor between the claimant and the putative jurisdiction, rather than between the defendant and the putative jurisdiction, which is what Article 5(3) and the Brussels Regulation more generally is concerned with: para 20. The Court of Appeal referred at para 22 to the articulation of the principle by Advocate General Darmon in *Dumez*, para 52, that:

> 'the place where the damage occurs is, for indirect victims, the place where the initial damage manifested itself, in other words the place where the damage to the direct victim occurred.'

Fn 72 On the application of Case C-364/93 *Marinari v Lloyds Bank* [1995] ECR I-2719 to competition damages claims, see *Deutsche Bahn v Morgan Crucible* [2013] CAT 18, upheld on appeal at [2013] EWCA Civ 1484, discussed in the update to footnote 71 above. The Tribunal considered that in accepting jurisdiction it was not construing Article 5(3) in a manner that encompassed a situation where adverse consequences of a harmful event were felt elsewhere, as on the facts of that case the relevant damage for jurisdictional purposes was all sustained in England.

Fn 73 In *Bord Na Mona Horticulture v British Industries* [2012] EWHC 3346 (Comm), para 91, the High Court considered an argument based on the Court of Justice's judgment in Cases C-509/09&C-161/10 *E-Date Advertising v X and Martinez v MGM*, EU:C:2011:685, [2011] ECR I-10269, [2012] 1 CMLR 163. It observed that, if it were relevant to consider the claimant's 'centre of interest' for the purposes of a claim for damages for breach of competition law, this is the place where the claimant is habitually resident, not the place where it made its purchases.

Characterisation under Article 5(1) or Article 5(3). A recast 'Brussels II **16.022** Regulation' (Regulation 1215/2012 on jurisdiction and the recognition and enforcement of judgments in civil and commercial matters (recast), OJ 2012 L351/1) was adopted on 20 December 2012 and entered into force on 10 January 2015: see the update to paragraph 16.015, above. The reference to Article 5(1) of the Brussels I Regulation should be read as Article 7(1) of the Brussels II Regulation, and the reference to Article 5(3) of Brussels I as Article 7(3) of Brussels II.

In *Ryanair v Esso Italiana* [2013] EWCA Civ 1450 the Court of Appeal rejected an attempt to characterise a claim for repayment of an overcharge that resulted from a breach of competition law as a claim for breach of contract. It held that the relevant contract must be capable, on a proper construction, of encompassing a claim based on a breach of competition law. In that case, the relevant contract contained a clause which stipulated the consequences of a contract price or fee failing to comply with applicable laws, and a non-exclusive jurisdiction clause in favour of the courts of England and Wales. The contract price clause was held, on a proper construction, not to be capable of encompassing a breach of competition law, and the Court refused to imply a term into the contract that prices would not be inflated as a result of breaches of competition law: paras 36–39. The appropriate claim (which Ryanair had pleaded in the alternative) was breach of statutory duty rather than breach of contract, and the Court considered that the jurisdiction clause was not capable of founding jurisdiction in England and Wales over a claim for breach of statutory duty, in circumstances where there was no analogous breach of contract claim, and the claim was against an Italian company, in respect of its participation in Italy with other Italian suppliers of fuel oil in Italy in arrangements, which the Italian NCA had found to be in breach Article 101: paras 42 et seq. The Court was concerned with jurisdiction under Article 23 of Brussels I, rather than Article 5(1), but its approach to the breach of contract claim appears equally applicable to an analysis under Article 5(1).

(b) Jurisdiction over defendants based outside the territory

16.023 **Co-defendants.** A recast 'Brussels II Regulation' (Regulation 1215/2012 on jurisdiction and the recognition and enforcement of judgments in civil and commercial matters (recast), OJ 2012 L351/1) was adopted on 20 December 2012 and entered into force on 10 January 2015: see the update to paragraph 16.015, above. The reference to Article 2 of the Brussels I Regulation should be read as Article 4 of the Brussels II Regulation, and the reference to Article 6(1) of Brussels I as Article 8(1) of Brussels II.

In a preliminary ruling on a number of questions referred to it by the Landgericht Dortmund, the Court of Justice in Case C-352/13 *Cartel Damage Claims Hydrogen Peroxide (CDC) v Evonik Degussa and others*, EU:C:2015:335, [2015] 5 CMLR 285 held that in the context of a follow-on damages action brought against defendants domiciled in different Member States, and relying upon a decision from the European Commission finding that those defendants have participated in a single and continuous infringement of competition law, there would be a risk of irreconcilable judgments, within Article 6, if separate actions were to be brought against those defendants in different Member States: para 25.

Fn 82 In *Bord Na Mona Horticulture v British Polythene Industries* [2012] EWHC 3346 (Comm), paras 78–83, the High Court doubted whether the reasoning in Case C-103/05 *Reisch Montage* [2006] ECR I-6827 applies to cases where the action against the anchor defendant is substantively unsustainable rather than merely precluded as a matter of national procedural law.

16.024 **Co-defendants in competition law cases.** A recast 'Brussels II Regulation' (Regulation 1215/2012 on jurisdiction and the recognition and enforcement of judgments in civil and commercial matters (recast), OJ 2012 L351/1) was adopted on 20 December 2012 and entered into force on 10 January 2015: see the update to paragraph 16.015, above. The reference to Article 2 of the Brussels I Regulation should be read as Article 4 of the Brussels II Regulation, and the reference to Article 6(1) of Brussels I as Article 8(1) of Brussels II.

16.025 **Cases after *Provimi*.** A recast 'Brussels II Regulation' (Regulation 1215/2012 on jurisdiction and the recognition and enforcement of judgments in civil and commercial matters (recast), OJ 2012 L351/1) was adopted on 20 December 2012 and entered into force on 10 January 2015: see the update to paragraph 16.015, above. The reference to Article 2 of the Brussels I Regulation should be read as Article 4 of the Brussels II Regulation, and the reference to Article 6(1) of Brussels I as Article 8(1) of Brussels II.

Declining jurisdiction. A recast 'Brussels II Regulation' (Regulation 1215/ 2012 on jurisdiction and the recognition and enforcement of judgments in civil and commercial matters (recast), OJ 2012 L351/1) was adopted on 20 December 2012 and entered into force on 10 January 2015: see the update to paragraph 16.015, above. The reference to Article 23 of the Brussels I Regulation should be read as Article 25 of the Brussels II Regulation; Article 27 of Brussels I as Article 29 of Brussels II; and Article 28 of Brussels I as Article 30 of Brussels II. **16.026**

Fn 99 The reference to Article 6(1) of Brussels I should be read as Article 8(1) of Brussels II.

Fn 100 See also the English Court of Appeal's analysis in *Starlight Shipping Company v Allianz Marine & Aviation Versicherungs & Ors* [2012] EWCA Civ 1714, paras 41–49, where the court considered whether or not two actions were 'mirror images' of each other for the purpose of applying Article 27 of the Brussels I Regulation.

Fn 103 In *CDC Project 14 v Shell and others*, judgment of the District Court of the Hague of 1 May 2013, Case No C/09/414499/HA ZA 12-293, the Court refused to stay proceedings in the Netherlands under Article 28 of the Brussels I Regulation before pleadings had closed, as it was not yet clear whether there was a risk of reaching a judgment that was irreconcilable with the judgment that might be reached in proceedings brought in England and Wales.

Fn 105 The reference to Article 31 of Brussels I should be read as Article 35 of Brussels II.

Disputes involving parties from non-contracting countries. A recast 'Brussels II Regulation' (Regulation 1215/2012 on jurisdiction and the recognition and enforcement of judgments in civil and commercial matters (recast), OJ 2012 L351/1) was adopted on 20 December 2012 and entered into force on 10 January 2015: see the update to paragraph 16.015, above. The Brussels II Regulation will in particular extend the rules on related actions to disputes involving parties from non-contracting countries. Where a Member State court is seised of a dispute involving the *same cause of action* between the *same parties* as proceedings already pending before a court of a third State, Article 33 provides that the Member State court may stay the proceedings before it if it is expected that the court of the third State will give a judgment capable of recognition and, where applicable, of enforcement in that Member State; and a stay is necessary for the proper administration of justice. It may continue the proceedings at any time if the action in the third State is stayed or discontinued; if it appears that the proceedings in the court of the third State are unlikely to be concluded within a reasonable time; or if the continuation of the proceedings is required for the proper administration of justice. Where a Member State court is seised of *related proceedings*, between different parties, relating to proceedings already pending before a court of a third State, Article 34 provides that the Member State court **16.027**

may stay the proceedings before it if it is expedient to hear and determine the related actions together to avoid the risk of irreconcilable judgments; it is expected that the court of the third State will give a judgment capable of recognition and, where applicable, of enforcement in that Member State; and the court of the Member State is satisfied that a stay is necessary for the proper administration of justice. It may continue the proceedings at any time if there ceases to be a risk of irreconcilable judgments; if the proceedings in the court of the third State are stayed or discontinued; it appears to the court of the Member State that the proceedings in the court of the third State are unlikely to be concluded within a reasonable time; or the continuation of the proceedings is required for the proper administration of justice.

The reference in the main text to Article 22 of the Brussels I Regulation should be read as Article 24 of the Brussels II Regulation.

Fn 106 The reference to Article 4 of Brussels I should be read as Article 6 of Brussels II, and Article 22 of Brussels I as Article 24 of Brussels II.

(c) Choice of applicable law

16.031 **Rome Convention and scope of applicable law.**
Fn 113 The 15th Edition of Collins (ed), *Dicey, Morris and Collins on The Conflict of Laws* (2012) is now available. The relevant part in the new edition is Chapter 32.

4. Establishing the Existence of an Infringement

16.035 **Nature of the cause of action under Articles 101 and 102.** Although a claim for damages for breach of Article 101 or 102 has traditionally been characterised in English law as a claim in tort for breach of statutory duty, in *W H Newson Holding & Ors v IMI and others* [2012] EWHC 3680 (Ch), the High Court refused to strike out a claim brought under s 47A of the Competition Act 1998 for the tort of unlawful means conspiracy, in circumstances where the follow-on claim (see paragraph 16.038 of the main text, and the updates thereto, below) was based on a finding that Article 101 is infringed by an agreement that has as its object the prevention, restriction or distortion of competition. The Court of Appeal upheld the High Court's conclusion that such a cause of action is potentially available under s 47A, but considered that the Commission decision relied upon in that case did not contain findings of the requisite intent to injure the particular claimants: *W H Newson Holding and others v IMI and others* [2013] EWCA Civ 1377. See also *Air Canada and others v Emerald Supplies* [2015] EWCA Civ 1024, paras 111 et seq, a stand-alone claim (see paragraph 16.037 of the main text) brought by indirect purchasers, in which the Court of Appeal held, following *W H Newson*, that the requisite intent to injure the particular claimants could not be established in circumstances where it was possible that the alleged victims would be in a position to pass on any overcharges imposed on them, thereby avoiding any loss themselves.

The claimant's task.   Directive 2014/104 on certain rules governing actions for   **16.036** damages under national law for infringements of the competition law provisions of the Member States and of the European Union, OJ 2014 L349/1, includes a requirement that Member States shall ensure claimants are able to claim and obtain full compensation for harm they suffer as a result of breaches of national competition law as well as EU law: Article 3. The deadline for national implementation is 27 December 2016.

Follow-on actions: binding elements of the decision.   Directive 2014/104 on   **16.038** certain rules governing actions for damages under national law for infringements of the competition law provisions of the Member States and of the European Union, OJ 2014 L349/1, includes a requirement that where a NCA has taken a decision finding an infringement of either EU or national competition laws, the national courts of that Member State are also bound not to take a decision running counter to it. This will make NCA 'infringement decisions' binding upon national courts, in the same way that Commission decisions are binding under Article 16 of Regulation 1/2003. See Article 9(1). In addition, Member States shall ensure that a final decision by a NCA in another Member State may, in accordance with national law, be presented before the national courts as at least *prima facie* evidence that an infringement of competition law has occurred and, as appropriate, may be assessed along with any other evidence adduced by the parties: Article 9(2).

See also the Supreme Court's judgment in *Deutsche Bahn v Morgan Crucible Company* [2014] UKSC 24, considering what the relevant 'decision' is for the purposes of bringing a monetary claim before the Competition Appeal Tribunal under section 47A of the Competition Act 1998. The Court held that it is the individual decision taken against the individual addressee which is binding, and as against non-appealing addressees that means it is binding in the form adopted by the Commission. The Court considered the difficulties which might arise in determining causation and quantum as against non-appealing addressees where other addressees had appealed successfully, and accepted that a non-appealing addressee may in theory be fully liable for the cartel, but considered that:

> '… if there was really no cartel (or a more limited cartel than found by the Commission Decision), it might be difficult for a Claimant to prove that it had suffered any loss caused thereby. Further, in the case of a whistle-blower like the present Appellant, a hypothesis of no cartel is self-evidently unreal. Finally, of course, the situation is likely to remain hypothetical in most cases, as it did in the present.'

See para 27. The Commission submitted observations to the Supreme Court, pursuant to Article 15(3) of Regulation 1/2003 (discussed in paragraph 15.051 of the main text), which are available on the *Amicus Curiae* section of the DG Comp website.

Fn 132 See also *Bord Na Mona Horticulture v British Industries* [2012] EWHC 3346 (Comm), paras 42–43.

16.039 **Fault.** In line with the views that the Commission expressed in the White Paper on Damages Acts for Breach of the EU antitrust rules, discussed in the main text, Directive 2014/104 on certain rules governing actions for damages under national law for infringements of the competition law provisions of the Member States and of the European Union, OJ 2014 L349/1, does not contain any provision that would relieve infringers from liability on grounds of absence of fault. Departing from its view in the White Paper, the Commission did not propose a provision to relieve infringers from liability where they made an 'excusable error'.

Fn 138 The Court of Justice confirmed in Case C-681/11 *Schenker*, EU:C:2013:404, [2013] 5 CMLR 831 that if Member States do establish conditions of intention or negligence for the imposition of a fine, those conditions must be at least as stringent as those in Article 23 of Regulation 1/2003: paras 35–36. Disagreeing with Advocate General Kokott's Opinion of 28 February 2013, the Court held that reliance by an undertaking on legal advice or a previous NCA decision that its conduct was not contrary to EU competition law is not sufficient to show that an infringement was not committed intentionally or negligently. To avoid a finding that an infringement was committed intentionally or negligently an undertaking must show that it could not have been aware of the anti-competitive nature of its conduct. If an undertaking characterised its conduct wrongly in law, then it cannot show that it could not have been aware of the anti-competitive nature of its conduct: para 38.

16.040 **Access to evidence held by competition authorities.** The Court of Justice held in Case C-536/11 *Bundeswettbewerbsbehörde v Donau Chemie*, EU:C:2013:366, [2013] 5 CMLR 658 that where a potential damages claimant seeks access to documents which form part of the file in public law proceedings concerning the application of Article 101, it is incompatible with European law, in particular the principle of effectiveness, for such access to be made subject to the consent of the parties to those proceedings. A domestic rule to that effect would be liable to make it impossible or excessively difficult to protect the right to compensation conferred on parties adversely affected by an infringement of Article 101. It must be possible for a national court to balance the competing interests in each individual case, in order to determine whether access should be granted or not, in the same way as in respect of leniency materials following Case C-360/09 *Pfleiderer v Bundeskartellampt* [2011] ECR I-5161.

Directive 2014/104 on certain rules governing actions for damages under national law for infringements of the competition law provisions of the Member States and of the European Union, OJ 2014 L349/1, includes significant provisions on access-ing evidence held by competition authorities. The main provisions are:

(a) a complete prohibition on disclosure of leniency statements and settlement sub-missions, together with a requirement that such information shall be inadmis-sible in a damages action before the national court where a party has obtained it through access to the file (or otherwise be given equivalent protection to ensure the effectiveness of the prohibition on disclosure): Articles 6(6) and 7(1);

(b) a temporary prohibition on disclosure of information prepared specifically for the proceedings before a competition authority; information drawn up by the competition authority and sent to the parties during the course of proceedings; and settlement submissions that have been withdrawn; until after the proceedings are closed, together with a requirement that such infor-mation shall be inadmissible in a damages action before the national court, where a party has obtained it through access to the file, until after the pro-ceedings before the competition authority are closed (or otherwise be given equivalent protection to ensure the effectiveness on the temporary prohibi-tion on disclosure): Article 6(5) and 7(2).

The prohibitions apply to documents/information relating to investigations by the Commission, as well as to investigations by national competition authorities. The deadline for national implementation is 27 December 2016.

Regulation 773/2004 was amended by Regulation 2015/1348 (OJ 2015 L208/3) to reflect the new Directive. Article 16a in particular has been added to provide that the Commission shall grant access to leniency corporate statements or settlement submissions only for the purposes of exercising rights of defence before it, and that information taken from such statements and submissions may be used by the party who has gained access only where it is necessary for the exercise of its rights of defence in proceedings before the EU courts; or before the Courts of Member States in cases concerning the allocation of fines imposed jointly and severally, or the review of a decision by the NCA finding an infringement of Article 101.

The scope for a litigant to gain access to documents by way of request under Regulation 1049/2001 has been restricted by the Court of Justice judgment in Case C-365/12P *Commission v EnBW Energie Baden-Württemberg ('EnBW')*, EU:C:2014:112, [2014] 4 CMLR 30, together with a number of General Court judgments which consider the public interest in disclosure: see the update to para-graph 16.046, below.

Request from the national court to the Commission.   Directive 2014/104 on   **16.041** certain rules governing actions for damages under national law for infringements of the competition law provisions of the Member States and of the European Union, OJ 2014 L349/1, includes significant provisions on accessing evidence held by competition authorities: see the update to paragraph 16.040, above.

Fn 145 The General Court suspended the Commission's decision to transmit the information, while the challenge was pending: Order of the President of 29 November 2012. The High Court subsequently withdrew its request to the Commission under Article 15(1) of Regulation 1/2003, as the Court of Appeal confirmed in *National Grid Electricity Transmission v ABB* [2013] EWCA Civ 1234 that the English High Court has power to order disclosure of documents notwithstanding the French law prohibition on them being provided directly (without recourse to the special procedures for the taking of evidence abroad laid down in Regulation 1206/2001).

16.042 **Disclosure by a defendant of documents emanating from the Commission.** Directive 2014/104 on certain rules governing actions for damages under national law for infringements of the competition law provisions of the Member States and of the European Union, OJ 2014 L349/1, includes significant provisions restricting access to documents forming part of the file: see the update to paragraph 16.040, above. Regulation 773/2004 was amended by Regulation 2015/1348 (OJ 2015 L208/3) to reflect the new Directive: see the update to paragraph 16.040, above.

16.043 **Material provided to NCAs under national leniency programmes.** The Court of Justice held in Case C-536/11 *Bundeswettbewerbsbehörde v Donau Chemie*, EU:C:2013:366, [2013] 5 CMLR 658 that where a potential damages claimant seeks access to documents which form part of the file in public law proceedings concerning the application of Article 101, it is incompatible with European law, in particular the principle of effectiveness, for such access to be made subject to the consent of the parties to those proceedings. A domestic rule to that effect would be liable to make it impossible or excessively difficult to protect the right to compensation conferred on parties adversely affected by an infringement of Article 101. It must be possible for a national court to balance the competing interests in each individual case, in order to determine whether access should be granted or not, in the same way as in respect of leniency materials following Case C-360/09 *Pfleiderer v Bundeskartellampt* [2011] ECR I-5161.

The ability of third parties to access leniency and settlement procedure information will be circumscribed by Directive 2014/104 on certain rules governing actions for damages under national law for infringements of the competition law provisions of the Member States and of the European Union, OJ 2014 L349/1. See the update to paragraph 16.040, above.

Fn 148 On Case C-536/11 *Bundeswettbewerbsbehörde v Donau Chemie*, EU:C:2013:366, [2013] 5 CMLR 658, see the update to the main paragraph, above.

Fn 149 The Court of Justice in Case C-365/12P *Commission v EnBW Energie Baden-Württemberg ('EnBW')*, EU:C:2014:112, [2014] 4 CMLR 30 has overturned the General Court judgment. See the update to paragraph 16.046, below.

Material provided to the Commission under EU leniency programme. The **16.044**
ability of third parties to access leniency and settlement procedure information
from the Commission will be circumscribed by Directive 2014/104 on certain
rules governing actions for damages under national law for infringements of the
competition law provisions of the Member States and of the European Union,
OJ 2014 L349/1. See the update to paragraph 16.040, above. Regulation 773/
2004 was amended by Regulation 2015/1348 (OJ 2015 L208/3) to reflect the
new Directive: see the update to paragraph 16.040, above.

Request for disclosure from Commission under Regulation 1049/2001. The **16.045**
scope for a litigant to gain access to documents by way of request under
Regulation 1049/2001 has been restricted by the Court of Justice judgment in
Case C-365/12P *Commission v EnBW Energie Baden-Württemberg ('EnBW')*,
EU:C:2014:112, [2014] 4 CMLR 30, together with a number of General Court
judgments which consider the public interest in disclosure: see the update to
paragraph 16.046, below.

In Case T-534/11 *Schenker v Commission*, EU:T:2014:854 the General Court considered the application of Regulation 1049/2001 to a request for disclosure of a
Commission decision. The Commission's obligation to respond to the request
within a mandatory timeframe under Article 8 of Regulation 1049/2001 must
be reconciled with its obligation not to disclose information covered by professional secrecy: this means that the Commission must endeavour to complete a
non-confidential version of the decision in the shortest possible timeframe and in
any event within a reasonable timeframe, established on the basis of the specific
circumstances of each case: paras 129–130; and, within the mandatory timeframe,
the Commission must disclose all parts of its decision in respect of which requests
for confidential treatment are not still outstanding: paras 137–138.

Fn 163 The Court of Justice in Case C-365/12P *Commission v EnBW Energie
Baden-Württemberg ('EnBW')*, EU:C:2014:112, [2014] 4 CMLR 30, has overturned the General Court judgment. See the update to paragraph 16.046, below.

Regulation 1049/2001: exceptions to the obligation to disclose. The Court **16.046**
of Justice in Case C-365/12P *Commission v EnBW Energie Baden-Württemberg
('EnBW')*, EU:C:2014:112, [2014] 4 CMLR 30, at paras 79 et seq, held that
by analogy with the approach taken in respect of requests for documents on
merger proceedings (Case C-404/10 P *Commission v Éditions Odile Jacob*,
EU:C:2013:808, [2013] 4 CMLR 11; and Case C-477/10 P *Commission v Agrofert
Holding*, EU:C:2012:394, [2012] 5 CMLR 510, discussed in paragraph 8.184
of the main text), and on State aid proceedings (Case C-139/07P *Commission v
Technische Glaswerke Ilmenau*, EU:C:2010:376, [2010] ECR I-5885, discussed
in paragraphs 16.046 et seq of the main text), the Commission is entitled to
apply a general presumption that disclosure of documents on its file in an antitrust investigation would undermine the protection of the commercial interests

of the undertakings involved in those proceedings, as well as the protection of the purpose of investigations relating to such proceedings, within the meaning of the first and third indents of Article 4(2) of Regulation 1049/2001. Otherwise, the restrictive rules on access to the file in Regulation 1/2003 and Regulation 773/2004 could be undermined: paras 88–90. It is not necessary to examine each document individually and determine the application of the exceptions to each: para 93. It is also entitled to apply a presumption that disclosure of its internal documents (such as background notes on the evidence, correspondence with other competition authorities, and consultations with other departments in the Commission) would seriously undermine the Commission's decision-making process, within the meaning of the second paragraph of Article 4(3) of Regulation 1049/2001, in circumstances where an appeal against the Commission's decision is still ongoing, and the possibility remains that the Commission may be called upon to re-open its investigation: para 114. The presumptions can be rebutted if there is evidence that it would be in the public interest to disclose the documents, but the Court held that a general statement that disclosure is required for the purposes of bringing a claim for compensation in the national courts will not suffice: a requestor has to establish that particular documents are necessary for that purpose in order for its rights to compensation to constitute an overriding public interest in disclosure: paras 107 and 132.

The General Court in Case T-181/10 *Reagens v Commission*, EU:T:2014:139, [2014] 4 CMLR 960 held that the Commission could not rely on the first indent of Article 4(2) of Regulation 1049/2001 as a basis for refusing access to a non-confidential version of an undertaking's request for a reduction in the fine imposed upon it on grounds of inability to pay, or the first, standard form, questionnaire sent by the Commission to the undertaking in response to that request, nor could it rely on the third indent of Article 4(2) to refuse access to the first standard form questionnaire: paras 106 and 129. It upheld the Commission's refusal to provide access to the undertaking's responses to the questionnaires, and to the Commission's second questionnaire. The General Court did not consider the Court of Justice's judgment in *EnBW*.

See also Case T-561/12 *Beninca v Commission*, EU:T:2013:558, [2014] 4 CMLR 549, in which the General Court confirmed that the Commission's internal documents prepared in the course of merger control proceedings may fall within the exception in Article 4(3) of Regulation 1049/2001. That exception will apply where the Commission's decision-making process may be prejudiced by disclosure of the document, and in particular in circumstances where its investigation has closed but its decision is under appeal and the possibility remains that it will be required to re-open its proceedings. The request was for disclosure of an internal Commission memorandum which related to M.6166 *NYSE Euronext/Deutsche Börse* (1 February 2012), at the time of the request under appeal in Case T-175/12 *Deutsche Börse v Commission*, EU:T:2015:148, [2015] 4 CMLR 1187. Similarly, in

Case T-456/13 *Sea Handling v Commission*, EU:T:2015:185, para 63, the General Court confirmed that the Commission is entitled to apply a general presumption that disclosure of documents on its file in a State aid investigation would undermine the protection of the purpose of investigations relating to such proceedings, within the meaning of the third indent of Article 4(2) of Regulation 1049/2001.

In Case T-623/13 *Unión de Almacenistas de Hierros de España v Commission*, EU:T:2015:268 the General Court applied *EnBW* to information exchanged between ECN members, and held that the Commission is entitled to apply a general presumption that documents submitted to it by a NCA under Article 11(4) of Regulation 1/2003 are within the scope of the exemptions from disclosure in Articles 4(2) first and third indent, of Regulation 1049/2001, as their disclosure would harm the commercial interests of third parties and the objectives on NCA investigations: para 64.

A number of General Court judgments have also considered the public interest in disclosing documents. In Case T-380/08 *Netherlands v Commission*, EU:T:2013:480, regarding Article 4(2) first indent and third indent of Regulation 1049/2001, the General Court considered that a victim's right to claim compensation for a breach of competition law is a private interest for the purposes of rebutting the presumption, not a public interest. It is a matter for the court seised of a damages claim to decide what evidence is required, under the law applicable to the dispute, and to request the transmission of information by the Commission under Article 15(1) of Regulation 1/2003 if appropriate: paras 79 et seq. In Case T-181/10 *Reagens v Commission*, EU:T:2014:139, [2014] 4 CMLR 960 the General Court held that the rights of defence of an addressee of a Commission infringement decision are also a private interest, not a public interest that justifies disclosure. The request had been made by one addressee of the Commission's decision in COMP/38589 *Heat Stabilisers*, decision of 11 November 2009, for disclosure of the request by another undertaking for a reduction in its fine. The General Court held that even if the documents were to prove necessary to the undertaking's appeal against the Commission's decision, that is irrelevant to the question of disclosure under Regulation 1049/2001: paras 142 et seq. (In Reagens' substantive appeal, the General Court subsequently refused to order measures of inquiry to obtain those documents: Case T-30/10 *Reagens v Commission*, EU:C:2014:253, at paras 56 et seq.)

In Case T-534/11 *Schenker v Commission*, EU:T:2014:854 the General Court considered the application of Regulation 1049/2001 to a request for disclosure of a Commission decision. The Commission's obligation to respond to the request within a mandatory timeframe under Article 8 of Regulation 1049/2001 must be reconciled with its obligation not to disclose information covered by professional secrecy: this means that the Commission must endeavour to complete a non-confidential version of the decision in the shortest possible timeframe and in any event within a reasonable timeframe, established on the basis of the specific circumstances of each case: paras 129–130; and, within the mandatory timeframe, the Commission must disclose all parts of its decision in respect of which requests for confidential treatment are not still outstanding: paras 137–138.

Fn 165 For a more recent example, see Case T-516/11 *MasterCard v Commission*, EU:T:2014:759, in particular paras 71–72, and 87. The Commission's refusal to disclose documents prepared by a third party, as part of a study it had commissioned into the costs and benefits of merchants accepting different methods of payment, was overturned. The Commission had not provided sufficient evidence to justify its conclusion that disclosure would seriously undermine its decision-making processes, under the first indent of Article 4(3) of Regulation 1049/2001, or would undermine the commercial interests of the third party, under the first indent of Article 4(2).

Fn 166 See also Case T-516/11 *MasterCard v Commission*, EU:T:2014:759, referred to in the update to Fn 165, above.

16.047 **Regulation 1049/2001: obligation to examine individual documents requested.** The Court of Justice in Case C-365/12P *Commission v EnBW Energie Baden-Württemberg ('EnBW')*, EU:C:2014:112, [2014] 4 CMLR 30, at paras 79 et seq, held that by analogy with the approach taken in respect of requests for documents on merger proceedings (Case C-404/10 P *Commission v Éditions Odile Jacob*, EU:C:2013:808, [2013] 4 CMLR 11; and Case C-477/10 P *Commission v Agrofert Holding*, EU:C:2012:394, [2012] 5 CMLR 510, discussed in paragraph 8.184 of the main text), and on State aid proceedings (Case C-139/07P *Commission v Technische Glaswerke Ilmenau*, EU:C:2010:376, [2010] ECR I-5885, discussed in paragraphs 16.046 et seq of the main text), the Commission is entitled to apply a general presumption that disclosure of documents on its file in an antitrust investigation would undermine the protection of the commercial interests of the undertakings involved in those proceedings, as well as the protection of the purpose of investigations relating to such proceedings, within the meaning of the first and third indents of Article 4(2) of Regulation 1049/2001. Otherwise, the restrictive rules on access to the file in Regulation 1/2003 and Regulation 773/2004 could be undermined: paras 88–90. It confirmed that it is not necessary to examine each document individually and determine the application of the exceptions to each: para 93. The Commission is also entitled to apply a presumption that disclosure of its internal documents (such as background notes on the evidence, correspondence with other competition authorities, and consultations with other departments in the Commission) would seriously undermine the Commission's decision-making process, within the meaning of the second paragraph of Article 4(3) of Regulation 1049/2001, in circumstances where an appeal against the Commission's decision is still ongoing, and the possibility remains that the Commission may be called upon to re-open its investigation: para 114.

The General Court has subsequently held in Case T-181/10 *Reagens v Commission*, EU:T:2014:139, [2014] 4 CMLR 960, that the Commission could not rely on the first indent of Article 4(2) of Regulation 1049/2001 as a basis for refusing access to a non-confidential version of an undertaking's request for a reduction in the fine imposed upon it on grounds of inability to pay, or the first, standard form, questionnaire sent by the Commission to the undertaking in response to that request, nor could it rely on the third indent of Article 4(2) to refuse access to the first standard form questionnaire: paras 106 and 129. It upheld the Commission's refusal to provide access to the undertaking's responses to the questionnaires, and to the Commission's second questionnaire. The General Court did not consider the Court of Justice's judgment in Case C-365/12P *Commission v EnBW Energie Baden-Württemberg ('EnBW')*, EU:C:2014:112, [2014] 4 CMLR 30, regarding the need for an individual assessment of the documents.

Fn 180 See also Case T-561/12 *Beninca v Commission*, EU:T:2013:558, [2014] 4 CMLR 549, in which the General Court confirmed that the Commission's internal documents prepared in the course of merger control proceedings may fall within the exception in Article 4(3) of Regulation 1049/2001. That exception will apply where the Commission's decision-making process may be prejudiced by disclosure of the document, and in particular in circumstances where its investigation has closed but its decision is under appeal and the possibility remains that it will be required to re-open its proceedings. The request was for disclosure of an internal Commission memorandum which related to M.6166 *NYSE Euronext/Deutsche Börse* (1 February 2012), at the time of the request under appeal in Case T-175/12 *Deutsche Börse v Commission*, EU:T:2015:148, [2015] 4 CMLR 1187. Similarly, in Case T-456/13 *Sea Handling v Commission*, EU:T:2015:185, para 63, the General Court confirmed that the Commission is entitled to apply a general presumption that disclosure of documents on its file in a State aid investigation would undermine the protection of the purpose of investigations relating to such proceedings, within the meaning of the third indent of Article 4(2) of Regulation 1049/2001.

5. Declarations of Invalidity

Effect on resulting agreements. In *Deutsche Bank and others v Unitech Global and* **16.054** *another* [2013] EWHC 2793 (Comm), paras 25–33 the High Court rejected the contention that the invalidity of a horizontal agreement can affect the validity of vertical, implementing agreements. The Court held that even if competition law was breached in the process by which the London Interbank Offered Rate (known as 'LIBOR') was set, and the 'horizontal' LIBOR agreements between the banks were void, that would not affect the validity of the 'vertical' credit and swap agreements which were based upon LIBOR. In particular, this approach was held to be consistent with the Court of Appeal's judgment in *Courage v Crehan* [1999] ECC 455: para 30.

16.057 **Non-compliance with conditions for block exemption.**   On 21 March 2014 the Commission adopted Regulation 316/2014 on the application of Article 101(3) of the Treaty on the Functioning of the European Union to categories of technology transfer agreements, OJ 2014 L93/17. It entered into force on 1 May 2014, and replaces Regulation 772/2004 which expired on 30 April 2014.

Fn 223 The reference to Article 4 of Regulation 772/2004 should be read as Article 4 in Regulation 316/2014.

Fn 224 The reference to Article 5 of Regulation 772/2004 should be read as Article 5 in Regulation 316/2014.

6. Injunctive Relief

16.060 **Development of English case law.**   The Consumer Rights Act 2015 amended s 47A of the Competition Act 1998: s 81 and Sch 8. The Competition Appeal Tribunal now has power to grant injunctions, as well as the High Court: see para 4 of Sch 8, substituting a new s 47A(3)(c).

16.061 **Mandatory injunctions.**   In *Chemistree Homecare v Abbvie* [2013] EWHC 264 (Ch), the High Court refused an injunction as the claimant had failed to show there was a real prospect of success on either dominance or abuse, or that the balance of convenience supported granting the injunction (upheld in *Chemistree Homecare v Abbvie* [2013] EWCA Civ 1338, where the Court of Appeal agreed that dominance could not be established).

In *Dahabshiil Transfer Services v Barclays Bank* [2013] EWHC 3379 (Ch) the High Court granted an interim injunction to prevent Barclays from withdrawing its banking services from certain 'money service businesses', who remit money internationally and provide foreign exchange services. The Court held that there was a serious issue to be tried as to whether Barclays' decision to withdraw its banking services from certain of these businesses was abusive, or whether the risk that money service businesses present (in particular of money laundering and financing of terrorism) and Barclays' assessment of these particular businesses' risk profiles was an objective justification for the decision.

7. Actions for Damages

(a) Introduction

16.064 **Guidance on quantification of damages.**   The Commission has adopted a Communication on quantifying harm in actions for damages based on breaches of Article 101 or 102 TFEU (COM(2013) 3440, OJ 2013 C167/19), and an accompanying Practical Guide (SWD(2013) 205) ('Quantification Guide'). Updated paragraph references to the Quantification Guide are given in the updates to paragraphs 16.077 et seq, below.

Consultation on collective redress.   On 11 June 2013 the Commission adopted   **16.065** a Recommendation on common principles for injunctive and compensatory collective redress mechanisms in the Member States concerning violations of rights granted under Union law, OJ 2013 L201/60. The particular recommendations are discussed in the update to paragraph 16.068, below.

In the UK, the Consumer Rights Act 2015 amended the Competition Act 1998 to provide for collective redress mechanisms: s 81 and Sch 8, in particular see paras 5–12 of Sch 8. The Competition Appeal Tribunal's rules have been updated to include collective proceedings and collective settlements: Competition Appeal Tribunal Rules 2015 (SI/2015/1648).

(b) The potential parties to the suit

(i) Potential claimants

Who can sue?   In Case C-557/12 *Kone v ÖBB-Infrastruktur*, EU:C:2014:1317,   **16.066** the Court of Justice confirmed that potential claimants also include those who purchased from non-infringing undertakings, where it is established that:

(a) in the circumstances of the case and in particular given the specific aspects of the relevant market, the cartel at issue was liable to have the effect of enabling the non-infringing undertakings to offer higher prices than they would have done under conditions of normal competition (known as 'umbrella pricing'); and

(b) those circumstances, and the specific aspects of the relevant market, could not be ignored by the members of that cartel.

It is for the national court to determine whether those conditions are satisfied.

The Court of Justice confirmed in Case C-199/11 *Europese Gemeenschap v Otis*, EU:C:2012:684, [2013] 4 CMLR 141 that the Commission is not precluded from bringing a civil action in a Member State to seek to recover the damages it has suffered as a result of a breach of competition law. The Court was asked whether it was compatible with Article 47 of the Charter of Fundamental Rights for the Commission to bring an action for damages in the courts of a Member State where it would be relying on its own infringement decision to establish liability, and Article 16(1) of Regulation 1/2003 would prevent the defendant from contesting the decision. It held that the Commission has authority to appear in Member State proceedings in these circumstances, and that the defendant's rights under Article 47 of the Charter are adequately protected by its right to appeal the Commission's decision in the European Courts under Article 263 TFEU, and its right to contest causation and damage in the Member State court.

16.067 Indirect purchasers. Directive 2014/104 on certain rules governing actions for damages under national law for infringements of the competition law provisions of the Member States and of the European Union, OJ 2014 L349/1, includes provision that compensation of harm should be capable of being claimed by anyone who suffered it, irrespective of whether they are direct or indirect purchasers, and that Member States should recognise a passing-on defence: see Articles 12–13. The Directive also provides that where a claim is brought by an indirect purchaser, the claimant should bear the burden of proving the loss was passed on to him: Article 14. The deadline for national implementation is 27 December 2016.

On the link between the passing-on defence and the standing of indirect purchasers, see also the Supreme Court of Canada's judgment in *Pro-Sys Consultants v Microsoft*, 2013 SCC 57. The Court rejected the passing-on defence in the context of a claim for restitution following a breach of competition law, and dismissed the argument that in doing so it was precluding the possibility of claims being brought by indirect purchasers.

16.068 Collective redress. On 11 June 2013 the Commission adopted a Recommendation on common principles for injunctive and compensatory collective redress mechanisms in the Member States concerning violations of rights granted under Union law, OJ 2013 L201/60 ('the Collective Redress Recommendation'). The recommendations include:

(a) representative entities should not be confined to public bodies, but should include designated bodies: para 4;

(b) claimant parties should be constituted on an 'opt-in' basis, and persons should be able to join the claimant at any point prior to judgment on, or settlement of, the claim: paras 21 and 23, respectively;

(c) claimant parties should declare the source of their funding at the start of proceedings, and provision should be made to deal with third party funding: paras 14–16;

(d) collective alternative dispute resolution mechanisms should be available, and use of such mechanisms should be subject to the parties' consent: paras 25–26;

(e) the losing party should pay the legal costs of the winner, and provision should be made to ensure that lawyers' remuneration is not calculated in such a way that it creates incentives to litigate unnecessarily: paras 13 and 29–30.

In the UK, the Consumer Rights Act 2015 amended the Competition Act 1998 to provide for collective redress mechanisms: s 81 and Sch 8, in particular see paras 5–12 of Sch 8. The Competition Appeal Tribunal's rules have been updated to include collective proceedings and collective settlements: Competition Appeal Tribunal Rules 2015 (SI/2015/1648).

(c) Causation and quantum of loss

Causation. Directive 2014/104 on certain rules governing actions for damages **16.074** under national law for infringements of the competition law provisions of the Member States and of the European Union, OJ 2014 L349/1, includes a requirement that Member States should apply a rebuttable presumption that an infringement of competition law caused harm: Article 17(2). The deadline for national implementation is 27 December 2016.

In Case C-557/12 *Kone v ÖBB-Infrastruktur*, EU:C:2014:1317, the Court of Justice held that Article 101 precludes a provision of national law which categorically excludes a claim for damages being brought by an undertaking that purchased from a non-infringing undertaking, in circumstances where the cartel has enabled the non-infringing undertaking to charge higher prices than it would have done in conditions of normal competition (known as 'umbrella pricing'), on the basis that there was an inadequate causal link between the cartel and the pricing decision of the non-infringing undertaking. The victim of umbrella pricing must be able to claim damages from the infringing undertaking(s) where it is established that:

(a) in the circumstances of the case and, in particular given the specific aspects of the relevant market, the cartel at issue was liable to have the effect of enabling the non-infringing undertakings to offer higher prices than they would have done under conditions of normal competition; and

(b) those circumstances, and the specific aspects of the relevant market, could not be ignored by the members of that cartel.

It is for the national court to determine whether those conditions are satisfied.

Causation: loss of a chance. In *Albion Water v Dŵr Cymru Cyfyngedig* [2013] **16.075** CAT 6, paras 205–220 the UK Competition Appeal Tribunal awarded damages to Albion Water based on business that it would have tendered for, had Dŵr Cymru supplied it with an input product at a price that was not unfair and did not impose an unlawful margin squeeze. The Tribunal was satisfied in this case that the claimant would have had a substantial chance of winning the contract had it bid for it, and reduced the damages claimed by one third on account of the uncertainty as to whether it would in fact have won or not.

Directive 2014/104 on certain rules governing actions for damages under national law for infringements of the competition law provisions of the Member States and of the European Union, OJ 2014 L349/1, includes a requirement that Member States should ensure that claimants are able to claim and obtain 'full compensation' for the harm they have suffered, and states that the provisions by which it would require Member States to recognise a passing-on defence are without prejudice to the ability of a claimant to claim for loss of profits: Articles 3 and 12(3). The deadline for national implementation is 27 December 2016.

16.076 **Extent of damages recoverable.** In Case C-557/12 *Kone v ÖBB-Infrastruktur*, EU:C:2014:1317, the Court of Justice confirmed that Article 101 precludes a provision of national law which categorically excludes a claim for damages being brought by an undertaking that purchased from a non-infringing undertaking, in circumstances where the cartel has enabled the non-infringing undertaking to charge higher prices than it would have done in conditions of normal competition (known as 'umbrella pricing'). The victim of umbrella pricing must be able to claim damages from the infringing undertakings where it is established that:

(a) in the circumstances of the case and, in particular given the specific aspects of the relevant market, the cartel at issue was liable to have the effect of enabling the non-infringing undertakings to offer higher prices than they would have done under conditions of normal competition; and

(b) those circumstances, and the specific aspects of the relevant market, could not be ignored by the members of that cartel.

It is for the national court to determine whether those conditions are satisfied.

16.077 **Assessing quantum: the draft Guidance Paper.** Directive 2014/104 on certain rules governing actions for damages under national law for infringements of the competition law provisions of the Member States and of the European Union, OJ 2014 L349/1, includes a requirement that Member States should ensure that there is a rebuttable presumption that harm was caused by an infringement of competition law, and that the burden and standard of proof required for the quantification of harm does not render the exercise of the claimant's right to compensation practically impossible or excessively difficult: Article 17. The deadline for national implementation is 27 December 2016. The Commission has also published a Communication on quantifying harm in actions for damages based on breaches of Article 101 or 102 TFEU (COM(2013) 3440, OJ 2013 C167/19), and an accompanying Practical Guide (SWD(2013) 205) ('Quantification Guide'). The references given in the main text to the draft Guidance Paper should now be read as follows:

Fn 294 The reference to para 6 of the draft Guidance Paper should be read as para 6 of the Quantification Guide.

Fn 295 The reference to para 11 of the draft Guidance Paper should be read as paras 11–12 of the Quantification Guide.

Fn 296 The reference to para 17 of the draft Guidance Paper should be read as para 20 of the Quantification Guide.

Fn 297 The reference to para 25 of the draft Guidance Paper should be read as para 29 of the Quantification Guide. The Quantification Guide sets out at Section IV guidance on the choice of method.

Comparator-based methods.   Directive 2014/104 on certain rules governing   **16.078**
actions for damages under national law for infringements of the competition law
provisions of the Member States and of the European Union, OJ 2014 L349/1,
includes a requirement that Member States should ensure that there is a rebuttable presumption that harm was caused by an infringement of competition law,
and that the burden and standard of proof required for the quantification of
harm does not render the exercise of the claimant's right to compensation practically impossible or excessively difficult: Article 17. The deadline for national
implementation is 27 December 2016. The Commission has also published a
Communication on quantifying harm in actions for damages based on breaches
of Article 101 or 102 TFEU (COM(2013) 3440, OJ 2013 C167/19), and an accompanying Practical Guide (SWD(2013) 205) ('Quantification Guide'). The
Quantification Guide sets out comparator-based methods in Section 2(II), and
references given in the main text to the draft Guidance Paper should now be read
as follows:

Fn 298 The reference to para 47 of the draft Guidance Paper should be read as para
53 of the Quantification Guide.

Fn 299 The reference to para 61 of the draft Guidance Paper should be read as para
67 of the Quantification Guide.

Fn 300 The discussion of regression analyses is at paras 69 et seq of the
Quantification Guide.

Fn 301 The worked example of a comparator model in the hypothetical flour
cartel is at paras 32 et seq.

The use of economic models.   Directive 2014/104 on certain rules governing   **16.079**
actions for damages under national law for infringements of the competition law
provisions of the Member States and of the European Union OJ 2014 L349/1,
includes a requirement that Member States should ensure that there is a rebuttable presumption that harm was caused by an infringement of competition
law, and that the burden and standard of proof required for the quantification
of harm does not render the exercise of the claimant's right to compensation
practically impossible or excessively difficult: Article 17. The deadline for national implementation is 27 December 2016. The Commission has also published a Communication on quantifying harm in actions for damages based on
breaches of Article 101 or 102 TFEU (COM(2013) 3440, OJ 2013 C167/19),
and an accompanying Practical Guide (SWD(2013) 205) ('Quantification
Guide'). The Quantification Guide sets out simulation modelling methods in
Section 2(III)(A), and references given in the main text to the draft Guidance
Paper should now be read as follows:

Fn 302 The reference to para 88 of the draft Guidance Paper should be read as
para 100 of the Quantification Guide.

Fn 303 The reference to para 92 of the draft Guidance Paper should be read as para 104 of the Quantification Guide.

16.080 **Cost-based methods.** Directive 2014/104 on certain rules governing actions for damages under national law for infringements of the competition law provisions of the Member States and of the European Union OJ 2014 L349/1, includes a requirement that Member States should ensure that there is a rebuttable presumption that harm was caused by an infringement of competition law, and that the burden and standard of proof required for the quantification of harm does not render the exercise of the claimant's right to compensation practically impossible or excessively difficult: Article 17. The deadline for national implementation is 27 December 2016. The Commission has also published a Communication on quantifying harm in actions for damages based on breaches of Article 101 or 102 TFEU (COM(2013) 3440, OJ 2013 C167/19), and an accompanying Practical Guide (SWD(2013) 205) ('Quantification Guide'). The Quantification Guide sets out cost-based and finance-based modelling methods in Section 2(III)(B), and references given in the main text to the draft Guidance Paper should now be read as follows:

Fn 304 The reference to para 94 of the draft Guidance Paper should be read as para 107 of the Quantification Guide.

16.081 **Prices inflated by cartel: examples in national courts.**
Fn 306 The UK Government has not pursued the proposal in its consultation paper, discussed in the footnote to the main text, that there should be a rebuttable presumption that loss has been suffered: paras 4.36–4.37 of the Government's Response to the consultation paper *Private Actions in Competition Law: A Consultation on Options for Reform* (January 2013). However, Directive 2014/104 on certain rules governing actions for damages under national law for infringements of the competition law provisions of the Member States and of the European Union OJ 2014 L349/1, includes a requirement that Member States should ensure that there is a rebuttable presumption that harm was caused by an infringement of competition law: Article 17(2). The deadline for national implementation is 27 December 2016.

16.082 **Prices inflated by cartels: the draft Guidance Paper.** Directive 2014/104 on certain rules governing actions for damages under national law for infringements of the competition law provisions of the Member States and of the European Union OJ 2014 L349/1, includes a requirement that Member States should ensure that there is a rebuttable presumption that harm was caused by an infringement of competition law, and that the burden and standard of proof required for the quantification of harm does not render the exercise of the claimant's right to compensation practically impossible or excessively difficult: Article 17. The deadline for national implementation is 27 December 2016. The Commission has also published a Communication on quantifying harm in actions for damages based on breaches of Article 101 or 102 TFEU (COM(2013) 3440, OJ 2013 C167/19), and an accompanying Practical Guide (SWD(2013) 205) ('Quantification Guide'). The Quantification Guide sets out guidance on quantifying the harm caused by cartels in Section 3, and references given in the main text to the draft Guidance Paper should now be read as follows:

Fn 307 The reference to paras 120 et seq of the draft Guidance Paper should be read as paras 141 et seq of the Quantification Guide.

Fn 308 The reference to para 125 of the draft Guidance Paper should be read as para 145 of the Quantification Guide.

Losses arising from exclusionary conduct.   Directive 2014/104 on certain rules   **16.083** governing actions for damages under national law for infringements of the competition law provisions of the Member States and of the European Union OJ 2014 L349/1 includes a requirement that Member States should ensure that there is a rebuttable presumption that harm was caused by an infringement of competition law, and that the burden and standard of proof required for the quantification of harm does not render the exercise of the claimant's right to compensation practically impossible or excessively difficult: Article 17. The deadline for national implementation is 27 December 2016. The Commission has also published a Communication on quantifying harm in actions for damages based on breaches of Article 101 or 102 TFEU (COM(2013) 3440, OJ 2013 C167/19), and an accompanying Practical Guide (SWD(2013) 205) ('Quantification Guide'). The Quantification Guide sets out guidance on quantifying the harm caused by exclusionary conduct in Section 4, and references given in the main text to the draft Guidance Paper should now be read as follows:

Fn 309 The reference to para 168 of the draft Guidance Paper should be read as para 188 of the Quantification Guide.

Exemplary damages.   In *Albion Water v Dŵr Cymru Cyfyngedig* [2013] CAT 6,   **16.085** paras 286–355, the Tribunal declined to award exemplary damages, notwithstanding 'a conspicuous and reprehensible failure of corporate governance': para 286.

'Passing-on' defence.   Directive 2014/104 on certain rules governing actions for   **16.087** damages under national law for infringements of the competition law provisions of the Member States and of the European Union OJ 2014 L349/1, includes a requirement that Member States should recognise a passing-on defence, and should ensure that compensation for harm can be claimed by anyone who suffered it, including indirect purchasers: Articles 12–14. Member States should also ensure that their courts have the power to estimate which share of an overcharge was passed on, and that the burden and standard of proof required for the quantification of harm do not render the exercise of the claimant's right to compensation practically impossible or excessively difficult: Articles 12(5) and 17(1). The deadline for national implementation is 27 December 2016. The Directive also requires that the Commission shall issue guidelines for national courts on how to estimate the share the overcharge which was passed on to the indirect purchaser: Article 16 of the Draft Damages Directive.

In addition to the consideration given to the passing-on defence in Member States, discussed in paragraph 16.088 of the main text (and the update thereto, below), the Supreme Court of Canada rejected the defence in the context of a claim for restitution following a breach of competition law in *Pro-Sys Consultants v Microsoft*, 2013 SCC 57.

16.088 **Treatment of the passing-on defence in the Member States.** In the UK, the passing-on defence was also raised in *Cooper Tire & Rubber Company and others v Shell Chemicals UK and others*, a damages claim arising from the Commission's decision in COMP/38638 *Butadiene Rubber*, decision of 29 November 2006, and in *National Grid Electricity Transmission v ABB and others*, which arose from the Commission's decision in COMP/38899 *Gas Insulated Switchgear*, decision of 24 January 2007. Both cases also settled before trial.

The issues associated with the existence of a passing-on defence have been noted by the Competition Appeal Tribunal in the context of a jurisdictional challenge under Article 5(3) of the Brussels I Regulation: see *Deutsche Bahn v Morgan Crucible* [2013] CAT 18, discussed in the update to paragraph 16.021, above.

In addition to the consideration given to the passing-on defence in Member States, the Supreme Court of Canada rejected the defence in the context of a claim for restitution following a breach of competition law in *Pro-Sys Consultants v Microsoft*, 2013 SCC 57.

Fn 341 The possibility of a purchasers passing on any overcharge was considered by the Court of Appeal to be sufficient to preclude a cartelist from having the requisite intent to injure that purchaser, for the purposes of a damages claim for unlawful means conspiracy: *W H Newson Holding and others v IMI and others* [2013] EWCA Civ 1377.

16.089 **Passing on defence: the draft Guidance Paper.** Directive 2014/104 on certain rules governing actions for damages under national law for infringements of the competition law provisions of the Member States and of the European Union, OJ 2014 L349/1 includes a requirement that Member States should recognise a passing-on defence, and should ensure that compensation for harm can be claimed by anyone who suffered it, including indirect purchasers: Articles 12–14. Member States should also ensure that their courts have the power to estimate which share of an overcharge was passed on, and that the burden and standard of proof required for the quantification of harm do not render the exercise of the claimant's right to compensation practically impossible or excessively difficult: Articles 12(5) and 17(1). The deadline for national implementation is 27 December 2016. The Directive also requires that the Commission shall issue guidelines for national courts on how to estimate the share the overcharge which was passed on to the indirect purchaser: Article 16.

The Commission has published a Communication on quantifying harm in actions for damages based on breaches of Article 101 or 102 TFEU (COM(2013) 3440, OJ 2013 C167/19), and an accompanying Practical Guide (SWD(2013) 205) ('Quantification Guide'). The Quantification Guide sets out guidance on assessing the impact of pass-on in Section 3(II)(A)(3), and references given in the main text to the draft Guidance Paper, should now be read as follows:

Fn 347 The reference to para 143 of the draft Guidance Paper should be read as para 162 of the Quantification Guide.

Fn 348 The reference to paras 149 et seq of the draft Guidance Paper should be read as paras 168 et seq of the Quantification Guide.

Fn 349 The reference to para 155 of the draft Guidance Paper should be read as paras 175 et seq of the Quantification Guide.

(d) Limitation periods

Limitation period for bringing claims. See also *Arcadia Group Brands and others v Visa Inc and others* [2015] EWCA Civ 883, in which the claimants' claim was restricted to the damage that they had suffered within the limitation period under domestic law. The claimants had sought to recover an overcharge they allegedly had suffered as a result of the level of the multilateral interchange fees imposed by Visa, dating back to 1977. The Court of Appeal upheld the finding that the elements necessary to complete the cause of action had been known to the claimants, and that time had begun to run from the date on which that knowledge was acquired. They were therefore not able to rely on s 32 of the Limitation Act 1980 in order to claim damages beyond the six year limitation period. **16.090**

Directive 2014/104 on certain rules governing actions for damages under national law for infringements of the competition law provisions of the Member States and of the European Union OJ 2014 L349/1 includes a requirement that Member States should ensure that their limitation periods for bringing private damages actions should be at least five years, and that time should not begin to run until the infringement has ceased and a claimant has knowledge of, or can reasonably be expected to have knowledge of: the behaviour and the fact that it constitutes an infringement of Union or national competition law; the fact that the infringement caused harm to him; and the identity of the infringer: Article 10. The deadline for national implementation is 27 December 2016.

Limitation periods in follow-on actions. Directive 2014/104 on certain rules governing actions for damages under national law for infringements of the competition law provisions of the Member States and of the European Union, OJ 2014 **16.091**

L349/1, includes a requirement that Member States shall ensure that their limitation periods for bringing private damages actions should be at least five years, and that time should not begin to run until the infringement has ceased and a claimant has knowledge of, or can reasonably be expected to have knowledge of: the behaviour and the fact that it constitutes an infringement of Union or national competition law; the fact that the infringement caused harm to him; and the identity of the infringer: Article 10. In addition, where a competition authority investigates the behaviour in question, the limitation period should be suspended (or, depending on national law, interrupted) until at least one year after the infringement decision has become final or the proceedings are otherwise terminated: Article 10(4). The deadline for national implementation is 27 December 2016.

In the UK, the Consumer Rights Act 2015 amended the Competition Act 1998 to provide for essentially the same limitation period to apply in the Competition Appeal Tribunal as in the High Court, subject to any provision in the Tribunal rules which defers the date on which time begins to run: s 81 and Sch 8, para 8, and in particular s 47E(7) of the Competition Act 1998, as amended, which provides for the continued application of the Tribunal rules.

8. Reliance on Articles 101 and 102 as a Defence

16.094 **Litigation to bring about an unlawful licence.** The Court of Justice in Case C-170/13 *Huawei v ZTE* EU:C:2015:477 confirmed that a refusal by the proprietor of a standard essential patent ('SEP') to grant a licence on fair, reasonable and non-discriminatory ('FRAND') terms, in circumstances where the patent has acquired SEP status as a result of the proprietor having irrevocably undertaken to the standard-setting body that it will license on FRAND terms, may also in principle be contrary to Article 102: para 53. The proprietor's undertaking does not, however, deprive it of its right to bring an action before the courts of a Member State to enforce its patent, so long as it complies with specific requirements when it does so. These are to notify the alleged infringer of the SEP and its breach; to make a specific, written offer of a licence on FRAND terms specifying the royalty and the way in which it has been calculated. The alleged infringer must respond in good faith, and without delay. If it does not accept the offer, it must promptly make a written counter-offer that corresponds to FRAND terms, and if its counter-offer is rejected and it is using the teachings of the SEP then from the point of rejection it must provide appropriate security. The parties may agree to submit the determination of the amount of the royalty to a third party. If the proprietor has complied with the requirements incumbent upon it, or if the alleged infringer has failed to comply with the requirements incumbent upon it, then it is not an abuse of the proprietor's dominant position for it to commence litigation to enforce its patent.

Following the Commission's investigation into alleged abusive conduct in relation to the intellectual property rights used in international telecoms standards, in COMP/39985 *Motorola – enforcement of ETSI standards essential patents*, decision of 29 April 2014, the Commission found that Motorola had breached Article 102 by seeking an injunction in Germany against Apple for breach of its standard essential patents (which were essential to meeting the European Telecommunications Standardisation Institute's (ETSI) GPRS standard, part of the GSM standard, which is a key industry standard for mobile and wireless communications), in circumstances where it had committed to license on FRAND terms, and where Apple was willing to enter into a licence agreement and to be bound by a determination by the German Court of the FRAND terms. However, in view of the novelty of the infringement finding, no fine has been imposed.

The Commission accepted commitments from Samsung in COMP/39939 *Samsung – enforcement of ETSI standards essential patents*, decision of 29 April 2014. In its preliminary assessment, the Commission considered that Samsung had infringed Article 102 by seeking injunctions against Apple in several Member States to enforce its patents that were essential to complying with ETSI's 3G UMTS standard (a key standard for mobile and wireless communications), and that Samsung had committed to license on FRAND terms. The Commission accepted commitments under which Samsung agrees, in essence, for a period of five years not to seek an injunction before any court or tribunal in the EEA for infringement of its standard essential patents implemented in mobile devices against a potential licensee that agrees to, and complies with, a particular framework set out in the commitments decision for determining the terms of a licence.

Article 102: unlawful refusal of a licence.   See also the update to paragraph **16.095** 16.094, above.

17

STATE AIDS

1. Introduction

Legislative developments. In July 2013, the Council adopted Regulation 733/ **17.003**
2013, amending Regulation 994/98 (the Enabling Regulation) and increasing
the categories of aid in respect of which the Commission is able to adopt block
exemption regulations: OJ 2013 L217/28; see the update to paragraph 17.070,
below. On the same day it adopted Regulation 734/2013, amending Regulation
659/99 (the Procedural Regulation), in particular increasing the Commission's
powers to gather information in State aid cases: OJ 2013 L204/15; see the update
to paragraph 17.075, below.

2. The Concept of an Aid

(a) An advantage

The test to be applied. In order to assess whether or not an undertaking has re- **17.010**
ceived an advantage by reason of a State measure, the Commission is required to
make a complete analysis of all the relevant elements of the State intervention and
its context. In Case T-525/08 *Poste Italiane v Commission*, EU:T:2013:481, the
General Court annulled a Commission decision finding that Poste Italiane had
received an economic advantage from the interest rates that the Italian Treasury
paid for funds deposited with it, which the Commission found were higher than
the interest rate that a private borrower would be prepared to pay. The General
Court held that for the purposes of determining whether the market economy
investor principle was satisfied in relation to the interest payments received, the
Commission should not have focused exclusively on the higher interest rate that
Poste Italiane received, but should have looked at the State intervention as a
whole, particularly at the fact that Poste Italiane was legally obliged to place the
funds with the Treasury. The Commission had failed to consider the alternative
rate of return that would have been available to Poste Italiane had it been it free
to pursue alternative investment strategies in the absence of that legal obligation

to place the funds with the Treasury. Provided that the Treasury's interest rate did not exceed the rate of return available under such alternative investment strategies, no advantage would be conferred: paras 66–68. It followed that the Commission had not established to the requisite legal standard that Poste Italiane had received an economic advantage.

An advantage does not arise where the State merely compensates an undertaking for the expropriation of its property, doing so at rates that do not exceed the market value of the property expropriated: SA.32225 *Expropriation compensation of Nedalco*, OJ 2013 C335/01.

In Case T-488/11 *Sarc v Commission*, EU:T:2014:497, at paras 111 et seq, the General Court dismissed a challenge to a Commission decision not to open a formal State aid investigation into a licensing arrangement involving a public body and a commercial operator, which was arrived at through exclusive negotiations rather than as the outcome of a competitive process. It rejected expert and other evidence put forward by the complainant to show that the arrangement conferred an advantage on the licensee.

In Case T-425/11 *Greece v Commission*, EU:T:2014:768 the General Court upheld the appeal against a Commission decision concerning the system of admission fees for Greek casinos. It held that in a system where all operators are required to remit 80 per cent of the fees they have charged for admission, to the State, and some operators remit lower amounts than others as a consequence of their admission fees being lower, there is no advantage to any of those operators. On appeal, Case C-530/14P, not yet decided.

See also SA.38517 *Micula v Romania (ICSID arbitration award)*, decision of 30 March 2015. Two Swedish investors had made investments in Romania, under an investment incentive scheme, prior to Romania's accession to the EU. Upon accession, Romania abolished the scheme, which comprised a State aid, four years ahead of its scheduled expiry. An arbitral tribunal found that this early termination breached the two investors' legitimate expectations, and a bilateral investment treaty between Sweden and Romania, and ordered Romania to compensate the investors for the loss of the full benefit of the scheme. In its decision, the Commission found that the payment made by Romania pursuant to the arbitral award was itself an unlawful State aid, as it conferred an advantage equivalent to that provided by the abolished scheme. On appeal, Cases T-646/14 and 704/14, not yet decided.

17.011 **Compensation for public service obligations: the *Altmark* criteria.**
Fn 58 See also, eg Joined Cases T-295&309/12 *Germany v Commission*, EU:T:2014:675. On further appeal, Case C-446/14P, not yet decided.

Fn 59 For a recent example of an aid that did not satisfy the *Altmark* criteria, but was lawful under Article 106(2), see SA.38788 *Compensation to Post Office Limited for costs incurred in providing SGEIs 2015-2018*, decision of 19 March 2015.

The 'market economy investor' principle. The market economy investor   **17.012**
principle must be applied at the point in time when the State measure that may
be characterised as a State aid is adopted. Thus all the elements of a State aid
set out in paragraph 17.009 of the main text must be present. In Joined Cases
T-425&444/04 *RENV France and Orange v Commission*, EU:T:2015:450, paras
202 et seq, the General Court considered the application of the principle to a
chain of events in which the French State had declared that it would provide
support for a particular undertaking, and had adopted an actual measure five
months later after market confidence in the undertaking had stabilised. The
Court held that the Commission erred by applying the market economy investor principle to the declarations by the French State, because although the
declarations had conferred an advantage there was not sufficient evidence to
enable the Commission to conclude that they were a grant of State resources.
The principle had to be applied to the subsequent measure. The Court also held
that the Commission erred by applying the principle to the subsequent measure
by reference to the factual situation pertaining before the declarations were
made, as the measure had to be assessed by reference to the context in which
it was adopted. The Court dismissed the Commission's argument that the declarations had 'contaminated' the market. On further appeal, Case C-486/15P,
not yet decided.

In Case C-73/11P *Frucona Košice v Commission*, EU:C:2013:32, [2013] 2 CMLR
719, the Court of Justice held that the market economy investor principle can be
relied on by the State to demonstrate that it is not conferring an advantage on
an undertaking in financial difficulties where it allows the undertaking to enter
arrangements for partial payment of its tax debts, rather than resorting to bankruptcy procedures.

The General Court's judgment in Case T-29/10 *Netherlands & ING Groep v
Commission*, EU:T:2012:98, discussed in the main text, was upheld on appeal
in Case C-224/12P *Commission v Netherlands and ING Groep*, EU:C:2014:213,
[2014] 3 CMLR 987. The Court of Justice dismissed the Commission's argument
that the market economy investor principle could not be applied in circumstances
where the State had granted a State aid to 'bail out' a bank, by acquiring securities, and had subsequently renegotiated the conditions under which the bank was
able to redeem those securities. Although a private investor would not find itself
in a situation in which it had provided State aid to a bank, any holder of securities
might wish to renegotiate the redemption conditions on their securities. The application of the market economy investor principle depends not on the way in which
an advantage is conferred, but on the classification of the intervention as a decision
adopted by a shareholder of the undertaking in question: para 31. It therefore applies to determining whether a renegotiation of redemption conditions was a further State aid. Thus the fact that the State's investment arose from an exceptional
State intervention, which was itself a State aid, did not mean that its subsequent

decision with regard to its investment was not taken on a commercial basis in its capacity as shareholder.

Fn 61 For a further example of the approach taken by a national court, see *R (Sky Blue Sports and Leisure) v Coventry City Council* [2014] EWHC 2089 (Admin). See also the interim decision in the same case, [2014] EWHC 1747 (Admin) at para 42, in which the High Court held that in a challenge to an investment decision by a public authority brought by way of a judicial review challenge, the Court '… will not enter into a conflict of evidence between experts as to whether the decision was in fact justified'.

For examples of the General Court's approach to expert evidence, see Case T-488/11 *Sarc v Commission*, EU:T:2014:497 (expert evidence relied on by a complainant in seeking to show that there has been a grant of State aid), discussed in the update to paragraph 17.010, above; and Joined Cases T-31&321/12 *Spain v Commission*, EU:T:2014:604, at paras 49–50 (contemporaneous assessments by independent consultants, engaged by the Member State, of the expected profitability of an investment).

Fn 68 The Court of Justice dismissed the further appeal in Joined Cases C-533&536/12P *SNCM v Corsica Ferries France and Commission*, EU:C:2014: 2142.

Fn 69 In Case C-73/11P *Frucona Košice v Commission*, EU:C:2013:32, [2013] 2 CMLR 719, the Court of Justice overturned the General Court's judgment, and remitted the case, as the General Court had failed to consider what impact the duration of bankruptcy proceedings (and consequent delay in recovery) would have on a private creditor. The remitted case is not yet decided, but the Commission has adopted a further decision remedying the deficiencies found by the Court, and reaching the same conclusion: SA.18211 *Frucona Košice*, OJ 2014 L176/38 (on appeal, Case T-103/14, not yet decided).

The Court of Justice dismissed the appeal in Case C-405/11P *Buczek Automotive v Commission*, EU:C:2013:186.

In SA.35131 *Intervention de la Wallonie en faveur de la Sonaca*, OJ 2013 C293/01, the Commission accepted that the debt to equity conversion of a debt owed to the Walloon Region by a Belgian aeronautics company would not constitute State aid because a private investor would have been prepared to do likewise in the same circumstances.

Fn 72 See also SA.35378 *Financing of Berlin Brandenburg Airport*, decision of 19 December 2012, in which a capital injection of €1.2 billion by the State to enable the construction of an airport to be finalised would be made on terms that would be acceptable to a private investor operating under normal market conditions.

The application of the market economy investor principle to public undertakings.   **17.014**
Fn 79 The General Court has confirmed that this does not require the Commission
to compare the expected profitability of the scheme in question with the average
profitability of undertakings in the sector in which the scheme operates: Joined
Cases T-319&321/12 *Spain v Commission*, EU:T:2014:604, at paras 43 et seq. The
Court upheld the Commission's comparison, in that case, between the expected
profitability of the scheme and the cost of capital of the vehicle used for its delivery,
calculated using the capital asset pricing model.

The Transparency Directive.   The Commission adopted, on 21 May 2014, a   **17.015**
Communication amending the Communications from the Commission on EU
Guidelines for the application of State aid rules in relation to the rapid deployment of broadband networks, on Guidelines on regional State aid for 2014–2020,
on State aid for films and other audiovisual works, on Guidelines on State aid to
promote risk finance investments and on Guidelines on State aid to airports and
airlines: OJ 2014 C198/30. In order to promote consistency and simplicity, the
transparency requirements in the various guidelines have been made consistent
with one another.

(b) Granted by a Member State or through State resources

Bodies caught.   **17.017**
Fn 95 See also Case T-251/11 *Austria v Commission*, EU:T:2014:1060, paras 69
et seq.

Imputability of the measure to the State.   In Case T-305/13 *SACE v*   **17.018**
Commission, EU:T:2015:435, paras 48–49, the General Court held that it is not
necessary to show that a public undertaking's conduct would have been different
if it had acted autonomously, in order to show that a measure is imputable to the
State. The public undertaking's interests may be aligned with the general public
interest, and in such a case the objectives pursued by a measure will not offer any
indication as to the involvement, or not, of public authorities in the undertaking's decision to adopt that measure. On further appeal, Case C-472/15P, not yet
decided.

Fn 99 A further example of the application of the test laid down by the Court
of Justice in Case C-482/99 *France v Commission (Stardust Marine)* [2002] ECR
I-4397, discussed in the main text, is the General Court judgment in Case T-468/08
Tisza Erőmű v Commission, EU:T:2014:235, at paras 166 et seq. The General Court
upheld the Commission's conclusion that decisions of a State-owned electricity
operator, by which it reserved all or a substantial part of the generation capacities
of various power plants and agreed to purchase a minimum quantity of electricity
from each, under a power purchasing agreement, were imputable to the State. Even
though the parties negotiated individual purchases, the power purchase agreement
provided a minimum purchase obligation and a defined price-setting mechanism,

such that there was a transfer of resources by the State independently of those individual negotiations.

Fn 100 A further example is Case T-387/11 *Nitrogénművek Vegyipari Zrt (Hungarian Development Bank) v Commission*, EU:T:2013:98, paras 58–66.

Fn 101 The Court of Justice has reversed the General Court's judgment in Cases T-50/06, etc, *RENV v Commission*, EU:T:2012:134, noted in the footnote of the main text, and remitted the case: Case C-272/12P *Commission v Ireland*, EU:C:2013:812, [2014] 2 CMLR 895. The Court held that the Council's authorisation of certain excise duty exemptions, pursuant to its powers under EU legislation harmonising such duties, does not oust the Commission's powers to examine whether or not those exemptions constitute State aid to their beneficiaries: paras 49–50. The Court's judgment appears to be distinguishable from Case T-351/02 *Deutsche Bahn* [2006] ECR II-1047 discussed in the main text, since the excise duty exemptions at issue in *Commission v Ireland* were national measures, albeit authorised by the Council at the request of the Member States wishing to grant the exemptions; whereas *Deutsche Bahn* concerned a difference in tax treatments which was effectively mandated by EU legislation and applied generally across the EU.

17.019 **State resources.**   In Case C-262/12 *Vent De Colère v Ministre de l'Écologie*, EU:C:2013:851, [2014] 2 CMLR 1025, the Court of Justice held, replying to questions referred by the French Conseil d'État for a preliminary ruling, that a French scheme which requires electricity distributors to purchase electricity generated by wind turbines at a higher price than they would otherwise need to pay for electricity, and which recovers the cost differential from electricity consumers, does involve the use of State resources. The Court held that the scheme was distinguishable from that which it considered in Case C-379/98 *PreussenElecktra* [2001] ECR I-2099, discussed in paragraph 17.016 and 17.019 of the main text, because the French scheme applied a compulsory levy to electricity consumers' bills, in an amount that could be determined by the Minister for Energy, and the revenues raised were administered by a public body to compensate electricity distributors for their additional costs of purchasing wind-generated electricity.

In the *French vegetables* cases (Cases T-139/09 *France v Commission*, T-243/09 *Fédération de l'organisation économique fruits et légumes (Fedecom) v Commission*, EU:T:2012:497, and T-328/09 *Producteurs de légumes de France v Commission*, EU:T:2012:498), measures that were financed by a combination of funds provided by a particular industrial institution, and funds provided by way of voluntary contributions from farmers' organisations, involved the use of State resources in circumstances where the State was represented on the committees that decided how the money should be spent, such that it was able to guide the use of the resources.

For an example of the application of Case C-345/02 *Pearle and Others* [2004] ECR I-7139, discussed in the main text, see Case C-677/11 *Doux Élevage v Ministère de l'Agriculture*, EU:C:2013:348, [2013] 3 CMLR 1136. The Court of Justice considered a decision of the French Agriculture Ministry by which it extended, to all traders in a particular economic sector, an agreement that required traders to pay a compulsory levy to a trade organisation. The trade organisation was neither part of, nor controlled by, the State, and carried out various representational and promotional activities to advance the interests of the sector. The Court noted that the funds received by the organisation by way of the levy were not State resources because they did not go through the State budget or any other State body, and the State did not relinquish any of its own resources. It held that as the State had no power to use the funds, or control how the organisation spent them, they could not be considered State resources: paras 32 and 36 et seq.

'Granted directly or indirectly through State resources'. As to what is required **17.021** to constitute 'a sufficiently direct connection between the measure in question and the [State's] loss of revenue', in Joined Cases C-399&401/10P *Bouygues Télécom v Commission*, EU:C:2013:175, [2013] 3 CMLR 127, the Court of Justice held that the State's offer of a shareholder loan could itself constitute State aid, at least where that offer and its public announcement advantaged the recipient in terms of its economic position, even if the loan agreement was never signed and the loan was never actually provided.

(c) Favouring certain undertakings or the production of certain goods

Favouring certain undertakings. Where a Member State concludes an agreement **17.022** with an economic operator which does not involve any State aid for the purposes of Article 107, the fact that, subsequently, conditions external to the agreement change in such a way that the operator in question is in an advantageous position vis-à-vis other operators that have not concluded a similar agreement is not a sufficient basis on which to conclude that, together, the agreement and the subsequent modification of the conditions external to that agreement can be regarded as constituting State aid. Nor does the fact that such an agreement has been concluded with only one operator necessarily mean that the measure at issue is selective, as it may be the result of only one operator being interested in taking up an offer that is made available to all: Case T-499/10 *MOL v Commission*, EU:T:2013:592, at paras 64 and 66. The General Court held in that case that an agreement extending the period in which a mining undertaking was granted mineral extraction rights was not a State aid, in circumstances where the original grant of extraction rights was not an aid, and where the option of an extension was available to all undertakings even though only one particular undertaking had concluded an extension agreement, and subsequent legislative changes meant that other operators were no longer able to obtain such favourable terms for their mineral extraction rights. Further appeal dismissed, Case C-15/14P *Commission v MOL*, EU:C:2015:362.

Fn 118 See also SA.23008 *Alleged State aid to SZP and VZP (Slovak health insurance)*, decision of 15 October 2014. The Commission concluded, following a formal investigation, that the Slovak compulsory health insurance system is non-economic in nature, and that State-owned insurers operating in that system could not be considered to be undertakings within Article 107. On appeal, Case T-216/15, not yet decided.

Fn 119 The analysis was adopted by the Court of Justice in Case C-15/14P *Commission v MOL*, EU:C:2015:362, at para 60.

17.023 **Difference in treatment not always favouring certain undertakings.** Where a Member State concludes an agreement with an economic operator which does not involve any State aid for the purposes of Article 107, the fact that, subsequently, conditions external to the agreement change in such a way that the operator in question is in an advantageous position vis-à-vis other operators that have not concluded a similar agreement is not a sufficient basis on which to conclude that, together, the agreement and the subsequent modification of the conditions external to that agreement can be regarded as constituting State aid. Nor does the fact that such an agreement has been concluded with only one operator necessarily mean that the measure at issue is selective, as it may be the result of only one operator being interested in taking up an offer that is made available to all: Case T-499/10 *MOL v Commission*, EU:T:2013:592, at paras 64 and 66. The General Court held in that case that an agreement extending the period in which a mining undertaking was granted mineral extraction rights was not a State aid in circumstances where the original grant of extraction rights was not an aid, and where the option of an extension was available to all undertakings even though only one particular undertaking had concluded an extension agreement, and subsequent legislative changes meant that other operators were no longer able to obtain such favourable terms for their mineral extraction rights. Further appeal dismissed, Case C-15/14P *Commission v MOL*, EU:C:2015:362

Fn 138 See also Case T-219/10 *Autogrill España v Commission*, EU:T:2014:939, paras 52 et seq; and Case T-399/11 *Banco Santander v Commission*, EU:T:2014:938, paras 56 et seq, in which the General Court held that tax legislation which provided that 'goodwill' obtained by an undertaking as a result of acquiring a shareholding of at least 5 per cent in a foreign company, should be deductible for corporation tax purposes, was not selective. It was aimed at a particular category of economic transactions, rather than a particular category of undertakings or production, and so applied to all undertakings. On further appeal, Case C-21/15P, not yet decided.

(d) **Distorting competition**

17.024 **Distorting competition.** The General Court held in Case T-58/13 *Club Hotel Loutraki v Commission*, EU:T:2015:1, paras 88–89, that as the Commission is not required to carry out an economic analysis of the actual situation on the relevant markets; of the market share of the recipients of the aid; of the position of competing undertakings; or of trade flows between Member States, when determining whether the measures at issue 'distort' or 'threaten to distort competition' within the meaning of Article 107(1), it is also not required to define the relevant market. It dismissed a complaint that the Commission had found an aid to be compatible with the internal market by assessing two measures jointly, which the appellant argued each referred to two separate markets. On further appeal, Case C-131/15, not yet decided.

(e) Affecting inter-State trade

Effect on trade between Member States.   **17.025**
Fn 156 On 29 April 2015, the Commission took seven decisions finding that measures granting support to purely local operations were outside the scope of Article 107: see SA.37963 *Alleged State aid to Glenmore Lodge*; SA.37432 *Funding to public hospitals in the Hradec Králové Region*; SA.37904 *Alleged State aid to medical centre in Durmersheim*; SA.33149 *Alleged unlawful State aid for the Städtische Projekt "Wirtschaftsbüro Gaarden" – Kiel*; SA.38035 *Alleged aid to a specialised rehabilitation clinic for orthopaedic medicine and trauma surgery*; SA.39403 *Investment in the port of Lauwersoog*; and SA.38208 *Alleged State aid to UK member-owned golf clubs.*

De minimis: **block exemption.**   On 18 December 2013 the Commission adopted   **17.027**
a new *de minimis* aid block exemption Regulation: Commission Regulation 1407/2013, OJ 2013 L352/1 ('the *de minimis* Regulation'). The *de minimis* Regulation replaced Regulation 1998/2006 with effect from 1 January 2014. The main provisions include:

(a) the *de minimis* thresholds under the previous Regulation, of €200,000 per undertaking over a three-year period, or €100,000 for undertakings in the road freight transport sector, have been retained: Article 3 of the *de minimis* Regulation;

(b) the *de minimis* Regulation does not exclude from its scope 'undertakings in difficulty', which are now entitled to receive *de minimis* aid;

(c) greater clarity on aspects of the calculation of *de minimis* aid, in particular aids in the form of loans and guarantees: Article 4 of the *de minimis* Regulation.

The Commission also adopted, on 18 December 2013, a new block exemption for *de minimis* aid in the agricultural sector: Commission Regulation 1408/2013, OJ 2013 L352/9. Regulation 1408/2013 came into effect from 1 January 2014 and has replaced Regulation 1535/2007. Regulation 1408/2013 has raised the *de minimis* threshold in this sector to cover aids not exceeding €15,000 (raised from €7,500) per beneficiary over a period of three years or 1 per cent (previously 0.75 per cent) of the value of the Member State's agricultural output.

17.028   **Calculating the amount of the advantage.**

Fn 172   The General Court in Case T-89/09 *Pollmeier Massivholz v Commission*, EU:T:2015:153, para 169, held that the Commission must apply its State aid in the Form of Guarantees Notice (discussed in paragraph 17.038 of the main text) when quantifying aid in the form of a State guarantee in order to determine whether it is *de minimis*. It dismissed the Commission's argument that, because *de minimis* aid is not notifiable, it must determine first whether it is *de minimis* and only if it is not apply the Notice to quantify the guarantee. On further appeal, Cases 242&246/15P, not yet decided.

Fn 174   See the update to paragraph 17.104, below.

(f)   Particular applications

17.029   **Examples of State aids.**

Fn 195   A new framework for State aid for research and development and innovation ('R&D&I Framework') was published in June 2014, OJ 2014 C198/1. The new R&D&I Framework is applicable from 1 July 2014.

17.030   **Tax measures and levies.**

Fn 201   See also Case T-275/11 *TF1 v Commission*, EU:T:2013:535, in which the General Court held that, although there was a relationship between the State aid provided to a public service broadcaster by way of budgetary grants, and the introduction of two new taxes on advertising and electronic communications respectively, those taxes could not be regarded as an integral part of the aid measure because the revenue from the taxes was not hypothecated to the aid, and it did not impact directly on the amount of aid provided: paras 65 and 81. Similarly, see Joined Cases T-533/10&151/11 *DTS and Telfónica v Commission*, EU:T:2014:629 also concerning a tax which could not be considered integral to the financing measure in favour of a public service broadcaster (on further appeal, Case C-449/14P, not yet decided).

Fn 202   See also Case T-219/10 *Autogrill España v Commission*, EU:T:2014:939, paras 52 et seq; and Case T-399/11 *Banco Santander v Commission*, EU:T:2014:938, paras 56 et seq, in which the General Court held that tax legislation which provided that 'goodwill' obtained by an undertaking as a result of acquiring a shareholding of at least 5 per cent in a foreign company should be deductible for corporation tax purposes, was not selective. It was aimed at a particular category of economic transactions, rather than a particular category of undertakings or production, and so applied to all undertakings. On further appeal, Case C-21/15P *Commission v Banco Santander*, not yet decided.

17.031   **Tax measures: differential taxation.**   On the cancellation, or special rescheduling, of tax debt, see Case C-73/11P *Frucona Košice v Commission*, EU:C:2013:32, [2013] 2 CMLR 719. Although the Court of Justice overturned the General

Court's judgment and remitted the case, it accepted that in principle entering such an arrangement rather than invoking bankruptcy procedures could constitute a State aid, unless the State can demonstrate that a hypothetical 'market economy investor', if owed the same amount of money by that undertaking, would be prepared to do the same in pursuing his own commercial interests. Remitted case not yet decided.

In addition to the measures listed in the main text, the Commission is investigating whether 'tax rulings' by tax authorities, consisting in comfort letters provided to taxpayers as to how tax will be calculated or special tax provisions will be applied, may also constitute a State aid. In particular, it is conducting an enquiry into the tax rulings practices of Member States, which it extended on 17 December 2014 to all Member States: see Press Release IP/14/2742 (17 December 2014). It has opened formal investigations into rulings by the tax authorities of Ireland, the Netherlands and Luxembourg approving transfer pricing arrangements adopted by certain multinational undertakings (Fiat, Apple, Starbucks and Amazon) for allocating taxable profit between subsidiaries located in different countries: SA.38373; SA.38374; SA.38375; and SA.38944; see also Commission Press Releases IP/14/663 (11 June 2014); and IP/14/1105 (7 October 2014). It has adopted a tax transparency package, which includes a proposal for a Directive amending Directive 2011/16 as regards mandatory automatic exchange of information in the field of taxation (COM(2015) 135 final.

Fn 205 The Court of Justice held in Case C-522/13 *Ministerio de Defensa and Navantia v Concello de Ferrol*, EU:C:2014:2262 that an exemption from a property tax for a plot of land that is owned by the State but made available to a State-owned company, which produces goods and services from that plot of land that may be traded between Member States on markets open to competition, may constitute a State aid.

In SA.25338 *Corporate tax exemption of Dutch public enterprises*, decision of 2 May 2013, the Commission formally asked the Netherlands under Article 108(1) to abolish its long-standing exemption of public undertakings from corporation tax, at least insofar as those undertakings engage in economic activities, as defined by EU law (such as publicly owned ports and airports). The Member State accepted the Commission's request: OJ 2013 C204/11.

Fn 210 In SA.33726 *Deferral of payment of the milk levy in Italy*, OJ 2013 L309/40, the Commission found that Italy granted an unlawful State aid by adopting a law that granted milk producers a six-month deferral of the date on which they were due to pay to the Italian Government an instalment in respect of a levy that the State had paid to the EU budget on their behalf. The Commission concluded that the deferment was an unlawful aid, equivalent to an interest-free loan: paras 13, second indent, and 28.

17.033 **Tax measures: objective justification by the logic of the tax system.**   In Case T-379/09 *Italy v Commission*, EU:T:2012:422, the General Court dismissed an argument by Italy that the 'logic of the system' of excise duties on diesel justified the laying down of a rate for diesel used for heating glasshouses that was lower than the rate provided for other users of diesel for agricultural purposes. The fact that diesel duties fell more heavily on glasshouse operators, who use large amounts of diesel, was a natural consequence of applying a tax to that commodity. To the extent that the lower rate was intended to 'level the playing field' between glasshouse growers and outdoor growers, this did not show that the lower rate was not a selective advantage, but was an argument that was relevant (if at all) to whether or not the lower rate was justified such that it might be authorised under Article 107(3).

If a State grants a tax exemption, the fact that there is a system of authorisation in place by which undertakings obtain the benefit of the exemption does not in itself make the tax exemption selective. However, in order to be justified, the degree of latitude granted to the authorities in deciding whether to grant the exemption or not must be limited to verifying whether the undertaking meets the conditions laid down in order to pursue an identifiable tax objective, and the criteria to be applied by those authorities must be inherent in the nature of the tax regime: Case C-6/12 *P Oy*, EU:C:2013:525, [2014] 1 CMLR 403, paras 23–24. The Court did not have sufficient information available to it to assess whether the Finnish tax rules at issue in that case (under which the tax authorities could grant individual authorisations for tax losses to be carried forwards into future tax years, in cases where companies had changed ownership, if special reasons were shown) were justified by the logic of the Finnish taxation scheme.

Fn 220 See also Case T-219/10 *Autogrill España v Commission*, EU:T:2014:939, paras 52 et seq; and Case T-399/11 *Banco Santander v Commission* EU:T:2014:938, paras 56 et seq, in which the General Court held that tax legislation which provided that 'goodwill' obtained by an undertaking as a result of acquiring a shareholding of at least 5 per cent in a foreign company should be deductible for corporation tax purposes, was not selective. It was aimed at a particular category of economic transactions, rather than a particular category of undertakings or production, and so applied to all undertakings. On further appeal, Case C-21/15P *Commission v Banco Santander*, not yet decided.

Fn 222 See also Case T-251/11 *Austria v Commission*, EU:T:2014:1060, paras 111 et seq, in which the General Court held that an exception, for energy-intensive businesses, from an obligation to purchase energy generated from renewable sources could not be justified as remedying distortions of competition.

17.036 **Sale of land and buildings.**   See also SA.26212 *Forest land swaps*, decision of 5 September 2014, OJ 2015 L80/100, paras 138 et seq, in which the Commission concluded that the principles applicable to the sale of land and buildings apply equally to transactions in which they are swapped. It found that a measure which allowed privately owned land to be swapped for publicly-owned forest land was an unlawful State aid, as the system for valuing the land had resulted in a systematic overvaluation of the privately owned land; in both under- and overvaluation of the publicly owned land; and an advantage being conferred on the private party in 80 per cent of the transactions.

Fn 240 On the review by the EU Courts of the Commission's assessments of whether, and to what extent, a sale of land has been at an undervalue, see also, eg Case T-89/09 *Pollmeier Massivholz v Commission*, EU:T:2015:153, paras 191 et seq.

The provision of infrastructure. The Court of Justice in Case C-288/11P **17.037** *Mitteldeutsche Flughafen and Flughafen Leipzig-Halle v Commission*, EU:C:2012:821, [2013] 2 CMLR 483, paras 46 et seq, confirmed that an airport operator's construction of an additional runway at an existing airport could not be divorced from its economic activity of operating a passenger airport, but was to be treated as part of the costs that an airport operator would normally have to bear itself for the purpose of carrying out that activity. The UK Department for Communities and Local Government issued guidance following this judgment (document ERDF-GN-1-010), which is available on the 'ERDF: national guidance' section of the gov.uk website. The provision of public funds for infrastructure projects may, however, avoid constituting State aid if it can be structured in such a way as to exclude the possibility of any net advantage to the recipient: see, for example, the Commission decision in the *German incubators* case, OJ 2005 L295/44.

Fn 244 On 20 February 2014, the Guidelines on financing of airports and start-up aid to airlines departing from regional airports (OJ 2005 C312/01) were replaced by Guidelines on State aid to airports and airlines, OJ 2014 C99/3. The new guidelines do not contain a separate section on airport infrastructure, as did paras 55–67 of the 2005 guidelines referred to in the footnote, and this form of aid will fall to be considered by reference to the general provisions.

State guarantees. **17.038**
Fn 245 See also Case T-487/11 *Banco Privado Português v Commission*, EU:T:2014:1077, para 56.

Fn 246 The General Court's judgment in Case T-154/10 *France v Commission*, EU:T:2012:452, was upheld on appeal: Case C-559/12P *France v Commission*, EU:C:2014:217, [2014] 3 CMLR 903.

Fn 248 The General Court in Case T-89/09 *Pollmeier Massivholz v Commission*, EU:T:2015:153, para 169, held that the Commission must apply its State aid in the Form of Guarantees Notice when quantifying aid in order to determine whether it is *de minimis* (see paragraph 17.027 of the main text). It dismissed the Commission's argument that, because *de minimis* aid is not notifiable, it must first determine whether it is *de minimis* and only if it is not apply the Notice to quantify the guarantee. On further appeal, Cases 242&246/15P, not yet decided.

3. Aids that are Compatible with the Internal Market

17.040 **Article 107(2)(a) Social aids to individual consumers.**
Fn 264 On 18 February 2014 the Commission published new Guidelines on State aid to airports and airlines, OJ 2014 C99/3. The Guidelines entered into force on 4 April 2014, and they replace both the 1994 and 2005 guidelines which had previously applied (Guidelines on the Application of Articles 92 and 93 of the EC Treaty and Article 61 of the EEA Agreement to State aids in the aviation sector (OJ 1994 C350/5); and Communication on Community guidelines on financing of airports and start-up aid to airlines departing from regional airports (OJ 2005 C312/1); respectively). The reference to para 24 of the 1994 guidelines should be read as a reference to para 156 of the new Guidelines.

17.041 **Article 107(2)(b)—Disasters and exceptional occurrences.**
Fn 267 See also Case SA.35482 *Actions urgentes en faveur des populations touchées par les séismes*, decision of 19 December 2012, in which the Commission relied on Article 107(2)(b) to authorise an aid scheme worth €2.66 billion to support the recovery of the Italian agricultural sector from the damage caused by the earthquakes of May 2012.

Fn 273 See also, eg SA.33083 *Aid measures linked to the 1990 earthquake in Sicily and the 1994 floods in Northern Italy*, decision of 14 August 2015, in which the Commission found that measures which reduced the tax liabilities and social security contributions of undertakings in areas affected by natural disasters had benefited undertakings that had suffered no losses (being available to any undertaking within the affected geographical areas), and overcompensated undertakings beyond the losses they had suffered (being available without proof of the extent of any losses suffered): see paras 123 et seq.

4. Aids that may be Compatible with the Internal Market

(a) Generally

17.044 **The exercise of the Commission's discretion.**
Fn 289 See also SA.28599 *Aid for the deployment of digital terrestrial television – Spain*, decision of 19 June 2013; and SA.27408 *DTT roll out in Castilla La Mancha*, decision of 1 October 2014.

Fn 294 The appeal against the General Court's judgment in Joined Cases T-394/08, etc, *Regione autonoma della Sardegna v Commission* [2011] ECR II-6255 was dismissed by the Court of Justice in C-630/11P *HGA v Commission*, EU:C:2013:387.

See also Case SA.33984 *Green Investment Bank*, decision of 17 October 2012, in which the Commission was asked to approve the provision of State resources to establish a bank that would make available sources of credit or investment finance that the market has so far failed to make available for particular categories of projects or borrowers. The Commission authorised the aid to the bank, but did not, at the same time, authorise aids to any of the downstream recipients of the loans and investments that the bank will make, requiring instead that the State aid compatibility of those loans be assessed on a case-by-case basis. In addition, it considered that the arrangements must not be indefinite, but must lapse once a market in the relevant form of loans or investments has been created. Similarly, in SA.36904 *MLB development segment and creation of the Latvian Single Development Institution*, decision of 9 June 2015, the Commission authorised aid to a bank that would make available financing for SMEs and other undertakings facing difficulty in raising finance, while noting that any financing granted which itself falls within Article 107 (in particular, for falling outside the *de minimis* rules) would require to be notified separately.

Operating aid. 17.045
Fn 296 See also, eg Case T-177/10 *Alcoa Trasformazioni v Commission*. EU:T:2014:897, para 92, where a preferential electricity tariff for aluminium smelters, which are very energy intensive, was held to be an operating aid. On further appeal, Case C-604/14P, not yet decided.

(b) Article 107(3)(a)

Guidelines on national regional aid: Article 107(3)(a) and (c). On 19 June 17.048
2013 the Commission adopted new Guidelines on regional State aid for 2014–2020, OJ 2013 C209/1 ('the 2014–2020 Guidelines'). These prolonged the existing Guidelines on National Regional Aid for 2007–2013 until 30 June 2014, after which the new Guidelines came into effect: paras 186 et seq of the 2014–2020 Guidelines. In broad terms, the 2012–2020 Guidelines focus the Commission's resources on the larger regional aid measures, and on aid for investments by larger enterprises in the more developed of the assisted areas.

Areas eligible for regional aid. On 19 June 2013 the Commission adopted 17.050
new Guidelines on regional State aid for 2014–2020, OJ 2013 C209/1 ('the 2014–2020 Guidelines'). These prolonged the existing Guidelines on National Regional Aid for 2007–2013 until 30 June 2014, after which the new Guidelines came into effect: paras 186 et seq of the 2014–2020 Guidelines. The 2014–2020 Guidelines will increase the proportion of the EU population living in areas eligible for regional aid, to 47.2 per cent: para 148 and footnote 52 of the 2014–2020 Guidelines. A safety net is also provided, to ensure that no Member State loses more than 50 per cent of its entitlement under the 2007–2013 Guidelines: paras 163–166 of the 2014–2020 Guidelines.

Disadvantaged regions. On 19 June 2013 the Commission adopted new 17.051
Guidelines on regional State aid for 2014–2020, OJ 2013 C209/1 ('the 2014–2020

Guidelines'). These prolonged the existing Guidelines on National Regional Aid for 2007–2013 until 30 June 2014, after which the new Guidelines came into effect: paras 186 et seq of the 2014–2020 Guidelines.

17.052 **Areas entitled to aid at lower rates under Article 103(3)(c).** On 19 June 2013 the Commission adopted new Guidelines on regional State aid for 2014–2020, OJ 2013 C209/1 ('the 2014–2020 Guidelines'). These prolonged the existing Guidelines on National Regional Aid for 2007–2013 until 30 June 2014, after which the new Guidelines came into effect: paras 186 et seq of the 2014–2020 Guidelines.

17.053 **Other aspects of entitlement to regional aid.** On 19 June 2013 the Commission adopted new Guidelines on regional State aid for 2014–2020, OJ 2013 C209/1 ('the 2014–2020 Guidelines'). These prolonged the existing Guidelines on National Regional Aid for 2007–2013 until 30 June 2014, after which the new Guidelines came into effect: paras 186 et seq of the 2014–2020 Guidelines.

(c) **Article 107(3)(b)**

17.056 **Article 107(3)(b): aid to remedy a serious disturbance or for an important project.** On 20 June 2014 the Commission published a Communication on the criteria for the analysis of the compatibility with the internal market of State aid to promote the execution of important projects of common European interest, OJ 2014 C188/4. The Communication sets out the criteria that the Commission will use to assess whether a particular project is eligible for the application of Article 107(3)(b) and explains the Commission's approach to the assessment of State aid for such projects. The Communication will apply from 1 July 2014 until 31 December 2020.

17.057 **Temporary measures following the 2008 financial crisis.** The General Court has considered several cases on Article 107(3)(b), following the 2008 financial crisis and the Commission's various communications on the application of the State aid rules to measures adopted in response to the crisis.

In Case T-391/11 *ABN Amro v Commission*, EU:T:2014:186, the General Court considered a Commission decision that the Dutch State granted a State aid by acquiring certain of ABN Amro's subsidiaries, but that the aid was compatible with the internal market subject to the imposition of conditions. The conditions include a prohibition on ABN Amro making any further acquisitions (other than of a specified type and specified size), for a period of three years, extended to five years if the Dutch State continues to own more than 50 per cent of ABN Amro at the end of the three-year period. The General Court dismissed the appeal against the scope and duration of that prohibition, which it held was consistent with the Commission's communications and with the principle of proportionality. The objective of the prohibition was to ensure that the aid granted was the minimum necessary to restore a bank to financial viability, and to avoid distortions of competition.

In Case T-457/09 *Westfälisch-Lippischer Sparkassen- und Giroverband v Commission*, EU:T:2014:683, paras 196 et seq, the General Court confirmed that the Rescue Guidelines (OJ 2004 C244/2) (discussed in paragraph 17.064 et seq of the main text) can be applied in circumstances where a firm is in difficulty as a result of a serious disturbance in the economy, provided it meets the definition of being 'in difficulty'. The Court dismissed a complaint that the Commission erred in considering the Rescue Guidelines when determining whether Article 107(3)(b) was met.

In Case T-487/11 *Banco Privado Português v Commission*, EU:T:2014:1077 the General Court upheld a decision requiring Portugal to recover aid granted pursuant to a guarantee it had provided following the 2008 financial crisis. Although the Commission had granted a provisional and urgent authorisation of the guarantee in March 2009, in accordance with the Rescue Guidelines, that authorisation was subject to the State submitting a restructuring plan for the bank within six months. That condition was not met, and the aid was extended beyond the six-month period, and the Commission was therefore justified in concluding in 2010 that the aid did not meet Article 107(3)(b).

On 3 February 2015 the Commission published a policy brief 'State aid to European banks: returning to viability', evaluating the effectiveness of the restructuring measures adopted in the aftermath of the 2008 financial crisis.

Fn 325 The most recent overview of national State aid measures adopted in response to the financial and economic crisis is Commission MEMO/13/337 (16 April 2013).

(d) Article 107(3)(c)

Article 107(3)(c): aid for development of certain economic activities or areas.   **17.058**

Fn 329 The framework that the Commission uses to assess the compatibility of an aid with the internal market, under Article 107(3)(c), does not have to be the same as that used to assess whether the measure should be categorised as an aid under Article 107(1): Case T-385/12 *Orange v Commission*, EU:T:2015:117, paras 88–89. On further appeal, Case C-211/15P, not yet decided.

Guidelines and rules on sectoral aid.   **17.062**

Fn 348 Following the expiry of the Commission Communication on certain legal aspects relating to cinematographic and other audiovisual works, OJ 2002 C43/6, on 13 November 2013 the Commission adopted a new Communication on State aid for films and other audiovisual works: OJ 2013 C332/1. On 12 September 2014 it published 'State aid rules for films and other audiovisual works' (2014) 13 Competition Policy Brief.

Fn 349 On 26 January 2013 the Commission published new EU Guidelines for the application of State aid rules in relation to the rapid deployment of broadband networks: OJ 2013 C25/1. The new guidelines came into force from 27 January 2013, and will be applied to all decisions taken after that date in respect of notified aid, including aids granted and notified prior to that date, and in respect of unlawful aid granted after that date: paras 87–88 of the Guidelines. The 2009 guidelines will still apply to unlawful aid granted while they were in force.

On 8 May 2014 the Commission published a handbook on the application of the State aid rules to broadband deployments: 'Handbook for decision makers – the broadband State aid rules explained': see Commission Press Release IP/14/535 (8 May 2014). On 24 September 2014 it published a 'Guide to High-Speed Broadband Investment'.

Fn 350 For an example of a case in which the Protocol was considered by the General Court, see Case T-520/09 *TF1 v Commission*, EU:T:2012:352.

Fn 354 The Framework on State aid for shipbuilding, OJ 2011 C364/9, was extended until 30 June 2014: Communication from the Commission concerning the prolongation of the application of the Framework on State aid to shipbuilding, OJ 2013 C357/1. Since 1 July 2014, shipbuilding has been covered by the Guidelines on regional State aid for 2014–2020, OJ 2013 C209/1.

Fn 356 On 1 July 2014 the Commission published new Guidelines for State aid in the agricultural and forestry sectors and in rural areas 2014 to 2020: OJ 2014 C204/1. At the same time, the Commission also published a new block exemption regulation for State aid in the agricultural and forestry sectors and in rural areas: Commission Regulation 702/2014, OJ 2014 L193/1. The Regulation entered into force on 1 July 2014, replacing Regulation 1857/2006, and will apply until 31 December 2020.

Fn 358 On 18 February 2014 the Commission published new Guidelines on State aid to airports and airlines, OJ 2014 C99/3. The Guidelines entered into force on 4 April 2014, and they replace both the 1994 and 2005 guidelines which had previously applied (Guidelines on the Application of Articles 92 and 93 of the EC Treaty and Article 61 of the EEA Agreement to State aids in the aviation sector (OJ 1994 C350/5); and Communication on Community guidelines on financing of airports and start-up aid to airlines departing from regional airports (OJ 2005 C312/1); respectively). The new Guidelines set out the conditions for assessing the compatibility of investment aid for airports, operating aid for airports, and start-up aid for airlines for new routes, with the State aid rules. In relation to operating aid, the possibility of authorising operating aid for airports with fewer than 3 million passengers a year is preserved for a 'transitional period' of 10 years from the date of publication of the Guidelines: see Section 5.1.2 of the new Guidelines. See also 'New State aid rules for a competitive aviation industry' (2014) 2 Competition Policy Brief.

The Commission has not proposed any amendments to the 2004 Guidelines on State aid to maritime transport.

Guidelines on horizontal aid.   **17.063**
Fn 361 A new framework for State aid for research and development and innovation ('R&D&I Framework') was published in June 2014, OJ 2014 C198/1. The new R&D&I Framework applies from 1 July 2014.

Fn 362 New Guidelines on State aid for environmental protection and energy were adopted in April 2014: OJ 2014 C200/1. The new Guidelines apply from 1 July 2014 to 31 December 2020, and cover a number of situations that were not specifically addressed in the 2008 guidelines, OJ 2008 C82/1, such as aid to energy infrastructure projects, generation adequacy measures, and support for energy intensive users (so as to mitigate the burdens on them of environmental levies or measures increasing the price of electricity). They also set out a framework for aid to renewable electricity.

For an example of the application of the guidelines in practice, see Case T-251/11 *Austria v Commission*, EU:T:2014:1060, para 183, in which the General Court upheld a Commission decision finding that the requirements set out in the guidelines were not met in respect of an exception, for energy-intensive businesses, from an obligation to purchase energy generated from renewable sources.

Fn 365 In January 2014 the Commission published new Guidelines on State aid to promote risk finance investments, OJ 2014 C19/4. The Guidelines replace the Risk Capital Guidelines, OJ 2006 C194/2, and will apply to the assessment of all risk finance aid awarded from 1 July 2014 until 31 December 2020. The purpose of the Guidelines is to set out principles for the assessment of risk finance measures which do not satisfy all the conditions laid down in the General Block Exemption Regulation.

Fn 369 In December 2012 the Commission published a new Communication on Short-term Export-credit Insurance: OJ 2012 C392/1. This Communication replaces the previous Communication and applies from 1 January 2013 until 31 December 2018.

Aid for rescuing and restructuring firms in difficulty.   The General Court held   **17.064**
that the Rescue Guidelines (OJ 2004 C244/2) can be applied in circumstances where a firm is in difficulty as a result of a serious disturbance in the economy, provided it meets the definition of being 'in difficulty': Case T-457/09 *Westfälisch-Lippischer Sparkassen- und Giroverband v Commission*, EU:T:2014:683, paras 196 et seq. The Court dismissed a complaint that the Commission erred in considering the Rescue Guidelines when determining whether Article 107(3)(b) was met (discussed in paragraph 17.057 of the main text).

On 9 July 2014 the Commission adopted new Guidelines on State aid for rescuing and restructuring non-financial undertakings in difficulty, OJ 2014 C249/1 ('the Revised Rescue Guidelines'). The Revised Rescue Guidelines, which entered into force on 1 August 2014, introduce the concept of 'temporary restructuring support', which enables loans and guarantees to be granted to SMEs for up to 18 months on simplified terms: see Section 2.3 of the Revised Rescue Guidelines. Like the previous Rescue Guidelines, the Revised Rescue Guidelines require Member States granting rescue or restructuring aid to demonstrate that the aid is needed to prevent hardship or address market failure by restoring the long-term viability of the undertaking concerned. They also require investors in an aid beneficiary to pay a fair share of the costs of the undertaking's restructuring. See also 'New rules on rescue and restructuring aid for industry: the right incentives for innovation and growth' (2014) 9 EU Competition Policy Brief.

Fn 370 The Revised Rescue Guidelines apply to all firms except those in the coal or steel sectors, or those covered by specific rules for financial institutions, without prejudice to any sector-specific rules relating to undertakings in difficulty in a particular sector: para 18 of the Revised Rescue Guidelines.

Fn 371 The reference to para 4 of the Rescue Guidelines should be read as a reference to para 6 of the Revised Rescue Guidelines.

Fn 372 The reference to para 9 of the Rescue Guidelines should be read as a reference to para 20 of the Revised Rescue Guidelines. For an example of the application of this provision, see Case T-209/11 *MB System v Commission*, EU:T:2013:338.

Fn 373 The reference to Chapter 4, and in particular para 79, of the Rescue Guidelines should be read as a reference to Chapter 6, and in particular paras 104–106, of the Revised Rescue Guidelines.

17.065 **Distinction between rescue and restructuring aid.** On 9 July 2014 the Commission adopted new Guidelines on State aid for rescuing and restructuring non-financial undertakings in difficulty, OJ 2014 C249/1 ('the Revised Rescue Guidelines'); see the update to paragraph 17.064, above.

On the requirement that rescue aid must be granted only for a period of six months, and be of a temporary and reversible nature, see Case T-487/11 *Banco Privado Português v Commission*, EU:T:2014:1077 in which the General Court upheld a decision requiring Portugal to recover aid granted pursuant to a guarantee it had provided following the 2008 financial crisis. Although the Commission had granted a provisional and urgent authorisation of the guarantee in March 2009, that authorisation was subject to the State submitting a restructuring plan for the bank within six months. That condition was not met, and the aid was extended beyond the six-month period without the Commission being notified. The General Court held that the Commission was therefore justified in concluding in 2010 that the aid did not meet Article 107(3)(b), and it did not breach Article 108(2) by requiring that the aid should be recovered. In particular, the Court held that the requirement that rescue aid should be temporary and reversible means that 'any advantage granted provisionally by means of rescue aid, in any form whatsoever, must be repaid if the conditions for authorisation to which its provisional grant is subject are not or are no longer met': para 102. In a parallel reference made to the Court of Justice for a preliminary ruling, by the Portuguese national court, the Court likewise confirmed, in Case C-667/13 *Estado português v Banco Privado Português*, EU:C:2015:151, para 74, that the temporal limitation on rescue aid and the obligation to notify the Commission of subsequent extensions are necessary conditions for aid to be declared compatible with the internal market and not mere procedural requirements.

Fn 374 The reference to para 25(b) of the Rescue Guidelines should be read as a reference to para 44 of the Revised Rescue Guidelines, which clarify that the aid can be approved only where it is the failure of the beneficiary that would be likely to involve serious social hardship or severe market failure.

Fn 375 The reference to para 15 of the Rescue Guidelines should be read as a reference to para 55 of the Revised Rescue Guidelines.

Fn 376 The reference to para 30 of the Rescue Guidelines should be read as a reference to para 121 of the Revised Rescue Guidelines.

Fn 377 The reference to para 16 of the Rescue Guidelines should be read as a reference to para 45 of the Revised Rescue Guidelines.

For an example of a Commission decision finding restructuring aid to be unlawful, see SA.35888, SA.37220 and SA.38225 *Restructuring aid for Cyprus Airways*, decision of 9 January 2015. The Commission concluded that the assumptions in the restructuring plan were not sufficiently prudent; that the plan did not address the circumstances that led to the undertaking's difficulties; that the proposed contribution by the undertaking did not meet the requisite threshold; and that there were no exceptional circumstances that justified the payment of a second restructuring aid within a ten-year period (aid having previously been given in 2007).

Fn 378 The reference to para 16 of the Rescue Guidelines should be read as a reference to para 45 of the Revised Rescue Guidelines.

Fn 379 The reference to para 31 of the Rescue Guidelines should be read as a reference to Section 3.6.2 of the Revised Rescue Guidelines.

Other conditions for rescue and restructuring aid. On 9 July 2014 the **17.066** Commission adopted new Guidelines on State aid for rescuing and restructuring non-financial undertakings in difficulty, OJ 2014 C249/1 ('the Revised Rescue Guidelines'); see the update to paragraph 17.064, above.

Fn 380 The reference to paras 43–44 of the Rescue Guidelines should be read as a reference to paras 64 and 111 of the Revised Rescue Guidelines.

Fn 382 The reference to paras 38–39 of the Rescue Guidelines should be read as a reference to paras 77–82 of the Revised Rescue Guidelines.

Fn 383 The reference to Section 3.3 (paras 72–73) of the Rescue Guidelines should be read as a reference to Section 3.6 (paras 70–71) of the Revised Rescue Guidelines.

Fn 384 The reference to para 12 of the Rescue Guidelines should be read as a reference to para 21 of the Revised Rescue Guidelines.

Fn 386 The reference to Section 3.2.4 (paras 55–56) of the Rescue Guidelines should be read as a reference to Chapter 4 (paras 97–98) of the Revised Rescue Guidelines.

(f) Aid authorised by the Council

17.068 **Authorisation by the Council: Article 107(3)(e).**
Fn 394 The appeal in Case C-167/11P *Cantierenavale De Poli v Commission*, was dismissed by Order of 22 March 2012. The appeal in Case C-200/11P *Italy v Commission*, was also dismissed by Order of 22 March 2012.

Fn 395 See also Council Decision 2010/787 on State aid to facilitate the closure of uncompetitive coal mines; and the Commission's decision in SA.39570 *Closure of the Paskov mine*, decision of 12 February 2015, approving a measure by which the Czech Republic contributed to the funding of workers' severance payments and to payments for those who had been exposed to occupational health risks.

17.069 **Authorisation by the Council: Article 108(2).** A decision of the Council to authorise a specific measure does not oust the power of the Commission to examine whether or not that measure constitutes State aid to its beneficiaries, if that decision is not taken pursuant to Article 108(2): see Case C-272/12P *Commission v Ireland*, EU:C:2013:812, [2014] 2 CMLR 895, at paras 49–50, in which the General Court held that the Council's authorisation of certain Member States' excise duty exemptions, pursuant to its powers under EU legislation harmonising such duties, did not preclude the Commission from subsequently examining whether or not those exemptions constituted State aid to the undertakings that benefited from them.

Fn 401 The breadth of the Council's discretion to authorise aids under Article 108(2) was also considered in Cases C-111/10, etc, *Commission v Council*, EU:C:2013:785, in which the Court of Justice held that the Council did not exceed the boundaries of its powers by authorising aids that Poland, Hungary, Lithuania and Latvia had previously agreed with the Commission they would bring to an end after a fixed period, in circumstances where the aids were granted under a new aid scheme and were assessed by the Council following a lapse of time since the Commission had considered the previous schemes.

17.070 **The Enabling Regulation, and the General Block Exemption Regulation.** On 22 July 2013, the Council adopted Regulation 733/2013, amending Regulation

994/98 (the Enabling Regulation): OJ 2013 L217/28. The amended Regulation increases the Commission's power to adopt block exemption regulations, so as to cover additional categories of aid including:

(a) culture and heritage conservation;
(b) making good the damage caused by natural disasters;
(c) making good the damage caused by certain adverse weather conditions in fisheries;
(d) forestry;
(e) the promotion of certain food products;
(f) conservation of marine and freshwater biological resources;
(g) sports;
(h) residents of remote regions for transport, when such aid has a social character and does not discriminate as to the identity of the carrier;
(i) certain broadband infrastructure;
(j) infrastructure in support of the objectives listed in the amended Regulation and in support of other objectives of common interest, in particular the Europe 2020 objectives.

These new categories of aid are areas where the Commission has acquired solid case experience and where there is limited potential distortion of competition: see Press Release IP/13/728 (23 July 2013).

On 17 June 2014, following the expansion in Regulation 733/2013 of the list of categories of aid which the Commission has power to exempt, the Commission adopted a new General Block Exemption Regulation ('the Revised GBER'): Regulation 651/2014, OJ 2014 L187/1. The Revised GBER entered into force on 1 July 2014 and will apply until 31 December 2020. The Revised GBER extends the categories of aid covered, to include:

(a) aid to make good the damage caused by certain natural disasters;
(b) social aid for transport for residents of remote regions;
(c) aid for broadband infrastructures
(d) aid for culture and heritage conservation;
(e) aid for sport and multifunctional recreational infrastructures; and
(f) aid for local infrastructures: Article 1(g)–1(l) of the Revised GBER.

It also widens the scope of the categories that were already covered by the previous GBER (Regulation 800/2008, OJ 2008 L214/3), which it replaces, in particular by increasing the relevant value thresholds below which notification is not required: Article 4 of the Revised GBER.

The Commission has also adopted a new block exemption regulation for State aid in the agricultural and forestry sectors and in rural areas: Commission Regulation 702/2014, OJ 2014 L193/1. The Regulation entered into force on 1 July 2014, replacing Regulation 1857/2006, and will apply until 31 December 2020.

Fn 404 In September 2012 the Commission published detailed guidance on the practical application of the General Block Exemption Regulation, in the form of answers to 'frequently asked questions', which is available in the State Aid section of the DG Comp website.

(g) Article 106(2)

17.071 **Exemptions for services of general economic interest: Article 106(2).** Although Member States have a broad discretion as to which services they recognise as services of general economic interest (SGEI), the General Court held in Case T-79/10 *Colt Télécommunications France v Commission*, EU:T:2013:463 that they must nonetheless be able to demonstrate the justification for considering the service in question a SGEI, and that there is a market failure justifying State intervention (ie that the service would otherwise either not be provided at all, or would not be provided under the same conditions as respects price or quality): paras 119–120 and 149 et seq. Further, in Joined Cases T-533/10&151/11 *DTS and Telfónica v Commission*, EU:T:2014:629, at paras 152 et seq the General Court held that the aid must not have a substantial effect on trade and competition, which is disproportionate to the objectives pursued by the Member State (on further appeal, Case C-449/14P, not yet decided). See also Case T-57/11 *Castelnou Energía v Commission*, EU:T:2014:1021, paras 147 et seq.

The General Court held in Case T-57/11 *Castelnou Energía v Commission*, EU:T:2014:1021, paras 187 et seq, that if a measure falls within Article 106(2), and does not pursue environmental protection objectives, the Commission does not have to assess the compatibility of the measure with EU environmental rules. To do so would encroach on the Member States' discretion to identify the services they will regard as SGEIs.

For a further example of a case in which the General Court found that the Commission did not have sufficient information to approve aid under Article 106(2) without opening a formal investigation, see Case T-137/10 *Coordination bruxelloise d'Institutions sociales et de santé ('CBI') v Commission*, EU:T:2012:584, in which the General Court annulled the Commission decision in Case NN54/2009 approving aid to public hospitals in Belgium.

Fn 408 See also, eg Joined Cases T-295&309/12 *Germany v Commission*, EU:T:2014:675, at paras 47–53, in which the General Court held that in the absence of EU measures harmonising the service considered to be an SGEI, the Commission's power to review a Member State's decision that that service is an SGEI is limited to determining whether there has been a manifest error of assessment. On further appeal, Case C-446/14P, not yet decided.

17.072 **Relationship between Article 106(2) and the *Altmark* criteria.**
Fn 415 For a recent example of an aid that did not satisfy the *Altmark* criteria, as it had not been shown in particular that the costs for which the recipient was being

compensated were those of an efficient undertaking, see SA.38788 *Compensation to Post Office Limited for costs incurred in providing SGEIs 2015-2018*, decision of 19 March 2015, para 68.

SGEI Communication, Article 106(2) Framework and Article 106(2) **17.073**
Decision. On the requirement that there must be mechanisms for ensuring that the undertaking is not over-compensated, see for example SA.33037 *Retroactive compensation of SIMET SpA for public transport services provided between 1987 and 2003*, OJ 2014 L114/48, in which the Commission found the provision of monetary compensation to a bus service operator could not be regarded as permissible compensation for carrying out an SGEI as (a) the parameters for calculating the amount of the compensation were not established in advance: paras 94 and 126; and (b) the possibility of over-compensation could not be ruled out, as it was not possible to establish the net costs of providing the services because the operator was not implementing a separate accounting method capable of identifying those costs: para 128. In contrast, see SA.38788 *Compensation to Post Office Limited for costs incurred in providing SGEIs 2015-2018*, decision of 19 March 2015, paras 111 et seq, in which the Commission found that the provision of compensation to a provider of universal postal services did not exceed the net cost of delivering the services, and that the Member State had adopted strict safeguards to avoid overcompensation.

Fn 417 The Commission issued a Staff Working Document, in April 2013 (SWD(2013) 53/final 2, *'Guide to the application of the European Union rules on state aid, public procurement and the internal market to services of general economic interest, and in particular to social services of general interest'*, which is available on the State Aid section of the DG Comp website.

Fn 420 See, eg SA.23008 *Alleged State aid to SZP and VZP (Slovak health insurance)*, decision of 15 October 2014. The Commission concluded, following a formal investigation, that the Slovak compulsory health insurance system is non-economic in nature, and that State-owned insurers could not be considered to be undertakings within Article 107. On appeal, Case T-216/15, not yet decided.

Fn 421 See also Case SA.33989 *Poste Italiane*, decision of 21 November 2012.

5. Supervision under Article 108

Procedures under Article 108 and Regulation 659/1999. On 22 July 2013, **17.075**
the Council adopted Regulation 734/2013, amending Regulation 659/99 (the Procedural Regulation): OJ 2013 L204/15. The main amendments include:

(a) Powers for the Commission to request information from Member States other than the notifying Member State, or from an undertaking or association of undertakings, in circumstances where the information provided to it by the notifying Member State is not sufficient: Article 6a of Regulation 659/99 as amended.

(b) Where the Commission requests information from an undertaking or association of undertakings, the power to impose fines and periodic penalty payments for the provision of incorrect or misleading information: Article 6b of Regulation 659/99 as amended.

(c) Clarification of the process for submitting a complaint to the Commission, in particular to provide that the Commission shall notify a complainant if it reaches the view that the facts and law put forward do not provide sufficient grounds to show, on the basis of a *prima facie* examination, the existence of unlawful aid or misuse of aid. The complainant is then to be provided with a period in which it may provide further comments. If it does not receive further comments, the Commission may treat the complaint as withdrawn: Article 20(2) of Regulation 659/99 as amended.

(d) Power for the Commission to conduct sector inquiries in the same way as in Article 101/102 cases: Article 20a of Regulation 659/99 as amended (see paragraph 13.021 and the update thereto on sector inquiries).

(e) Power for the Commission to transmit information in its possession, or opinions, to national courts in the same way as it does under Article 15 of Regulation 1/2003 in Article 101/102 cases: Article 23a of Regulation 659/99 as amended (see paragraph 15.047, and the update thereto on Article 15 of Regulation 1/2003).

The references in the main text to the Regulation 659/99 (the Procedural Regulation) will not be altered by the amendments, save where otherwise indicated in the update to the relevant paragraph.

As part of the procedural reforms, the Commission has adopted a mandatory complaints form that persons wishing to submit a complaint regarding alleged unlawful State aid must use: see Press Release IP/14/404 (9 April 2014). The form is available on the DGCOMP website, and is designed to assist the Commission in obtaining the basic information that it needs to be able to make an initial assessment of the complaint. Completion of the form is made mandatory by Commission Regulation 372/2014, OJ 2014 L109/14, which amended Regulation 794/2004. As well as requiring completion of the form, the amendments also make it a requirement for any person submitting a complaint to demonstrate that they are an 'interested party' as defined in Article 1(h) of Regulation 659/1999 (ie a Member State or an individual, undertaking or association of undertakings whose interests might be affected by the alleged unlawful State aid). A complainant or any other person submitting information to the Commission in connection with a State aid complaint or investigation must indicate which information they consider to be confidential and the reasons for such confidentiality, and provide a non-confidential version.

The Commission has issued a Staff Working Document, in May 2014, (SWD(2014) 179 final) *'Common methodology for State aid evaluation'*, which explains the principles by reference to which *ex post* evaluations of aid are to be carried out, where they are required. Such evaluations are now required in respect of certain large aid schemes under the Revised GBER (discussed in the update to paragraph 17.070, above); and certain schemes under the revised guidelines on broadband; and aviation (see the updates to paragraph 17.062, above); regional aid (see the update to paragraph 17.048 et seq, above); risk finance; research, development and innovation; and environment and energy (see the updates to paragraph 17.063, above). See also 'State aid evaluation' (2014) 7 EU Competition Policy Brief.

On 29 April 2015, the Commission opened its first sector inquiry using its new powers. It is investigating measures adopted by Member States to ensure that adequate capacity to produce electricity is available at all times, in order to avoid blackouts: see Press Release IP/15/4891 (29 April 2015).

Concept of an existing aid. **17.076**
Fn 431 With regard to the 10 Member States that acceded to the EU on 1 May 2004, and the Accession Treaty which provides that certain aid measures are to be regarded as existing aid from the date of accession, the Court of Justice has confirmed that any aid measures granted before the date of accession and continuing after that date which do not fall within any of the categories of 'existing aids', as defined in the Accession Treaty, are to be treated as new aids (as though they had been granted on the date of accession): Case C-672/13 *OTP Bank v Magyar Állam*, EU:C:2015:185, paras 60 et seq.

Fn 439 In Case T-542/11 *Alouminion v Commission*, EU:T:2014:859 the General Court annulled a Commission decision which had concluded that interim measures granted by a national court, suspending temporarily a purported termination of a contract under which existing aid had been granted, amounted to a new aid. The national court's judgment did not have either the purpose or effect of altering the substance of the existing aid, but merely ruled on an interim basis that the effects of the purported termination of the contract were to be suspended. On further appeal, Case C-590/14P, not yet decided.

In Case T-291/11 *Portovesme v Commission*, EU:T:2014:896, paras 114 et seq, the General Court upheld the Commission's conclusion that a new aid was granted in circumstances where a preferential electricity tariff previously granted by an energy supplier was placed on a legislative footing and subsidised by the State. On further appeal, Case 606/14P, not yet decided.

(b) Notification of new aids

Time limit for review of new aid. Where a Member State has failed to notify the **17.084**
Commission of a new aid, there is no time limit applicable to the Commission's

review. However, where a complaint is submitted by a third party regarding an alleged aid, the Commission must conduct a diligent and impartial examination of the complaints in the interests of sound administration of the fundamental rules of the Treaty relating to State aid: eg Case T-512/11 *Ryanair v Commission*, EU:T:2014:989, para 68. In that case, the General Court observed that a period of 24 months 'considerably exceed[ed] the period normally required for a preliminary investigation': para 71.

Fn 475 The General Court judgment in Case T-79/10 *Colt Télécommunications France v Commission*, EU:T:2013:463, illustrates that the time taken by a Member State to submit a complete notification can impact significantly on the time taken by the Commission to review a new aid. In that case, France had notified the proposed aid measure in June 2008, but subsequently the Commission sent further information requests and it was not until France provided supplementary information in August 2009 that the Commission considered the notification to be complete. The Commission reached its decision within two months of that date. On appeal, the General Court held that the Commission's preliminary examination only commenced once it received the completed notification in August 2009 (para 50), and that it had therefore been completed within the required timeframe. The General Court also rejected a complaint that the length of the discussions between the Commission and France meant that the Commission should have opened a formal investigation under Article 108(2). The Commission enjoys a certain margin of discretion in determining whether or not a case presents 'serious difficulties' for the purposes of Article 108(2), and the mere fact that the Commission had initiated a dialogue with the French State does not in itself indicate there are such difficulties, nor did the number of requests sent by the Commission: paras 55–56 and 59. The Court did note that the content of discussions between the Commission and the notifying Member State during this phase of the proceedings may, in certain circumstances, reveal such difficulties: para 58. It found, however, that the content of the discussions in this case did not do so.

17.086 **Preliminary examination of a notification.** In Case C-646/11P *Falles Fagligt Forbund (3F) v Commission*, EU:C:2013:36, at para 32, the Court of Justice held that the fact that the Commission's preliminary examination has been of longer duration than two months is an indicator that the Commission may have had serious doubts as to the compatibility of the aid, but is not, of itself, sufficient to lead to a conclusion that the Commission was required to open the formal investigation procedure.

The Commission may enter into a dialogue as part of its preliminary examination of the aid in order to endeavour to overcome any difficulties encountered. By implication, the Commission may conclude that there is no State aid following that dialogue and the receipt of commitments to modify the aid. The fact that the Member State offered commitments to modify the aid should not be interpreted as meaning that the Commission had serious doubts about its compatibility with the internal market and should therefore have opened a formal investigation: Case T-58/13 *Club Hotel Loutraki v Commission*, EU:T:2015:1, paras 41–44. On further appeal, Case C-131/15, not yet decided.

Fn 482 See also Case T-79/10 *Colt Télécommunications France v Commission*, EU:T:2013:463, discussed in the update to paragraph 17.084 and footnote 475, above.

(c) The formal investigation procedure under Article 108(2)

Final decision under Article 108(2).   **17.091**
Fn 510 The Court of Justice in Case C-288/11 *Mitteldeutsche Flughafen and Flughafen Leipzig-Halle v Commission*, EU:C:2012:821, [2013] 2 CMLR 483, dismissed the appeal against the General Court's judgment in Cases T-443&455/08 *Freistaat Sachsen and Land Sachsen-Anhalt v Commission*, [2011] ECR II-1311.

Conditional positive decisions.   **17.092**
Fn 511 The Court of Justice dismissed the appeal in Case C-287/12P *Ryanair v Commission*, EU:C:2013:395, [2013] CMLR 1348 against the General Court's judgment in Case T-123/09 *Ryanair v Commission*, EU:T:2012:164 (upholding the General Court's conclusion that the Commission had not given a condition clearance decision: see paras 67 et seq).

Article 109. A further example of legislation is Regulation 1370/2007 of the **17.096** European Parliament and of the Council on public passenger transport services by rail and by road, OJ 2007 L315/1, which repealed Council Regulations 1191/69 and 1107/70. In relation to the application of those particular Regulations, see Cases C-516/12, etc, *Compagnia Trasporti Pubblici (CTP) v Regione Campania*, EU:C:2014:220.

7. Unlawful Aid and Misuse of Aid

In general.   **17.097**
Fn 532 Complaints must be submitted on a mandatory form: see the update to paragraph 17.075, above.

Request for information and information injunction. On 22 July 2013, **17.100** the Council adopted Regulation 734/2013, amending Regulation 659/99 (the Procedural Regulation): OJ 2013 L204/15. The amendments include, in particular, an expansion of the Commission's power to request information from other sources: see the update to paragraph 17.075, above.

Fn 543 For an example of a challenge to an information injunction, see Case T-570/08 *RENV Deutsche Post v Commission*, EU:T:2013:589. The Commission has recently issued information injunctions to Estonia and Poland in connection with its enquiry into Member States' tax rulings practices (see the update to paragraph 17.031, above): see Press Release IP/15/5140 (8 June 2015).

17.104 **Recovery decision.** If the Commission does attempt to quantify the amount of aid to be recovered, it must assess the actual value of the benefit received from the aid by the beneficiary as accurately as possible. This will not necessarily be the same as the full value of the unlawful aid. In Case T-473/12 *Aer Lingus v Commission*, EU:T:2015:78, paras 97 et seq the General Court held that in circumstances where the unlawful aid consisted of a differential charge to excise duty, and the excise duty was intended to be passed on to the beneficiary's customers, it could not be assumed that the benefit received is equal to the difference between the charge to which the beneficiary has been subject, and the charge to which other undertakings have been subject. Rather, the benefit is the possibility, for the beneficiary, of offering more attractive prices as a result of being subject to the lower charges, and thereby increasing its turnover. It was therefore necessary in that case to determine the extent to which the charge, and the economic benefit of being charged at a lower rate, was passed on by the beneficiary to its customers in order to identify the economic benefit it had enjoyed. On further appeal, Case 164/15P, not yet decided.

Fn 557 As to the extent to which the Commission's decision and other statements of position are binding on the national authorities when calculating the amount to be recovered from each beneficiary of an aid measure, see Case C-69/13 *Mediaset v Ministero dello Sviluppo economico*, EU:C:2014:71, [2014] 3 CMLR 169, discussed in the update to paragraph 17.116, below.

On the Commission's methods for calculating the amount of the unlawful advantage, in the context of a recovery decision, see the update to the main paragraph, above.

Fn 558 The appeal, on other grounds, against the General Court's judgment in Cases T-394/08, etc, *Regione autonomadella Sardegna v Commission* [2011] ECR II-6255 was dismissed by the Court of Justice in C-630/11P *HGA v Commission*, EU:C:2013:387.

17.105 **Recovery where recipient's assets have been sold.** It is also necessary to determine whether there is economic continuity between the recipient and the purchaser, such that recovery could be sought from the purchaser. See, eg SA.315501 *Nürburgring*, decision of 1 October 2014, paras 231 et seq; and SA.35546 *Restructuring aid to Viana shipyards*, decision of 7 May 2015, paras 146 et seq.

17.106 **Interest and tax.** In Case C-89/14 *A2A v Agenzia delle Entrate*, EU:C:2015:537, the Court of Justice ruled that a Member State can apply compound interest in a recovery measure, in circumstances where the Commission decision finding that the State aid was unlawful was taken prior to the adoption of the Implementing Regulation, but the recovery measure was taken after.

Defences open to the Member State: absolute impossibility. In Case C-63/14 **17.109** *France v Commission*, EU:C:2015:458, paras 52 et seq, the Court of Justice held that where recovering an unlawful aid might lead to social unrest, and jeopardise public order, a Member State can rely upon a defence of absolute impossibility only where it could not cope with the consequences of that unrest using all the means at its disposal. The Court dismissed an argument by France that, if it were to seek to recover aid unlawfully paid to the shipping company, SNCM, it would lead to the undertaking being liquidated, to strikes, and to the port of Marseille being blocked for a long period, impacting upon public order and on the region's economy.

In Case SA.20829 *Scheme concerning the municipal real estate tax exemption granted to real estate used by non commercial entities for specific purposes*, decision of 19 December 2012, OJ 2013 L166/24, at paras 191 et seq, the Commission accepted that recovery may be impossible where there are significant difficulties in quantifying how much aid has been paid. It accepted that it would be impossible to recover aid granted by way of exemptions from municipal real estate taxes, where those exemptions had been found to be incompatible with State aid rules but only insofar as the relevant land/building was used for economic activities, because of the difficulties in assessing retrospectively the proportion of each property that was used for economic activities. Similarly, in SA.33083 *Aid measures linked to the 1990 earthquake in Sicily and the 1994 floods in Northern Italy*, decision of 14 August 2015, at paras 148 et seq, the Commission accepted that recovery would be impossible where the unlawful aid was granted in response to natural disasters that occurred more than 10 years ago, and national law does not require undertakings to retain business and accounting records for more than 10 years.

If the recipient of the aid has gone into liquidation and its assets have been sold, it is also necessary to determine whether there is economic continuity between the recipient and the purchaser, such that recovery could be sought from the purchaser. See, eg SA.315501 *Nürburgring*, decision of 1 October 2014, paras 231 et seq; and SA.35546 *Restructuring aid to Viana shipyards*, decision of 7 May 2015, paras 146 et seq.

Fn 582 See also Case C-263/12 *Commission v Greece*, EU:C:2013:673, paras 34 et seq.

The position of the recipient of the aid. See also SA.38517 *Micula v Romania* **17.110** *(ICSID arbitration award)*, decision of 30 March 2015. Two Swedish investors had made investments in Romania, under an investment incentive scheme, prior to Romania's accession to the EU. Upon accession, Romania abolished the scheme, which comprised a State aid, four years ahead of its scheduled expiry. An arbitral tribunal found that this early termination breached the two investors' legitimate expectations, and a bilateral investment treaty between Sweden and Romania, and ordered Romania to compensate the investors for the loss of the full benefit of the scheme. In its decision, the Commission found that the payment made by Romania pursuant to the arbitral award was itself an unlawful State aid, as it conferred an advantage equivalent to that provided by the abolished scheme. On appeal, Cases T-646/14 and 704/14, not yet decided.

17.111 **Legitimate expectation as a defence.**
Fn 595 In *Exemption from excise duty on mineral oils used as fuel for alumina production in Gardanne, in the Shannon region and in Sardinia implemented by France, Ireland and Italy respectively*, Commission decision 2006/323/EC, OJ 2006 L119/12, the Commission accepted that the authorisation by the Council of the excise duty exemptions in issue, which were found to be an unlawful State aid, under EU legislation on the harmonisation of excise duties was an exceptional circumstance. The Commission considered that the beneficiaries of the exemptions would have had reasonable grounds for believing that the exemptions were compatible with the State aid rules, and it ordered recovery only of the aid paid from the date on which its decision to launch a formal investigation was published in the Official Journal: paras 95–100.

8. Judicial Remedies

(a) National Courts

17.114 **Existing aids.**
Fn 614 In the light of the judgment of the Court of Justice in Case C-284/12 *Deutsche Lufthansa*, EU:C:2013:755, [2014] 2 CMLR 667, discussed in the update to paragraph 17.115, below, the Dutch courts' approach in *City of Alkmaar*, judgment of 7 October 2005, NJ 2006, 131; RvdW 2005, 111; and *UPC Nederland*, Amsterdam Court of Appeal, judgment of 18 January 2007, 1252/06 KG, discussed in the footnote to the main text, should not be relied on as a guide to how national courts should decide what interim measures to impose in a case concerning an alleged aid which is the subject of a formal investigation by the Commission.

17.115 **New aids (including alterations to existing aids).** In Case C-284/12 *Deutsche Lufthansa v Flughafen Frankfurt-Hahn*, EU:C:2013:755, [2014] 2 CMLR 667, the Court of Justice held that, in circumstances where the Commission has initiated a formal procedure under Article 108(2) in respect of a State measure which has not been notified and is being implemented, a national court hearing an application for the cessation of the implementation of that measure, and the recovery of payments already made, must safeguard the rights of individuals faced with a possible breach of Article 108 until the final decision of the Commission: para 28.

To that end, the Court held that a national court must adopt all necessary measures with a view to drawing the appropriate conclusions from an infringement of the obligation to suspend the implementation of the measure: para 42. The national court may:

(a) suspend the implementation of the measure in question and order the recovery of payments already made: para 43;
(b) order provisional measures in order to safeguard both the interests of the parties concerned and the effectiveness of the Commission's decision to initiate the formal examination procedure: para 43;
(c) seek clarification from the Commission and, in accordance with the second and third paragraphs of Article 267 TFEU, may or must refer a question to the Court for a preliminary ruling, where it has doubts as to whether the measure at issue constitutes State aid, or as to the validity or interpretation of the decision to initiate the formal investigation procedure: para 44.

Where the Commission has not yet initiated the formal investigation procedure, and has therefore not yet given a preliminary decision as to whether the measure under consideration involves State aid, the position is different. In that event, it is for the national court to decide whether or not the measure falls within Article 107(1) and ought to have been notified: para 34.

See also Case C-27/13 *Flughafen Lübeck v Air Berlin*, Order of 4 April 2014.

Fn 618 See also Case C-672/13 *OTP Bank v Magyar Állam*, EU:C:2015:185, paras 74–76.

Enforcement of Commission decisions. In respect of Commission decisions **17.116** formally to investigate under Article 108(2), and the duties of national courts seised of proceedings while those investigations are ongoing, see Case C-284/12 *Deutsche Lufthansa v Flughafen Frankfurt-Hahn*, discussed in the update to paragraph 17.115, above.

Where the Commission has taken a final decision that an aid measure was unlawful, but has not specified in the decision the recipients of the aid and/or the amounts to be recovered from each of them, a national court called upon to determine those matters will be bound by the Commission's decision, but not by any subsequent statements that the Commission has made in the execution of that decision. In Case C-69/13 *Mediaset v Ministero dello Sviluppo economico*, EU:C:2014:71, [2014] 3 CMLR 169 the Commission had engaged in correspondence with the Italian Republic to ensure the immediate and effective execution of its decision. The Court held that statements in that correspondence could not be binding on the national court: para 28. However, the principle of sincere cooperation requires that they be taken into account by the national court as a factor in the assessment of the dispute before it: para 31.

(b) The EU courts

(i) Reviewable acts

17.118 **Generally.**   In addition to the decisions of the Commission which have been challenged in the field of State aids, listed in the main text, a decision requiring the provision of information by a Member State (an 'information injunction'; see paragraph 17.100 of the main text) about the income and expenditure of a beneficiary of putative aid, as part of the procedure under Article 108(2), has also been held to be admissible: Case T-570/08 *RENV Deutsche Post v Commission*, EU:T:2013:589.

Fn 641   See, however, Case T-517/12 *Alro v Commission*, EU:T:2014:890, para 44. Although a decision to initiate the formal investigation procedure in relation to a measure which is already being implemented can itself be challenged under Article 263 TFEU, a decision to initiate a formal investigation in relation to a measure which is no longer in the course of implementation does not produce binding legal effects and therefore is not challengeable.

(ii) Applicants before the EU Courts

17.119 **Actions by the Commission.**   Where a Member State fails to take the necessary action to recover unlawful State aid, the Commission may ultimately ask the Court of Justice to impose a fine. In Case C-610/10 *Commission v Spain*, EU:C:2012:781, the Court of Justice fined Spain €20 million for its long-standing failure to recover aid which had been granted to certain producers of stainless steel products and electrical appliances for use in the home. In addition, Spain was required to pay a daily fine of €50,000 for each further day for which it failed to comply with the Court's previous judgment ordering recovery of the aid. Spain's failure to fulfil its obligations had persisted for more than 10 years since the date of delivery of that judgment, and for more than 22 years since the date on which the relevant Commission decision was adopted. In Case C-184/11 *Commission v Spain*, EU:C:2014:316, the Court fined Spain €30 million for its failure to recover aid which had been granted through certain tax credit schemes.

Fn 658   See, for example, Case C-674/13 *Commission v Germany* EU:C:2015:302 in which the Commission referred Germany to the Court for its failure to recover in full aid granted to Deutsche Post, notwithstanding that appeals against the Commission's decision are still pending (Cases T-143&152/12, not yet decided) as the decision has not been suspended (see paragraph 17.132 of the main text).

17.120 **Actions by Member States and regional bodies.**
Fn 661   The General Court's judgment in Case T-154/10 *France v Commission*, EU:T:2012:452, was upheld on appeal: Case C-559/12P *France v Commission*, EU:C:2014:217, [2014] 3 CMLR 903.

Actions by private parties against decisions prohibiting aid.   In several State **17.121**
aid cases the Court of Justice has considered the applicability of the fourth paragraph of Article 263 TFEU, which permits challenges to regulatory acts which
do not entail implementing measures and are of direct concern to the applicant,
to a State aid decision.

In Case C-274/12P *Telefónica v Commission*, EU:C:2013:852, the Court upheld
the General Court's judgment that Telefónica did not have standing to challenge
a Commission decision which found that a Spanish tax scheme was an unlawful
State aid. Agreeing with Advocate General Kokott, the Court held that 'the question whether a regulatory act entails implementing measures should be assessed
by reference to the position of the person pleading the right to bring proceedings
under the final limb of the fourth paragraph of Article 263 TFEU': para 30. On
that basis, it held that even though Telefónica had been a beneficiary of the Spanish
tax scheme, the part of the Commission's decision under challenge did not identify
Telefónica as a beneficiary and order recovery from it, and as such it required implementing measures (eg the issue of a tax liability notice by the Spanish authorities).
Telefónica would be able to challenge any implementing measures in the national
courts, including on the basis that the Commission's decision is unlawful, which
would cause a reference to be made to the Court for a preliminary ruling: para 59.

In Case C-132/12P *Stichting Woonpunt v Commission*, EU:C:2014:100, and Case
C-133/12P *Stichting Woonlinie v Commission*, EU:C:2014:105, the Court of Justice
considered a Commission decision which found that an existing aid was compatible
with the internal market, subject to amendments proposed by the Member State.
The Court of Justice held that in that case the decision under challenge entailed
the Member State implementing its proposed amendments to the scheme, and the
applicants therefore did not have standing under the fourth paragraph of Article
263 TFEU. In Case T-601/11 *Dansk Automat Brancheforening v Commission*,
EU:T:2014:839, paras 58–60, the General Court applied this case to a situation
in which the Commission had declared a new aid to be compatible with the internal market as notified. It held that as the decision under challenge entailed the
Member State enacting, and implementing, legislation the applicants did not have
standing under the fourth paragraph of Article 263 TFEU. On further appeal,
Case C-563/14P, not yet decided.

Fn 674 For a further example of applicants being found to be individually concerned by a decision because they formed part of an identifiable 'closed circle of operators' whose interests were affected by the decision, see Case C-132/12P *Stichting
Woonpunt v Commission*, EU:C:2014:100.

Fn 676 Where a trade association asserts that it has standing on the basis that its
members are directly and individually concerned by the decision, it must submit
evidence to demonstrate this: see, eg Case T-156/10 *Confederación de Cooperativas*

Agrarias de España v Commission, Order of 23 January 2014, EU:T:2014:41, paras 48–50.

17.122 Challenge by complainants to refusal to open formal procedure. Where the person bringing the appeal against a refusal to open a formal complaint seeks not only to secure the procedural rights available under Article 108(2), but also challenges the merits of a decision which finds an aid to be compatible with the internal market, he must establish that he is directly and individually concerned within the meaning of that test laid down in Case C-25/62 *Plaumann v Commission* [1963] ECR 95, [1964] CMLR 29 if the latter arguments are to be admissible. See, eg Case T-57/11 *Castelnou Energía v Commission*, EU:T:2014:1021, paras 28 et seq, in which the General Court held that the challenge was admissible as the appellant's competitive position was more seriously affected by the contested measure than other competitors'. The test of direct and individual concern is discussed in paragraph 17.123 of the main text, and the updates thereto, below.

See also the recent judgments of the Court of Justice on the applicability of the fourth paragraph of Article 263 TFEU, which permits challenges to regulatory acts which do not entail implementing measures and are of direct concern to the applicant, to a State aid decision, discussed in the update to paragraph 17.121, above.

On the factors relevant to determining whether the Commission's initial review revealed serious difficulties with the aid in question, the Court of Justice held in Case C-646/11P *Falles Fagligt Forbund (3F) v Commission*, EU:C:2013:36, at para 32, that the fact that the Commission's preliminary examination has been of longer duration than two months is an indicator that the Commission may have had serious doubts as to the compatibility of the aid, but is not, of itself, sufficient to lead to a conclusion that the Commission was required to open the formal investigation procedure. In Case T-304/08 *Smurfit Kappa Group v Commission*, EU:T:2012:351, para 26, the General Court held that if the examination carried out by the Commission is insufficient or incomplete, this may be evidence of serious difficulties. In Case T-58/13 *Club Hotel Loutraki v Commission*, EU:T:2015:1, paras 41–44, the General Court held that as the Commission may enter into a dialogue as part of its preliminary examination of the aid, in order to endeavour to overcome any difficulties encountered, by implication the Commission may conclude that there is no State aid following that dialogue and the receipt of commitments to modify the aid. The fact that the Member State offered commitments to modify the aid should not be interpreted as meaning that the Commission had serious doubts about its compatibility with the internal market. On further appeal, Case C-131/15, not yet decided. In Case T-57/11 *Castelnou Energía v Commission* EU:T:2014:1021, paras 81 et seq, the General Court held that the number and seriousness of objections raised against an aid at national level cannot be taken into consideration, as to do so would be tantamount to making the initiation of a formal investigation depend on the level of opposition to the national scheme rather than on the serious difficulties encountered by the Commission. However, the nature of those objections may indicate serious difficulties with the measure. In that case, the General Court considered, and dismissed, an argument by Greenpeace-España that the Commission had not adequately assessed the environmental implications of the aid: paras 113–114.

For examples of the General Court annulling the Commission's decision not to open the formal procedure, see Case T-304/08 *Smurfit Kappa Group v Commission*, EU:T:2012:351 in which it held that the Commission's decision was based on a misapprehension that the Regional Aid Guidelines precluded it from doing so in circumstances where the thresholds relating to market share and increase in production capacity were not exceeded; and Case T-512/11 *Ryanair v Commission*, EU:T:2014:989 in which the Commission's review had taken 24 months, and there were doubts as to the manner in which the measure would actually apply in practice such that the Commission did not have the information necessary to assess whether that measure was selective.

Another route open to complainants for challenging the Commission's failure to take a decision, within a reasonable time, to open a formal investigation into the State aid complaint is a complaint to the European Ombudsman alleging maladministration by the Commission in its handling of the complaint. The Ombudsman has taken a number of decisions on such complaints: see, eg Case 1184/2012/(ER) PMC (decision summary published 24 April 2014); and Case 2521/2011/(MF)JF (decision summary published 30 July 2014).

Fn 681 The Court of Justice dismissed the appeal in Case C-615/11P *Commission v Ryanair*, EU:C:2013:310, [2013] 3 CMLR 1074, against the General Court's judgment in Case T-442/07 *Ryanair v Commission* [2011] ECR II-333.

Fn 682 See also Case T-304/08 *Smurfit Kappa Group v Commission*, EU:T:2012:351; Case T-362/10 *Vtesse Networks v Commission*, EU:T:2014:928, para 47; and Case T-512/11 *Ryanair v Commission*, EU:T:2014:989, para 28.

Fn 686 The Court of Justice dismissed the appeal in Case C-646/11P *Falles Fagligt Forbund (3F) v Commission*, EU:C:2013:36; see in particular paras 32–36.

Challenge by complainants to decision following formal investigation. The requirement to show direct and individual concern, discussed in the main text, must also be met where the person brings an appeal against a refusal to open a formal complaint, in which he seeks not only to secure the procedural rights available under Article 108(2), but also challenges the merits of a decision which finds an aid to be compatible with the internal market. See, eg Case T-57/11 *Castelnou Energía v Commission*, EU:T:2014:1021, paras 28 et seq. **17.123**

See also the recent judgments of the Court of Justice on the applicability of the fourth paragraph of Article 263 TFEU, which permits challenges to regulatory acts which do not entail implementing measures and are of direct concern to the applicant, to a State aid decision, discussed in the update to paragraph 17.121, above.

Fn 692 See also Case T-182/10 *AISCAT v Commission*, EU:T:2013:9; and Case T-601/11 *Dansk Automat Brancheforening v Commission*, EU:T:2014:839, paras 38 et seq (on further appeal, Case C-563/14P, not yet decided).

(iii) The grounds of annulment

17.126 **Lack of reasoning.**
Fn 707 The Court of Justice dismissed the appeal in Case C-405/11P *Buczek Automotive v Commission*, EU:C:2013:186.

17.128 **Review of the exercise of the Commission's discretion.**
Fn 722 See also Case T-387/11 *Nitrogénművek Vegyipari Zrt (Hungarian Development Bank) v Commission*, EU:T:2013:98, para 25, where the General Court held that 'in order to establish that the Commission committed a manifest error in assessing the facts such as to justify the annulment of the contested decision, the evidence adduced by the applicant must be sufficient to make the factual assessments used in the decision at issue implausible'.

Fn 725 The Court of Justice upheld the appeal on other grounds in Case C-73/11P *Frucona Košice v Commission*, EU:C:2013:32, [2013] 2 CMLR 719.

(iv) Interim relief

17.132 **Member States.**
Fn 737 In Case C-674/13 *Commission v Germany*, EU:C:2015:302 the Commission referred Germany to the Court for its failure to recover in full aid granted to Deutsche Post, notwithstanding that appeals against the Commission's decision are still pending (Cases T-143&152/12, not yet decided), as the decision has not been suspended.

Fn 738 See also Case T-366/13R *France v Commission*, Order of 29 August 2013, in which the General Court refused France's application for interim measures, seeking to suspend the effect of the Commission's order requiring the recovery of unlawful aid from the shipping company SNCM. France had argued that implementation of the recovery order would entail the liquidation of SNCM. The General Court considered, however, that France's interest as a Member State was in protecting general interests at a national level: para 25, whereas SNCM was able to protect its own interests by bringing proceedings in the national courts for the suspension of its obligation to repay the aid, on the ground that repayment would be likely to cause it to suffer serious irreparable harm: paras 44 et seq.